PHILIP'S ROAD

2019 BIG ATLAS BRITAIN & IRELAND

CONTENTS

www.philips-maps.co.uk

First published in 2009 by Philip's
a division of Octopus Publishing Group Ltd
www.octopusbooks.co.uk
Carmelite House, 50 Victoria Embankment
London EC4Y 0DZ
An Hachette UK Company
www.hachette.co.uk

Tenth edition 2018
First impression 2018

ISBN 978-1-84907-472-8

Cartography by Philip's
Copyright © 2018 Philip's

This product includes mapping data licensed from Ordnance Survey®, with the permission of the Controller of Her Majesty's Stationery Office. © Crown copyright 2018. All rights reserved. Licence number 100011710

The map of Ireland on pages XIV-XV is based upon the Crown Copyright and is reproduced with the permission of Land & Property Services under delegated authority from the Controller of Her Majesty's Stationery Office, © Crown Copyright and database right 2018, PMLPA No 100503, and on Ordnance Survey Ireland by permission of the Government © Ordnance Survey Ireland / Government of Ireland Permit number 9130.

Information for National Parks, Areas of Outstanding Natural Beauty, National Trails and Country Parks in Wales supplied by the Countryside Council for Wales.

Information for National Parks, Areas of Outstanding Natural Beauty, National Trails and Country Parks in England supplied by Natural England. Data for Regional Parks, Long Distance Footpaths and Country Parks in Scotland provided by Scottish Natural Heritage.

Gaelic name forms used in the Western Isles provided by Comhairle nan Eilean.

Data for the National Nature Reserves in England provided by Natural England. Data for the National Nature Reserves in Wales provided by Countryside Council for Wales. Darparwyd data'n ymwneud â Gwarchodfeydd Natur Cenedlaethol Cymru gan Gyngor Cefn Gwlad Cymru.

Information on the location of National Nature Reserves in Scotland was provided by Scottish Natural Heritage.

Data for National Scenic Areas in Scotland provided by the Scottish Executive Office. Crown copyright material is reproduced with the permission of the Controller of HMSO and the Queen's Printer for Scotland. Licence number C02W0003960.

Printed in China

*Data from Nielsen Total Consumer Market 2016 weeks 1–52

Inside back cover: **County and unitary authority boundaries**

Road map symbols

M6	Motorway, toll motorway
4 5	Motorway junction – full, restricted access
S S	Motorway service area – full, restricted access
	Motorway under construction
A453	Primary route – dual, single carriageway
S	Service area, roundabout, multi-level junction
4 5	Numbered junction – full, restricted access
	Primary route under construction
	Narrow primary route
Derby	Primary destination
A34	A road – dual, single carriageway
	A road under construction, narrow A road
B2135	B road – dual, single carriageway
	B road under construction, narrow B road
	Minor road – over 4 metres, under 4 metres wide
	Minor road with restricted access
2	Distance in miles
	Scenic route
TOLL	Toll, steep gradient – arrow points downhill
	Tunnel
	National trail – England and Wales
	Long distance footpath – Scotland
	Railway with station
	Level crossing, tunnel
	Preserved railway with station
	National boundary
	County / unitary authority boundary
	Car ferry, catamaran
	Passenger ferry, catamaran
	Hovercraft
CALAIS	Ferry destination
Ferry	Car ferry – river crossing
	Principal airport, other airport
	National park
	Area of Outstanding Natural Beauty – England and Wales National Scenic Area – Scotland forest park / regional park / national forest
	Woodland
	Beach
	Linear antiquity
	Roman road
1066	Hillfort, battlefield – with date
795	Viewpoint, nature reserve, spot height – in metres
	Golf course, youth hostel, sporting venue
	Camp site, caravan site, camping and caravan site
P&R	Shopping village, park and ride
29	Adjoining page number – road maps

Relief

Feet	metres
3000	914
2600	792
2200	671
1800	549
1400	427
1000	305
0	0

Road map scale 1: 200 000 • 3·15 miles to 1 inch

0 1 2 3 4 5 6 miles
0 1 2 3 4 5 6 7 8 9 10 km

Parts of Scotland 1: 250 000 • 3.94 miles to 1 inch

0 1 2 3 4 5 6 7 8 miles
0 1 2 3 4 5 6 7 8 9 10 11 12 km

Orkney and Shetland Islands 1:340 000, approximately 5.25 miles to 1 inch

Approach map symbols

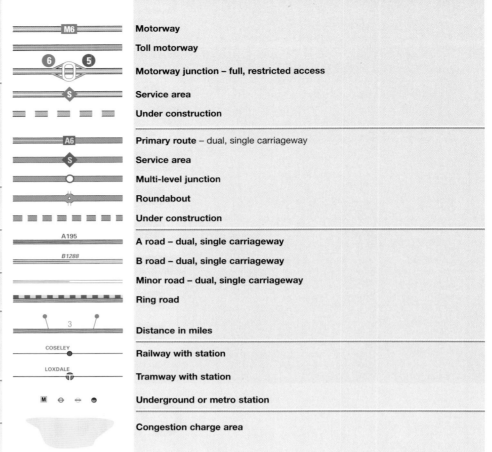

M6	Motorway
	Toll motorway
6 5	Motorway junction – full, restricted access
S	Service area
	Under construction
A6	Primary route – dual, single carriageway
S	Service area
	Multi-level junction
	Roundabout
	Under construction
A195	A road – dual, single carriageway
B1288	B road – dual, single carriageway
	Minor road – dual, single carriageway
	Ring road
3	Distance in miles
COSELEY	Railway with station
LOXDALE	Tramway with station
M	Underground or metro station
	Congestion charge area

Town plan symbols

	Motorway
	Primary route – dual, single carriageway
	A road – dual, single carriageway
	B road – dual, single carriageway
	Minor through road
	One-way street
	Pedestrian roads
	Shopping streets
	Railway with station
City Hall	Tramway with station
	Bus or railway station building
	Shopping precinct or retail park
	Park
	Building of public interest
	Theatre, cinema
P	Parking, shopmobility
Bank	Underground station
West St	Metro station
H	Hospital, Police station
PO	Post office

Tourist information

✝ Abbey, cathedral or priory	⛪ Church	House and garden	Safari park
Ancient monument	Country park England and Wales Scotland	Motor racing circuit	Theme park
Aquarium		Museum	Tourist information centre
Art gallery	Farm park	Picnic area	🄸 open all year
Bird collection or aviary	Garden	Preserved railway	🄸 open seasonally
	Historic ship	Race course	Zoo
Castle	House	Roman antiquity	Other place of interest

Motorway service areas

Motorway service area

Restricted motorway junctions

M1 Junction 34

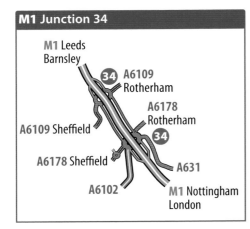

M1 Junctions 6, 6A
M25 Junctions 21, 21A

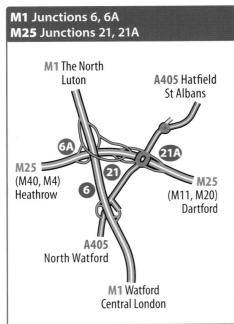

M4 Junctions 25, 25A, 26

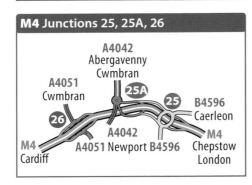

M5 Junction 11A

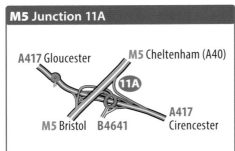

M8 Junctions 8, 9 · M73 Junctions 1, 2 · M74 Junctions 2A, 3, 3A, 4

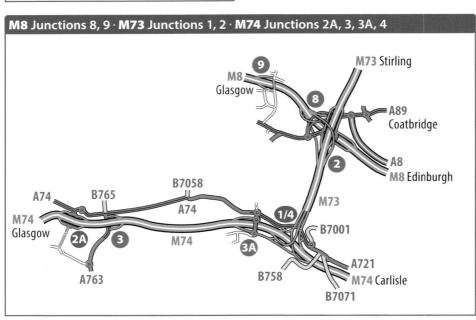

M1	Northbound	Southbound
2	No exit	No access
4	No exit	No access
6A	No exit. Access from M25 only	No access. Exit to M25 only
7	No exit. Access from A414 only	No access. Exit to A414 only
17	No access. Exit to M45 only	No exit. Access from M45 only
19	No exit to A14	No access from A14
21A	No access	No exit
23A		Exit to A42 only
24A	No exit	No access
35A	No access	No exit
43	No access. Exit to M621 only	No exit. Access from M621 only
48	No exit to A1(M) southbound	

M3	Eastbound	Westbound
8	No exit	No access
10	No access	No exit
13	No access to M27 eastbound	
14	No exit	No access

M4	Eastbound	Westbound
1	Exit to A4 eastbound only	Access from A4 westbound only
2	Access from A4 eastbound only	Access to A4 westbound only
21	No exit	No access
23	No access	No exit
25	No exit	No access
25A	No exit	No access
29	No exit	No access
38		No access
39	No exit or access	No exit
41	No access	No exit
41A	No exit	No access
42	Access from A483 only	Exit to A483 only

M5	Northbound	Southbound
10	No exit	No access
11A	No access from A417 eastbound	No exit to A417 westbound

M6	Northbound	Southbound
3A	No access.	Access from M6 eastbound only
4A	No exit. Access from M42 southbound only	No access. Exit to M42 only
5	No access	No exit
10A	No access. Exit to M54 only	No exit. Access from M54 only
11A	No exit. Access from M6 Toll only	No access. Exit to M6 Toll only
20	No exit to M56 eastbound	No access from M56 westbound
24	No exit	No access
25	No access	No exit
30	No exit. Access from M61 northbound only	No access. Exit to M61 southbound only
31A	No access	No exit
45	No access	No exit

M6 Toll	Northbound	Southbound
T1		No exit
T2	No exit, no access	No access
T5	No exit	No access
T7	No access	No exit
T8	No access	No exit

M8	Eastbound	Westbound
6	No exit	No access
6A	No access	No exit
7	No Access	No exit
7A	No exit. Access from A725 northbound only	No access. Exit to A725 southbound only
8	No exit to M73 northbound	No access from M73 southbound
9	No access	No exit
13	No exit southbound	Access from M73 southbound only
14	No access	No exit
16	No exit	No access
17	No exit	
18		No exit
19	No exit to A814 eastbound	No access from A814 westbound
20	No exit	No access
21	No access from M74	No exit
22	No exit. Access from M77 only	No access. Exit to M77 only
23	No exit	No access
25	Exit to A739 northbound only. Access from A739 southbound only	
25A	No exit	No access
28	No exit	No access
28A	No exit	No access

M9	Eastbound	Westbound
1A	No exit	No access
2	No access	No exit
3	No access	No access
6	No access	No exit
8	No exit	No access

M11	Northbound	Southbound
4	No exit	No access
5	No access	No exit
9	No access	No exit
13	No access	No exit
14	No exit to A428 westbound	No exit. Access from A14 westbound only

M20	Eastbound	Westbound
2	No access	No exit
3	No exit Access from M26 eastbound only	No access Exit to M26 westbound only
11A	No access	No exit

M23	Northbound	Southbound
7	No exit to A23 southbound	No access from A23 northbound
10A	No exit	No access

M25	Clockwise	Anticlockwise
5	No exit to M26 eastbound	No access from M26 westbound
19	No access	No exit
21	No exit to M1 southbound. Access from M1 southbound only	No exit to M1 southbound. Access from M1 southbound only
31	No exit	No access

M27	Eastbound	Westbound
10	No exit	No access
12	No access	No exit

M40	Eastbound	Westbound
3	No exit	No access
7	No exit	No access
8	No exit	No access
13	No exit	No access
14	No access	No exit
16	No access	No exit

M42	Northbound	Southbound
1	No exit	No access
7	No access Exit to M6 northbound only	No exit. Access from M6 northbound only
7A	No access. Exit to M6 southbound only	No exit
8	No exit. Access from M6 southbound only	Exit to M6 northbound only. Access from M6 southbound only

M45	Eastbound	Westbound
M1 J17	Access to M1 southbound only	No access from M1 southbound
With A45	No access	No exit

M48	Eastbound	Westbound
M4 J21	No exit to M4 westbound	No access from M4 eastbound
M4 J23	No access from M4 westbound	No exit to M4 eastbound

M11 Junctions 13, 14

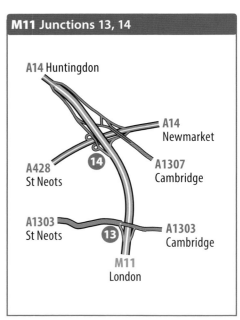

M49	Southbound	Northbound
18A	No exit to M5 northbound	No access from M5 southbound

M53	Northbound	Southbound
11	Exit to M56 eastbound only. Access from M56 westbound only	Exit to M56 eastbnd only. Access from M56 westbound only

M56	Eastbound	Westbound
2	No exit	No access
3	No access	No exit
4	No exit	No access
7		No access
8	No exit or access	No exit
9	No access from M6 northbound	No access to M6 southbound
15	No exit to M53	No access from M53 northbound

M57	Northbound	Southbound
3	No exit	No access
5	No exit	No access

M58	Eastbound	Westbound
1	No exit	No access

M60	Clockwise	Anticlockwise
2	No exit	No access
3	No exit to A34 northbound	No exit to A34 northbound
4	No access from M56	No exit to M56
5	No exit to A5103 southbound	No exit to A5103 northbound
14	No exit	No access
16	No exit	No access
20	No access	No exit
22		No access
25	No access	
26		No exit or access
27	No exit	No access

M61	Northbound	Southbound
2	No access from A580 eastbound	No exit to A580 westbound
3	No access from A580 eastbound. No access from A666 southbound	No exit to A580 westbound
M6 J30	No exit to M6 southbound	No access from M6 northbound

M62	Eastbound	Westbound
23	No access	No exit

M65	Eastbound	Westbound
9	No access	No exit
11	No exit	No access

M66	Northbound	Southbound
1	No access	No exit

M67	Eastbound	Westbound
1A	No access	No exit
2	No exit	No access

M69	Northbound	Southbound
2	No exit	No access

M73	Northbound	Southbound
2	No access from M8 eastbound	No exit to M8 westbound

M74	Northbound	Southbound
3	No access	No exit
3A	No exit	No access
7	No exit	No access
9	No exit or access	
10		No exit
11	No exit	No access
12	No access	No exit

M77	Northbound	Southbound
4	No exit	No access
6	No exit	No access
7	No exit	
8	No access	No access

M80	Northbound	Southbound
4A	No access	No exit
6A	No exit	No access
8	Exit to M876 northbound only. No access	Access from M876 southbound only. No exit

M90	Northbound	Southbound
1	Access from A90 northbound only	No access. Exit to A90 southbound only
2A	No access	No access
7	No exit	No access
8	No access	No access
10	No access from A912	No exit to A912

M180	Eastbound	Westbound
1	No access	No exit

M621	Eastbound	Westbound
2A	No exit	No access
4	No exit	
5	No access	No access
6	No exit	No access

M876	Northbound	Southbound
2	No access	No exit

A1(M)	Northbound	Southbound
2	No access	No exit
3		No access
5	No exit	No exit, no access
14	No access	No exit
40	No access	No exit
43	No exit. Access from M1 only	No access. Exit to M1 only
57	No access	No exit
65	No access	No exit

A3(M)	Northbound	Southbound
1	No exit	No access
4	No access	No exit

A38(M) with Victoria Rd, (Park Circus) Birmingham	
Northbound	No exit
Southbound	No access

A48(M)	Northbound	Southbound
M4 Junc 29	Exit to M4 eastbound only	Access from M4 westbound only
29A	Access from A48 eastbound only	Exit to A48 westbound only

A57(M)	Eastbound	Westbound
With A5103	No access	No exit
With A34	No access	No exit

A58(M)	Southbound
With Park Lane and Westgate, Leeds	No access

A64(M)	Eastbound	Westbound
With A58 Clay Pit Lane, Leeds	No access from A58	No exit to A58

A74(M)	Northbound	Southbound
18	No access	No exit
22		No exit to A75

A194(M)	Northbound	Southbound
A1(M) J65 Gateshead Western Bypass	Access from A1(M) northbound only	Exit to A1(M) southbound only

M3 Junctions 13, 14 · M27 Junction 4

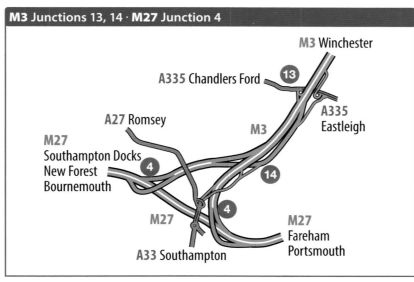

M6 Junctions 3A, 4A · M42 Junctions 7, 7A, 8, 9
M6 Toll Junctions T1, T2

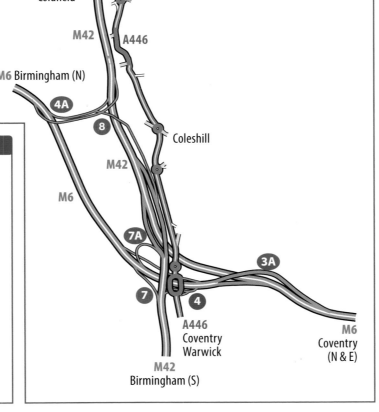

M6 Junction 20 · M56 Junction 9

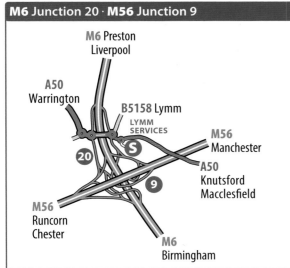

M62 Junctions 32A, 33 · A1(M) Junctions 40, 41

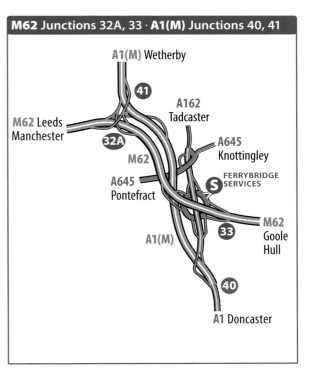

Dash Cam Hell – the perils of Britain's country roads

By Stephen Mesquita
Philip's On the Road Correspondent

Part fallen off tractor

If, like most people, you live in a town or suburb, your driving life is probably well structured (even if it doesn't feel like it).

You'll be used to doing most of your driving in built-up areas, controlled by speed limits, traffic lights, one-way streets, white lines and all the other props of urban motoring. Or on motorways and dual carriageways getting from A to B. You'll spend time in traffic jams.

It's when you decide to take a holiday and live the rural dream that your experiences behind the wheel will change beyond recognition. You may be expecting a pastoral idyll of empty roads, breathing in the sweet scent of country meadows and hearing nothing but the larks warbling overhead.

Forget it! You're entering a motoring free-for-all. However carefree it may feel to be bowling along country lanes, you've entered a zone which the stats show is far more hazardous that the one you're used to.

To give you a flavour of what to expect, here are some stills taken from my dash cam video last August. Nothing here is staged. I made no special journeys to take this footage. It's all recorded just as it happened. And here's the crunch: many country roads barely have room for two 'normal-sized' cars. They certainly don't have room for two normal-sized cars and a bicycle, a jogger, a deer or for one normal-sized car and a farm vehicle. And country roads aren't always straight. Some of these inconvenient extras loom up suddenly as you come round a corner.

We've split Country Road Hazards into four different categories

1 Other drivers

Driving on the wrong side of the road

As we all know, everyone drives on the wrong side of the road – except you, of course. So it's always best to assume on blind bends that something will come round at least partly on your side of the road. At least take bends slowly and give yourself a better than evens chance of evading the oncoming car.

Pulling out without looking

Country roads often contain hidden exits. The exit is hidden to the motorist on the road and the road is hidden to the motorist trying to exit. The result – unexpected pulling out and hoping for the best.

2 Other vehicles

On the farm

The time when you are on your summer holiday is the time of maximum activity on the farm – which means that the narrow country roads bear the brunt of all the paraphernalia of modern farming. And many of the 21st century vehicles are monsters which can take up the whole road. My simple advice: don't argue with them!

White vans and Ute's

The countryside is full of busy people: not only farmers, but builders and maintenance people, plumbers and electricians and delivery vehicles. The car of choice on the farm is no longer the modest Landrover. It's what the Australians call a ute (utility truck). They are bulky. All these drivers know the roads and drive accordingly.

Driver using phone

Large cars

Cars are getting bigger and country roads aren't. That means that, on many country roads, there often isn't even room for you and another car to pass easily. If in doubt, slow down – or even stop altogether.

3 Two wheels and two feet

Cyclists

As a very occasional cyclist, I have to be careful what I say here. There is no doubt that cyclists are a major hazard on country roads – to themselves and to motorists. It's difficult to overtake cyclists safely on roads with bends – especially if they are a group. However cautiously you are driving, if you see a cyclist, double the caution, especially if they are a family group of occasional cyclists. And be patient – cyclists have as much right to use the roads as motorists and are far more vulnerable.

Joggers

As for cyclists, so joggers. Why jog on a busy country road? I can't answer that one.

Dog walkers

There is usually not room for a roadside dog, its walker and two passing cars. The side of the road holds numerous distractions for Fido. It all adds up to alarm bells ringing for the passing motorist.

Cylist 'walking' two dogs ↘

Gardeners

We country folk are responsible for cutting back roadside hedges where they might obscure visibility. This is a less than enjoyable occupation, especially if you live on a bend.

← Man with wheelbarrow

Social chit-chatterers

It's the country. The pace of life is different here. Priorities aren't the same. So why not stand in the middle of the road, having a gossip? Or, better still, stop your car and have a natter with a pedestrian? That'll teach those townies about life in the country. To make things more interesting, this sometimes happens on horseback.

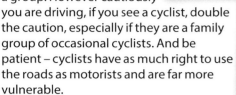

Dash cams
what are they, how do they work and do you need one?

The message

This truck failed to stop at a passing place on a country road just two miles from my house and forced me to jump a deep ditch with an Olympian prowess which I never knew I possessed, to get out of my car. It was then that I decided to invest in a dashcam.

When the truck driver stopped in the hedge and refused to drive on, I stupidly tried to drive past and ended up writing off a door on the bar at the back of his truck. A passing policeman wasn't much help – he told me I should have refused to move. Even though the truck driver admitted it was his fault, it still ended up as joint liability on my insurance.

When I reported the accident, the first question I was asked was 'do you have a dash cam'. That's the moment when I became a dash cam convert.

You can see from the pictures in this article what a dash cam does. You attach it with a suction pad to your windscreen and it records the road ahead of you on a video loop which erases the oldest clip to record the latest one. If you need to, you can then download the footage to your computer.

You can get a simple dash cam for as little as £25 – or with all sorts of bells and whistles, such as front- and back-facing recordings, for more.

One thing to remember: if you drive badly, you'll have a silent witness.

4 Four feet/two wings

Wildlife

If you hit a deer, it can do serious damage to your car. 42,000 deer are killed by cars every year. 400 motorists are injured every year – some of them fatally. May-June and October–November are particularly hazardous.

And that's just the start of it: add in squirrels, rabbits, hares, badgers, hedgehogs and foxes – not to mention domestic pets, such as cats and dogs. The quieter the time of day or night, the more likely it is there will be animals on the road.

When I drive on a narrow country road to catch an early train, I impose a 30mph speed limit on myself. On a number of occasions (but, sadly, not always) this has saved an animal and, once or twice, my car from suffering damage.

Birdlife

As above: pheasants can damage your car. I once got one stuck in the front grille, resulting in some wag posting a notice on my car 'Meals on Wheels'. If you drive at night, watch out for owls.

The official view

Brake before the bend, not on it

- 59% of all fatalities occur on country roads. These roads often have sharp bends and blind bends which can hide unexpected hazards. Stay in control and give yourself time to react because you never know what's around the corner. THINK! Brake before the bend, not on it.

The facts

- 59% of all fatalities occur on country roads
- Three people die each day on average on country roads
- The number of people killed on country roads is nearly 10 times higher than on motorways
- In 2015, 10,307 people were killed or seriously injured on country roads in Great Britain

The law

You must not drive faster than the speed limit for the type of road and your type of vehicle. The speed limit is the absolute maximum and it doesn't mean it's safe to drive at this speed in all conditions.

The best drivers read the road ahead and anticipate potential hazards. Look out for upcoming bends, hidden dips, blind summits and concealed entrances.

Country roads often have sharp bends. To stay in control and give yourself time to react to unexpected hazards, brake before the bend, not in it.

Overgrown verges, bushes and trees on country roads can block your view and potentially obscure an oncoming hazard. Always drive at a speed which will allow you to stop in the distance you can see to be clear (double that on a single track road). Allow more time to stop on wet or slippy surfaces.

The speed limit is a limit not a target. The national speed limit on single carriage roads is 60mph, but there will be times you need to drive under that in order to drive correctly for the conditions. In fact, most people do on these roads – the average free flow speed is 48mph.

If you get stuck behind a slow-moving vehicle be patient. Dips in roads, bends and other junctions joining your road often hide oncoming vehicles, so unless it's absolutely safe, don't overtake.

If passing more vulnerable road users such as horse riders, cyclists and walkers, pass wide and slow.

Even if you're familiar with a country road, never take it for granted as the conditions can be different every time.

For the full article and further information, visit http://think.direct.gov.uk/country-roads.html

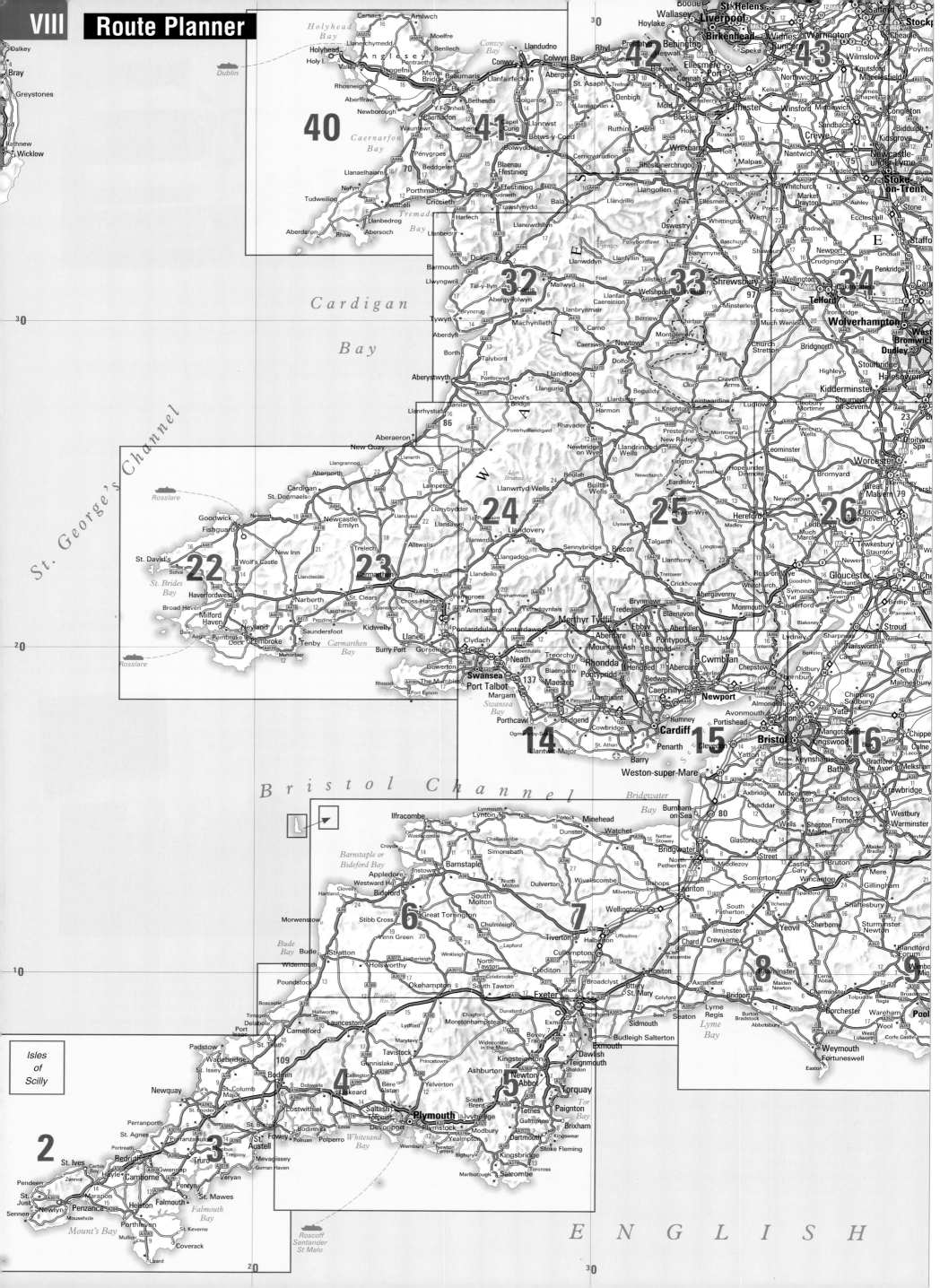

Scale 1:1000000 1cm = 10km 1 inch = 15.78 miles

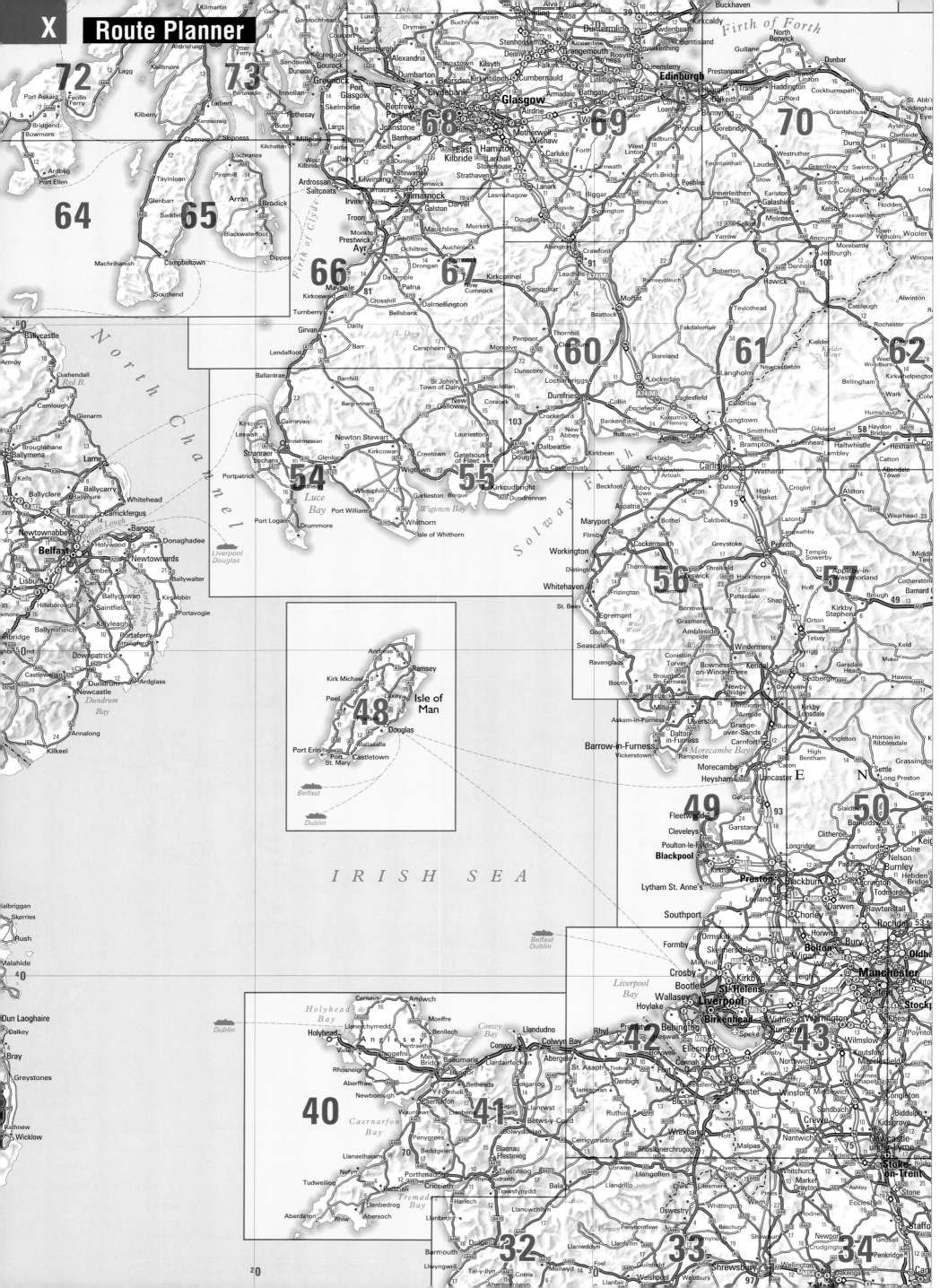

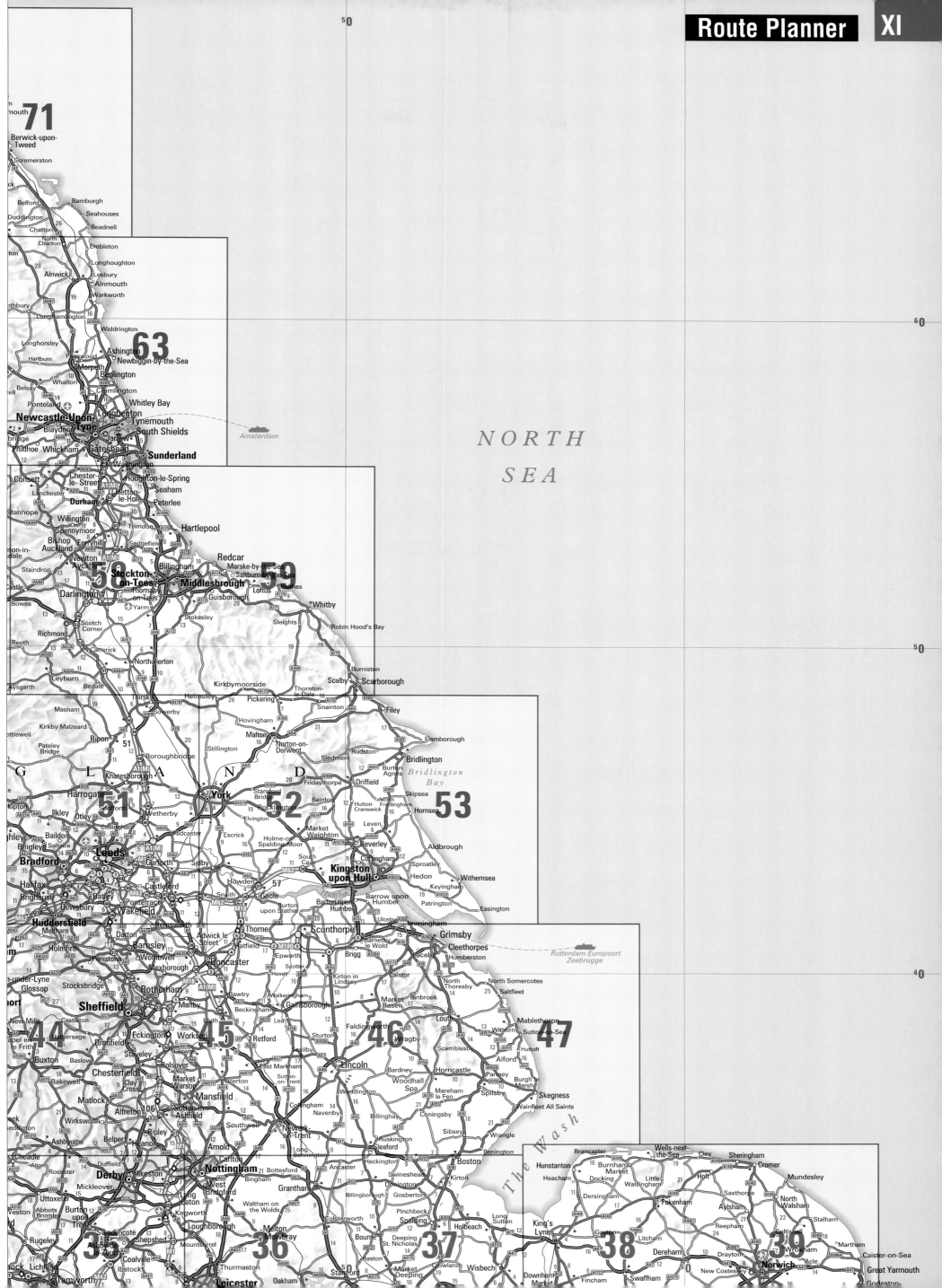

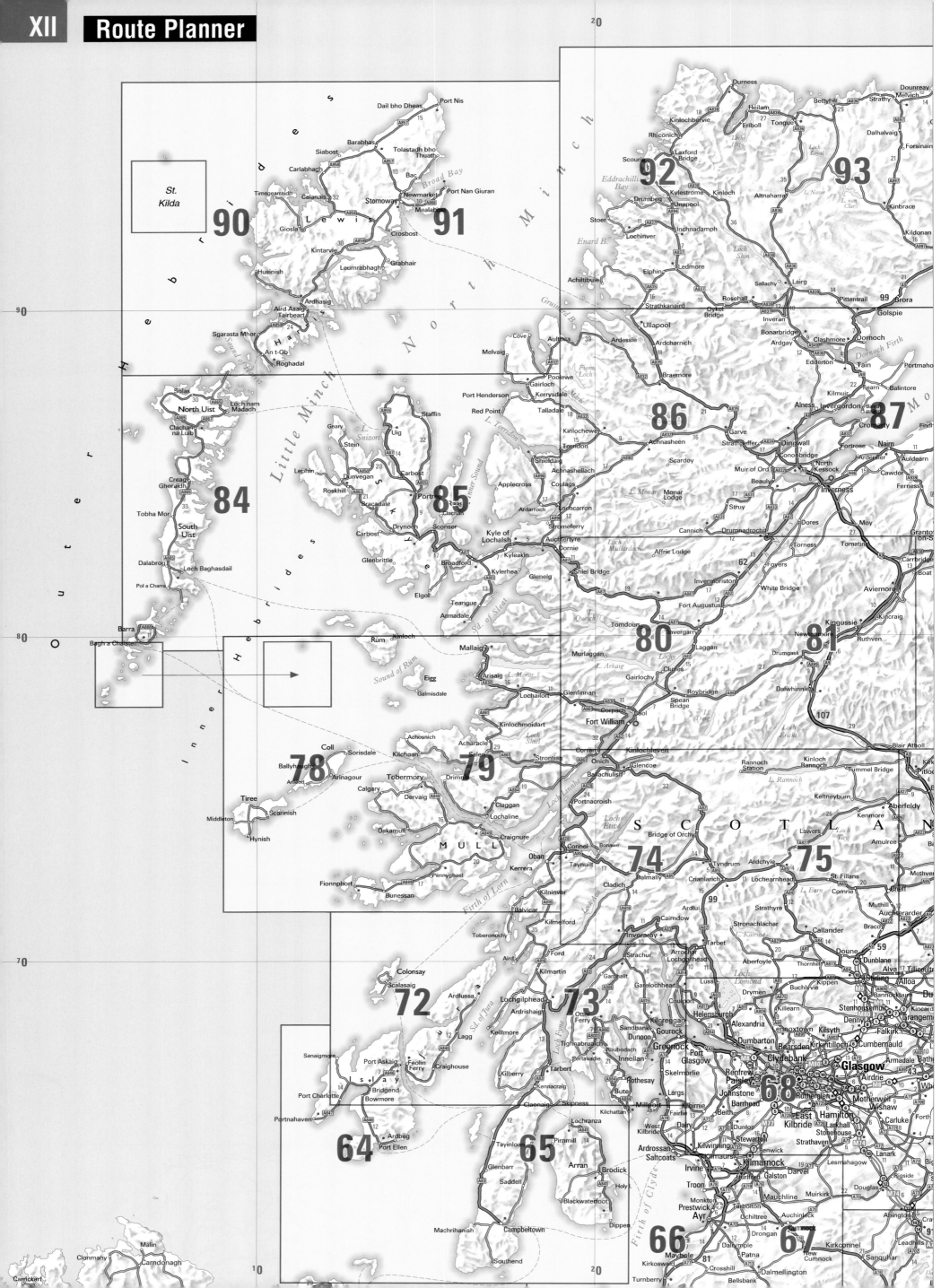

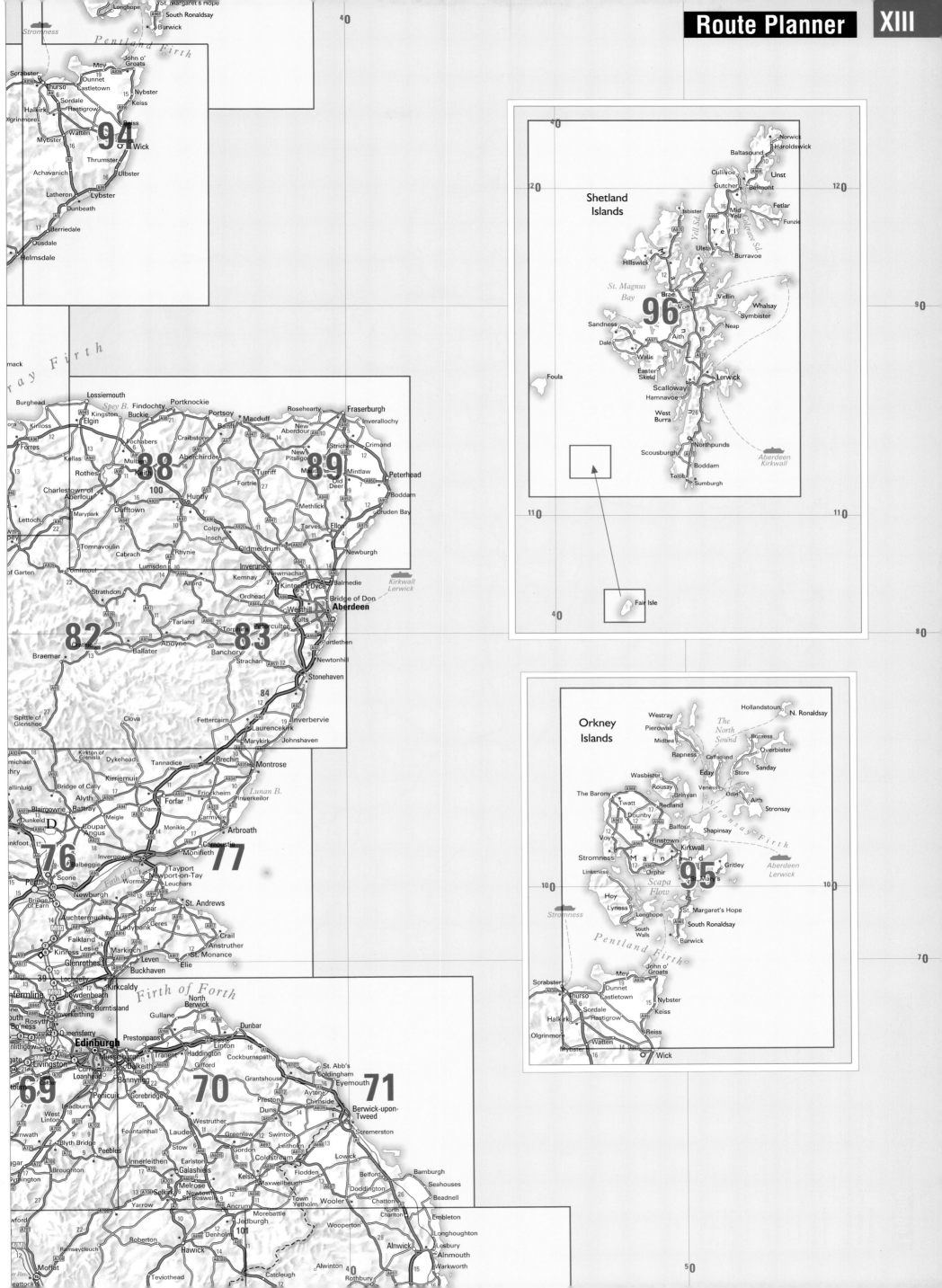

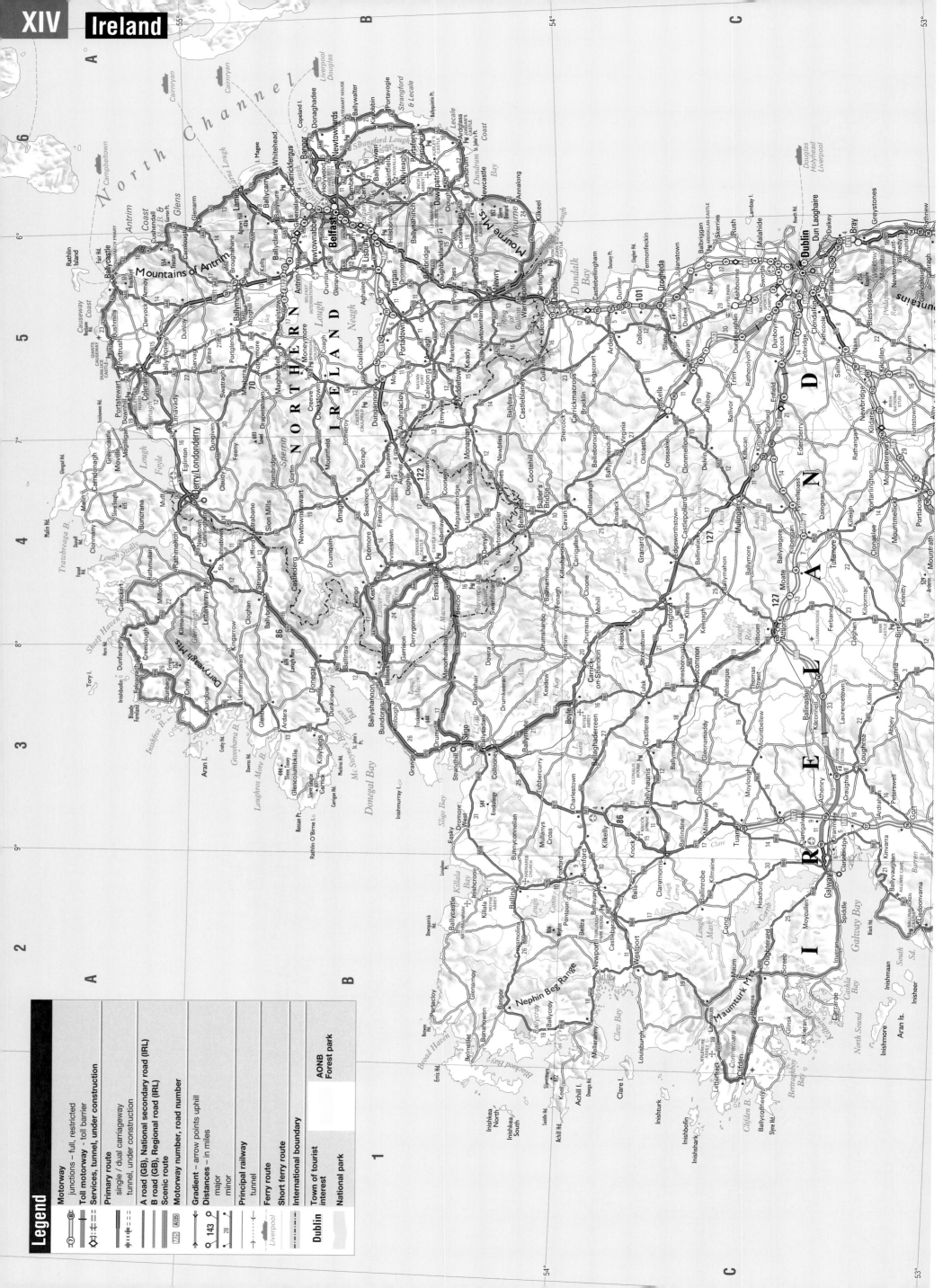

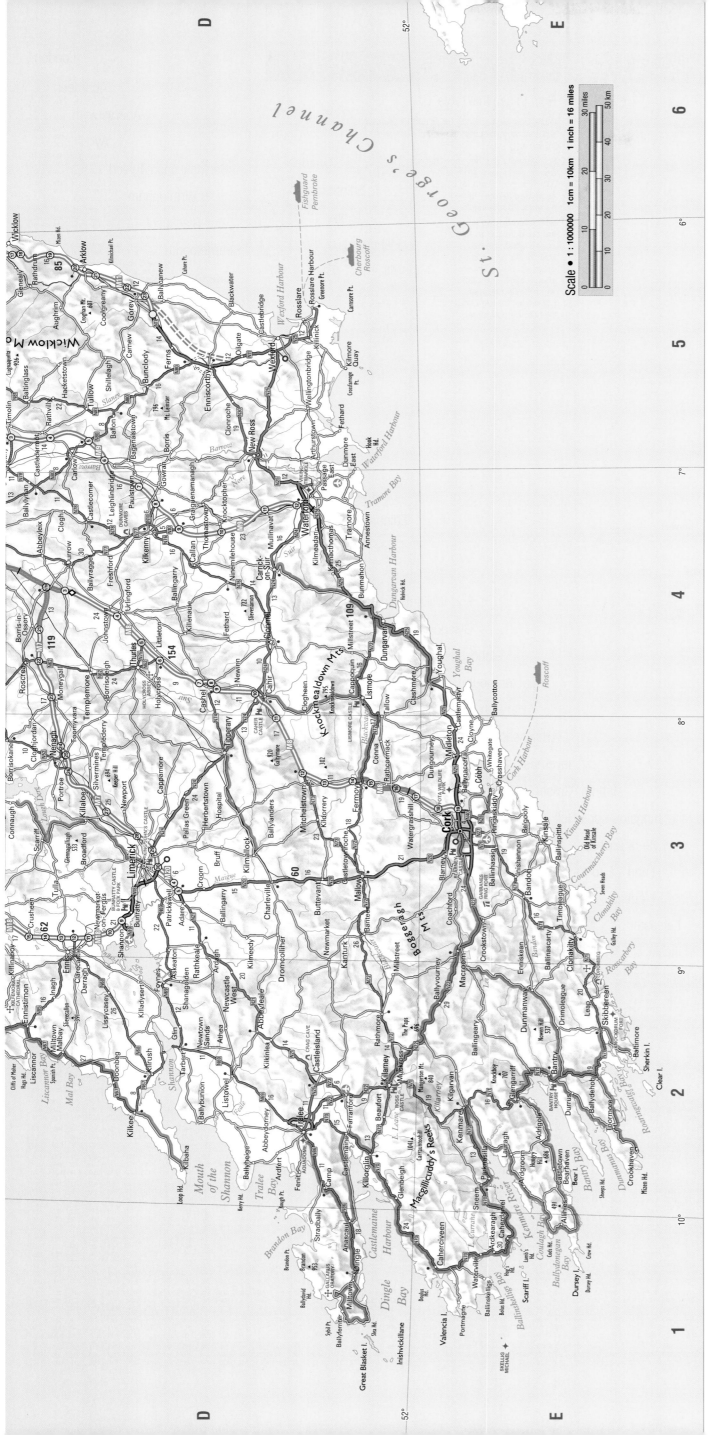

St. George's Channel

Wicklow Mts.

Mouth of the Shannon

Dingle Bay

Bantry Bay

Scale ● 1 : 1000000   1cm = 10km   1 inch = 16 miles

30 miles · 50 km

Fishguard / Pembroke

Rosslare Harbour · Cherbourg / Roscoff

Distance table

How to use this table

Distances are shown in miles and kilometres with estimated journey times in hours and minutes.

For example: the distance between Dover and Fishguard is 331 miles or 533 kilometres with an estimated journey time of 6 hours, 20 minutes.

Estimated driving times are based on an average speed of 60mph on Motorways and 40mph on other roads. Drivers should allow extra time when driving at peak periods or through areas likely to be congested.

Supporting

THINK!

Travel safe –
Don't drive tired

Map of Great Britain showing cities including John o' Groats, Kyle of Lochalsh, Inverness, Braemar, Aberdeen, Fort William, Dundee, Oban, Edinburgh, Glasgow, Ayr, Berwick-upon-Tweed, Stranraer, Carlisle, Newcastle upon Tyne, Blackpool, Leeds, York, Kingston upon Hull, Manchester, Liverpool, Doncaster, Holyhead, Sheffield, Lincoln, Shrewsbury, Nottingham, Norwich, Great Yarmouth, Leicester, Birmingham, Aberystwyth, Cambridge, Gloucester, Fishguard, Swansea, Oxford, Harwich, Cardiff, Bristol, London, Exeter, Bournemouth, Southampton, Portsmouth, Brighton, Dover, Plymouth, Land's End.

Example detail from the table

Dover				523 / 842 / 9:10
Dundee			56 / 90 / 1:30	462 / 744 / 8:10
Edinburgh		450 / 724 / 8:00	518 / 834 / 9:10	248 / 399 / 4:40
Exeter	230 / 370 / 4:30	399 / 642 / 7:30	460 / 740 / 8:30	331 / 533 / 6:20
Fishguard	486 / 782 / 9:30	560 / 901 / 10:20	144 / 232 / 3:30	127 / 204 / 3:10	596 / 959 / 11:00
Fort William					

(Full national distance matrix follows in the original, listing mileage, kilometres and journey times between each pair of the towns shown.)

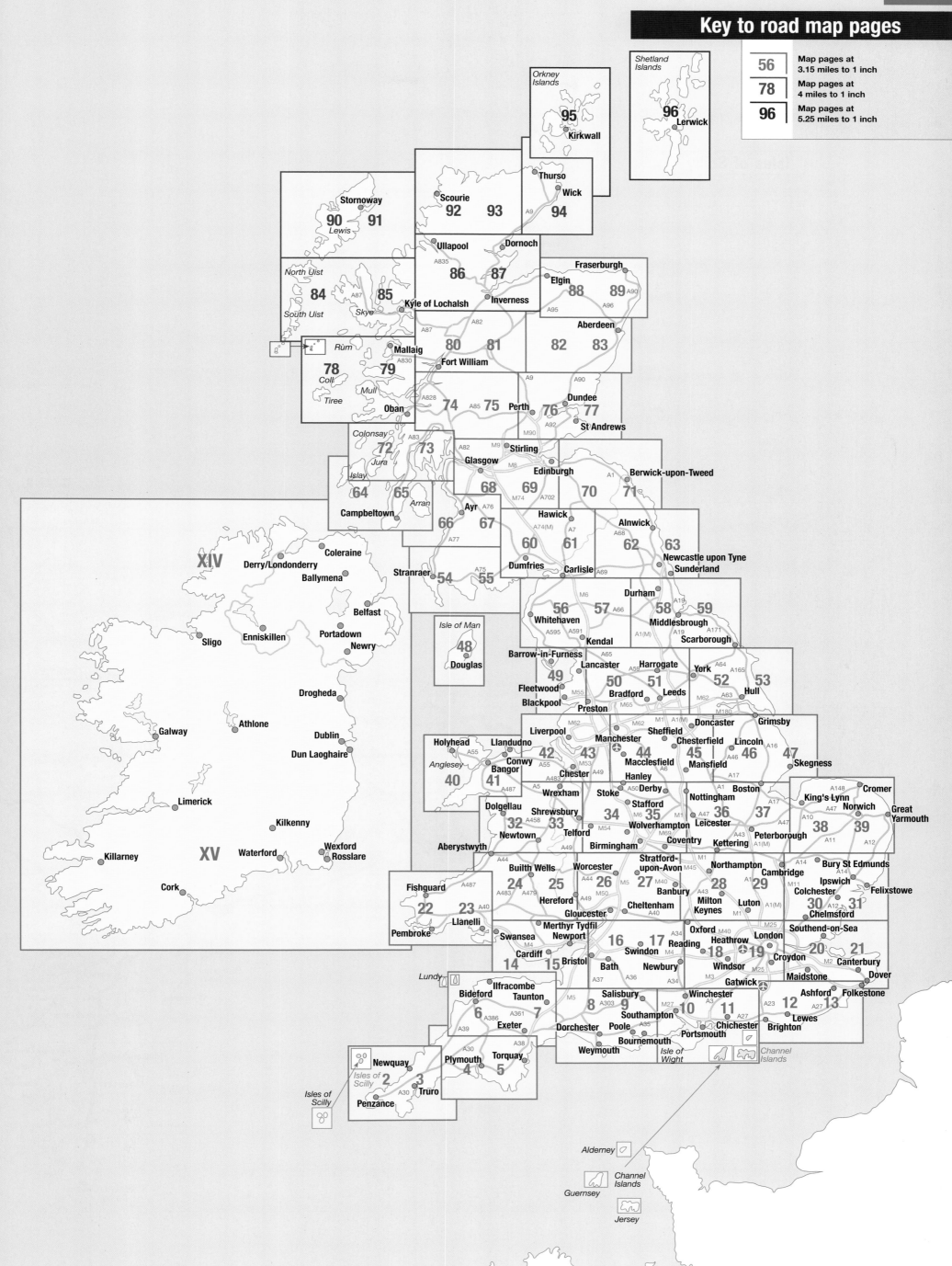

Key to road map pages

56	Map pages at 3.15 miles to 1 inch
78	Map pages at 4 miles to 1 inch
96	Map pages at 5.25 miles to 1 inch

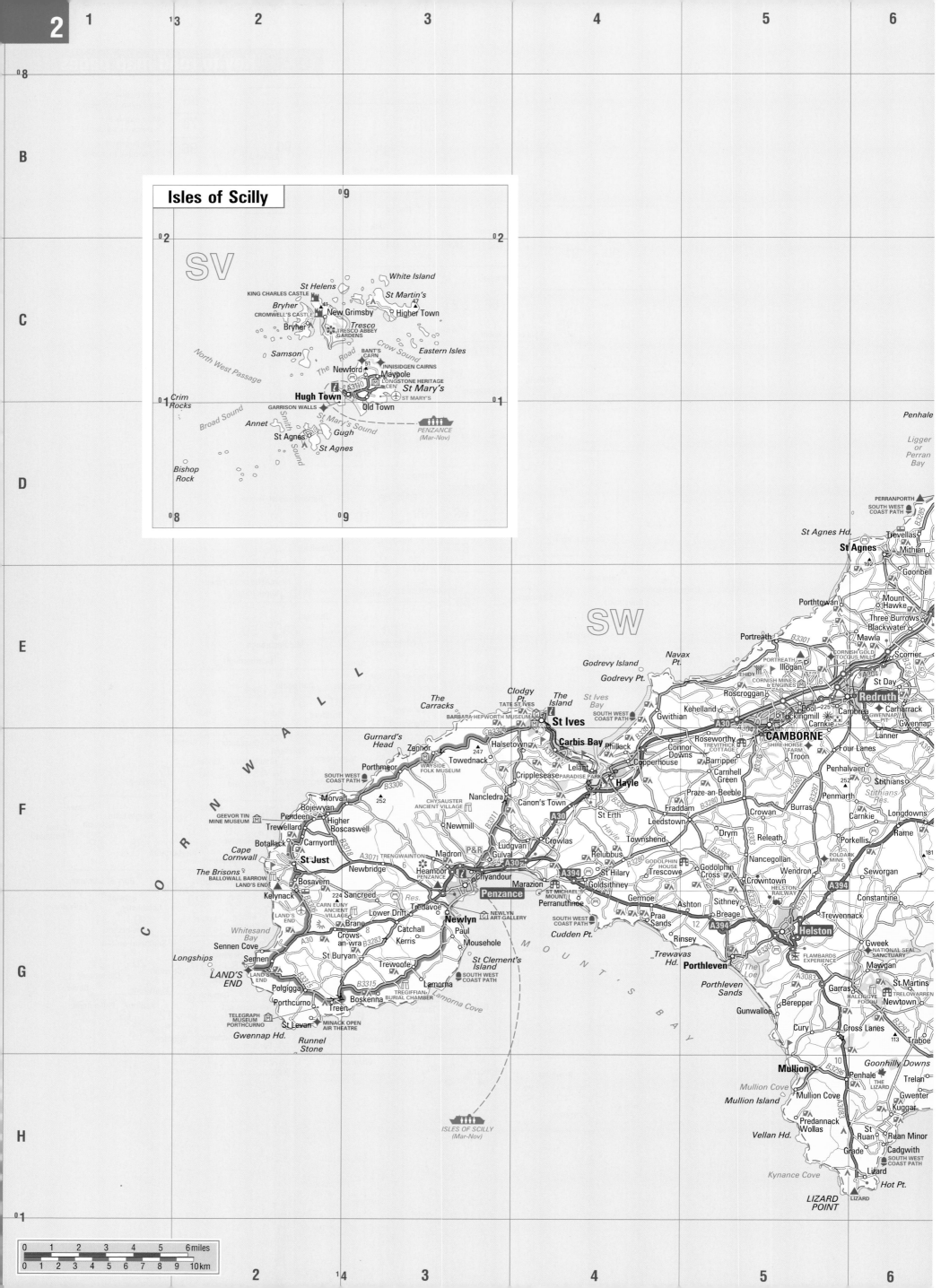

Isles of Scilly

White Island
St Helens
KING CHARLES CASTLE
St Martin's
Bryher
CROMWELL'S CASTLE
New Grimsby
Higher Town
Bryher
Tresco
TRESCO ABBEY GARDENS
Samson
Eastern Isles
Crow Sound
North West Passage
BANT'S CARN
INNISIDGEN CAIRNS
Newford
Maypole
The Road
LONGSTONE HERITAGE CEN
St Mary's
Hugh Town
ST MARY'S
Crim Rocks
GARRISON WALLS
Old Town
Broad Sound
Annet
Gugh
St Mary's Sound
PENZANCE (Mar-Nov)
St Agnes
Smith Sound
St Agnes
Bishop Rock

SV

SW

CORNWALL

Penhale
Ligger or Perran Bay
PERRANPORTH
SOUTH WEST COAST PATH
St Agnes Hd.
Trevellas
St Agnes
Mithian
Goonbell
Porthtowan
Mount Hawke
Three Burrows
Blackwater
Mawla
Portreath
PORTREATH
CORNISH GOLD TOLGUS MILL
Scorrier
Godrevy Island
Navax Pt.
TEHIDY
Illogan
CORNISH MINES & ENGINES
St Day
Godrevy Pt.
Roscroggan
Bool 225
Tuckingmill
Carharrack
Redruth
Clodgy Pt.
The Island
St Ives Bay
SOUTH WEST COAST PATH
Gwithian
Kehelland
Crofthandy
Gwennap
The Carracks
TATE ST IVES
BARBARA HEPWORTH MUSEUM
St Ives
Connor Downs
TREVITHICK COTTAGE
CAMBORNE
SHIRE-HORSE FARM
Carnkie
Lanner
Gurnard's Head
Halsetown
Carbis Bay
Philack
Copperhouse
Roseworthy
Barripper
Four Lanes
Zennor
Towednack
Lelant
Hayle
Praze-an-Beeble
Troon
Penhalvaen
WAYSIDE FOLK MUSEUM
247
Cripplesease
PARADISE PARK
Carnhell Green
Stithians
Porthmeor
SOUTH WEST COAST PATH
Nancledra
Canon's Town
St Erth
Fraddam
Leedstown
Crowan
Releath
Porkellis
Stithians Res.
Morvah
B3306
252
Newmill
Relubbus
Drym
Townshend
Carnkie
Rame
Bojewyan
GEEVOR TIN MINE MUSEUM
Higher Boscaswell
CHYSAUSTER ANCIENT VILLAGE
Ludgvan
Gulval
Crowlas
GODOLPHIN HOUSE
Godolphin Cross
Nancegollan
Longdowns
Pendeen
Trewellard
Madron
Townsend
St Hilary
Trescowe
Wendron
Sewogan
Carnyorth
TRENGWAINTON
Heamoor
P&R
Crowntown
HELSTON RAILWAY
Botallack
Cape Cornwall
St Just
Newbridge
PENZANCE
Chyandour
Marazion
ST MICHAEL'S MOUNT
Goldsithney
Germoe
Ashton
Sithney
The Brisons
BALLOWALL BARROW
LAND'S END
Bosavern
CARN EUNY ANCIENT VILLAGE
Sancreed
Newlyn
NEWLYN ART-GALLERY
Perranuthnoe
Praa Sands
Rinsey
Helston
Kelynack
224
Tredavoe
SOUTH WEST COAST PATH
Cudden Pt.
Breage
Trewennack
Lower Drift
Catchall
Paul
Mousehole
Gweek
NATIONAL SEAL SANCTUARY
Crows-an-wra
Brane
Kerris
St Clement's Island
Trewavas Hd.
Porthleven
The Loe
FLAMBARDS EXPERIENCE
Mawgan
Whitesand Bay
Sennen Cove
St Buryan
Trewoofe
Lamorna
Porthleven Sands
Garras
St Martins
Longships
Sennen
Boskenna
SOUTH WEST COAST PATH
Gunwalloe
MALLIGGYE FOGOU
Newtown
LAND'S END
B3315
TREGIFFIAN BURIAL CHAMBER
Lamorna Cove
Berepper
Cross Lanes
Traboe
Polgigga
Porthcurno
Treen
Cury
113
TELEGRAPH MUSEUM PORTHCURNO
MINACK OPEN AIR THEATRE
Goonhilly Downs
St Levan
Mullion
Penhale
Trelan
Gwennap Hd.
Runnel Stone
Mullion Cove
THE LIZARD
Gwenter
Mullion Island
Mullion Cove
Predannack Wollas
Kuggar
Vellan Hd.
St Ruan
Ruan Minor
Cadgwith
Grade
SOUTH WEST COAST PATH
Kynance Cove
Lizard
Hot Pt.
LIZARD POINT
LIZARD

MOUNT'S BAY

ISLES OF SCILLY (Mar-Nov)

0 1 2 3 4 5 6 miles
0 1 2 3 4 5 6 7 8 9 10km

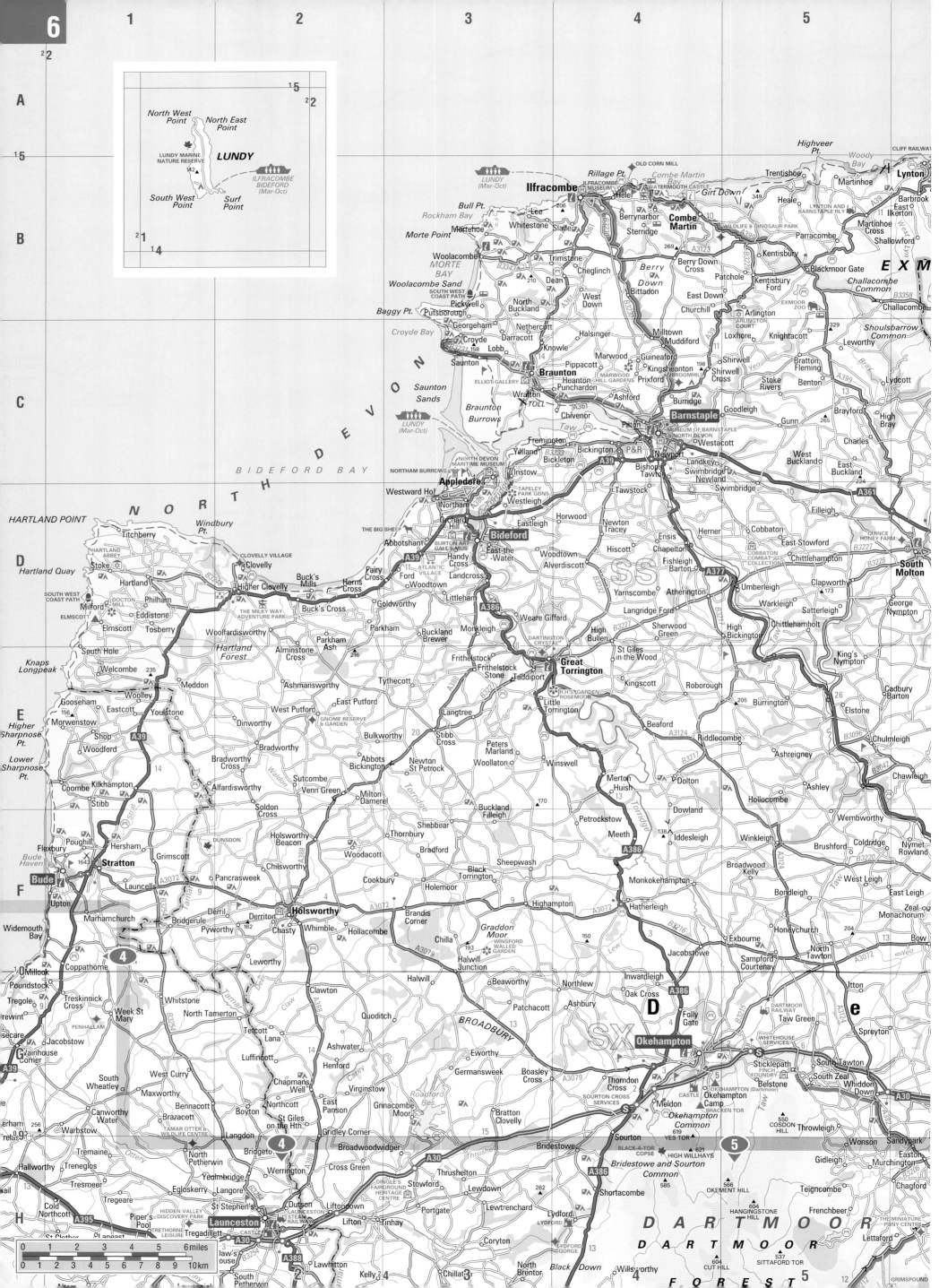

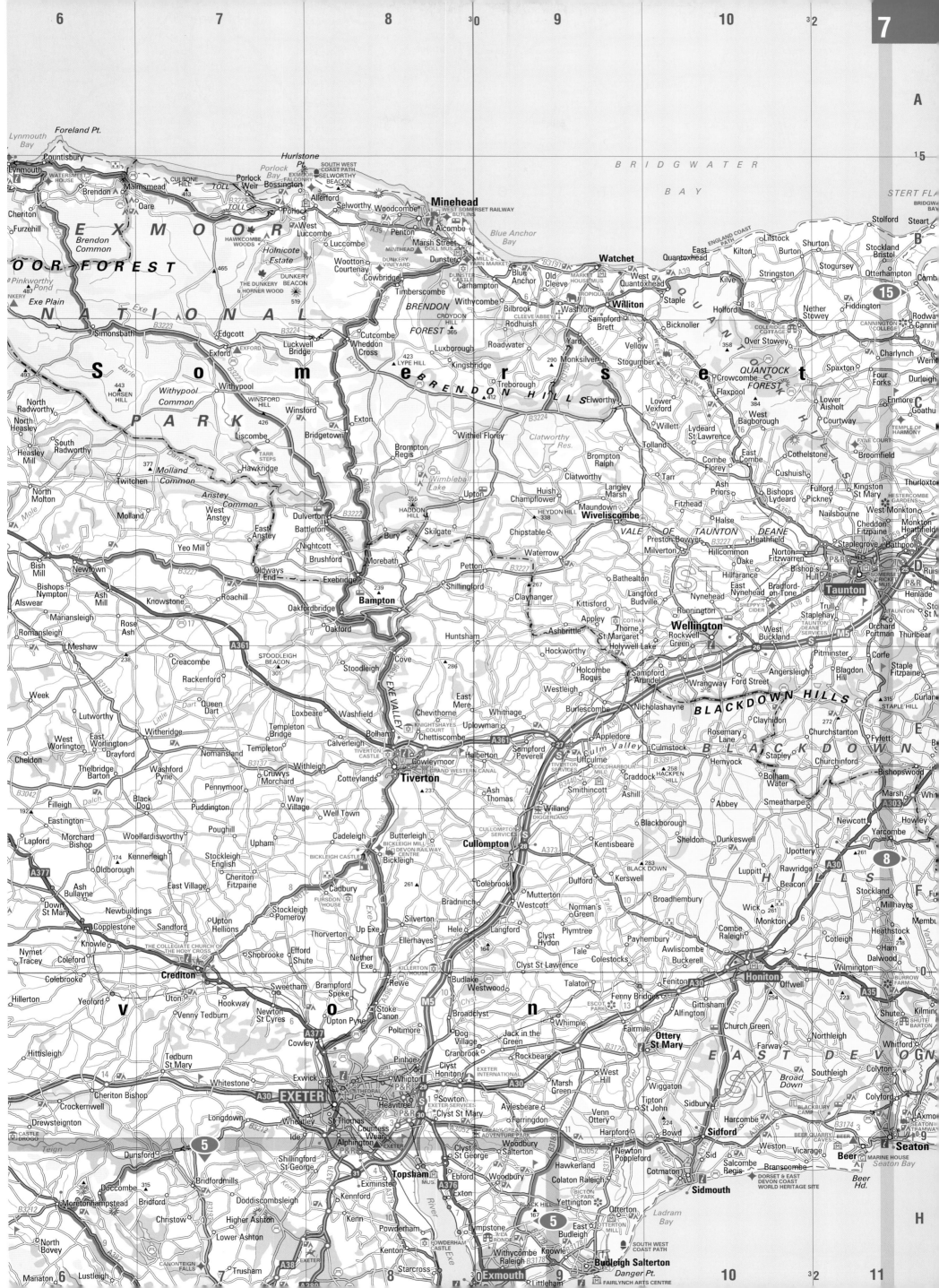

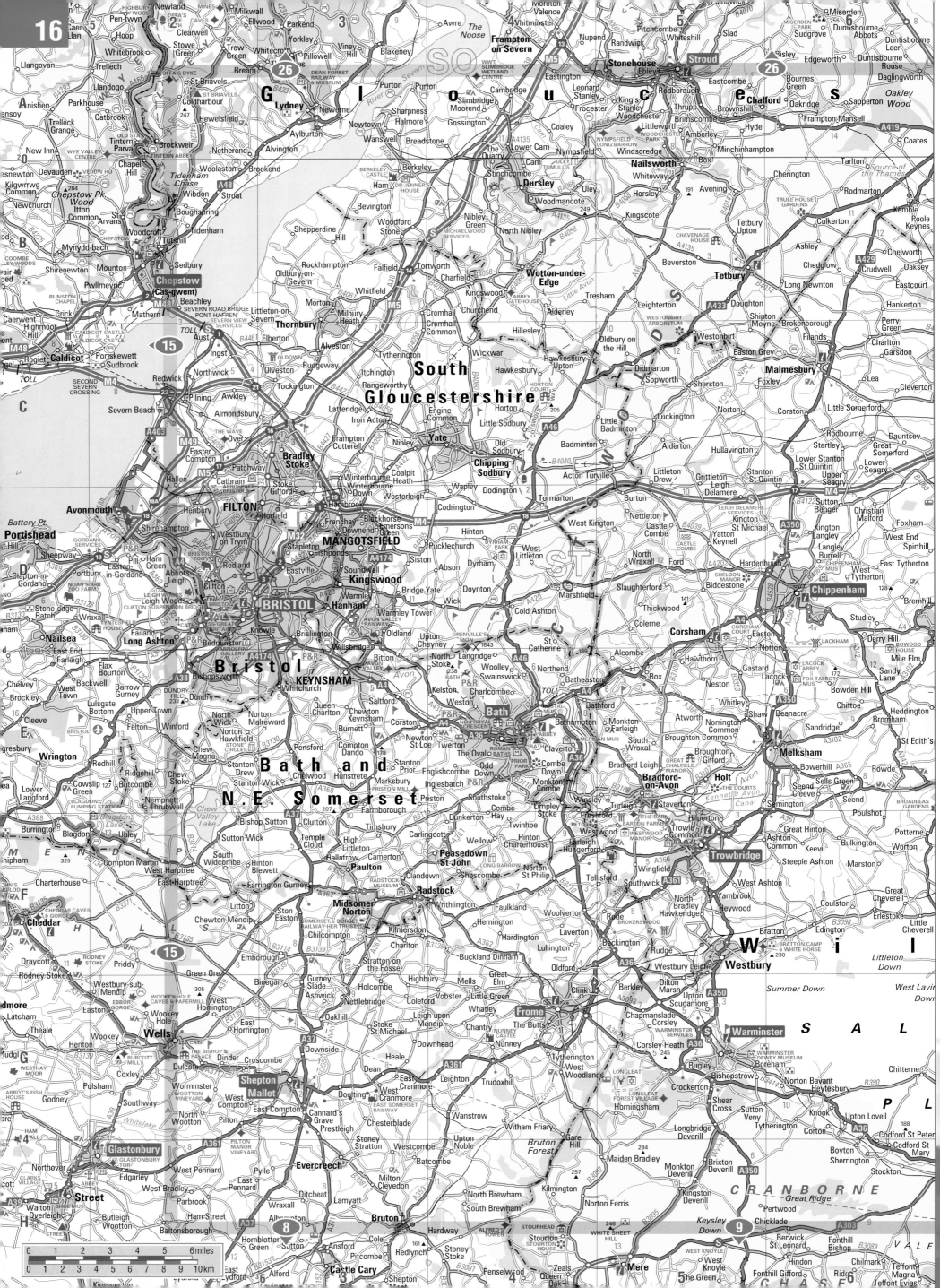

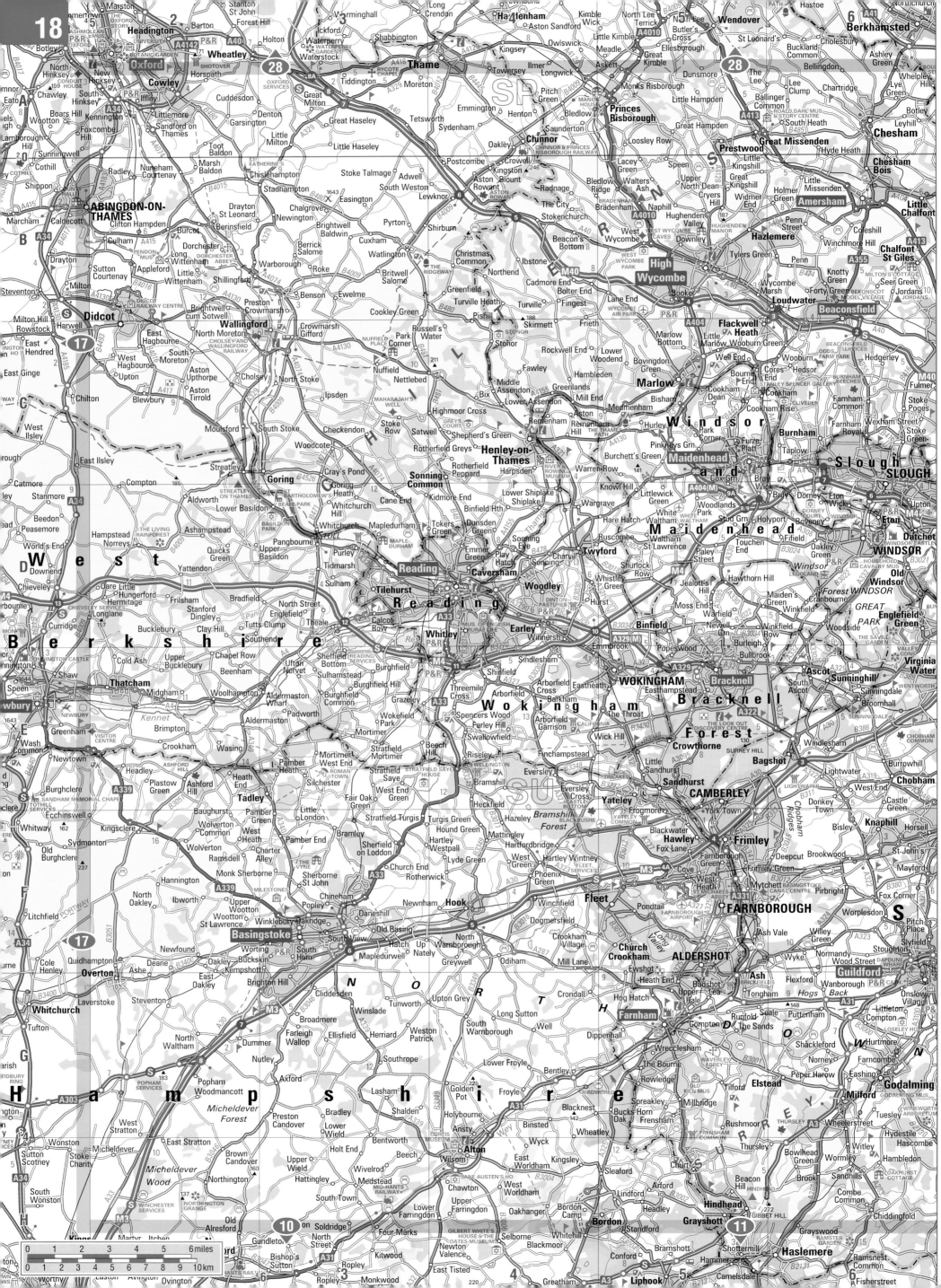

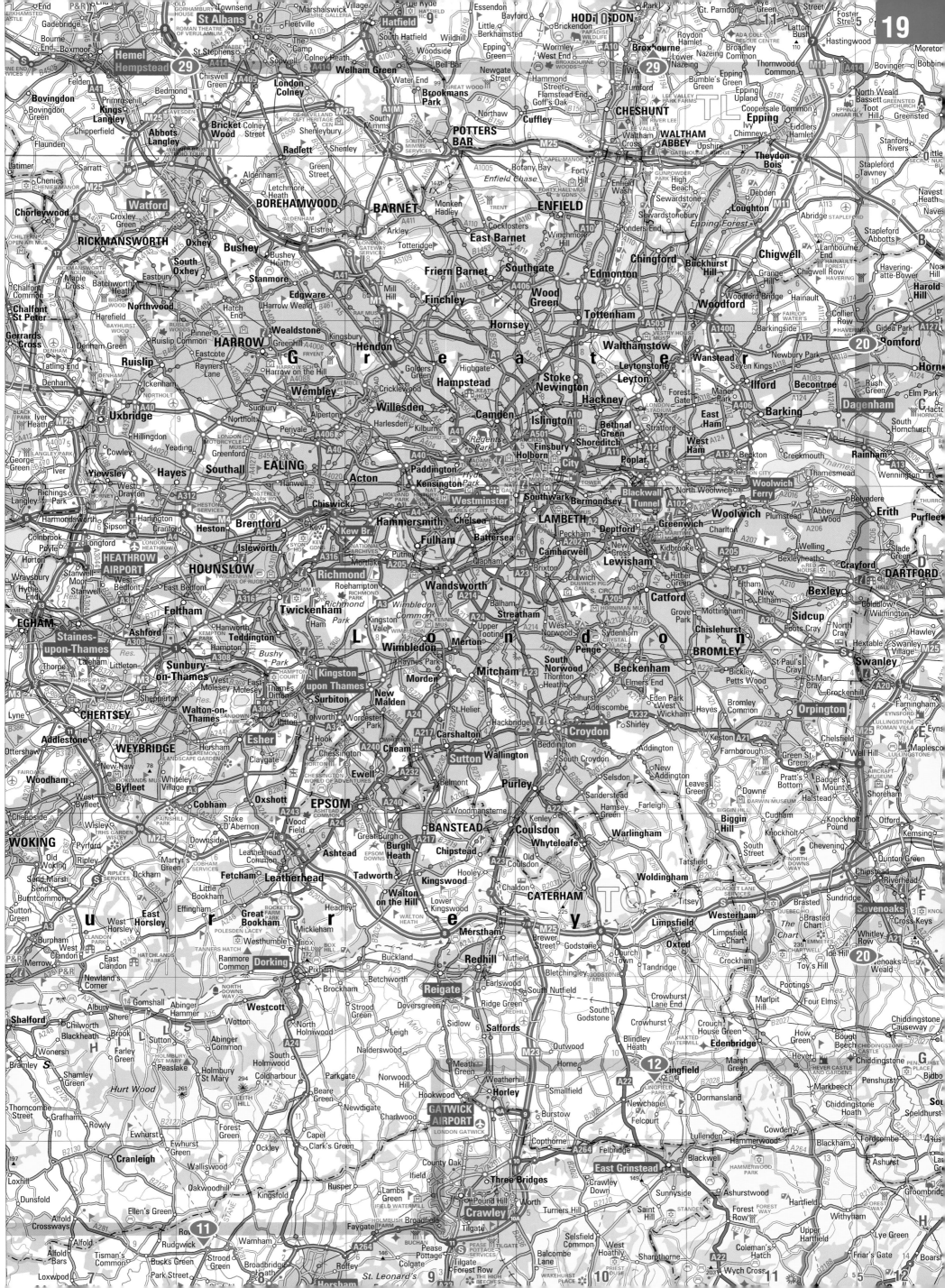

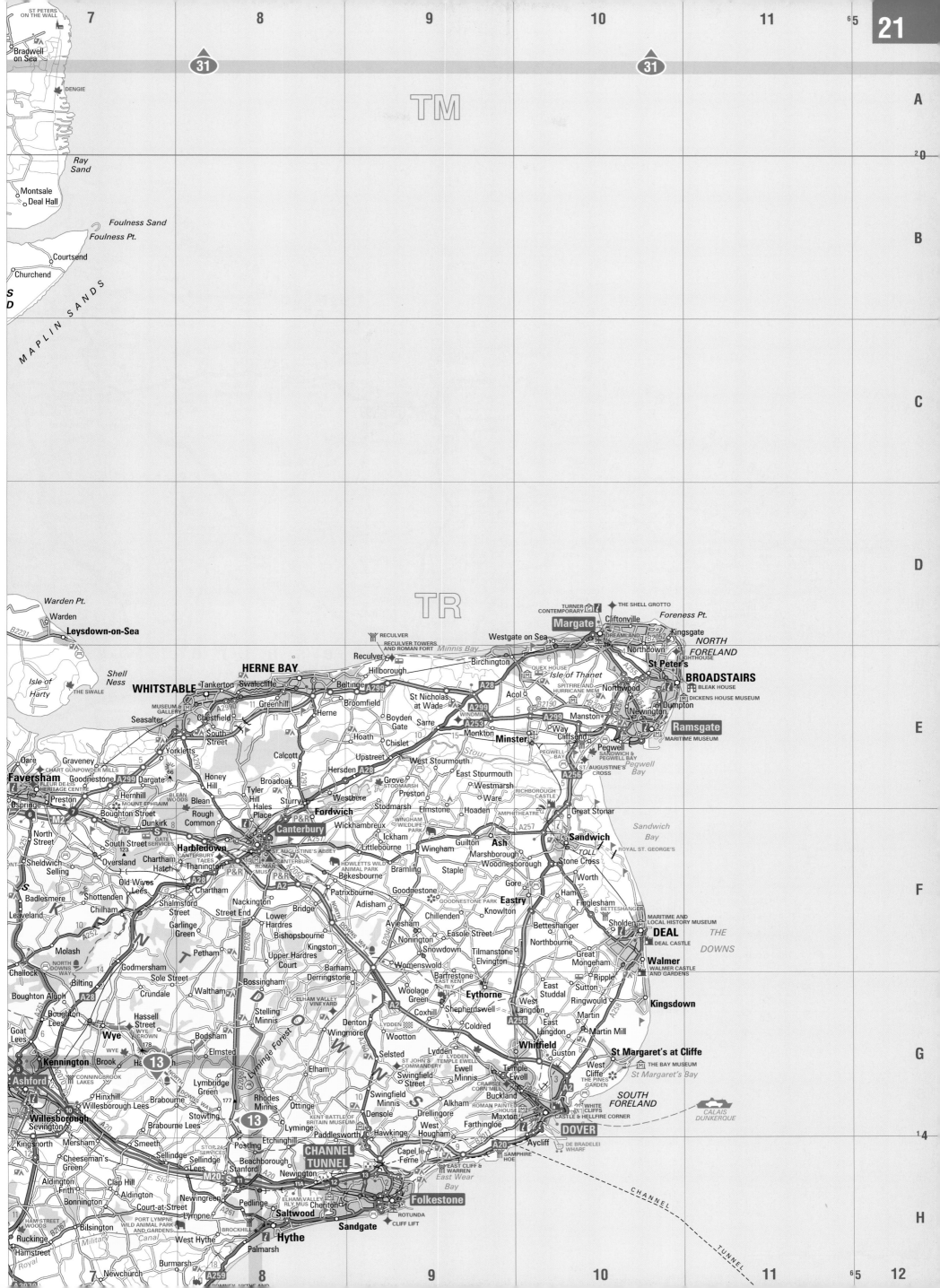

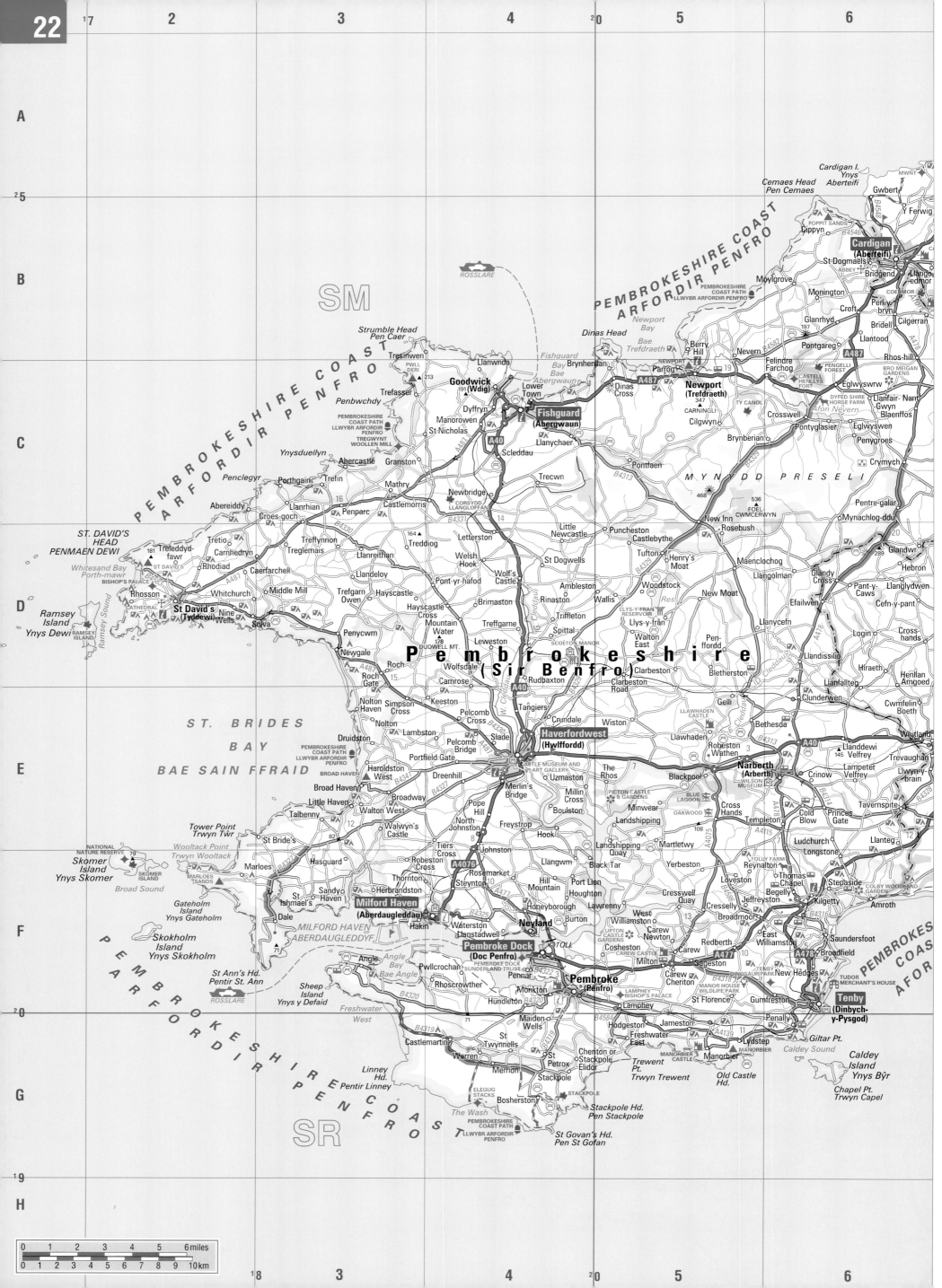

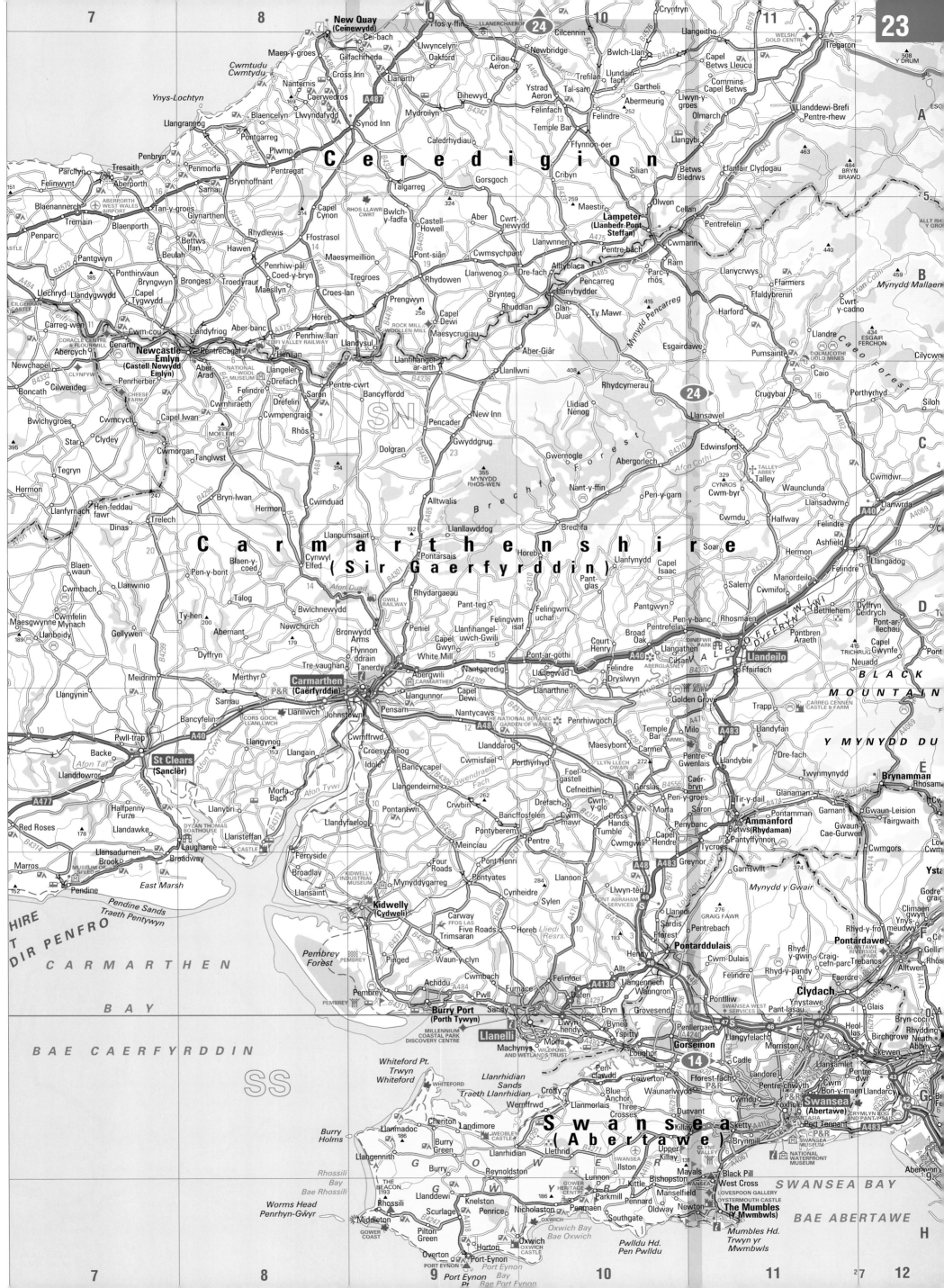

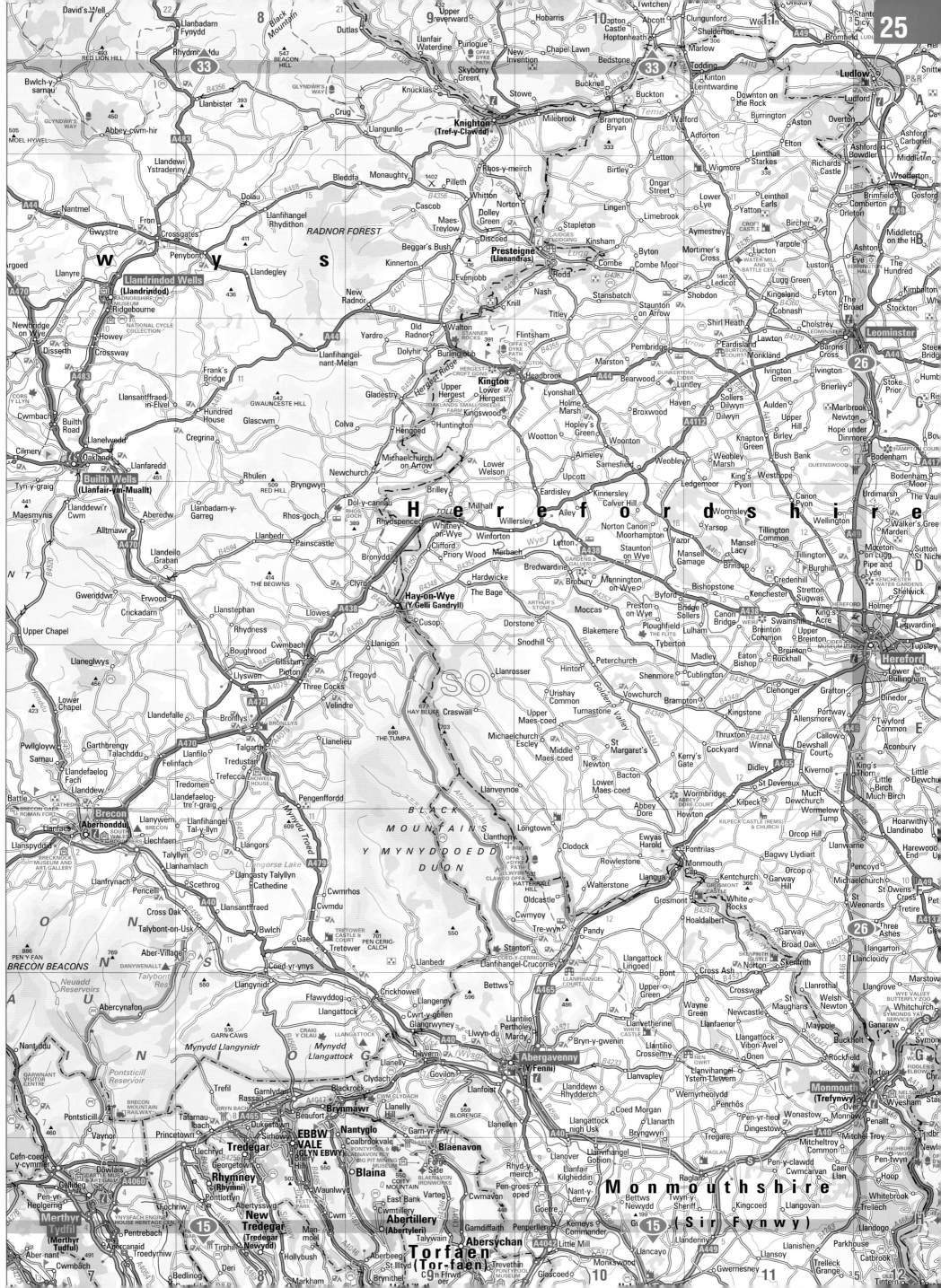

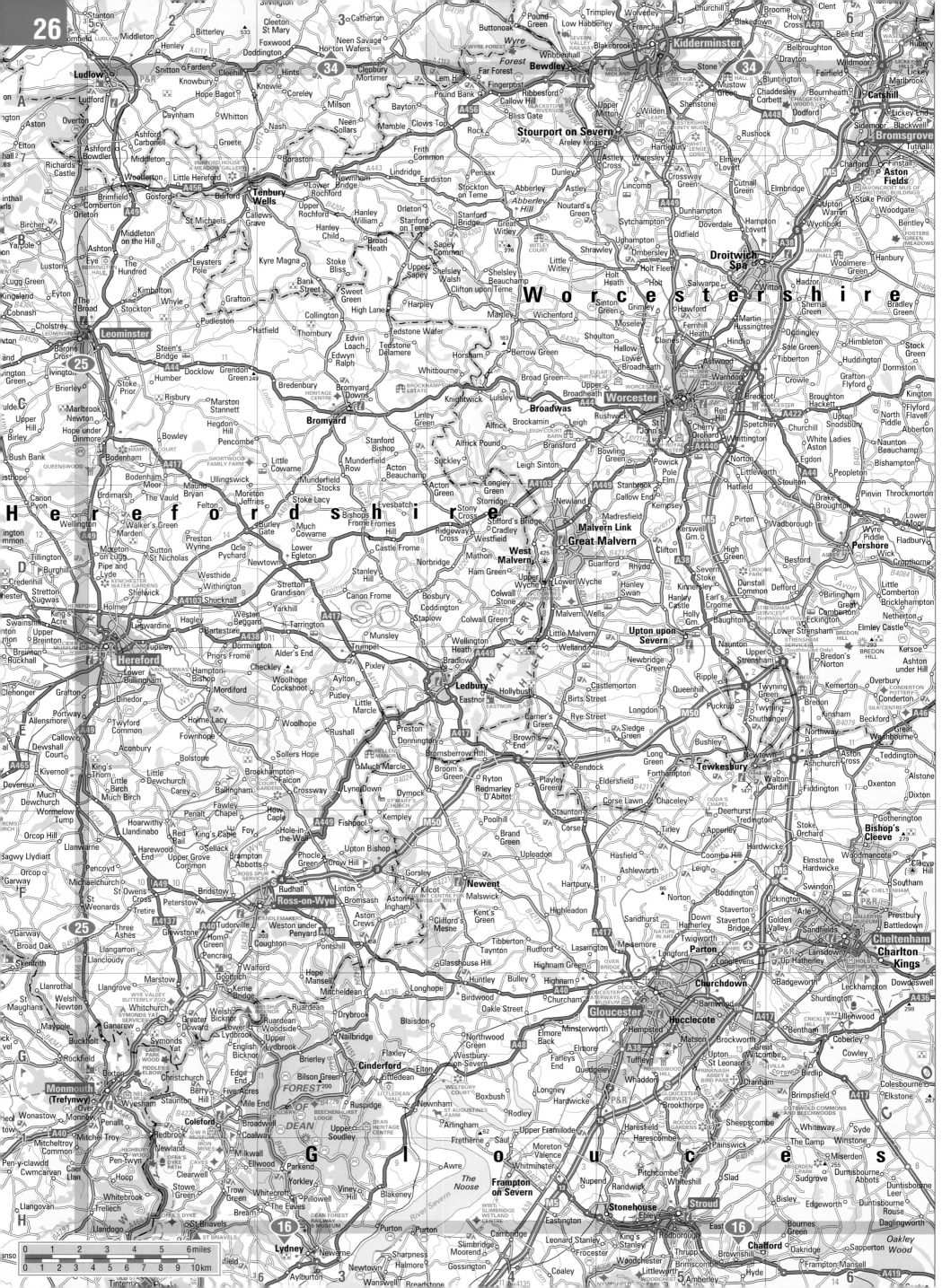

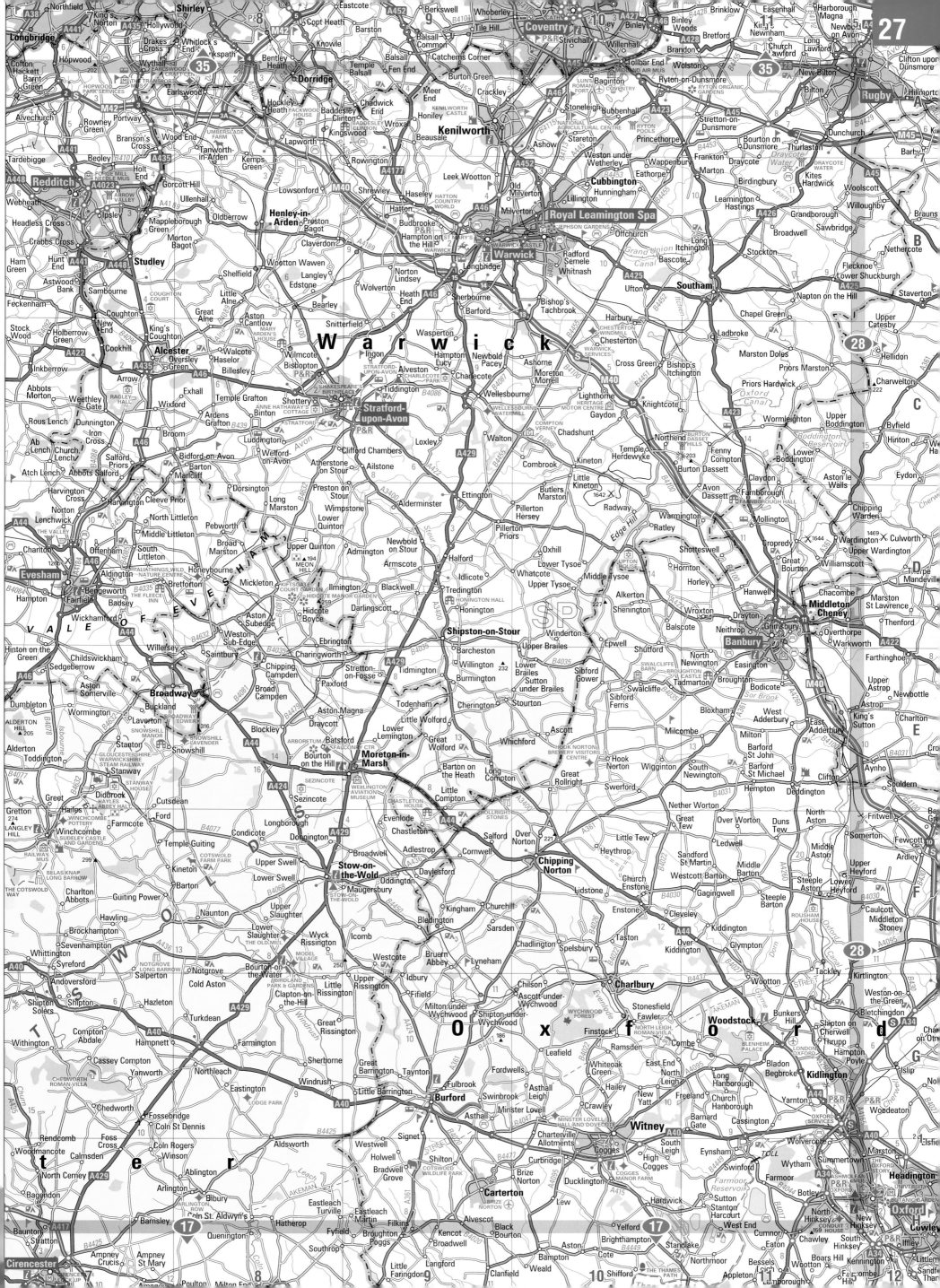

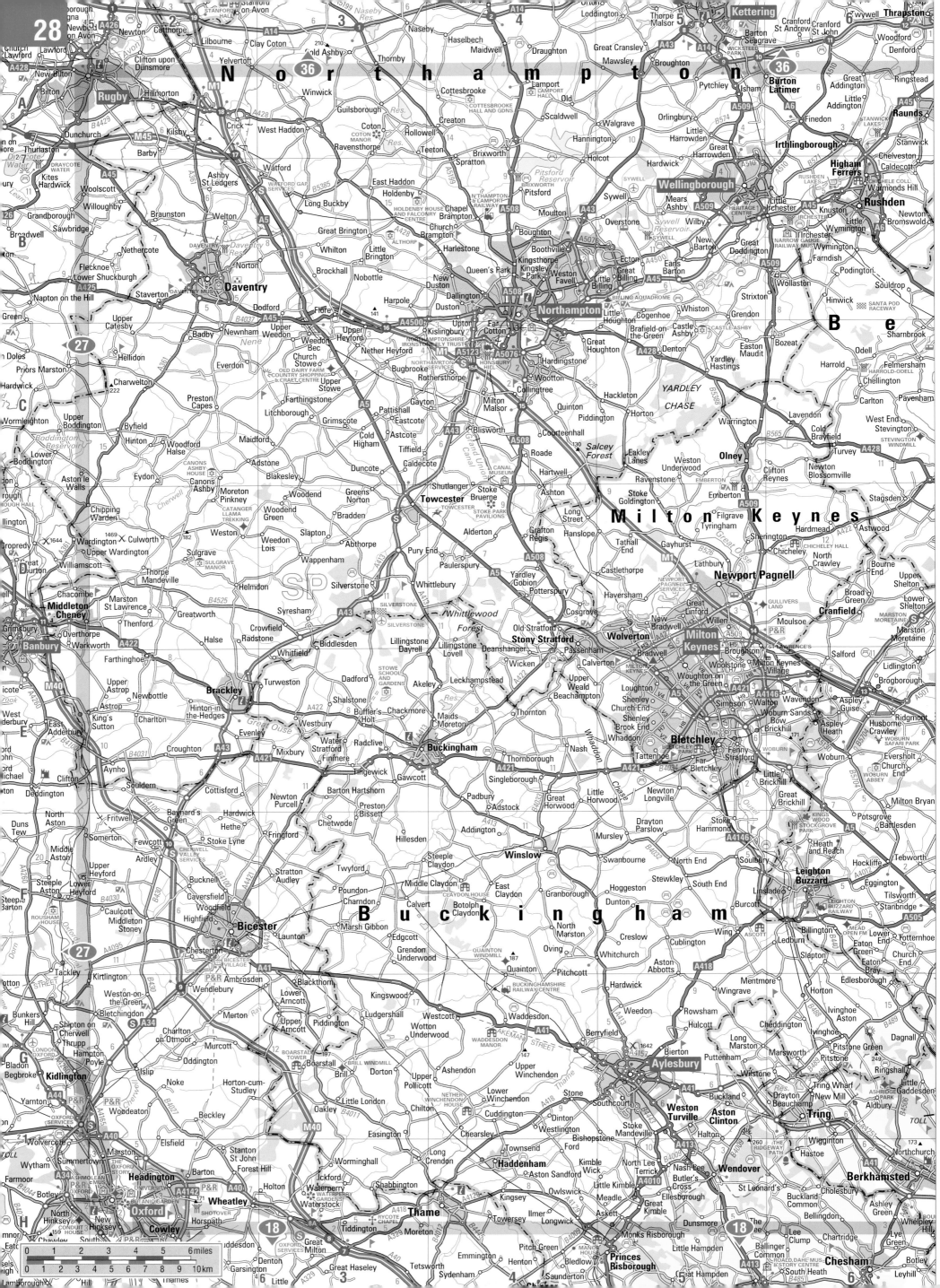

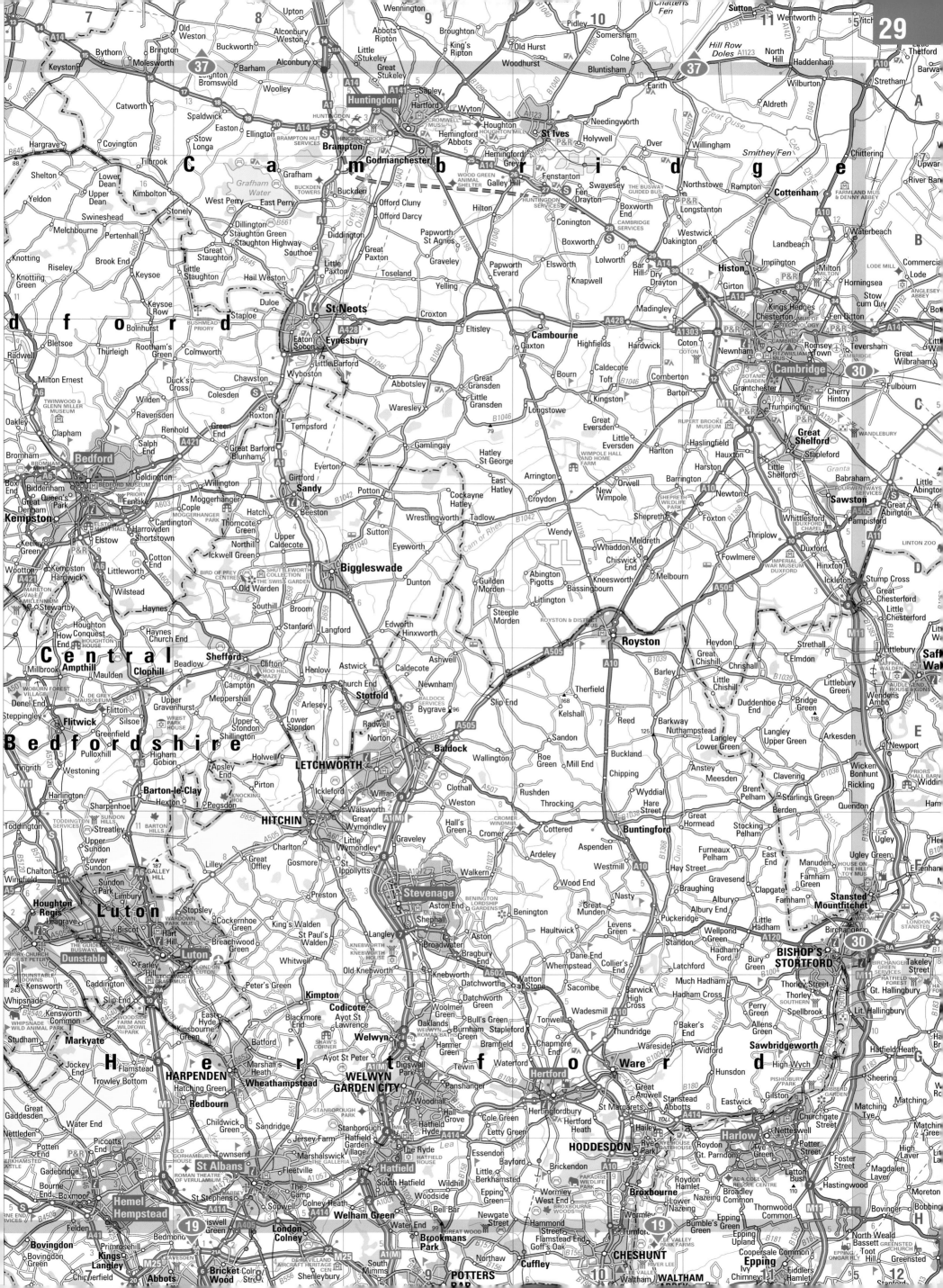

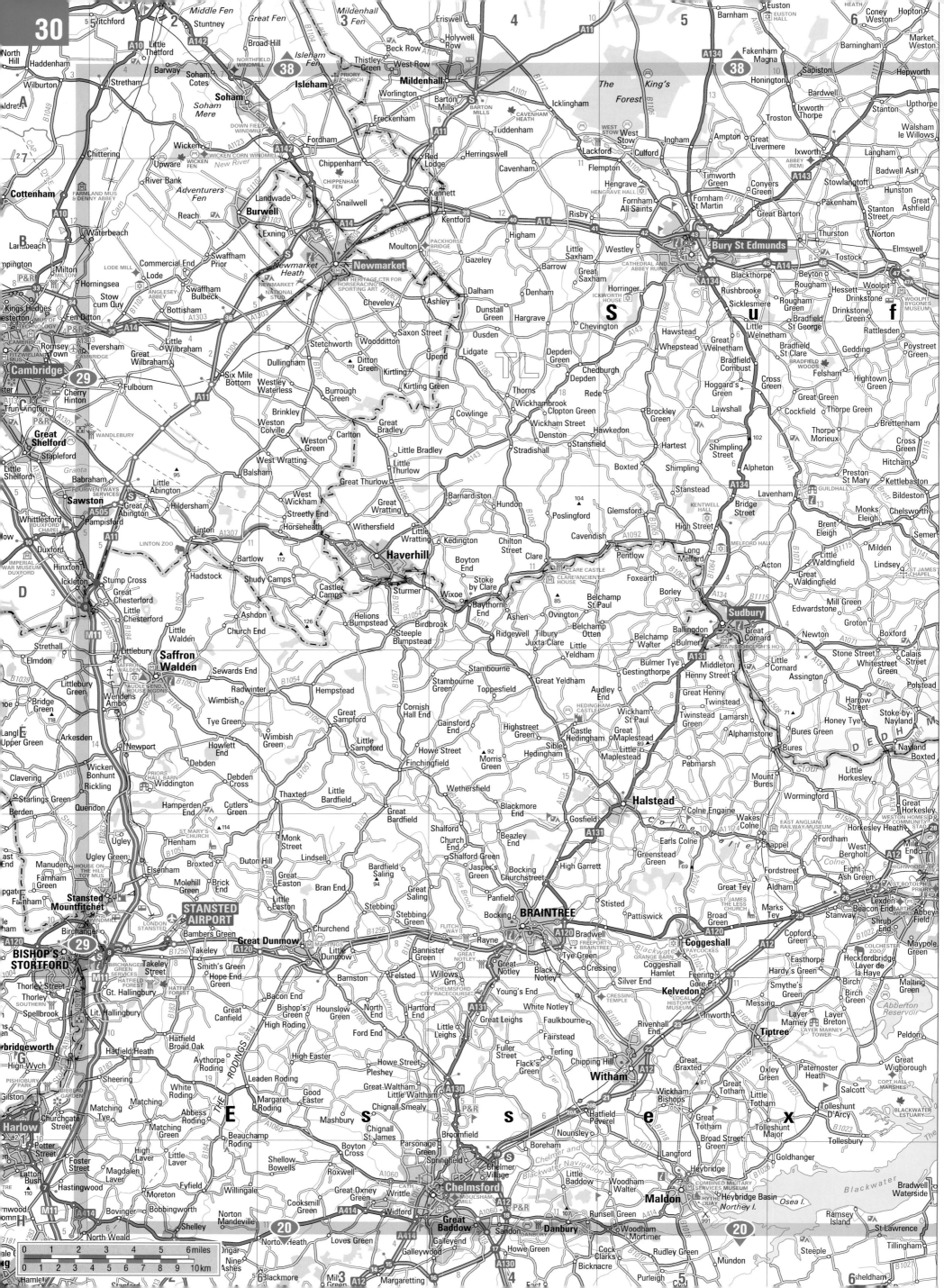

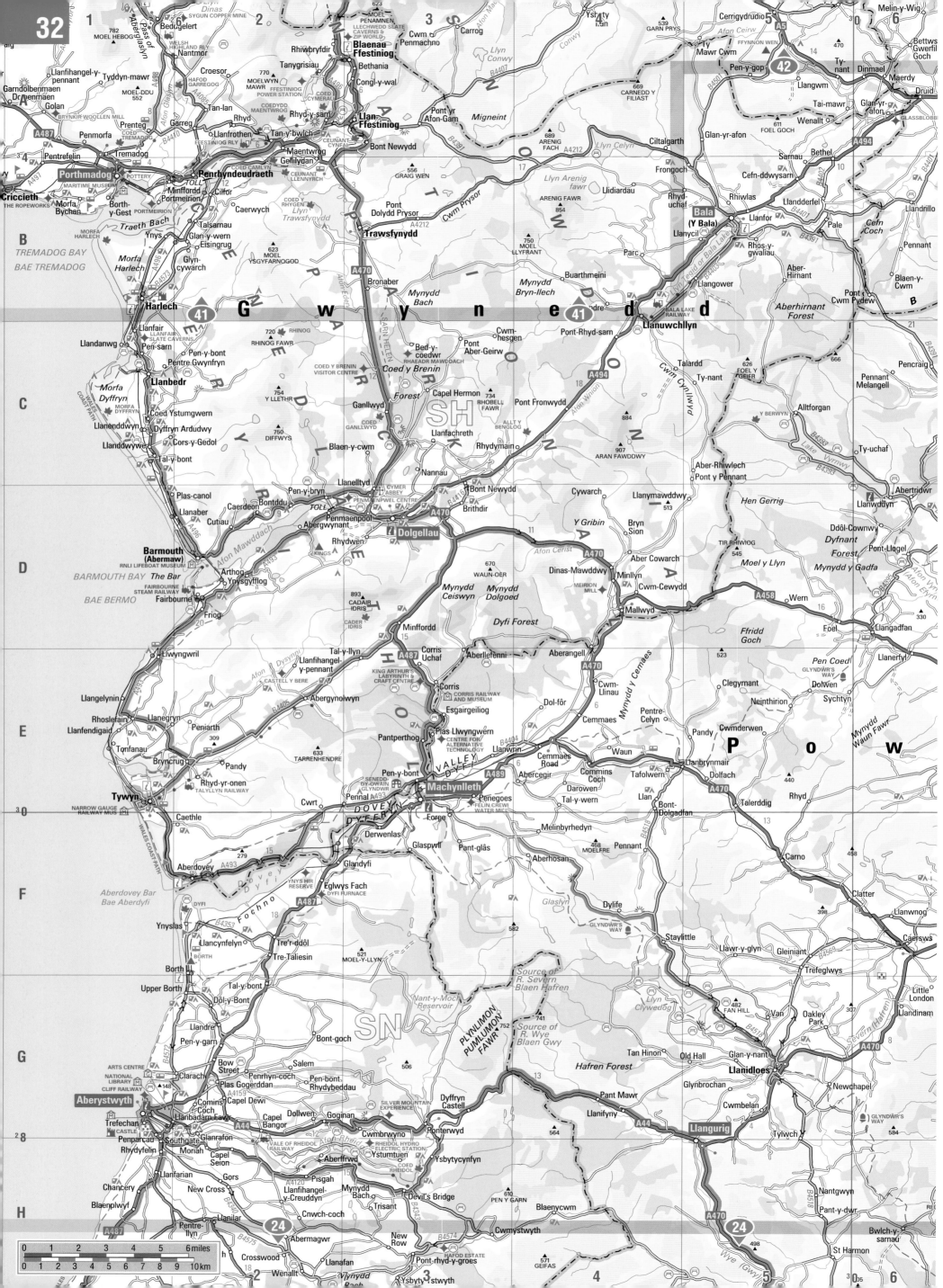

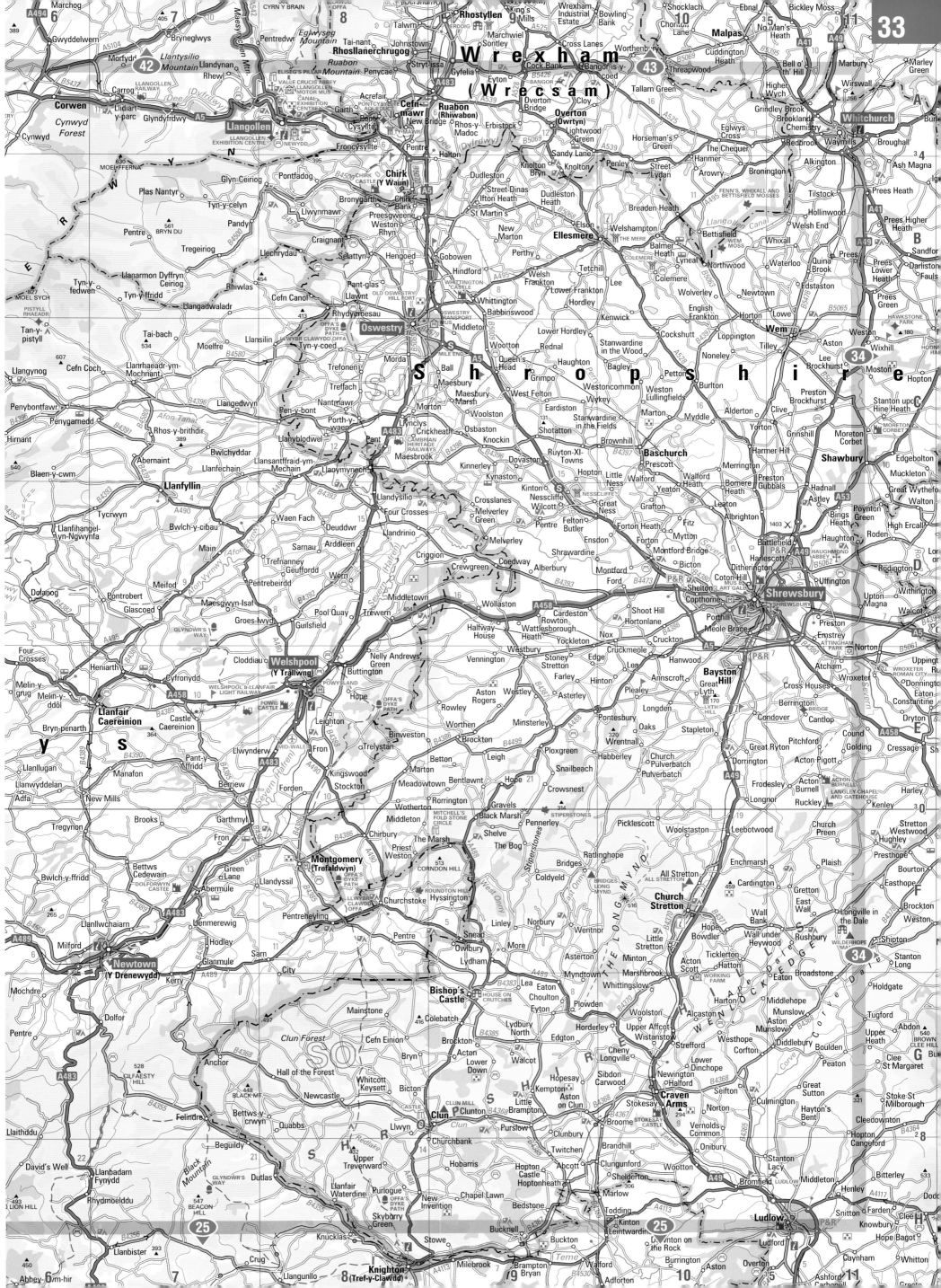

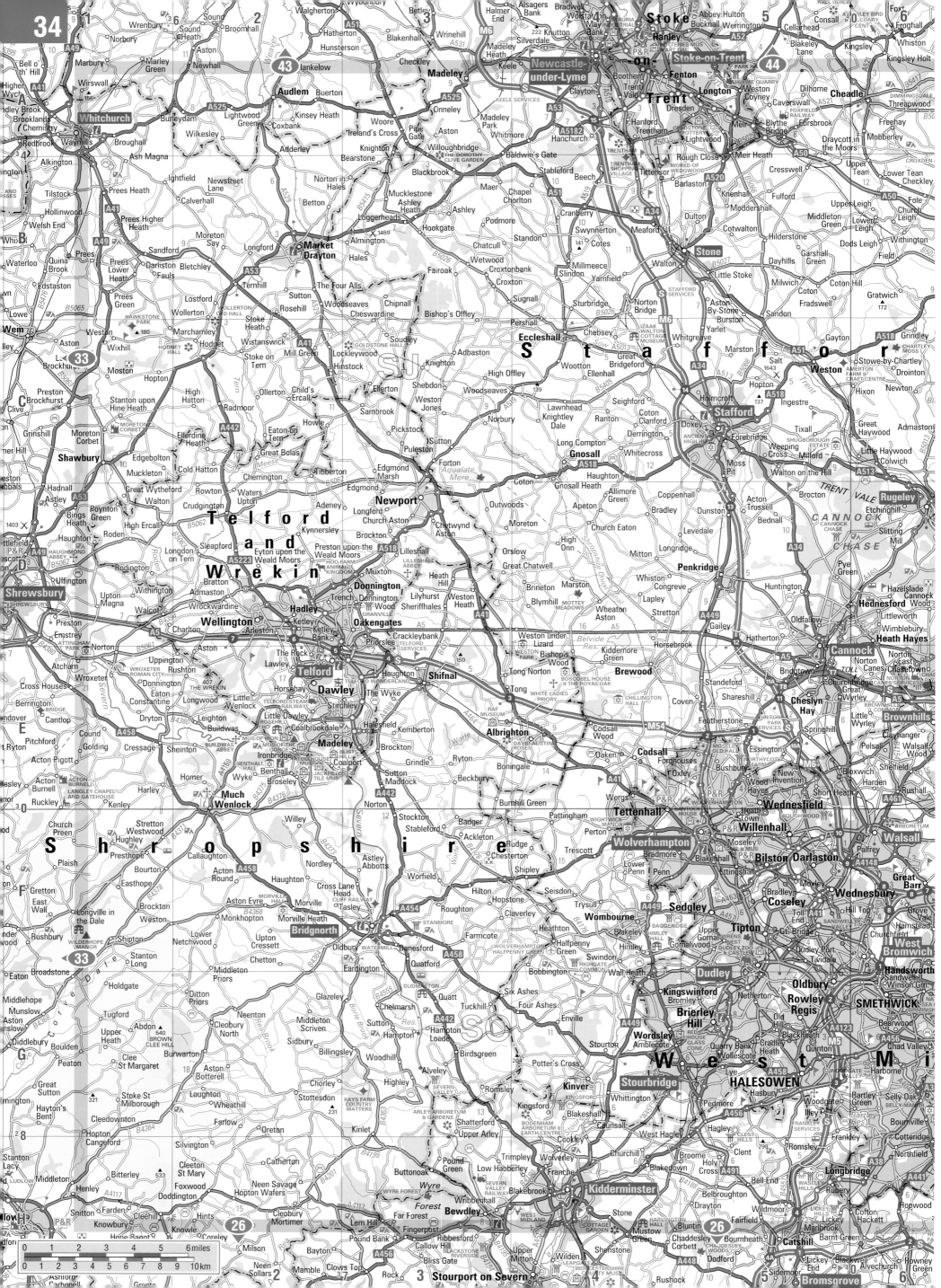

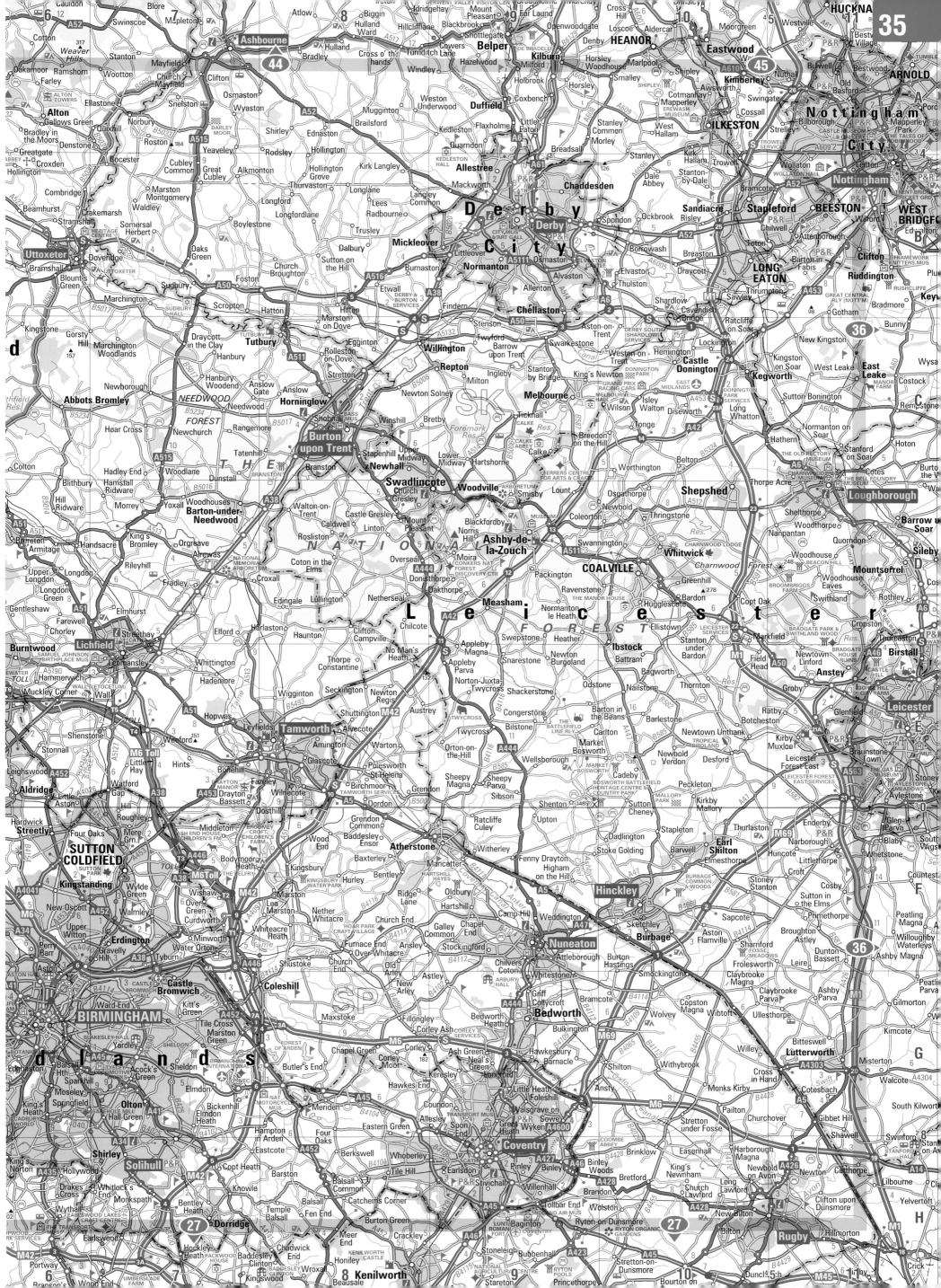

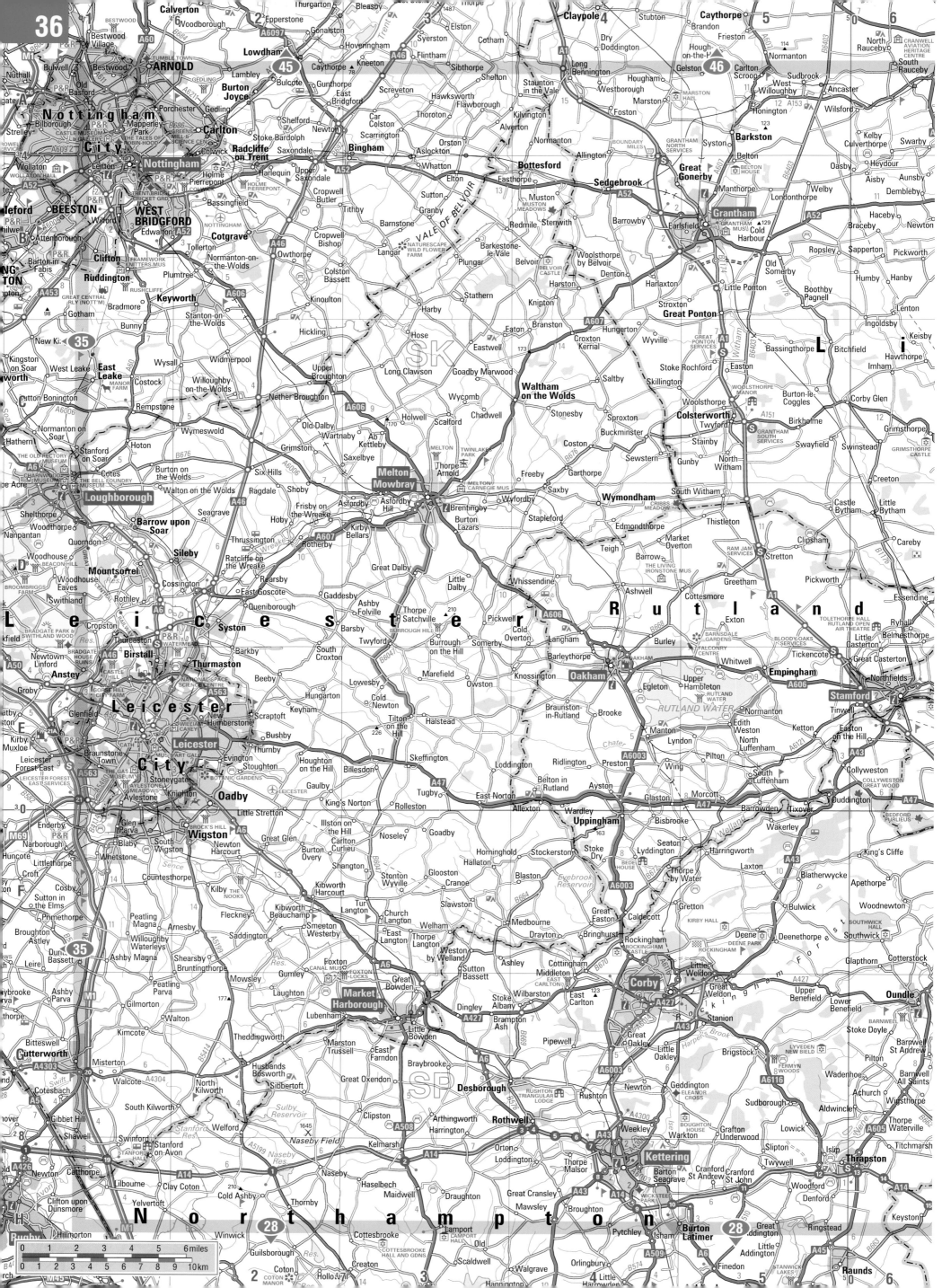

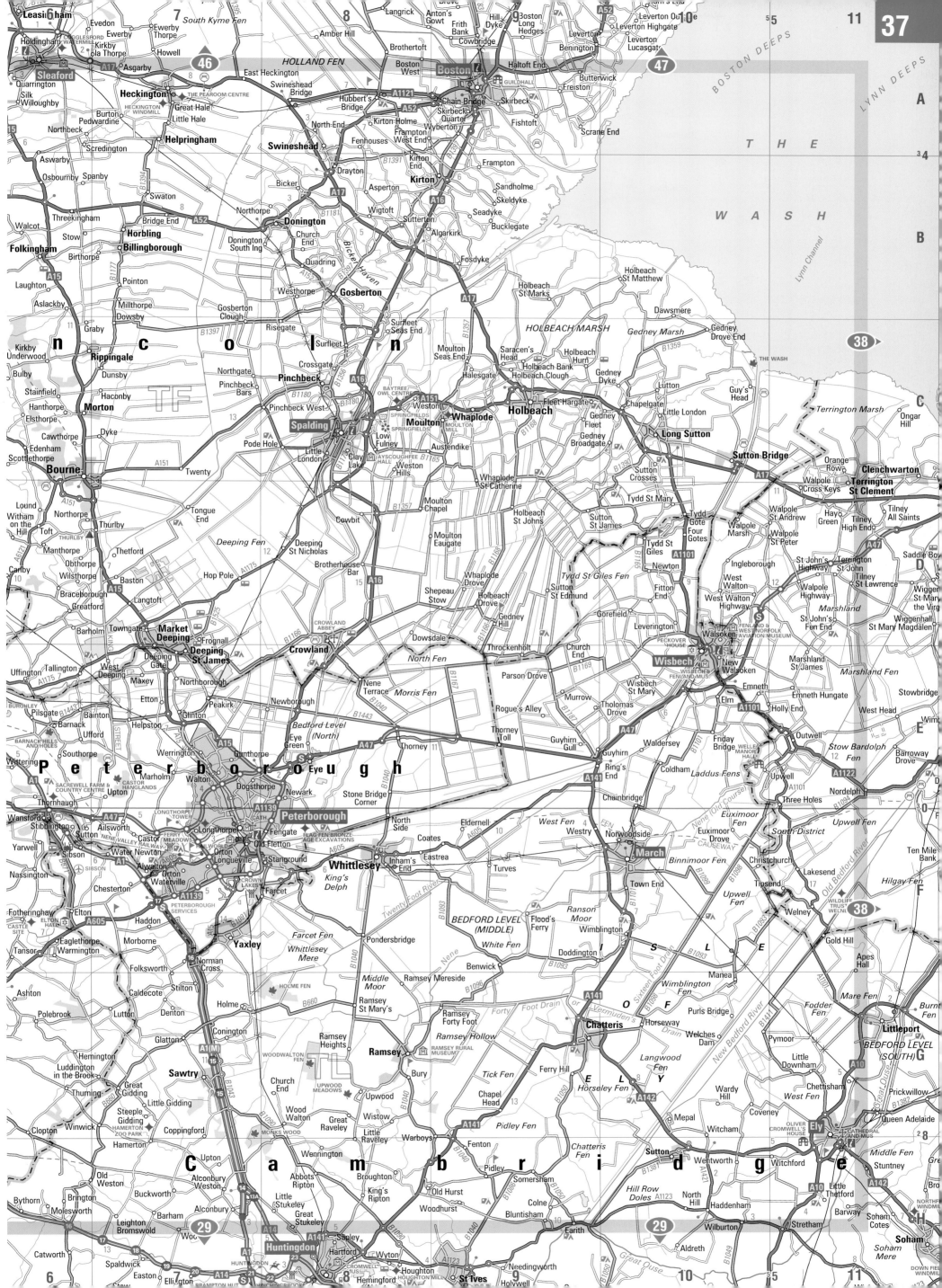

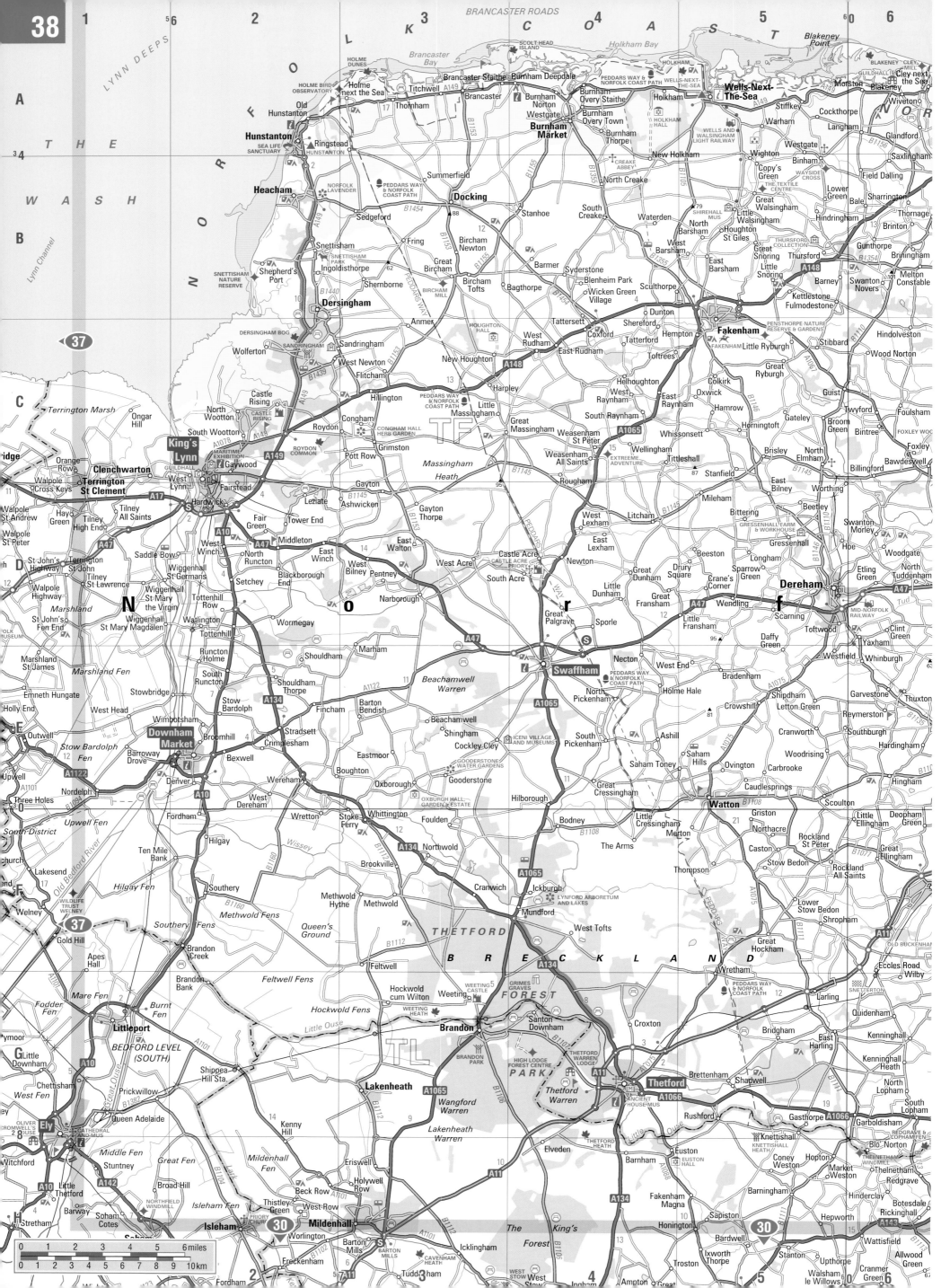

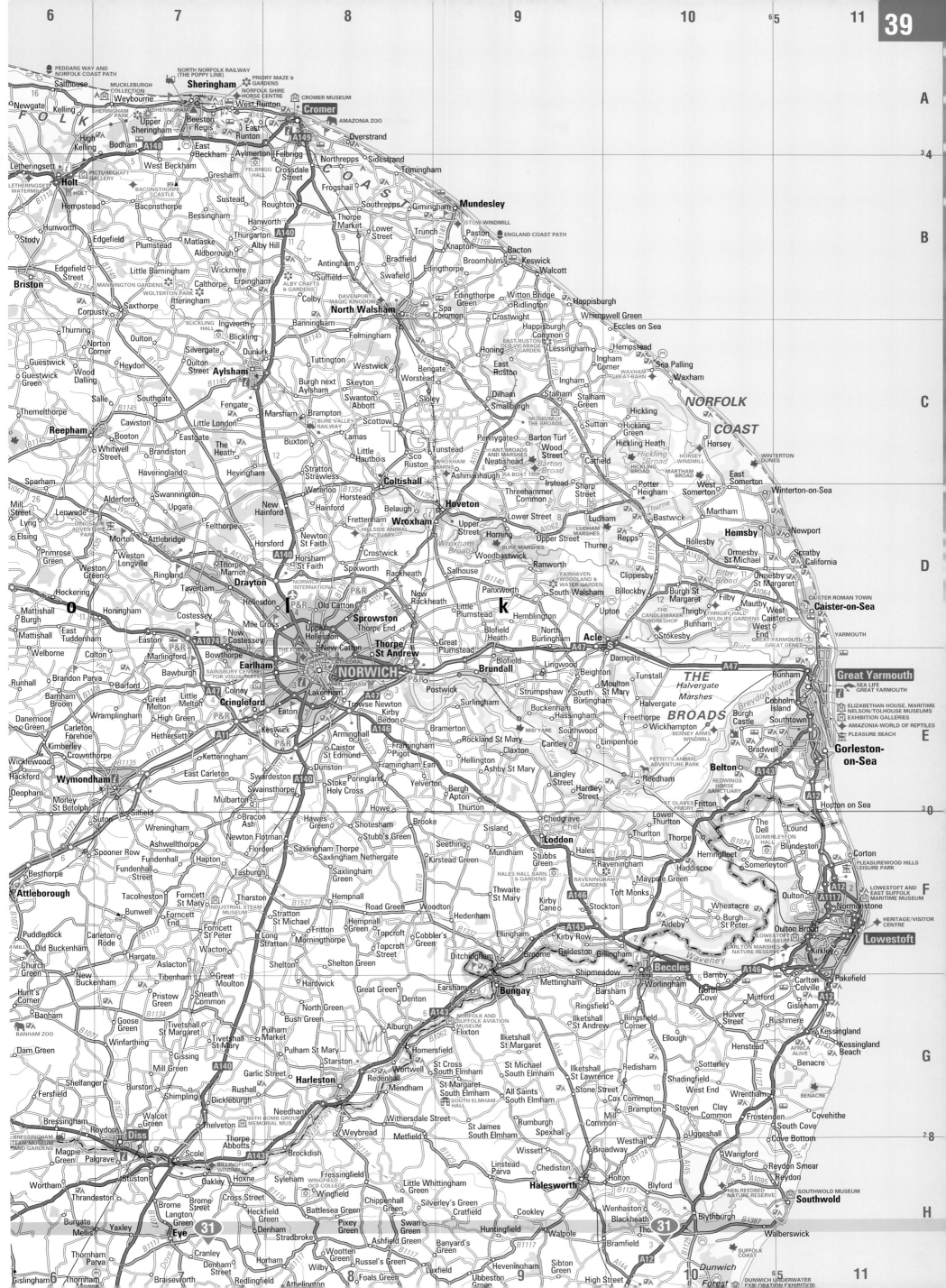

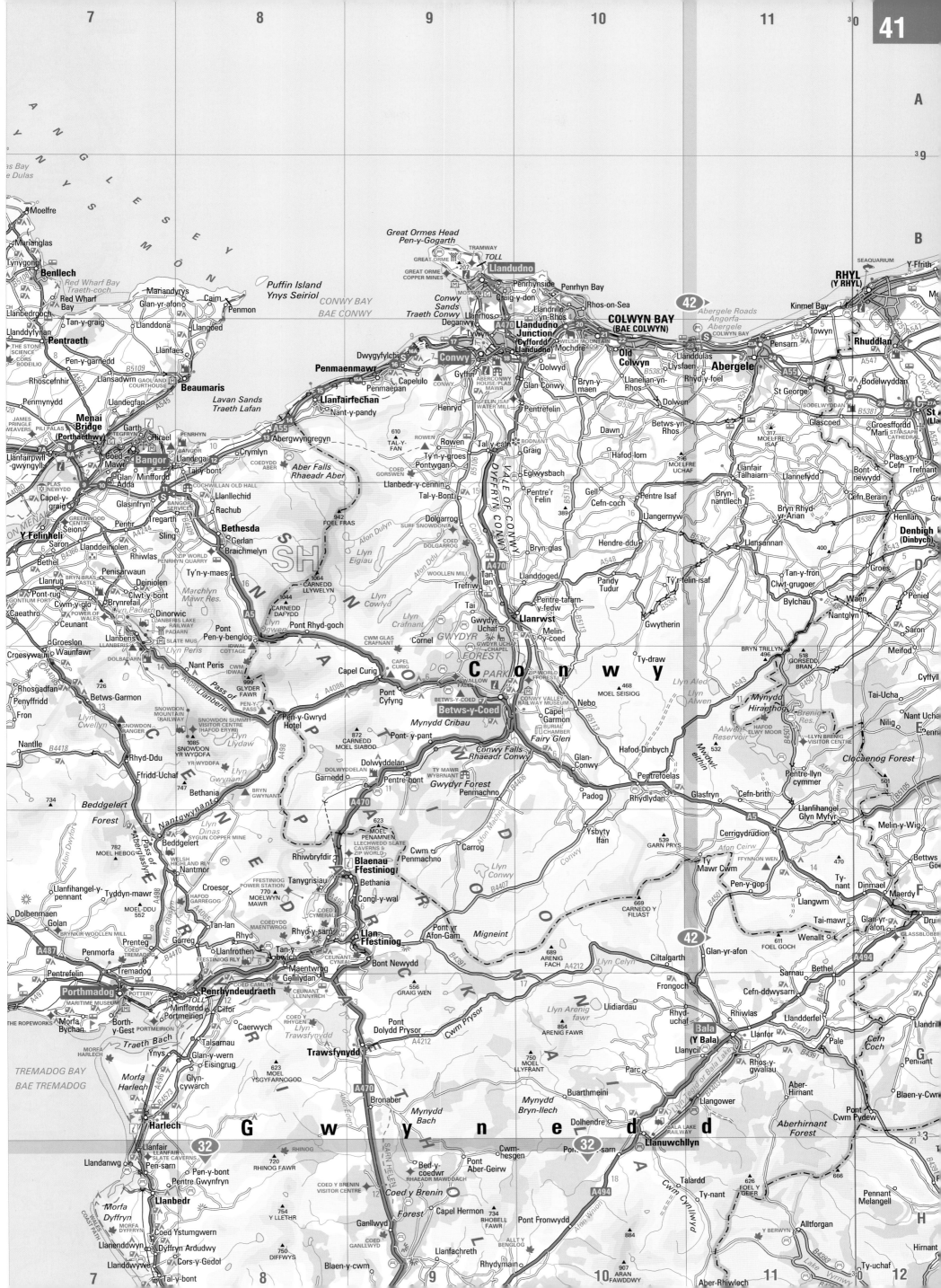

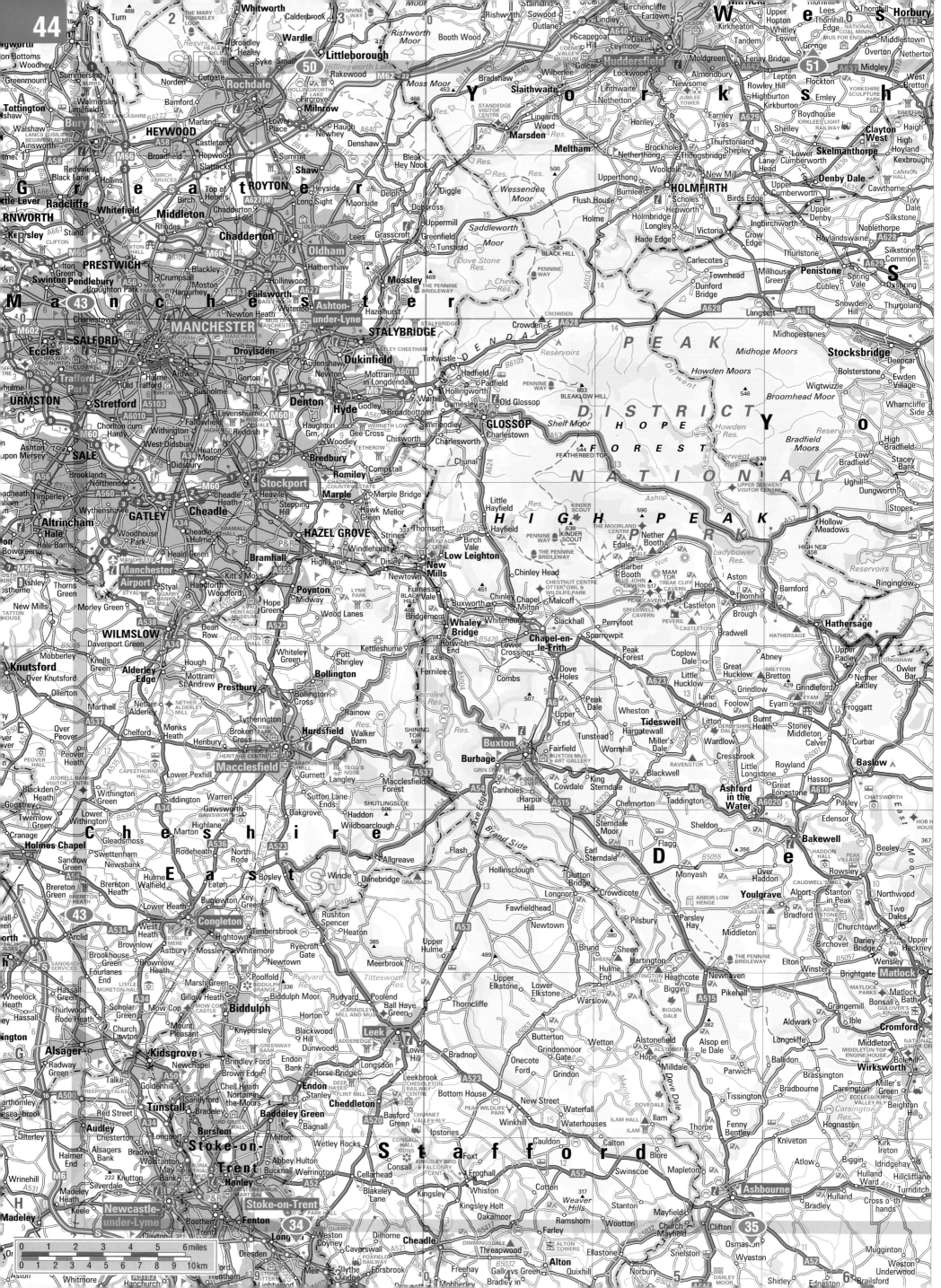

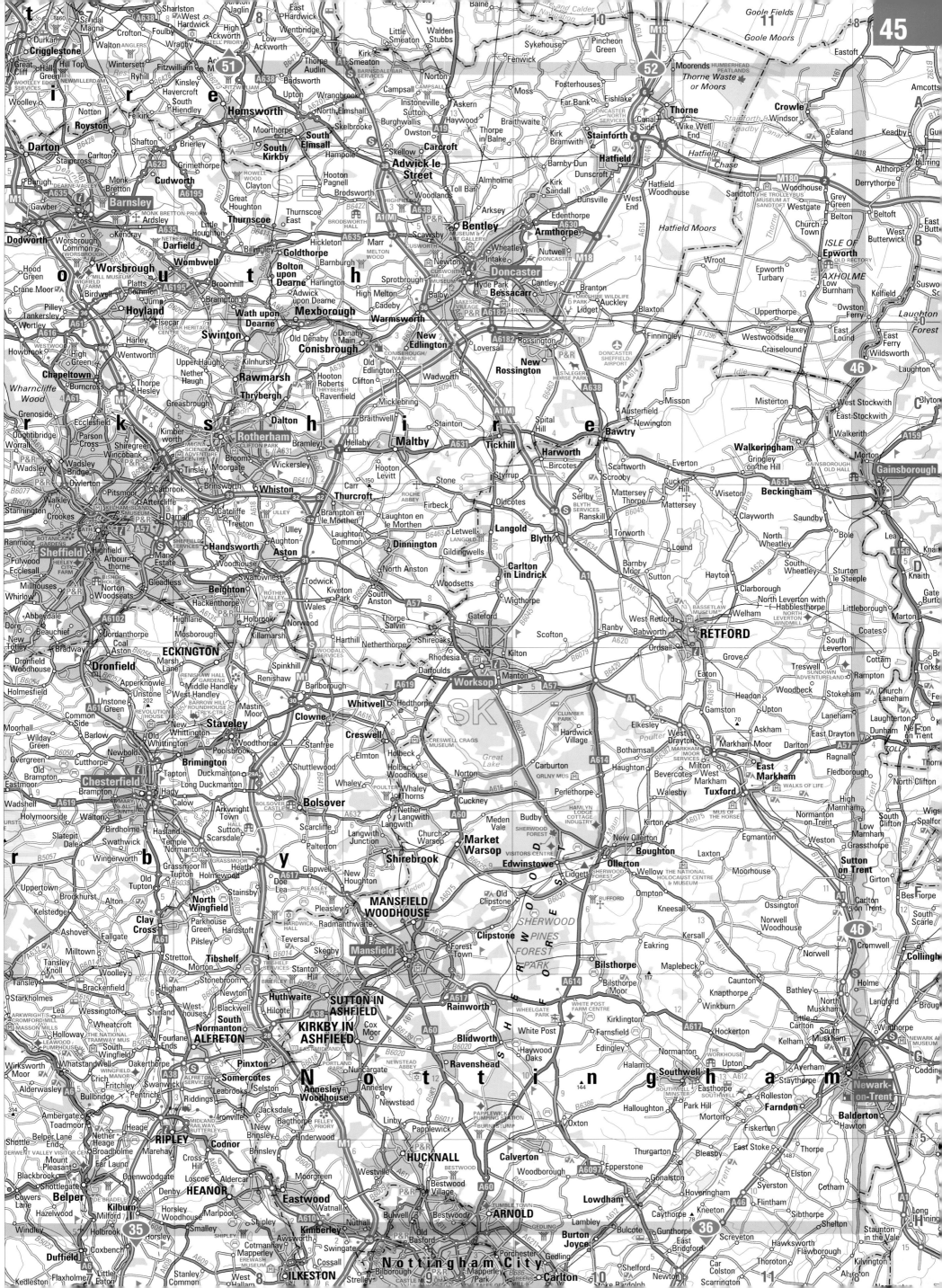

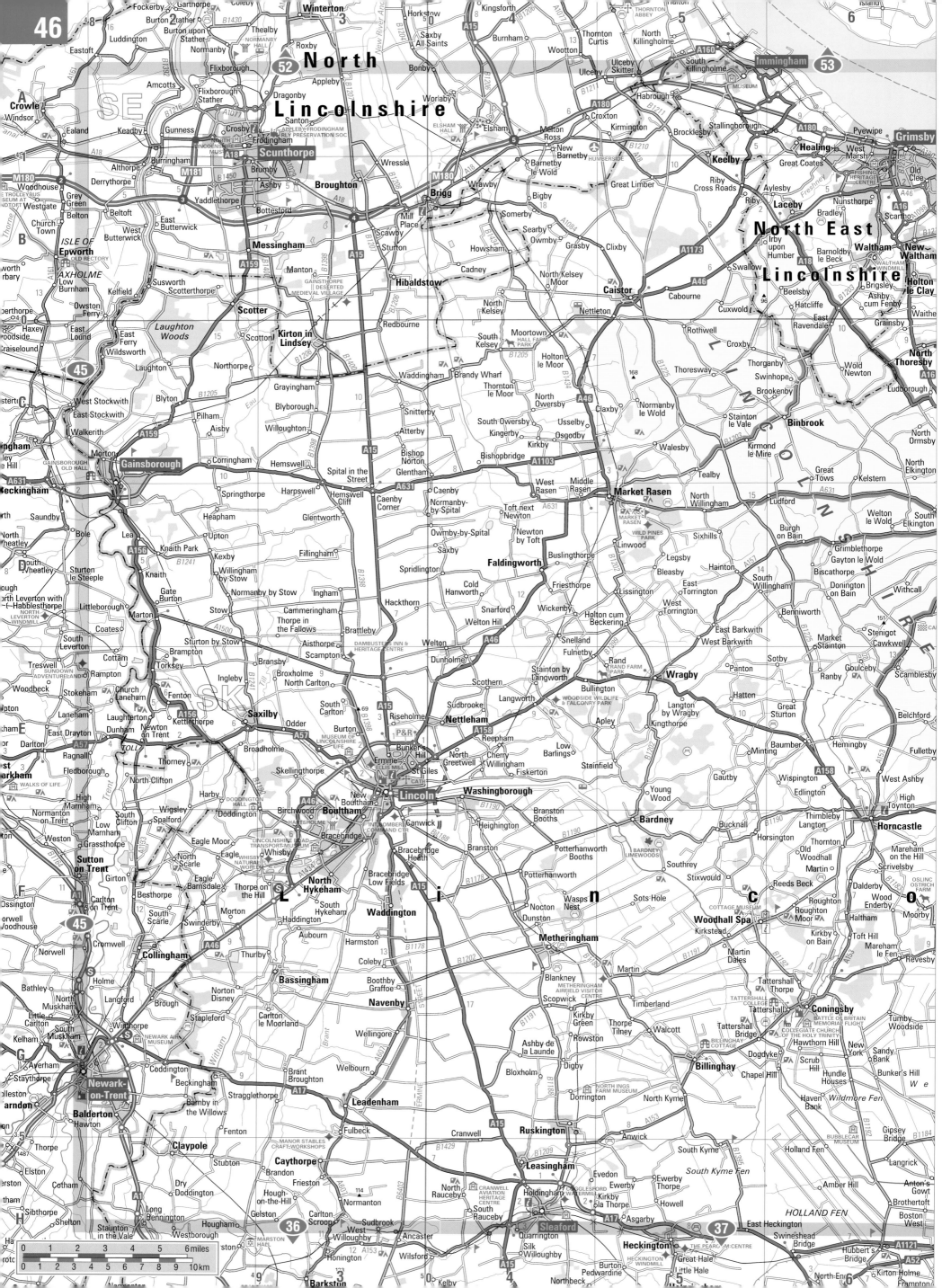

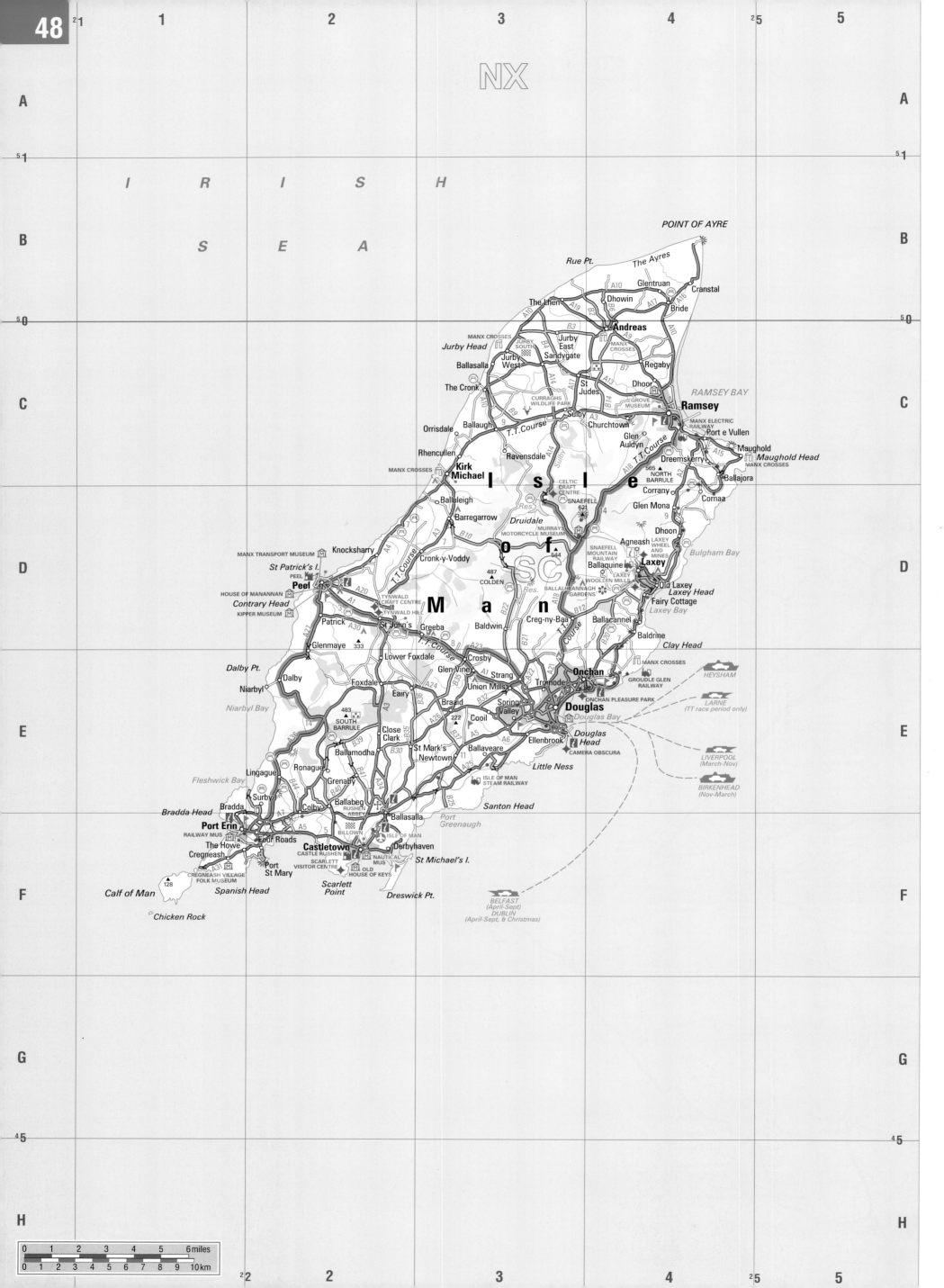

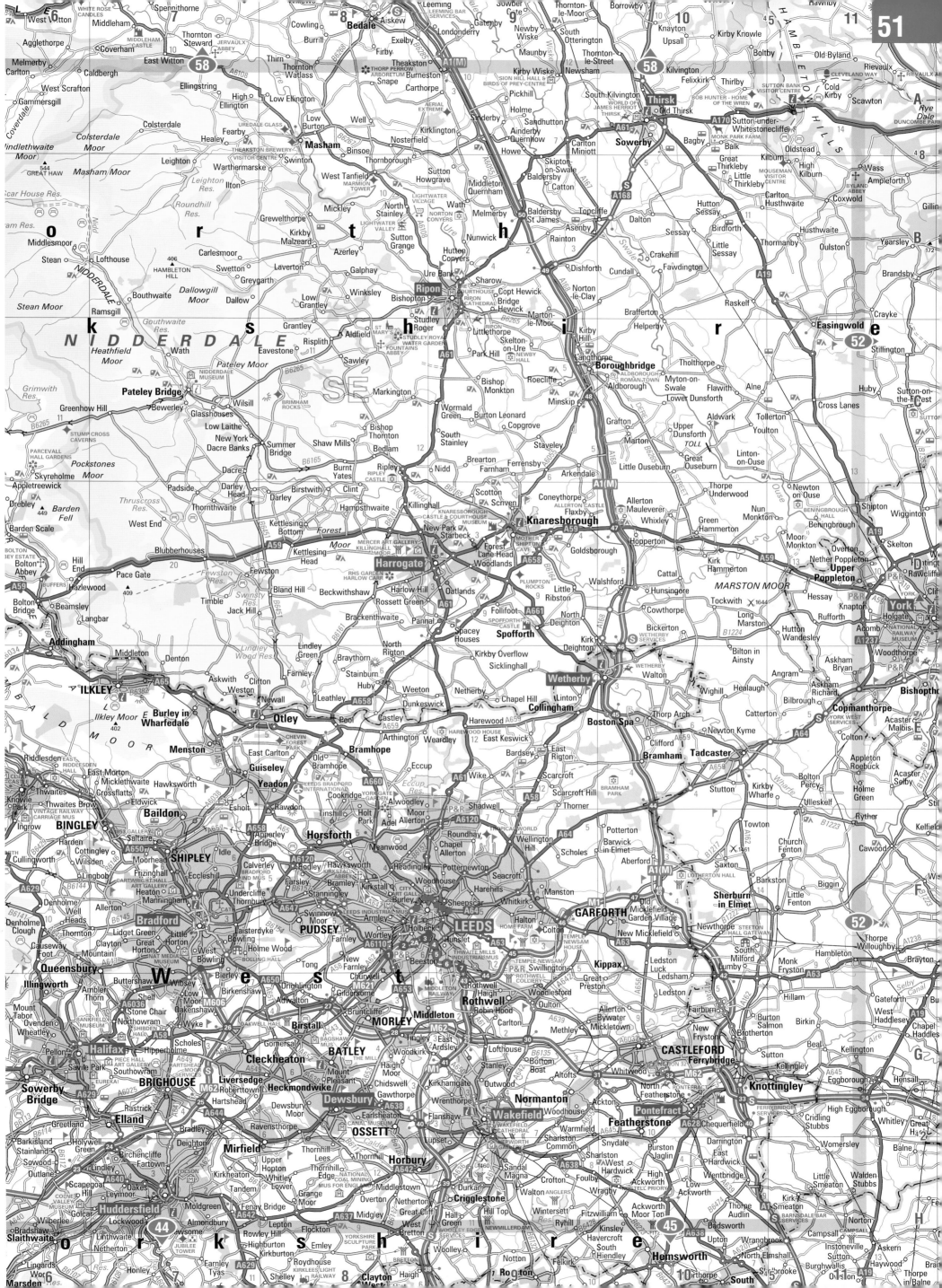

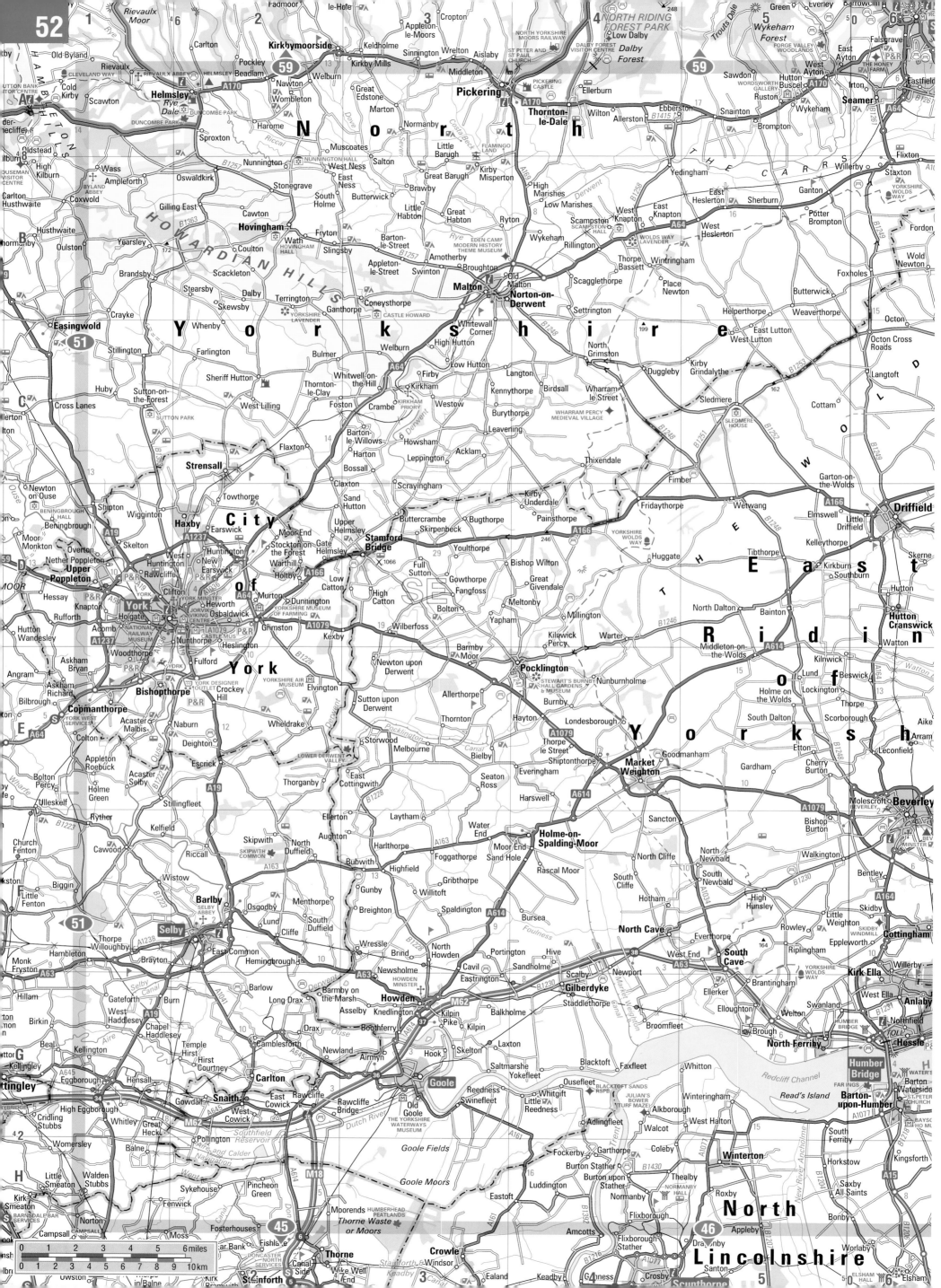

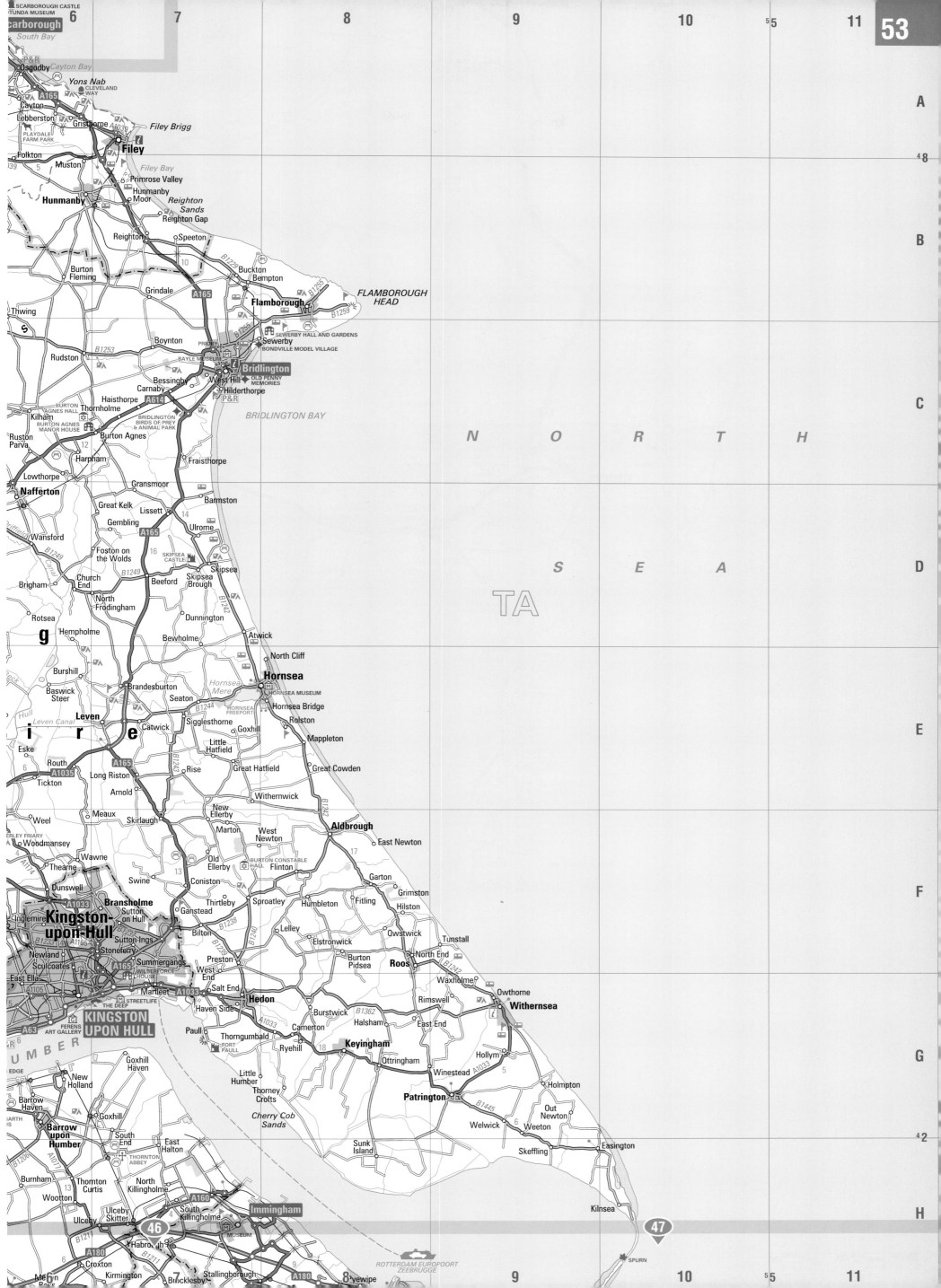

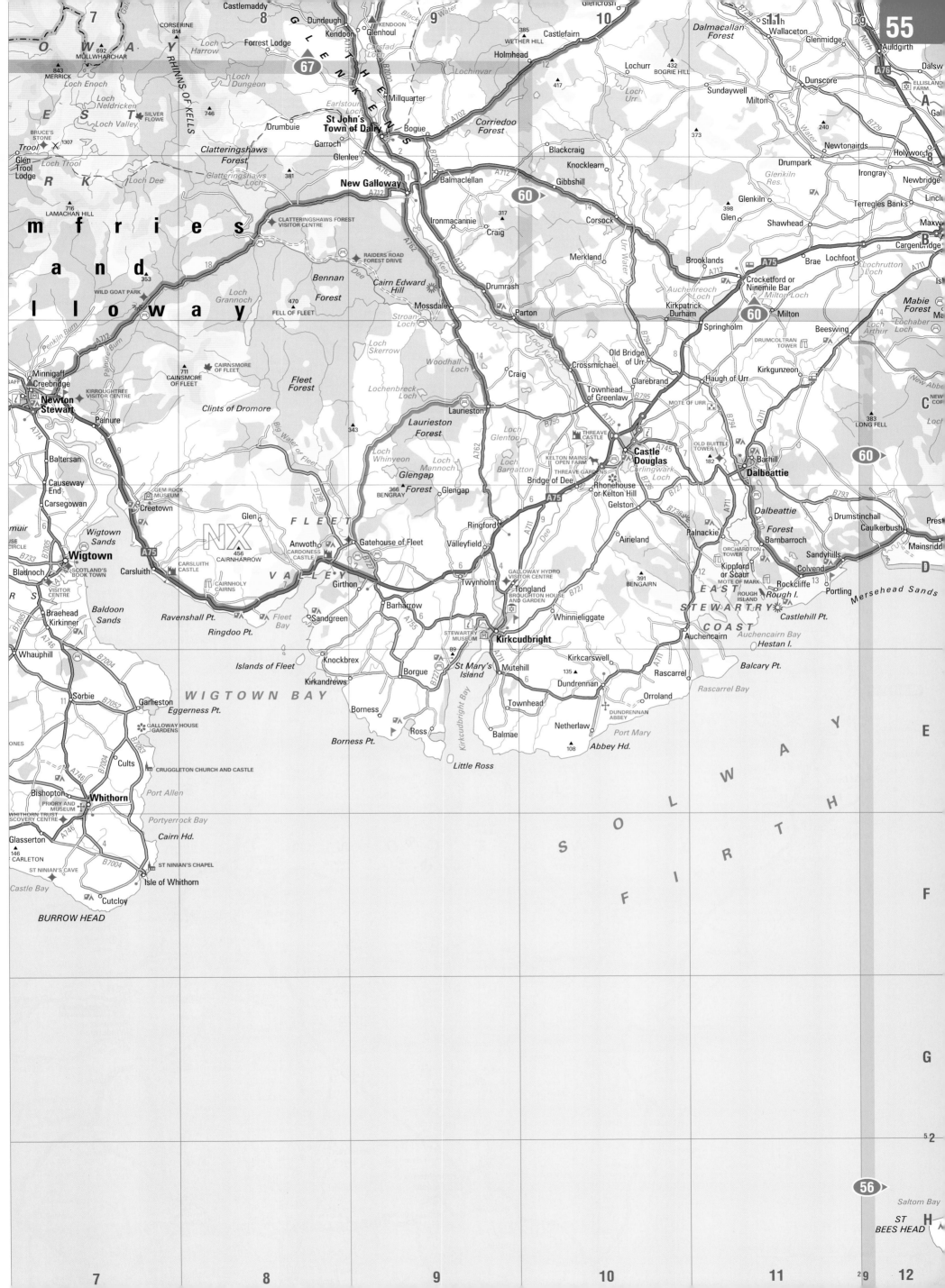

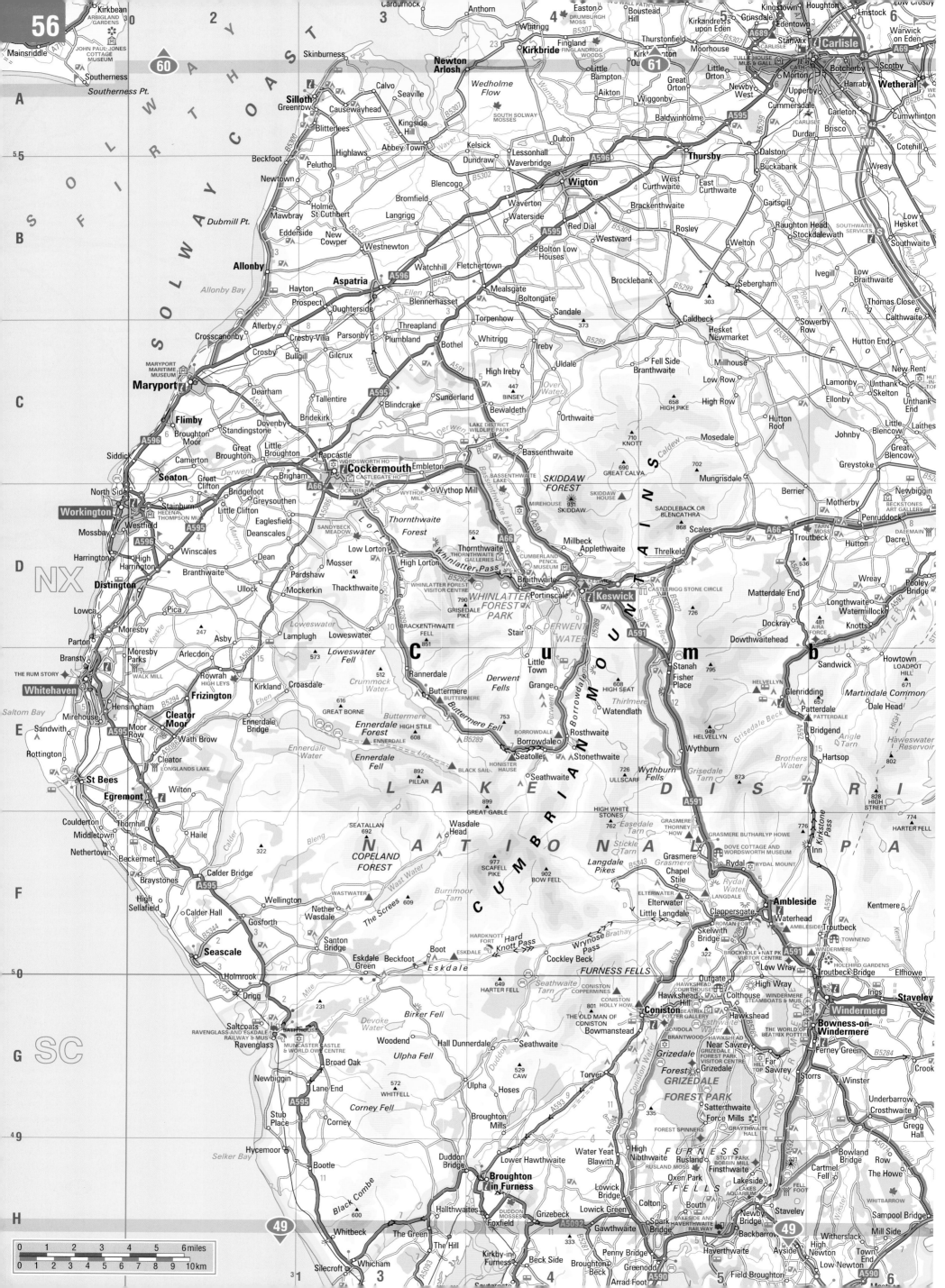

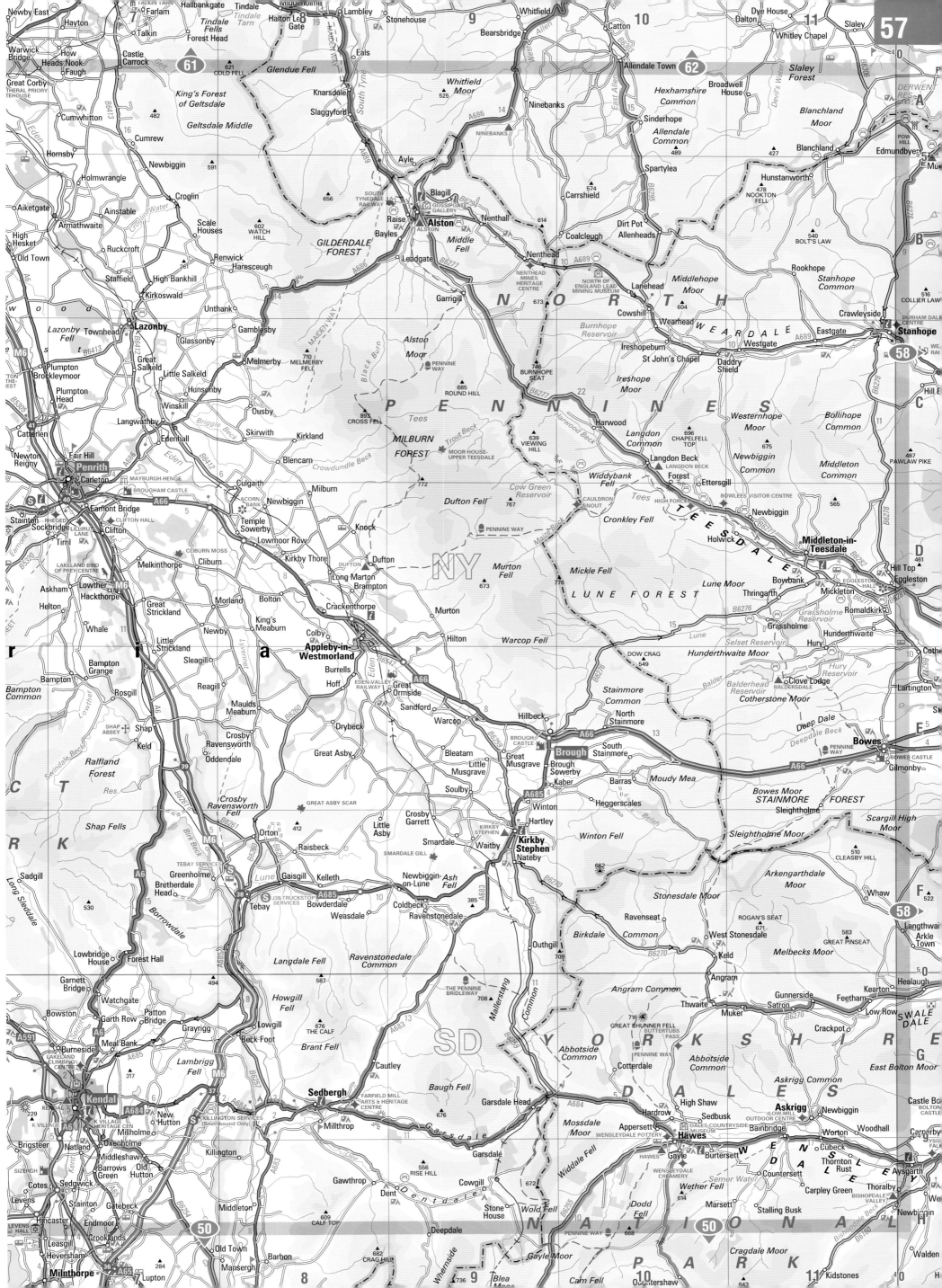

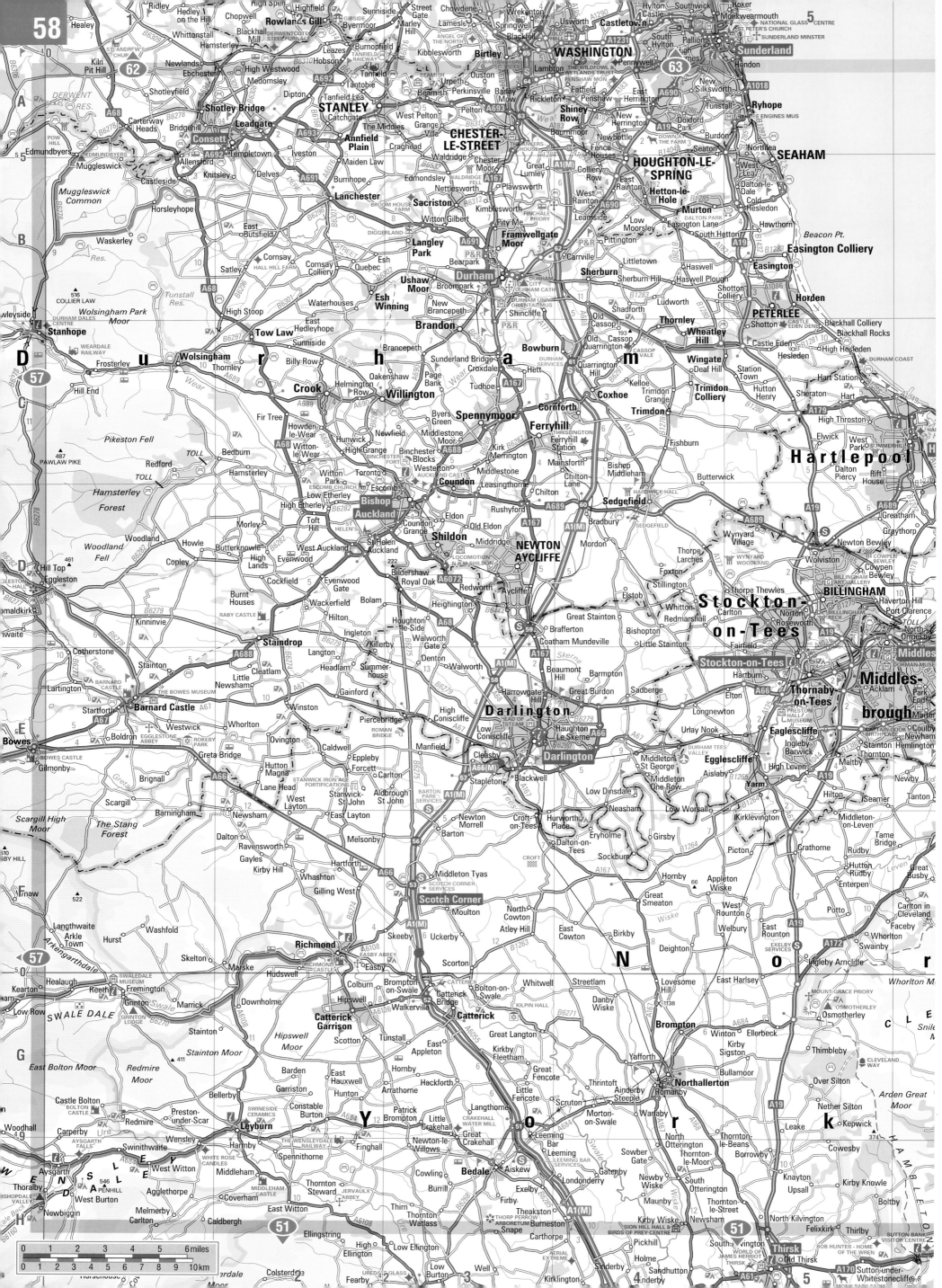

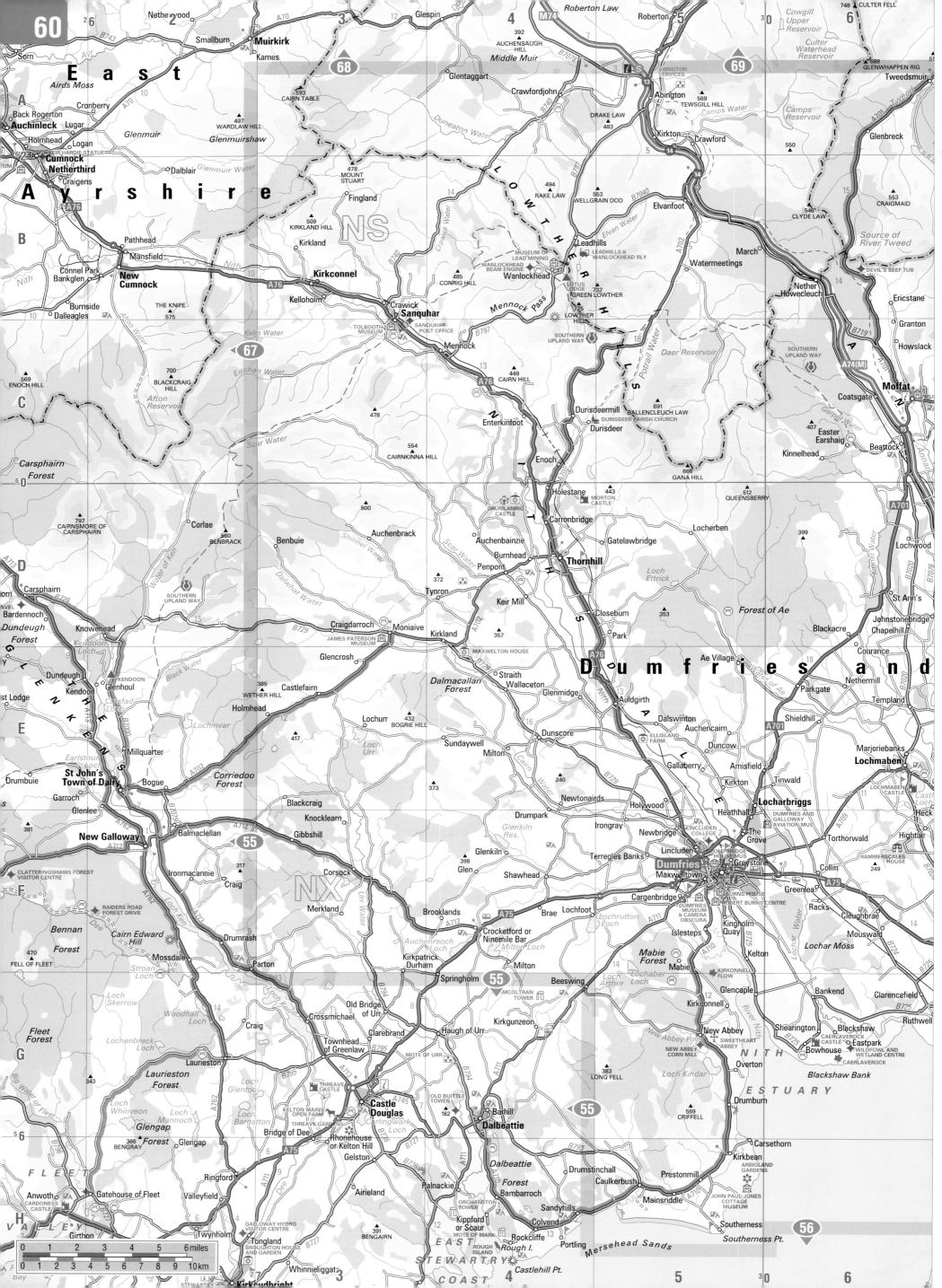

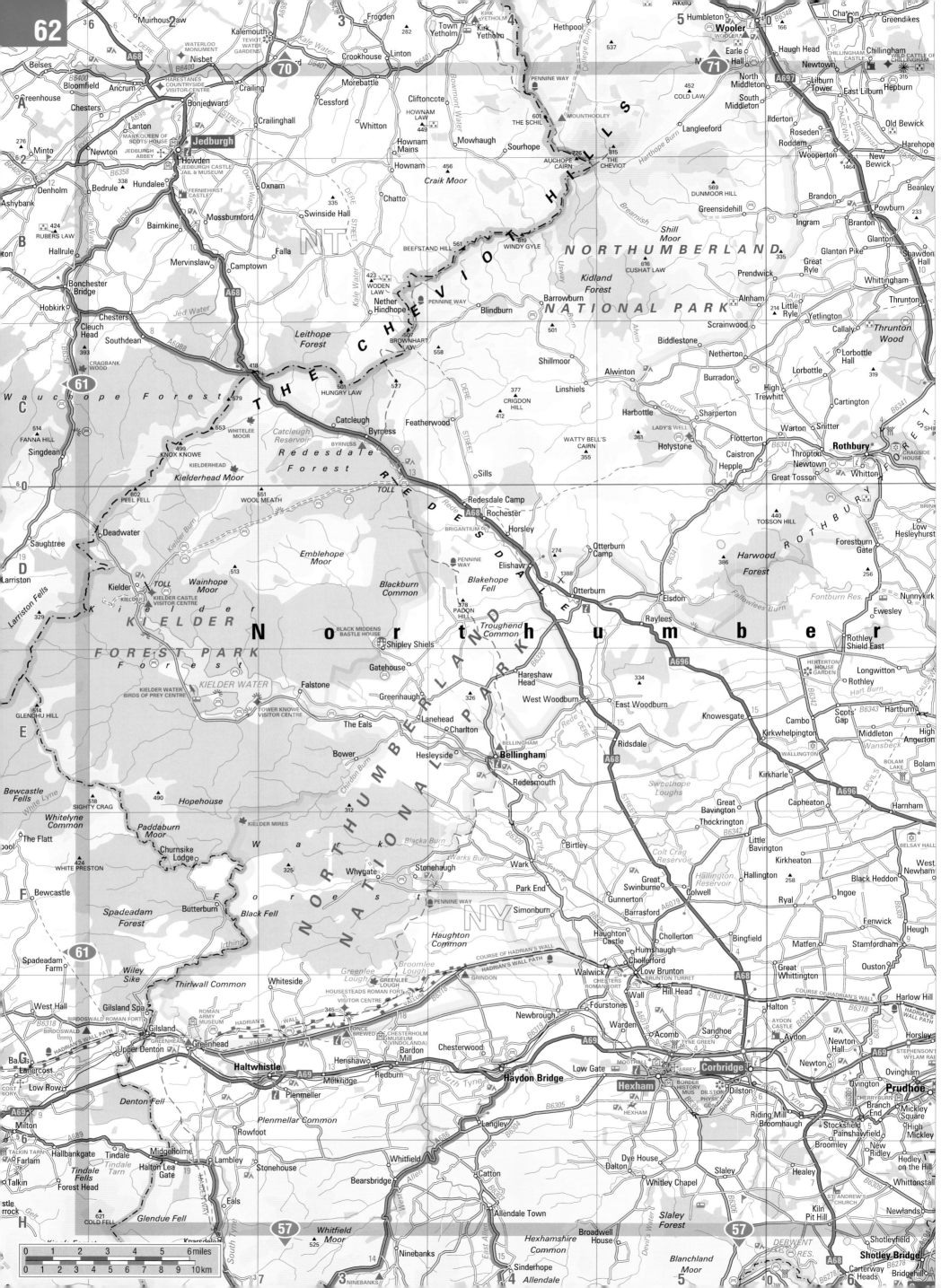

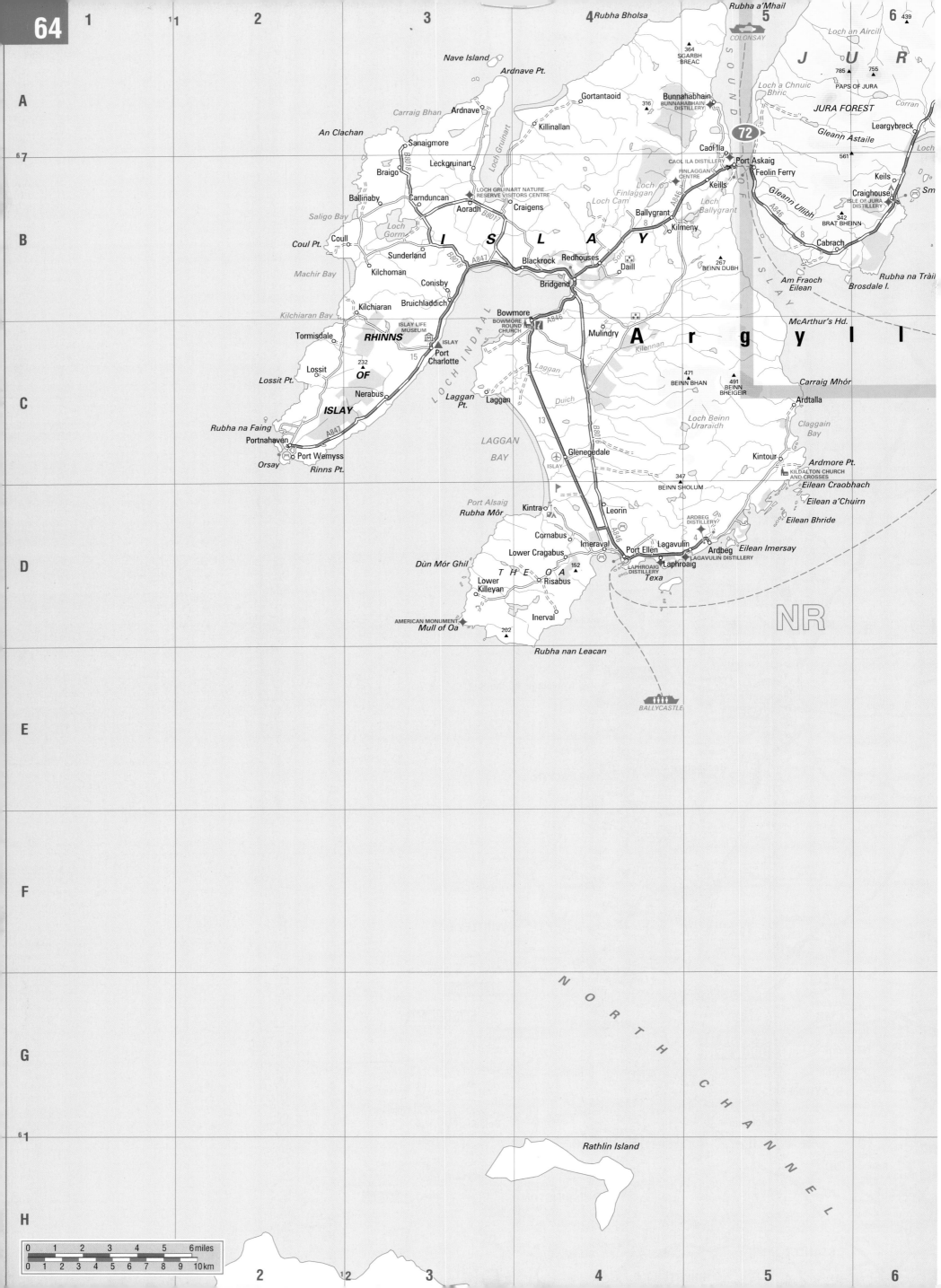

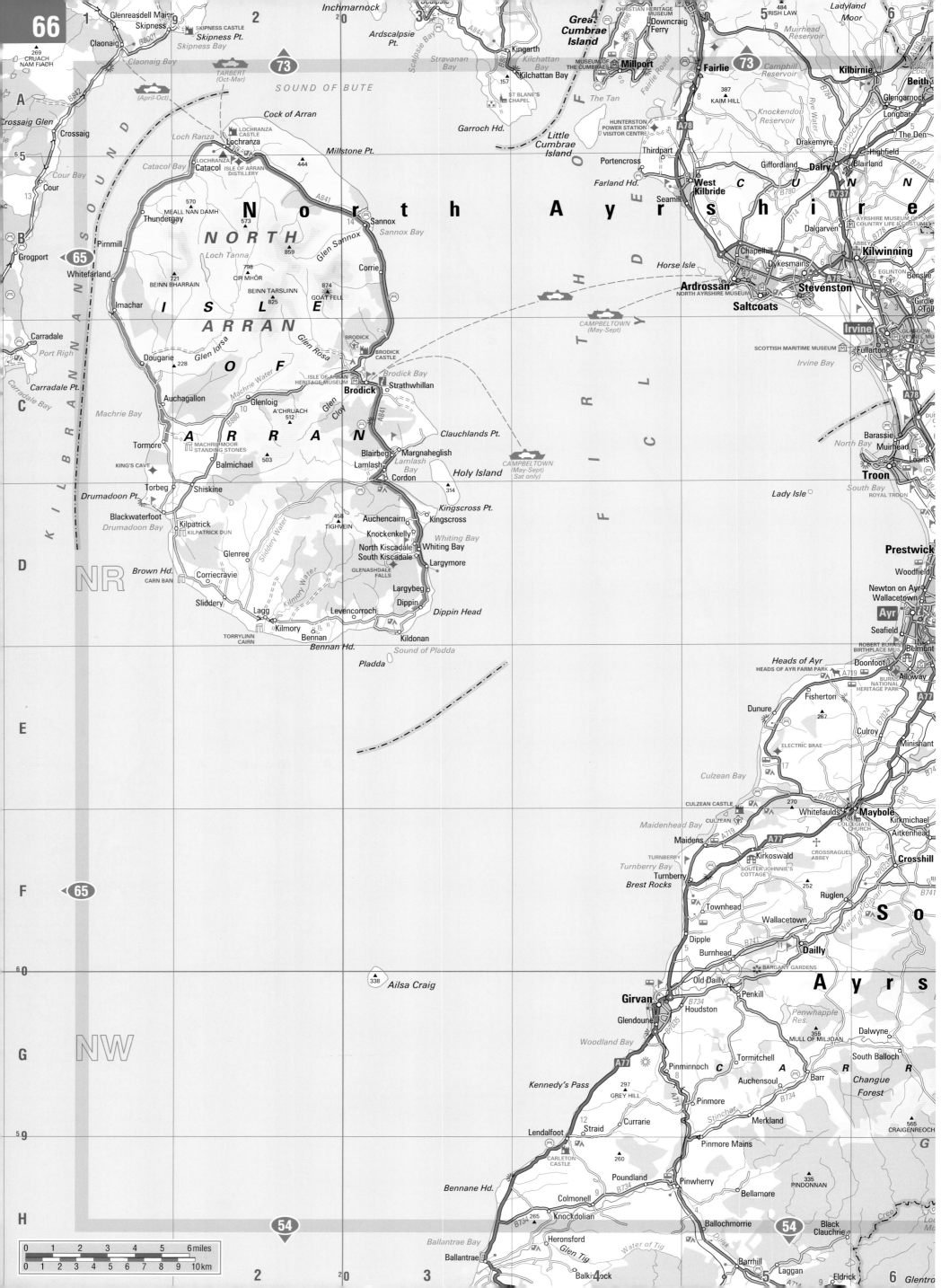

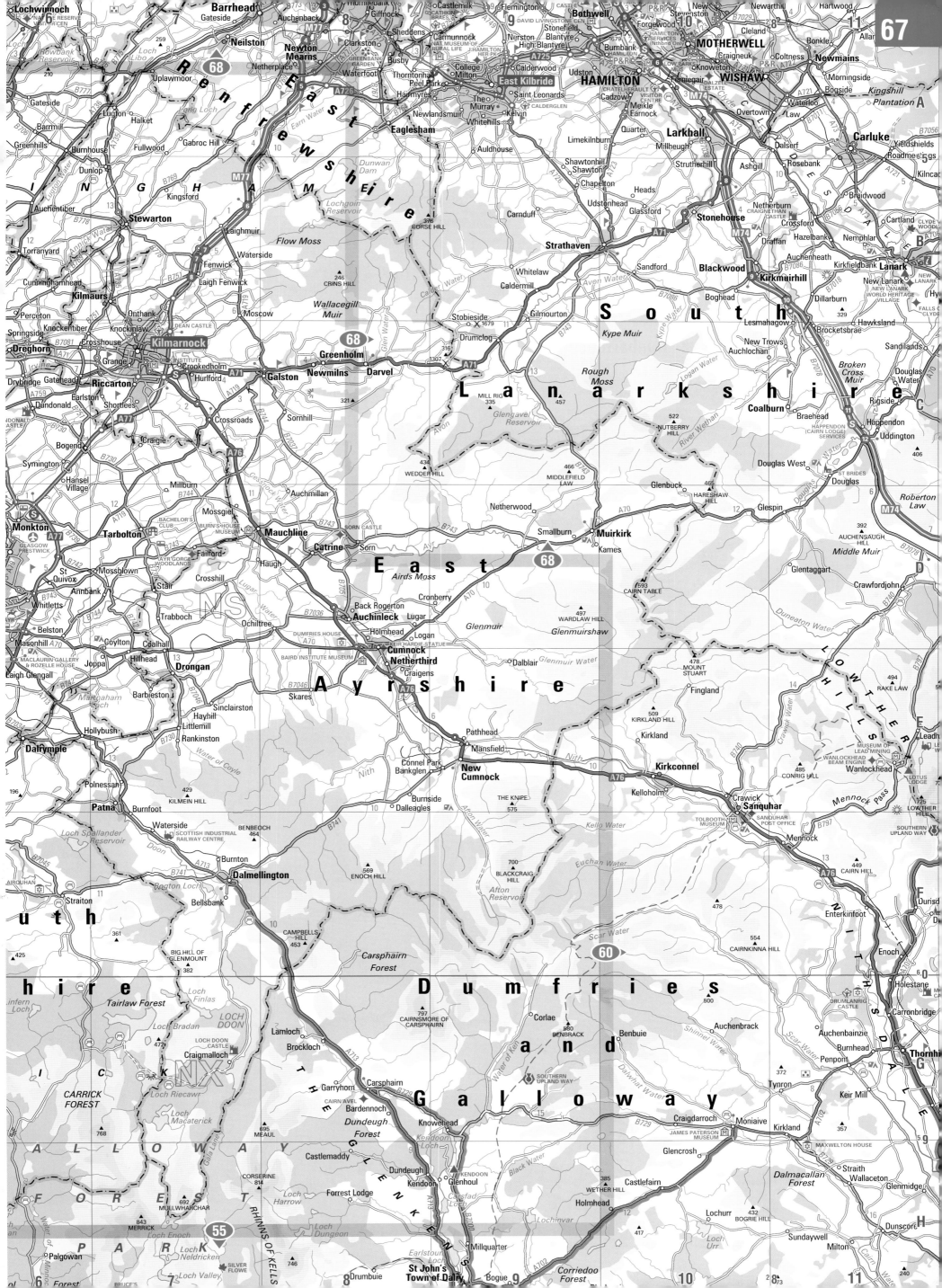

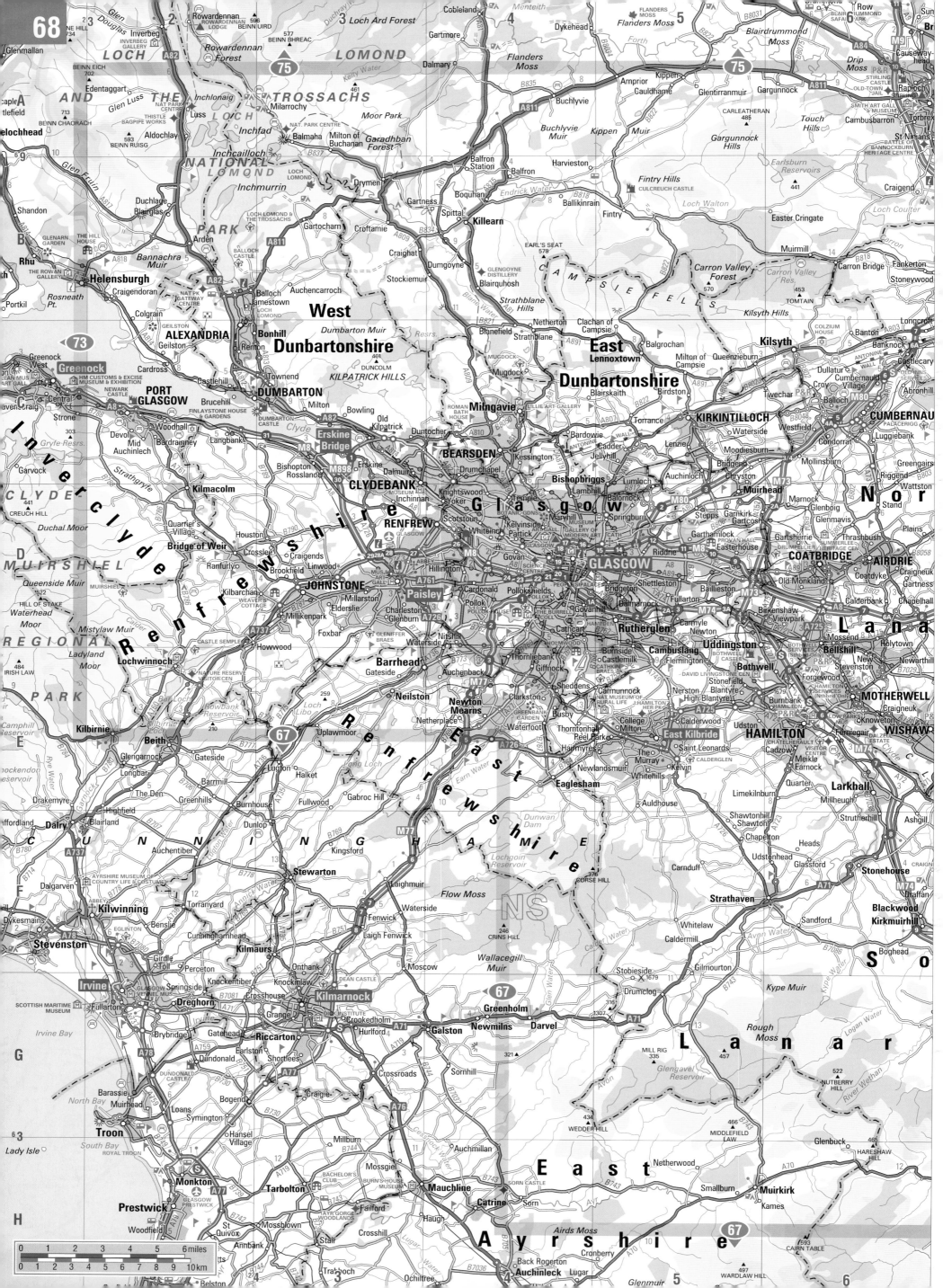

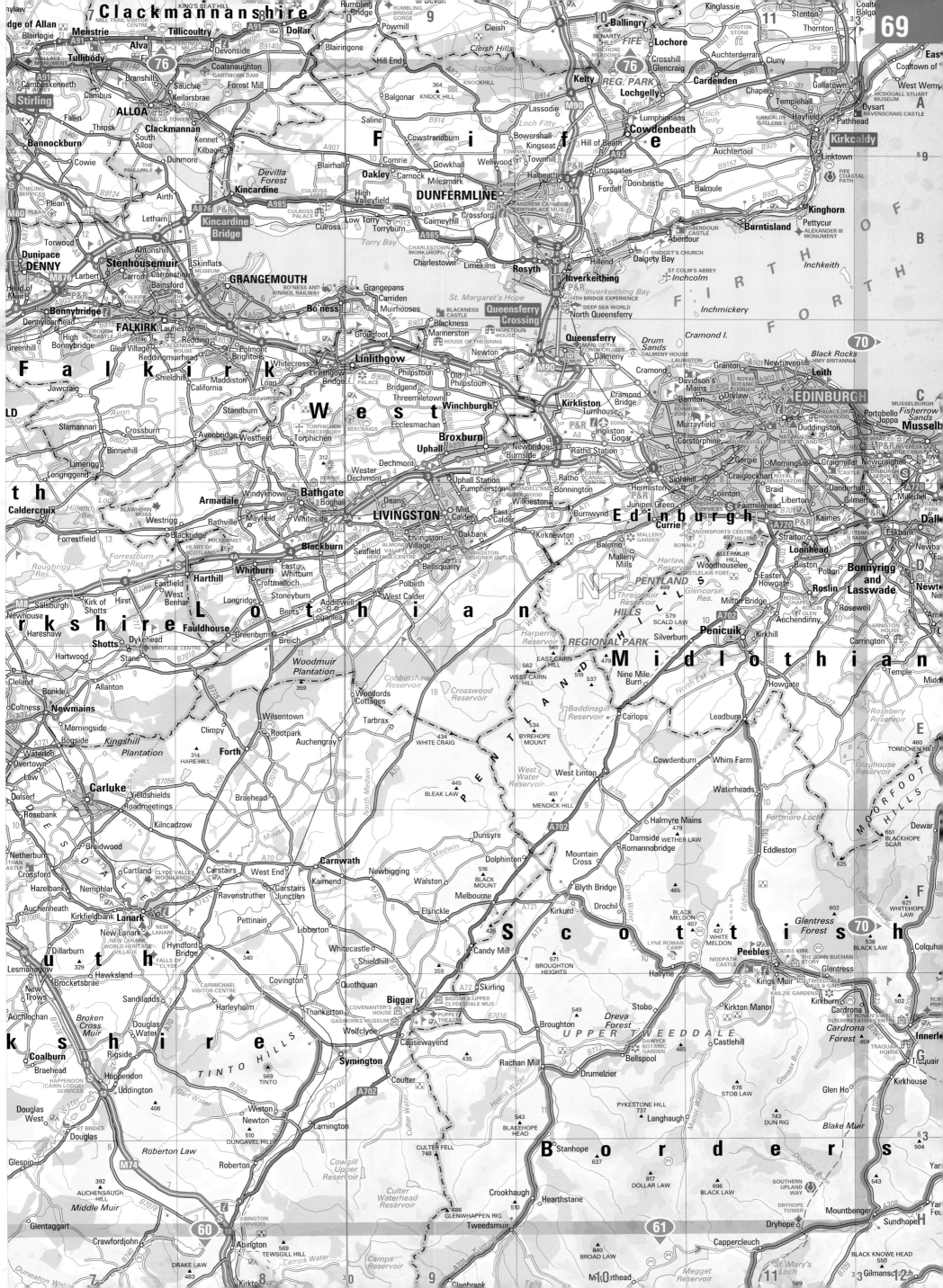

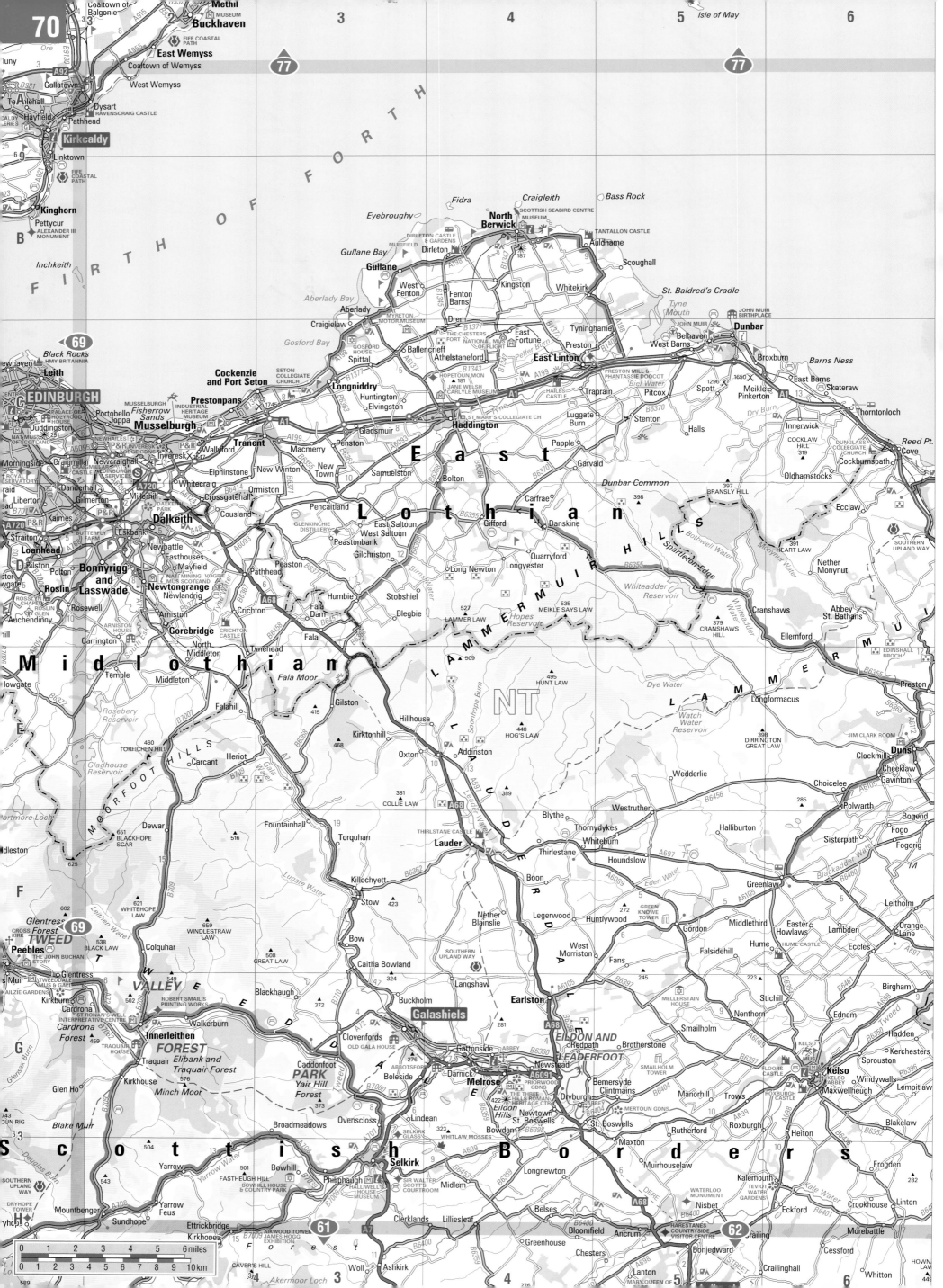

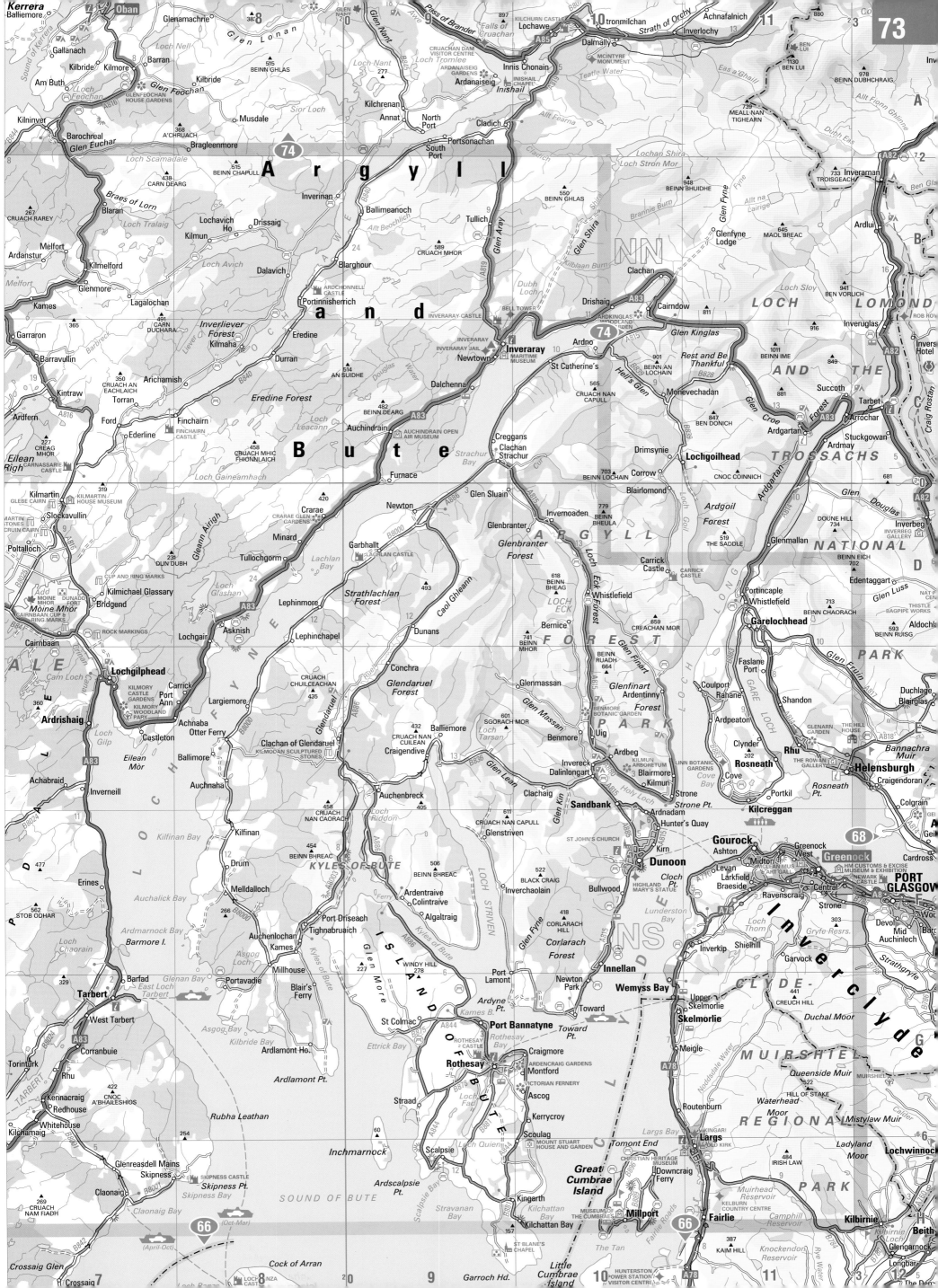

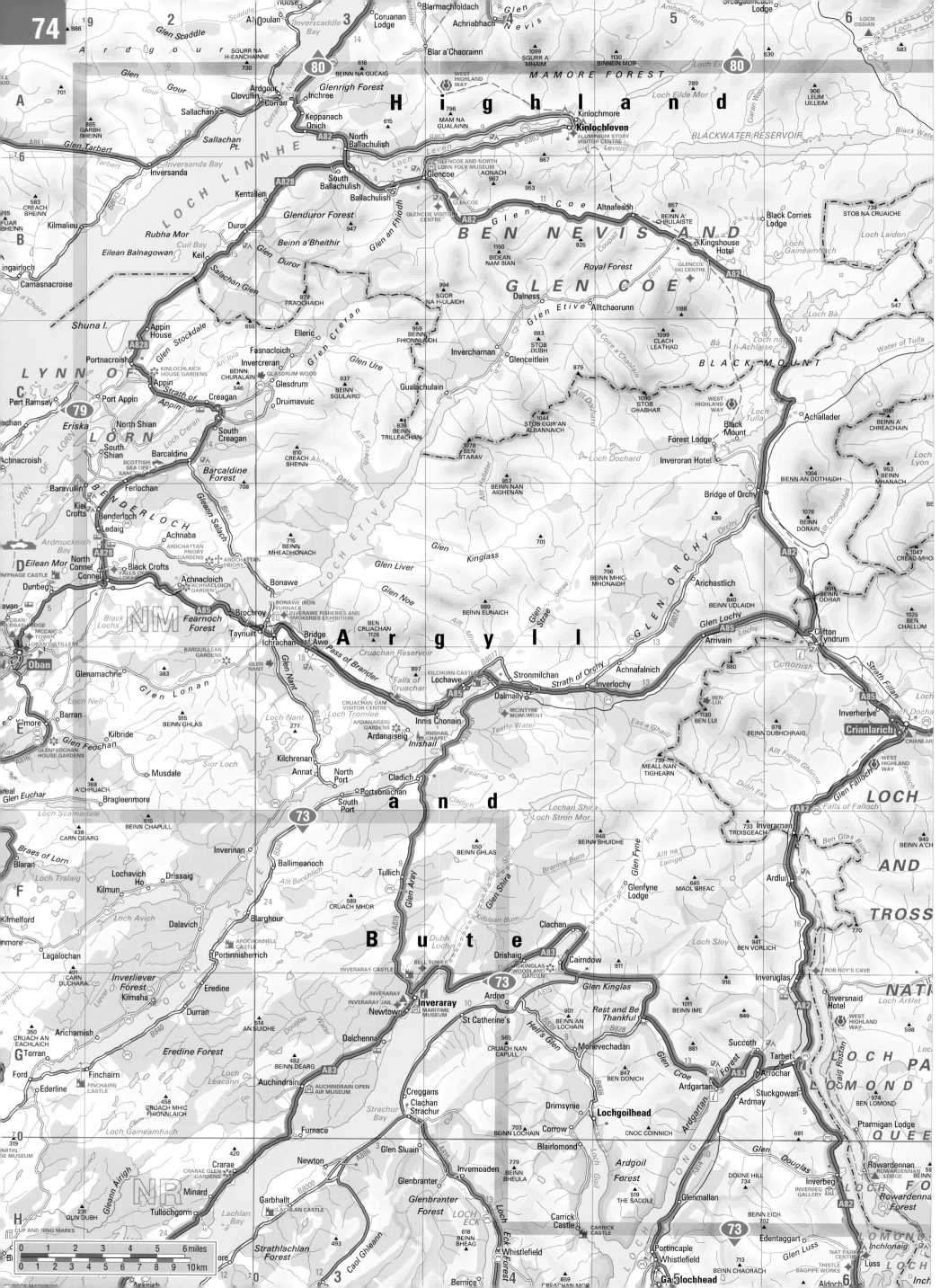

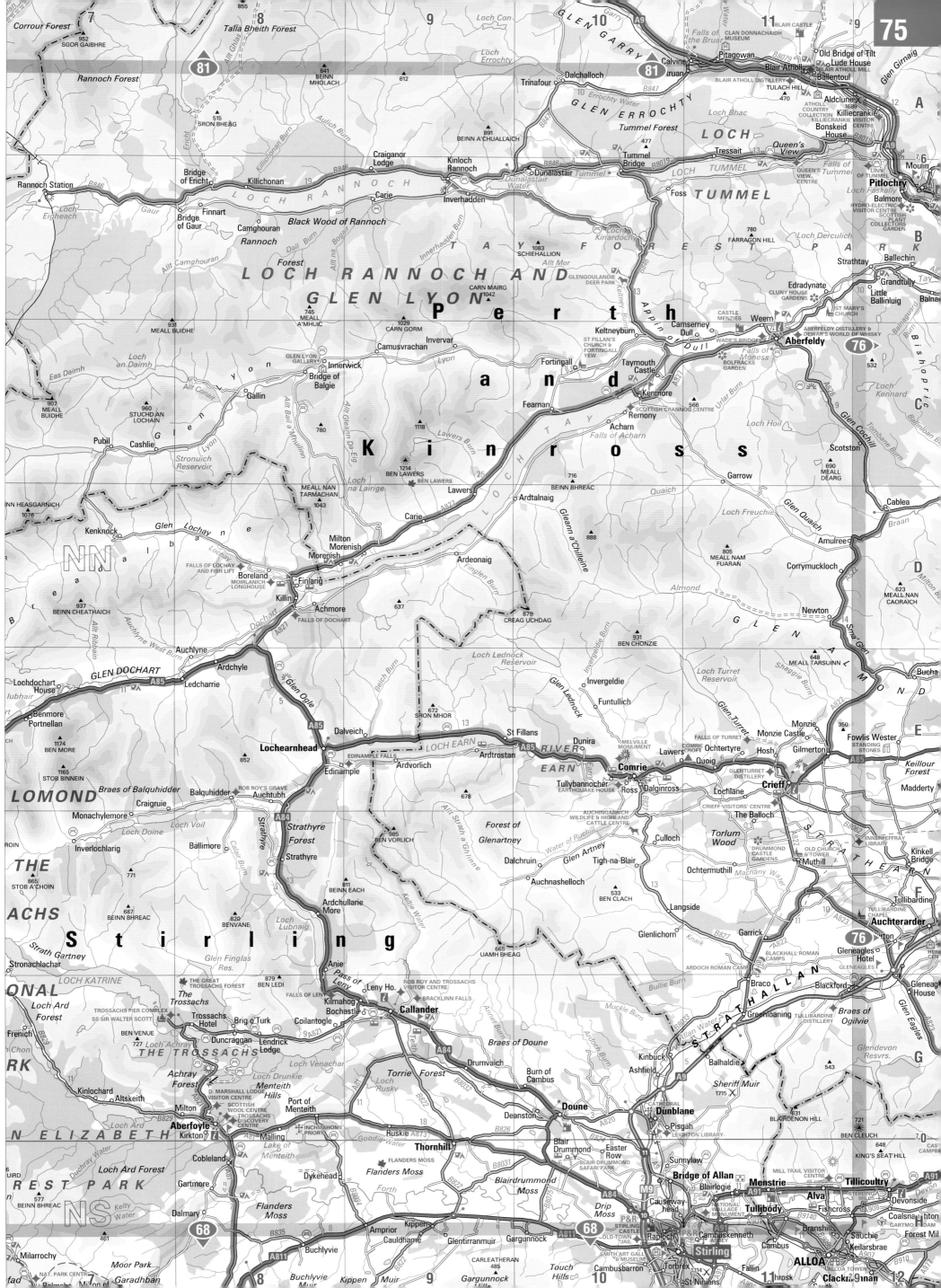

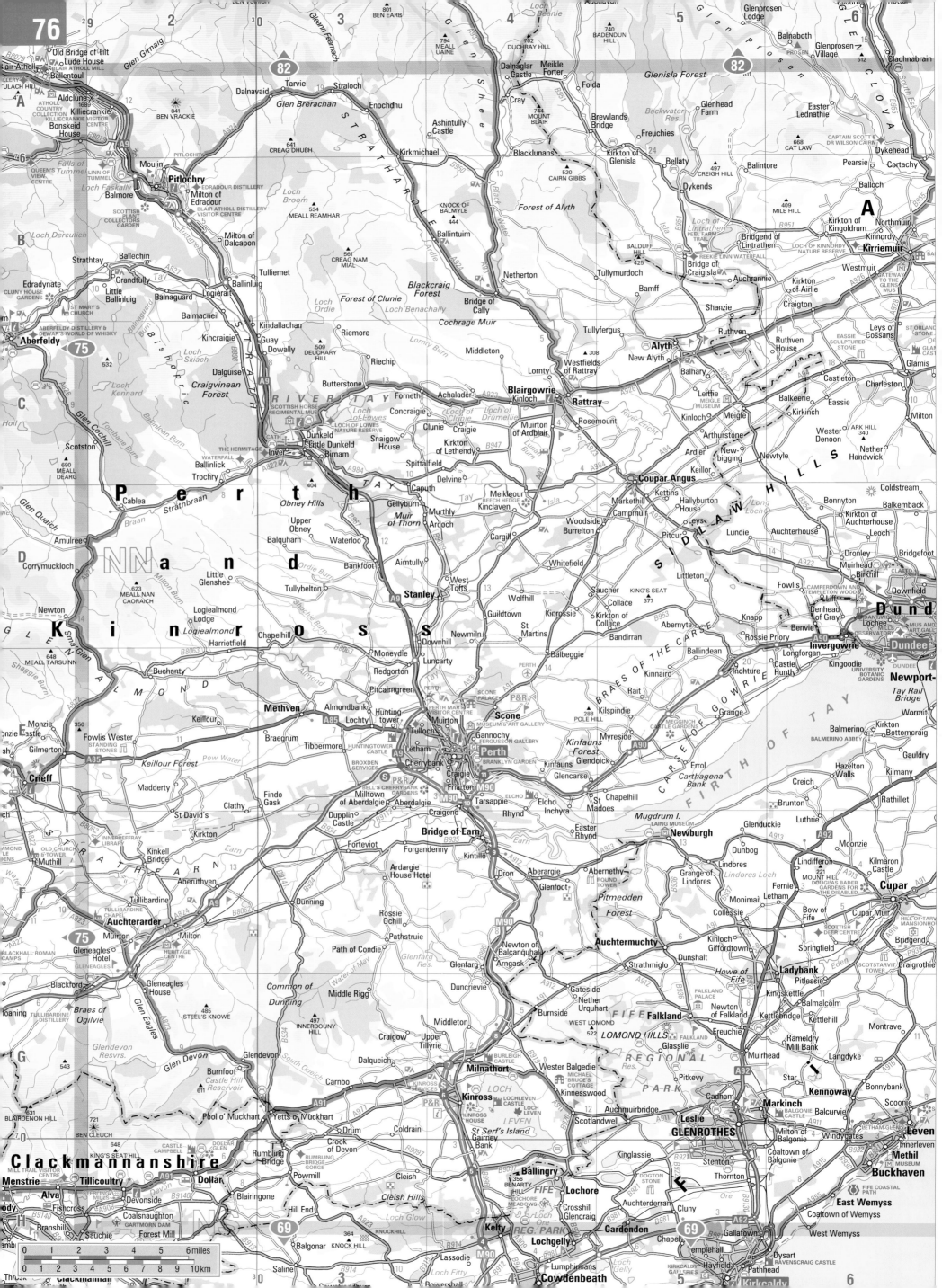

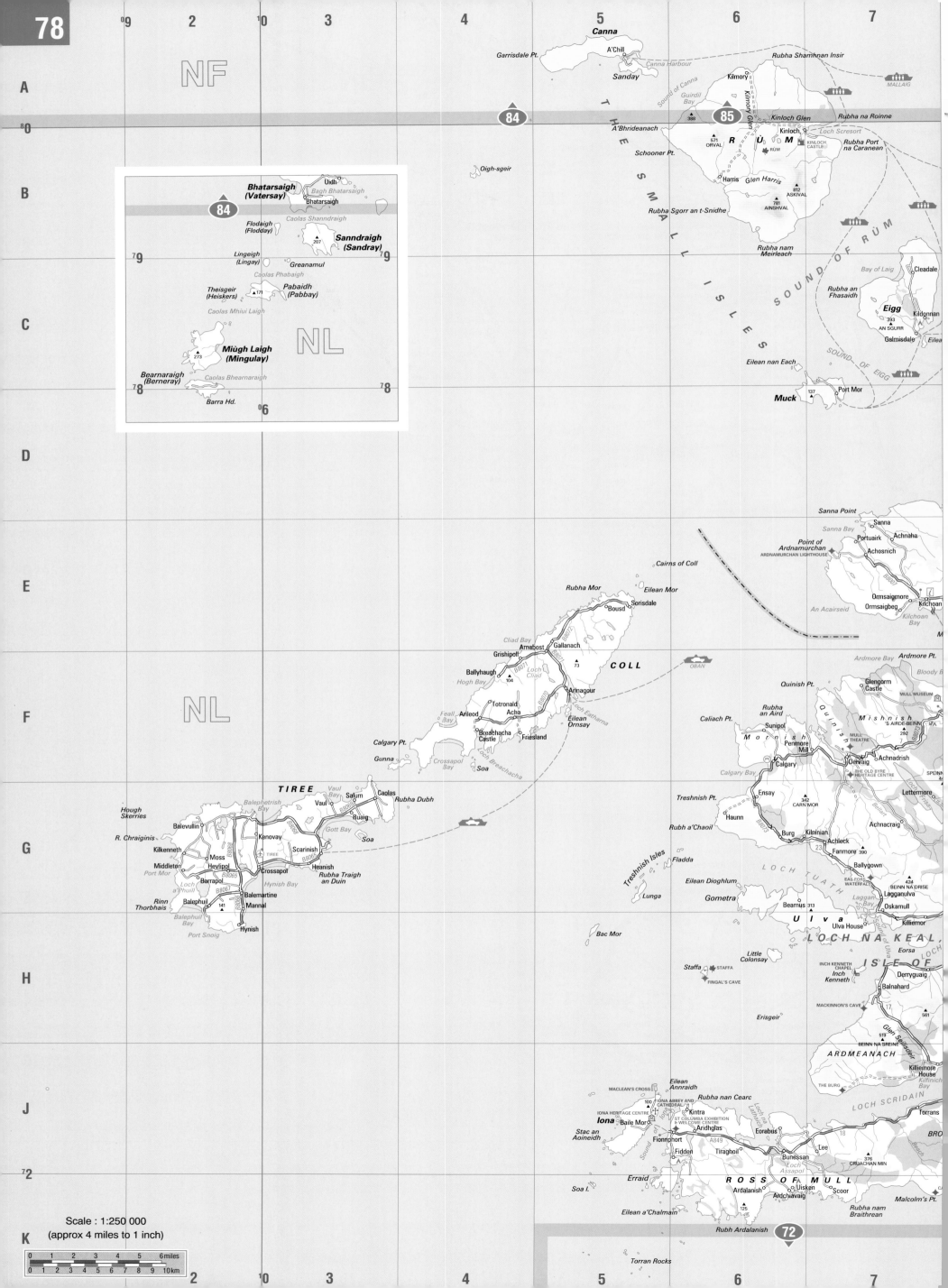

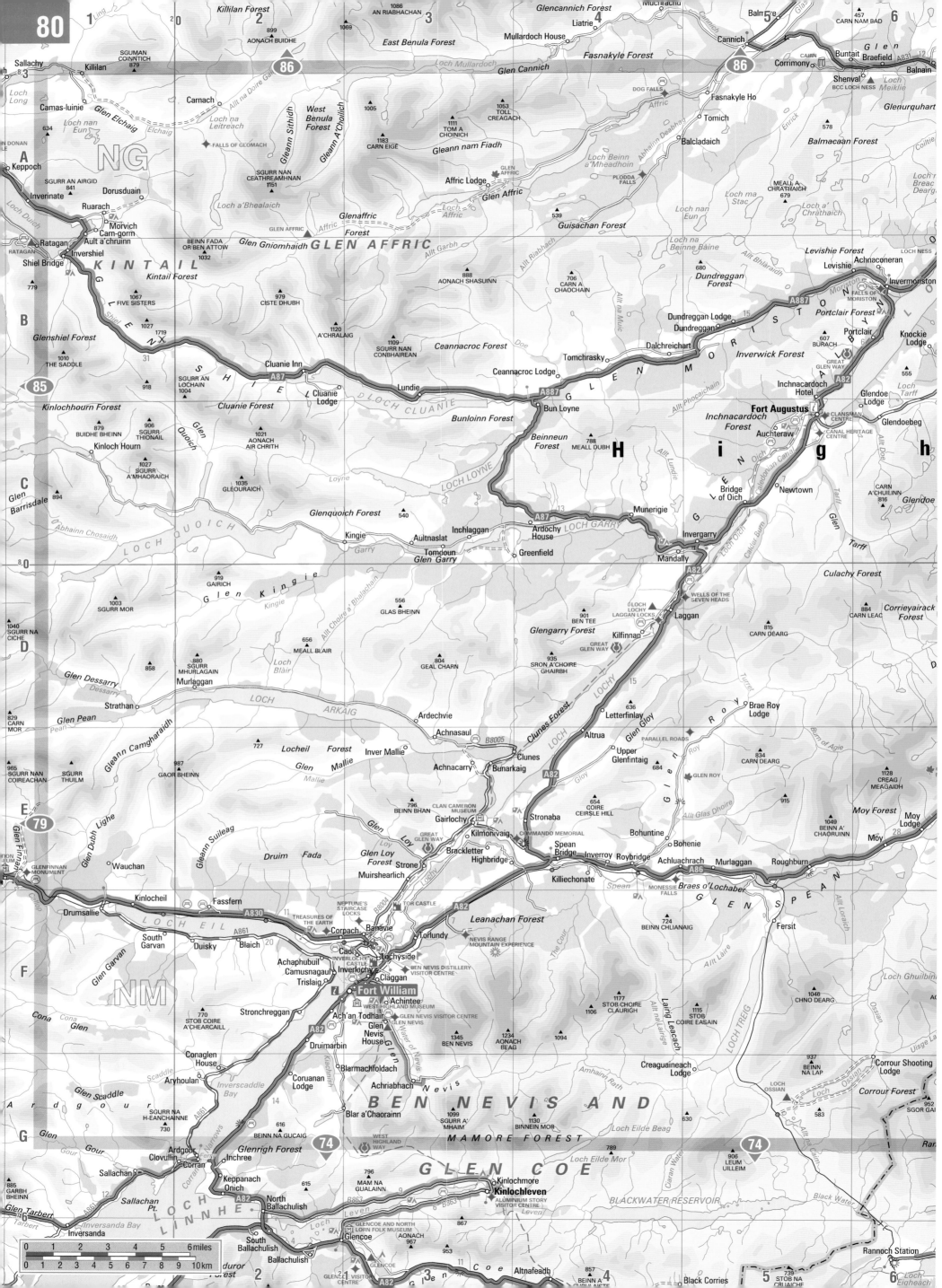

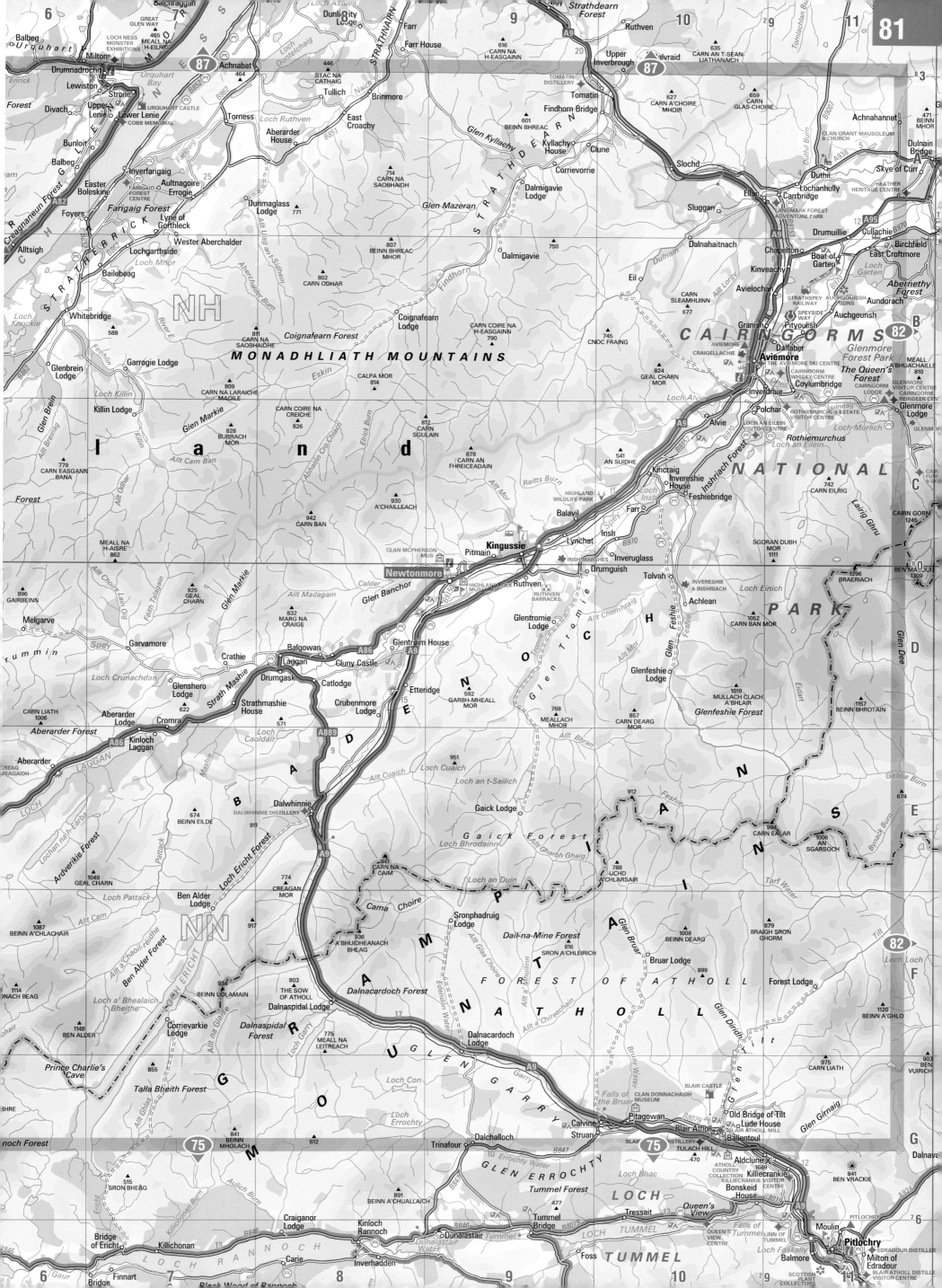

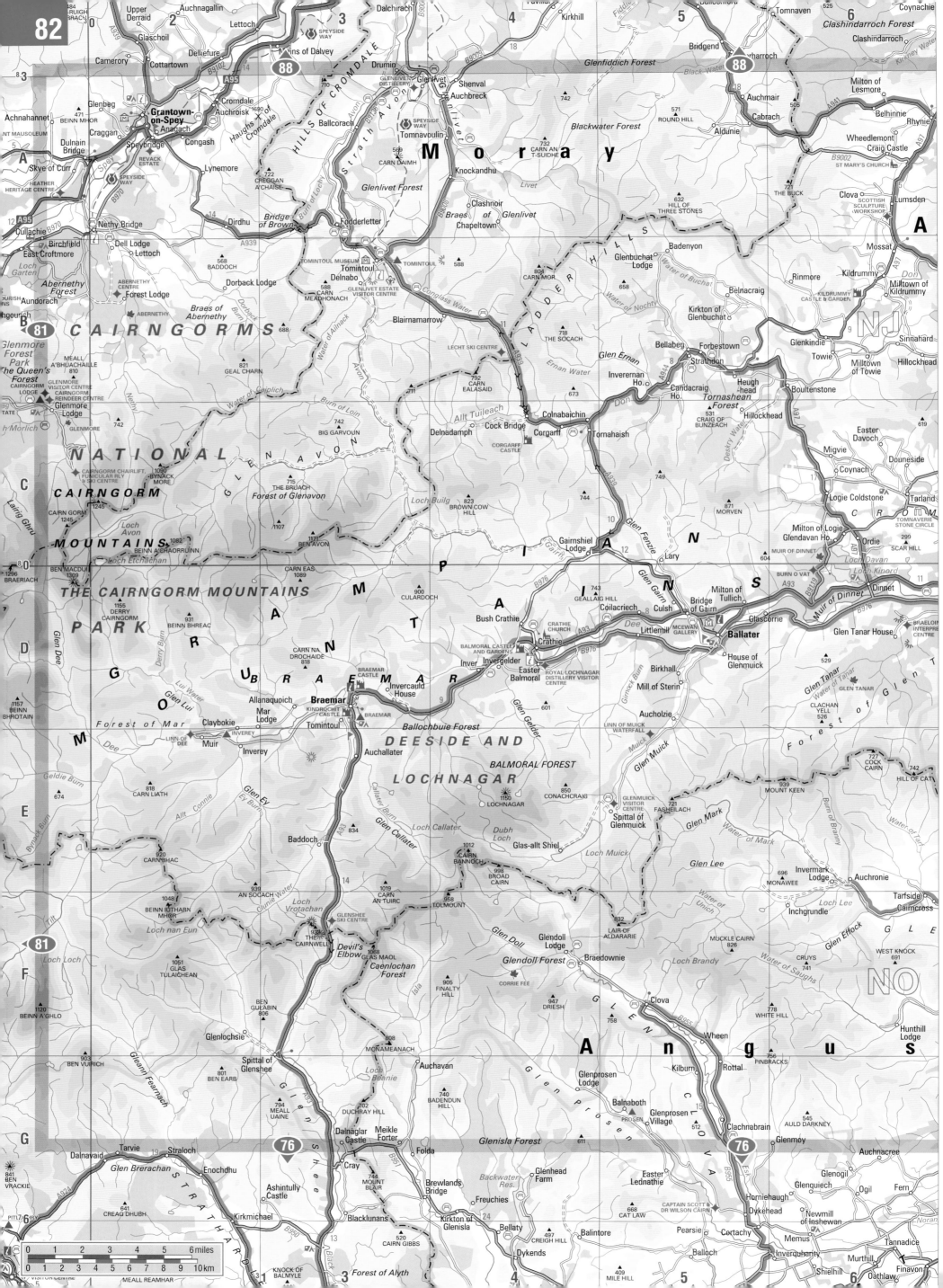

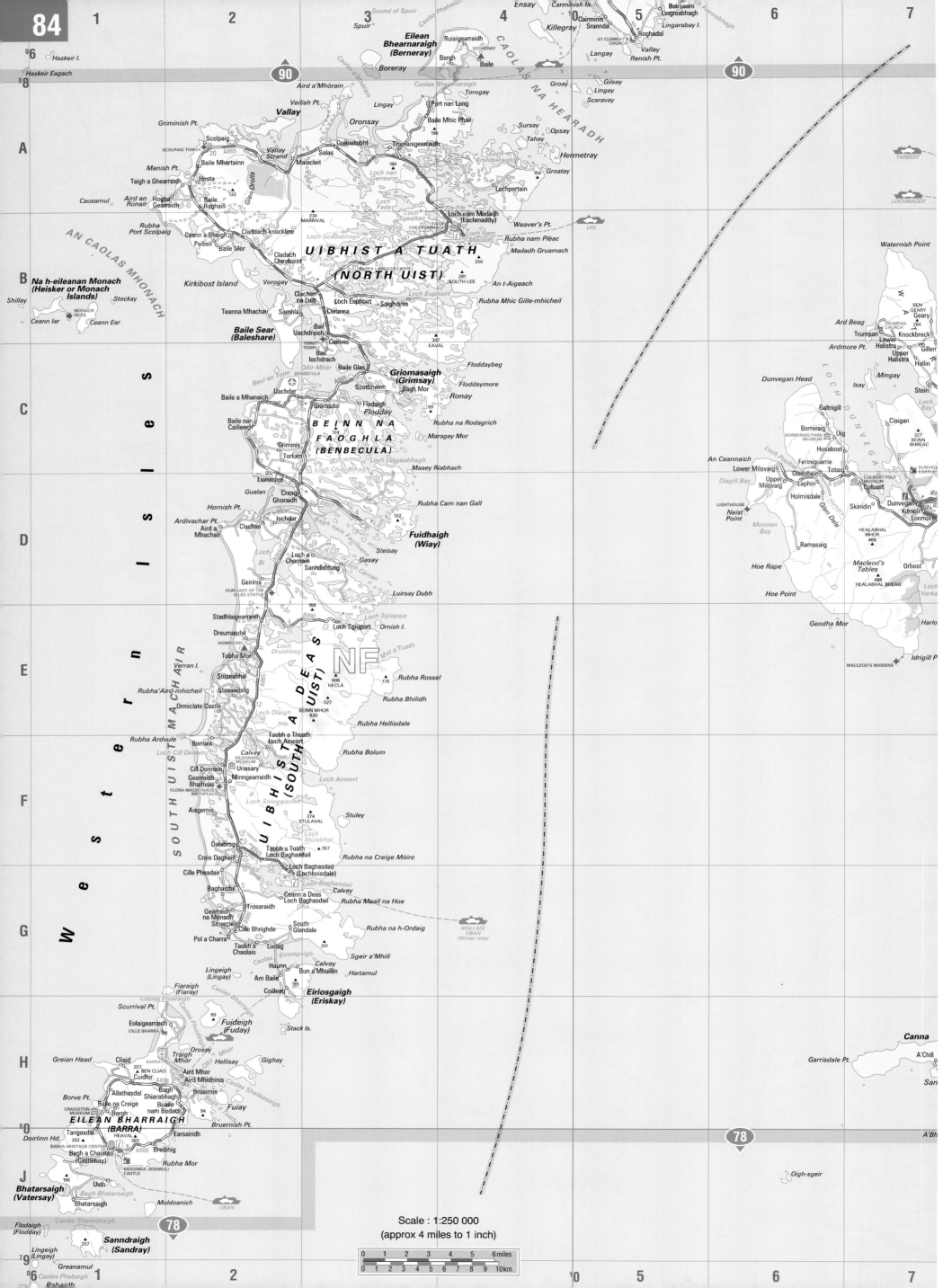

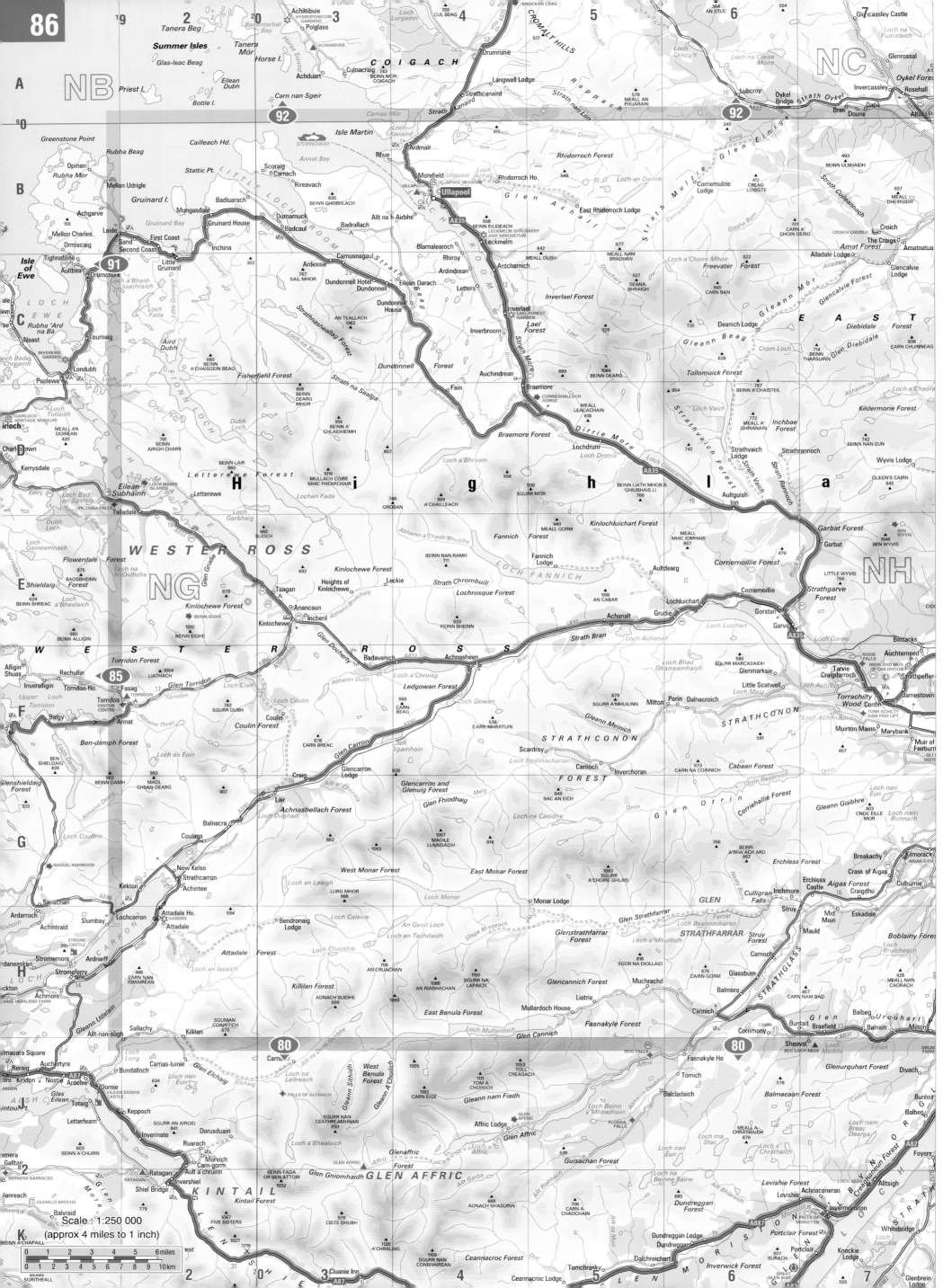

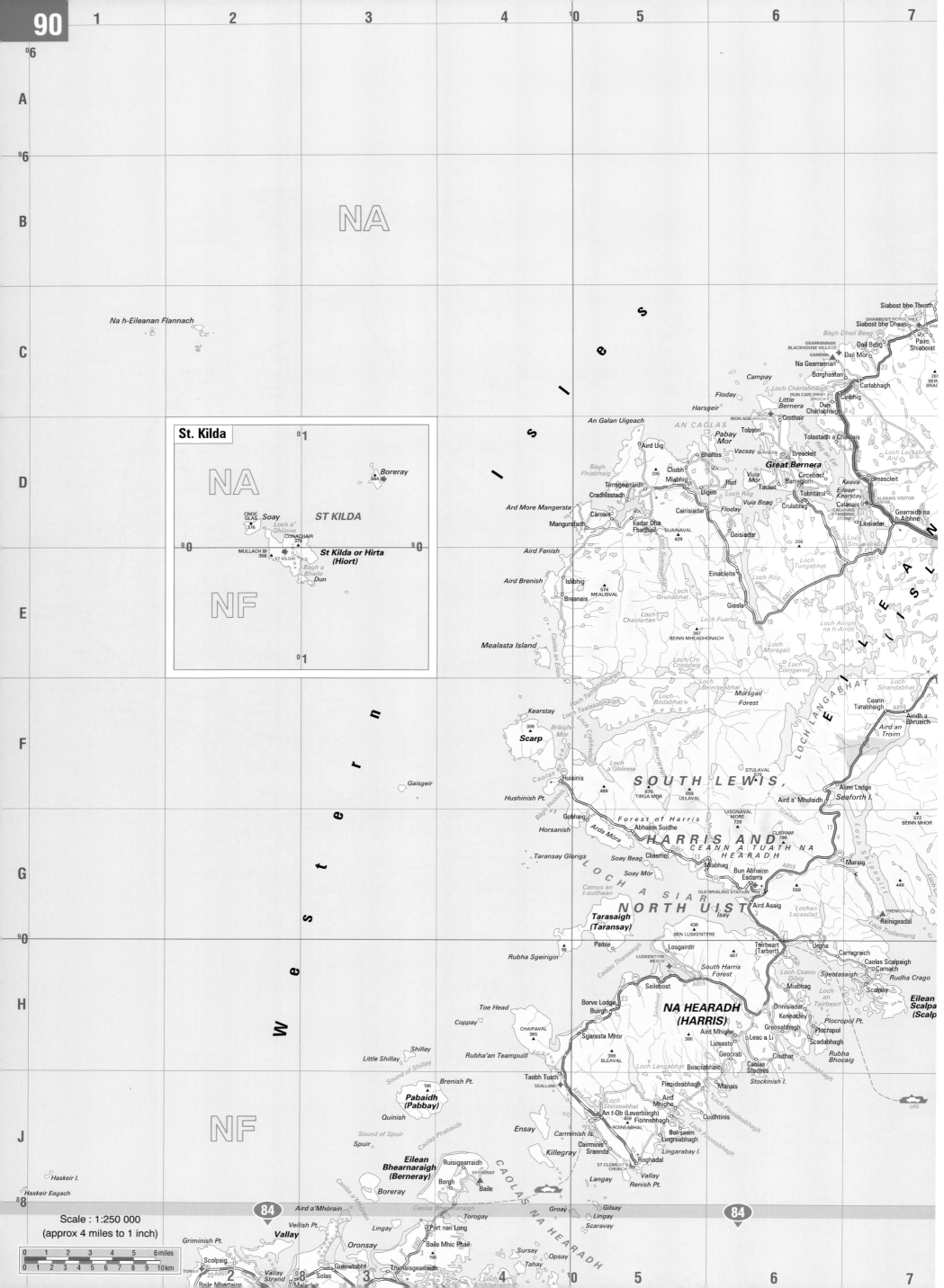

St. Kilda

NA

NF

St KILDA

Boreray

Soay
CNOC
GLAS
376
Loch a'
Ghlinne
CONACHAIR
376
MULLACH BI
358
ST KILDA
St Kilda or Hirta
(Hiort)
Bágh a
Bhaile
Dun

NA

NF

W e s t e r n

Na h-Eileanan Flannach

Na Gearrannan

Siabost bho Thuath
SHAWBOST NORSE MILL
Siabost bho Dheas
Bágh Dhail Beag
Pairc
Shiabost
GEARRANNAN
BLACKHOUSE VILLAGE
GARENIN
Dail Beag
Dail Mór
Borghastan
Campay
Loch Chàrlabhaigh
DUN CARLOWAY
BROCH
Carlabhagh
Floday
Little
Bernera
Ciribhig
Harsgeir
IRON AGE HOUSE
An Galan Uigeach
Aird Uig
Pabay
Mór
Vacsay
Tobson
Breacleit
Tolastadh a Chaolais
Cliobh
Bhaltos
Miabhig
Great Bernera
Circebost
Breascleit
Vuia
Mór
Riof
Tacleit
Barraglom
Keava
Eilean
Kearstay
Crulabhig
Uigen
Loch Róg
Tobhtarol
CALANAIS VISITOR CENTRE
CALANAIS
STANDING STONE
Circebost
Timsgearraidh
Cradhlastadh
Eadar Dha
Fhadhail
Vuia Beag
Gearraidh na
h-Aibhne
Càrnais
Floday
Cairisiadar
Linsiadar
Ard More Mangersta
Geisiadar
Loch
Tungabhat
Mangurstadh
256
SUAINAVAL
429
Einacleite
Loch Róg
Aird Fenish
Aird Brenish
Islibhig
574
MEALISVAL
Giosla
Loch
Grunabhat
Giosla
Breanais
Loch
Chaolartan
BEINN MHEADHONACH
397
Loch
Morsgail
Loch Airigh
na h-Airde
Mealasta Island
Loch Cro
Criosdaig
Loch
Coingerod
SOUTH LEWIS,

Loch Langabhat

E I L E A N

Loch Strandabhat

Loch Beinisebhal

Morsgail
Forest

Ceann
Tarabhaigh
Airidh a
Bhruaich

Loch Tamnabhaigh

Aird an
Troim

Kearstay
308
Bràighe
Mór

Loch Tealasbhaigh

Loch Bódabhat
Reasort

Loch Crabhlat
Scarp
489
STULAVAL
575
Aline Lodge

Gaisgeir
Huisinis
Aird a' Mhulaidh
Seaforth I.
679
TIRGA MÓR
659
ULLAVAL
UISGNAVAL
MORE
729
572
BEINN MHOR
Hushinish Pt.
Gobhaig
Forest of Harris
Horsanish
Abhainn Suidhe
HARRIS AND
CLISHAM
799
Arda Móra
CEANN A TUATH NA
HEARADH
Taransay Glorigs
Cliasmol
Soay Beag
Miabhag
559
449
Soay Mór
Bun Abhainn
Eadarra
Camus an
t-suithean
OLD WHALING STATION
NORTH UIST
Aird Asaig
Isay
Reinigeadal
Tarasaigh
(Taransay)
Lochan
Lacasdail
Loch Trollamaraig
Paible
BEN LUSKENTYRE
436
Urgha
Carragraich
99
Rubha Sgeirigin
LUSKENTYRE
BEACH
Losgaintir
Tàirbeart
(Tarbert)
Caolas Scalpaigh
Carnach
467
South Harris
Dibig
Loch Ceann
Dibig
Sgeotasaigh
Rubha Crago
Caolas Tharasaigh
Seilebost
South Harris
Forest
Miabhag
Loch
an
Tairbeart
Scalpay
Eilean
Scalpa
(Scalp
Toe Head
Borve Lodge
23
Drinisiadar
Coppay
Buirgh
Seilebost
NA HEARADH
(HARRIS)
Kennacley
Plocrapol Pt.
CHAIPAVAL
365
Sgarasta Mhor
Aird Mhighe
386
Greosabhagh
Leac a Li
Plocrapol
Scadabhagh
Rubha
Bhocaig
Little Shillay
Shillay
Liceasto
Geocrab
Cluthar
398
BLEAVAL
Loch Langabhat
Caolas
Stocinis
Greosabhagh
Rubha'an Teampuill
Taobh Tuath
SEALLAM!
Beacrabhaic
Fleoideabhagh
Stockinish I.
Brenish Pt.
196
Manais
Aird
Loch
Steiseabhat
Cuidhtinis
Pabaidh
(Pabbay)
An t-Ob (Leverburgh)
ROINEABHAL
459
Bòrseam
Quinish
Fionnsbhagh
Lingreabhagh
Lingarabay I.
Ensay
Carminish Is.
Sound of Spuir
Spuir
Killegray
Cairminis
Srannda
Langay
ST CLEMENT'S
CHURCH
Roghadal
Valley
Eilean
Bhearnaraigh
(Berneray)
Ruisigearraidh
BERNERAY
Renish Pt.
Boreray
Borgh
Baile
Gilsay
Haskeir I.
Groay
Scaravay
Caolas a'Mhòrain
CAOLAS NA HEARADH
Haskeir Eagach

Scale : 1:250 000
(approx 4 miles to 1 inch)

0 1 2 3 4 5 6miles
0 1 2 3 4 5 6 7 8 9 10km

Aird a'Mhòrain
Valley
Lingay
Torogay
Veilish Pt.
Port nan Long
Griminish Pt.
Baile Mhic Phail
Sursay
Opsay
Scolpaig
Valley
Strand
Oronsay
190
Tahay
TOWER
A865
Baile Mhartainn
Solas
Greinetobht
Trumaisgearraidh
Malacleit

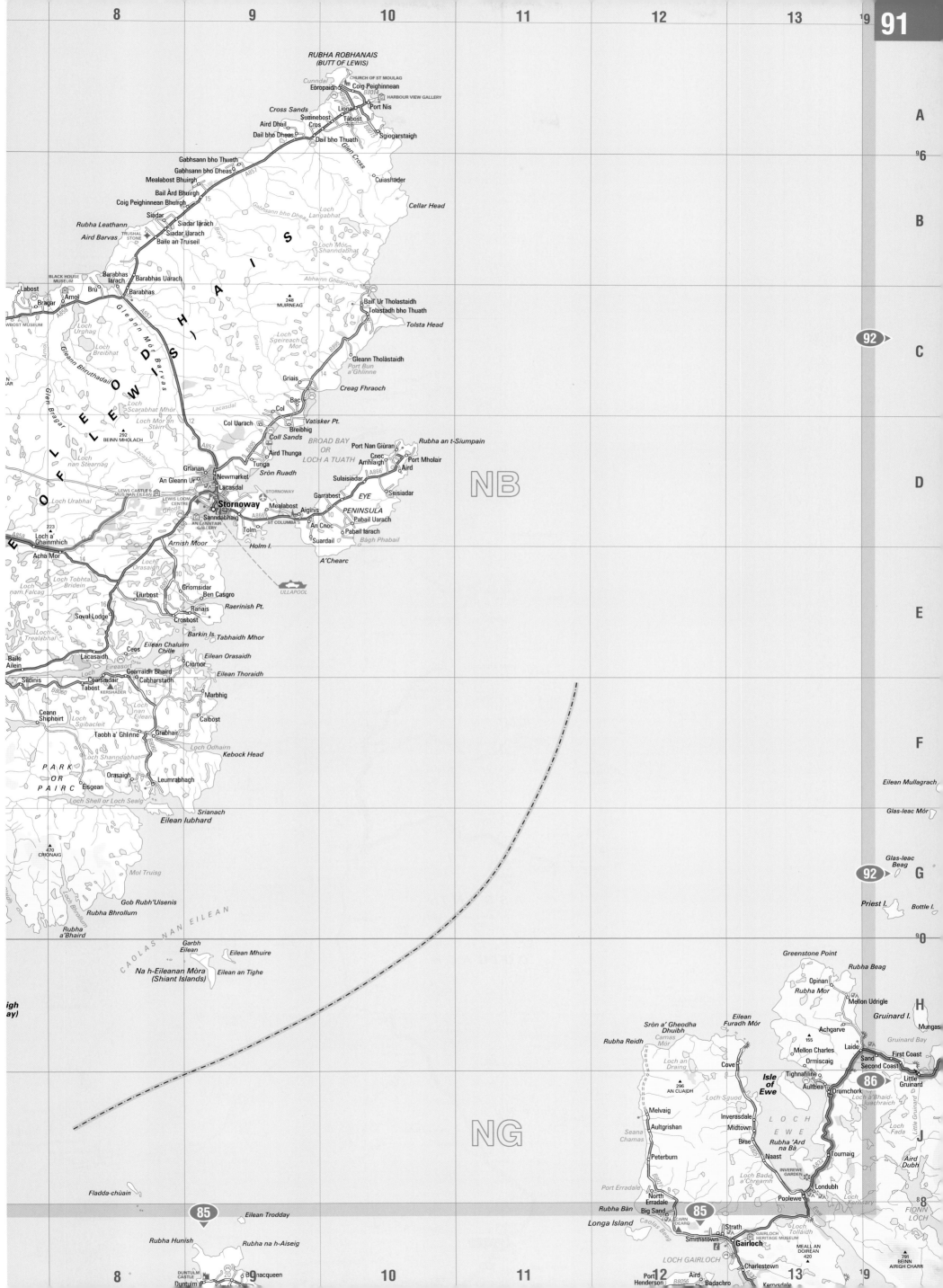

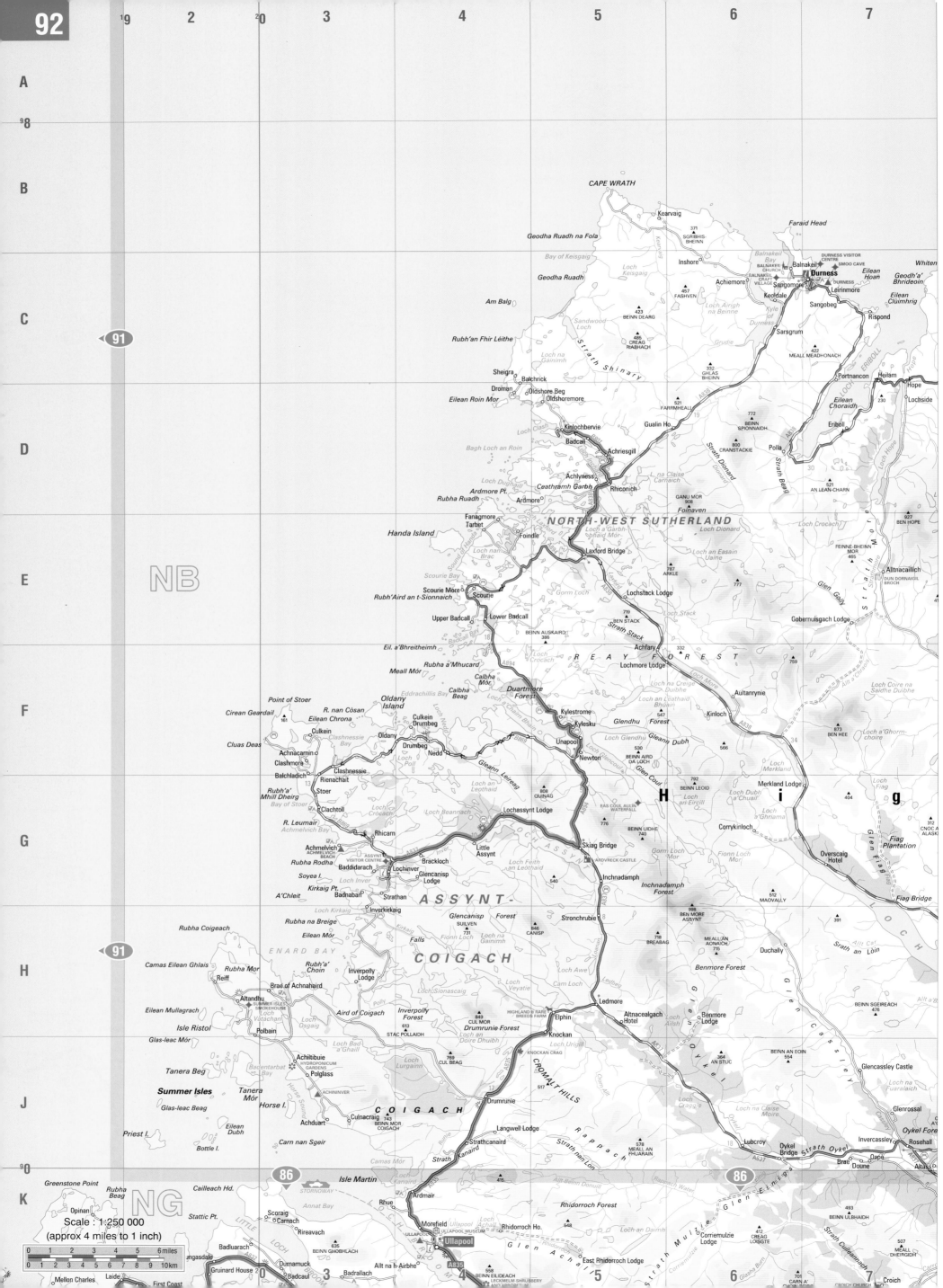

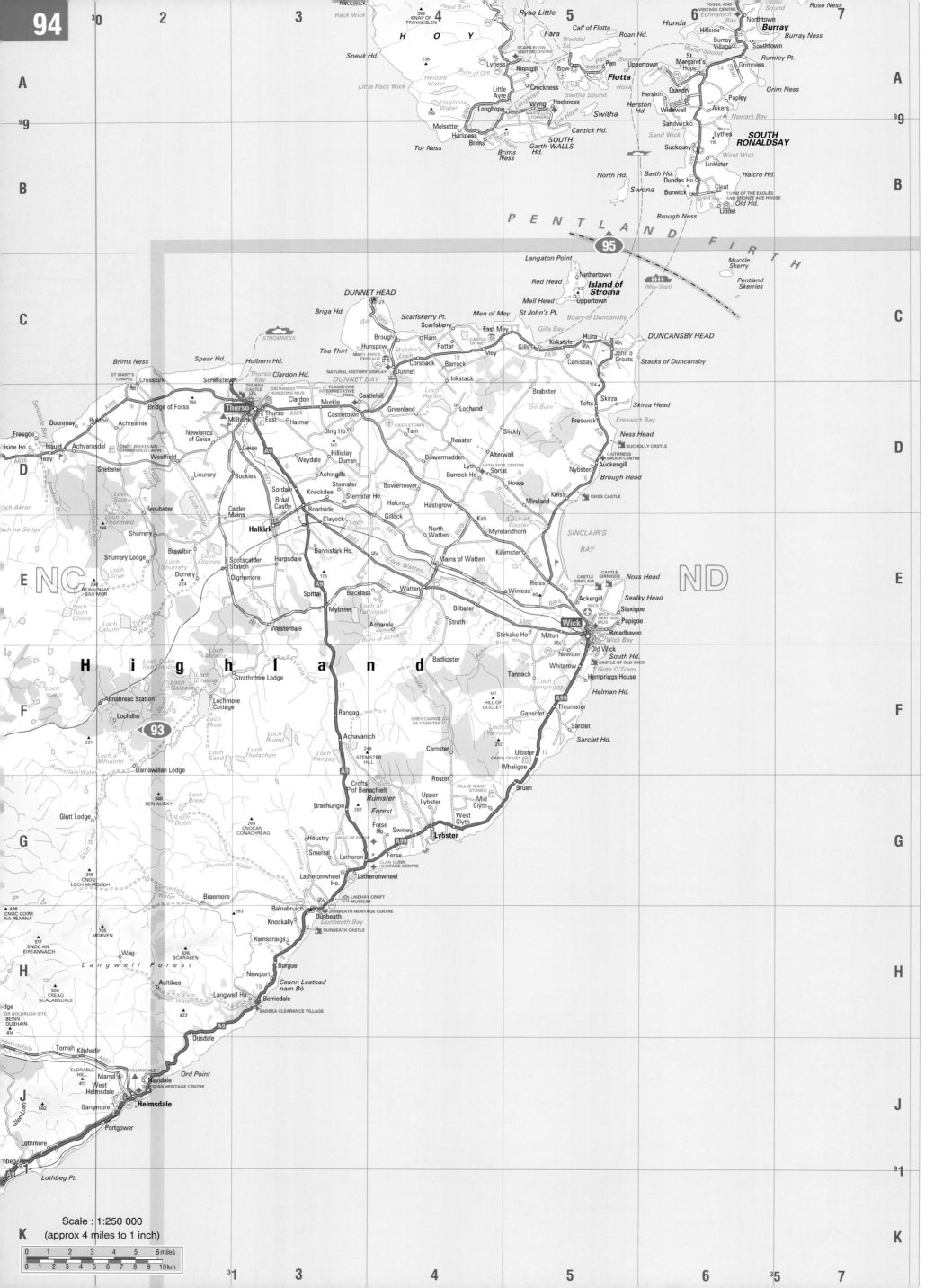

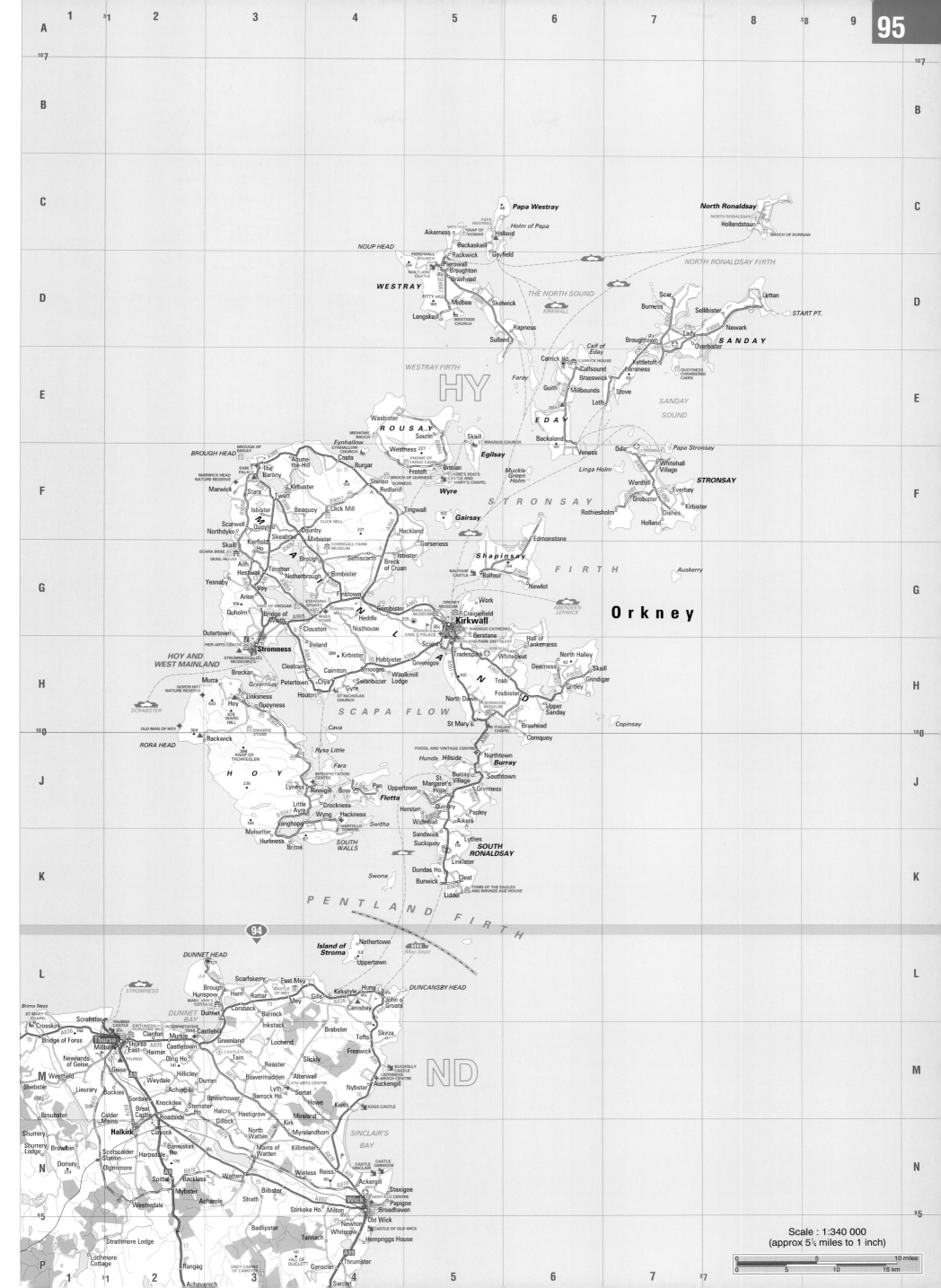

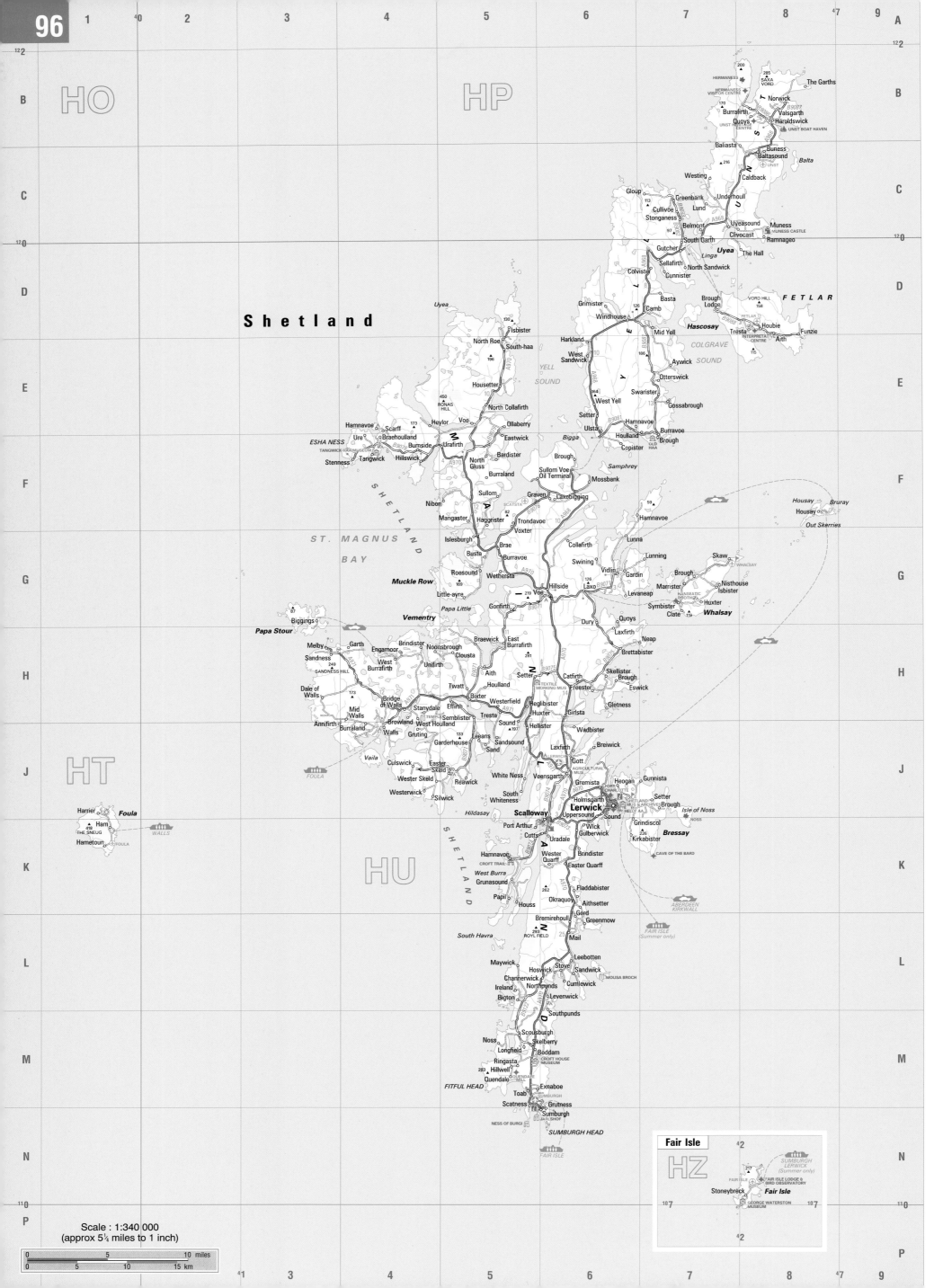

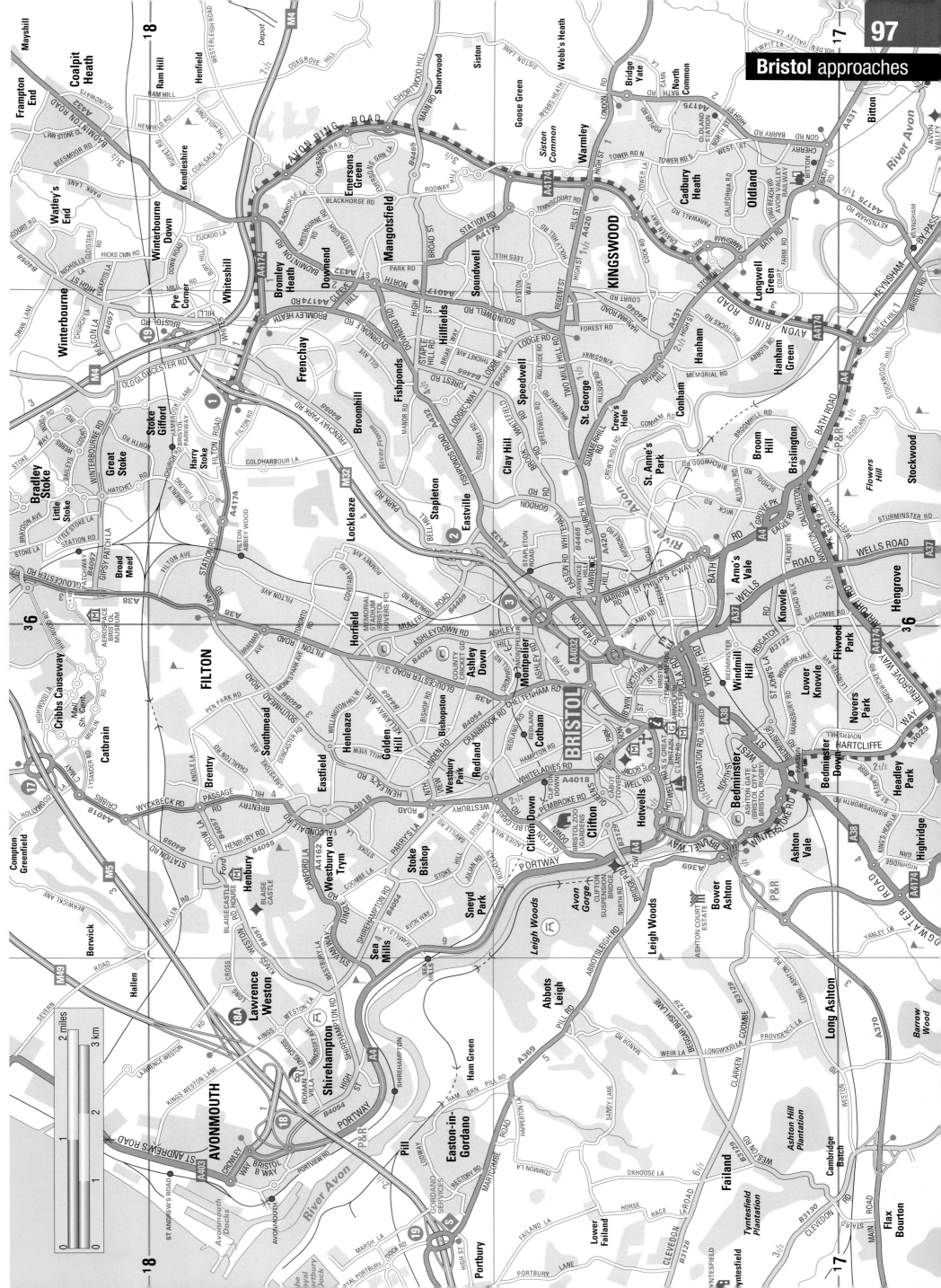

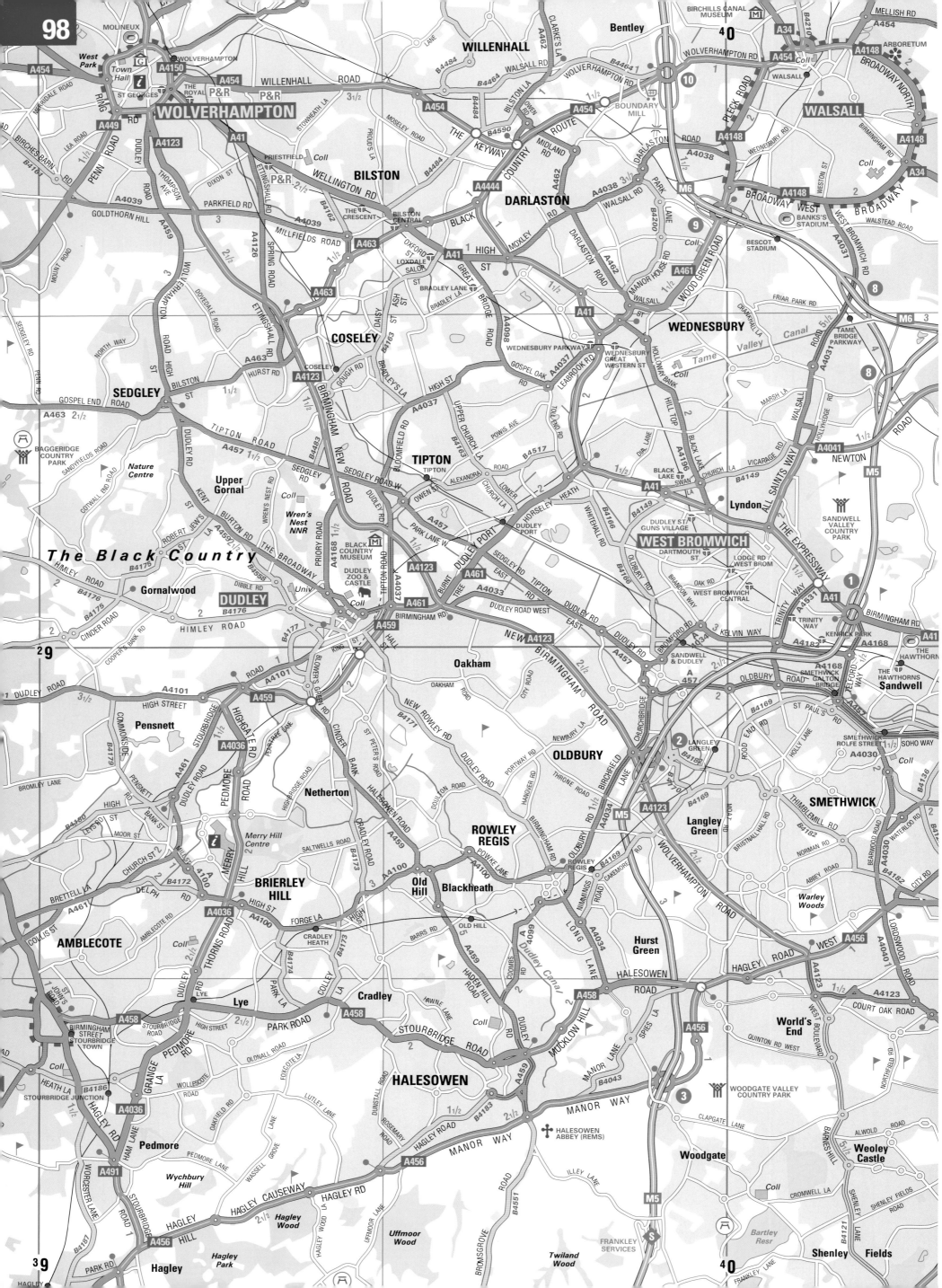

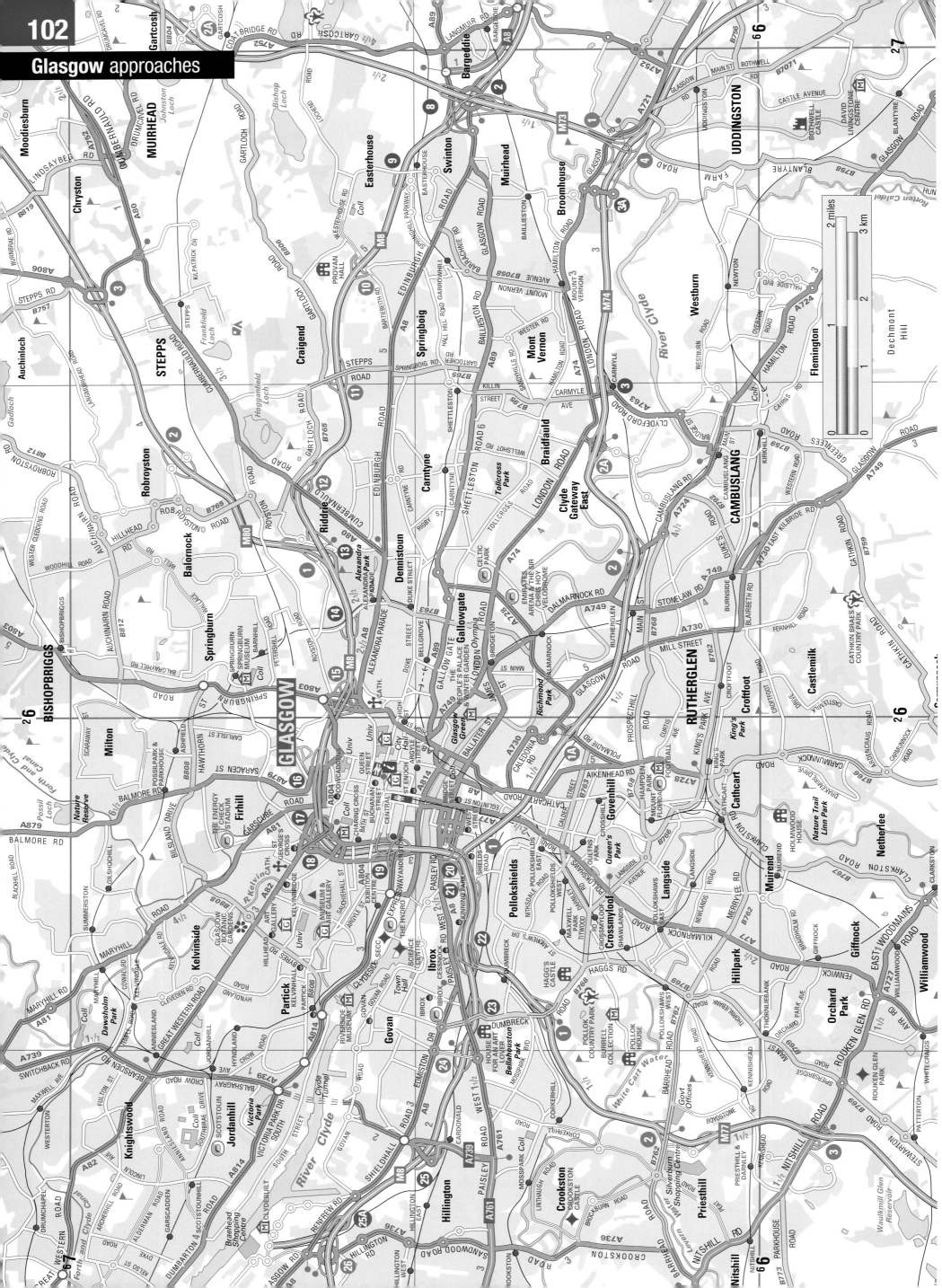

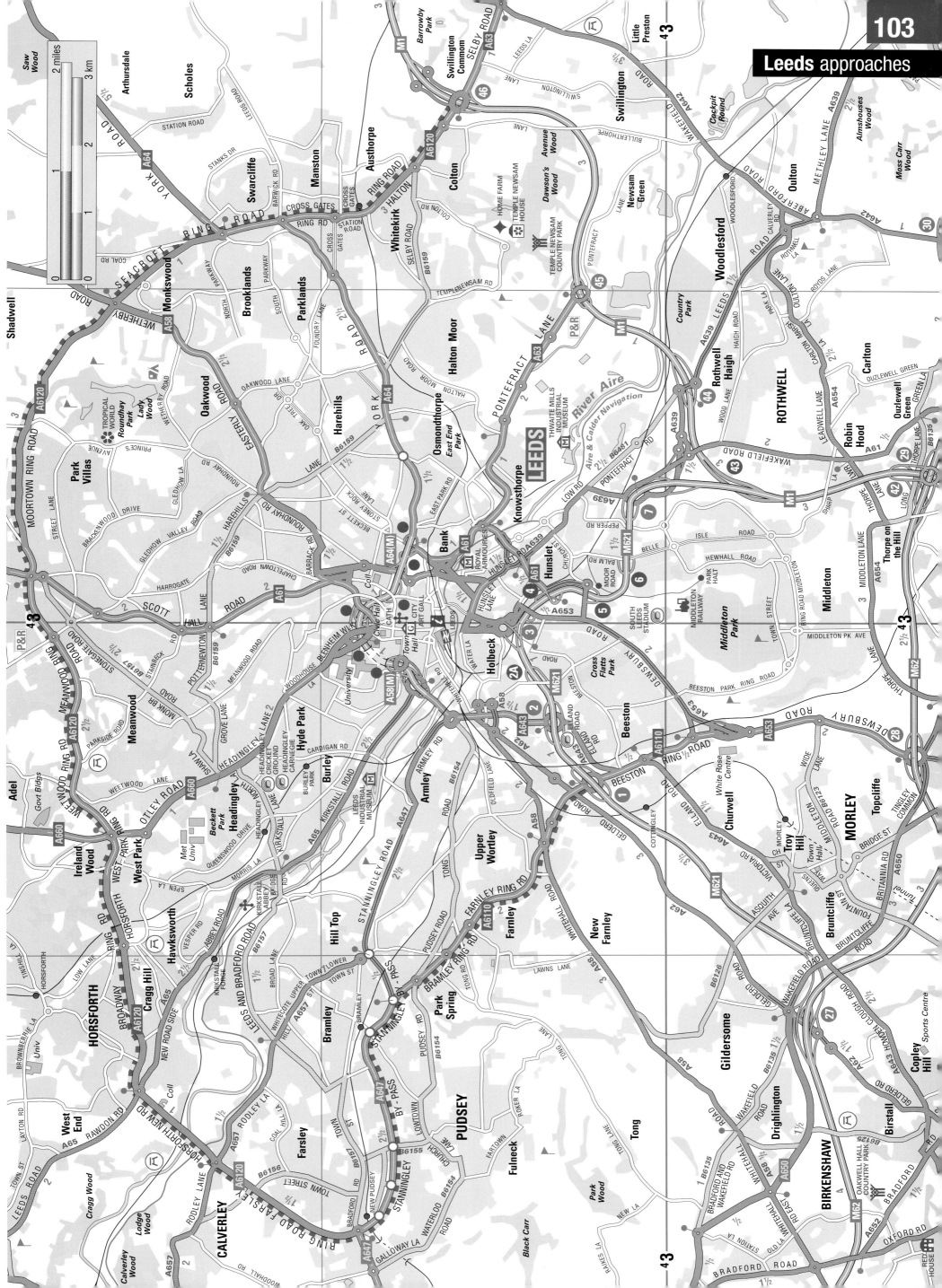

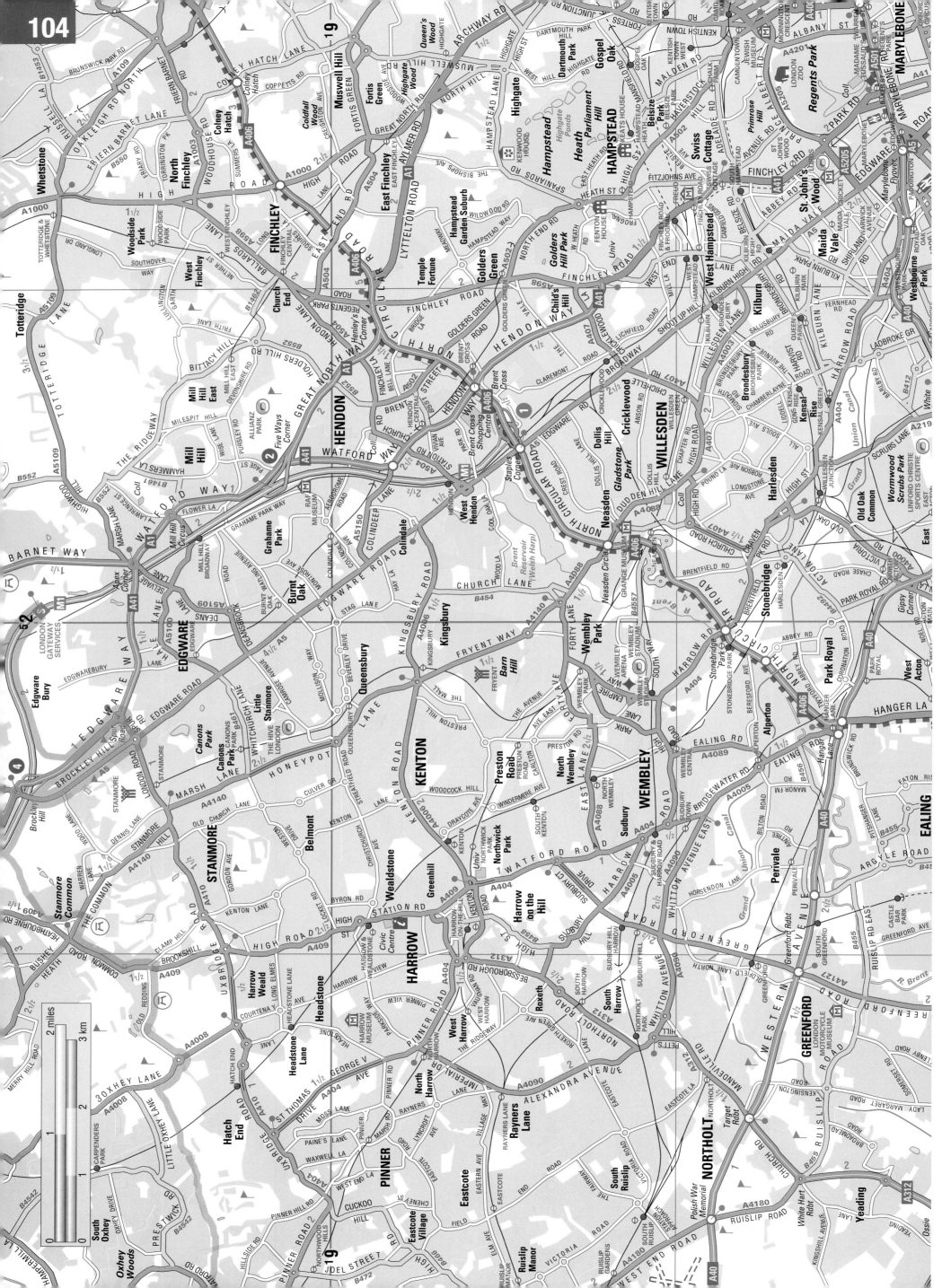

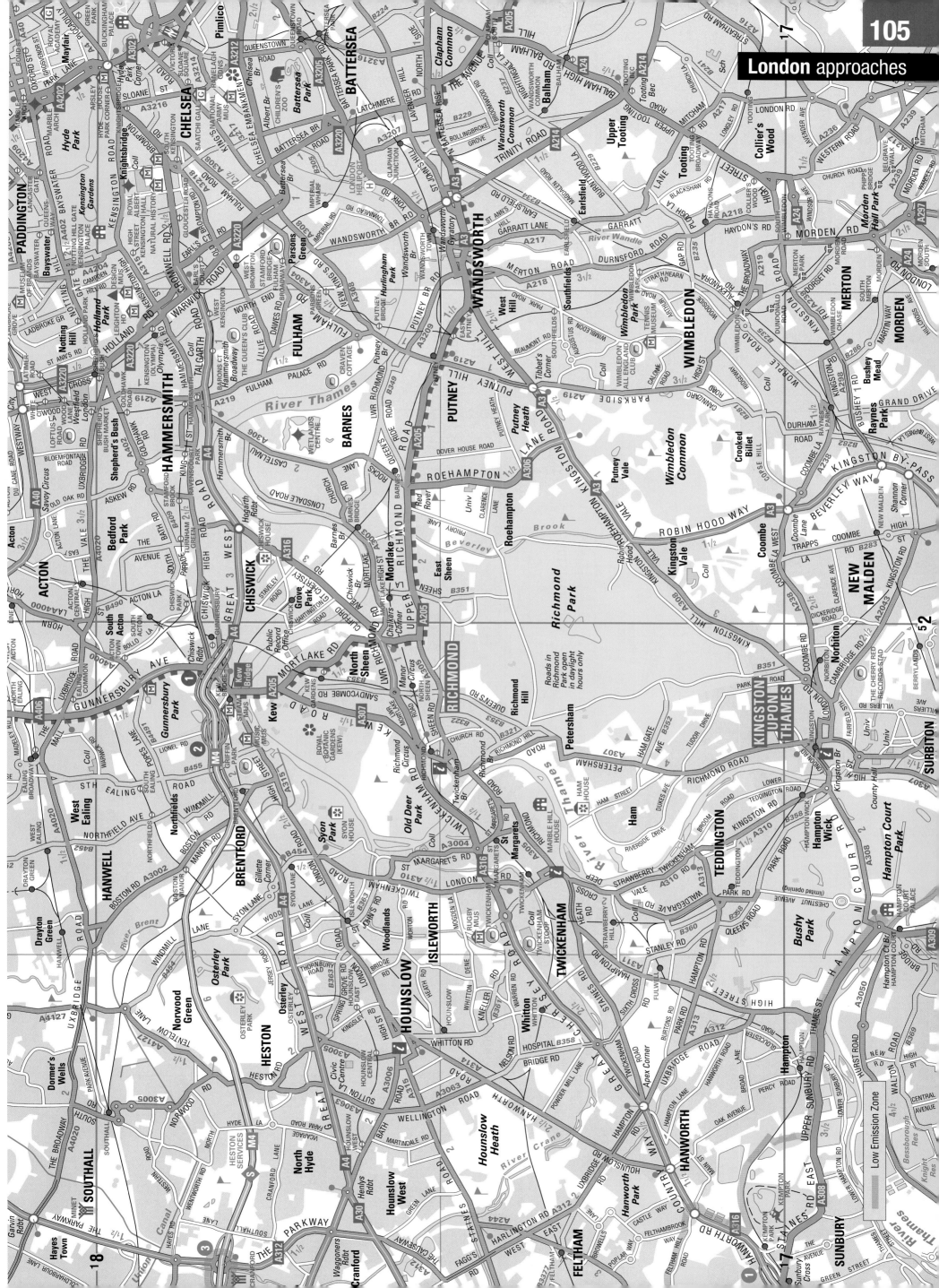

Bath

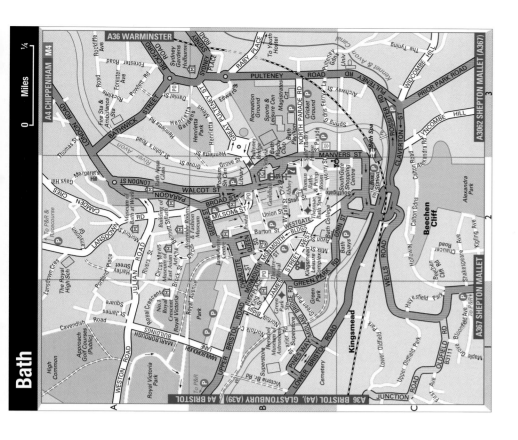

Blackpool

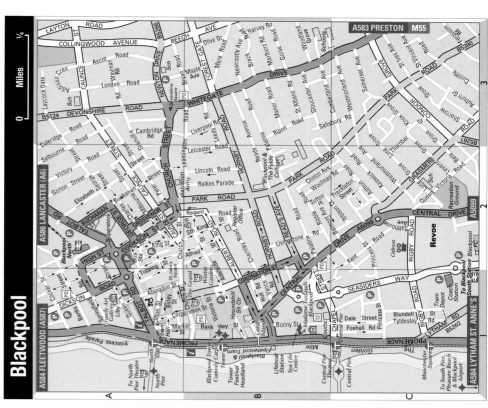

Aberdeen

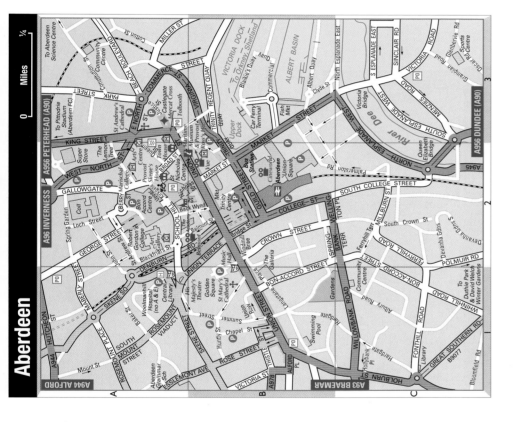

Town plan symbols

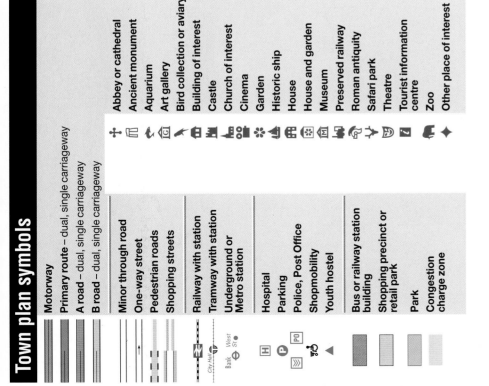

Motorway	
Primary route – dual, single carriageway	
A road – dual, single carriageway	
B road – dual, single carriageway	
Minor through road	
One-way street	
Pedestrian roads	
Shopping streets	
Railway with station	
Tramway with station	
Underground or Metro station	
Hospital	
Parking	
Police, Post Office	
Shopmobility	
Youth hostel	
Bus or railway station building	
Shopping precinct or retail park	
Park	
Congestion charge zone	

Abbey or cathedral	
Ancient monument	
Aquarium	
Art gallery	
Bird collection or aviary	
Building of interest	
Castle	
Church of interest	
Cinema	
Garden	
Historic ship	
House	
House and garden	
Museum	
Preserved railway	
Roman antiquity	
Safari park	
Theatre	
Tourist information centre	
Zoo	
Other place of interest	

Birmingham

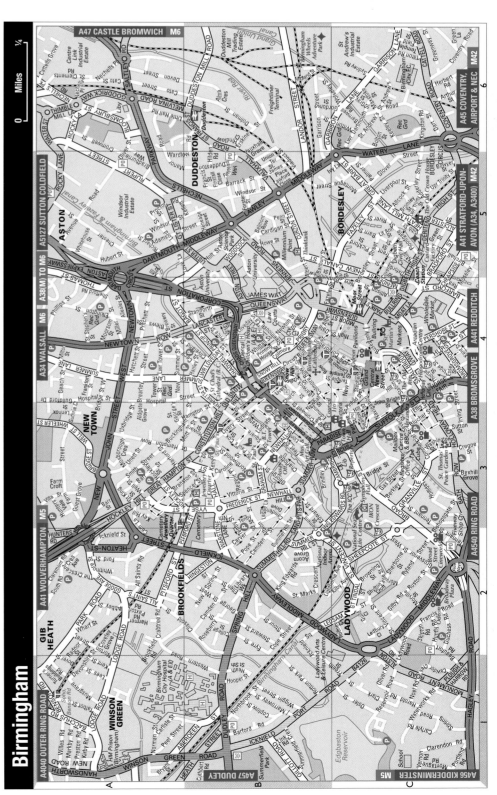

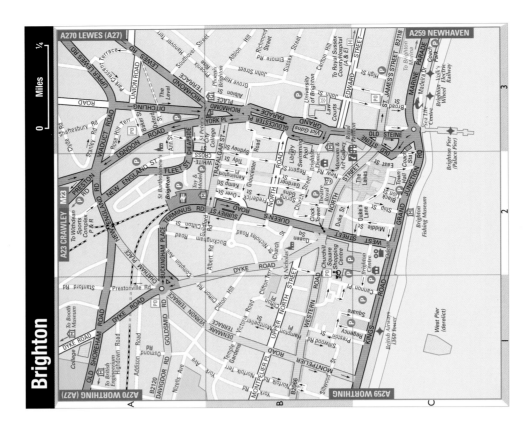

Brighton

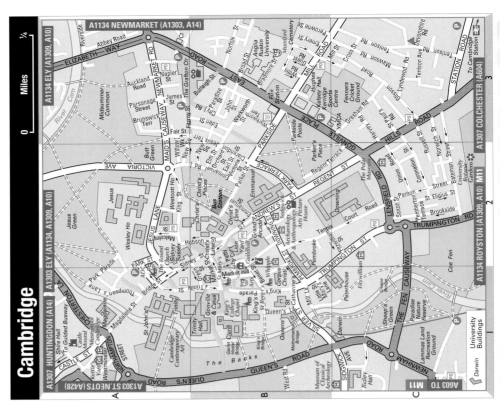

Cambridge

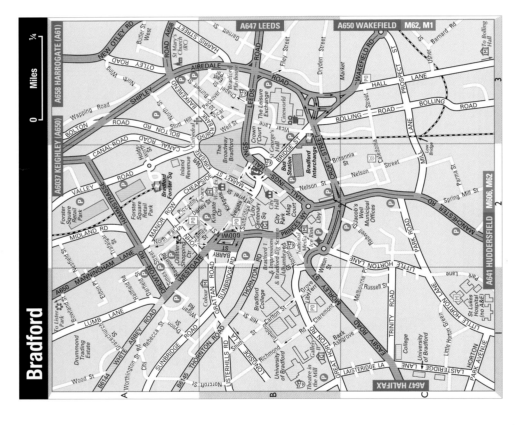

Bradford

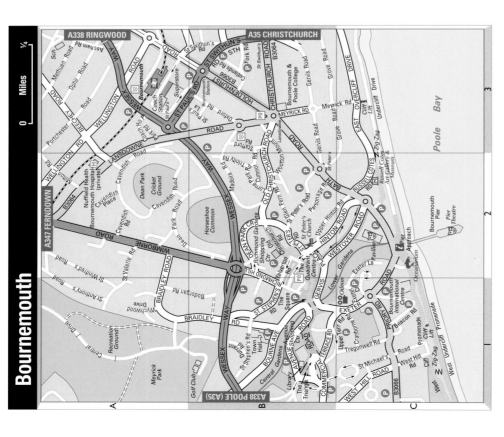

Bournemouth

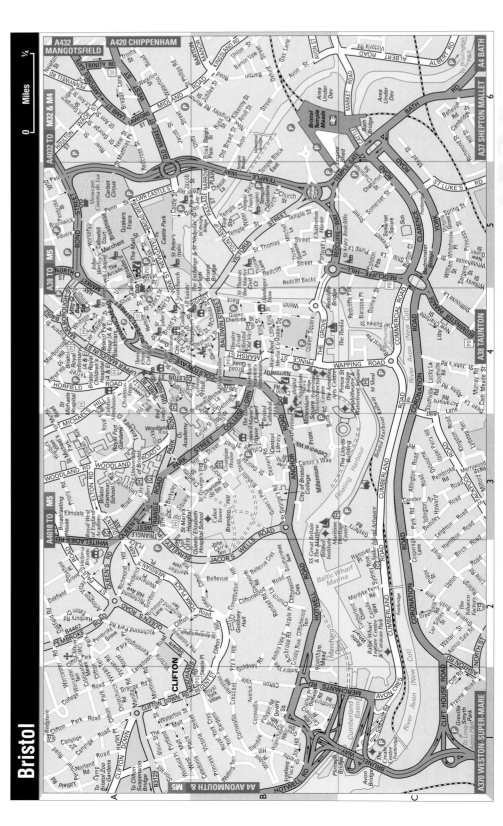

Bristol

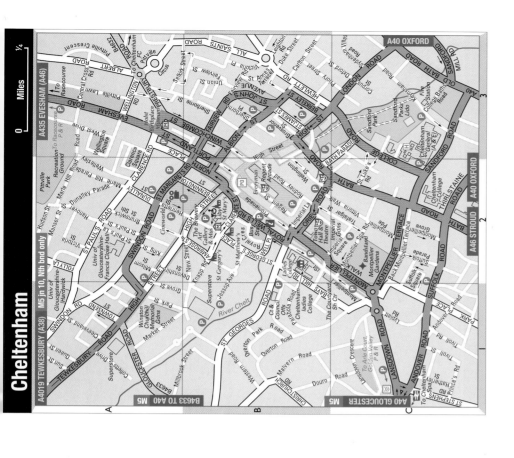

Cheltenham

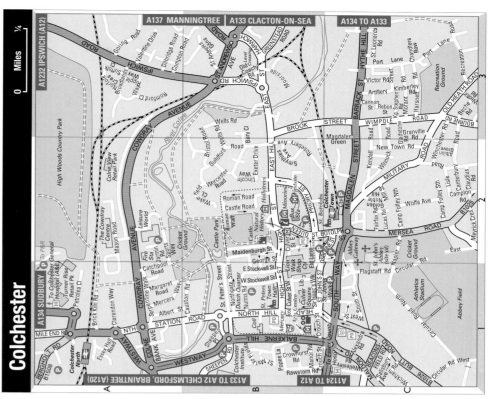

Colchester

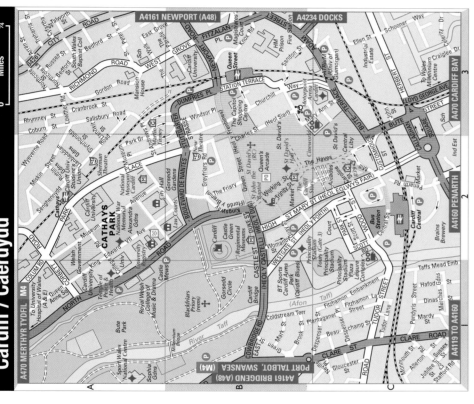

Cardiff / Caerdydd

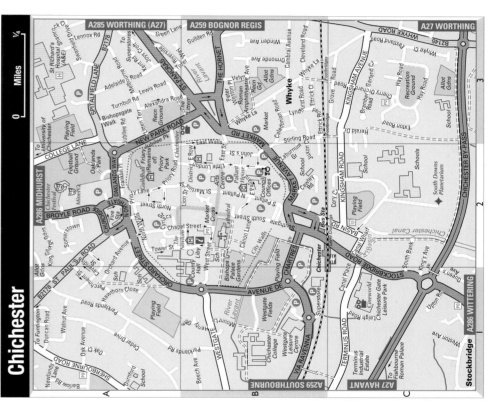

Chichester

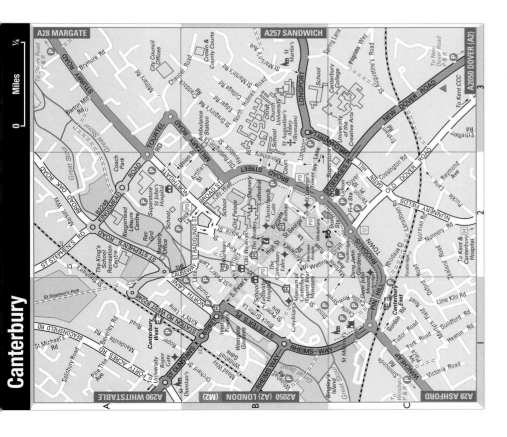

Canterbury

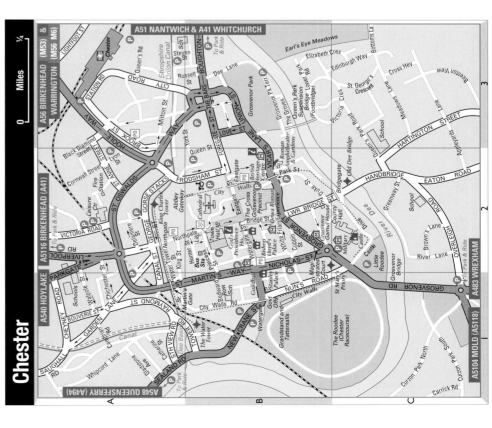

Chester

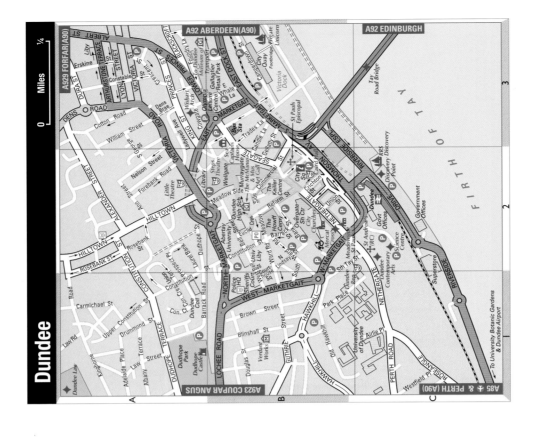

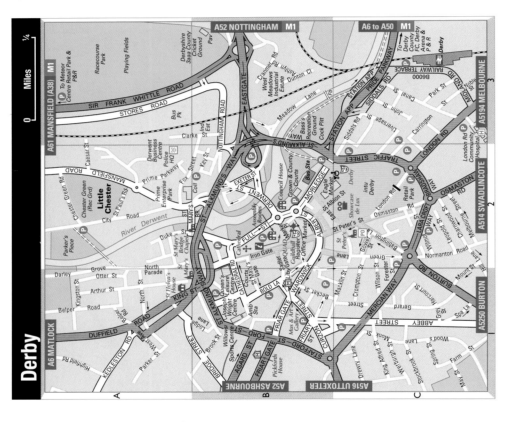

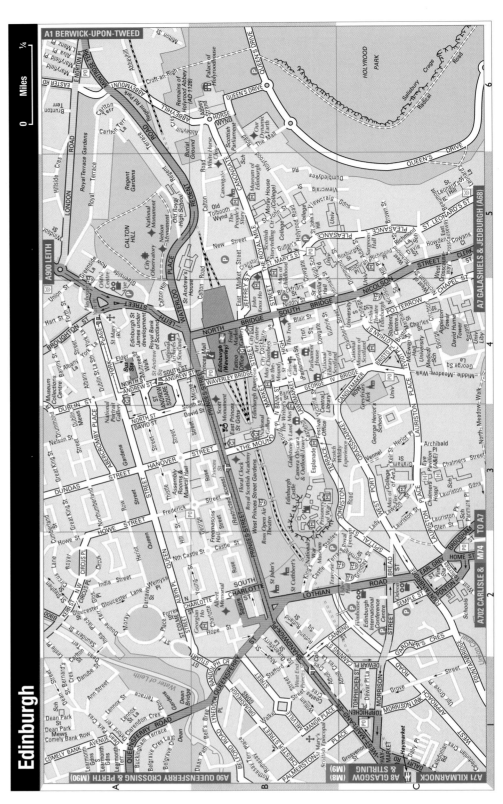

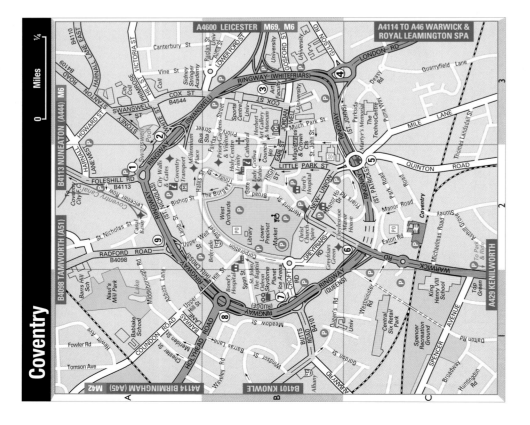

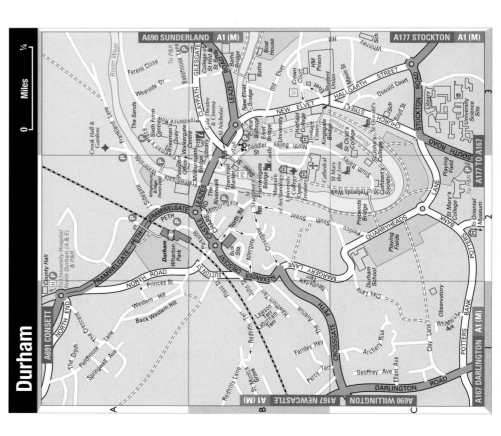

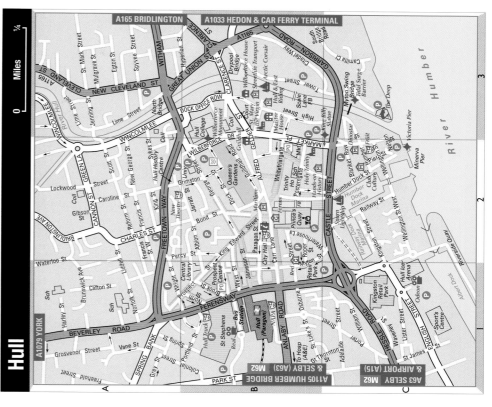

Hull

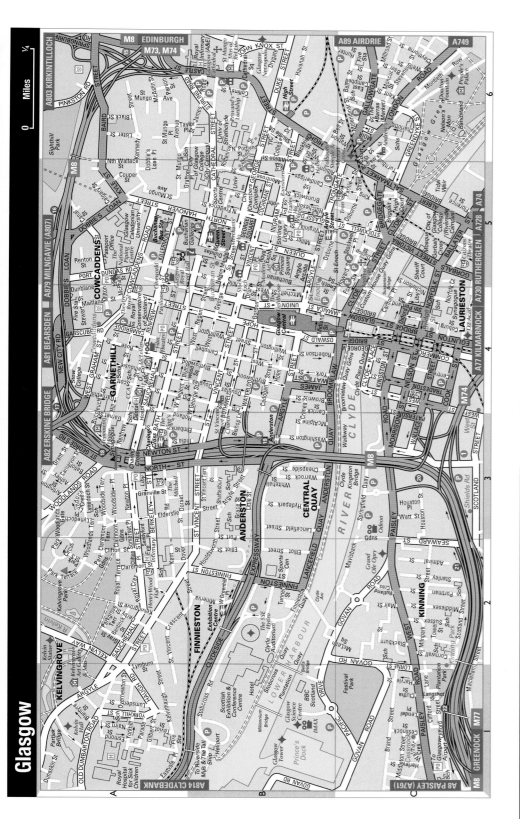

Glasgow

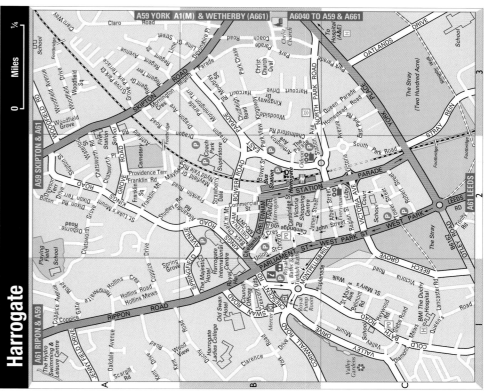

Harrogate

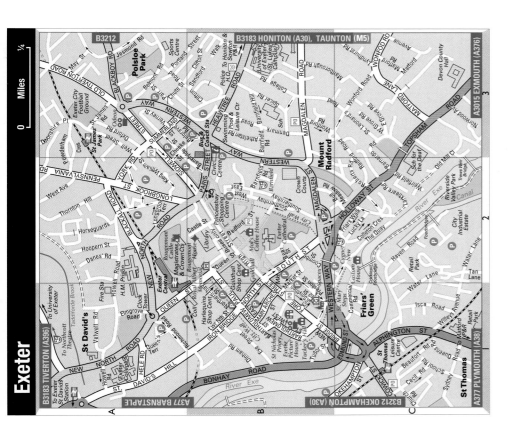

Exeter

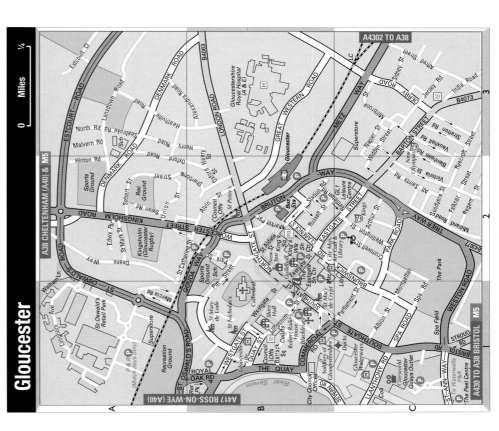

Gloucester

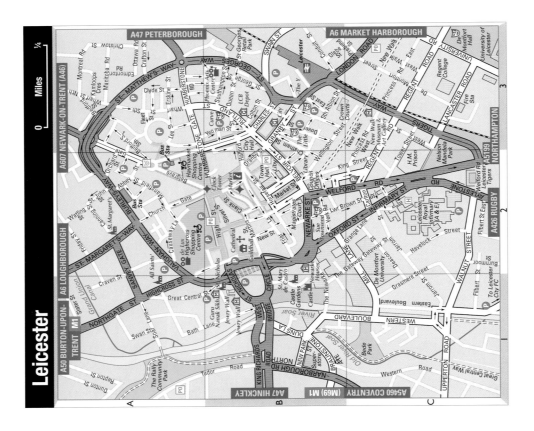

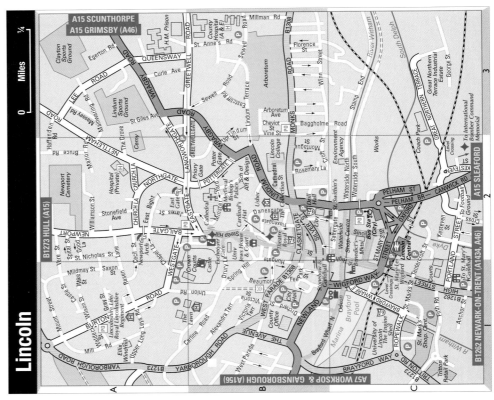

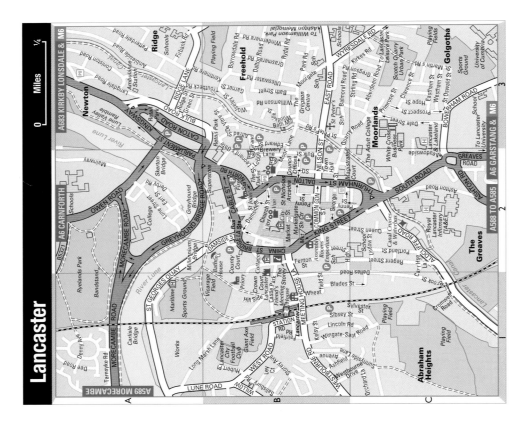

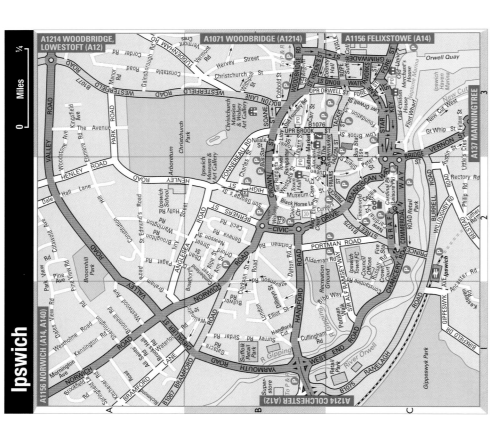

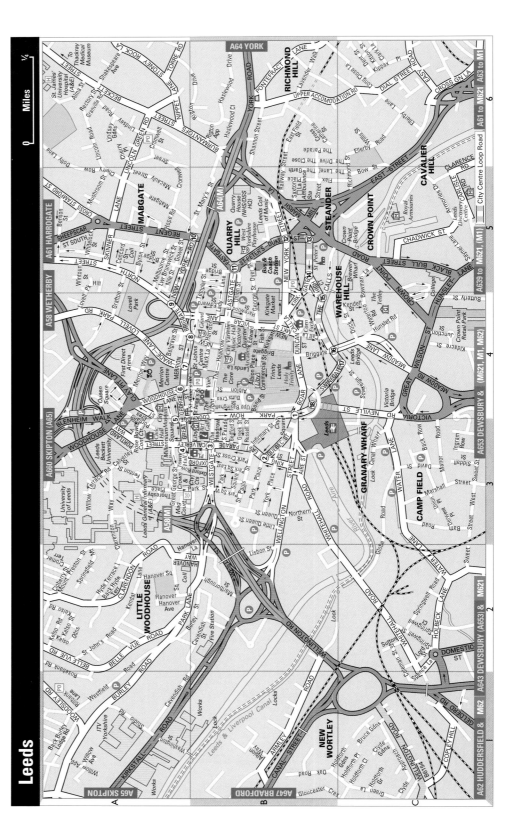

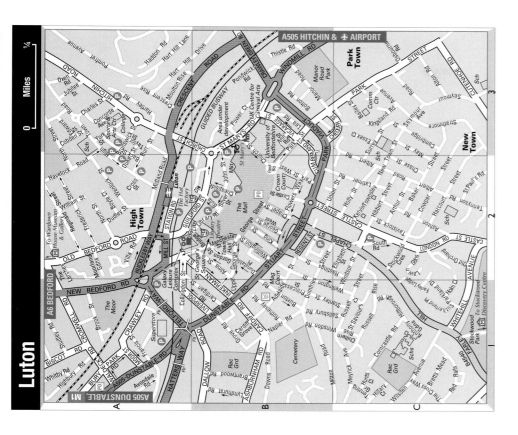

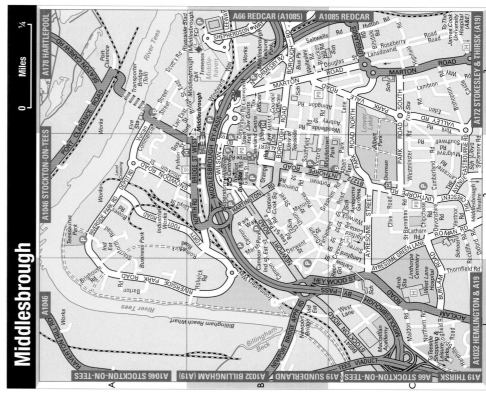

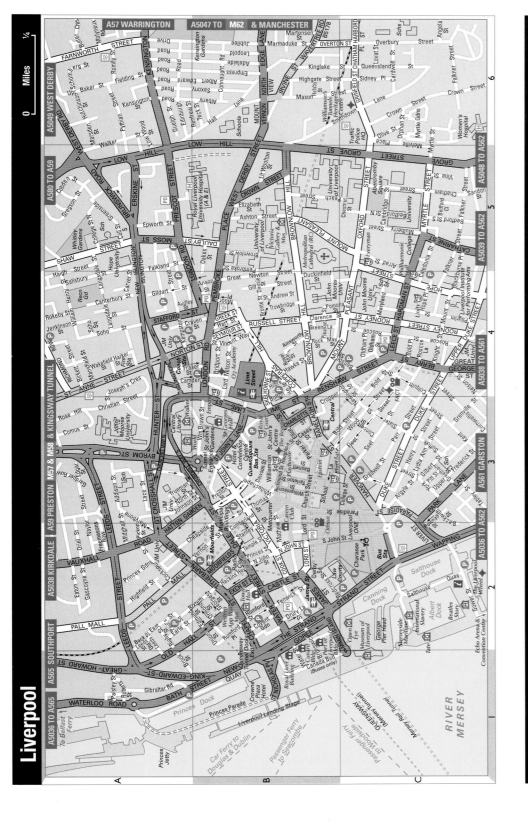

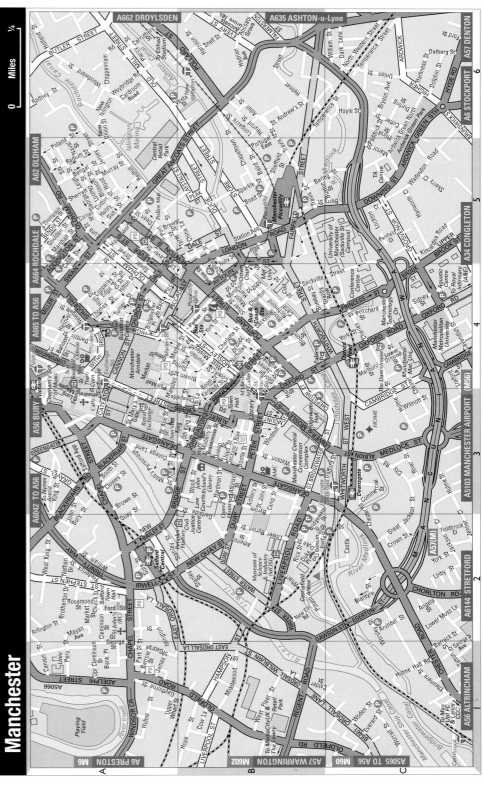

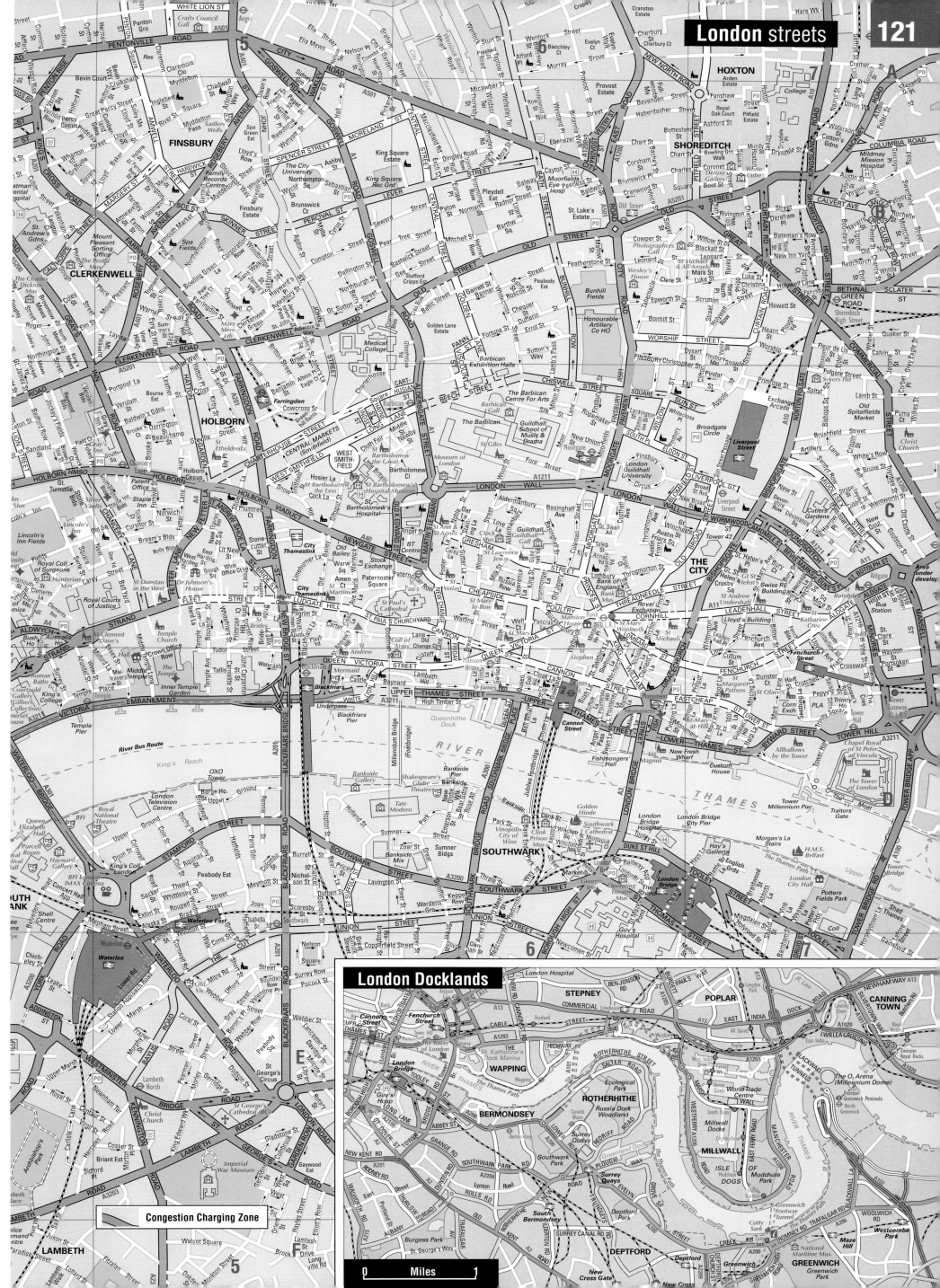

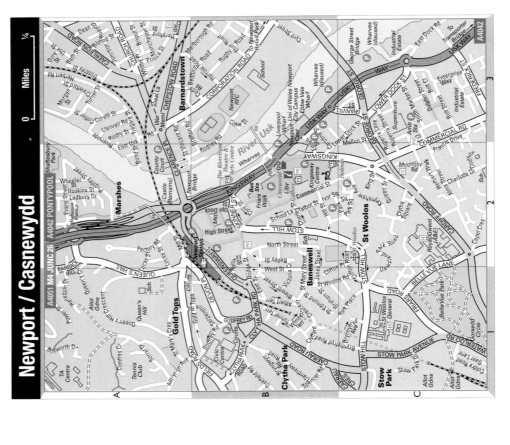

Newport / Casnewydd

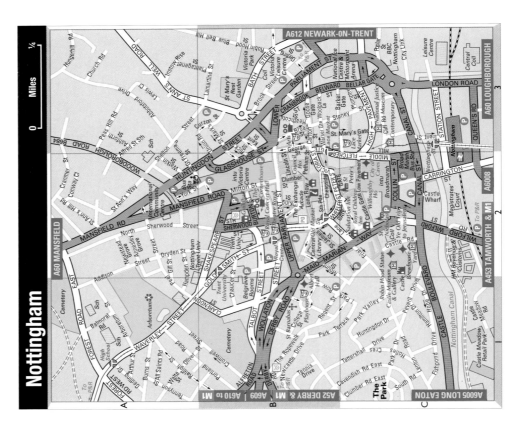

Nottingham

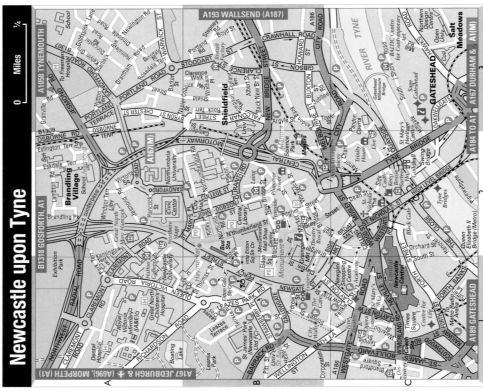

Newcastle upon Tyne

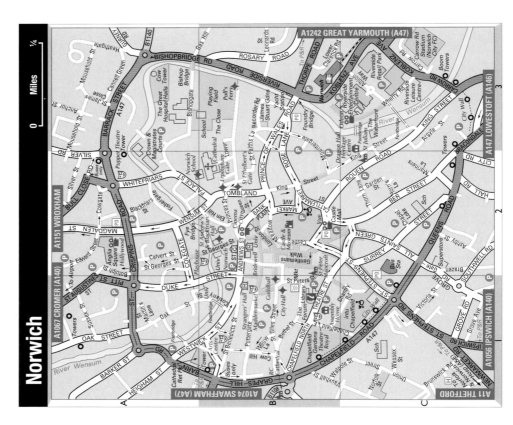

Norwich

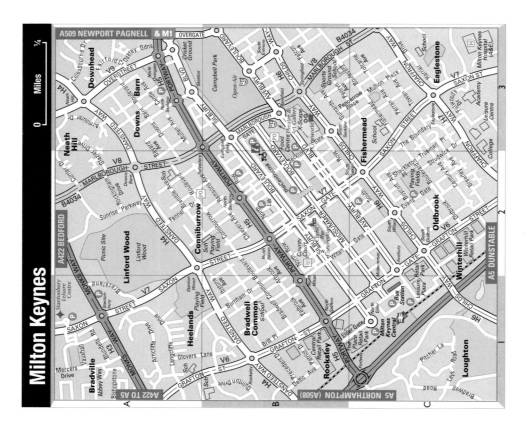

Milton Keynes

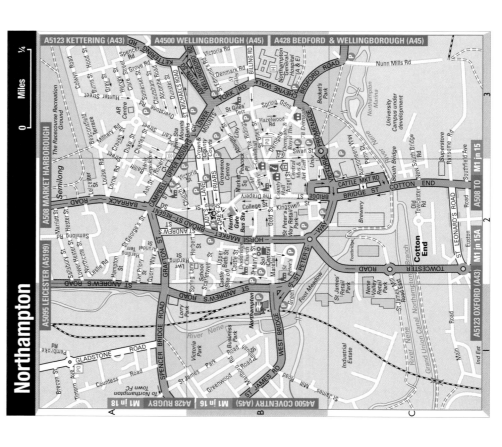

Northampton

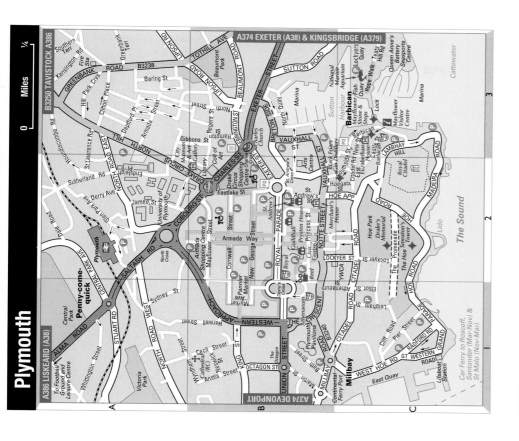

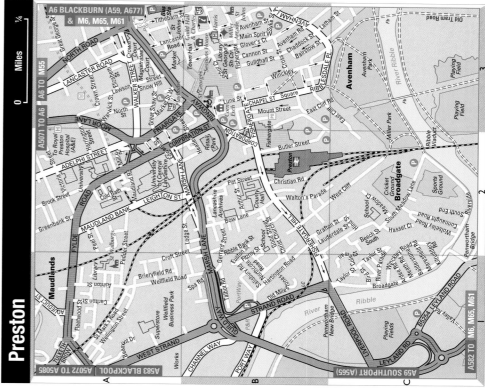

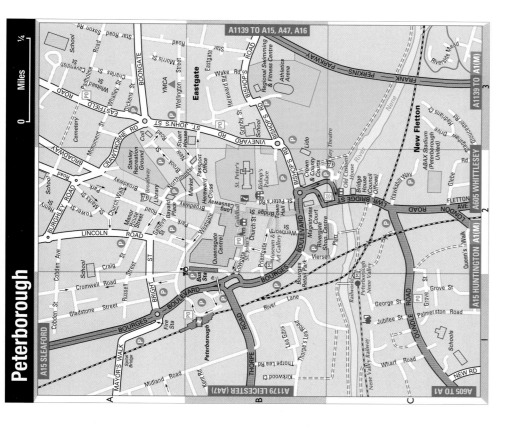

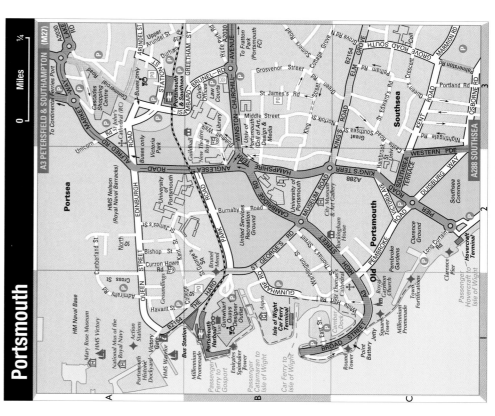

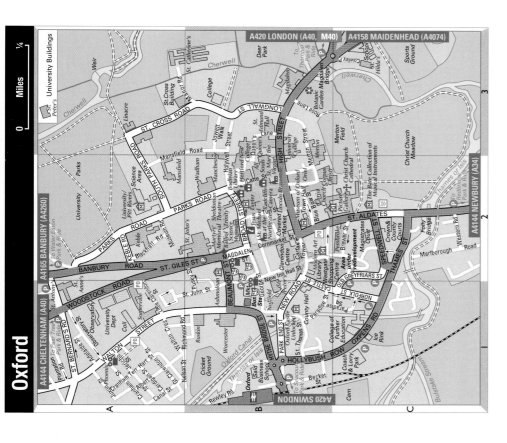

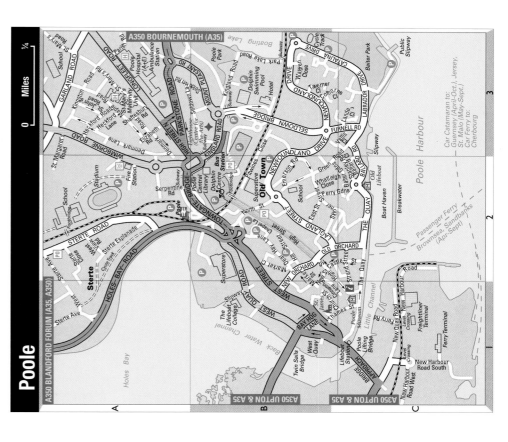

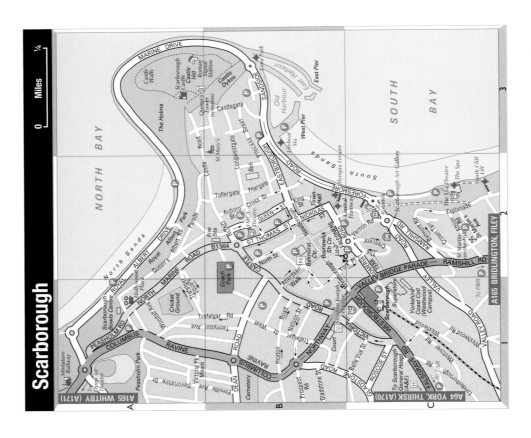

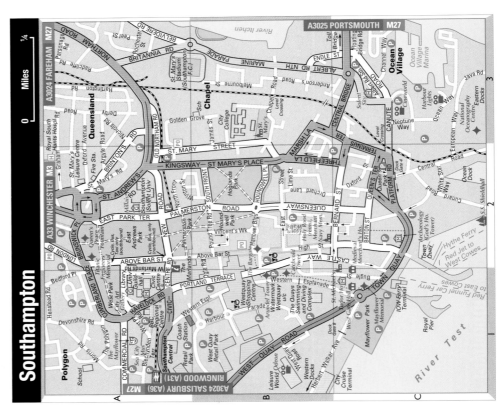

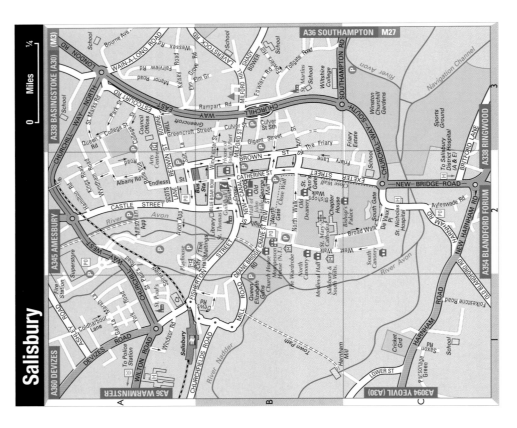

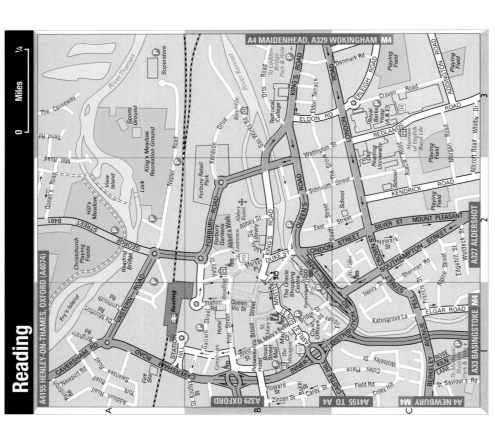

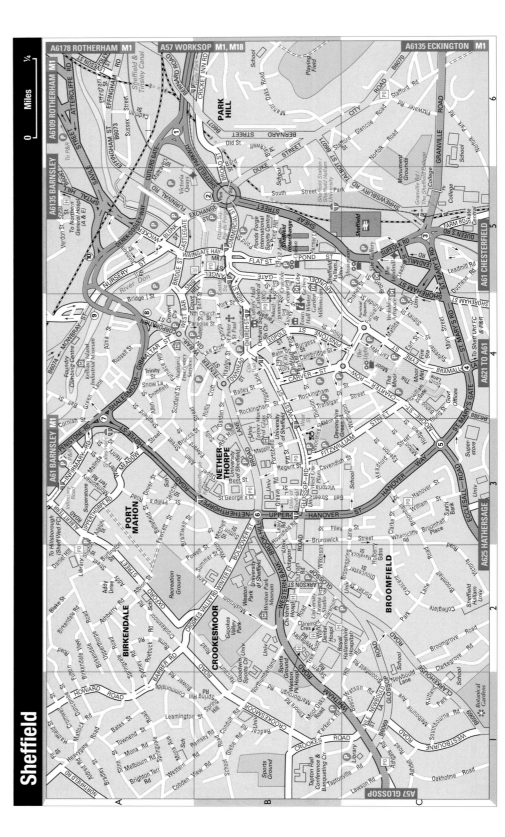

Southend-on-Sea page 20 • **Stoke-on-Trent (Hanley)** page 44 • **Stratford-upon-Avon** page 27 • **Sunderland** page 63 • **Swansea** page 14 • **Swindon** page 17

125

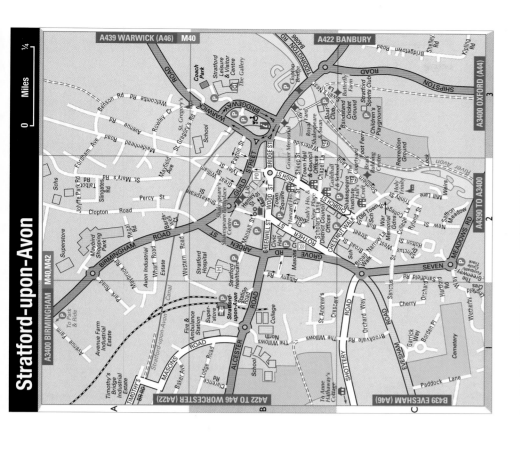

Stratford-upon-Avon

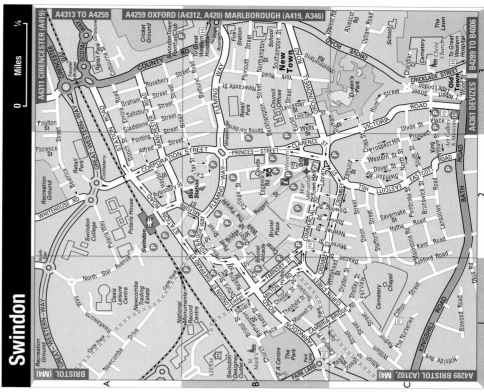

Swindon

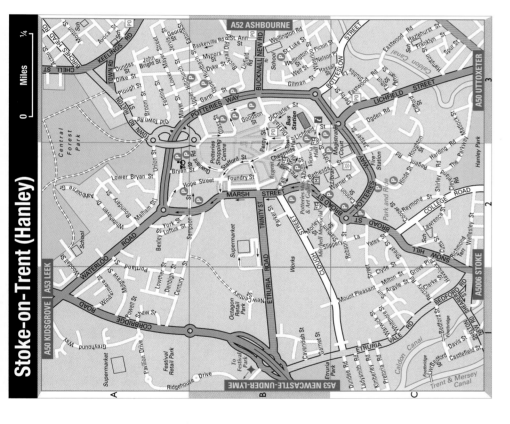

Stoke-on-Trent (Hanley)

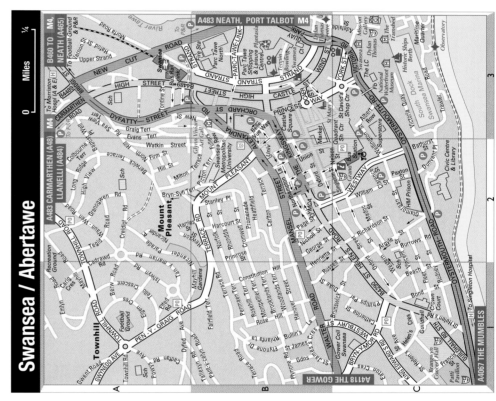

Swansea / Abertawe

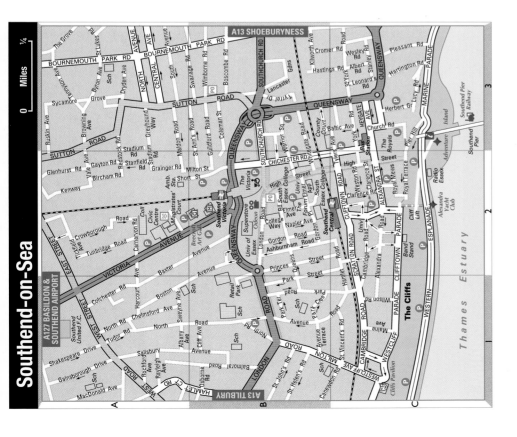

Southend-on-Sea

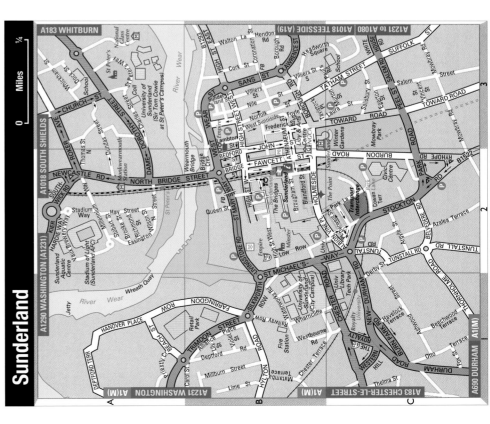

Sunderland

126

Telford page 34 • **Torquay** page 5 • **Winchester** page 10 • **Windsor** page 18 • **Worcester** page 26 • **York** page 52

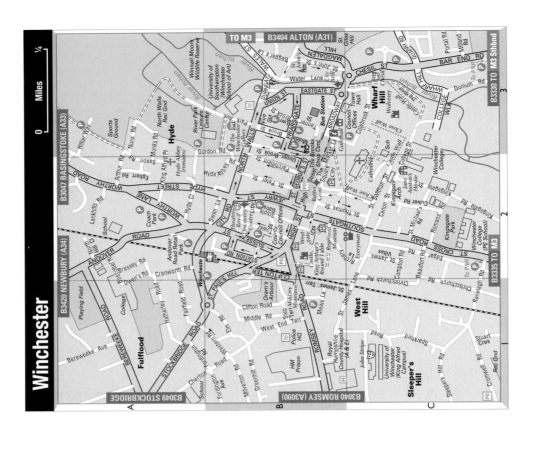

Winchester

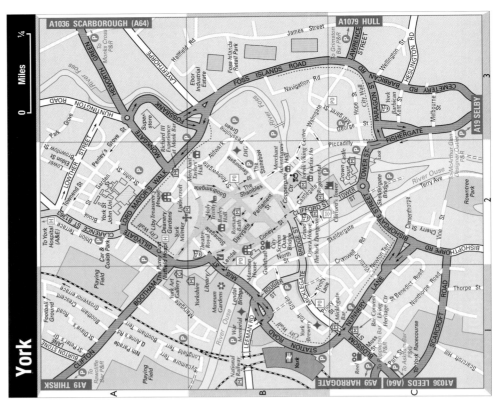

York

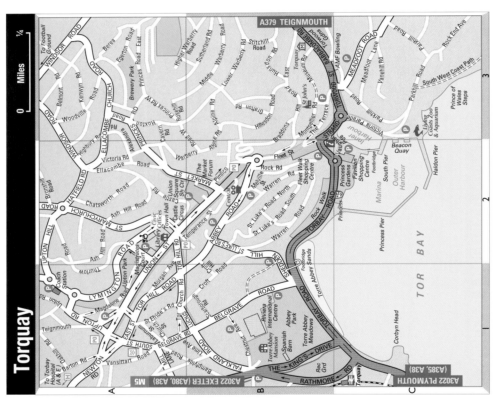

Torquay

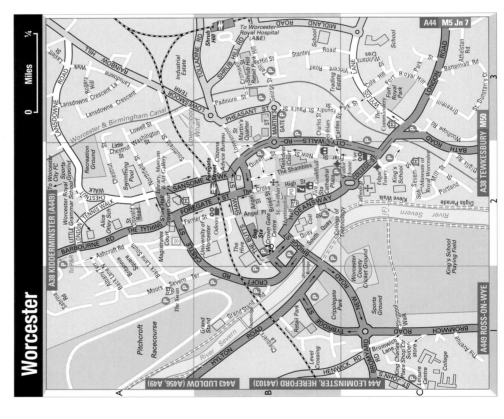

Worcester

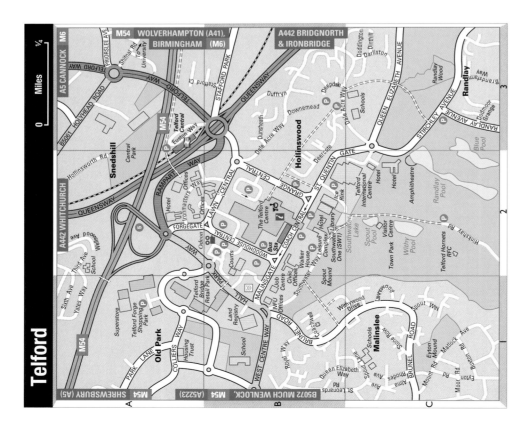

Telford

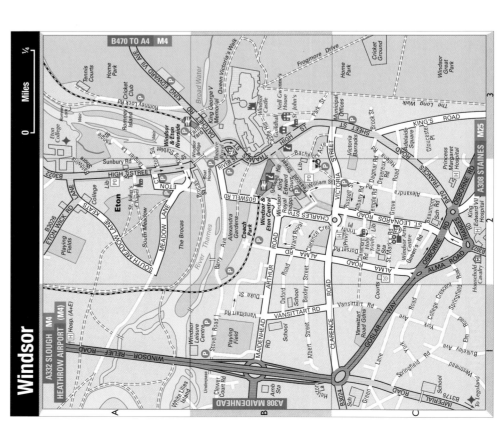

Windsor

Town plan indexes

Bibb Way B1
Birkfield Dr C1
Black Horse La B2
Bolton La B3
Bond St C3
Bowthorpe Cl B2
Bramford La A1
Bramford Rd A1
Bridge St C2
Brookfield Rd A1
Brooks Hall Rd A1
Broomhill Park A1
Broomhill Rd A1
Broughton Rd A2
Bulwer Rd B1
Burrell Rd C2
Bus Station B3
Butter Market B2
Buttermarket Shopping Ctr,The B3
Cardinal Park Leisure Park C2
Carr St B3
Cecil Rd B2
Cecilia St C2
Chancery Rd C2
Charles St B2
Chevallier St A1
Christchurch Mansion & Wolsey Art Gallery 🏛 B3
Christchurch Park A3
Christchurch St B3
Cineworld 🎞 C2
Civic Centre B2
Civic Dr B2
Clarkson St B1
Cobbold St B3
Commercial Rd C2
Constable Rd A3
Constantine Rd C1
Constitution Hill A2
Corder Rd A3
Corn Exchange B2
Cotswold Ave A2
Council Offices C2
County Hall B3
Crown Court C2
Crown St B2
Cullingham Rd B1
Cumberland St B2
Curriers La B2
Dale Hall La A2
Dales View Rd A1
Dalton Rd B2
Dillwyn St B1
Elliot St B1
Elm St B2
Elsmere Rd A3
Falcon St C2
Felaw St C3
Fire Station C2
Flint Wharf C3
Fonnereau Rd B2
Fore St C3
Foundation St C3
Franciscan Way C2
Friars St C2
Gainsborough Rd A3
Gatacre Rd B1
Geneva Rd B2
Gippeswyk Ave C1
Gippeswyk Park C1
Grafton Way C2
Graham Rd A1
Great Whip St C3
Grimwade St C3
Handford Cut B1
Handford Rd B1
Henley Rd A2
Hervey St B3
High St B2
Holly Rd A2
Information Ctr ℹ B3
Ipswich Haven Marina ✦ C3
Ipswich Museum & Art Gallery 🏛 B2
Ipswich School A2
Ipswich Station ⇌ C2
Ipswich Town FC (Portman Road) C2
Ivry St A2
Kensington Rd A1
Kesteven Rd C1
Key St C3
Kingsfield Ave A3
Kitchener Rd A1
Little's Cr C2
London Rd B1
Low Brook St C3
Lower Orwell St C3
Luther Rd C2
Magistrates Court B2
Manor Rd A3
Mornington Ave A1
Museum St B2
Neale St B3
New Cardinal St C2
New Cut East C3
New Cut West C3
New Wolsey 🎭 B2
Newson St B2
Norwich Rd A1/B1
Oban St B2
Old Custom Ho ⌂ C3
Old Foundry Rd B3
Old Merchant's House ⌂ C3
Orford St B2
Paget Rd A2
Park Rd A3
Park View Rd A2
Peter's St C2
Philip Rd C2
Pine Ave A2
Pine View Rd A2
Police Station ▣ B2
Portman Rd B2
Portman Walk C1
Post Office ✉ B2
Princes St C2
Prospect St B1
Queen St B2
Ranelagh Rd C1
Recreation Ground B1
Rectory Rd C2
Regent Theatre 🎭 B3
Retail Park C1
Retail Park C2
Richmond Rd A1
Rope Walk C3
Rose La C2
Russell Rd C2
St Edmund's Rd A2
St George's St B2
St Helen's St B3
Sherrington Rd A1
Shopmobility B2
Silent St C2
Sir Alf Ramsey Way C1
Sirdar Rd B1
Soane St B3
Springfield La A1
Star La C3
Stevenson Rd B1
Suffolk College C3
Suffolk Retail Park B1
Superstore B1
Surrey Rd B1
Tacket St C3
Tavern St B3
Tower Ramparts B2
Tower Ramparts Shopping Centre B2
Tower St B3
Town Hall ⌂ B2
Tuddenham Rd A3
University C3
Upper Brook St B3
Upper Orwell St B3
Valley Rd A2
Vermont Cr B3
Vermont Rd B3
Vernon St C3
Warrington Rd A2
Waterloo Rd A1
Waterworks St C3
Wellington St B1
West End Rd B1
Westerfield Rd A3
Westgate St B2
Westholme Rd A1
Westwood Ave A1
Willoughby Rd C2
Withipoll St B3
Woodbridge Rd B3
Woodstone Ave A3
Yarmouth Rd B1

Lancaster 118

Aberdeen Rd C3
Adult College,The C3
Aldcliffe Rd C2
Alfred St B3
Ambleside Rd A3
Ambulance Sta A3
Ashfield Ave B1
Ashton Rd C2
Assembly Rooms Emporium ⌂ B2
Balmoral Rd B3
Bath House ⛫ B2
Bath Mill La B3
Bath St B3
Blades St B1
Borrowdale Rd B3
Bowerham Rd C3
Brewery La B2
Bridge La B2
Brook St C1
Bulk Rd A3
Bulk St B2
Bus Station B2
Cable St B2
Canal Cruises & Waterbus ✦ C2
Carlisle Bridge A1
Carr House La C2
Castle ♜ B1
Castle Park B1
Caton Rd A3
China St B2
Church St B2
City Museum 🏛 B2
Clarence St C3
Common Gdn St B2
Coniston Rd A3
Cott Museum 🏛 B2
Council Offices B2
County Court B2
Cromwell Rd C1
Crown Court B1
Dale St C3
Dallas Rd B1/C1
Dalton Rd B3
Dalton Sq B2
Damside St B2
De Vitre St B3
Dee Rd A1
Denny Ave A1
Derby Rd A2
Dukes,The B2
Earl St A2
East Rd B3
Eastham St C1
Edward St B3
Fairfield Rd B1
Fenton St B2
Firbank Rd A3
Fire Station B2
Friend's Meeting House ⌂ B1
Garnet St B3
George St B2
Giant Axe Field B1
Grand 🎭 B2
Grasmere Rd B3
Greaves Rd C2
Green St A3
Gregson Ctr,The B3
Gregson Rd C3
Greyhound Bridge A2
Greyhound Bridge Rd A2
High St B2
Hill Side B1
Hope St C3
Hubert Pl B1
Information Ctr ℹ B2
Kelsy St B1
Kentmere Rd B3
King St B2
Kingsway A3
Kirkes Rd C3
Lancaster and Lakeland Ⓗ C3
Lancaster City Football Club B1
Lancaster Sta ⇌ B1
Langdale Rd A3
Ley Ct B1
Library B2
Lincoln Rd B1
Lindow St C2
Lodge St B2
Long Marsh La B1
Lune Rd A1
Lune St A2
Lune Valley Ramble A3
Mainway A2
Maritime Mus 🏛 A1
Marketgate Shopping Centre B2
Market St B2
Meadowside C2
Meeting House La B1
Millennium Bridge A2
Moor La B2
Moorgate B3
Morecambe Rd A1/A2
Nelson St B2
North Rd B2
Orchard La C1
Owen Rd A2
Park Rd B3
Parliament St A3
Patterdale Rd A3
Penny St B2
Police Station ▣ B2
Portland St C2
Post Office ✉ B2
Primrose St C3
Priory ⛪ B1
Prospect St C3
Quarry Rd B3
Queen St C2
Regent St C2
Ridge La A3
Ridge St A3
Royal Lancaster Infirmary (A&E) Ⓗ C2
Rydal Rd B3
Ryelands Park A1
St Georges Quay A1
St John's ⛪ B2
St Leonard's Gate B2
St Martin's Rd C3
St Nicholas Arcades Shopping Centre B2
St Oswald St C3
St Peter's ✝ B3
St Peter's Rd B3
Salisbury Rd B1
Scotch Quarry Urban Park C3
Sibsey St B1
Skerton Bridge A2
South Rd C2
Station Rd B1
Stirling Rd C3
Storey Ave B1
Sunnyside La C1
Sylvester St C1
Tarnsyke Rd A1
Thurnham St C2
Town Hall B2
Troutbeck Rd B3
Ulleswater Rd B3
Univ of Cumbria C3
Vicarage Field B1
Vue 🎞 B2
West Rd B1
Westbourne Dr C1
Westbourne Rd B1
Westham St C3
Wheatfield St B1
White Cross Business Park C2
Williamson Rd B3
Willow La B1
Windermere Rd B3
Wingate-Saul Rd B1
Wolseley St B3
Woodville St B3
Wyresdale Rd C3

Leeds 118

Aire St B3
Albion Pl B4
Albion St B4
Albion Way B1
Alma St A6
Ambulance Sta B5
Arcades ⌂ B4
Armley Rd B1
Armories Dr C5
Back Burley Lodge Rd A1
Back Hyde Terr A2
Back Row C3
Bath Rd C3
Beckett St A6
Bedford St B3
Belgrave St A4
Belle Vue Rd A2
Benson St A5
Black Bull St C5
Blenheim Walk A3
Boar La B4
Bond St B4
Bow St C5
Bowman La C4
Brewery ✦ C4
Brewery Wharf C5
Bridge St A5/B5
Briggate B4
Bruce Gdns C1
Burley Rd A1
Burley St B1
Burmantofs St B6
Bus & Coach Sta B5
Butterly St C4
Butts Cr B4
Byron St A5
Call La B4
Calls,The B5
Calverley St A3/B3
Canal St B1
Canal Wharf C3
Carlisle Rd C5
Cavendish Rd A1
Cavendish St A2
Chadwick St C5
Cherry Pl A6
Cherry Row A5
City Museum 🏛 A4
City Varieties Music Hall 🎭 B4
City Sq B3
Civic Hall ⌂ A3
Clarence Road C5
Clarendon Rd A2
Clarendon Way A3
Clark La C5
Clay Pit La A4
Cloberry St A2
Close,The B6
Clyde Approach C1
Clyde Gdns C1
Coleman St C2
Commercial St B4
Concord St A5
Cookridge St A4
Copley Hill C1
Core,The B4
Corn Exchange ⌂ B4
Cromer Terr A2
Cromwell St A5
Cross Catherine St B6
Cross Green La C6
Cross Stamford St A5
Crown & County Courts A3
Crown Point Bridge C5
Crown Point Rd C4
Crown Point Retail Park C4
David St C3
Dent St C6
Derwent Pl C3
Dial St C6
Dock St C4
Dolly La A6
Domestic St C2
Drive,The B6
Duke St B5
Duncan St B4
Dyer St B5
East Field St B6
East Pde B3
East St C5
Eastgate B5
Easy Rd C6
Edward St B4
Ellerby La C6
Ellerby Rd C6
Fenton St A3
Fire Station B2
First Direct Arena A4
Fish St B4
Flax Place B6
Garth,The B5
Gelderd Rd C1
George St B4
Globe Rd C2
Gloucester Cr B1
Gower St A5
Grafton St A4
Grand Theatre 🎭 B4
Granville Rd A6
Great George St A3
Great Wilson St C4
Greek St B3
Green La C1
Hanover Ave A2
Hanover La A2
Hanover Sq A2
Hanover Way A2
Harewood St B4
Harrison St B4
Haslewood Cl B6
Haslewood Drive B6
Headrow,The B3/B4
High Court B5
Holbeck La C2
Holdforth Cl C1
Holdforth Gdns B1
Holdforth Gr C1
Holdforth Pl C1
Holy Trinity ⛪ B4
Hope Rd A5
Hunslet La C4
Hunslet Rd C4
Hyde Terr A2
Infirmary St B3
Information Ctr ℹ B3
Ingram Row C3
ITV Yorkshire A1
Junction St C4
Kelso Gdns A2
Kelso Rd A2
Kelso St A2
Kendal La A2
Kendell St C4
Kidacre St C4
King Edward St B4
King St B3
Kippax Pl C6
Kirkgate B4
Kirkgate Market B4
Kirkstall Rd A1
Kitson St C6
Lady La B4
Lands La B4
Lane,The B5
Lavender Walk B6
Leeds Art Gallery 🏛 B3
Leeds Beckett Univ A3
Leeds Bridge C4
Leeds Coll of Music B5
Leeds Discovery Centre ⌂ C5
Leeds General Infirmary (A&E) Ⓗ A3
Leeds Station ⇌ B3
Library B3/B4
Light,The B4
Lincoln Green Rd A6
Lincoln Rd A6
Lindsey Gdns A6
Lindsey Rd A6
Lisbon St B3
Little Queen St B3
Long Close La C6
Lord St C2
Lovell Park A4
Lovell Park Hill A4
Lovell Park Rd A4
Lower Brunswick St A5
Mabgate A5
Macauly St A5
Magistrates Court A3
Manor Rd C3
Mark La B4
Marlborough St B2
Marsh La B5
Marshall St C3
Meadow La C4
Meadow Rd C4
Melbourne St A5
Merrion Centre A4
Merrion St A4
Merrion Way A4
Mill St B5
Millennium Sq A3
Mount Preston St A2
Mushroom St A5
Neville St C4
New Briggate A4/B4
New Market St B4
New York Rd A5
New York St B5
Nile St A5
Nippet La A6
North St A4
Northern St B3
Oak Rd B1
Oxford Pl B3
Oxford Row A3
Parade,The B6
Park Cross St B3
Park La A2
Park Pl B3
Park Row B4
Park Sq B3
Park Sq East B3
Park Sq West B3
Park St B3
Police Station ▣ A3
Pontefract La B6
Portland Cr A3
Portland Way A3
Post Office ✉ B4/B5
Quarry House (NHS/DSS HQ) B5
Quebec St B3
Queen St B3
Railway St B5
Rectory St A6
Regent St A5
Richmond St C5
Rigton Approach B6
Rigton Dr B6
Rillbank La A1
Rosebank Rd A1
Rose Bowl Conference Ctr A3
Royal Armouries 🏛 C5
Russell St B3
St Anne's Cathedral (RC) ✝ A4
St Anne's St B4
St James' Hosp Ⓗ A6
St John's Rd A2
St Johns Centre B4
St Mary's St B5
St Pauls St B3
St Peter's ⛪ B5
Saxton La B5
Sayner La C5
Shakespeare Ave A6
Shannon St B6
Sheepscar St South A5
Siddall St C3
Skinner La A5
South Pde B3
Sovereign St C4
Spence La C2
Springfield Mount A2
Springwell Ct C2
Springwell Rd C2
Springwell St C2
Stoney Rock La A6
Studio Rd A1
Sutton St C2
Sweet St C3
Sweet St West C3
Swinegate B4
Templar St B5
Tetley,The 🏛 C4
Thoresby Place A3
Torre Rd A6
Town Hall ⌂ A3
Union Pl C3
Union St B5
University of Leeds A3
Upper Accomodation Rd B6
Upper Basinghall St B4
Vicar La B4
Victoria Bridge C4
Victoria Quarter B4
Victoria Rd C4
Vue 🎞 B4
Wade La A4
Washington St A1
Water La C3
Waterloo Rd C4
Wellington Rd B2/C1
Wellington St B3
West St B2
West Yorkshire Playhouse 🎭 B5
Westfield Rd A1
Westgate B3
Whitehall Rd B3/C2
Whitelock St A5
Willis St C6
Willow Approach A1
Willow Ave A1
Willow Terrace Rd A3
Wintoun St A5
Woodhouse La A3/A4
Woodsley Rd A1
York Pl B3
York Rd B6

Leicester 118

Abbey St A2
All Saints' ⛪ A1
Aylestone Rd C2
Bath La A1
Bede Park C1
Bedford St A3
Bedford St South A3
Belgrave Gate A2
Belvoir St B2
Braunstone Gate B1
Burleys Way A2
Burnmoor St C2
Bus Station A2
Canning St A2
Carlton St C2
Castle ♜ B1
Castle Gardens B1
Cathedral ✝ B2
Causeway La A2
Charles St B3
Chatham St B2
Christow St A3
Church Gate A2
City Gallery 🏛 B3
City Hall B3
Clank St B2
Clock Tower ✦ B2
Clyde St A3
Colton St B3
Conduit St B3
Council Offices B2
Crafton St A3
Craven St A1
Crown Courts B3
Curve 🎭 B3
De Lux 🎞 A2
De Montfort Hall 🎭 C3
De Montfort St C3
De Montfort Univ C1
Deacon St C2
Dover St B3
Duns La B1
Dunton St A1
East St B3
Eastern Boulevard C1
Edmonton Rd A3
Erskine St A3
Filbert St C1
Filbert St East C2
Fire Station C3
Fleet St A3
Friar La B2
Friday St A2
Gateway St C2
Gateway,The C2
Glebe St B3
Granby St B3
Grange La C2
Grasmere St C1
Great Central St A1
Guildhall ⌂ B2
Guru Nanak Sikh Museum 🏛 B1
Halford St B2
Havelock St C2
Haymarket Shopping Ctr A2
High St A2
Highcross Shopping Ctr A2
Highcross St A1
HM Prison C2
Horsefair St B2
Humberstone Gate B2
Humberstone Rd A3
Infirmary St C2
Information Ctr ℹ B2
Jarrom St C2
Jewry Wall 🏛⌂ B1
Kamloops Cr A3
King Richards Rd B1
King St B2
Lancaster Rd C3
LCB Depot 🏛 B3
Lee St A3
Leicester Royal Infirmary (A&E) Ⓗ C2
Leicester Station ⇌ B3
Library B2
London Rd C3
Lower Brown St B2
Magistrates Court B2
Manitoba Rd A3
Mansfield St A2
Market ✦ B2
Market St B2
Mill La C2
Montreal Rd A3
Narborough Rd North B1
Nelson Mandela Pk C2
New Park St B1
New St B2
New Walk C3
New Walk Museum & Art Gallery 🏛 C3
Newarke Houses 🏛 B2
Newarke St B2
Newarke,The B1
Northgate St A1
Orchard St A2
Ottawa Rd A3
Oxford St C2
Phoenix Arts Ctr 🎞 B3
Police Station ▣ A3
Post Office ✉ A1/B2/C3
Prebend St C3
Princess Rd East C3
Princess Rd West C3
Queen St B3
Rally Com Pk,The A2
Regent College C3
Regent Rd C2/C3
Repton St A1
Rutland St B3
St Georges Ret Pk B3
St George St B3
St Georges Way B3
St John St A2
St Margaret's ⛪ A2
St Margaret's Way A2
St Martins B2
St Mary de Castro ⛪ B1
St Matthew's Way A3
St Nicholas ⛪ B1
St Nicholas Circle B1
Sanvey Gate A2
Silver St B2
Slater St A1
Soar La A1
South Albion St B3
Southampton St B3
Sue Townsend Theatre 🎭 B2
Swain St B3
Swan St A1
Tigers Way C3
Tower St C3
Town Hall B2
Tudor Rd B1
Univ of Leicester C3
University Rd C3
Upper Brown St 🎭 B2
Upperton Rd C1
Vaughan Way A2
Walnut St C2
Watling St A2
Welford Rd B2
Welford Rd Leicester Tigers C2
Wellington St B2
West Bridge B1
West St C3
West Walk C3
Western Boulevard C1
Western Rd C1
Wharf St North A3
Wharf St South A3
Y Theatre,The 🎭 B3
Yeoman St B3
York Rd B2

Lincoln 118

Alexandra Terr B1
Anchor St C1
Arboretum B3
Arboretum Ave B3
Avenue,The B1
Baggholme Rd B3
Bailgate A2
Beaumont Fee B1
Brayford Way C1
Brayford Wharf East C1
Brayford Wharf North B1
Bruce Rd A2
Burton Rd A1
Bus Station (City) C2
Canwick Rd C2
Cardinal's Hat ✦ B2
Carline Rd B1
Castle ♜ B1
Castle St A1
Cathedral ✝ B2
Cathedral St B2
Cecil St A2
Chapel La A2
Cheviot St B3
Church La A2
City Hall B1
Clasketgate B2
Clayton Sports Gd A3
Coach Park C2
Collection,The 🏛 B2
County Hospital (A&E) Ⓗ B3
County Office B1
Courts C1
Croft St B2
Cross St C2
Crown Courts B1
Curle Ave A3
Danesgate B2
Drill Hall 🎭 B2
Drury La B1
East Bight A2
East Gate ⛫ A2
Eastcliff Rd B3
Eastgate B2
Egerton Rd A3
Ellis Windmill A1
Engine Shed,The 🎭 C1
Environment Agency C2
Exchequer Gate ✦ B2
Firth Rd C1
Flaxengate B2
Florence St B3
George St C3
Good La A2
Gray St A1
Great Northern Terr C3
Great Northern Terr Ind Est C3
Greetwell Rd B3
Greetwellgate B3
Grove,The A3
Haffenden Rd A2
High St B2/C1
HM Prison A3
Hosp (Private) Ⓗ A2
Hungate B2
James St A2
Jews House & Ct ⌂ B2
Kesteven St C2
Langworthgate A2
Lawn,The 🏛 B1
Lee Rd A3
Library B2
Lincoln Central Station ⇌ C2
Lincoln College B2
Lincolnshire Life/ Royal Lincolnshire Regiment Mus 🏛 A1
Lindum Rd B2
Lindum Sports Gd A3
Lindum Terr B3
Mainwaring Rd A3
Manor Rd A2
Market C2
Massey Rd A3
Medieval Bishop's Palace ⌂ B2
Mildmay St A1
Mill Rd A1
Millman Rd B3
Minster Yard B2
Monks Rd B3
Montague St B2
Mount St A1
Nettleham Rd A2
Newland B1
Newport A2
Newport Arch ⛫ A2
Newport Cemetery A2
Northgate A2
Odeon 🎞 C1
Orchard St B1
Oxford St C2
Park St B1
Pelham Bridge C2
Pelham St C2
Police Station ▣ B1
Portland St C2
Post Office ✉ A1/B3/C2
Potter Gate B2
Priory Gate B2
Queensway A3
Rasen La A1
Ropewalk C1
Rosemary La B2
St Anne's Rd B3
St Benedict's ⛪ C1
St Giles Ave A3
St Mark's Shopping Centre C1
St Marks St C1
St Mary-Le-Wigford ⛪ C1
St Mary's St C2
St Nicholas St A2
St Swithin's ⛪ B2
Saltergate C1
Saxon St A1
School of Art & Design B2
Sewell Rd B3
Silver St B2
Sincil St C2
Spital St A2
Spring Hill B1
Stamp End C3
Steep Hill B2
Stonebow & Guildhall ⌂ C2
Stonefield Ave A2
Tentercroft St C1
Theatre Royal 🎭 B2
Tritton Rd C1
Tritton Retail Park C1
Union Rd B1
Univ of Lincoln C1
Upper Lindum St B3
Upper Long Leys Rd A1
Usher 🏛 B2
Vere St A2
Victoria St B1
Victoria Terr B1
Vine St B3
Wake St A1
Waldeck St A1
Waterside North C2
Waterside Shopping Centre C2
Waterside South C2
West Pde B1
Westgate A2
Wigford Way C1
Williamson St A2
Wilson St A1
Winn St B3
Wragby Rd A3
Yarborough Rd A1

Liverpool 119

Abercromby Sq C5
Acc Liverpool ✦ C2
Addison St A3
Adelaide Rd B6
Ainsworth St B4
Albany Rd B6
Albert Dock C2
Albert Edward Rd B6
Angela St C6
Anson St B4
Argyle St C3
Arrad St C4
Ashton St B5
Audley St A4
Back Leeds St A2
Basnett St B3
Bath St A1
Beacon,The ✦ B3
Beatles Story 🏛 C2
Beckwith St C3
Bedford Close C5
Bedford St North C5
Bedford St South C5
Benson St C4
Berry St C4
Birkett St A4
Bixteth St B2
Blackburne Place C4
Bluecoat 🎭 B3
Bold Place C4
Bold St C4
Bolton St B3
Bridport St B4
Bronte St B4
Brook St A1
Brownlow Hill B4/B5
Brownlow St B5
Brunswick Rd A5
Brunswick St B1
Bus Station C2
Butler Cr A6
Byrom St A3
Caledonia St C4
Cambridge St C5
Camden St A4
Canada Blvd B1
Canning Dock C2
Canterbury St A4
Cardwell St C6
Carver St A4
Cases St B3
Castle St B2
Catherine St C5
Cavern Club ⌂ B3
Central Library A3
Central Station ⇌ B3
Chapel St B2
Charlotte St B3
Chatham Place C6
Chatham St C5
Cheapside B2
Cherasse Park C2
Chestnut St C5
Christian St A3
Church St B3
Churchill Way North A3
Churchill Way South B3
Clarence St B4
Coach Station A4
Cobden St A5
Cockspur St A2
College St C3
College St North A5
College St South A5
Colquitt St C4
Comus St A3
Concert St C3
Connaught Rd B6
Cook St B2
Copperas Hill B4
Cornwallis St C3
Covent Garden B2
Craven St A4
Cropper St B3
Crown St B5/C6
Cumberland St B2
Cunard Building ⌂ B1
Dale St B2
Dansie St B4
Daulby St B5
Dawson St B3
Derby Sq B2
Drury La B2
Duckinfield St B4
Duke St C3
Earle St A2
East St A2
Eaton St A2
Edgar St A3
Edge La B6
Edinburgh Rd A6
Edmund St B2
Elizabeth St B5
Elliot St B3
Empire Theatre 🎭 B4
Empress Rd B6
Epstein Theatre 🎭 B3
Epworth St A5
Erskine St A5
Everyman Theatre 🎭 C5
Exchange St East B2
FACT ✦🎞 C4
Falkland St A5
Falkner St C5/C6
Farnworth St A6
Fenwick St B2
Fielding St A6
Fire Sta A4
Fleet St C3
Fraser St A4
Freemasons Row A2
Gardner Row A3
Gascoyne St A2
George Pier Head C1
George St B2
Gibraltar Road A1
Gilbert St C3
Gildart St A4
Gill St B4
Goree B2
Gower St C2
Gradwell St C3
Great Crosshall St A3
Great George St C4
Great Howard St A1
Great Newton St B4
Greek St B4
Green La B4
Greenside A5
Greetham St C3
Gregson St A5
Grenville St C3
Grinfield St C6
Grove St C5
Guelph St A6
Hackins Hey B2
Haigh St A4
Hall La B6
Hanover St B3
Harbord St C6
Hardman St C4
Harker St A4
Hart St B4
Hatton Garden A2
Hawke St B4
Helsby St B6
Henry St C3
Highfield St A2
Highgate St B6
Hilbre St B4
HM Customs & Excise National Mus 🏛 C2
Hope Place C4
Hope St C4
Hope University A5
Houghton St B3
Hunter St A3
Hutchinson St A6
Information Ctr ℹ B4/C2
Institute for the Performing Arts C4
Int Slavery 🏛 C2
Irvine St B6
Irwell St B2
Islington A4
James St B2
James St Station ⇌ B2
Jenkinson St A4
John Moores Univ A2/A3/A4/B4/C4
Johnson St A3
Jubilee Drive B6
Kempston St A4
Kensington A6
Kensington Gdns B6
Kensington St A6
Kent St C3
King Edward St A1
Kinglake St B6
Knight St C4
Lace St A3
Langsdale St A4
Law Courts C2
Leece St C4
Leeds St A2
Leopold Rd B6
Lime St B3
Lime St Station ⇌ B4
Little Woolton St B5
Liver St C2
Liverpool Landing Stage B1
Liverpool Institute for Performing Arts C4
Liverpool ONE C2
Liverpool Wheel, The C2
London Rd A4/B4
Lord Nelson St B4
Lord St B2
Lovat St C6
Low Hill A5
Low Wood St A6
Lydia Ann St C3
Mansfield St A4
Marmaduke St B6
Marsden St A6
Martensen St B6
Marybone A3
Maryland St C4
Mason St B6
Mathew St B2
May St B4
Melville Place C6
Merseyside Maritime Museum 🏛 C2
Metquarter B3
Metropolitan Cathedral (RC) ✝ B5
Midghall St A2
Molyneux Rd A6
Moor Place B4
Moorfields B2
Moorfields Sta ⇌ B2
Moss St A5
Mount Pleasant B4/B5
Mount St C4
Mount Vernon B6
Mulberry St C5
Municipal Bldgs B2
Mus of Liverpool 🏛 C2
Myrtle Gdns C6
Myrtle St C5
Naylor St A2
Nelson St C4
New Islington A4
New Quay B1
Newington St C3
North John St B2
North St A3
North View B6
Norton St A4
O2 Academy B4
Oakes St B5
Odeon 🎞 B2
Old Hall St A1
Old Leeds St A2
Oldham Place C4
Oldham St C4
Olive St C6
Open Eye Gallery 🏛 C2
Oriel St A2
Ormond St B2
Orphan St C6
Overbury St C6
Overton St B6
Oxford St C5
Paisley St A1
Pall Mall A2
Paradise St C3
Park La C3
Parker St B3
Parr St C3
Peach St B5
Pembroke Place B4
Pembroke St B5
Philharmonic Hall 🎭 C5
Pickop St A2
Pilgrim St C4
Pitt St C3
Playhouse Theatre 🎭 B3
Pleasant St B4
Police HQ ▣ C2
Police Station A4/A6/B4
Pomona St B4
Port of Liverpool Building ⌂ B2
Post Office ✉ A2/A4/A5/B2/B3/B4/C4
Pownall St C2
Prescot St A5
Preston St B3
Princes Dock A1
Princes Gdns A2
Princes Jetty A1
Princes Pde B1
Princes St B2
Pythian St A6
Queen Sq Bus Sta B3
Queensland St C6
Queensway Tunnel (Docks exit) B1
Queensway Tunnel (Entrance) B3
Radio City B2
Ranelagh St B3

Middlesbrough • Milton Keynes • Newcastle upon Tyne • Newport • Northampton • Norwich 133

Crown St C2
Dalberg St C6
Dale St A4/B5
Dancehouse,The C4
Dantzic St A4
Dark La C6
Dawson St C2
Dean St A5
Deansgate A3/B3
Deansgate Castlefield C3
Deansgate Sta C3
Dolphin St C6
Downing St C5
Ducie St B5
Duke Pl B2
Duke St B2
Durling St C6
East Ordsall La A2/B1
Edge St A4
Egerton St C2
Ellesmere St C1
Everard St C1
Every St B6
Exchange Sq A4
Fairfield St B5
Faulkner St B4
Fennel St A3
Ford St A2
Ford St C6
Fountain St B4
Frederick St A2
Gartside St B2
Gaythorne St A1
George Leigh St A5
George St A1
George St B4
Gore St A2
Goulden St A5
Granby Row B4
Gravel St A3
Great Ancoats St A5
Great Bridgewater St B3
Great George St A1
Great Jackson St C2
Great Marlborough St C4
Greengate A3
Grosvenor St C5
Gun St A5
Hadrian Ave B6
Hall St B3
Hampson St B1
Hanover St A4
Hanworth Cl C5
Hardman St B3
Harkness St C6
Harrison St B6
Hart St B4
Helmet St B6
Henry St A5
Heyrod St B6
High St A4
Higher Ardwick C6
Hilton St A4/A5
Holland St A6
HOME C3
Hood St A5
Hope St B1
Hope St B4
Houldsworth St A5
Hoyle St C6
Hulme Hall Rd C1
Hulme St A1
Hulme St C3
Hyde Rd C6
Information Ctr B4
Irwell St A2
Islington St A2
Jackson Cr C2
Jackson's Row B3
James St A1
Jenner Cl C2
Jersey St A5
John Dalton St B3
John Ryland's Library B3
John St A2
Kennedy St B3
Kincardine Rd C5
King St A3
King St West A3
Law Courts B3
Laystall St B5
Lever St A5
Library B3
Linby St C2
Little Lever St A4
Liverpool Rd B2
Liverpool St B1
Lloyd St B3
Lockton Cl C5
London Rd B5
Long Millgate A3
Longacre St B6
Loom St A5
Lower Byrom St B2
Lower Mosley St B3
Lower Moss La C2
Lower Ormond St C4
Loxford La C4
Luna St A5
Major St B4
Manchester Arndale A4
Manchester Art Gallery B4
Manchester Central Convention Complex B3
Manchester Metropolitan University B4/C4
Manchester Piccadilly Station B5
Manchester Technology Ctr C4
Mancunian Way C3
Manor St C5
Marble St A4
Market St A2
Market St A4
Market St A4
Marsden St A3
Marshall St A5
Mayan Ave A2
Medlock St C3
Middlewood St B1
Miller St A4
Minshull St B4
Mosley St A4
Mount St B3
Mulberry St B3
Murray St A5
Museum of Science & Industry (MOSI) B2
Nathan Dr A2
National Football Museum A4
Naval St A5
New Bailey St A2
New Elm Rd B2
New Islington A6
New Islington Station B6
New Quay St B2
New Union St A6
Newgate St A4
Newton St A5
Nicholas St B4
North Western St C6
Oak St A4
Odeon A4
Old Mill St A6
Oldfield Rd A1/C1
Oldham Rd A5
Oldham St A4
Opera House B3
Ordsall La C1
Oxford Rd C4
Oxford Rd C4
Oxford St B4
Paddock St C6
Palace Theatre B4
Pall Mall A3
Palmerston St B6
Park St A1
Parker St B4
Peak St B5
Penfield Cl C5
Peoples' History Museum B2
Peru St A1
Peter St B3
Piccadilly A4
Piccadilly B5
Piccadilly Gdns B4
Piercy St A6
Poland St A5
Police Museum A5
Police Sta B3/B5
Pollard St B6
Port St A5
Portland St B4
Portugal St East B5
Post Office A1/A2/A4/A5/B3/B4
Potato Wharf B2
Princess St B3/C4
Pritchard St C4
Quay St A2
Quay St B2
Queen St B3
Radium St A5
Redhill St A5
Regent Rd B1
Retail Park A5
Rice St B2
Richmond St B4
River St C3
Roby St B5
Rodney St A6
Roman Fort B2
Rosamond St A2
Royal Exchange A3
Sackville St B4
St Andrew's St B6
St Ann St A3
St Ann's A3
St George's Ave C1
St James St B4
St John St B3
St John's Cathedral (RC) A2
St Mary's B3
St Mary's Gate A3
St Mary's Parsonage A3
St Peter's Sq B3
St Stephen St A2
Salford Approach A3
Salford Central A2
Sheffield St B5
Shepley St B5
Sherratt St A5
Shopmobility A4
Shudehill A4
Shudehill A4
Sidney St C4
Silk St A5
Silver St B4
Skerry Cl C5
Snell St B6
South King St B3
Sparkle St B5
Spear St A4
Spring Gdns A4
Stanley St A2/B2
Station Approach B5
Store St B5
Swan St A4
Tariff St B5
Tatton St C1
Temperance St B6/C6
Thirsk St C6
Thomas St A4
Thompson St A5
Tib La B3
Tib St A4
Town Hall (Manchester) B3
Town Hall (Salford) A2
Trafford St C3
Travis St B5
Trinity Way A2
Turner St A4
Union St C6
Univ of Manchester (Sackville St Campus) C5
Univ of Salford A1
Upper Brook St C5
Upper Cleminson St A1
Upper Wharf St A1
Vesta St B6
Victoria A4
Victoria Station A4
Wadesdon Rd C5
Water St B2
Watson St B3
West Fleet St B1
West King St A2
West Mosley St B4
Weybridge Rd A6
Whitworth St B4
Whitworth St West C3
Wilburn St B1
William St A2
William St C6
Wilmott St C3
Windmill St B3
Windsor Cr A1
Withy Gr A4
Woden St C1
Wood St B3
Woodward St A6
Worrall St C1
Worsley St C2
York St B4
York St C2
York St C4

Middlesbrough 119

Abingdon Rd C3
Acklam Rd C1
Albert Park C2
Albert Rd B2
Albert Terr C2
Ambulance Station C1
Aubrey St C3
Avenue,The C2
Ayresome Gdns C2
Ayresome Green La C1
Ayresome St C2
Barton Rd A1
Bilsdale Rd C3
Bishopton Rd C3
Borough Rd B2/B3
Bowes Rd A2
Breckon Hill Rd B3
Bridge St East B3
Bridge St West B2
Brighouse Rd A1
Burlam Rd C1
Bus Station B2
Cannon Park B1
Cannon Park Way B2
Cannon St B1
Captain Cook Sq B2
Carlow St C1
Castle Way C3
Chipchase Rd C2
Cineworld B3
Cleveland Centre B2
Clive Rd C2
Commercial St A2
Corporation Rd B2
Costa St C2
Council Offices B3
Crescent Rd C2
Crescent,The C2
Cumberland Rd C2
Depot Rd A2
Derwent St B2
Devonshire Rd C2
Diamond Rd B2
Dorman Mus C2
Douglas St B3
Eastbourne Rd C2
Eden Rd C3
Fire Sta A3
Forty Foot Rd A2
Gilkes St B2
Gosford St A2
Grange Rd B2
Gresham Rd B2
Harehills Rd C1
Harford St C2
Hartington Rd B2
Haverton Hill Rd A1
Hey Wood St B1
Highfield Rd C3
Hillstreet Centre B2
Holwick Rd B1
Hutton Rd C3
Ironmasters Way B1
Lambton Rd C3
Lancaster Rd C2
Lansdowne Rd C3
Latham Rd C2
Law Courts B2/B3
Lees Rd B2
Leeway B3
Library B2/C2
Linthorpe Cemetery C1
Linthorpe Rd B2
Lloyd St B2
Longford St C2
Longlands Rd C3
Lower East St A3
Lower Lake C3
Macmillan Acad C1
Maldon Rd C1
Manor St B2
Marsh St B2
Marton Rd B3
Middlehaven B3
Middlesbrough By-Pass B2/C1
Middlesbrough College B3
Middlesbrough Leisure Park B3
Middlesbrough Station B2
Middletown Park C2
MIMA B3
Mulgrave Rd C2
Newport Bridge B1
Newport Bridge Approach Rd B1
Newport Rd B2
North Ormesby Rd B3
North Rd B2
Northern Rd C1
Outram St B2
Oxford Rd C2
Park La C2
Park Rd North C2
Park Rd South C2
Park Vale Rd C3
Parliament Rd B1
Police Station A2
Port Clarence Rd A3
Portman St B2
Post Office B3/C1/C2
Princes Rd B2
Python A2
Riverside Park Rd A1
Riverside Stadium (Middlesbrough FC) B3
Rockliffe Rd C2
Romaldkirk Rd B1
Roman Rd C2
Roseberry Rd C3
St Barnabas' Rd C2
St Paul's Rd B2
Saltwells Rd B3
Scott's Rd A3
Seaton Carew Rd A3
Shepherdson Way B3
Shopmobility B2
Snowdon Rd A2
South West Ironmasters Park B1
Southfield Rd B2
Southwell Rd C2
Springfield Rd C1
Startforth Rd A2
Stockton Rd C1
Stockton St A2
Superstore B2
Surrey St C2
Sycamore Rd C2
Tax Offices B3
Tees Viaduct C1
Teessaurus Park A2
Teesside Tertiary College C3
Temenos B3
Thornfield Rd C1
Town Hall B2
Transporter Bridge (Toll) A3
Union St B2
Univ of Teesside B2
Upper Lake C2
Valley Rd C3
Ventnor Rd C2
Victoria Rd B2
Vulcan St A2
Warwick St C2
Wellesley Rd B3
West La B1
West Lane Hosp C1
Westminster Rd C2
Wilson St B2
Windward Way B3
Woodlands Rd B2
York Rd C3

Milton Keynes 122

Abbey Way A1
Arbrook Ave B1
Armourer Dr A3
Arncliffe Dr A1
Avebury C2
Avebury Blvd C2
Bankfield B3
Bayard Ave A2
Belvedere A2
Bishopstone A1
Blundells Rd A1
Boundary,The C3
Boycott Ave C2
Bradwell Common Blvd B1
Bradwell Rd C1
Bramble Ave A2
Brearley Ave C2
Breckland A1
Brill Place B1
Burnham Dr B1
Bus Station C1
Campbell Park B3
Cantle Ave A3
Central Retail Park C1
Century Ave C2
Chaffron Way C3
Childs Way C1
Christ the Cornerstone B2
Cineworld B2
Civic Offices B2
Cleavers Ave B2
Colesbourne Dr A3
Conniburrow Blvd B2
County Court B2
Currier Dr A2
Dansteed Way A2/A3/B1
Deltic Ave B1
Downs Barn A2
Downs Barn Blvd A3
Eaglestone C3
Eelbrook Ave B1
Elder Gate B1
Evans Gate C2
Fairford Cr A3
Falcon Ave B3
Fennel Dr A2
Fishermead Blvd C3
Food Centre B3
Fulwoods Dr C3
Glazier Dr A2
Glovers La A1
Grafton Gate C1
Grafton St A1/C2
Gurnards Ave B3
Harrier Dr C3
Ibstone Ave B1
Information Ctr B2
Langcliffe Dr A1
Leisure Centre C3
Leisure Plaza C1
Leys Rd C1
Library B2
Linford Wood A2
Marlborough Gate B3
Marlborough St A2/B3
Mercers Dr A1
Midsummer C2
Midsummer Blvd B2
Milton Keynes Central C1
Milton Keynes Hospital (A&E) C3
Monks Way A1
Mullen Ave A3
Mullion Pl C3
Neath Hill A3
North Elder C1
North Grafton B1
North Overgate A3
North Row B2
North Saxon B2
North Secklow B2
North Skeldon A3
North Witan B1
Oakley Gdns A3
Oldbrook Blvd C2
Open-Air Theatre B3
Overgate A3
Overstreet A3
Patriot Dr B1
Pencarrow Pl B3
Penryn Ave B3
Perran Ave C3
Pitcher La C1
Place Retail Pk,The C1
Police Station B2
Portway B2
Post Office A2/B2/B3
Precedent Dr B1
Quinton Dr B1
Ramsons Ave B2
Retail Park C2
Rockingham Dr A2
Rooksley B1
Saxon Gate B2
Saxon St A1/C3
Secklow Gate B2
Shackleton Pl C2
Shopmobility B2
Silbury Blvd B2
Skeldon A3
South Enmore B3
South Grafton C2
South Row C2
South Saxon C2
South Secklow B3
South Witan C2
Springfield B3
Stanton Wood A1
Stantonbury A1
Stantonbury Leisure Centre A1
Strudwick Dr C2
Sunrise Parkway A2
Theatre & Art Gallery B3
theCentre:mk B2
Tolcarne Ave C3
Tourist Information Centre B3
Towan Ave C3
Trueman Pl C2
Vauxhall A1
Winterhill Retail Pk C2
Witan Gate B2
X-Scape B3

Newcastle upon Tyne 122

Albert St B3
Argyle St B3
Back New Bridge St B3
BALTIC Centre for Contemporary Art C3
Barker St A3
Barrack Rd B1
Bath La B1
Bessie Surtees House C2
Bigg Market C2
Biscuit Factory B3
Black Gate C2
Blackett St B2
Blandford Sq C1
Boating Lake A1
Boyd St B3
Brandling Park A2
Bus Station B2
Buxton St B3
Byron St A3
Camden St B2
Castle Keep C2
Central C1
Central Library B2
Central Motorway B2
Chester St A3
City Hall B2
City Rd B3/C3
City Walls C1
Civic Centre A2
Claremont Rd A1
Clarence St B3
Clarence Walk B3
Clayton St C1/B1
Clayton St West C1
Close,The C2
Coach Station C1
College St B2
Collingwood St C2
Copland Terr B3
Coppice Way B3
Corporation St B1
Courts C3
Crawhall Rd B3
Dean St C2
Dental Hospital A1
Dinsdale Pl A3
Dinsdale Rd A3
Discovery C1
Doncaster Rd A3
Durant Rd B2
Eldon Sq B1
Ellison Pl B2
Empire B1
Eskdale Terr A2
Eslington Terr A2
Exhibition Park A1
Falconar St B3
Fenkle St C1
Forth Banks C1
Forth St C1
Gallowgate B1
Gate,The B1
Gateshead Millennium Bridge C3
Gibson St B3
Goldspink La A3
Grainger Market B2
Grainger St B2
Grantham Rd A3
Granville Rd A3
Great North Children's Hosp A1
Great North Mus:Hancock A2
Grey St B2
Groat Market C2
Guildhall C2
Hancock St A2
Hanover St C2
Hatton Gallery A1
Hawks Rd C3
Haymarket B2
Heber St B1
Helmsley Rd A3
High Bridge C2
High Level Bridge C2
Hillgate C3
Howard St B3
Hutton Terr A3
Information Ctr C3
intu Eldon Sq Shopping Centre B2
Jesmond A2
Jesmond Rd A2/A3
John Dobson St B2
John George Joicey Museum C2
Jubilee Rd B3
Kelvin Gr A3
Kensington Terr A2
Laing Gallery B2
Lambton Rd A2
Leazes Cr B1
Leazes La B1
Leazes Park B1
Leazes Park Rd B1
Leazes Terr B1
Library A2
Live C2
Low Friar St C1
Manor Chare C2
Manors B2
Manors Station B2
Market St B2
Melbourne St B2
Mill Rd C3
Monument B2
Monument Mall Shopping Centre B2
Morpeth St A2
Mosley St C2
Napier St A3
New Bridge St B2/B3
Newcastle Central Station C1
Newcastle Univ A1
Newgate Shopping Centre C1
Newgate St B1
Newington Rd A3
Northern Design Centre C3
Northern Stage Theatre A2
Northumberland Rd B2
Northumberland St B2
Northumbria Univ A2
Northwest Radial Rd A1
O2 Academy C1
Oakwellgate C3
Open Univ C3
Orchard St C1
Osborne Rd A2
Osborne Terr A3
Pandon C3
Pandon Bank B3
Park Terr A1
Percy St B1
Pilgrim St B2
Pipewellgate C2
Pitt St B1
Plummer Tower A2
Police Station B1
Portland Rd A3/B3
Portland Terr A3
Post Office B1/B2
Pottery La C1
Prudhoe Pl B1
Prudhoe St B1
Quayside C2
Queen Elizabeth II Bridge C2
Queen Victoria Rd A1
Richardson Rd A1
Ridley Pl B2
Rock Terr B3
Rosedale Terr A3
Royal Victoria Infirmary A1
Sage Gateshead C3
St Andrew's St B1
St James B1
St James' Blvd C1
St James' Park (Newcastle Utd FC) B1
St Mary's Heritage Centre C3
St Mary's (RC) C1
St Mary's Place B2
St Nicholas C2
St Nicholas St C2
St Thomas' St B1
Sandyford Rd A2/A3
Science Park B2
Shield St B3
Shieldfield B3
Shopmobility B1
Side,The C2
Simpson Terr B3
South Shore Rd C3
South St C1
Starbeck Ave A3
Stepney Rd B3
Stoddart St B3
Stowell St B1
Strawberry Pl B1
Swing Bridge C2
Temple St C1
Terrace Pl B1
Theatre Royal B2
Times Sq C1
Tower St B3
Trinity House C2
Tyne Bridge C2
Tyne Bridges C2
Tyne Theatre & Opera House C1
Tyneside B2
Victoria Sq A2
Warwick St A3
Waterloo St C1
Wellington St B1
Westgate Rd C1/C2
Windsor Terr A2
Worswick St B2
Wretham Pl B3

Newport Casnewydd 122

Albert Terr B1
Allt-yr-Yn Ave A1
Alma St C2
Ambulance Station C3
Bailey St B2
Barrack Hill A2
Bath St A3
Bedford Rd B3
Belle Vue La C1
Belle Vue Park C1
Bishop St A3
Blewitt St B1
Bolt Cl C3
Bolt St C3
Bond St A2
Bosworth Dr A1
Bridge St B1
Bristol St A3
Bryngwyn Rd B1
Brynhyfryd Ave C1
Brynhyfryd Rd C1
Bus Station B2
Caerau Cres C1
Caerau Rd B1
Caerleon Rd A3
Capel Cres C2
Cardiff Rd C2
Caroline St B3
Castle (Remains) A2
Cedar Rd B3
Charles St B2
Charlotte Dr C2
Chepstow Rd A3
Church Rd A3
Cineworld B2
Civic Centre B1
Clarence Pl A2
Clifton Pl B1
Clifton Rd C1
Clyffard Cres B1
Clytha Park Rd B1
Clytha Sq C2
Coldra Rd C1
Collier St A3
Colne St B3
Comfrey Cl A1
Commercial Rd C3
Commercial St B2
Corelli St A3
Corn St B2
Corporation Rd B3
Coulson Cl C2
County Court A2
Courts A1
Courts B1
Crawford St A3
Cyril St B3
Dean St A3
Devon Pl B1
Dewsland Park Rd C2
Dolman B2
Dolphin St C3
East Dock Rd C3
East St B1
East Usk Rd A3
Ebbw Vale Wharf B3
Emlyn St B2
Enterprise Way C3
Eton Rd B3
Evans St A2
Factory Rd A2
Fields Rd B1
Francis Dr C2
Frederick St C3
Friars Rd C1
Friars Walk B2
Gaer La C1
George St C3
George St Bridge C3
Godfrey Rd B1
Gold Tops B1
Gore St A3
Gorsedd Circle C1
Grafton Rd A3
Graham St B1
Granville St C3
Harlequin Dr A1
Harrow Rd B3
Herbert Rd A3
Herbert Walk C2
Hereford St A3
High St B2
Hill St B2
Hoskins St A2
Information Ctr B2
Ivor Sq B2
Jones St B1
Junction Rd A3
Keynshaw Ave C2
King St C2
Kingsway B2
Kingsway Centre B2
Ledbury Dr A2
Library A3
Library, Museum & Art Gallery B2
Liverpool Wharf B3
Llanthewy Rd B1
Llanvair Rd A3
Locke St A2
Lower Dock St C3
Lucas St A2
Manchester St A3
Market B2
Marlborough Rd B3
Mellon St C3
Mill St A2
Morgan St A3
Mountjoy Rd C2
Newport Bridge A2
Newport Ctr B2
Newport RFC B3
Newport Station B2
North St B2
Oakfield Rd B1
Park Sq C2
Police Sta A3/C2
Post Office B2/C3
Power St A1
Prince St A3
Pugsley St A2
Queen St C2
Queen's Cl A1
Queen's Hill A1
Queen's Hill Cres A1
Queensway B2
Railway St B2
Riverfront Theatre & Arts Ctr,The B2
Riverside A3
Rodney Rd A2
Royal Gwent (A&E) C2
Rudry St A3
Rugby Rd B3
Ruperra La C3
Ruperra St C3
St Edmund St B1
St Mark's Cres A1
St Mary St B1
St Vincent Rd A3
St Woolos C2
St Woolos General (no A&E) C1
St Woolos Rd B1
School La B2
Serpentine Rd B1
Shaftesbury Park A2
Sheaf La A3
Skinner St B2
Sorrel Dr A1
South Market St C3
Spencer Rd B1
Stow Hill B2/C1/C2
Stow Park Ave C1
Stow Park Dr C1
TA Centre A1
Talbot St B2
Tennis Club A1
Tregare St A3
Trostrey St A3
Tunnel Terr B1
Turner St A3
Univ of Wales Newport City Campus B3
Upper Dock St B2
Usk St A3
Usk Way B3/C3
Victoria Cr B1
War Memorial A3
Waterloo Rd C1
West St B1
Wharves B2
Wheeler St A2
Whitby Pl A3
Windsor Terr B1
York Pl C1

Northampton 122

78 Derngate B3
Abington Sq B3
Abington St B3
Alcombe St A3
All Saints' B2
Ambush St B1
Angel St B2
AR Centre A3
Arundel St A2
Ash St A2
Auctioneers Way C2
Bailiff St A2
Barrack Rd A2
Beaconsfield Terr A3
Becket's Park C3
Bedford Rd B3
Billing Rd B3
Brecon St A1
Brewery C2
Bridge St B2
Broad St B2
Burns St A3
Bus Station B2
Campbell St A2
Castle (Site of) B2
Castle St B2
Cattle Market Rd C2
Central Museum & Art Gallery B2
Charles St A3
Cheyne Walk B3
Church La A2
Clare St A3
Cloutsham St A3
College St B2
Colwyn Rd A3
Cotton End C2
Countess Rd A1
County Hall B2
Court A2
Craven St A3
Crown & County Courts B3
Denmark Rd B3
Derngate B3
Derngate & Royal Theatres B3
Doddridge Church B2
Drapery,The B2
Duke St A3
Dunster St A3
Earl St A3
Euston Rd C2
Fire Station A3
Foot Meadow B2
Gladstone Rd A1
Gold St B2
Grafton St A2
Gray St A3
Green St B1
Greenwood Rd B1
Greyfriars B2
Grosvenor Centre B2
Grove Rd A3
Guildhall B2
Hampton St A2
Harding Terr A2
Hazelwood Rd B3
Herbert St B2
Hervey St A3
Hester St A2
Holy Sepulchre A2
Hood St A3
Horse Market B2
Hunter St A3
Information Ctr B2
Kettering Rd A3
Kingswell St B2
Lady's La B2
Leicester St A2
Leslie Rd A2
Library B3
Lorne Rd A2
Lorry Park A1
Louise Rd A2
Lower Harding St A2
Lower Hester St A2
Lower Mounts B3
Lower Priory St A2
Main Rd C1
Marefair B2
Market Sq B2
Marlboro Rd B1
Marriott St A2
Military Rd A3
Mounts Baths Leisure Ctr A3
Nene Valley Ret Pk C1
New South Bridge Rd C2
Northampton General Hospital (A&E) B3
Northampton Marina C3
Northampton Station B1
Northcote St A2
Nunn Mills Rd C3
Old Towcester Rd C2
Overstone Rd A3
Peacock Pl B2
Pembroke Rd A1
Penn Court C2
Police Station B3
Post Office A1/B3
Quorn Way A2
Ransome Rd C3
Regent Sq A2
Ridings,The B3
Robert St A2
St Andrew's Rd B1
St Andrew's St A2
St Edmund's Rd B3
St George's St A2
St Giles B3
St Giles St B3
St Giles' Terr B3
St James Park Rd B1
St James Rd B1
St James Retail Pk C1
St James' Mill Rd B1
St James' Mill Rd East C1
St Leonard's Rd C2
St Mary's St B2
St Michael's Rd A3
St Peter's B2
St Peter's Way Shopping Prec B2
St Peter's Way B2
Salisbury St A2
Scarletwell St B2
Semilong Rd A2
Sheep St B2
Sol Central (Leisure Ctr) B2
Somerset St A3
South Bridge C2
Southfield Ave C2
Spencer Bridge Rd A1
Spencer Rd A3
Spring Gdns B3
Spring La B2
Superstore C2
Swan St B3
Tintern Ave A1
Towcester Rd C2
Upper Bath St B2
Upper Mounts A2
Victoria Park A1
Victoria Prom B2
Victoria Rd A3
Victoria St A2
Wellingborough Rd B3
West Bridge B1
York Rd B3

Norwich 122

Albion Way C3
All Saints Green C2
Anchor St A3
Anglia Sq A2
Argyle St C3
Arts Centre B1
Ashby St C2
Assembly House B1
Bank Plain B2
Barker St A1
Barn Rd A1
Barrack St A3
Ber St C2
Bethel St B1
Bishop Bridge A3
Bishopbridge Rd A3
Bishopgate A3
Blackfriars St A2
Botolph St A2
Bracondale C3
Brazen Gate C2
Bridewell B2
Brunswick Rd C1
Bull Close Rd A2
Bus Station C2
Calvert St A2
Cannell Green A3
Carrow Rd C3
Castle & Mus B2
Castle Mall B2
Castle Meadow B2
Cathedral B2
Cath Retail Park A1
Cattlemarket St B2
Chantry Rd C1
Chapel Loke C2
Chapelfield East B1
Chapelfield Gdns B1
Chapelfield North B1
Chapelfield Rd B1
Cinema City B2
City Hall B1
City Rd C2
City Wall C1/C3
Close,The B3
Colegate A2
Coslany St B1
Cow Hill B1
Cow Tower A3
Cowgate A2
Crown & Magistrates' Courts A2
Dragon Hall Heritage Centre C3
Duke St A1
Edward St A2
Elm Hill B2
Erpingham Gate B2
Fishergate A2
Forum,The B1
Foundry Bridge B3
Fye Bridge A2
Garden St C2
Gas Hill B3
Gentlemans Walk B2
Grapes Hill B1
Great Hospital Halls,The A3
Grove Ave C1
Grove Rd C1
Guildhall B1
Gurney Rd A3
Hall Rd C2
Heathgate A3
Heigham St A1
Hollywood A2
Horn's La C2
Information Ctr B1
intu Chapelfield C1
Ipswich Rd C1
James Stuart Gdns B3
King St B2
King St C3
Koblenz Ave C3
Library B1
London St B2
Lower Cl B3
Lower Clarence Rd B3
Maddermarket B1
Magdalen St A2
Mariners La C2
Market B2
Market Ave B2
Mountergate B3
Mousehold St A3
Newmarket Rd C1
Norfolk St C1
Norwich City FC C3
Norwich Gallery B2
Norwich School B2
Norwich Station B3
Oak St A1
Odeon C3
Palace St A2
Pitt St A1
Playhouse B2
Police Station B1
Post Office A2/B2/B3/C1
Pottergate B1
Prince of Wales Rd B2
Princes St B2
Pull's Ferry B3
Puppet Theatre A2
Queen St B2
Queens Rd C2
RC Cathedral B1
Recorder Rd B3
Riverside Entertainment Ctr C3
Riverside L Ctr C3
Riverside Rd B3
Riverside Retail Pk C3
Rosary Rd B3
Rose La B3
Rouen Rd C2
St Andrews St B2
St Augustines St A1
St Benedicts St B1
St Ethelbert's Gate B2
St Faiths La B3
St Georges St A2

Parsonage Green C1
Playhouse Theatre A2
Post Office A2/B2/C2
Poultry Cross B2
Queen Elizabeth Gdns B1
Queen's Rd A3
Rampart Rd B3
St Ann St B2
St Ann's Gate B2
St Marks Rd A3
St Martins B3
St Mary's Cathedral B2
St Nicholas Hosp C2
St Paul's A1
St Paul's Rd A1
St Thomas B2
Salisbury & South Wiltshire Mus B2
Salisbury Sta A1
Salt La A3
Saxon Rd C1
Scots La A2
Shady Bower B3
South Canonry C2
South Gate C2
Southampton Rd B2
Spire View A1
Sports Ground C3
Tollgate Rd B3
Town Path B1
Wain-a-Long Rd A3
Wardrobe,The B2
Wessex Rd A3
West Walk C2
Wilton Rd A1
Wiltshire College B3
Winchester St B3
Windsor Rd A1
Winston Churchill Gdns C3
Wyndham Rd A2
YHA B3
York Rd A1

Scarborough 124

Aberdeen Walk B2
Albert Rd A2
Albion Rd C2
Auborough St B2
Balmoral Ctr B2
Belle Vue St C1
Belmont Rd C2
Brunswick Shopping Centre B2
Castle Dykes B3
Castle Hill A3
Castle Rd B2
Castle Walls A3
Castlegate B3
Cemetery B1
Central Tramway B2
Coach Park B1
Columbus Ravine A1
Court B1
Crescent,The C2
Cricket Ground A1
Cross St B2
Crown Terr C2
Dean Rd B1
Devonshire Dr A1
East Harbour B3
East Pier B3
Eastborough B2
Elmville Ave B1
Esplanade C2
Falconers Rd B2
Falsgrave Rd C1
Fire Station B2
Foreshore Rd B2
Friargate B2
Gladstone Rd B1
Gladstone St B1
Hollywood Plaza A1
Holms,The A3
Hoxton Rd B1
King St B2
Library B2
Lifeboat Station B3
Londesborough Rd C1
Longwestgate B3
Marine Dr A3
Luna Park B3
Miniature Railway A1
Nelson St B1
Newborough B2
Nicolas St B2
North Marine Rd A1
North St B2
Northway B1
Old Harbour B3
Olympia Leisure B2
Peasholm Park A1
Peasholm Rd A1
Police Station B1
Post Office B2
Princess St B3
Prospect Rd B1
Queen St B2
Queen's Parade A2
Queen's Tower (Remains) A3
Ramshill Rd C2
Roman Signal Station A3
Roscoe St C1
Rotunda Mus C2
Royal Albert Dr A2
Royal Albert Park A2
St Martin-on-the-Hill C2
St Martin's Ave C2
St Mary's B3
St Thomas St B2
Sandside B3
Scarborough C1
Scarborough Art Gallery C2
Scarborough Bowls Centre A1
Scarborough Castle A3
Shopmobility C2
Somerset Terr C2
South Cliff Lift C2
Spa Theatre,The C2
Spa,The C2
Stephen Joseph Theatre B1
Tennyson Ave B1
Tollergate B2
Town Hall B2
Trafalgar Rd B1
Trafalgar Square A1
Trafalgar St West B1
Valley Bridge Par C2
Valley Rd C1
Vernon Rd C2
Victoria Pk Mount A1
Victoria Rd B1
West Pier B3
Westborough C1
Westover Rd C1
Westwood C1
Woodall Ave A1
YMCA Theatre B2
York Pl B2
Yorkshire Coast College (Westwood Campus) C1

Sheffield 124

Addy Dr A2
Addy St A2
Adelphi St A3
Albert Terrace Rd A3
Albion St A2
Aldred Rd A1
Allen St A4
Alma St A4
Angel St B5
Arundel Gate B5
Arundel St C4
Ashberry Rd A2
Ashdell Rd C1
Ashgate Rd C1
Athletics Centre B2
Attercliffe Rd A6
Bailey St B4
Ball St A4
Balm Green B4
Bank St B4
Barber Rd A2
Bard St B5
Barker's Pool B4
Bates St A1
Beech Hill Rd C1
Beet St B3
Bellefield St A3
Bernard Rd A6
Bernard St B6
Birkendale A2
Birkendale Rd A2
Birkendale View A1
Bishop St C4
Blackwell Pl B6
Blake St A2
Blonk St A5
Bolsover St B2
Botanical Gdns C1
Bower Rd A1
Bradley St A1
Bramall La C4
Bramwell St A3
Bridge St A4/A5
Brighton Terr Rd A1
Broad La B3
Broad St B6
Brocco St A3
Brook Hill B3
Broomfield Rd C1
Broomgrove Rd C2
Broomhall Pl C3
Broomhall Rd C2
Broomhall St C3
Broomspring La C2
Brown St C5
Brunswick St B3
Burgess St B4
Burlington St A2
Burns Rd A2
Cadman St A6
Cambridge St B4
Campo La B4
Carver St B4
Castle Square B5
Castlegate A5
Cathedral B4
Cathedral (RC) B4
Cavendish St B3
Charles St C4
Charter Row C4
Children's Hosp B2
Church St B4
City Hall B4
City Hall B4
City Rd C6
Claremont Cr B2
Claremont Pl B2
Clarke St C3
Clarkegrove Rd C2
Clarkehouse Rd C1
Clarkson St B2
Cobden View Rd A1
Collegiate Cr C2
Commercial St B5
Commonside A1
Conduit Rd B1
Cornish St A3
Corporation St A4
Court B4
Cricket Inn Rd B6
Cromwell St A1
Crookes Rd B1
Crookes Valley Park B2
Crookes Valley Rd B2
Crookesmoor Rd A2
Crown Court A4
Crucible Theatre B5
Cutlers' Hall B4
Cutlers Gate A6
Daniel Hill A2
Dental Hospital B2
Derek Dooley Way A5
Devonshire Green B3
Devonshire St B3
Division St B4
Dorset St C2
Dover St A3
Duchess Rd C5
Duke St B5
Duncombe St A1
Durham Rd B2
Earl St C4
Earl Way C4
Ecclesall Rd C3
Edward St B3
Effingham Rd A6
Effingham St A6
Egerton St C3
Eldon St B3
Elmore Rd B1
Exchange St B5
Eyre St C4
Fargate B4
Farm Rd C5
Fawcett St A3
Filey St B3
Fir St A1
Fire Station C4
Fitzalan Sq/Ponds Forge B5
Fitzwater Rd C6
Fitzwilliam Gate C4
Fitzwilliam St B3
Flat St B5
Foley St A6
Foundry Climbing Centre A4
Fulton Rd A1
Furnace Hill A4
Furnival Rd A5
Furnival Sq C4
Furnival St C4
Garden St B3
Gell St B3
Gibraltar St A4
Glebe Rd B1
Glencoe Rd C6
Glossop Rd B2/B3/C1
Gloucester St C2
Government Offices C4
Granville Rd C6
Granville Rd / The Sheffield Coll C5
Graves Gallery B5
Greave Rd B3
Green La A4
Hadfield St A1
Hanover St C3
Hanover Way C3
Harcourt Rd B1
Harmer La B5
Havelock St C2
Hawley St B4
Haymarket B5
Headford St C3
Heavygate Rd A1
Henry St A3
High St B4
Hodgson St C3
Holberry Gdns C2
Hollis Croft B4
Holly St B4
Hounsfield Rd B3
Howard Rd A1
Hoyle St A3
Hyde Park A6
Infirmary Rd A3
Infirmary Rd A3
Information Ctr B4
Jericho St A3
Johnson St A5
Kelham Island Industrial Mus A4
Lawson Rd C1
Leadmill Rd C5
Leadmill St C5
Leadmill,The C5
Leamington St A1
Leavy Rd B3
Lee Croft B4
Leopold St B4
Leveson St A6
Library A2/B5/C1
Light,The C4
Lyceum Theatre B5
Malinda St A3
Maltravers St A5
Manor Oaks Rd B6
Mappin St B3
Marlborough Rd B1
Mary St C4
Matilda St C4
Matlock Rd A1
Meadow St A3
Melbourn Rd A1
Melbourne Ave C1
Millennium Galleries B5
Milton St C3
Mitchell St B3
Mona Ave A1
Mona Rd A1
Montgomery Terrace Rd A3
Montgomery Theatre B4
Monument Grounds C6
Moor Oaks Rd B1
Moor,The C4
Moor,The C4
Moor Market C4
Moore St C3
Mowbray St A4
Mushroom La B2
National Emergency Service A4
Netherthorpe Rd B3
Netherthorpe Rd B3
Newbould La C1
Nile St C1
Norfolk Park Rd C6
Norfolk Rd C6
Norfolk St B4
North Church St B4
Northfield Rd A1
Northumberland Rd B1
Nursery St A5
O2 Academy B5
Oakholme Rd C1
Octagon B2
Odeon B5
Old St B6
Orchard Square B4
Orchard Square Shopping Ctr B4
Oxford St A2
Paradise St B4
Park La C2
Park Sq B5
Parker's Rd B1
Pearson Building (Univ) C2
Penistone Rd A3
Pinstone St B4
Pitt St B3
Police Station B5
Pond Hill B5
Pond St B5
Ponds Forge Int Sports Ctr B5
Portobello St B3
Post Office A2/B3/B4/B5/C1/C3/C6
Powell St A2
Queen St B4
Queen's Rd C5
Ramsey Rd B1
Red Hill B3
Redcar Rd B1
Regent St B3
Rockingham St B4
Roebuck Rd A2
Royal Hallamshire Hospital C2
Russell St A4
Rutland Park C1
St George's Cl B3
St Mary's Gate C3
St Mary's Rd C4/C5
St Peter & St Paul Cathedral B4
St Philip's Rd A3
Savile St A5
School Rd B1
Scotland St A4
Severn Rd B1
Shalesmoor A4
Shalesmoor A3
Sheaf St B5
Sheffield Hallam University B5
Sheffield Ice Sports Centre – Skate Central C5
Sheffield Interchange B5
Sheffield Parkway A6
Sheffield Sta C5
Sheffield Sta/ Sheffield Hallam University B5
Sheffield University B2
Shepherd St A3
Shipton St A2
Shopmobility B3
Shoreham St C4
Showroom C5
Shrewsbury Rd C5
Sidney St C4
Site Gallery C5
Slinn St A1
Smithfield A4
Snig Hill A5
Snow La A4
Solly St B3
South La C4
South Street Park B5
Southbourne Rd C1
Spital Hill A5
Spital St A5
Spring Hill B1
Spring Hill Rd B1
Springvale Rd A1
Stafford Rd C6
Stafford St B6
Suffolk Rd C5
Summer St B2
Sunny Bank C3
Superstore A3/C3
Surrey St B4
Sussex St A6
Sutton St B3
Sydney Rd A2
Sylvester St C4
Talbot St B5
Tapton Hall Conference & Banqueting Ctr B1
Taptonville Rd B1
Tenter St B4
Town Hall B4
Townend St A1
Townhead St B4
Trafalgar St B4
Tree Root Walk B2
Trinity St A4
Trippet La B4
Turner Museum of Glass B3
Union St B4
University Drama Studio B2
Univ of Sheffield B3
Upper Allen St A3
Upper Hanover St B3
Upperthorpe Rd A2/A3
Verdon St A5
Victoria Rd C2
Victoria St B3
Waingate B5
Watery St A3
Watson Rd C1
Wellesley Rd B2
Wellington St C3
West Bar A4
West Bar Green A4
West One Plaza B3
West St B3
West St B3
Westbourne Rd C1
Western Bank B2
Western Rd A1
Weston Park B2
Weston Pk Hosp B2
Weston Pk Mus B2
Weston St B2
Wharncliffe Rd C3
Whitham Rd B1
Wicker A5
Wilkinson St B2
William St C3
Winter Garden B4
Winter St B2
York St B4
Yorkshire Artspace C5
Young St C4

Southampton 124

Above Bar St A2
Albert Rd North B3
Albert Rd South C3
Anderson's Rd B3
Archaeology Museum (God's House Tower) C2
Argyle Rd A2
Arundel Tower B1
Bargate,The B2
BBC Regional Ctr A1
Bedford Pl A1
Belvidere Rd A3
Bernard St C2
Blechynden Terr A1
Brinton's Rd A2
Britannia Rd A3
Briton St C2
Brunswick Pl A2
Bugle St C1
Canute Rd C3
Castle Way C2
Catchcold Tower B1
Central Bridge C3
Central Rd C2
Channel Way C3
Chapel Rd B3
Cineworld C3
City Art Gallery A1
City College B3
City Cruise Terminal C1
Civic Centre A1
Civic Centre Rd A1
Coach Station B1
Commercial Rd A1
Cumberland Pl A1
Cunard Rd C2
Derby Rd A3
Devonshire Rd A1
Dock Gate 4 C2
Dock Gate 8 B1
East Andrews Park A2
East Park Terr A2
East St B2
Emirates Spinnaker Tower B1
Endle St B3
European Way C2
Fire Station A2
Floating Bridge Rd C3
Golden Gr A3
Graham Rd A2
Guildhall A1
Hanover Bldgs B2
Harbour Lights C3
Harbour Pde B1
Hartington Rd A3
Havelock Rd A1
Henstead Rd A1
Herbert Walker Ave B1
High St B2
Hoglands Park B2
Holy Rood (Rems), Merchant Navy Memorial B2
Houndwell Park B2
Houndwell Pl B2
Hythe Ferry C2
Information Ctr A1
Isle of Wight Ferry Terminal C1
James St B3
Java Rd C2
Kingsway A2
Leisure World B1
Library A1
Lime St B2
London Rd A2
Marine Pde B3
Marlands Shop Ctr, The A1
Marsh La B2
Mayflower Meml C1
Mayflower Park C1
Mayflower Theatre, The A1
Medieval Merchant's House C1
Melbourne St B3
Millais A2
Morris Rd A1
National Oceanography Centre C3
Neptune Way C3
New Rd A2
Nichols Rd A3
North Front A2
Northam Rd A3
Ocean Dock C2
Ocean Village Marina C3
Ocean Way C3
Odeon B1
Ogle Rd B1
Old Northam Rd A2
Orchard La B2
Oxford Ave A2
Oxford St C2
Palmerston Park A2
Palmerston Rd A2
Parsonage Rd A3
Peel St A3
Platform Rd C2
Polygon,The A1
Portland Terr B1
Post Office A2/A3/B2
Pound Tree Rd B2
Quays Swimming & Diving Complex, The B1
Queen's Park C2
Queen's Peace Fountain A2
Queen's Terr C2
Queensway B2
Radcliffe Rd A3
Rochester St A3
Royal Pier C1
Royal South Hants Hospital A2
St Andrew's Rd A2
St Mary's B3
St Mary St A2
St Mary's Leisure Ctr A2
St Mary's Pl B2
St Mary's Rd A2
St Mary's Stadium (Southampton FC) A3
St Michael's C1
Sea City Mus A1
Solent Sky C3
South Front B2
Southampton Central Station A1
Southampton Solent University A2
SS Shieldhall C2
Terminus Terrace C2
Threefield La B2
Titanic Engineers' Memorial A2
Town Quay C1
Town Walls B2
Tudor House C1
Vincent's Walk B2
West Gate Hall C1
West Marlands Rd A1
West Park A1
West Park Rd A1
West Quay Rd B1
West Quay Retail Pk B1
Western Esplanade B1
Westquay Shop Ctr B1
White Star Way C2
Winton St A2

Southend-on-Sea 125

Adventure Island C3
Albany Ave A1
Albert Rd C3
Alexandra Rd C2
Alexandra St C2
Alexandra Yacht Club C2
Ashburnham Rd B2
Ave Rd B1
Avenue Terr B1
Balmoral Rd B1
Baltic Ave B3
Baxter Ave A2/B2
Beecroft Art Gallery B2
Bircham Rd A2
Boscombe Rd B3
Boston Ave A1/B2
Bournemouth Park Rd A3
Browning Ave A3
Bus Station C3
Byron Ave A3
Cambridge Rd C1/C2
Canewdon Rd B1
Carnarvon Rd A2
Central Ave A3
Chelmsford Ave A1
Chichester Rd B2
Church Rd C3
Civic Centre A2
Clarence Rd C2
Clarence St C2
Cliff Ave B1
Cliffs Pavilion C1
Clifftown Parade C2
Clifftown Rd C2
Colchester Rd A1
Coleman St B3
College Way B2
County Court B3
Cromer Rd B3
Crowborough Rd A2
Dryden Ave A3
East St A2
Elmer App B2
Elmer Ave B2
Forum,The B2
Gainsborough Dr A1
Gayton Rd A2
Glenhurst Rd A2
Gordon Pl B2
Gordon Rd B2
Grainger Rd A2
Greyhound Way A3
Grove,The A3
Guildford Rd B3
Hamlet Ct Rd B1
Hamlet Rd C1
Harcourt Ave A1
Hartington Rd C3
Hastings Rd B3
Herbert Gr C3
Heygate Ave C3
High St B2/C2
Information Ctr C3
Kenway A2
Kilworth Ave B3
Lancaster Gdns B3
London Rd B1
Lucy Rd C3
MacDonald Ave A1
Magistrates' Court A2
Maine Ave C1
Maldon Rd A2
Marine Parade C3
Marine Rd C1
Milton Rd B1
Milton St B2
Napier Ave B2
North Ave A3
North Rd A1/B1
Odeon B2
Osborne Rd B1
Park Cres B1
Park Rd B1
Park St B1
Park Terr B1
Pier Hill C3
Pleasant Rd C3
Police Station A2
Post Office B2/B3
Princes St B2
Queens Rd B2
Queensway B2/B3/C3
Radio Essex C2
Rayleigh Ave A1
Redstock Rd A2
Rochford Ave A1
Royal Mews C2
Royal Terr C2
Royals Shopping Centre,The C3
Ruskin Ave A3
St Ann's Rd B3
St Helen's Rd B1
St John's Rd B1
St Leonard's Rd C3
St Lukes Rd A3
St Vincent's Rd C1
Salisbury Ave A1/B1
Scratton Rd C2
Shakespeare Dr A1
Shopmobility B2
Short St A2
South Ave A3
South Essex Coll B2
Southchurch Rd B3
Southend Central B2
Southend Pier Railway C3
Southend United FC A1
Southend Victoria B2
Stadium Rd A2
Stanfield Rd A2
Stanley Rd C3
Sutton Rd A3/B3
Swanage Rd B3
Sweyne Ave A1
Sycamore Gr A3
Tennyson Ave A3
Tickfield Ave A2
Tudor Rd A1
Tunbridge Rd A2
Tylers Ave B3
Tyrrel Dr B3
Univ of Essex B2/C2
Vale Ave A2
Victoria Ave A2
Victoria Shopping Centre,The B2
Warrior Sq B3
Wesley Rd C3
West Rd A1
West St A1
Westcliff Ave C1
Westcliff Parade C1
Western Esplanade C1
Weston Rd C2
Whitegate Rd B3
Wilson Rd C1
Wimborne Rd B3
York Rd C3

Stoke-on-Trent (Hanley) 125

Acton St A3
Albion St B2
Argyle St C1
Ashbourne Gr A2
Avoca St A3
Baskerville Rd B3
Bedford Rd C1
Bedford St C1
Bethesda St B2
Bexley St A2
Birches Head Rd A3
Botteslow St C3
Boundary St A2
Broad St C2
Broom St A3
Bryan St A2
Bucknall New Rd B3
Bucknall Old Rd B3
Bus Station B3
Cannon St C2
Castlefield St C1
Cavendish St B1
Central Forest Pk A2
Charles St B3
Cheapside B2
Chell St A3
Clarke St C1
Cleveland Rd C2
Clifford St C3
Clough St B2
Clyde St C1
College Rd C2
Cooper St C2
Corbridge Rd A1
Cutts St C2
Davis St C1
Denbigh St A1
Derby St C3
Dilke St A3
Dundas St A3
Dundee Rd C1
Dyke St B3
Eastwood Rd C3
Eaton St A3
Etruria Park B1
Etruria Rd B1
Etruria Vale Rd C1
Festing St A3
Festival Retail Park A1
Fire Station C2
Foundry St B2
Franklyn St C3
Garnet St B1
Garth St B3
George St A3
Gilman St B3
Glass St B3
Goodson St B3
Greyhound Way A1
Grove Pl C1
Hampton St C3
Hanley Park C2
Hanley Park C2
Harding Rd C2
Hassall St B3
Havelock Pl C1
Hazlehurst St C3
Hinde St C2
Hope St B2
Houghton St C2
Hulton St A3
Information Ctr B3
Jasper St C2
Jervis St A3
John Bright St A3
John St B2
Keelings Rd A3
Kimberley Rd C1
Ladysmith Rd C1
Lawrence St C2
Leek Rd C3
Library C2
Lichfield St C3
Linfield Rd B3
Loftus St A2
Lower Bedford St C1
Lower Bryan St A2
Lower Mayer St A3
Lowther St A1
Magistrates Court C2
Malham St A2
Marsh St B2
Matlock St C3
Mayer St A3
Milton St C1
Mitchell Memorial Theatre B2
Morley St B2
Moston St A3
Mount Pleasant C1
Mulgrave St A1
Mynors St B3
Nelson Pl B3
New Century St B1
Octagon Retail Pk B1
Ogden Rd C3
Old Hall St B3
Old Town Rd A3
Pall Mall B2
Palmerston St C3
Park and Ride C2
Parker St B2
Parkway,The C2
Pavilion Dr A1
Pelham St C3
Percy St B2
Piccadilly B2
Picton St B3
Plough St A3
Police Station C2
Portland St A1
Post Office A3/B3/C3
Potteries Museum & Art Gallery B2
Potteries Shopping Centre B2
Potteries Way C2
Powell St A1
Pretoria Rd C1
Quadrant Rd B2
Ranelagh St C2
Raymond St C2
Rectory Rd C1
Regent Rd C2
Regent Theatre B2
Richmond Terr C2
Ridgehouse Dr A1
Robson St C2
St Ann St B3
St Luke St B3
Sampson St B2
Shaw St A1
Sheaf St C2
Shearer St C1
Shelton New Rd C1
Shirley Rd C2
Slippery La B2
Snow Hill C2
Spur St C3
Stafford St B2
Statham St B2
Stubbs La C3
Sun St C1
Supermarket A1/B2
Talbot St C3
Town Hall B2
Town Rd A3
Trinity St B2
Union St A2
Upper Hillchurch St A3
Upper Huntbach St B3
Victoria Hall Theatre B3
Warner St C2
Warwick St C1
Waterloo Rd A1
Waterloo St B3
Well St B3
Wellesley St C2
Wellington Rd B3
Wellington St B3
Whitehaven Dr A2
Whitmore St C1
Windermere St A1
Woodall St A1
Yates St C2
York St A2

Stratford-upon-Avon 125

Albany Rd B1
Alcester Rd B1
Ambulance Station B1
Arden St B2
Avenue Farm A1
Ave Farm Ind Est A1
Avenue Rd A3
Avon Industrial Est A2
Baker Ave A1
Bandstand C3
Benson Rd A3
Birmingham Rd A2
Boat Club B3
Borden Pl C1
Brass Rubbing Centre C2
Bridge St B2
Bridgetown Rd C3
Bridgeway B3
Broad St C2
Broad Walk C2
Brookvale Rd C1
Bull St C2
Butterfly Farm C3
Cemetery C1
Chapel La B2
Cherry Orchard C1
Chestnut Walk B2
Children's Playground C3
Church St C2
Civic Hall B2
Clarence Rd B1
Clopton Bridge B3
Clopton Rd A2
College B1
College La C2
College St C2
Com Sports Centre B1
Council Offices (District) B2
Courtyard,The C2
Cox's Yard B3
Cricket Ground C3
Ely Gdns B2
Ely St B2
Evesham Rd C1
Fire Station B1
Foot Ferry C3
Fordham Ave A2
Gallery,The B3
Garrick Way C1
Gower Memorial B3
Great William St B2
Greenhill St B2
Greenway,The C2
Grove Rd B2
Guild St B2
Guildhall & School B2
Hall's Croft C2
Harvard House B2
Henley St B2
High St B2
Holton St C2
Holy Trinity C2
Information Ctr B3
Jolyffe Park Rd A2
Kipling Rd C3
Library B2
Lodge Rd B1
Maidenhead Rd A3
Mansell St B2
Masons Court B2
Masons Rd A1
Maybird Sh Pk A2
Maybrook Rd A1
Mayfield Ave A2
Meer St B2
Mill La C2
Moat House Hotel B3
Narrow La C2
Nash's House & New Place B2
New St C2
Old Town C2
Orchard Way C1
Paddock La C1
Park Rd A1
Payton St B2
Percy St A2
Police Station B2
Post Office B2
Recreation Ground C2
Regal Road A2
Rother St B2
Rowley Cr A3
Royal Shakespeare Theatre B3
Ryland St C2
Saffron Meadow C2
St Andrew's Cr B1
St Gregory's A3
St Gregory's Rd A3
St Mary's Rd A2
Sanctus Dr C2
Sanctus St C1
Sandfield Rd C2
Scholars La B2
Seven Meadows Rd C2
Shakespeare Ctr B2
Shakespeare Inst C2
Shakespeare St B2
Shakespeare's Birthplace B2
Sheep St B2
Shelley Rd C3
Shipston Rd C3
Shottery Rd C1
Slingates Rd A2
Southern La C2
Station Rd B1
Stratford Healthcare B2
Stratford Hosp B2
Stratford Leisure & Visitor Centre B3
Stratford Sports Club B1
Stratford-upon-Avon Station B1
Swan Theatre B3
Swan's Nest La B3
Talbot Rd A2
Tiddington Rd B3
Timothy's Bridge Industrial Estate A1
Timothy's Bridge Rd A1
Town Hall & Council Offices B2
Town Sq B2
Trinity St C2
Tyler St B2
War Memorial Gdns B3
Warwick Rd B3
Waterside B3
Welcombe Rd A3
West St C2
Western Rd A2
Wharf Rd A2
Willows North,The B1
Willows,The B1
Wood St B2

Sunderland 125

Albion Pl C2
Alliance Pl B1
Argyle St C2
Ashwood St C1
Athenaeum St B2
Azalea Terr C2
Beach St A1
Bedford St B2
Beechwood Terr C1
Belvedere Rd C2
Blandford St B2
Borough Rd B3
Bridge Cr B2
Bridge St B2
Bridges,The B2
Brooke St A2
Brougham St B2
Burdon Rd C2
Burn Park C1
Burn Park Rd C1
Burn Park Tech Pk C1
Carol St B1
Charles St A3
Chester Rd C1
Chester Terr B1
Church St A3
Civic Centre C2
Cork St B3
Coronation St B3
Cowan Terr C2
Dame Dorothy St A2
Deptford Rd B1
Deptford Terr A1
Derby St C2
Derwent St C2
Dock St A3
Dundas St A2
Durham Rd C1
Easington St A2
Egerton St C3
Empire B3
Empire Theatre B2
Farringdon Row B1
Fawcett St B2
Fire Station B1
Fox St C1
Foyle St B3
Frederick St B3
Hanover Pl A1
Havelock Terr C1
Hay St A2
Headworth Sq B3
Hendon Rd B3
High St East B3
High St West B2/B3
Holmeside B2
Hylton Rd B1
Information Ctr B2
John St B3
Kier Hardie Way A2
Lambton St B3
Laura St C3
Lawrence St B3
Library & Arts Ctr B3
Lily St B1
Lime St B1
Livingstone Rd B2
Low Row B2
Matamba Terr B1
Millburn St B1
Millennium Way A2
Minster B2
Monkwearmouth Sta Mus A2
Mowbray Park C3
Mowbray Rd C3
Murton St C3
National Glass Centre A3
New Durham Rd C1
Newcastle Rd A2
Nile St B3
Norfolk St B3
North Bridge St A2
Northern Gallery for Contemporary Art B3
Otto Terr C1
Park La C2
Park Lane C2
Park Rd C2
Paul's Rd B3
Peel St C3
Police Station B2
Priestly Cr A1
Queen St B2
Railway Row B1
Retail Park B1
Richmond St A2
Roker Ave A2
Royalty Theatre C1
Royalty,The C1
Ryhope Rd C2
St Mary's Way B2
St Michael's Way B2
St Peter's A3
St Peter's A2
St Peter's Way A3
St Vincent St C3
Salem Rd C3
Salem St C3
Salisbury St C3
Sans St B3
Shopmobility B2
Silkworth Row B1

Abbreviations used in the index

Aberdeen	**Aberdeen City**	Dumfries	**Dumfries and**
Aberds	**Aberdeenshire**		**Galloway**
Ald	**Alderney**	Dundee	**Dundee City**
Anglesey	**Isle of Anglesey**	Durham	**Durham**
Angus	**Angus**	E Ayrs	**East Ayrshire**
Argyll	**Argyll and Bute**	E Dunb	**East**
Bath	**Bath and North East**		**Dunbartonshire**
	Somerset	E Loth	**East Lothian**
Bedford	**Bedford**	E Renf	**East Renfrewshire**
Bl Gwent	**Blaenau Gwent**	E Sus	**East Sussex**
Blackburn	**Blackburn with**	E Yorks	**East Riding of**
	Darwen		**Yorkshire**
Blackpool	**Blackpool**	Edin	**City of Edinburgh**
Bmouth	**Bournemouth**	Essex	**Essex**
Borders	**Scottish Borders**	Falk	**Falkirk**
Brack	**Bracknell**	Fife	**Fife**
Bridgend	**Bridgend**	Flint	**Flintshire**
Brighton	**City of Brighton and**	Glasgow	**City of Glasgow**
	Hove	Glos	**Gloucestershire**
Bristol	**City and County of**	Gtr Man	**Greater Manchester**
	Bristol	Guern	**Guernsey**
Bucks	**Buckinghamshire**	Gwyn	**Gwynedd**
C Beds	**Central**	Halton	**Halton**
	Bedfordshire	Hants	**Hampshire**
Caerph	**Caerphilly**	Hereford	**Herefordshire**
Cambs	**Cambridgeshire**	Herts	**Hertfordshire**
Cardiff	**Cardiff**	Highld	**Highland**
Carms	**Carmarthenshire**	HrtIpI	**Hartlepool**
Ceredig	**Ceredigion**	Hull	**Hull**
Ches E	**Cheshire East**	IoM	**Isle of Man**
Ches W	**Cheshire West and**	IoW	**Isle of Wight**
	Chester	Invclyd	**Inverclyde**
Clack	**Clackmannanshire**	Jersey	**Jersey**
Conwy	**Conwy**	Kent	**Kent**
Corn	**Cornwall**	Lancs	**Lancashire**
Cumb	**Cumbria**	Leicester	**City of Leicester**
Darl	**Darlington**	Leics	**Leicestershire**
Denb	**Denbighshire**	Lincs	**Lincolnshire**
Derby	**City of Derby**	London	**Greater London**
Derbys	**Derbyshire**	Luton	**Luton**
Devon	**Devon**	M Keynes	**Milton Keynes**
Dorset	**Dorset**	M Tydf	**Merthyr Tydfil**

Mbro	**Middlesbrough**	Poole	**Poole**	Swansea	**Swansea**
Medway	**Medway**	Powys	**Powys**	Swindon	**Swindon**
Mers	**Merseyside**	Ptsmth	**Portsmouth**	T&W	**Tyne and Wear**
Midloth	**Midlothian**	Reading	**Reading**	Telford	**Telford and Wrekin**
Mon	**Monmouthshire**	Redcar	**Redcar and**	Thurrock	**Thurrock**
Moray	**Moray**		**Cleveland**	Torbay	**Torbay**
N Ayrs	**North Ayrshire**	Renfs	**Renfrewshire**	Torf	**Torfaen**
N Lincs	**North Lincolnshire**	Rhondda	**Rhondda Cynon Taff**	V Glam	**The Vale of**
N Lanark	**North Lanarkshire**	Rutland	**Rutland**		**Glamorgan**
N Som	**North Somerset**	S Ayrs	**South Ayrshire**	W Berks	**West Berkshire**
N Yorks	**North Yorkshire**	S Glos	**South**	W Dunb	**West**
NE Lincs	**North East**		**Gloucestershire**		**Dunbartonshire**
	Lincolnshire	S Lanark	**South Lanarkshire**	W Isles	**Western Isles**
Neath	**Neath Port Talbot**	S Yorks	**South Yorkshire**	W Loth	**West Lothian**
Newport	**City and County of**	Scilly	**Scilly**	W Mid	**West Midlands**
	Newport	Shetland	**Shetland**	W Sus	**West Sussex**
Norf	**Norfolk**	Shrops	**Shropshire**	W Yorks	**West Yorkshire**
Northants	**Northamptonshire**	Slough	**Slough**	Warks	**Warwickshire**
Northumb	**Northumberland**	Som	**Somerset**	Warr	**Warrington**
Nottingham	**City of Nottingham**	Soton	**Southampton**	Wilts	**Wiltshire**
Notts	**Nottinghamshire**	Staffs	**Staffordshire**	Windsor	**Windsor and**
Orkney	**Orkney**	Stirling	**Stirling**		**Maidenhead**
Oxon	**Oxfordshire**	Stockton	**Stockton-on-Tees**	Wokingham	**Wokingham**
Pboro	**Peterborough**	Stoke	**Stoke-on-Trent**	Worcs	**Worcestershire**
Pembs	**Pembrokeshire**	Suff	**Suffolk**	Wrex	**Wrexham**
Perth	**Perth and Kinross**	Sur	**Surrey**	York	**City of York**
Plym	**Plymouth**				

Index to road maps of Britain

How to use the index

Example   Thornton-le-Beans N Yorks   58 G4

— grid square
— page number
— county or unitary authority

Bowderdale Cumb 57 F8
Bowdon Gtr Man 43 D10
Bower Northumb 62 E3
Bower Hinton Som 8 C3
Bowerchalke Wilts 9 B9
Bowerhill Wilts 16 E6
Bowermadden Highld 94 D4
Bowers Gifford Essex 20 C4
Bowershall Fife 69 A9
Bowertower Highld 94 D4
Bowes Durham 57 E11
Bowgreave Lancs 49 E4
Bowgreen Gtr Man 43 D10
Bowhill Borders 70 H3
Bowhouse Dumfries 60 G6
Bowland Bridge Cumb 56 H6
Bowley Hereford 26 C2
Bowlhead Green Sur 18 H6
Bowling W Dunb 68 C3
Bowling W Yorks 51 F7
Bowling Bank Wrex 43 H6
Bowling Green Worcs 26 C5
Bowmanstead Cumb 56 G5
Bowmore Argyll 64 C4
Bowness-on-Solway Cumb 61 G8
Bowness-on-Windermere Cumb 56 G6
Bowsden Northumb 71 F8
Bowside Lodge Highld 93 C11
Bowston Cumb 57 G6
Bowthorpe Norf 39 E7
Box Glos 16 A5
Box Wilts 16 E5
Box End Bedford 29 D7
Boxbush Glos 26 G4
Boxford Suff 30 D6
Boxford W Berks 17 D11
Boxgrove W Sus 11 D8
Boxley Kent 20 F4
Boxmoor Herts 29 H7
Boxted Essex 30 E6
Boxted Suff 30 C5
Boxted Cross Essex 31 E7
Boxted Heath Essex 31 E7
Boxworth Cambs 29 B10
Boxworth End Cambs 29 B10
Boyden Gate Kent 21 E9
Boylestone Derbys 35 B7
Boyndie Aberds 89 B6
Boynton E Yorks 53 C7
Boysack Angus 77 C9
Boyton Corn 6 G2
Boyton Suff 31 D10
Boyton Wilts 16 H6
Boyton Cross Essex 30 H3
Boyton End Suff 30 D4
Bozeat Northants 28 C6
Brù W Isles 91 C8
Braaid IoM 48 E3
Braal Castle Highld 94 D3
Brabling Green Suff 31 B9
Brabourne Kent 13 B9
Brabourne Lees Kent 13 B9
Brabster Highld 94 D5
Bracadale Highld 85 E8
Bracara Highld 79 B10
Braceborough Lincs 37 D6
Bracebridge Lincs 46 F3
Bracebridge Heath Lincs 46 F3
Bracebridge Low Fields Lincs 46 F3
Braceby Lincs 36 B6
Bracewell Lancs 50 E4
Brackenfield Derbys 45 G7
Brackenthwaite Cumb 56 B4
Brackenthwaite N Yorks 51 D8
Bracklesham W Sus 11 E7
Brackletter Highld 80 E3
Brackley Argyll 65 D8
Brackley Northants 28 E2
Brackloch Highld 92 G4
Bracknell Brack 18 E5
Braco Perth 75 G11
Bracobrae Moray 88 C5
Bracon Ash Norf 39 F7
Bracorina Highld 79 B10
Bradbourne Derbys 44 G6
Bradbury Durham 58 D4
Bradda IoM 48 F1
Bradden Northants 28 D3
Braddock Corn 4 E2
Bradeley Stoke 44 G2
Bradenham Bucks 18 B5
Bradenham Norf 38 E5
Bradenstoke Wilts 17 D7
Bradfield Essex 31 E8
Bradfield Norf 39 B8
Bradfield W Berks 18 D3
Bradfield Combust Suff 30 C5
Bradfield Green Ches E 43 G9
Bradfield Heath Essex 31 F8
Bradfield St Clare Suff 30 C6
Bradfield St George Suff 30 B6
Bradford Corn 4 D2
Bradford Derbys 44 F6
Bradford Devon 6 F3
Bradford Northumb 71 G10
Bradford W Yorks 51 F7
Bradford Abbas Dorset 8 C4
Bradford Leigh Wilts 16 E5
Bradford-on-Avon Wilts 16 E5
Bradford-on-Tone Som 7 D10
Bradford Peverell Dorset 8 E5
Brading IoW 10 F5
Bradley Derbys 44 H6
Bradley Hants 18 G3
Bradley NE Lincs 46 B6
Bradley Staffs 34 D4
Bradley W Mid 34 F5
Bradley W Yorks 51 G7
Bradley Green Worcs 26 B6
Bradley in the Moors Staffs 35 A6
Bradley Stoke S Glos 16 C3
Bradlow Hereford 26 E4
Bradmore Notts 36 B1
Bradmore W Mid 34 F4
Bradninch Devon 7 F9
Bradnop Staffs 44 G4
Bradpole Dorset 8 E3
Bradshaw Gtr Man 43 A10
Bradshaw W Yorks 44 A4
Bradstone Devon 4 C4
Bradwall Green Ches E 43 F10
Bradway S Yorks 45 D7
Bradwell Derbys 44 D5
Bradwell Essex 30 F5
Bradwell M Keynes 28 E5
Bradwell Norf 39 E11
Bradwell Staffs 44 H2
Bradwell Grove Oxon 27 H9
Bradwell on Sea Essex 31 H7
Bradwell Waterside Essex 30 H6
Bradworthy Devon 6 E2
Bradworthy Cross Devon 6 E2
Brae Dumfries 60 F4
Brae Highld 91 J13
Brae Highld 92 J7
Brae Shetland 96 G5
Brae of Achnahaird Highld 92 H3
Brae Roy Lodge Highld 80 D5
Braeantra Highld 87 D8
Braedownie Angus 82 F4
Braefield Highld 86 H7
Braegrum Perth 76 E3
Braehead Dumfries 55 D7
Braehead Orkney 95 D5
Braehead Orkney 95 H6
Braehead S Lanark 69 E8
Braehead S Lanark 69 G7
Braehead of Lunan Angus 77 B9
Braehoulland Shetland 96 F4
Braehungie Highld 94 G3
Braelangwell Lodge Highld 87 B8
Braemar Aberds 82 D3
Braemore Highld 86 D4
Braemore Highld 94 G2
Braes of Enzie Moray 88 C3
Braeside Invclyd 73 F11
Braeswick Orkney 95 E7
Braewick Shetland 96 H5
Brafferton Darl 58 D3
Brafferton N Yorks 51 B10
Brafield-on-the-Green Northants 28 C5
Bragar W Isles 91 C7
Bragbury End Herts 29 F9
Bragleenmore Argyll 74 E2
Braichmelyn Gwyn 41 D8
Braid Edin 69 D11
Braides Lancs 49 D4
Braidley N Yorks 50 A6
Braidwood S Lanark 69 F7
Braigo Argyll 64 B3
Brailsford Derbys 35 A8
Brainshaugh Northumb 63 C8
Braintree Essex 30 F4
Braiseworth Suff 31 A8
Braishfield Hants 10 B2
Braithwaite Cumb 56 D4
Braithwaite S Yorks 45 A10
Braithwaite W Yorks 50 E6
Braithwell S Yorks 45 C9
Bramber W Sus 11 C10
Bramcote Notts 35 B11
Bramcote Warks 35 G10
Bramdean Hants 10 B5
Bramerton Norf 39 E8
Bramfield Herts 29 G9
Bramfield Suff 31 A10
Bramford Suff 31 D8
Bramhall Gtr Man 44 D2
Bramham W Yorks 51 E10
Bramhope W Yorks 51 E8
Bramley Hants 18 F3
Bramley S Yorks 45 C8
Bramley Sur 19 G7
Bramley W Yorks 51 F8
Bramling Kent 21 F9
Brampford Speke Devon 7 G8
Brampton Cambs 29 A9
Brampton Cumb 57 D8
Brampton Cumb 61 G11
Brampton Derbys 45 E7
Brampton Hereford 25 E11
Brampton Lincs 46 E2
Brampton Norf 39 C8
Brampton S Yorks 45 B8
Brampton Suff 39 G10
Brampton Abbotts Hereford 26 F3
Brampton Ash Northants 36 G3
Brampton Bryan Hereford 25 A10
Brampton en le Morthen S Yorks 45 D8
Bramshall Staffs 35 B6
Bramshaw Hants 10 C1
Bramshill Hants 18 E4
Bramshott Hants 11 A7
Bran End Essex 30 F3
Branault Highld 79 E8
Brancaster Norf 38 A3
Brancaster Staithe Norf 38 A3
Brancepeth Durham 58 C3
Branch End Northumb 62 G6
Branchill Moray 87 F13
Brand Green Glos 26 F4
Branderburgh Moray 88 A2
Brandesburton E Yorks 53 E7
Brandeston Suff 31 B9
Brandhill Shrops 33 H10
Brandis Corner Devon 6 F3
Brandiston Norf 39 C7
Brandon Durham 58 C3
Brandon Lincs 46 H3
Brandon Northumb 62 B6
Brandon Suff 38 G3
Brandon Warks 35 H10
Brandon Bank Cambs 38 G2
Brandon Creek Norf 38 F2
Brandon Parva Norf 39 E6
Brandsby N Yorks 52 B1
Brandy Wharf Lincs 46 C4
Brane Corn 2 G3
Branksome Poole 9 E9
Branksome Park Poole 9 E9
Bransby Lincs 46 E2
Branscombe Devon 7 H10
Bransford Worcs 26 C4
Bransgore Hants 9 E10
Branshill Clack 69 A7
Bransholme Hull 53 F7
Branson's Cross Worcs 27 A7
Branston Leics 36 C4
Branston Lincs 46 F4
Branston Staffs 35 C8
Branston Booths Lincs 46 F4
Branstone IoW 10 F4
Bransty Cumb 56 E1
Brant Broughton Lincs 46 G3
Brantham Suff 31 E8
Branthwaite Cumb 56 C4
Branthwaite Cumb 56 D2
Brantingham E Yorks 52 G5
Branton Northumb 62 B6
Branton S Yorks 45 B10
Branxholm Park Borders 61 B10
Branxholme Borders 61 B10
Branxton Northumb 71 G7
Brassey Green Ches W 43 F8
Brassington Derbys 44 G6
Brasted Kent 19 F11
Brasted Chart Kent 19 F11
Brathens Aberds 83 D8
Bratoft Lincs 47 F8
Brattleby Lincs 46 D3
Bratton Telford 34 D2
Bratton Wilts 16 F6
Bratton Clovelly Devon 6 G3
Bratton Fleming Devon 6 C5
Bratton Seymour Som 8 B5
Braughing Herts 29 F10
Braunston Northants 28 B2
Braunston-in-Rutland Rutland 36 E4
Braunstone Town Leicester 36 E1
Braunton Devon 6 C3
Brawby N Yorks 52 B3
Brawl Highld 93 C11
Brawlbin Highld 94 E2
Bray Windsor 18 D6
Bray Shop Corn 4 D4
Bray Wick Windsor 18 D5
Braybrooke Northants 36 G3
Braye Ald 11
Brayford Devon 6 C5
Braystones Cumb 56 F2
Braythorn N Yorks 51 E8
Brayton N Yorks 52 F2
Brazacott Corn 6 G1
Breach Kent 20 E5
Breachacha Castle Argyll 78 F4
Breachwood Green Herts 29 F8
Breacleit W Isles 90 D6
Breaden Heath Shrops 33 B10
Breadsall Derbys 35 B9
Breadstone Glos 16 A4
Breage Corn 2 G5
Breakachy Highld 86 G7
Bream Glos 26 H3
Breamore Hants 9 C10
Brean Som 15 F8
Breanais W Isles 90 E4
Brearton N Yorks 51 C9
Breascleit W Isles 90 D7
Breaston Derbys 35 B10
Brechfa Carms 23 C10
Brechin Angus 77 A8
Breck of Cruan Orkney 95 G4
Breckan Orkney 95 H3
Breckrey Highld 85 B10
Brecon = Aberhonddu Powys 25 F7
Bredbury Gtr Man 44 C3
Brede E Sus 13 E7
Bredenbury Hereford 26 C3
Bredfield Suff 31 C9
Bredgar Kent 20 E5
Bredhurst Kent 20 E4
Bredicot Worcs 26 C6
Bredon Worcs 26 E6
Bredon's Norton Worcs 26 E6
Bredwardine Hereford 25 D10
Breedon on the Hill Leics 35 C10
Breibhig W Isles 84 J1
Breibhig W Isles 91 D9
Breich W Loth 69 D8
Breightmet Gtr Man 43 B10
Breighton E Yorks 52 F3
Breinton Hereford 25 E11
Breinton Common Hereford 25 D11
Breiwick Shetland 96 J6
Bremhill Wilts 16 D6
Bremirehoull Shetland 96 L6
Brenchley Kent 12 B5
Brendon Devon 7 B6
Brenkley T&W 63 F8
Brent Eleigh Suff 30 D6
Brent Knoll Som 15 F9
Brent Pelham Herts 29 E11
Brentford London 19 D8
Brentingby Leics 36 D3
Brentwood Essex 20 B2
Brenzett Kent 13 D9
Brereton Staffs 35 D6
Brereton Green Ches E 43 F10
Brereton Heath Ches E 44 F2
Bressingham Norf 39 G6
Bretby Derbys 35 C8
Bretford Warks 35 H10
Bretforton Worcs 27 D7
Bretherdale Head Cumb 57 F7
Bretherton Lancs 49 G4
Brettabister Shetland 96 H6
Brettenham Norf 38 G5
Brettenham Suff 30 C6
Bretton Derbys 44 E6
Bretton Flint 42 F6
Brewer Street Sur 19 F10
Brewlands Bridge Angus 76 A4
Brewood Staffs 34 E4
Briach Moray 87 F13
Briants Puddle Dorset 9 E7
Brick End Essex 30 F2
Brickendon Herts 29 H10
Bricket Wood Herts 19 A8
Bricklehampton Worcs 26 D6
Bride IoM 48 B4
Bridekirk Cumb 56 C3
Bridell Pembs 22 B6
Bridestowe Devon 4 C6
Brideswell Aberds 88 E5
Bridford Devon 5 C9
Bridfordmills Devon 5 C9
Bridge Kent 21 F8
Bridge End Lincs 37 B7
Bridge Green Essex 29 E11
Bridge Hewick N Yorks 51 B9
Bridge of Alford Aberds 83 B7
Bridge of Allan Stirling 75 H10
Bridge of Avon Moray 88 E1
Bridge of Awe Argyll 74 E3
Bridge of Balgie Perth 75 C8
Bridge of Cally Perth 76 B4
Bridge of Canny Aberds 83 D8
Bridge of Craigisla Angus 76 B5
Bridge of Dee Dumfries 55 D10
Bridge of Don Aberdeen 83 B11
Bridge of Dun Angus 77 B9
Bridge of Dye Aberds 83 E8
Bridge of Earn Perth 76 F4
Bridge of Ericht Perth 75 B8
Bridge of Feugh Aberds 83 D9
Bridge of Forss Highld 93 C13
Bridge of Gairn Aberds 82 D5
Bridge of Gaur Perth 75 B8
Bridge of Muchalls Aberds 83 D10
Bridge of Oich Highld 80 C5
Bridge of Orchy Argyll 74 D5
Bridge of Waith Orkney 95 G3
Bridge of Walls Shetland 96 H4
Bridge of Weir Renfs 68 D2
Bridge Sollers Hereford 25 D11
Bridge Street Suff 30 D5
Bridge Trafford Ches W 43 E7
Bridge Yate S Glos 16 D3
Bridgefoot Angus 76 D6
Bridgefoot Cumb 56 D2
Bridgehampton Som 8 B4
Bridgehill Durham 58 A1
Bridgemary Hants 10 D4
Bridgemont Derbys 44 D4
Bridgend Aberds 83 B7
Bridgend Aberds 88 E5
Bridgend Angus 83 G7
Bridgend Argyll 64 B4
Bridgend Argyll 65 E8
Bridgend Argyll 73 D7
Bridgend = Pen-y-bont ar Ogwr Bridgend 14 D5
Bridgend Cumb 56 E5
Bridgend Fife 76 F6
Bridgend Moray 88 E3
Bridgend N Lanark 68 C5
Bridgend Pembs 22 B6
Bridgend W Loth 69 C9
Bridgend of Lintrathen Angus 76 B5
Bridgerule Devon 6 F1
Bridges Shrops 33 F9
Bridgeton Glasgow 68 D5
Bridgetown Corn 4 C4
Bridgetown Som 7 C8
Bridgham Norf 38 G5
Bridgnorth Shrops 34 F3
Bridgtown Staffs 34 E5
Bridgwater Som 15 H9
Bridlington E Yorks 53 C7
Bridport Dorset 8 E3
Bridstow Hereford 26 F2
Brierfield Lancs 50 F4
Brierley Glos 26 G3
Brierley Hereford 25 C11
Brierley S Yorks 45 A8
Brierley Hill W Mid 34 G5
Briery Hill Bl Gwent 25 H8
Brig o'Turk Stirling 75 G8
Brigg N Lincs 46 B4
Briggswath N Yorks 59 F9
Brigham Cumb 56 C2
Brigham E Yorks 53 D6
Brighouse W Yorks 51 G7
Brighstone IoW 10 F3
Brightgate Derbys 44 G6
Brighthampton Oxon 17 A10
Brightling E Sus 12 D5
Brightlingsea Essex 31 G7
Brighton Brighton 12 F2
Brighton Corn 3 D8
Brighton Hill Hants 18 G3
Brightons Falk 69 C8
Brightwalton W Berks 17 D11
Brightwell Suff 31 D9
Brightwell Baldwin Oxon 18 B3
Brightwell cum Sotwell Oxon 18 B2
Brignall Durham 58 E1
Brigsley NE Lincs 46 B6
Brigsteer Cumb 57 H6
Brigstock Northants 36 G5
Brill Bucks 28 G3
Brilley Hereford 25 D9
Brimaston Pembs 22 D4
Brimfield Hereford 26 B2
Brimington Derbys 45 E8
Brimley Devon 5 D8
Brimpsfield Glos 26 G6
Brimpton W Berks 18 E2
Brims Orkney 95 K3
Brimscombe Glos 16 A5
Brimstage Mers 42 D6
Brinacory Highld 79 B10
Brind E Yorks 52 F3
Brindister Shetland 96 H4
Brindister Shetland 96 K6
Brindle Lancs 50 G2
Brindley Ford Stoke 44 G2
Brineton Staffs 34 D4
Bringhurst Leics 36 F4
Brington Cambs 37 H6
Brinian Orkney 95 F5
Briningham Norf 38 B6
Brinkhill Lincs 47 E7
Brinkley Cambs 30 C3
Brinklow Warks 35 H10
Brinkworth Wilts 17 C7
Brinmore Highld 81 A8
Brinscall Lancs 50 G2
Brinsea N Som 15 E10
Brinsley Notts 45 H8
Brinsop Hereford 25 D11
Brinsworth S Yorks 45 D8
Brinton Norf 38 B6
Brisco Cumb 56 A6
Brisley Norf 38 C5
Brislington Bristol 16 D3
Bristol Bristol 16 D2
Briston Norf 39 B6
Britannia Lancs 50 G4
Britford Wilts 9 B10
Brithdir Gwyn 32 D3
British Legion Village Kent 20 F4
Briton Ferry Neath 14 B3
Britwell Salome Oxon 18 B3
Brixham Torbay 5 F10
Brixton Devon 5 F6
Brixton London 19 D10
Brixton Deverill Wilts 16 H5
Brixworth Northants 28 A4
Brize Norton Oxon 27 H10
Broad Blunsdon Swindon 17 B8
Broad Campden Glos 27 E8
Broad Chalke Wilts 9 B9
Broad Green C Beds 28 D6
Broad Green Essex 30 F5
Broad Green Worcs 26 C4
Broad Haven Pembs 22 E3
Broad Heath Worcs 26 B3
Broad Hill Cambs 38 H1
Broad Hinton Wilts 17 D8
Broad Laying Hants 17 E11
Broad Marston Worcs 27 D8
Broad Oak Carms 23 D10
Broad Oak Cumb 56 G3
Broad Oak Dorset 8 E3
Broad Oak Dorset 9 C6
Broad Oak E Sus 12 D5
Broad Oak E Sus 13 E7
Broad Oak Hereford 25 F11
Broad Oak Mers 43 C8
Broad Street Kent 20 F5
Broad Street Green Essex 30 H5
Broad Town Wilts 17 D7
Broadbottom Gtr Man 44 C3
Broadbridge W Sus 11 D7
Broadbridge Heath W Sus 11 A10
Broadclyst Devon 7 G8
Broadfield Gtr Man 44 A2
Broadfield Lancs 49 G5
Broadfield Pembs 22 F6
Broadfield W Sus 12 C1
Broadford Highld 85 F11
Broadford Bridge W Sus 11 B9
Broadhaugh Borders 61 C10
Broadhaven Highld 94 E5
Broadheath Gtr Man 43 D10
Broadhembury Devon 7 F10
Broadhempston Devon 5 E9
Broadholme Derbys 45 H7
Broadholme Lincs 46 E2
Broadland Row E Sus 13 E7
Broadlay Carms 23 F8
Broadley Lancs 50 H4
Broadley Moray 88 B3
Broadley Common Essex 29 H11
Broadmayne Dorset 8 F6
Broadmeadows Borders 70 G3
Broadmere Hants 18 G3
Broadmoor Pembs 22 F5
Broadoak Kent 21 E8
Broadrashes Moray 88 C4
Broadsea Aberds 89 B9
Broadstairs Kent 21 E10
Broadstone Poole 9 E9
Broadstone Shrops 33 G11
Broadtown Lane Wilts 17 D7
Broadwas Worcs 26 C4
Broadwater Herts 29 F9
Broadwater W Sus 11 D10
Broadway Carms 23 F7
Broadway Pembs 22 E3
Broadway Som 8 C2
Broadway Suff 39 H9
Broadway Worcs 27 E7
Broadwell Glos 26 G2
Broadwell Glos 27 F9
Broadwell Oxon 17 A9
Broadwell Warks 27 B11
Broadwell House Northumb 57 A11
Broadwey Dorset 8 F5
Broadwindsor Dorset 8 D3
Broadwood Kelly Devon 6 F5
Broadwoodwidger Devon 4 C5
Brobury Hereford 25 D10
Brochel Highld 85 D10
Brochloch Dumfries 67 G8
Brochroy Argyll 74 D3
Brockamin Worcs 26 C4
Brockbridge Hants 10 C5
Brockdam Northumb 63 A7
Brockdish Norf 39 H8
Brockenhurst Hants 10 D2
Brocketsbrae S Lanark 69 G7
Brockford Street Suff 31 B8
Brockhall Northants 28 B3
Brockham Sur 19 G8
Brockhampton Glos 27 F7
Brockhampton Hereford 26 E2
Brockholes W Yorks 44 A5
Brockhurst Derbys 45 F7
Brockhurst Hants 10 D5
Brocklebank Cumb 56 B5
Brocklesby Lincs 46 A5
Brockley N Som 15 E10
Brockley Green Suff 30 C5
Brockleymoor Cumb 57 C6
Brockton Shrops 33 E9
Brockton Shrops 33 G9
Brockton Shrops 34 E3
Brockton Shrops 34 F1
Brockton Telford 34 D3
Brockweir Glos 15 A11
Brockwood Hants 10 B5
Brockworth Glos 26 G5
Brocton Staffs 34 D5
Brodick N Ayrs 66 C3
Brodsworth S Yorks 45 B9
Brogaig Highld 85 B9
Brogborough C Beds 28 E6
Broken Cross Ches E 44 E2
Broken Cross Ches W 43 E9
Brokenborough Wilts 16 C6
Bromborough Mers 42 D6
Brome Suff 39 H7
Brome Street Suff 39 H7
Bromeswell Suff 31 C10
Bromfield Cumb 56 B3
Bromfield Shrops 33 H10
Bromham Bedford 29 C7
Bromham Wilts 16 E6
Bromley London 19 E11
Bromley W Mid 34 G5
Bromley Common London 19 E11
Bromley Green Kent 13 C8
Brompton Medway 20 E4
Brompton N Yorks 52 A5
Brompton N Yorks 58 G4
Brompton-on-Swale N Yorks 58 G3
Brompton Ralph Som 7 C9
Brompton Regis Som 7 C8
Bromsash Hereford 26 F3
Bromsberrow Hth. Glos 26 E4
Bromsgrove Worcs 26 A6
Bromyard Hereford 26 C3
Bromyard Downs Hereford 26 C3
Bronaber Gwyn 41 G9
Brongest Ceredig 23 B8
Bronington Wrex 33 B10
Bronllys Powys 25 E8
Bronnant Ceredig 24 B3
Bronwydd Arms Carms 23 D9
Bronydd Powys 25 D9
Bronygarth Shrops 33 B8
Brook Carms 23 F7
Brook Hants 10 B2
Brook Hants 10 C1
Brook IoW 10 F2
Brook Kent 13 B9
Brook Sur 18 H6
Brook Sur 19 G7
Brook End Bedford 29 B7
Brook Hill Hants 10 C1
Brook Street Kent 13 C8
Brook Street Kent 20 G2
Brook Street W Sus 12 D2
Brooke Norf 39 F8
Brooke Rutland 36 E4
Brookenby Lincs 46 C6
Brookend Glos 16 B2
Brookfield Renfs 68 D3
Brookhouse Lancs 49 C5
Brookhouse Green Ches E 44 F2
Brookland Kent 13 D8
Brooklands Dumfries 60 F4
Brooklands Gtr Man 43 C10
Brooklands Shrops 33 A11
Brookmans Park Herts 19 A9
Brooks Powys 33 F7
Brooks Green W Sus 11 B10
Brookthorpe Glos 26 G5
Brookville Norf 38 F3
Brookwood Sur 18 F6
Broom C Beds 29 D8
Broom S Yorks 45 C8
Broom Warks 27 C7
Broom Worcs 34 H5
Broom Green Norf 38 C5
Broom Hill Dorset 9 D9
Broome Norf 39 F9
Broome Shrops 33 G10
Broome Park Northumb 63 B7
Broomedge Warr 43 D10
Broomer's Corner W Sus 11 B10
Broomfield Aberds 89 E9
Broomfield Essex 30 G4
Broomfield Kent 20 F5
Broomfield Kent 21 E8
Broomfield Som 7 C11
Broomfleet E Yorks 52 G4
Broomhall Ches E 43 H9
Broomhall Windsor 18 E6
Broomhaugh Northumb 62 G6
Broomhill Norf 38 E2
Broomhill Northumb 63 C8
Broomhill S Yorks 45 B8
Broomholm Norf 39 B9
Broomley Northumb 62 G6
Broompark Durham 58 B3
Broom's Green Glos 26 E4
Broomy Lodge Hants 9 C11
Brora Highld 93 J12
Broseley Shrops 34 E2
Brotherhouse Bar Lincs 37 D8
Brotherstone Borders 70 G5
Brothertoft Lincs 46 H6
Brotherton N Yorks 51 G10
Brotton Redcar 59 E7
Broubster Highld 93 C13
Brough Cumb 57 E9
Brough Derbys 44 D5
Brough E Yorks 52 G5
Brough Highld 94 C4
Brough Notts 46 G2
Brough Orkney 95 G4
Brough Shetland 96 F7
Brough Shetland 96 F6
Brough Shetland 96 G7
Brough Shetland 96 H6
Brough Shetland 96 J7
Brough Lodge Shetland 96 D7
Brough Sowerby Cumb 57 E9
Broughall Shrops 34 A1
Broughton Borders 69 G10
Broughton Cambs 37 H8
Broughton Flint 42 F6
Broughton Hants 10 A2
Broughton Lancs 49 F5
Broughton M Keynes 28 D5
Broughton N Lincs 46 B3
Broughton N Yorks 50 D5
Broughton N Yorks 52 B3
Broughton Northants 36 H4
Broughton Orkney 95 D5
Broughton Oxon 27 E11
Broughton V Glam 14 D5
Broughton Astley Leics 35 F11
Broughton Beck Cumb 49 A2
Broughton Common Wilts 16 E5
Broughton Gifford Wilts 16 E5
Broughton Hackett Worcs 26 C6
Broughton in Furness Cumb 56 H4
Broughton Mills Cumb 56 G4
Broughton Moor Cumb 56 C2
Broughton Park Gtr Man 44 B2
Broughton Poggs Oxon 17 A9
Broughtown Orkney 95 D7
Broughty Ferry Dundee 77 D7
Browhouses Dumfries 61 G8
Browland Shetland 96 H4
Brown Candover Hants 18 H2
Brown Edge Lancs 42 A6
Brown Edge Staffs 44 G3
Brown Heath Ches W 43 F7
Brownhill Aberds 89 D8
Brownhill Aberds 89 D6
Brownhill Blackburn 50 F2
Brownhill Shrops 33 C10
Brownhills Fife 77 F8
Brownhills W Mid 34 E6
Brownlow Ches E 44 F2
Brownlow Heath Ches E 44 F2
Brownmuir Aberds 83 F9
Brown's End Glos 26 E4
Brownshill Glos 16 A5
Brownston Devon 5 F7
Brownyside Northumb 63 A7
Broxa N Yorks 59 G10
Broxbourne Herts 29 H10
Broxburn E Loth 70 C5
Broxburn W Loth 69 C9
Broxholme Lincs 46 E3
Broxted Essex 30 F2
Broxton Ches W 43 G7
Broxwood Hereford 25 C10
Broyle Side E Sus 12 E3
Bruairnis W Isles 84 H2
Bruan Highld 94 G5
Bruar Lodge Perth 81 F10
Brucehill W Dunb 68 C2
Bruera Ches W 43 F7
Bruern Abbey Oxon 27 F9
Bruichladdich Argyll 64 B3
Bruisyard Suff 31 B10
Brumby N Lincs 46 B2
Brund Staffs 44 F5
Brundall Norf 39 E9
Brundish Suff 31 B9
Brundish Street Suff 31 A9
Brunery Highld 79 D10
Brunshaw Lancs 50 F4
Brunswick Village T&W 63 F8
Bruntcliffe W Yorks 51 G8
Bruntingthorpe Leics 36 F2
Brunton Fife 76 E6
Brunton Northumb 63 A8
Brunton Wilts 17 F9
Brushford Devon 6 F5
Brushford Som 7 D8
Bruton Som 8 A5
Bryanston Dorset 9 D7
Brydekirk Dumfries 61 F7
Bryher Scilly 2 C2
Brymbo Wrex 42 G5
Brympton Som 8 C4
Bryn Carms 23 F10
Bryn Gtr Man 43 B8
Bryn Neath 14 B4
Bryn Shrops 33 G8
Bryn-coch Neath 14 B3
Bryn Du Anglesey 40 C5
Bryn Gates Gtr Man 43 B8
Bryn-glas Conwy 41 D10
Bryn Golau Rhondda 14 C5
Bryn-Iwan Carms 23 C8
Bryn-mawr Gwyn 40 G4
Bryn-nantllech Conwy 42 F2
Bryn-penarth Powys 33 E7
Bryn Rhyd-yr-Arian Conwy 42 F2
Bryn Saith Marchog Denb 42 G3
Bryn Sion Gwyn 32 D4
Bryn-y-gwenin Mon 25 G10
Bryn-y-maen Conwy 41 C10
Bryn-yr-eryr Gwyn 40 F5
Brynamman Carms 24 G4
Brynberian Pembs 22 C6
Brynbryddan Neath 14 B3
Brynbuga = Usk Mon 15 A9
Bryncae Rhondda 14 C5
Bryncethin Bridgend 14 C5
Bryncir Gwyn 40 F6
Bryncroes Gwyn 40 G4
Bryncrug Gwyn 32 E2
Bryneglwys Denb 42 H4
Brynford Flint 42 E4
Bryngwran Anglesey 40 C5
Bryngwyn Ceredig 23 B7
Bryngwyn Mon 25 H10
Bryngwyn Powys 25 D8
Brynhenllan Pembs 22 C5
Brynhoffnant Ceredig 23 A8
Brynithel Bl Gwent 15 A8
Brynmawr Bl Gwent 25 G8
Brynmenyn Bridgend 14 C5
Brynmill Swansea 14 B2
Brynna Rhondda 14 C5
Brynrefail Anglesey 40 B6
Brynrefail Gwyn 41 D7
Brynsadler Rhondda 14 C6
Brynsiencyn Anglesey 40 D6
Brynteg Anglesey 40 B6
Brynteg Ceredig 23 B9
Buaile nam Bodach W Isles 84 H2
Bualintur Highld 85 F9
Buarthmeini Gwyn 41 G10
Bubbenhall Warks 27 A10
Bubwith E Yorks 52 F3
Buccleuch Borders 61 B9
Buchanhaven Aberds 89 D11
Buchanty Perth 76 E2
Buchlyvie Stirling 68 A4
Buckabank Cumb 56 B5
Buckden Cambs 29 B8
Buckden N Yorks 50 B5
Buckenham Norf 39 E9
Buckerell Devon 7 F10
Buckfast Devon 5 E8
Buckfastleigh Devon 5 E8
Buckhaven Fife 76 H6
Buckholm Borders 70 G3
Buckholt Mon 26 G2
Buckhorn Weston Dorset 9 B6
Buckhurst Hill Essex 19 B11
Buckie Moray 88 B4
Buckies Highld 94 D3
Buckingham Bucks 28 E3
Buckland Bucks 28 G5
Buckland Devon 5 G7
Buckland Glos 27 E7
Buckland Hants 10 E2
Buckland Herts 29 E10
Buckland Kent 21 G10
Buckland Oxon 17 B10
Buckland Sur 19 F9
Buckland Brewer Devon 6 D3
Buckland Common Bucks 28 H6
Buckland Dinham Som 16 F4
Buckland Filleigh Devon 6 F3
Buckland in the Moor Devon 5 D8
Buckland Monachorum Devon 4 E5
Buckland Newton Dorset 8 D5
Buckland St Mary Som 8 C1
Bucklebury W Berks 18 D2
Bucklegate Lincs 37 B9
Bucklerheads Angus 77 D7
Bucklers Hard Hants 10 E3
Bucklesham Suff 31 D9
Buckley = Bwcle Flint 42 F5
Bucklow Hill Ches E 43 D10
Buckminster Leics 36 C4
Bucknall Lincs 46 F5
Bucknall Stoke 44 H3
Bucknell Oxon 28 F2
Bucknell Shrops 25 A10
Buckpool Moray 88 B4
Buck's Cross Devon 6 D2
Bucks Green W Sus 11 A9
Bucks Horn Oak Hants 18 G5
Buck's Mills Devon 6 D2
Bucksburn Aberdeen 83 C10
Buckshaw Village Lancs 50 G1
Buckskin Hants 18 F3
Buckton E Yorks 53 B7
Buckton Hereford 25 A10
Buckton Northumb 71 G9
Buckworth Cambs 37 H7
Budbrooke Warks 27 B9
Budby Notts 45 F10
Budd's Titson Corn 4 A3
Bude Corn 6 F1
Budlake Devon 7 G8
Budle Northumb 71 G10
Budleigh Salterton Devon 7 H9
Budock Water Corn 3 F6
Buerton Ches E 34 A2
Buffler's Holt Bucks 28 E3
Bugbrooke Northants 28 C3
Buglawton Ches E 44 F2
Bugle Corn 3 D9
Bugley Wilts 16 G5
Bugthorpe E Yorks 52 D3
Buildwas Shrops 34 E2
Builth Road Powys 25 C7
Builth Wells = Llanfair-ym-Muallt Powys 25 C7
Buirgh W Isles 90 H5
Bulby Lincs 37 C6
Bulcote Notts 36 A2
Buldoo Highld 93 C12
Bulford Wilts 17 G8
Bulford Camp Wilts 17 G8
Bulkeley Ches E 43 G8
Bulkington Warks 35 G9
Bulkington Wilts 16 F6
Bulkworthy Devon 6 E2
Bull Hill Hants 10 E2
Bullamoor N Yorks 58 G4
Bullbridge Derbys 45 G7
Bullbrook Brack 18 E5
Bulley Glos 26 G4
Bullgill Cumb 56 C2
Bullington Hants 17 G11
Bullington Lincs 46 E4
Bull's Green Herts 29 G9
Bullwood Argyll 73 F10
Bulmer Essex 30 D5
Bulmer N Yorks 52 C2
Bulmer Tye Essex 30 E5
Bulphan Thurrock 20 C3
Bulverhythe E Sus 13 F6
Bulwark Aberds 89 D9
Bulwell Nottingham 45 H9
Bulwick Northants 36 F5
Bumble's Green Essex 29 H11
Bun Abhainn Eadarra W Isles 90 G6
Bun a'Mhuillin W Isles 84 G2
Bun Loyne Highld 80 C4
Bunacaimb Highld 79 C9
Bunarkaig Highld 80 E3
Bunbury Ches E 43 G8
Bunbury Heath Ches E 43 G8
Bunchrew Highld 87 G9
Bundalloch Highld 85 F13
Buness Shetland 96 C8
Bunessan Argyll 78 J6
Bungay Suff 39 G9
Bunker's Hill Lincs 46 E3
Bunker's Hill Lincs 46 G6
Bunkers Hill Oxon 27 G11
Bunloit Highld 81 A7
Bunnahabhain Argyll 64 A5
Bunny Notts 36 C1
Buntait Highld 86 H6
Buntingford Herts 29 F10
Bunwell Norf 39 F7
Burbage Derbys 44 E4
Burbage Leics 35 F10
Burbage Wilts 17 E9
Burchett's Green Windsor 18 C5
Burcombe Wilts 9 A9
Burcot Oxon 18 B2
Burcott Bucks 28 F5
Burdon T&W 58 A4
Bures Suff 30 E6
Bures Green Suff 30 E6
Burford Ches E 43 G9
Burford Oxon 27 G9
Burford Shrops 26 B2
Burg Argyll 78 G6
Burgar Orkney 95 F4
Burgate Hants 9 C10
Burgate Suff 39 H6
Burgess Hill W Sus 12 E2
Burgh Suff 31 C9
Burgh by Sands Cumb 61 H9
Burgh Castle Norf 39 E10
Burgh Heath Sur 19 F9
Burgh le Marsh Lincs 47 F9
Burgh Muir Aberds 83 A9
Burgh next Aylsham Norf 39 C8
Burgh on Bain Lincs 46 D6
Burgh St Margaret Norf 39 D10
Burgh St Peter Norf 39 F10
Burghclere Hants 17 E11
Burghead Moray 87 E14
Burghfield W Berks 18 E3
Burghfield Common W Berks 18 E3
Burghfield Hill W Berks 18 E3
Burghill Hereford 25 D11
Burghwallis S Yorks 45 A9
Burham Kent 20 E4
Buriton Hants 10 B6
Burland Ches E 43 G9
Burlawn Corn 3 B8
Burleigh Brack 18 E5
Burlescombe Devon 7 E9
Burleston Dorset 9 E6
Burley Hants 9 D11
Burley Rutland 36 D4
Burley W Yorks 51 F8
Burley Gate Hereford 26 D2
Burley in Wharfedale W Yorks 51 E7
Burley Lodge Hants 9 D11
Burley Street Hants 9 D11
Burleydam Ches E 34 A2
Burlingjobb Powys 25 C9
Burlow E Sus 12 E4
Burlton Shrops 33 C10
Burmarsh Kent 13 C9
Burmington Warks 27 E9
Burn N Yorks 52 G1
Burn of Cambus Stirling 75 G10
Burnaston Derbys 35 B8
Burnbank S Lanark 68 E6
Burnby E Yorks 52 E4
Burncross S Yorks 45 C7
Burneside Cumb 57 G7
Burness Orkney 95 D7
Burneston N Yorks 58 H4
Burnett Bath 16 E3
Burnfoot Borders 61 B11
Burnfoot Borders 61 B10
Burnfoot E Ayrs 67 F7
Burnfoot Perth 76 G2
Burnham Bucks 18 C6
Burnham N Lincs 53 H6
Burnham Deepdale Norf 38 A4
Burnham Green Herts 29 G9
Burnham Market Norf 38 A4
Burnham Norton Norf 38 A4
Burnham-on-Crouch Essex 20 B6
Burnham-on-Sea Som 15 G9
Burnham Overy Staithe Norf 38 A4
Burnham Overy Town Norf 38 A4
Burnham Thorpe Norf 38 A4
Burnhead Dumfries 60 D4
Burnhead S Ayrs 66 F5
Burnhervie Aberds 83 B9
Burnhill Green Staffs 34 E3
Burnhope Durham 58 B2
Burnhouse N Ayrs 67 A6
Burniston N Yorks 59 G11
Burnlee W Yorks 44 B5
Burnley Lancs 50 F4
Burnley Lane Lancs 50 F4
Burnmouth Borders 71 D8
Burnopfield Durham 63 H7
Burnsall N Yorks 50 C6
Burnside Angus 77 B8
Burnside E Ayrs 67 E8
Burnside Fife 76 G4
Burnside S Lanark 68 D5
Burnside Shetland 96 F4
Burnside W Loth 69 C9
Burnside of Duntrune Angus 77 D7
Burnswark Dumfries 61 F7
Burnt Heath Derbys 44 E6
Burnt Houses Durham 58 D2
Burnt Yates N Yorks 51 C8
Burntcommon Sur 19 F7
Burnthouse Corn 3 F6
Burntisland Fife 69 B11
Burnton E Ayrs 67 F7
Burntwood Staffs 35 E6
Burnwynd Edin 69 D10
Burpham Sur 19 F7
Burpham W Sus 11 D9
Burradon Northumb 62 C5
Burradon T&W 63 F8
Burrafirth Shetland 96 B8
Burraland Shetland 96 F5
Burraland Shetland 96 J4
Burras Corn 2 F5
Burravoe Shetland 96 F7
Burravoe Shetland 96 G5
Burray Village Orkney 95 J5
Burrells Cumb 57 E8
Burrelton Perth 76 D5
Burridge Devon 6 C4
Burridge Hants 10 C4
Burrill N Yorks 58 H3
Burringham N Lincs 46 B2
Burrington Devon 6 E5
Burrington Hereford 25 A11
Burrington N Som 15 F10
Burrough Green Cambs 30 C3
Burrough on the Hill Leics 36 D3
Burrow-bridge Som 8 B2
Burrowhill Sur 18 E6
Burry Swansea 23 G9
Burry Green Swansea 23 G9
Burry Port = Porth Tywyn Carms 23 F9
Burscough Lancs 43 A7
Burscough Bridge Lancs 43 A7
Bursea E Yorks 52 F4
Burshill E Yorks 53 E6
Bursledon Hants 10 D3
Burslem Stoke 44 H2
Burstall Suff 31 D7
Burstock Dorset 8 D3
Burston Norf 39 G7
Burston Staffs 34 B5
Burstow Sur 12 B2
Burstwick E Yorks 53 G8
Burtersett N Yorks 57 H10
Burtle Som 15 G9
Burton Ches W 42 E6
Burton Ches W 43 F8
Burton Dorset 9 E10
Burton Lincs 46 E3
Burton Northumb 71 G10
Burton Pembs 22 F4
Burton Som 7 B10
Burton Wilts 16 D5
Burton Agnes E Yorks 53 C7
Burton Bradstock Dorset 8 F3
Burton Dassett Warks 27 C10
Burton Fleming E Yorks 53 B6
Burton Green W Mid 35 H8
Burton Green Wrex 42 G6
Burton Hastings Warks 35 F10
Burton-in-Kendal Cumb 49 B5
Burton in Lonsdale N Yorks 50 B2
Burton Joyce Notts 36 A2
Burton Latimer Northants 28 A6
Burton Lazars Leics 36 D3
Burton-le-Coggles Lincs 36 C5
Burton Leonard N Yorks 51 C9
Burton on the Wolds Leics 36 C1
Burton Overy Leics 36 F2
Burton Pedwardine Lincs 37 A7
Burton Pidsea E Yorks 53 F8
Burton Salmon N Yorks 51 G10
Burton Stather N Lincs 52 H4
Burton upon Stather N Lincs 52 H4
Burton upon Trent Staffs 35 C8
Burtonwood Warr 43 C8
Burwardsley Ches W 43 G8
Burwarton Shrops 34 G2
Burwash E Sus 12 D5
Burwash Common E Sus 12 D5
Burwash Weald E Sus 12 D5
Burwell Cambs 30 B2
Burwell Lincs 47 E7
Burwen Anglesey 40 A6
Burwick Orkney 95 K5
Bury Cambs 37 G8
Bury Gtr Man 44 A2
Bury Som 7 D8
Bury W Sus 11 C9
Bury Green Herts 29 F11
Bury St Edmunds Suff 30 B5
Burythorpe N Yorks 52 C3
Busby E Renf 68 E4
Buscot Oxon 17 B9
Bush Bank Hereford 25 C11
Bush Crathie Aberds 82 D4
Bush Green Norf 39 G8
Bushbury W Mid 34 E5
Bushby Leics 36 E2
Bushey Herts 19 B8
Bushey Heath Herts 19 B8
Bushley Worcs 26 E5
Bushton Wilts 17 D7
Buslingthorpe Lincs 46 D4
Busta Shetland 96 G5
Butcher's Cross E Sus 12 D4
Butcombe N Som 15 E11
Butetown Cardiff 15 D7
Butleigh Som 8 A4
Butleigh Wootton Som 15 H11
Butler's Cross Bucks 28 H5
Butler's End Warks 35 G8
Butlers Marston Warks 27 C11
Butley Suff 31 C10
Butley High Corner Suff 31 D10
Butt Green Ches E 43 G9
Butterburn Cumb 62 F2
Buttercrambe N Yorks 52 D3
Butterknowle Durham 58 D2
Butterleigh Devon 7 F8
Buttermere Cumb 56 E3
Buttermere Wilts 17 E10
Buttershaw W Yorks 51 G7
Butterstone Perth 76 C3
Butterton Staffs 44 G4
Butterwick Durham 58 D4
Butterwick Lincs 47 H7
Butterwick N Yorks 52 B5
Butterwick N Yorks 52 B3
Buttington Powys 33 E8
Buttonoak Worcs 34 H3
Butt's Green Hants 10 B2
Buttsash Hants 10 D3
Buxhall Suff 31 C7
Buxhall Fen Street Suff 31 C7
Buxley Borders 71 E7
Buxted E Sus 12 D3
Buxton Derbys 44 E4
Buxton Norf 39 C8
Buxworth Derbys 44 D4
Bwcle = Buckley Flint 42 F5
Bwlch Powys 25 F8
Bwlch-Llan Ceredig 23 A10
Bwlch-y-cibau Powys 33 D7
Bwlch-y-fadfa Ceredig 23 B9
Bwlch-y-ffridd Powys 33 F6
Bwlch-y-sarnau Powys 25 A7
Bwlchgwyn Wrex 42 G5
Bwlchnewydd Carms 23 D8
Bwlchtocyn Gwyn 40 H5
Bwlchyddar Powys 33 C7
Bwlchygroes Pembs 23 C7
Byermoor T&W 63 H7
Byers Green Durham 58 C3
Byfield Northants 28 C2
Byfleet Sur 19 E7
Byford Hereford 25 D10
Bygrave Herts 29 E9
Byker T&W 63 G8
Bylchau Conwy 42 F2
Byley Ches W 43 F10
Bynea Carms 23 G10
Byrness Northumb 62 C3
Bythorn Cambs 37 H6
Byton Hereford 25 B10
Byworth W Sus 11 B8

C

Cabharstadh W Isles 91 E8
Cablea Perth 76 D2
Cabourne Lincs 46 B5
Cabrach Argyll 72 G3
Cabrach Moray 82 A5
Cabrich Highld 87 G8
Cabus Lancs 49 E4
Cackle Street E Sus 12 D3
Cadbury Devon 7 F8
Cadbury Barton Devon 6 E5
Cadder E Dunb 68 C5
Caddington C Beds 29 G7
Caddonfoot Borders 70 G3
Cade Street E Sus 12 D5
Cadeby Leics 35 E10
Cadeby S Yorks 45 B9
Cadeleigh Devon 7 F8
Cadgwith Corn 2 H6
Cadham Fife 76 G5
Cadishead Gtr Man 43 C10
Cadle Swansea 14 B2
Cadley Lancs 49 F5
Cadley Wilts 17 E9
Cadley Wilts 17 F9
Cadmore End Bucks 18 B4
Cadnam Hants 10 C1
Cadney N Lincs 46 B4
Cadole Flint 42 F5
Cadoxton V Glam 15 E7
Cadoxton-Juxta-Neath Neath 14 B3
Cadshaw Blackburn 50 H3
Cadzow S Lanark 68 E6
Caeathro Gwyn 41 D7
Caehopkin Powys 24 G5
Caenby Lincs 46 D4
Caenby Corner Lincs 46 D3
Caér-bryn Carms 23 E10
Caer Llan Mon 25 H11
Caerau Bridgend 14 B4
Caerau Cardiff 15 D7
Caerdeon Gwyn 32 D2
Caerdydd = Cardiff Cardiff 15 D7
Caerfarchell Pembs 22 D2
Caerffili = Caerphilly Caerph 15 C7
Caerfyrddin = Carmarthen Carms 23 D9
Caergeiliog Anglesey 40 C5
Caergwrle Flint 42 G6
Caergybi = Holyhead Anglesey 40 B4
Caerleon = Caerllion Newport 15 B9
Caerllion = Caerleon Newport 15 B9
Caernarfon Gwyn 40 D6
Caerphilly = Caerffili Caerph 15 C7
Caersws Powys 32 F6
Caerwedros Ceredig 23 A8
Caerwent Mon 15 B10
Caerwych Gwyn 41 G8
Caerwys Flint 42 E4
Caethle Gwyn 32 F2
Caim Anglesey 41 B8
Caio Carms 24 E3
Cairinis W Isles 84 B3
Cairisiadar W Isles 90 D5
Cairminis W Isles 90 J5
Cairnbaan Argyll 73 D7
Cairnbanno Ho. Aberds 89 D8
Cairnborrow Aberds 88 D4
Cairnbrogie Aberds 89 F8
Cairnbulg Castle Aberds 89 B10
Cairncross Angus 82 F6
Cairncross Borders 71 D7
Cairndow Argyll 74 F4
Cairness Aberds 89 B10
Cairneyhill Fife 69 B9
Cairnfield Ho. Moray 88 B4
Cairngaan Dumfries 54 F4
Cairngarroch Dumfries 54 E3
Cairnhill Aberds 89 E6
Cairnie Aberds 83 C10
Cairnie Aberds 88 D4
Cairnorrie Aberds 89 D8
Cairnpark Aberds 83 B10
Cairnryan Dumfries 54 C3
Cairnton Orkney 95 H4
Caister-on-Sea Norf 39 D11
Caistor Lincs 46 B5
Caistor St Edmund Norf 39 E8
Caistron Northumb 62 C5
Caitha Bowland Borders 70 F3
Calais Street Suff 30 E6
Calanais W Isles 90 D7
Calbost W Isles 91 F9
Calbourne IoW 10 F3
Calceby Lincs 47 E7
Calcot Row W Berks 18 D3
Calcott Kent 21 E8
Caldback Shetland 96 C8
Caldbeck Cumb 56 C5
Caldbergh N Yorks 58 H1
Caldecote Cambs 29 C10
Caldecote Cambs 37 G7
Caldecote Herts 29 E9
Caldecote Northants 28 C3
Caldecott Northants 28 B6
Caldecott Oxon 17 B11
Caldecott Rutland 36 F4
Calder Bridge Cumb 56 F2
Calder Hall Cumb 56 F2
Calder Mains Highld 94 E2
Calder Vale Lancs 49 E5
Calderbank N Lanark 68 D6
Calderbrook Gtr Man 50 H5
Caldercruix N Lanark 69 D7
Caldermill S Lanark 68 F5
Calderwood S Lanark 68 E5
Caldhame Angus 77 C7
Caldicot Mon 15 C10
Caldwell Derbys 35 D8
Caldwell N Yorks 58 E2
Caldy Mers 42 D5
Caledrhydiau Ceredig 23 A9
Calfsound Orkney 95 E6
Calgary Argyll 78 F6
Califer Moray 87 F13
California Falk 69 C8
California Norf 39 D11
Calke Derbys 35 C9
Callakille Highld 85 C11
Callaly Northumb 62 C6
Callander Stirling 75 G9
Callaughton Shrops 34 F2
Callestick Corn 3 D6
Calligarry Highld 85 H11
Callington Corn 4 E4
Callow Hereford 25 E11
Callow End Worcs 26 D5
Callow Hill Wilts 17 C7
Callow Hill Worcs 26 A4
Callows Grave Worcs 26 B2
Calmore Hants 10 C2
Calmsden Glos 27 H7
Calne Wilts 17 D7
Calow Derbys 45 E8
Calshot Hants 10 D3
Calstock Corn 4 E5
Calstone Wellington Wilts 17 E7
Calthorpe Norf 39 B7
Calthwaite Cumb 56 B6
Calton N Yorks 50 D5
Calton Staffs 44 G5
Calveley Ches E 43 G8
Calver Derbys 44 E6
Calver Hill Hereford 25 D10
Calverhall Shrops 34 B2
Calverleigh Devon 7 E8
Calverley W Yorks 51 F8
Calvert Bucks 28 F3
Calverton M Keynes 28 E4
Calverton Notts 45 H10
Calvine Perth 81 G10
Calvo Cumb 56 A3
Cam Glos 16 B4
Camas-luinie Highld 80 A1
Camasnacroise Highld 79 F11
Camastianavaig Highld 85 E10
Camasunary Highld 85 G10
Camault Muir Highld 87 G8
Camb Shetland 96 D7
Camber E Sus 13 E8
Camberley Sur 18 E5
Camberwell London 19 D10
Camblesforth N Yorks 52 G2
Cambo Northumb 62 E6
Cambois Northumb 63 E9
Camborne Corn 2 E5
Cambourne Cambs 29 C10
Cambridge Cambs 29 C11
Cambridge Glos 16 A4
Cambridge Town Southend 20 C6
Cambus Clack 69 A7
Cambusavie Farm Highld 87 B10
Cambusbarron Stirling 68 A6
Cambuskenneth Stirling 69 A7
Cambuslang S Lanark 68 D5
Cambusmore Lodge Highld 87 B10
Camden London 19 C9
Camelford Corn 4 C2
Camelsdale Sur 11 A7
Camerory Highld 87 H13
Camer's Green Worcs 26 E4
Camerton Bath 16 F3
Camerton Cumb 56 C2
Camerton E Yorks 53 G8
Camghouran Perth 75 B8
Cammachmore Aberds 83 D11
Cammeringham Lincs 46 D3
Camore Highld 87 B10
Camp Hill Warks 35 F9
Campbeltown Argyll 65 F8
Camperdown T&W 63 F8
Campmuir Perth 76 D5
Campsall S Yorks 45 A9
Campsey Ash Suff 31 C10
Campton C Beds 29 E8
Camptown Borders 62 B2
Camrose Pembs 22 D4
Camserney Perth 75 C11
Camster Highld 94 F4
Camuschoirk Highld 79 E10
Camuscross Highld 85 G11
Camusnagaul Highld 80 F2
Camusnagaul Highld 86 C3
Camusrory Highld 79 B11
Camusteel Highld 85 D12
Camusterrach Highld 85 D12
Camusvrachan Perth 75 C9
Canada Hants 10 C1
Canadia E Sus 12 E6
Canal Side S Yorks 45 A10
Candacraig Ho. Aberds 82 B5
Candlesby Lincs 47 F8
Candy Mill S Lanark 69 F9
Cane End Oxon 18 D3
Canewdon Essex 20 B5
Canford Bottom Dorset 9 D9
Canford Cliffs Poole 9 F9
Canford Magna Poole 9 E9
Canham's Green Suff 31 B7
Canholes Derbys 44 E4
Canisbay Highld 94 C5
Cann Dorset 9 B7
Cann Common Dorset 9 B7
Cannard's Grave Som 16 G3
Cannich Highld 86 H6
Cannington Som 15 H8
Cannock Staffs 34 E5
Cannock Wood Staffs 34 D6
Canon Bridge Hereford 25 D11
Canon Frome Hereford 26 D3
Canon Pyon Hereford 25 D11
Canonbie Dumfries 61 F9
Canons Ashby Northants 28 C2
Canonstown Corn 2 F4
Canterbury Kent 21 F8
Cantley Norf 39 E9
Cantley S Yorks 45 B10
Cantlop Shrops 33 E11
Canton Cardiff 15 D7
Cantraybruich Highld 87 G10
Cantraydoune Highld 87 G10
Cantraywood Highld 87 G10
Cantsfield Lancs 50 B2
Canvey Island Essex 20 C4
Canwick Lincs 46 F3
Canworthy Water Corn 4 B3
Caol Highld 80 F3
Caol Ila Argyll 64 A5
Caolas Argyll 78 G3
Caolas Scalpaigh W Isles 90 H7
Caolas Stocinis W Isles 90 H6
Capel Sur 19 G8
Capel Bangor Ceredig 32 G2
Capel Betws Lleucu Ceredig 24 C3
Capel Carmel Gwyn 40 H3
Capel Coch Anglesey 40 B6
Capel Curig Conwy 41 E9
Capel Cynon Ceredig 23 B8
Capel Dewi Carms 23 D9
Capel Dewi Ceredig 23 B9
Capel Dewi Ceredig 32 G2
Capel Garmon Conwy 41 E10
Capel-gwyn Anglesey 40 C5
Capel Gwyn Carms 23 D9
Capel Gwynfe Carms 24 F4
Capel Hendre Carms 23 E10
Capel Hermon Gwyn 32 C3
Capel Isaac Carms 23 D10
Capel Iwan Carms 23 C7
Capel le Ferne Kent 21 H9
Capel Llanilltern Cardiff 14 C6
Capel Mawr Anglesey 40 C6
Capel St Andrew Suff 31 D10
Capel St Mary Suff 31 E7
Capel Seion Ceredig 32 H2
Capel Tygwydd Ceredig 23 B7
Capel Uchaf Gwyn 40 F6
Capel-y-graig Gwyn 41 D7
Capelulo Conwy 41 C9
Capenhurst Ches W 42 E6
Capernwray Lancs 49 B5
Capheaton Northumb 62 E6
Cappercleuch Borders 61 A8
Capplegill Dumfries 61 C7
Capton Devon 5 F9
Caputh Perth 76 D3
Car Colston Notts 36 A3
Carbis Bay Corn 2 F4
Carbost Highld 85 D9
Carbost Highld 85 E8
Carbrook S Yorks 45 D7
Carbrooke Norf 38 E5
Carburton Notts 45 E10
Carcant Borders 70 E2
Carcary Angus 77 B9
Carclaze Corn 3 D9
Carcroft S Yorks 45 A9
Cardenden Fife 69 A11
Cardeston Shrops 33 D9
Cardiff = Caerdydd Cardiff 15 D7
Cardigan = Aberteifi Ceredig 22 B6
Cardington Bedford 29 D7
Cardington Shrops 33 F11
Cardinham Corn 4 E2
Cardonald Glasgow 68 D4
Cardow Moray 88 D1
Cardrona Borders 70 G2
Cardross Argyll 68 C2
Cardurnock Cumb 61 H7
Careby Lincs 36 D6
Careston Castle Angus 77 B8
Carew Pembs 22 F5
Carew Cheriton Pembs 22 F5
Carew Newton Pembs 22 F5
Carey Hereford 26 E2
Carfrae E Loth 70 D4
Cargenbridge Dumfries 60 F5
Cargill Perth 76 D4
Cargo Cumb 61 H9
Cargreen Corn 4 E5
Carham Northumb 71 G7
Carhampton Som 7 B9
Carharrack Corn 2 E6
Carie Perth 75 B9
Carie Perth 75 D9
Carines Corn 3 D6
Carisbrooke IoW 10 F3
Cark Cumb 49 B3
Carlabhagh W Isles 90 C7
Carland Cross Corn 3 D7
Carlby Lincs 37 D6
Carlecotes S Yorks 44 B5
Carlesmoor N Yorks 51 B7
Carleton Cumb 56 A6
Carleton Cumb 57 D7
Carleton Lancs 49 F3
Carleton N Yorks 50 E5
Carleton Forehoe Norf 39 E6
Carleton Rode Norf 39 F7
Carlin How Redcar 59 E8
Carlingcott Bath 16 F3
Carlisle Cumb 61 H10
Carlops Borders 69 E10
Carlton Bedford 28 C6
Carlton Cambs 30 C3
Carlton Leics 35 E9
Carlton N Yorks 51 A6
Carlton N Yorks 52 G2
Carlton N Yorks 58 E2
Carlton N Yorks 59 H7
Carlton Notts 36 A2
Carlton S Yorks 45 A7
Carlton Stockton 58 D4
Carlton Suff 31 B10
Carlton W Yorks 51 G9
Carlton Colville Suff 39 G11
Carlton Curlieu Leics 36 F2
Carlton Husthwaite N Yorks 51 B10
Carlton in Cleveland N Yorks 58 F6
Carlton in Lindrick Notts 45 D9
Carlton le Moorland Lincs 46 G3
Carlton Miniott N Yorks 51 A9
Carlton on Trent Notts 45 F11
Carlton Scroop Lincs 36 A5
Carluke S Lanark 69 E7
Carmarthen = Caerfyrddin Carms 23 D9
Carmel Anglesey 40 B5
Carmel Carms 23 E10
Carmel Flint 42 E4
Carmel Guern 11
Carmel Gwyn 40 E6
Carmont Aberds 83 E10
Carmunnock Glasgow 68 E5
Carmyle Glasgow 68 D5
Carmyllie Angus 77 C8
Carn-gorm Highld 80 A1
Carnaby E Yorks 53 C7
Carnach Highld 80 A2
Carnach Highld 86 B3
Carnach W Isles 90 H7
Carnachy Highld 93 D10
Càrnais W Isles 90 D5
Carnbee Fife 77 G8
Carnbo Perth 76 G3
Carnbrea Corn 2 E5
Carnduff S Lanark 68 F5
Carnduncan Argyll 64 B3
Carne Corn 3 F8
Carnforth Lancs 49 B4
Carnhedryn Pembs 22 D3
Carnhell Green Corn 2 F5
Carnkie Corn 2 F5
Carnkie Corn 2 F6
Carno Powys 32 F5
Carnoch Highld 86 F5
Carnoch Highld 86 H6
Carnock Fife 69 B9
Carnon Downs Corn 3 E6
Carnousie Aberds 89 C6
Carnoustie Angus 77 D8
Carnwath S Lanark 69 F8
Carnyorth Corn 2 F2
Carperby N Yorks 58 H1
Carpley Green N Yorks 57 H11
Carr S Yorks 45 C9
Carr Hill T&W 63 G8
Carradale Argyll 65 E9
Carragraich W Isles 90 H6
Carrbridge Highld 81 A11
Carrefour Selous Jersey 11
Carreg-wen Pembs 23 B7
Carreglefn Anglesey 40 B5
Carrick Argyll 73 E8
Carrick Fife 77 E7
Carrick Castle Argyll 73 D10
Carrick Ho. Orkney 95 E6
Carriden Falk 69 B9
Carrington Gtr Man 43 C10
Carrington Lincs 47 G7
Carrington Midloth 70 D2
Carrog Conwy 41 F9
Carrog Denb 33 A7
Carron Falk 69 B7
Carron Moray 88 D2
Carron Bridge Stirling 68 B6
Carronbridge Dumfries 60 D4
Carronshore Falk 69 B7
Carrshield Northumb 57 B10
Carrutherstown Dumfries 61 F7
Carrville Durham 58 B4
Carsaig Argyll 72 E6
Carsaig Argyll 79 J8
Carscreugh Dumfries 54 D5
Carse Gray Angus 77 B7
Carse Ho. Argyll 72 G6
Carsegowan Dumfries 55 D7
Carseriggan Dumfries 54 C6
Carsethorn Dumfries 60 H5
Carshalton London 19 E9
Carsington Derbys 44 G6
Carskiey Argyll 65 H7
Carsluith Dumfries 55 D7
Carsphairn Dumfries 67 G8
Carstairs S Lanark 69 F8
Carstairs Junction S Lanark 69 F8
Carswell Marsh Oxon 17 B10
Carter's Clay Hants 10 B2
Carterton Oxon 27 H9
Carterway Heads Northumb 58 A1
Carthew Corn 3 D9
Carthorpe N Yorks 51 A9
Cartington Northumb 62 C6
Cartland S Lanark 69 F7
Cartmel Cumb 49 B3
Cartmel Fell Cumb 56 H6
Carway Carms 23 F9
Cary Fitzpaine Som 8 B4
Cas-gwent = Chepstow Mon 15 B11
Cascob Powys 25 B9
Cashlie Perth 75 C7
Cashmoor Dorset 9 C8
Casnewydd = Newport Newport 15 C9
Cassey Compton Glos 27 G7
Cassington Oxon 27 G11
Cassop Durham 58 C4
Castell Denb 42 F4
Castell-Howell Ceredig 23 B9

Castell-Nedd = Neath Neath 14 B3
Castell Newydd Emlyn = Newcastle Emlyn Carms 23 B8
Castell-y-bwch Torf 15 B8
Castellau Rhondda 14 C6
Casterton Cumb 50 B2
Castle Acre Norf 38 D4
Castle Ashby Northants 28 C5
Castle Bolton N Yorks 58 G1
Castle Bromwich W Mid 35 G7
Castle Bytham Lincs 36 D5
Castle Caereinion Powys 33 E7
Castle Camps Cambs 30 D3
Castle Carrock Cumb 61 H11
Castle Cary Som 8 A5
Castle Combe Wilts 16 D5
Castle Donington Leics 35 C10
Castle Douglas Dumfries 55 C10
Castle Eaton Swindon 17 B8
Castle Eden Durham 58 C5
Castle Forbes Aberds 83 B8
Castle Frome Hereford 26 D3
Castle Green Sur 18 E6
Castle Gresley Derbys 35 D8
Castle Heaton Northumb 71 F8
Castle Hedingham Essex 30 E4
Castle Hill Kent 12 B5
Castle Huntly Perth 76 E6
Castle Kennedy Dumfries 54 D4
Castle O'er Dumfries 61 D8
Castle Pulverbatch Shrops 33 E10
Castle Rising Norf 38 C2
Castle Stuart Highld 87 G10
Castlebay = Bagh a Chaisteil W Isles 84 J1
Castlebythe Pembs 22 D5
Castlecary N Lanark 68 C6
Castlecraig Highld 87 E11
Castlefairn Dumfries 60 E3
Castleford W Yorks 51 G10
Castlehill Borders 69 G11
Castlehill Highld 94 D3
Castlehill W Dunb 68 C2
Castlemaddy Dumfries 67 H8
Castlemartin Pembs 22 G4
Castlemilk Dumfries 61 F7
Castlemilk Glasgow 68 E5
Castlemorris Pembs 22 C4
Castlemorton Worcs 26 E4
Castleside Durham 58 B1
Castlethorpe M Keynes 28 D5
Castleton Angus 76 C6
Castleton Argyll 73 E7
Castleton Derbys 44 D5
Castleton Gtr Man 44 A2
Castleton N Yorks 59 F7
Castleton Newport 15 C8
Castletown Ches W 43 G7
Castletown Highld 87 G10
Castletown Highld 94 D3
Castletown IoM 48 F2
Castletown T&W 63 H9
Castleweary Borders 61 C10
Castley N Yorks 51 E8
Caston Norf 38 F5
Castor Pboro 37 F7
Catacol N Ayrs 66 B2
Catbrain S Glos 16 C2
Catbrook Mon 15 A11
Catchall Corn 2 G3
Catchems Corner W Mid 35 H8
Catchgate Durham 58 A2
Catcleugh Northumb 62 C3
Catcliffe S Yorks 45 D8
Catcott Som 15 H9
Caterham Sur 19 F10
Catfield Norf 39 C9
Catfirth Shetland 96 H6
Catford London 19 D10
Catforth Lancs 49 F4
Cathays Cardiff 15 D7
Cathcart Glasgow 68 D4
Cathedine Powys 25 F8
Catherington Hants 10 C5
Catherton Shrops 34 H2
Catlodge Highld 81 D8
Catlowdy Cumb 61 F10
Catmore W Berks 17 C11
Caton Lancs 49 C5
Caton Green Lancs 49 C5
Catrine E Ayrs 67 D8
Cat's Ash Newport 15 B9
Catsfield E Sus 12 E6
Catshill Worcs 26 A6
Cattal N Yorks 51 D10
Cattawade Suff 31 E8
Catterall Lancs 49 E4
Catterick N Yorks 58 G3
Catterick Bridge N Yorks 58 G3
Catterick Garrison N Yorks 58 G2
Catterlen Cumb 57 C6
Catterline Aberds 83 F10
Catterton N Yorks 51 E11
Catthorpe Leics 36 H1
Cattistock Dorset 8 E4
Catton N Yorks 51 B9
Catton Northumb 62 H4
Catwick E Yorks 53 E7
Catworth Cambs 29 A7
Caudlesprings Norf 38 E5
Caulcott Oxon 28 F2
Cauldcots Angus 77 C9
Cauldhame Stirling 68 A5
Cauldmill Borders 61 B11
Cauldon Staffs 44 H4
Caulkerbush Dumfries 60 H5
Caulside Dumfries 61 E10
Caunsall Worcs 34 G4
Caunton Notts 45 G11
Causeway End Dumfries 55 C7
Causeway Foot W Yorks 51 F6
Causeway-head Stirling 75 H10
Causewayend S Lanark 69 G9
Causewayhead Cumb 56 A3
Causey Park Bridge Northumb 63 D7
Causeyend Aberds 83 B11
Cautley Cumb 57 G8
Cavendish Suff 30 D5
Cavendish Bridge Leics 35 C10
Cavenham Suff 30 B4
Caversfield Oxon 28 F2
Caversham Reading 18 D4
Caverswall Staffs 34 A5
Cavil E Yorks 52 F3
Cawdor Highld 87 F11
Cawkwell Lincs 46 E6
Cawood N Yorks 52 F1
Cawsand Corn 4 F5
Cawston Norf 39 C7
Cawthorne S Yorks 44 B6
Cawthorpe Lincs 37 C6
Cawton N Yorks 52 B2
Caxton Cambs 29 C10
Caynham Shrops 26 A2
Caythorpe Lincs 46 H3
Caythorpe Notts 45 H10
Cayton N Yorks 53 A6
Ceann a Bhaigh W Isles 84 B2
Ceann a Deas Loch Baghasdail W Isles 84 G2
Ceann Shiphoirt W Isles 91 F7
Ceann Tarabhaigh W Isles 90 F7
Ceannacroc Lodge Highld 80 B4
Cearsiadair W Isles 91 E8
Cefn Berain Conwy 42 F2
Cefn-brith Conwy 42 G2
Cefn Canol Powys 33 B8
Cefn-coch Conwy 41 D10
Cefn Coch Powys 33 C7
Cefn-coed-y-cymmer M Tydf 25 H7
Cefn Cribbwr Bridgend 14 C4
Cefn Cross Bridgend 14 C4
Cefn-ddwysarn Gwyn 32 B5
Cefn Einion Shrops 33 G8
Cefn-gorwydd Powys 24 D6
Cefn-mawr Wrex 33 A8
Cefn-y-bedd Flint 42 G6
Cefn-y-pant Carms 22 D6
Cefneithin Carms 23 E10
Cei-bach Ceredig 23 A9
Ceinewydd = New Quay Ceredig 23 A8
Ceint Anglesey 40 C6
Cellan Ceredig 24 D3
Cellarhead Staffs 44 H3
Cemaes Anglesey 40 A5
Cemmaes Powys 32 E4
Cemmaes Road Powys 32 E4
Cenarth Carms 23 B7
Cenin Gwyn 40 F6
Central Invclyd 73 F11
Ceos W Isles 91 E8
Ceres Fife 77 F7
Cerne Abbas Dorset 8 D5
Cerney Wick Glos 17 B7
Cerrigceinwen Anglesey 40 C6
Cerrigydrudion Conwy 42 H2
Cessford Borders 62 A3
Ceunant Gwyn 41 D7
Chaceley Glos 26 E5
Chacewater Corn 3 E6
Chackmore Bucks 28 E3
Chacombe Northants 27 D11
Chad Valley W Mid 34 G6
Chadderton Gtr Man 44 B3
Chadderton Fold Gtr Man 44 B2
Chaddesden Derby 35 B9
Chaddesley Corbett Worcs 26 A5
Chaddleworth W Berks 17 D11
Chadlington Oxon 27 F10
Chadshunt Warks 27 C10
Chadwell Leics 36 C3
Chadwell St Mary Thurrock 20 D3
Chadwick End W Mid 27 A9
Chadwick Green Mers 43 C8
Chaffcombe Som 8 C2
Chagford Devon 5 C8
Chailey E Sus 12 E2
Chain Bridge Lincs 37 A9
Chainbridge Cambs 37 E10
Chainhurst Kent 20 G4
Chalbury Dorset 9 D9
Chalbury Common Dorset 9 D9
Chaldon Sur 19 F10
Chaldon Herring Dorset 9 F6
Chale IoW 10 G3
Chale Green IoW 10 G3
Chalfont Common Bucks 19 B7
Chalfont St Giles Bucks 18 B6
Chalfont St Peter Bucks 19 B7
Chalford Glos 16 A5
Chalgrove Oxon 18 B3
Chalk Kent 20 D3
Challacombe Devon 6 B5
Challoch Dumfries 54 C6
Challock Kent 21 F7
Chalton C Beds 29 F7
Chalton Hants 10 C6
Chalvington E Sus 12 F4
Chancery Ceredig 32 H1
Chandler's Ford Hants 10 B3
Channel Tunnel Kent 21 H8
Channerwick Shetland 96 L6
Chantry Som 16 G4
Chantry Suff 31 D8
Chapel Fife 69 A11
Chapel Allerton Som 15 F10
Chapel Allerton W Yorks 51 F9
Chapel Amble Corn 3 B8
Chapel Brampton Northants 28 B4
Chapel Chorlton Staffs 34 B4
Chapel-en-le-Frith Derbys 44 D4
Chapel End Warks 35 F9
Chapel Green Warks 27 B11
Chapel Green Warks 35 G8
Chapel Haddlesey N Yorks 52 G1
Chapel Head Cambs 37 G9
Chapel Hill Aberds 89 E10
Chapel Hill Lincs 46 G6
Chapel Hill Mon 15 B11
Chapel Hill N Yorks 51 E9
Chapel Lawn Shrops 33 H9
Chapel-le-Dale N Yorks 50 B3
Chapel Milton Derbys 44 D4
Chapel of Garioch Aberds 83 A9
Chapel Row W Berks 18 E2
Chapel St Leonards Lincs 47 E9
Chapel Stile Cumb 56 F5
Chapelgate Lincs 37 C10
Chapelhall N Lanark 68 D6
Chapelhill Dumfries 60 D6
Chapelhill Highld 87 D11
Chapelhill N Ayrs 66 B5
Chapelhill Perth 76 D3
Chapelhill Perth 76 E5
Chapelknowe Dumfries 61 F9
Chapelton Angus 77 C9
Chapelton Devon 6 D4
Chapelton Highld 81 B11
Chapelton S Lanark 68 F5
Chapeltown Blackburn 50 H3
Chapeltown Moray 82 A4
Chapeltown S Yorks 45 C7
Chapmans Well Devon 6 G2
Chapmanslade Wilts 16 G5
Chapmore End Herts 29 G10
Chappel Essex 30 F5
Chard Som 8 D2
Chardstock Devon 8 D2
Charfield S Glos 16 B4
Charford Worcs 26 B6
Charing Kent 20 G6
Charing Cross Dorset 9 C10
Charing Heath Kent 20 G6
Charingworth Glos 27 E9
Charlbury Oxon 27 G10
Charlcombe Bath 16 E4
Charlecote Warks 27 C9
Charles Devon 6 C5
Charles Tye Suff 31 C7
Charlesfield Dumfries 61 G7
Charleston Angus 76 C6
Charleston Renfs 68 D3
Charlestown Aberdeen 83 C11
Charlestown Corn 3 D9
Charlestown Derbys 44 C4
Charlestown Dorset 8 G5
Charlestown Fife 69 B9
Charlestown Gtr Man 44 B2
Charlestown Highld 85 A13
Charlestown Highld 87 G9
Charlestown W Yorks 50 G5
Charlestown of Aberlour Moray 88 D2
Charlesworth Derbys 44 C4
Charleton Devon 5 G8
Charlton Hants 17 G10
Charlton Herts 29 F8
Charlton London 19 D11
Charlton Northants 28 E2
Charlton Northumb 62 E4
Charlton Som 16 F3
Charlton Telford 34 D1
Charlton W Sus 11 C7
Charlton Wilts 9 B8
Charlton Wilts 16 C6
Charlton Wilts 17 F8
Charlton Worcs 27 D7
Charlton Abbots Glos 27 F7
Charlton Adam Som 8 B4
Charlton-All-Saints Wilts 9 B10
Charlton Down Dorset 8 E5
Charlton Horethorne Som 8 B5
Charlton Kings Glos 26 F6
Charlton Mackerell Som 8 B4
Charlton Marshall Dorset 9 D7
Charlton Musgrove Som 8 B6
Charlton on Otmoor Oxon 28 G2
Charltons Redcar 59 E7
Charlwood Sur 19 G9
Charlynch Som 7 C11
Charminster Dorset 8 E5
Charmouth Dorset 8 E2
Charndon Bucks 28 F3
Charney Bassett Oxon 17 B10
Charnock Richard Lancs 50 H1
Charsfield Suff 31 C9
Chart Corner Kent 20 F4
Chart Sutton Kent 20 G5
Charter Alley Hants 18 F2
Charterhouse Som 15 F10
Charterville Allotments Oxon 27 G10
Chartham Kent 21 F8
Chartham Hatch Kent 21 F8
Chartridge Bucks 18 A6
Charvil Wokingham 18 D4
Charwelton Northants 28 C2
Chasetown Staffs 34 E6
Chastleton Oxon 27 F9
Chasty Devon 6 F2
Chatburn Lancs 50 E3
Chatcull Staffs 34 B3
Chatham Medway 20 E4
Chathill Northumb 71 H10
Chattenden Medway 20 D4
Chatteris Cambs 37 G9
Chattisham Suff 31 D7
Chatto Borders 62 B3
Chatton Northumb 71 H9
Chawleigh Devon 6 E6
Chawley Oxon 17 A11
Chawston Bedford 29 C8
Chawton Hants 18 H4
Cheadle Gtr Man 44 D2
Cheadle Staffs 34 A6
Cheadle Heath Gtr Man 44 D2
Cheadle Hulme Gtr Man 44 D2
Cheam London 19 E9
Cheapside Sur 19 F7
Chearsley Bucks 28 G4
Chebsey Staffs 34 C4
Checkendon Oxon 18 C3
Checkley Ches E 43 H10
Checkley Hereford 26 E2
Checkley Staffs 34 B6
Chedburgh Suff 30 C4
Cheddar Som 15 F10
Cheddington Bucks 28 G6
Cheddleton Staffs 44 G3
Cheddon Fitzpaine Som 8 B1
Chedglow Wilts 16 B6
Chedgrave Norf 39 F9
Chedington Dorset 8 D3
Chediston Suff 39 H9
Chedworth Glos 27 G7
Chedzoy Som 15 H9
Cheeklaw Borders 70 E6
Cheeseman's Green Kent 13 C9
Cheglinch Devon 6 B4
Cheldon Devon 7 E6
Chelford Ches E 44 E2
Chell Heath Stoke 44 G2
Chellaston Derby 35 B9
Chellington Bedford 28 C6
Chelmarsh Shrops 34 G3
Chelmer Village Essex 30 H4
Chelmondiston Suff 31 E9
Chelmorton Derbys 44 F5
Chelmsford Essex 30 H4
Chelsea London 19 D9
Chelsfield London 19 E11
Chelsworth Suff 30 D6
Cheltenham Glos 26 F6
Chelveston Northants 28 B6
Chelvey N Som 15 E10
Chelwood Bath 16 E3
Chelwood Common E Sus 12 D3
Chelwood Gate E Sus 12 D3
Chelworth Wilts 16 B6
Chelworth Green Wilts 17 B7
Chemistry Shrops 33 A11
Chenies Bucks 19 B7
Cheny Longville Shrops 33 G10
Chepstow = Cas-gwent Mon 15 B11
Chequerfield W Yorks 51 G10
Cherhill Wilts 17 D7
Cherington Glos 16 B6
Cherington Warks 27 E9
Cheriton Devon 7 B6
Cheriton Hants 10 B4
Cheriton Kent 21 H8
Cheriton Swansea 23 G9
Cheriton Bishop Devon 7 G6
Cheriton Fitzpaine Devon 7 F7
Cheriton or Stackpole Elidor Pembs 22 G4
Cherrington Telford 34 C2
Cherry Burton E Yorks 52 E5
Cherry Hinton Cambs 29 C11
Cherry Orchard Worcs 26 C5
Cherry Willingham Lincs 46 E4
Cherrybank Perth 76 E4
Chertsey Sur 19 E7
Cheselbourne Dorset 9 E6
Chesham Bucks 18 A6
Chesham Bois Bucks 18 B6
Cheshunt Herts 19 A10
Cheslyn Hay Staffs 34 E5
Chessington London 19 E8
Chester Ches W 43 F7
Chester-Le-Street Durham 58 A3
Chester Moor Durham 58 B3
Chesterblade Som 16 G3
Chesterfield Derbys 45 E7
Chesters Borders 62 A2
Chesters Borders 62 B2
Chesterton Cambs 29 B11
Chesterton Cambs 37 F7
Chesterton Glos 17 A7
Chesterton Oxon 28 F2
Chesterton Shrops 34 F3
Chesterton Staffs 44 H2
Chesterton Warks 27 C10
Chesterwood Northumb 62 G4
Chestfield Kent 21 E8
Cheston Devon 5 F7
Cheswardine Shrops 34 C3
Cheswick Northumb 71 F9
Chetnole Dorset 8 D5
Chettiscombe Devon 7 E8
Chettisham Cambs 37 G11
Chettle Dorset 9 C8
Chetton Shrops 34 F2
Chetwode Bucks 28 F3
Chetwynd Aston Telford 34 D3
Cheveley Cambs 30 B3
Chevening Kent 19 F11
Chevington Suff 30 C4
Chevithorne Devon 7 E8
Chew Magna Bath 16 E2
Chew Stoke Bath 16 E2
Chewton Keynsham Bath 16 E3
Chewton Mendip Som 16 F2
Chicheley M Keynes 28 D6
Chichester W Sus 11 D7
Chickerell Dorset 8 F5
Chicklade Wilts 9 A8
Chicksgrove Wilts 9 A8
Chidden Hants 10 C5
Chiddingfold Sur 18 H6
Chiddingly E Sus 12 E4
Chiddingstone Kent 19 G11
Chiddingstone Causeway Kent 20 G2
Chiddingstone Hoath Kent 12 B3
Chideock Dorset 8 E3
Chidham W Sus 11 D6
Chidswell W Yorks 51 G8
Chieveley W Berks 17 D11
Chignall St James Essex 30 H3
Chignall Smealy Essex 30 G3
Chigwell Essex 19 B11
Chigwell Row Essex 19 B11
Chilbolton Hants 17 H10
Chilcomb Hants 10 B4
Chilcombe Dorset 8 E4
Chilcompton Som 16 F3
Chilcote Leics 35 D8
Child Okeford Dorset 9 C7
Childer Thornton Ches W 42 E6
Childrey Oxon 17 C10
Child's Ercall Shrops 34 C2
Childswickham Worcs 27 E7
Childwall Mers 43 D7
Childwick Green Herts 29 G8
Chilfrome Dorset 8 E4
Chilgrove W Sus 11 C7
Chilham Kent 21 F7
Chilhampton Wilts 9 A9
Chilla Devon 6 F3
Chillaton Devon 4 C5
Chillenden Kent 21 F9
Chillerton IoW 10 F3
Chillesford Suff 31 C10
Chillingham Northumb 71 H9
Chillington Devon 5 G8
Chillington Som 8 C2
Chilmark Wilts 9 A8
Chilson Oxon 27 G10
Chilsworthy Corn 4 D5
Chilsworthy Devon 6 F2
Chilthorne Domer Som 8 C4
Chiltington E Sus 12 E2
Chilton Bucks 28 G3
Chilton Durham 58 D3
Chilton Oxon 17 C11
Chilton Cantelo Som 8 B4
Chilton Foliat Wilts 17 D10
Chilton Lane Durham 58 C4
Chilton Polden Som 15 H9
Chilton Street Suff 30 D4
Chilton Trinity Som 15 H8
Chilvers Coton Warks 35 F9
Chilwell Notts 35 B11
Chilworth Hants 10 C3
Chilworth Sur 19 G7
Chimney Oxon 17 A10
Chineham Hants 18 F3
Chingford London 19 B10
Chinley Derbys 44 D4
Chinley Head Derbys 44 D4
Chinnor Oxon 18 A4
Chipnall Shrops 34 B3
Chippenhall Green Suff 39 H8
Chippenham Cambs 30 B3
Chippenham Wilts 16 D6
Chipperfield Herts 19 A7
Chipping Herts 29 E10
Chipping Lancs 50 E2
Chipping Campden Glos 27 E8
Chipping Hill Essex 30 G5
Chipping Norton Oxon 27 F10
Chipping Ongar Essex 20 A2
Chipping Sodbury S Glos 16 C4
Chipping Warden Northants 27 D11
Chipstable Som 7 D9
Chipstead Kent 19 F11
Chipstead Sur 19 F9
Chirbury Shrops 33 F8
Chirk = Y Waun Wrex 33 B8
Chirk Bank Shrops 33 B8
Chirmorrie S Ayrs 54 B5
Chirnside Borders 71 E7
Chirnsidebridge Borders 71 E7
Chirton Wilts 17 F7
Chisbury Wilts 17 E9
Chiselborough Som 8 C3
Chiseldon Swindon 17 D8
Chiserley W Yorks 50 G6
Chislehampton Oxon 18 B2
Chislehurst London 19 D11
Chislet Kent 21 E9
Chiswell Green Herts 19 A8
Chiswick London 19 D9
Chiswick End Cambs 29 D10
Chisworth Derbys 44 C3
Chithurst W Sus 11 B7
Chittering Cambs 29 A11
Chitterne Wilts 16 G6
Chittlehamholt Devon 6 D5
Chittlehampton Devon 6 D5
Chittoe Wilts 16 E6
Chivenor Devon 6 C4
Chobham Sur 18 E6
Choicelee Borders 70 E6
Cholderton Wilts 17 G9
Cholesbury Bucks 28 H6
Chollerford Northumb 62 F5
Chollerton Northumb 62 F5
Cholmondeston Ches E 43 F9
Cholsey Oxon 18 C2
Cholstrey Hereford 25 C11
Chop Gate N Yorks 59 G6
Choppington Northumb 63 E8
Chopwell T&W 63 H7
Chorley Ches E 43 G8
Chorley Lancs 50 H1
Chorley Shrops 34 G2
Chorley Staffs 35 D6
Chorleywood Herts 19 B7
Chorlton cum Hardy Gtr Man 44 C2
Chorlton Lane Ches W 43 H7
Choulton Shrops 33 G9
Chowdene T&W 63 H8
Chowley Ches W 43 G7
Chrishall Essex 29 E11
Christchurch Cambs 37 F10
Christchurch Dorset 9 E10
Christchurch Glos 26 G2
Christchurch Newport 15 C9
Christian Malford Wilts 16 D6
Christleton Ches W 43 F7
Christmas Common Oxon 18 B4
Christon N Som 15 F9
Christon Bank Northumb 63 A8
Christow Devon 5 C9
Chryston N Lanark 68 C5
Chudleigh Devon 5 D9
Chudleigh Knighton Devon 5 D9
Chulmleigh Devon 6 E5
Chunal Derbys 44 C4
Church Lancs 50 G3
Church Aston Telford 34 D3
Church Brampton Northants 28 B4
Church Broughton Derbys 35 B8
Church Crookham Hants 18 F5
Church Eaton Staffs 34 D4
Church End C Beds 28 E6
Church End C Beds 28 F6
Church End C Beds 29 E8
Church End Cambs 37 E9
Church End Cambs 37 G8
Church End E Yorks 53 D6
Church End Essex 30 D2
Church End Essex 30 F4
Church End Hants 18 F3
Church End Lincs 37 B8
Church End Warks 35 F8
Church End Warks 35 F8
Church End Wilts 17 D7
Church Enstone Oxon 27 F10
Church Fenton N Yorks 51 F11
Church Green Devon 7 G10
Church Green Norf 39 F6
Church Gresley Derbys 35 D8
Church Hanborough Oxon 27 G11
Church Hill Ches W 43 F9
Church Houses N Yorks 59 G7
Church Knowle Dorset 9 F8
Church Laneham Notts 46 E2
Church Langton Leics 36 F3
Church Lawford Warks 35 H10
Church Lawton Ches E 44 G2
Church Leigh Staffs 34 B6
Church Lench Worcs 27 C7
Church Mayfield Staffs 35 A7
Church Minshull Ches E 43 F9
Church Norton W Sus 11 E7
Church Preen Shrops 33 F11
Church Pulverbatch Shrops 33 E10
Church Stoke Powys 33 F8
Church Stowe Northants 28 C3
Church Street Kent 20 D4
Church Stretton Shrops 33 F10
Church Town N Lincs 45 B11
Church Town Sur 19 F10
Church Village Rhondda 14 C6
Church Warsop Notts 45 F9
Churcham Glos 26 G4
Churchbank Shrops 33 H8
Churchbridge Staffs 34 E5
Churchdown Glos 26 G5
Churchend Essex 21 B7
Churchend Essex 30 F3
Churchend S Glos 16 B4
Churchfield W Mid 34 F6
Churchgate Street Essex 29 G11
Churchill Devon 6 B4
Churchill Devon 8 D2
Churchill N Som 15 F10
Churchill Oxon 27 F9
Churchill Worcs 26 C6
Churchill Worcs 34 H4
Churchinford Som 7 E11
Churchover Warks 35 G11
Churchstanton Som 7 E10
Churchstow Devon 5 G8
Churchtown Derbys 44 F6
Churchtown IoM 48 C4
Churchtown Lancs 49 E4
Churchtown Mers 49 H3
Churnsike Lodge Northumb 62 F2
Churston Ferrers Torbay 5 F10
Churt Sur 18 H5
Churton Ches W 43 G7
Churwell W Yorks 51 G8
Chute Standen Wilts 17 F10
Chwilog Gwyn 40 G6
Chyandour Corn 2 F3
Cilan Uchaf Gwyn 40 H4
Cilcain Flint 42 F4
Cilcennin Ceredig 24 B2
Cilfor Gwyn 41 G8
Cilfrew Neath 14 A3
Cilfynydd Rhondda 14 B6
Cilgerran Pembs 22 B6
Cilgwyn Carms 24 F4
Cilgwyn Gwyn 40 E6
Cilgwyn Pembs 22 C5
Ciliau Aeron Ceredig 23 A9
Cill Donnain W Isles 84 F2
Cille Bhrighde W Isles 84 G2
Cille Pheadair W Isles 84 G2
Cilmery Powys 25 C7
Cilsan Carms 23 D10
Ciltalgarth Gwyn 41 F10
Cilwendeg Pembs 23 C7
Cilybebyll Neath 14 A3
Cilycwm Carms 24 E4
Cimla Neath 14 B3
Cinderford Glos 26 G3
Cippyn Pembs 22 B6
Circebost W Isles 90 D6
Cirencester Glos 17 A7
Ciribhig W Isles 90 C6
City London 19 C10
City Powys 33 G8
City Dulas Anglesey 40 B6
Clachaig Argyll 73 E10
Clachan Argyll 72 B6
Clachan Argyll 72 H6
Clachan Argyll 74 F4
Clachan Argyll 79 G11
Clachan Highld 85 E10
Clachan W Isles 84 D2
Clachan na Luib W Isles 84 B3
Clachan of Campsie E Dunb 68 C5
Clachan of Glendaruel Argyll 73 E8
Clachan-Seil Argyll 72 B6
Clachan Strachur Argyll 73 C9
Clachaneasy Dumfries 54 B6
Clachanmore Dumfries 54 E3
Clachbreck Argyll 72 F6
Clachnabrain Angus 82 G5
Clachtoll Highld 92 G3
Clackmannan Clack 69 A8
Clacton-on-Sea Essex 31 G8
Cladach Chireboist W Isles 84 B2
Claddach-knockline W Isles 84 B2
Cladich Argyll 74 E3
Claggan Highld 79 G9
Claggan Highld 80 F3
Claigan Highld 84 C7
Claines Worcs 26 C5
Clandown Bath 16 F3
Clanfield Hants 10 C5
Clanfield Oxon 17 A9
Clanville Hants 17 G10
Claonaig Argyll 73 H7
Claonel Highld 93 J8
Clap Hill Kent 13 C9
Clapgate Dorset 9 D9
Clapgate Herts 29 F11
Clapham Bedford 29 C7
Clapham London 19 D9
Clapham N Yorks 50 C3
Clapham W Sus 11 D9
Clappers Borders 71 E8
Clappersgate Cumb 56 F5
Clapton Som 8 D3
Clapton-in-Gordano N Som 15 D10
Clapton-on-the-Hill Glos 27 G8
Clapworthy Devon 6 D5
Clara Vale T&W 63 G7
Clarach Ceredig 32 G2
Clarbeston Pembs 22 D5
Clarbeston Road Pembs 22 D5
Clarborough Notts 45 D11
Clardon Highld 94 D3
Clare Suff 30 D4
Clarebrand Dumfries 55 C10
Clarencefield Dumfries 60 G6
Clarilaw Borders 61 B11
Clark's Green Sur 19 H8
Clarkston E Renf 68 E4
Clashandorran Highld 87 G8
Clashcoig Highld 87 B9
Clashindarroch Aberds 88 E4
Clashmore Highld 87 C10
Clashmore Highld 92 F3
Clashnessie Highld 92 F3
Clashnoir Moray 82 A4
Clate Shetland 96 G7
Clathy Perth 76 F2
Clatt Aberds 83 A7
Clatter Powys 32 F5
Clatterford IoW 10 F3
Clatterin Bridge Aberds 83 F8
Clatworthy Som 7 C9
Claughton Lancs 49 E5
Claughton Lancs 50 C1
Claughton Mers 42 D6
Claverdon Warks 27 B8
Claverham N Som 15 E10
Clavering Essex 29 E11
Claverley Shrops 34 F3
Claverton Bath 16 E4
Clawdd-newydd Denb 42 G3
Clawthorpe Cumb 49 B5
Clawton Devon 6 G2
Claxby Lincs 46 C5
Claxby Lincs 47 E8
Claxton N Yorks 52 C2
Claxton Norf 39 E9
Clay Common Suff 39 G10
Clay Coton Northants 36 H1
Clay Cross Derbys 45 F7
Clay Hill W Berks 18 D2
Clay Lake Lincs 37 C8
Claybokie Aberds 82 D2
Claybrooke Magna Leics 35 G10
Claybrooke Parva Leics 35 G10
Claydon Oxon 27 C11
Claydon Suff 31 C8
Claygate Dumfries 61 F9
Claygate Kent 12 B6
Claygate Sur 19 E8
Claygate Cross Kent 20 F3
Clayhanger Devon 7 D9
Clayhanger W Mid 34 E6
Clayhidon Devon 7 E10
Clayhill E Sus 13 D7
Clayhill Hants 10 D2
Clayock Highld 94 E3
Claypole Lincs 46 H2
Clayton S Yorks 45 B8
Clayton Staffs 34 A4
Clayton W Sus 12 E1
Clayton W Yorks 51 F7
Clayton Green Lancs 50 G1
Clayton-le-Moors Lancs 50 F3
Clayton-le-Woods Lancs 50 G1
Clayton West W Yorks 44 A6
Clayworth Notts 45 D11
Cleadale Highld 78 C7
Cleadon T&W 63 G9
Clearbrook Devon 4 E6
Clearwell Glos 26 H2
Cleasby N Yorks 58 E3
Cleat Orkney 95 K5
Cleatlam Durham 58 E2
Cleator Cumb 56 E2
Cleator Moor Cumb 56 E2
Clebrig Highld 93 F8
Cleckheaton W Yorks 51 G7
Clee St Margaret Shrops 34 G1
Cleedownton Shrops 34 G1
Cleehill Shrops 34 H1
Cleethorpes NE Lincs 47 B7
Cleeton St Mary Shrops 34 H2
Cleeve N Som 15 E10
Cleeve Hill Glos 26 F6
Cleeve Prior Worcs 27 D7
Clegyrnant Powys 32 E5
Clehonger Hereford 25 E11
Cleish Perth 76 H3
Cleland N Lanark 69 E7
Clench Common Wilts 17 E8
Clenchwarton Norf 38 C1
Clent Worcs 34 H5
Cleobury Mortimer Shrops 34 H2
Cleobury North Shrops 34 G2
Cleongart Argyll 65 E7
Clephanton Highld 87 F11
Clerklands Borders 61 A11
Clestrain Orkney 95 H4
Cleuch Head Borders 61 B11
Cleughbrae Dumfries 60 F6
Clevancy Wilts 17 D7
Clevedon N Som 15 D10
Cleveley Oxon 27 F10
Cleveleys Lancs 49 E3
Cleverton Wilts 16 C6
Clevis Bridgend 14 D4
Clewer Som 15 F10
Cley next the Sea Norf 38 A6
Cliaid W Isles 84 H1
Cliasmol W Isles 90 G5
Cliburn Cumb 57 D7
Click Mill Orkney 95 F4
Cliddesden Hants 18 G3
Cliff End E Sus 13 E7
Cliffburn Angus 77 C9
Cliffe Medway 20 D4
Cliffe N Yorks 52 F2
Cliffe Woods Medway 20 D4
Clifford Hereford 25 D9
Clifford W Yorks 51 E10
Clifford Chambers Warks 27 C8
Clifford's Mesne Glos 26 F4
Cliffsend Kent 21 E10
Clifton Bristol 16 D2
Clifton C Beds 29 E8
Clifton Cumb 57 D7
Clifton Derbys 35 A7
Clifton Lancs 49 F4
Clifton N Yorks 51 E7
Clifton Northumb 63 E8
Clifton Nottingham 36 B1
Clifton Oxon 27 E11
Clifton S Yorks 45 C9
Clifton Stirling 74 D6
Clifton Worcs 26 D5
Clifton York 52 D1
Clifton Campville Staffs 35 D8
Clifton Green Gtr Man 43 B10
Clifton Hampden Oxon 18 B2
Clifton Reynes M Keynes 28 C6
Clifton upon Dunsmore Warks 35 H11
Clifton upon Teme Worcs 26 B4
Cliftoncote Borders 62 A4
Cliftonville Kent 21 D10
Climaen gwyn Neath 24 H4
Climping W Sus 11 D9
Climpy S Lanark 69 E8
Clink Som 16 G4
Clint N Yorks 51 D8
Clint Green Norf 38 D6
Clintmains Borders 70 G5
Cliobh W Isles 90 D5
Clippesby Norf 39 D10
Clipsham Rutland 36 D5
Clipston Northants 36 G3
Clipstone Notts 45 F9
Clitheroe Lancs 50 E3
Cliuthar W Isles 90 H6
Clive Shrops 33 C11
Clivocast Shetland 96 C8
Clixby Lincs 46 B5
Clocaenog Denb 42 G3
Clochan Moray 88 B4
Clock Face Mers 43 C8
Clockmill Borders 70 E6
Cloddiau Powys 33 E8
Clodock Hereford 25 F10
Clola Aberds 89 D10
Clophill C Beds 29 E7
Clopton Northants 37 G6
Clopton Suff 31 C9
Clopton Corner Suff 31 C9
Clopton Green Suff 30 C4
Close Clark IoM 48 E2
Closeburn Dumfries 60 D4
Closworth Som 8 C4
Clothall Herts 29 E9
Clotton Ches W 43 F8
Clough Foot W Yorks 50 G5
Cloughton N Yorks 59 G11
Cloughton Newlands N Yorks 59 G11
Clousta Shetland 96 H5
Clouston Orkney 95 G3
Clova Aberds 82 A6
Clova Angus 82 F5
Clove Lodge Durham 57 E11
Clovelly Devon 6 D2
Clovenfords Borders 70 G3
Clovenstone Aberds 83 B9
Clovullin Highld 74 A3
Clow Bridge Lancs 50 G4
Clowne Derbys 45 E8
Clows Top Worcs 26 A4
Cloy Wrex 33 A9
Cluanie Inn Highld 80 B2
Cluanie Lodge Highld 80 B2
Clun Shrops 33 G9
Clunbury Shrops 33 G9
Clunderwen Carms 22 E6
Clune Highld 81 A9
Clunes Highld 80 E4
Clungunford Shrops 33 H9
Clunie Aberds 89 C6
Clunie Perth 76 C4
Clunton Shrops 33 G9
Cluny Fife 76 H5
Cluny Castle Highld 81 D8
Clutton Bath 16 F3
Clutton Ches W 43 G7
Clwt-grugoer Conwy 42 F2
Clwt-y-bont Gwyn 41 D7
Clydach Mon 25 G9
Clydach Swansea 14 A2
Clydach Vale Rhondda 14 B5
Clydebank W Dunb 68 C3
Clydey Pembs 23 C7
Clyffe Pypard Wilts 17 D7
Clynder Argyll 73 E11
Clyne Neath 14 A4
Clynelish Highld 93 J11
Clynnog-fawr Gwyn 40 E6
Clyro Powys 25 D9
Clyst Honiton Devon 7 G8
Clyst Hydon Devon 7 F9
Clyst St George Devon 5 C10
Clyst St Lawrence Devon 7 F9
Clyst St Mary Devon 7 G8
Cnoc Amhlaigh W Isles 91 D10
Cnwch-coch Ceredig 32 H2
Coachford Aberds 88 D4
Coad's Green Corn 4 D3
Coal Aston Derbys 45 E7
Coalbrookdale Telford 34 E2
Coalbrookvale Bl Gwent 25 H8
Coalburn S Lanark 69 G7
Coalburns T&W 63 G7
Coalcleugh Northumb 57 B10
Coaley Glos 16 A4
Coalhall E Ayrs 67 E7
Coalhill Essex 20 B4
Coalpit Heath S Glos 16 C3
Coalport Telford 34 E2
Coalsnaughton Clack 76 H2
Coaltown of Balgonie Fife 76 H5
Coaltown of Wemyss Fife 76 H6
Coalville Leics 35 D10
Coalway Glos 26 G2
Coat Som 8 B3
Coatbridge N Lanark 68 D6
Coatdyke N Lanark 68 D6
Coate Swindon 17 C8
Coate Wilts 17 E7
Coates Cambs 37 F9
Coates Glos 16 A6
Coates Lancs 50 E4
Coates Notts 46 D2
Coates W Sus 11 C8
Coatham Redcar 59 D6
Coatham Mundeville Darl 58 D3
Coatsgate Dumfries 60 C6
Cobbaton Devon 6 D5
Cobbler's Green Norf 39 F8
Coberley Glos 26 G6
Cobham Kent 20 E3
Cobham Sur 19 E8
Cobholm Island Norf 39 E11
Cobleland Stirling 75 H8
Cobnash Hereford 25 B11
Coburty Aberds 89 B9
Cock Bank Wrex 42 H6
Cock Bridge Aberds 82 C4
Cock Clarks Essex 20 A5
Cockayne N Yorks 59 G7
Cockayne Hatley Cambs 29 D9
Cockburnspath Borders 70 C6
Cockenzie and Port Seton E Loth 70 C3
Cockerham Lancs 49 D4
Cockermouth Cumb 56 C3
Cockernhoe Green Herts 29 F8
Cockfield Durham 58 D2
Cockfield Suff 30 C6
Cockfosters London 19 B9
Cocking W Sus 11 C7
Cockington Torbay 5 E9
Cocklake Som 15 G10
Cockley Beck Cumb 56 F4
Cockley Cley Norf 38 E3
Cockshutt Shrops 33 C10
Cockthorpe Norf 38 A5
Cockwood Devon 5 C10
Cockyard Hereford 25 E11
Codda Corn 4 D2
Coddenham Suff 31 C8
Coddington Ches W 43 G7
Coddington Hereford 26 D4
Coddington Notts 46 G2
Codford St Mary Wilts 16 H6
Codford St Peter Wilts 16 H6
Codicote Herts 29 G9
Codmore Hill W Sus 11 B9
Codnor Derbys 45 H8
Codrington S Glos 16 D4
Codsall Staffs 34 E4
Codsall Wood Staffs 34 E4
Coed Duon = Blackwood Caerph 15 B7
Coed Mawr Gwyn 41 C7
Coed Morgan Mon 25 G10
Coed-Talon Flint 42 G5
Coed-y-bryn Ceredig 23 B8
Coed-y-paen Mon 15 B9
Coed-yr-ynys Powys 25 F8
Coed Ystumgwern Gwyn 32 C1
Coedely Rhondda 14 C6
Coedkernew Newport 15 C8
Coedpoeth Wrex 42 G5
Coedway Powys 33 D9
Coelbren Powys 24 G5
Coffinswell Devon 5 E9
Cofton Hackett Worcs 34 H6
Cogan V Glam 15 D7
Cogenhoe Northants 28 B5
Cogges Oxon 27 H10
Coggeshall Essex 30 F5
Coggeshall Hamlet Essex 30 F5
Coggins Mill E Sus 12 D4
Coig Peighinnean W Isles 91 A10
Coig Peighinnean Bhuirgh W Isles 91 B9
Coignafearn Lodge Highld 81 B8
Coilacriech Aberds 82 D5
Coilantogle Stirling 75 G8
Coilleag W Isles 84 G2
Coillore Highld 85 E8
Coity Bridgend 14 C5
Col W Isles 91 C9
Col Uarach W Isles 91 D9
Colaboll Highld 93 H8
Colan Corn 3 C7
Colaton Raleigh Devon 7 H9
Colbost Highld 84 D7
Colburn N Yorks 58 G2
Colby Cumb 57 D8
Colby IoM 48 E2
Colby Norf 39 B8
Colchester Essex 31 F7
Colcot V Glam 15 E7
Cold Ash W Berks 18 E2
Cold Ashby Northants 36 H2
Cold Ashton S Glos 16 D4
Cold Aston Glos 27 G8
Cold Blow Pembs 22 E6
Cold Brayfield M Keynes 28 C6
Cold Hanworth Lincs 46 D4
Cold Harbour Lincs 36 B5
Cold Hatton Telford 34 C2
Cold Hesledon Durham 58 B5
Cold Higham Northants 28 C3
Cold Kirby N Yorks 51 A11
Cold Newton Leics 36 E3
Cold Northcott Corn 4 C3
Cold Norton Essex 20 A5
Cold Overton Leics 36 D4
Coldbackie Highld 93 D9
Coldbeck Cumb 57 F9
Coldblow London 20 D2
Coldean Brighton 12 F2
Coldeast Devon 5 D9
Colden W Yorks 50 G5
Colden Common Hants 10 B3
Coldfair Green Suff 31 B11
Coldham Cambs 37 E10
Coldharbour Glos 16 A2
Coldharbour Kent 20 F2
Coldharbour Sur 19 G8
Coldingham Borders 71 D8
Coldrain Perth 76 G3
Coldred Kent 21 G9
Coldridge Devon 6 F5
Coldstream Angus 76 D6
Coldstream Borders 71 G7
Coldwaltham W Sus 11 C9
Coldwells Aberds 89 D11
Coldwells Croft Aberds 83 A7
Coldyeld Shrops 33 F9
Cole Som 8 A5
Cole Green Herts 29 G9
Cole Henley Hants 17 F11
Colebatch Shrops 33 G9
Colebrook Devon 7 F9
Colebrooke Devon 7 G6
Coleby Lincs 46 F3
Coleby N Lincs 52 H4
Coleford Devon 7 F6
Coleford Glos 26 G2
Coleford Som 16 G3
Colehill Dorset 9 D9
Coleman's Hatch E Sus 12 C3
Colemere Shrops 33 B10
Colemore Hants 10 A6
Coleorton Leics 35 D10
Colerne Wilts 16 D5
Cole's Green Suff 31 B9
Coles Green Suff 31 D7
Colesbourne Glos 26 G6
Colesden Bedford 29 C8
Coleshill Bucks 18 B6
Coleshill Oxon 17 B9
Coleshill Warks 35 G8
Colestocks Devon 7 F9
Colgate W Sus 11 A11
Colgrain Argyll 68 B2
Colinsburgh Fife 77 G7
Colinton Edin 69 D11
Colintraive Argyll 73 F9
Colkirk Norf 38 C5
Collace Perth 76 D5
Collafirth Shetland 96 G6
Collaton St Mary Torbay 5 F9
College Milton S Lanark 68 E5
Collessie Fife 76 F5
Collier Row London 20 B2
Collier Street Kent 20 G4
Collier's End Herts 29 F10
Collier's Green Kent 13 C6
Colliery Row T&W 58 B4
Collieston Aberds 89 F10
Collin Dumfries 60 F6
Collingbourne Ducis Wilts 17 F9
Collingbourne Kingston Wilts 17 F9
Collingham Notts 46 F2
Collingham W Yorks 51 E9
Collington Hereford 26 B3
Collingtree Northants 28 C4
Collins Green Warr 43 C8
Colliston Angus 77 C9
Collycroft Warks 35 G9
Collynie Aberds 89 E8
Collyweston Northants 36 E5
Colmonell S Ayrs 66 H4
Colmworth Bedford 29 C8
Coln Rogers Glos 27 H7
Coln St Aldwyn's Glos 27 H8
Coln St Dennis Glos 27 G7
Colnabaichin Aberds 82 C4
Colnbrook Slough 19 D7
Colne Cambs 37 H9
Colne Lancs 50 E4
Colne Edge Lancs 50 E4
Colne Engaine Essex 30 E5
Colney Norf 39 E7
Colney Heath Herts 29 H9
Colney Street Herts 19 A8
Colpy Aberds 89 E6
Colquhar Borders 70 F2
Colsterdale N Yorks 51 A7
Colsterworth Lincs 36 C5
Colston Bassett Notts 36 B2
Coltfield Moray 87 E14
Colthouse Cumb 56 G5
Coltishall Norf 39 D8
Coltness N Lanark 69 E7
Colton Cumb 56 H5
Colton N Yorks 51 E11
Colton Norf 39 E7
Colton Staffs 35 C6
Colton W Yorks 51 F9
Colva Powys 25 C9
Colvend Dumfries 55 D11
Colvister Shetland 96 D7
Colwall Green Hereford 26 D4
Colwall Stone Hereford 26 D4
Colwell Northumb 62 F5
Colwich Staffs 34 C6
Colwick Notts 36 A2
Colwinston V Glam 14 D5
Colworth W Sus 11 D8
Colwyn Bay = Bae Colwyn Conwy 41 C10
Colyford Devon 8 E1
Colyton Devon 8 E1
Combe Hereford 25 B10
Combe Oxon 27 G11
Combe W Berks 17 E10
Combe Common Sur 18 H6
Combe Down Bath 16 E4
Combe Florey Som 7 C10
Combe Hay Bath 16 F4
Combe Martin Devon 6 B4
Combe Moor Hereford 25 B10
Combe Raleigh Devon 7 F10
Combe St Nicholas Som 8 C2
Combeinteignhead Devon 5 D10
Comberbach Ches W 43 E9
Comberton Cambs 29 C10
Comberton Hereford 25 B11
Combpyne Devon 8 E1
Combridge Staffs 35 B6
Combrook Warks 27 C10
Combs Derbys 44 E4
Combs Suff 31 C7
Combs Ford Suff 31 C7
Combwich Som 15 G8
Comers Aberds 83 C8
Comins Coch Ceredig 32 G2
Commercial End Cambs 30 B2
Commins Capel Betws Ceredig 24 C3
Commins Coch Powys 32 E4
Common Edge Blackpool 49 F3
Common Side Derbys 45 E7
Commondale N Yorks 59 E7
Commonmoor Corn 4 E3
Commonside Ches W 43 E8
Compstall Gtr Man 44 C3
Compton Devon 5 E9
Compton Hants 10 B3
Compton Sur 18 G5
Compton Sur 18 G6
Compton W Berks 18 D2
Compton W Sus 11 C6
Compton Wilts 17 F8
Compton Abbas Dorset 9 C7
Compton Abdale Glos 27 G7
Compton Bassett Wilts 17 D7
Compton Beauchamp Oxon 17 C9
Compton Bishop Som 15 F9
Compton Chamberlayne Wilts 9 B9
Compton Dando Bath 16 E3
Compton Dundon Som 8 A3
Compton Martin Bath 15 F11
Compton Pauncefoot Som 8 B5
Compton Valence Dorset 8 E4
Comrie Fife 69 B9
Comrie Perth 75 E10
Conaglen House Highld 80 G2
Conchra Argyll 73 E9
Concraigie Perth 76 C4
Conder Green Lancs 49 D4
Conderton Worcs 26 E6
Condicote Glos 27 F8
Condorrat N Lanark 68 C6
Condover Shrops 33 E10
Coney Weston Suff 38 H5
Coneyhurst W Sus 11 B10
Coneysthorpe N Yorks 52 B3
Coneythorpe N Yorks 51 D9
Conford Hants 11 A7
Congash Highld 82 A2
Congdon's Shop Corn 4 D3
Congerstone Leics 35 E9
Congham Norf 38 C3
Congl-y-wal Gwyn 41 F9
Congleton Ches E 44 F2
Congresbury N Som 15 E10
Congreve Staffs 34 D5
Conicavel Moray 87 F12
Coningsby Lincs 46 G6
Conington Cambs 29 B10
Conington Cambs 37 G7
Conisbrough S Yorks 45 C9
Conisby Argyll 64 B3
Conisholme Lincs 47 C8
Coniston Cumb 56 G5
Coniston E Yorks 53 F7
Coniston Cold N Yorks 50 D5
Conistone N Yorks 50 C5
Connah's Quay Flint 42 F5
Connel Argyll 74 D2
Connel Park E Ayrs 67 E9
Connor Downs Corn 2 F4
Conon Bridge Highld 87 F8
Conon House Highld 87 F8
Cononley N Yorks 50 E5
Conordan Highld 85 E10
Consall Staffs 44 H3
Consett Durham 58 A2
Constable Burton N Yorks 58 G2
Constantine Corn 2 G6
Constantine Bay Corn 3 B7
Contin Highld 86 F7
Contlaw Aberdeen 83 C10
Conwy Conwy 41 C9
Conyer Kent 20 E6
Conyers Green Suff 30 B5
Cooden E Sus 12 F6
Cooil IoM 48 E3
Cookbury Devon 6 F3
Cookham Windsor 18 C5
Cookham Dean Windsor 18 C5
Cookham Rise Windsor 18 C5
Cookhill Worcs 27 C7
Cookley Suff 39 H9
Cookley Worcs 34 G4
Cookley Green Oxon 18 B3
Cookney Aberds 83 D10
Cookridge W Yorks 51 E8
Cooksbridge E Sus 12 E3
Cooksmill Green Essex 30 H3
Coolham W Sus 11 B10
Cooling Medway 20 D4
Coombe Corn 3 D8
Coombe Corn 6 E1
Coombe Hants 10 B5
Coombe Wilts 17 F8
Coombe Bissett Wilts 9 B10
Coombe Hill Glos 26 F5
Coombe Keynes Dorset 9 F7
Coombes W Sus 11 D10
Coopersale Common Essex 19 A11
Cootham W Sus 11 C9
Copdock Suff 31 D8
Copford Green Essex 30 F6
Copgrove N Yorks 51 C9
Copister Shetland 96 F6
Cople Bedford 29 D8
Copley Durham 58 D1
Coplow Dale Derbys 44 E5
Copmanthorpe York 52 E1
Coppathorne Corn 4 A3
Coppenhall Staffs 34 D5
Coppenhall Moss Ches E 43 G10
Copperhouse Corn 2 F4
Coppingford Cambs 37 G7
Copplestone Devon 7 F6
Coppull Lancs 43 A8
Coppull Moor Lancs 43 A8
Copsale W Sus 11 B10
Copster Green Lancs 50 F2
Copston Magna Warks 35 G10
Copt Heath W Mid 35 H7
Copt Hewick N Yorks 51 B9
Copt Oak Leics 35 D10
Copthorne Shrops 33 D10
Copthorne Sur 12 C2
Copy's Green Norf 38 B5
Copythorne Hants 10 C2
Corbets Tey London 20 C2
Corbridge Northumb 62 G5
Corby Northants 36 G4
Corby Glen Lincs 36 C5
Cordon N Ayrs 66 C3
Coreley Shrops 26 A3
Cores End Bucks 18 C6
Corfe Som 7 E11
Corfe Castle Dorset 9 F8
Corfe Mullen Dorset 9 E8
Corfton Shrops 33 G10
Corgarff Aberds 82 C4
Corhampton Hants 10 B5
Corlae Dumfries 67 G9
Corley Warks 35 G9
Corley Ash Warks 35 G8
Corley Moor Warks 35 G8
Cornaa IoM 48 D4
Cornabus Argyll 64 D4
Cornel Conwy 41 D9
Corner Row Lancs 49 F4
Corney Cumb 56 G3
Cornforth Durham 58 C4
Cornhill Aberds 88 C5
Cornhill-on-Tweed Northumb 71 G7
Cornholme W Yorks 50 G5
Cornish Hall End Essex 30 E3
Cornquoy Orkney 95 J6
Cornsay Durham 58 B2
Cornsay Colliery Durham 58 B2
Corntown Highld 87 F8
Corntown V Glam 14 D5
Cornwell Oxon 27 F9
Cornwood Devon 5 F7
Cornworthy Devon 5 F9
Corpach Highld 80 F2
Corpusty Norf 39 B7
Corran Highld 74 A3
Corran Highld 85 H13
Corranbuie Argyll 73 G7
Corrany IoM 48 D4
Corrie N Ayrs 66 B3
Corrie Common Dumfries 61 E8
Corriecravie N Ayrs 66 D2
Corriemoillie Highld 86 E6
Corriemulzie Lodge Highld 86 B6
Corrievarkie Lodge Perth 81 F7
Corrievorrie Highld 81 A9
Corrimony Highld 86 H6
Corringham Lincs 46 C2
Corringham Thurrock 20 C4
Corris Gwyn 32 E3
Corris Uchaf Gwyn 32 E3
Corrour Shooting Lodge Highld 80 G6
Corrow Argyll 74 G4
Corry Highld 85 F11
Corry of Ardnagrask Highld 87 G8
Corrykinloch Highld 92 G6
Corrymuckloch Perth 75 D11
Corrynachenchy Argyll 79 G9
Cors-y-Gedol Gwyn 32 C1
Corsback Highld 94 C4
Corscombe Dorset 8 D4
Corse Aberds 88 D6
Corse Glos 26 F4
Corse Lawn Worcs 26 E5
Corse of Kinnoir Aberds 88 D5
Corsewall Dumfries 54 C3
Corsham Wilts 16 D5
Corsindae Aberds 83 C8
Corsley Wilts 16 G5
Corsley Heath Wilts 16 G5
Corsock Dumfries 60 F3
Corston Bath 16 E3
Corston Wilts 16 C6
Corstorphine Edin 69 C10
Cortachy Angus 76 B6
Corton Suff 39 F11
Corton Wilts 16 G6
Corton Denham Som 8 B5
Coruanan Lodge Highld 80 G2
Corunna W Isles 84 B3
Corwen Denb 33 A6
Coryton Devon 4 C5
Coryton Thurrock 20 C4
Cosby Leics 35 F11
Coseley W Mid 34 F5
Cosgrove Northants 28 D4
Cosham Ptsmth 10 D5
Cosheston Pembs 22 F5
Cossall Notts 35 A10
Cossington Leics 36 D2
Cossington Som 15 G9
Costa Orkney 95 F4
Costessey Norf 39 D7
Costock Notts 36 C1
Coston Leics 36 C4
Cote Oxon 17 A10
Cotebrook Ches W 43 F8
Cotehill Cumb 56 A6
Cotes Cumb 57 H6
Cotes Leics 36 C1
Cotes Staffs 34 B4
Cotesbach Leics 35 G11
Cotgrave Notts 36 B2
Cothall Aberds 83 B10
Cotham Notts 45 H11
Cothelstone Som 7 C10
Cotherstone Durham 58 E1
Cothill Oxon 17 B11
Cotleigh Devon 7 F11
Cotmanhay Derbys 35 A10
Cotmaton Devon 7 H10
Coton Cambs 29 C11
Coton Northants 28 A3
Coton Staffs 34 B5
Coton Staffs 34 C4
Coton Clanford Staffs 34 C4
Coton Hill Shrops 33 D10
Coton Hill Staffs 34 B5
Coton in the Elms Derbys 35 D8
Cott Devon 5 E8
Cottam E Yorks 52 C5
Cottam Lancs 49 F5
Cottam Notts 46 E2
Cottartown Highld 87 H13
Cottenham Cambs 29 B11
Cotterdale N Yorks 57 G10
Cottered Herts 29 F10
Cotteridge W Mid 34 H6
Cotterstock Northants 36 F6
Cottesbrooke Northants 28 A4
Cottesmore Rutland 36 D5
Cotteylands Devon 7 E8
Cottingham E Yorks 52 F6
Cottingham Northants 36 F4
Cottingley W Yorks 51 F7
Cottisford Oxon 28 E2
Cotton Staffs 44 H4
Cotton Suff 31 B7
Cotton End Bedford 29 D7
Cottown Aberds 83 A7
Cottown Aberds 83 B9
Cottown Aberds 89 D8
Cotwalton Staffs 34 B5
Couch's Mill Corn 4 F2
Coughton Hereford 26 F2
Coughton Warks 27 B7
Coulaghailtro Argyll 72 G6
Coulags Highld 86 G2
Coulby Newham Mbro 58 E6
Coulderton Cumb 56 F1
Coulin Highld 86 F3
Coull Aberds 83 C7
Coull Argyll 64 B3
Coulport Argyll 73 E11
Coulsdon London 19 F9
Coulston Wilts 16 F6
Coulter S Lanark 69 G9
Coulton N Yorks 52 B2
Cound Shrops 34 E1
Coundon Durham 58 D3
Coundon W Mid 35 G9
Coundon Grange Durham 58 D3
Countersett N Yorks 57 H11
Countess Wilts 17 G8
Countess Wear Devon 5 C10
Countesthorpe Leics 36 F1
Countisbury Devon 7 B6
County Oak W Sus 12 C1
Coup Green Lancs 50 G1
Coupar Angus Perth 76 C5
Coupland Northumb 71 G8
Cour Argyll 65 D9
Courance Dumfries 60 D6
Court-at-Street Kent 13 C9
Court Henry Carms 23 D10
Courteenhall Northants 28 C4
Courtsend Essex 21 B7
Courtway Som 7 C11
Cousland Midloth 70 D2
Cousley Wood E Sus 12 C5
Cove Argyll 73 E11
Cove Borders 70 C6
Cove Devon 7 E8
Cove Hants 18 F5
Cove Highld 91 H13
Cove Bay Aberdeen 83 C11
Cove Bottom Suff 39 H10
Covehithe Suff 39 G11
Coven Staffs 34 E5
Coveney Cambs 37 G10
Covenham St Bartholomew Lincs 47 C7
Covenham St Mary Lincs 47 C7
Coventry W Mid 35 H9
Coverack Corn 3 H6
Coverham N Yorks 58 H2
Covesea Moray 88 A1
Covington Cambs 29 A7
Covington S Lanark 69 G8
Cow Ark Lancs 50 E2
Cowan Bridge Lancs 50 B2
Cowbeech E Sus 12 E5
Cowbit Lincs 37 D8
Cowbridge Lincs 47 H7
Cowbridge Som 7 B8
Cowbridge = Y Bont-Faen V Glam 14 D5
Cowdale Derbys 44 E4
Cowden Kent 12 B3
Cowdenbeath Fife 69 A10
Cowdenburn Borders 69 E11
Cowers Lane Derbys 45 H7
Cowes IoW 10 E3
Cowesby N Yorks 58 H5
Cowfold W Sus 11 B11
Cowgill Cumb 57 H9
Cowie Aberds 83 E10
Cowie Stirling 69 B7
Cowley Devon 7 G8
Cowley Glos 26 G6
Cowley London 19 C7
Cowley Oxon 18 A2
Cowleymoor Devon 7 E8
Cowling Lancs 50 H1
Cowling N Yorks 50 E5
Cowling N Yorks 58 H3
Cowlinge Suff 30 C4
Cowpe Lancs 50 G4
Cowpen Northumb 63 E8
Cowpen Bewley Stockton 58 D5
Cowplain Hants 10 C5
Cowshill Durham 57 B10
Cowslip Green N Som 15 E10
Cowstrandburn Fife 69 A9
Cowthorpe N Yorks 51 D10
Cox Common Suff 39 G9
Cox Green Windsor 18 D5
Cox Moor Notts 45 G9
Coxbank Ches E 34 A2
Coxbench Derbys 35 A9
Coxford Norf 38 C4
Coxford Soton 10 C2
Coxheath Kent 20 F4
Coxhill Kent 21 G9
Coxhoe Durham 58 C4
Coxley Som 15 G11
Coxwold N Yorks 51 B11
Coychurch Bridgend 14 D5
Coylton S Ayrs 67 D7
Coylumbridge Highld 81 B11
Coynach Aberds 82 C6
Coynachie Aberds 88 E4
Coytrahen Bridgend 14 C4
Crabadon Devon 5 F8
Crabbs Cross Worcs 27 B7
Crabtree W Sus 11 B11
Crackenthorpe Cumb 57 D8
Crackington Haven Corn 4 B2
Crackley Warks 27 A9
Crackleybank Shrops 34 D3
Crackpot N Yorks 57 G11
Cracoe N Yorks 50 C5
Craddock Devon 7 E9
Cradhlastadh W Isles 90 D5
Cradley Hereford 26 D4
Cradley Heath W Mid 34 G5
Crafthole Corn 4 F4
Cragg Vale W Yorks 50 G6
Craggan Highld 82 A2
Craggie Highld 87 H10
Craggie Highld 93 H11
Craghead Durham 58 A3
Crai Powys 24 F5
Craibstone Moray 88 C4
Craichie Angus 77 C8
Craig Dumfries 55 B9
Craig Dumfries 55 C9
Craig Highld 86 G3
Craig Castle Aberds 82 A6
Craig-cefn-parc Swansea 14 A2
Craig Penllyn V Glam 14 D5
Craig-y-don Conwy 41 B9
Craig-y-nos Powys 24 G5
Craiganor Lodge Perth 75 B9
Craigdam Aberds 89 E8
Craigdarroch Dumfries 60 D3
Craigdarroch Highld 86 F7
Craigdhu Highld 86 G7
Craigearn Aberds 83 B9
Craigellachie Moray 88 D2
Craigencross Dumfries 54 C3
Craigend Perth 76 E4
Craigend Stirling 68 B6
Craigendive Argyll 73 E9
Craigendoran Argyll 68 B2
Craigends Renfs 68 D3
Craigens Argyll 64 B3
Craigens E Ayrs 67 E8
Craighat Stirling 68 B3
Craighead Fife 77 G9
Craighlaw Mains Dumfries 54 C6
Craighouse Argyll 72 G4
Craigie Aberds 83 B11
Craigie Dundee 77 D7
Craigie Perth 76 C4
Craigie Perth 76 E4
Craigie S Ayrs 67 C7
Craigiefield Orkney 95 G5
Craigielaw E Loth 70 C3
Craiglockhart Edin 69 C11
Craigmalloch E Ayrs 67 G7
Craigmaud Aberds 89 C8
Craigmillar Edin 69 C11
Craigmore Argyll 73 G10
Craignant Shrops 33 B8
Craigneuk N Lanark 68 D6
Craigneuk N Lanark 68 E6
Craignure Argyll 79 H10
Craigo Angus 77 A9
Craigow Perth 76 G3
Craigrothie Fife 76 F6
Craigroy Moray 87 F14
Craigruie Stirling 75 E7
Craigston Castle Aberds 89 C7
Craigton Aberdeen 83 C10
Craigton Angus 76 B6
Craigton Angus 77 D8
Craigton Highld 87 B9
Craigtown Highld 93 D11
Craik Borders 61 C9
Crail Fife 77 G9
Crailing Borders 62 A2
Crailinghall Borders 62 A2
Craiselound N Lincs 45 C11
Crakehill N Yorks 51 B10
Crakemarsh Staffs 35 B6
Crambe N Yorks 52 C3
Cramlington Northumb 63 F8
Cramond Edin 69 C10
Cramond Bridge Edin 69 C10
Cranage Ches E 43 F10
Cranberry Staffs 34 B4
Cranborne Dorset 9 C9
Cranbourne Brack 18 D6
Cranbrook Devon 7 G9
Cranbrook Kent 13 C6
Cranbrook Common Kent 13 C6
Crane Moor S Yorks 45 B7
Crane's Corner Norf 38 D5
Cranfield C Beds 28 D6
Cranford London 19 D8
Cranford St Andrew Northants 36 H5
Cranford St John Northants 36 H5
Cranham Glos 26 G5
Cranham London 20 C2
Crank Mers 43 C8
Crank Wood Gtr Man 43 B9
Cranleigh Sur 19 H7
Cranley Suff 31 A8
Cranmer Green Suff 31 A7
Cranmore IoW 10 F2

Cranna Aberds 89 C6
Crannich Argyll 79 G8
Crannoch Moray 88 C4
Cranoe Leics 36 F3
Cransford Suff 31 B10
Cranshaws Borders 70 D5
Cranstal IoM 48 B4
Crantock Corn 3 C6
Cranwell Lincs 46 H4
Cranwich Norf 38 F3
Cranworth Norf 38 E5
Craobh Haven Argyll 72 C6
Crapstone Devon 4 E6
Crarae Argyll 73 D8
Crask Inn Highld 93 G8
Crask of Aigas Highld 86 G7
Craskins Aberds 83 C7
Craster Northumb 63 B8
Craswall Hereford 25 E9
Cratfield Suff 39 H9
Crathes Aberds 83 D9
Crathie Aberds 82 D4
Crathie Highld 81 D7
Crathorne N Yorks 58 F5
Craven Arms Shrops 33 G10
Crawcrook T&W 63 G7
Crawford Lancs 43 B7
Crawford S Lanark 60 A5
Crawfordjohn S Lanark 60 A4
Crawick Dumfries 60 B3
Crawley Hants 10 A3
Crawley Oxon 27 G10
Crawley W Sus 12 C1
Crawley Down W Sus 12 C2
Crawleyside Durham 57 B11
Crawshawbooth Lancs 50 G4
Crawton Aberds 83 F10
Cray N Yorks 50 B5
Cray Perth 76 A4
Crayford London 20 D2
Crayke N Yorks 52 B1
Crays Hill Essex 20 B4
Cray's Pond Oxon 18 C3
Creacombe Devon 7 E7
Creag Ghoraidh W Isles 84 D2
Creagan Argyll 74 C2
Creaguaineach Lodge Highld 80 G5
Creaksea Essex 20 B6
Creaton Northants 28 A4
Creca Dumfries 61 F8
Credenhill Hereford 25 D11
Crediton Devon 7 F7
Creebridge Dumfries 55 C7
Creech Heathfield Som 8 B1
Creech St Michael Som 8 B1
Creed Corn 3 E8
Creekmouth London 19 C11
Creeting Bottoms Suff 31 C8
Creeting St Mary Suff 31 C7
Creeton Lincs 36 C6
Creetown Dumfries 55 D7
Creg-ny-Baa IoM 48 D3
Creggans Argyll 73 C9
Cregneash IoM 48 F1
Cregrina Powys 25 C8
Creich Fife 76 E6
Creigiau Cardiff 14 C6
Cremyll Corn 4 F5
Creslow Bucks 28 F5
Cressage Shrops 34 E1
Cressbrook Derbys 44 E5
Cresselly Pembs 22 F5
Cressing Essex 30 F4
Cresswell Northumb 63 D8
Cresswell Staffs 34 B5
Cresswell Quay Pembs 22 F5
Creswell Derbys 45 E9
Cretingham Suff 31 B9
Cretshengan Argyll 72 G6
Crewe Ches E 43 G10
Crewe Ches W 43 G7
Crewgreen Powys 33 D9
Crewkerne Som 8 D3
Crianlarich Stirling 74 E6
Cribyn Ceredig 23 A10
Criccieth Gwyn 40 G6
Crich Derbys 45 G7
Crichie Aberds 89 D9
Crichton Midloth 70 D2
Crick Mon 15 B10
Crick Northants 28 A2
Crickadarn Powys 25 D7
Cricket Malherbie Som 8 C2
Cricket St Thomas Som 8 D2
Crickheath Shrops 33 C8
Crickhowell Powys 25 G9
Cricklade Wilts 17 B8
Cricklewood London 19 C9
Cridling Stubbs N Yorks 51 G11
Crieff Perth 75 E11
Criggion Powys 33 D8
Crigglestone W Yorks 51 H9
Crimond Aberds 89 C10
Crimonmogate Aberds 89 C10
Crimplesham Norf 38 E2
Crinan Argyll 72 D6
Cringleford Norf 39 E7
Cringles W Yorks 50 E6
Crinow Pembs 22 E6
Cripplesease Corn 2 F4
Cripplestyle Dorset 9 C9
Cripp's Corner E Sus 13 D6
Croasdale Cumb 56 E2
Crock Street Som 8 C2
Crockenhill Kent 20 E2
Crockernwell Devon 7 G6
Crockerton Wilts 16 G5
Crocketford or Ninemile Bar Dumfries 60 F4
Crockey Hill York 52 E2
Crockham Hill Kent 19 F11
Crockleford Heath Essex 31 F7
Crockness Orkney 95 J4
Croes-goch Pembs 22 C3
Croes-lan Ceredig 23 B8
Croes-y-mwyalch Torf 15 B9
Croeserw Neath 14 B4
Croesor Gwyn 41 F8
Croesyceiliog Carms 23 E9
Croesyceiliog Torf 15 B9
Croesywaun Gwyn 41 E7
Croft Leics 35 F11
Croft Lincs 47 F9
Croft Pembs 22 B6
Croft Warr 43 C9
Croft-on-Tees N Yorks 58 F3
Croftamie Stirling 68 B3
Croftmalloch W Loth 69 D8
Crofton W Yorks 51 H9
Crofton Wilts 17 E9
Crofts of Benachielt Highld 94 G3
Crofts of Haddo Aberds 89 E8
Crofts of Inverthernie Aberds 89 D7
Crofts of Meikle Ardo Aberds 89 D8
Crofty Swansea 23 G10
Croggan Argyll 79 J10
Croglin Cumb 57 B7
Croich Highld 86 B7
Crois Dughaill W Isles 84 F2
Cromarty Highld 87 E10
Cromblet Aberds 89 E7
Cromdale Highld 82 A2
Cromer Herts 29 F9
Cromer Norf 39 A8
Cromford Derbys 44 G6
Cromhall S Glos 16 B3
Cromhall Common S Glos 16 C3
Cromor W Isles 91 E9
Cromra Highld 81 D7
Cromwell Notts 45 F11
Cronberry E Ayrs 67 D9
Crondall Hants 18 G4
Cronk-y-Voddy IoM 48 D3
Cronton Mers 43 D7
Crook Cumb 56 G6
Crook Durham 58 C2
Crook of Devon Perth 76 G3
Crookedholm E Ayrs 67 C7
Crookes S Yorks 45 D7
Crookham Northumb 71 G8
Crookham W Berks 18 E2
Crookham Village Hants 18 F4
Crookhaugh Borders 69 H10
Crookhouse Borders 70 H6
Crooklands Cumb 49 A5
Cropredy Oxon 27 D11
Cropston Leics 36 D1
Cropthorne Worcs 26 D6
Cropton N Yorks 59 H8
Cropwell Bishop Notts 36 B2
Cropwell Butler Notts 36 B2
Cros W Isles 91 A10
Crosbost W Isles 91 E8
Crosby Cumb 56 C2
Crosby IoM 48 E3
Crosby N Lincs 46 A2
Crosby Garrett Cumb 57 F9
Crosby Ravensworth Cumb 57 E8
Crosby Villa Cumb 56 C2
Croscombe Som 16 G2
Cross Som 15 F10
Cross Ash Mon 25 G11
Cross-at-Hand Kent 20 G4
Cross Green Devon 4 C4
Cross Green Suff 30 C6
Cross Green Suff 30 C5
Cross Green Warks 27 C10
Cross-hands Carms 22 D6
Cross Hands Carms 23 E10
Cross Hands Pembs 22 E5
Cross Hill Derbys 45 H8
Cross Houses Shrops 33 E11
Cross in Hand E Sus 12 D4
Cross in Hand Leics 35 G11
Cross Inn Ceredig 23 A8
Cross Inn Ceredig 24 B2
Cross Inn Rhondda 14 C6
Cross Keys Kent 20 F2
Cross Lane Head Shrops 34 F3
Cross Lanes Corn 2 G5
Cross Lanes N Yorks 51 C11
Cross Lanes Wrex 43 H6
Cross o' th' hands Derbys 44 H6
Cross Oak Powys 25 F8
Cross of Jackston Aberds 89 E7
Cross Street Suff 39 H7
Cross Trickett's Dorset 9 D9
Crossaig Argyll 65 C9
Crossal Highld 85 E9
Crossapol Argyll 78 G2
Crossburn Falk 69 C7
Crossbush W Sus 11 D9
Crosscanonby Cumb 56 C2
Crossdale Street Norf 39 B8
Crossens Mers 49 H3
Crossflatts W Yorks 51 E7
Crossford Fife 69 B9
Crossford S Lanark 69 F7
Crossgate Lincs 37 C8
Crossgatehall E Loth 70 D2
Crossgates Fife 69 B10
Crossgates Powys 25 B7
Crossgill Lancs 50 C1
Crosshill E Ayrs 67 D7
Crosshill Fife 76 H4
Crosshill S Ayrs 66 F6
Crosshouse E Ayrs 67 C6
Crossings Cumb 61 F11
Crosskeys Caerph 15 B8
Crosskirk Highld 93 B13
Crosslanes Shrops 33 D9
Crosslee Borders 61 B9
Crosslee Renfs 68 D3
Crossmichael Dumfries 55 C10
Crossmoor Lancs 49 F4
Crossroads Aberds 83 D9
Crossroads E Ayrs 67 C7
Crossway Hereford 26 E3
Crossway Mon 25 G11
Crossway Powys 25 C7
Crossway Green Worcs 26 B5
Crossways Dorset 9 F6
Crosswell Pembs 22 C6
Crosswood Ceredig 24 A3
Crosthwaite Cumb 56 G6
Croston Lancs 49 H4
Crostwick Norf 39 D8
Crostwight Norf 39 C9
Crothair W Isles 90 D6
Crouch Kent 20 F3
Crouch Hill Dorset 8 C6
Crouch House Green Kent 19 G11
Croucheston Wilts 9 B9
Croughton Northants 28 E2
Crovie Aberds 89 B8
Crow Edge S Yorks 44 B5
Crow Hill Hereford 26 F3
Crowan Corn 2 F5
Crowborough E Sus 12 C4
Crowcombe Som 7 C10
Crowdecote Derbys 44 F5
Crowden Derbys 44 C4
Crowell Oxon 18 B4
Crowfield Northants 28 D3
Crowfield Suff 31 C8
Crowhurst E Sus 13 E6
Crowhurst Sur 19 G10
Crowhurst Lane End Sur 19 G10
Crowland Lincs 37 D8
Crowlas Corn 2 F4
Crowle N Lincs 45 A11
Crowle Worcs 26 C6
Crowmarsh Gifford Oxon 18 C3
Crown Corner Suff 31 A9
Crownhill Plym 4 F5
Crownland Suff 31 B7
Crownthorpe Norf 39 E6
Crowntown Corn 2 F5
Crows-an-wra Corn 2 G2
Crowshill Norf 38 E5
Crowsnest Shrops 33 E9
Crowthorne Brack 18 E5
Crowton Ches W 43 E8
Croxall Staffs 35 D7
Croxby Lincs 46 C5
Croxdale Durham 58 C3
Croxden Staffs 35 B6
Croxley Green Herts 19 B7
Croxton Cambs 29 B9
Croxton N Lincs 46 A4
Croxton Norf 38 G4
Croxton Staffs 34 B3
Croxton Kerrial Leics 36 C4
Croxtonbank Staffs 34 B3
Croy Highld 87 G10
Croy N Lanark 68 C6
Croyde Devon 6 C3
Croydon Cambs 29 D10
Croydon London 19 E10
Crubenmore Lodge Highld 81 D8
Cruckmeole Shrops 33 E10
Cruckton Shrops 33 D10
Cruden Bay Aberds 89 E10
Crudgington Telford 34 D2
Crudwell Wilts 16 B6
Crug Powys 25 A8
Crugmeer Corn 3 B8
Crugybar Carms 24 E3
Crulabhig W Isles 90 D6
Crumlin = Crymlyn Caerph 15 B8
Crumpsall Gtr Man 44 B2
Crundale Kent 21 G7
Crundale Pembs 22 E4
Cruwys Morchard Devon 7 E7
Crux Easton Hants 17 F11
Crwbin Carms 23 E9
Crya Orkney 95 H4
Cryers Hill Bucks 18 B5
Crymlyn = Crumlin Caerph 15 B8
Crymlyn Gwyn 41 C8
Crymych Pembs 22 C6
Crynant Neath 14 A3
Crynfryn Ceredig 24 B2
Cuaig Highld 85 C12
Cuan Argyll 72 B6
Cubbington Warks 27 B10
Cubeck N Yorks 57 H11
Cubert Corn 3 D6
Cubley S Yorks 44 B6
Cubley Common Derbys 35 B7
Cublington Bucks 28 F5
Cublington Hereford 25 E11
Cuckfield W Sus 12 D2
Cucklington Som 9 B6
Cuckney Notts 45 E9
Cuckoo Hill Notts 45 C11
Cuddesdon Oxon 18 A3
Cuddington Bucks 28 G4
Cuddington Ches W 43 E9
Cuddington Heath Ches W 43 H7
Cuddy Hill Lancs 49 F4
Cudham London 19 F11
Cudliptown Devon 4 D6
Cudworth S Yorks 45 B7
Cudworth Som 8 C2
Cuffley Herts 19 A10
Cuiashader W Isles 91 B10
Cuidhir W Isles 84 H1
Cuidhtinis W Isles 90 J5
Culbo Highld 87 E9
Culbokie Highld 87 F9
Culburnie Highld 86 G7
Culcabock Highld 87 G9
Culcairn Highld 87 E9
Culcharry Highld 87 F11
Culcheth Warr 43 C9
Culdrain Aberds 88 E5
Culduie Highld 85 D12
Culford Suff 30 A5
Culgaith Cumb 57 D8
Culham Oxon 18 B2
Culkein Highld 92 F3
Culkein Drumbeg Highld 92 F4
Culkerton Glos 16 B6
Cullachie Highld 81 A11
Cullen Moray 88 B5
Cullercoats T&W 63 F9
Cullicudden Highld 87 E9
Cullingworth W Yorks 51 F6
Cullipool Argyll 72 B6
Cullivoe Shetland 96 C7
Culloch Perth 75 F10
Culloden Highld 87 G10
Cullompton Devon 7 F9
Culmaily Highld 87 B11
Culmazie Dumfries 54 D6
Culmington Shrops 33 G10
Culmstock Devon 7 E10
Culnacraig Highld 92 J3
Culnaknock Highld 85 B10
Culpho Suff 31 D9
Culrain Highld 87 B8
Culross Fife 69 B8
Culroy S Ayrs 66 E6
Culsh Aberds 82 D5
Culsh Aberds 89 D8
Culshabbin Dumfries 54 D6
Culswick Shetland 96 J4
Cultercullen Aberds 89 F9
Cults Aberdeen 83 C10
Cults Aberds 88 E5
Cults Dumfries 55 E7
Culverstone Green Kent 20 E3
Culverthorpe Lincs 36 A6
Culworth Northants 28 D2
Culzie Lodge Highld 87 D8
Cumbernauld N Lanark 68 C6
Cumbernauld Village N Lanark 68 C6
Cumberworth Lincs 47 E9
Cuminestown Aberds 89 C8
Cumlewick Shetland 96 L6
Cummersdale Cumb 56 A5
Cummertrees Dumfries 61 G7
Cummingston Moray 88 B1
Cumnock E Ayrs 67 D8
Cumnor Oxon 17 A11
Cumrew Cumb 57 A7
Cumwhinton Cumb 56 A6
Cumwhitton Cumb 57 A7
Cundall N Yorks 51 B10
Cunninghamhead N Ayrs 67 B6
Cunnister Shetland 96 D7
Cupar Fife 76 F6
Cupar Muir Fife 76 F6
Cupernham Hants 10 B2
Curbar Derbys 44 E6
Curbridge Hants 10 C4
Curbridge Oxon 27 H10
Curdridge Hants 10 C4
Curdworth Warks 35 F7
Curland Som 8 C1
Curlew Green Suff 31 B10
Currarie S Ayrs 66 G4
Curridge W Berks 17 D11
Currie Edin 69 D10
Curry Mallet Som 8 B2
Curry Rivel Som 8 B2
Curtisden Green Kent 12 B6
Curtisknowle Devon 5 F8
Cury Corn 2 G5
Cushnie Aberds 89 B7
Cushuish Som 7 C10
Cusop Hereford 25 D9
Cutcloy Dumfries 55 F7
Cutcombe Som 7 C8
Cutgate Gtr Man 44 A2
Cutiau Gwyn 32 D2
Cutlers Green Essex 30 E2
Cutnall Green Worcs 26 B5
Cutsdean Glos 27 E7
Cutthorpe Derbys 45 E7
Cutts Shetland 96 K6
Cuxham Oxon 18 B3
Cuxton Medway 20 E4
Cuxwold Lincs 46 B5
Cwm Bl Gwent 25 H8
Cwm Denb 42 E3
Cwm Swansea 14 B2
Cwm-byr Carms 24 E3
Cwm-Cewydd Gwyn 32 D4
Cwm-cou Ceredig 23 B7
Cwm-Dulais Swansea 14 A2
Cwm-felin-fach Caerph 15 B7
Cwm Ffrwd-oer Torf 15 A8
Cwm-hesgen Gwyn 32 C3
Cwm-hwnt Rhondda 24 H6
Cwm Irfon Powys 24 D5
Cwm-Llinau Powys 32 E4
Cwm-mawr Carms 23 E10
Cwm-parc Rhondda 14 B5
Cwm Penmachno Conwy 41 F9
Cwm-y-glo Carms 23 E10
Cwm-y-glo Gwyn 41 D7
Cwmafan Neath 14 B3
Cwmaman Rhondda 14 B6
Cwmann Carms 23 B10
Cwmavon Torf 25 H9
Cwmbach Carms 23 D7
Cwmbach Carms 23 F9
Cwmbach Powys 25 C7
Cwmbach Powys 25 E8
Cwmbâch Rhondda 14 A6
Cwmbelan Powys 32 G5
Cwmbran = Cwmbrân Torf 15 B8
Cwmbrân = Cwmbran Torf 15 B8
Cwmbrwyno Ceredig 32 G3
Cwmcarn Caerph 15 B8
Cwmcarvan Mon 25 H11
Cwmcych Carms 23 C7
Cwmdare Rhondda 14 A5
Cwmderwen Powys 32 E5
Cwmdu Carms 24 E3
Cwmdu Powys 25 F8
Cwmdu Swansea 14 B2
Cwmduad Carms 23 C8
Cwmdwr Carms 24 E4
Cwmfelin Bridgend 14 C4
Cwmfelin M Tydf 14 A6
Cwmfelin Boeth Carms 22 E6
Cwmfelin Mynach Carms 23 D7
Cwmffrwd Carms 23 E9
Cwmgiedd Powys 24 G4
Cwmgors Neath 24 G4
Cwmgwili Carms 23 E10
Cwmgwrach Neath 14 A4
Cwmhiraeth Carms 23 C8
Cwmifor Carms 24 F3
Cwmisfael Carms 23 E9
Cwmllynfell Neath 24 G4
Cwmorgan Pembs 23 C7
Cwmpengraig Carms 23 C8
Cwmrhos Powys 25 F8
Cwmsychpant Ceredig 23 B9
Cwmtillery Bl Gwent 25 H9
Cwmwysg Powys 24 F5
Cwmyoy Mon 25 F9
Cwmystwyth Ceredig 24 A4
Cwrt Gwyn 32 E2
Cwrt-newydd Ceredig 23 B9
Cwrt-y-cadno Carms 24 D3
Cwrt-y-gollen Powys 25 G9
Cydweli = Kidwelly Carms 23 F9
Cyffordd Llandudno = Llandudno Junction Conwy 41 C9
Cyffylliog Denb 42 G3
Cyfronydd Powys 33 E7
Cymer Neath 14 B4
Cyncoed Cardiff 15 C7
Cynghordy Carms 24 D5
Cynheidre Carms 23 F9
Cynwyd Denb 33 A6
Cynwyl Elfed Carms 23 D8
Cywarch Gwyn 32 D4

D

Dacre Cumb 56 D6
Dacre N Yorks 51 C7
Dacre Banks N Yorks 51 C7
Daddry Shield Durham 57 C10
Dadford Bucks 28 E3
Dadlington Leics 35 F10
Dafarn Faig Gwyn 40 F6
Dafen Carms 23 F10
Daffy Green Norf 38 E5
Dagenham London 19 C11
Daglingworth Glos 26 H6
Dagnall Bucks 28 G6
Dail Beag W Isles 90 C7
Dail bho Dheas W Isles 91 A9
Dail bho Thuath W Isles 91 A9
Dail Mor W Isles 90 C7
Daill Argyll 64 B4
Dailly S Ayrs 66 F5
Dairsie or Osnaburgh Fife 77 F7
Daisy Hill Gtr Man 43 B9
Dalabrog W Isles 84 F2
Dalavich Argyll 73 B8
Dalbeattie Dumfries 55 C11
Dalblair E Ayrs 67 E9
Dalbog Angus 83 F7
Dalbury Derbys 35 B8
Dalby IoM 48 E2
Dalby N Yorks 52 B2
Dalchalloch Perth 75 A10
Dalchalm Highld 93 J12
Dalchenna Argyll 73 C9
Dalchirach Moray 88 E1
Dalchork Highld 93 H8
Dalchreichart Highld 80 B4
Dalchruin Perth 75 F10
Dalderby Lincs 46 F6
Dale Pembs 22 F3
Dale Abbey Derbys 35 B10
Dale Head Cumb 56 E6
Dale of Walls Shetland 96 H3
Dalelia Highld 79 E10
Daless Highld 87 H11
Dalfaber Highld 81 B11
Dalgarven N Ayrs 66 B5
Dalgety Bay Fife 69 B10
Dalginross Perth 75 E10
Dalguise Perth 76 C2
Dalhalvaig Highld 93 D11
Dalham Suff 30 B4
Dalinlongart Argyll 73 E10
Dalkeith Midloth 70 D2
Dallam Warr 43 C8
Dallas Moray 87 F14
Dalleagles E Ayrs 67 E8
Dallinghoo Suff 31 C9
Dallington E Sus 12 E5
Dallington Northants 28 B4
Dallow N Yorks 51 B7
Dalmadilly Aberds 83 B9
Dalmally Argyll 74 E4
Dalmarnock Glasgow 68 D5
Dalmary Stirling 75 H8
Dalmellington E Ayrs 67 F7
Dalmeny Edin 69 C10
Dalmigavie Highld 81 B9
Dalmigavie Lodge Highld 81 A9
Dalmore Highld 87 E9
Dalmuir W Dunb 68 C3
Dalnabreck Highld 79 E9
Dalnacardoch Lodge Perth 81 F9
Dalnacroich Highld 86 F6
Dalnaglar Castle Perth 76 A4
Dalnahaitnach Highld 81 A10
Dalnaspidal Lodge Perth 81 F8
Dalnavaid Perth 76 A3
Dalnavie Highld 87 D9
Dalnawillan Lodge Highld 93 E13
Dalness Highld 74 B4
Dalnessie Highld 93 H9
Dalqueich Perth 76 G3
Dalreavoch Highld 93 J10
Dalry N Ayrs 66 B5
Dalrymple E Ayrs 67 E6
Dalserf S Lanark 69 E7
Dalston Cumb 56 A5
Dalswinton Dumfries 60 E5
Dalton Dumfries 61 F7
Dalton Lancs 43 B7
Dalton N Yorks 51 B10
Dalton N Yorks 58 F2
Dalton Northumb 62 H5
Dalton Northumb 63 F7
Dalton S Yorks 45 C8
Dalton-in-Furness Cumb 49 B2
Dalton-le-Dale Durham 58 B5
Dalton-on-Tees N Yorks 58 F3
Dalton Piercy Hrtlpl 58 C5
Dalveich Stirling 75 E9
Dalvina Lo. Highld 93 E9
Dalwhinnie Highld 81 E8
Dalwood Devon 8 D1
Dalwyne S Ayrs 66 G6
Dam Green Norf 39 G6
Dam Side Lancs 49 E4
Damerham Hants 9 C10
Damgate Norf 39 E10
Damnaglaur Dumfries 54 F4
Damside Borders 69 F10
Danbury Essex 30 H4
Danby N Yorks 59 F8
Danby Wiske N Yorks 58 G4
Dandaleith Moray 88 D2
Danderhall Midloth 70 D2
Dane End Herts 29 F10
Danebridge Ches E 44 F3
Danehill E Sus 12 D3
Danemoor Green Norf 39 E6
Danesford Shrops 34 F3
Daneshill Hants 18 F3
Dangerous Corner Lancs 43 A8
Danskine E Loth 70 D4
Darcy Lever Gtr Man 43 B10
Darenth Kent 20 D2
Daresbury Halton 43 D8
Darfield S Yorks 45 B8
Darfoulds Notts 45 E9
Dargate Kent 21 E7
Darite Corn 4 E3
Darlaston W Mid 34 F5
Darley N Yorks 51 D8
Darley Bridge Derbys 44 F6
Darley Head N Yorks 51 D7
Darlingscott Warks 27 D9
Darlington Darl 58 E3
Darliston Shrops 34 B1
Darlton Notts 45 E11
Darnall S Yorks 45 D7
Darnick Borders 70 G4
Darowen Powys 32 E4
Darra Aberds 89 D7
Darracott Devon 6 C3
Darras Hall Northumb 63 F7
Darrington W Yorks 51 G10
Darsham Suff 31 B11
Dartford Kent 20 D2
Dartford Crossing Kent 20 D2
Dartington Devon 5 E8
Dartmeet Devon 5 D7
Dartmouth Devon 5 F9
Darton S Yorks 45 B7
Darvel E Ayrs 68 G4
Darwell Hole E Sus 12 E5
Darwen Blackburn 50 G2
Datchet Windsor 18 D6
Datchworth Herts 29 G9
Datchworth Green Herts 29 G9
Daubhill Gtr Man 43 B10
Daugh of Kinermony Moray 88 D2
Dauntsey Wilts 16 C6
Dava Moray 87 H13
Davenham Ches W 43 E9
Davenport Green Ches E 44 E2
Daventry Northants 28 B2
David's Well Powys 33 H6
Davidson's Mains Edin 69 C11
Davidstow Corn 4 C2
Davington Dumfries 61 C8
Daviot Aberds 83 A9
Daviot Highld 87 H10
Davoch of Grange Moray 88 C4
Davyhulme Gtr Man 43 C10
Dawley Telford 34 E2
Dawlish Devon 5 D10
Dawlish Warren Devon 5 D10
Dawn Conwy 41 C10
Daws Heath Essex 20 C5
Daw's House Corn 4 C4
Dawsmere Lincs 37 B10
Dayhills Staffs 34 B5
Daylesford Glos 27 F9
Ddôl-Cownwy Powys 32 D6
Ddrydwy Anglesey 40 C5
Deadwater Northumb 62 D2
Deaf Hill Durham 58 C4
Deal Kent 21 F10
Deal Hall Essex 21 B7
Dean Cumb 56 D2
Dean Devon 5 E8
Dean Devon 6 B4
Dean Dorset 9 C8
Dean Hants 10 C4
Dean Som 16 G3
Dean Prior Devon 5 E8
Dean Row Ches E 44 D2
Deanburnhaugh Borders 61 B9
Deane Gtr Man 43 B9
Deane Hants 18 F2
Deanich Lodge Highld 86 C6
Deanland Dorset 9 C8
Deans W Loth 69 D9
Deanscales Cumb 56 D2
Deanshanger Northants 28 E4
Deanston Stirling 75 G10
Dearham Cumb 56 C2
Debach Suff 31 C9
Debden Essex 19 B11
Debden Essex 30 E2
Debden Cross Essex 30 E2
Debenham Suff 31 B8
Dechmont W Loth 69 C9
Deddington Oxon 27 E11
Dedham Essex 31 E7
Dedham Heath Essex 31 E7
Deebank Aberds 83 D8
Deene Northants 36 F5
Deenethorpe Northants 36 F5
Deepcar S Yorks 44 C6
Deepcut Sur 18 F6
Deepdale Cumb 50 A3
Deeping Gate Lincs 37 E7
Deeping St James Lincs 37 E7
Deeping St Nicholas Lincs 37 D8
Deerhill Moray 88 C4
Deerhurst Glos 26 F5
Deerness Orkney 95 H6
Defford Worcs 26 D6
Defynnog Powys 24 F6
Deganwy Conwy 41 C9
Deighton N Yorks 58 F4
Deighton W Yorks 51 H7
Deighton York 52 E2
Deiniolen Gwyn 41 D7
Delabole Corn 4 C1
Delamere Ches W 43 F8
Delfrigs Aberds 89 F9
Dell Lodge Highld 82 B2
Delliefure Highld 87 H13
Delnabo Moray 82 B3
Delnadamph Aberds 82 C4
Delph Gtr Man 44 B3
Delves Durham 58 B2
Delvine Perth 76 C4
Dembleby Lincs 36 B6
Denaby Main S Yorks 45 C8
Denbigh = Dinbych Denb 42 F3
Denbury Devon 5 E9
Denby Derbys 45 H7
Denby Dale W Yorks 44 B6
Denchworth Oxon 17 B10
Dendron Cumb 49 B2
Denel End C Beds 29 E7
Denend Aberds 88 E6
Denford Northants 36 H5
Dengie Essex 20 A6
Denham Bucks 19 C7
Denham Suff 30 B4
Denham Suff 31 A8
Denham Street Suff 31 A8
Denhead Aberds 89 C9
Denhead Fife 77 F7
Denhead of Arbilot Angus 77 C8
Denhead of Gray Dundee 76 D6
Denholm Borders 61 B11
Denholme W Yorks 51 F6
Denholme Clough W Yorks 51 F6
Denio Gwyn 40 G5
Denmead Hants 10 C5
Denmore Aberdeen 83 B11
Denmoss Aberds 89 D6
Dennington Suff 31 B9
Denny Falk 69 B7
Denny Lodge Hants 10 D2
Dennyloanhead Falk 69 B7
Denshaw Gtr Man 44 A3
Denside Aberds 83 D10
Densole Kent 21 G9
Denston Suff 30 C4
Denstone Staffs 35 A7
Dent Cumb 57 H9
Denton Cambs 37 G7
Denton Darl 58 E3
Denton E Sus 12 F3
Denton Gtr Man 44 C3
Denton Kent 21 G9
Denton Lincs 36 B4
Denton N Yorks 51 E7
Denton Norf 39 G8
Denton Northants 28 C5
Denton Oxon 18 A2
Denton's Green Mers 43 C7
Denver Norf 38 E2
Denwick Northumb 63 B8
Deopham Norf 39 E6
Deopham Green Norf 38 F6
Depden Suff 30 C4
Depden Green Suff 30 C4
Deptford London 19 D10
Deptford Wilts 17 H7
Derby Derby 35 B9
Derbyhaven IoM 48 F2
Dereham Norf 38 D5
Deri Caerph 15 A7
Derril Devon 6 F2
Derringstone Kent 21 G9
Derrington Staffs 34 C4
Derriton Devon 6 F2
Derry Hill Wilts 16 D6
Derryguaig Argyll 78 H7
Derrythorpe N Lincs 46 B2
Dersingham Norf 38 B2
Dervaig Argyll 78 F7
Derwen Denb 42 G3
Derwenlas Powys 32 F3
Desborough Northants 36 G4
Desford Leics 35 E10
Detchant Northumb 71 G9
Detling Kent 20 F4
Deuddwr Powys 33 D8
Devauden Mon 15 B10
Devil's Bridge Ceredig 32 H3
Devizes Wilts 17 E7
Devol Invclyd 68 C2
Devonport Plym 4 F5
Devonside Clack 76 H2
Devoran Corn 3 F6
Dewar Borders 70 F2
Dewlish Dorset 9 E6
Dewsbury W Yorks 51 G8
Dewsbury Moor W Yorks 51 G8
Dewshall Court Hereford 25 E11
Dhoon IoM 48 D4
Dhoor IoM 48 C4
Dhowin IoM 48 B4
Dial Post W Sus 11 C10
Dibden Hants 10 D3
Dibden Purlieu Hants 10 D3
Dickleburgh Norf 39 G7
Didbrook Glos 27 E7
Didcot Oxon 18 C2
Diddington Cambs 29 B8
Diddlebury Shrops 33 G11
Didley Hereford 25 E11
Didling W Sus 11 C7
Didmarton Glos 16 C5
Didsbury Gtr Man 44 C2
Didworthy Devon 5 E7
Digby Lincs 46 G4
Digg Highld 85 B9
Diggle Gtr Man 44 B4
Digmoor Lancs 43 B7
Digswell Park Herts 29 G9
Dihewyd Ceredig 23 A9
Dilham Norf 39 C9
Dilhorne Staffs 34 A5
Dillarburn S Lanark 69 F7
Dillington Cambs 29 B8
Dilston Northumb 62 G5
Dilton Marsh Wilts 16 G5
Dilwyn Hereford 25 C11
Dinas Carms 23 C7
Dinas Gwyn 40 G4
Dinas Cross Pembs 22 C5
Dinas Dinlle Gwyn 40 E6
Dinas-Mawddwy Gwyn 32 D4
Dinas Powys V Glam 15 D7
Dinbych = Denbigh Denb 42 F3
Dinbych-y-Pysgod = Tenby Pembs 22 F6
Dinder Som 16 G2
Dinedor Hereford 26 E2
Dingestow Mon 25 G11
Dingle Mers 42 D6
Dingleden Kent 13 C7
Dingley Northants 36 G3
Dingwall Highld 87 F8
Dinlabyre Borders 61 D11
Dinmael Conwy 32 A6
Dinnet Aberds 82 D6
Dinnington S Yorks 45 D9
Dinnington Som 8 C3
Dinnington T&W 63 F8
Dinorwic Gwyn 41 D7
Dinton Bucks 28 G4
Dinton Wilts 9 A9
Dinwoodie Mains Dumfries 61 D7
Dinworthy Devon 6 E2
Dippen N Ayrs 66 D3
Dippenhall Sur 18 G5
Dipple Moray 88 C3
Dipple S Ayrs 66 F5
Diptford Devon 5 F8
Dipton Durham 58 A2
Dirdhu Highld 82 A2
Dirleton E Loth 70 B4
Dirt Pot Northumb 57 B10
Discoed Powys 25 B9
Diseworth Leics 35 C10
Dishes Orkney 95 F7
Dishforth N Yorks 51 B9
Disley Ches E 44 D3
Diss Norf 39 H7
Disserth Powys 25 C7
Distington Cumb 56 D2
Ditchampton Wilts 9 A9
Ditcheat Som 16 H3
Ditchingham Norf 39 F9
Ditchling E Sus 12 E2
Ditherington Shrops 33 D11
Dittisham Devon 5 F9
Ditton Halton 43 D7
Ditton Kent 20 F4
Ditton Green Cambs 30 C3
Ditton Priors Shrops 34 G2
Divach Highld 81 A6
Divlyn Carms 24 E4
Dixton Glos 26 E6
Dixton Mon 26 G2
Dobcross Gtr Man 44 B3
Dobwalls Corn 4 E3
Doc Penfro = Pembroke Dock Pembs 22 F4
Doccombe Devon 5 C8
Dochfour Ho. Highld 87 H9
Dochgarroch Highld 87 G9
Docking Norf 38 B3
Docklow Hereford 26 C2
Dockray Cumb 56 D5
Dockroyd W Yorks 50 F6
Dodburn Borders 61 C10
Doddinghurst Essex 20 B2
Doddington Cambs 37 F9
Doddington Kent 20 F6
Doddington Lincs 46 E3
Doddington Northumb 71 G8
Doddington Shrops 34 H2
Doddiscombsleigh Devon 5 C9
Dodford Northants 28 B3
Dodford Worcs 26 A6
Dodington S Glos 16 C4
Dodleston Ches W 42 F6
Dods Leigh Staffs 34 B6
Dodworth S Yorks 45 B7
Doe Green Warr 43 D8
Doe Lea Derbys 45 F8
Dog Village Devon 7 G8
Dogdyke Lincs 46 G6
Dogmersfield Hants 18 F4
Dogridge Wilts 17 C7
Dogsthorpe Pboro 37 E7
Dol-fôr Powys 32 E4
Dôl-y-Bont Ceredig 32 G2
Dol-y-cannau Powys 25 D9
Dolanog Powys 33 D6
Dolau Powys 25 B8
Dolau Rhondda 14 C5
Dolbenmaen Gwyn 41 F7
Dolfach Powys 32 E5
Dolfor Powys 33 G7
Dolgarrog Conwy 41 D9
Dolgellau Gwyn 32 D3
Dolgran Carms 23 C9
Dolhendre Gwyn 41 G10
Doll Highld 93 J11
Dollar Clack 76 H2
Dolley Green Powys 25 B9
Dollwen Ceredig 32 G2
Dolphin Flint 42 E4
Dolphinholme Lancs 49 D5
Dolphinton S Lanark 69 F10
Dolton Devon 6 E4
Dolwen Conwy 41 C10
Dolwen Powys 32 E5
Dolwyd Conwy 41 C10
Dolwyddelan Conwy 41 E9
Dolyhir Powys 25 C9
Doncaster S Yorks 45 B9
Dones Green Ches W 43 E9
Donhead St Andrew Wilts 9 B8
Donhead St Mary Wilts 9 B8
Donibristle Fife 69 B10
Donington Lincs 37 B8
Donington on Bain Lincs 46 D6
Donington South Ing Lincs 37 B8
Donisthorpe Leics 35 D9
Donkey Town Sur 18 E6
Donnington Glos 27 F8
Donnington Hereford 26 E4
Donnington Shrops 34 E1
Donnington Telford 34 D3
Donnington W Berks 17 E11
Donnington W Sus 11 D7
Donnington Wood Telford 34 D3
Donyatt Som 8 C2
Doonfoot S Ayrs 66 E6
Dorback Lodge Highld 82 B2
Dorchester Dorset 8 E5
Dorchester Oxon 18 B2
Dordon Warks 35 E8
Dore S Yorks 45 D7
Dores Highld 87 H8
Dorking Sur 19 G8
Dormansland Sur 12 B3
Dormanstown Redcar 59 D6
Dormington Hereford 26 D2
Dormston Worcs 26 C6
Dornal S Ayrs 54 B5
Dorney Bucks 18 D6
Dornie Highld 85 F13
Dornoch Highld 87 C10
Dornock Dumfries 61 G8
Dorrery Highld 94 E2
Dorridge W Mid 35 H7
Dorrington Lincs 46 G4
Dorrington Shrops 33 E10
Dorsington Warks 27 D8
Dorstone Hereford 25 D10
Dorton Bucks 28 G3
Dorusduain Highld 80 A1
Dosthill Staffs 35 F8
Dottery Dorset 8 E3
Doublebois Corn 4 E2
Dougarie N Ayrs 66 C1
Doughton Glos 16 B5
Douglas IoM 48 E3
Douglas S Lanark 69 G7
Douglas & Angus Dundee 77 D7
Douglas Water S Lanark 69 G7
Douglas West S Lanark 69 G7
Douglastown Angus 77 C7
Doulting Som 16 G3
Dounby Orkney 95 F3
Doune Highld 92 J7
Doune Stirling 75 G10
Doune Park Aberds 89 B7
Douneside Aberds 82 C6
Dounie Highld 87 B8
Dounreay Highld 93 C12
Dousland Devon 4 E6
Dovaston Shrops 33 C9
Dove Holes Derbys 44 E4
Dovenby Cumb 56 C2
Dover Kent 21 G10
Dovercourt Essex 31 E9
Doverdale Worcs 26 B5
Doveridge Derbys 35 B7
Doversgreen Sur 19 G9
Dowally Perth 76 C3
Dowbridge Lancs 49 F4
Dowdeswell Glos 26 G6
Dowlais M Tydf 25 H7
Dowland Devon 6 E4
Dowlish Wake Som 8 C2
Down Ampney Glos 17 B8
Down Hatherley Glos 26 F5
Down St Mary Devon 7 F6
Down Thomas Devon 4 F6
Downcraig Ferry N Ayrs 73 H10
Downderry Corn 4 F4
Downe London 19 E11
Downend IoW 10 F4
Downend S Glos 16 D3
Downend W Berks 17 D11
Downfield Dundee 76 D6
Downgate Corn 4 D4
Downham Essex 20 B4
Downham Lancs 50 E3
Downham Northumb 71 G7
Downham Market Norf 38 E2
Downhead Som 16 G3
Downhill Perth 76 D3
Downhill T&W 63 H9
Downholland Cross Lancs 42 B6
Downholme N Yorks 58 G2
Downies Aberds 83 D11
Downley Bucks 18 B5
Downside Som 16 G3
Downside Sur 19 F8
Downton Hants 10 E1
Downton Wilts 9 B10
Downton on the Rock Hereford 25 A11
Dowsby Lincs 37 C7
Dowsdale Lincs 37 D8
Dowthwaitehead Cumb 56 D5
Doxey Staffs 34 C5
Doxford Northumb 63 A7
Doxford Park T&W 58 A4
Doynton S Glos 16 D4
Draffan S Lanark 68 F6
Dragonby N Lincs 46 A3
Drakeland Corner Devon 5 F6
Drakemyre N Ayrs 66 A5
Drake's Broughton Worcs 26 D6
Drakes Cross Worcs 35 H6
Drakewalls Corn 4 D5
Draughton N Yorks 50 D6
Draughton Northants 36 H3
Drax N Yorks 52 G2
Draycote Warks 27 A11
Draycott Derbys 35 B10
Draycott Glos 27 E8
Draycott Som 15 F10
Draycott in the Clay Staffs 35 C7
Draycott in the Moors Staffs 34 A5
Drayford Devon 7 E6
Drayton Leics 36 F4
Drayton Lincs 37 B8
Drayton Norf 39 D7
Drayton Oxon 17 B11
Drayton Oxon 27 D11
Drayton Ptsmth 10 D5
Drayton Som 8 B3
Drayton Worcs 34 H5
Drayton Bassett Staffs 35 E7
Drayton Beauchamp Bucks 28 G6
Drayton Parslow Bucks 28 F5
Drayton St Leonard Oxon 18 B1
Dre-fach Carms 24 G3
Dre-fach Ceredig 23 B10
Drebley N Yorks 51 D6
Dreemskerry IoM 48 C4
Dreenhill Pembs 22 E4
Drefach Carms 23 C8
Drefach Carms 23 E10
Drefelin Carms 23 C8
Dreghorn N Ayrs 67 C6
Drellingore Kent 21 G9
Drem E Loth 70 C4
Dresden Stoke 34 A5
Dreumasdal W Isles 84 E2
Drewsteignton Devon 7 G6
Driby Lincs 47 E7
Driffield E Yorks 52 D6
Driffield Glos 17 B7
Drigg Cumb 56 G2
Drighlington W Yorks 51 G8
Drimnin Highld 79 F8
Drimpton Dorset 8 D3
Drimsynie Argyll 74 G4
Drinisiadar W Isles 90 H6
Drinkstone Suff 30 B6
Drinkstone Green Suff 30 B6
Drishaig Argyll 74 F4
Drissaig Argyll 73 B8
Drochil Borders 69 F10
Drointon Staffs 34 C6
Droitwich Spa Worcs 26 B5
Droman Highld 92 D4
Dron Perth 76 F4
Dronfield Derbys 45 E7
Dronfield Woodhouse Derbys 45 E7
Drongan E Ayrs 67 E7
Dronley Angus 76 D6
Droxford Hants 10 C5
Droylsden Gtr Man 44 C3
Druid Denb 32 A6
Druidston Pembs 22 E3
Druimarbin Highld 80 F2
Druimavuic Argyll 74 C3
Druimdrishaig Argyll 72 F6
Druimindarroch Highld 79 C9
Druimyeon More Argyll 65 C7
Drum Argyll 73 F8
Drum Perth 76 G3
Drumbeg Highld 92 F4
Drumblade Aberds 88 D5
Drumblair Aberds 89 D6
Drumbuie Dumfries 55 A8
Drumbuie Highld 85 E12
Drumburgh Cumb 61 H8
Drumburn Dumfries 60 G5
Drumchapel Glasgow 68 C4
Drumchardine Highld 87 G8
Drumchork Highld 91 J13
Drumclog S Lanark 68 G5
Drumderfit Highld 87 F9
Drumeldrie Fife 77 G7
Drumelzier Borders 69 G10
Drumfearn Highld 85 G11
Drumgask Highld 81 D8
Drumgley Angus 77 B7
Drumguish Highld 81 D9
Drumin Moray 88 E1
Drumlasie Aberds 83 C8
Drumlemble Argyll 65 G7
Drumligair Aberds 83 B11
Drumlithie Aberds 83 E9
Drummoddie Dumfries 54 E6
Drummond Highld 87 E9
Drummore Dumfries 54 F4
Drummuir Moray 88 D3
Drummuir Castle Moray 88 D3
Drumnadrochit Highld 81 A7
Drumnagorrach Moray 88 C5
Drumoak Aberds 83 D9
Drumpark Dumfries 60 E4
Drumphail Dumfries 54 C5
Drumrash Dumfries 55 B9
Drumrunie Highld 92 J4
Drums Aberds 89 F9
Drumsallie Highld 80 F1
Drumstinchall Dumfries 55 D11
Drumsturdy Angus 77 D7
Drumtochty Castle Aberds 83 F8
Drumtroddan Dumfries 54 E6
Drumuie Highld 85 D9
Drumuillie Highld 81 A11
Drumvaich Stirling 75 G9
Drumwhindle Aberds 89 E9
Drunkendub Angus 77 C9
Drury Flint 42 F5
Drury Square Norf 38 D5
Dry Doddington Lincs 46 H2
Dry Drayton Cambs 29 B10
Drybeck Cumb 57 E8
Drybridge Moray 88 B4
Drybridge N Ayrs 67 C6
Drybrook Glos 26 G3
Dryburgh Borders 70 G4
Dryhope Borders 61 A8
Drylaw Edin 69 C11
Drym Corn 2 F5
Drymen Stirling 68 B3
Drymuir Aberds 89 D9
Drynoch Highld 85 E9
Dryslwyn Carms 23 D10
Dryton Shrops 34 E1
Dubford Aberds 89 B8
Dubton Angus 77 B8
Duchally Highld 92 H6
Duchlage Argyll 68 B2
Duck Corner Suff 31 D10
Duckington Ches W 43 G7
Ducklington Oxon 27 H10
Duckmanton Derbys 45 E8
Duck's Cross Bedford 29 C8
Duddenhoe End Essex 29 E11
Duddingston Edin 69 C11
Duddington Northants 36 E5
Duddleswell E Sus 12 D3
Duddo Northumb 71 F8
Duddon Ches W 43 F8
Duddon Bridge Cumb 56 H4
Dudleston Shrops 33 B9
Dudleston Heath Shrops 33 B9
Dudley T&W 63 F8
Dudley W Mid 34 F5
Dudley Port W Mid 34 F5
Duffield Derbys 35 A9
Duffryn Neath 14 B4
Duffryn Newport 15 C8
Dufftown Moray 88 E3
Duffus Moray 88 B1
Dufton Cumb 57 D8
Duggleby N Yorks 52 C4
Duirinish Highld 85 E12
Duisdalemore Highld 85 G12
Duisky Highld 80 F2
Dukestown Bl Gwent 25 G8
Dukinfield Gtr Man 44 C3
Dulas Anglesey 40 B6
Dulcote Som 16 G2
Dulford Devon 7 F9
Dull Perth 75 C11
Dullatur N Lanark 68 C6
Dullingham Cambs 30 C3
Dulnain Bridge Highld 82 A1
Duloe Bedford 29 B8
Duloe Corn 4 F3
Dulsie Highld 87 G12
Dulverton Som 7 D8
Dulwich London 19 D10
Dumbarton W Dunb 68 C2
Dumbleton Glos 27 E7
Dumcrieff Dumfries 61 C7
Dumfries Dumfries 60 F5
Dumgoyne Stirling 68 B4
Dummer Hants 18 G2
Dumpford W Sus 11 B7
Dumpton Kent 21 E10
Dun Angus 77 B9
Dun Charlabhaigh W Isles 90 C6
Dunain Ho. Highld 87 G9
Dunalastair Perth 75 B10
Dunan Highld 85 F10
Dunans Argyll 73 D9
Dunball Som 15 G9
Dunbar E Loth 70 C5
Dunbeath Highld 94 H3
Dunbeg Argyll 79 H11
Dunblane Stirling 75 G10
Dunbog Fife 76 F5
Duncanston Highld 87 F8
Duncanstone Aberds 83 A7
Dunchurch Warks 27 A11
Duncote Northants 28 C3
Duncow Dumfries 60 E5
Duncraggan Stirling 75 G8
Duncrievie Perth 76 G4
Duncton W Sus 11 C8
Dundas Ho. Orkney 95 K5
Dundee Dundee 77 D7
Dundeugh Dumfries 67 H8
Dundon Som 8 A3
Dundonald S Ayrs 67 C6
Dundonnell Highld 86 C3
Dundonnell Hotel Highld 86 C3
Dundonnell House Highld 86 C4
Dundraw Cumb 56 B4
Dundreggan Highld 80 B5
Dundreggan Lodge Highld 80 B5
Dundrennan Dumfries 55 E10
Dundry N Som 16 E2
Dunecht Aberds 83 C9
Dunfermline Fife 69 B9
Dunfield Glos 17 B8
Dunford Bridge S Yorks 44 B5
Dungworth S Yorks 44 D6
Dunham Notts 46 E2
Dunham-on-the-Hill Ches W 43 E7
Dunham Town Gtr Man 43 D10
Dunhampton Worcs 26 B5
Dunholme Lincs 46 E4
Dunino Fife 77 F8
Dunipace Falk 69 B7
Dunira Perth 75 E10
Dunkeld Perth 76 C3
Dunkerton Bath 16 F4
Dunkeswell Devon 7 F10
Dunkeswick N Yorks 51 E9
Dunkirk Kent 21 F7
Dunkirk Norf 39 C8
Dunk's Green Kent 20 F3
Dunlappie Angus 83 G7
Dunley Hants 17 F11
Dunley Worcs 26 B4
Dunlichity Lodge Highld 87 H9
Dunlop E Ayrs 67 B7
Dunmaglass Lodge Highld 81 A7
Dunmore Argyll 72 G6
Dunmore Falk 69 B7
Dunnet Highld 94 C4
Dunnichen Angus 77 C8
Dunninald Angus 77 B10
Dunning Perth 76 F3
Dunnington E Yorks 53 D7
Dunnington Warks 27 C7
Dunnington York 52 D2
Dunnockshaw Lancs 50 G4
Dunollie Argyll 79 H11
Dunoon Argyll 73 F10
Dunragit Dumfries 54 D4
Dunrostan Argyll 72 E6
Duns Borders 70 E6
Duns Tew Oxon 27 F11
Dunsby Lincs 37 C7
Dunscore Dumfries 60 E4
Dunscroft S Yorks 45 B10
Dunsdale Redcar 59 E7
Dunsden Green Oxon 18 D4
Dunsfold Sur 19 H7
Dunsford Devon 5 C9
Dunshalt Fife 76 F5
Dunshillock Aberds 89 D9
Dunskey Ho. Dumfries 54 D3
Dunsley N Yorks 59 E9
Dunsmore Bucks 28 H5
Dunsop Bridge Lancs 50 D2
Dunstable C Beds 29 F7
Dunstall Staffs 35 C7
Dunstall Common Worcs 26 D5
Dunstall Green Suff 30 B4
Dunstan Northumb 63 B8
Dunstan Steads Northumb 63 A8
Dunster Som 7 B8
Duston Lincs 46 F4
Dunston Norf 39 E8
Dunston Staffs 34 D5
Dunston T&W 63 G8
Dunsville S Yorks 45 B10
Dunswell E Yorks 53 F6
Dunsyre S Lanark 69 F9
Dunterton Devon 4 D4
Duntisbourne Abbots Glos 26 H6
Duntisbourne Leer Glos 26 H6
Duntisbourne Rouse Glos 26 H6
Duntish Dorset 8 D5
Duntocher W Dunb 68 C3
Dunton Bucks 28 F5
Dunton C Beds 29 D9
Dunton Norf 38 B4
Dunton Bassett Leics 35 F11
Dunton Green Kent 20 F2
Dunton Wayletts Essex 20 B3
Duntulm Highld 85 A9
Dunure S Ayrs 66 E5
Dunvant Swansea 23 G10
Dunvegan Highld 84 D7
Dunwich Suff 31 A11
Dunwood Staffs 44 G3
Dupplin Castle Perth 76 F3
Durdar Cumb 56 A6
Durgates E Sus 12 C5
Durham Durham 58 B3
Durisdeer Dumfries 60 C4
Durisdeermill Dumfries 60 C4
Durkar W Yorks 51 H9
Durleigh Som 15 H8
Durley Hants 10 C4
Durley Wilts 17 E9
Durnamuck Highld 86 B3
Durness Highld 92 C7
Durno Aberds 83 A9
Duror Highld 74 B2
Durran Argyll 73 C8
Durran Highld 94 D3
Durrington W Sus 11 D10
Durrington Wilts 17 G8
Dursley Glos 16 B4
Durston Som 8 B1
Durweston Dorset 9 D7
Dury Shetland 96 G6
Duston Northants 28 B4
Duthil Highld 81 A11
Dutlas Powys 33 H8
Duton Hill Essex 30 F3
Dutson Corn 4 C4
Dutton Ches W 43 E8
Duxford Cambs 29 D11
Duxford Oxon 17 B10
Dwygyfylchi Conwy 41 C9
Dwyran Anglesey 40 D6
Dyce Aberdeen 83 B10
Dye House Northumb 62 H5
Dyffryn Bridgend 14 B4
Dyffryn Carms 23 D8
Dyffryn Pembs 22 C4
Dyffryn Ardudwy Gwyn 32 C1
Dyffryn Castell Ceredig 32 G3
Dyffryn Ceidrych Carms 24 F4
Dyffryn Cellwen Neath 24 H5
Dyke Lincs 37 C7
Dyke Moray 87 F12
Dykehead Angus 76 A6
Dykehead N Lanark 69 E7
Dykehead Stirling 75 H8
Dykelands Aberds 83 G9
Dykends Angus 76 B5
Dykeside Aberds 89 D7
Dykesmains N Ayrs 66 B5
Dylife Powys 32 F4
Dymchurch Kent 13 D9
Dymock Glos 26 E4
Dyrham S Glos 16 D4
Dysart Fife 70 A2
Dyserth Denb 42 E3

E

Eachwick Northumb 63 F7
Eadar Dha Fhadhail W Isles 90 D5
Eagland Hill Lancs 49 E4
Eagle Lincs 46 F2
Eagle Barnsdale Lincs 46 F2
Eagle Moor Lincs 46 F2
Eaglescliffe Stockton 58 E5
Eaglesfield Cumb 56 D2
Eaglesfield Dumfries 61 F8
Eaglesham E Renf 68 E4
Eaglethorpe Northants 37 F6
Eairy IoM 48 E2
Eakley Lanes M Keynes 28 C5
Eakring Notts 45 F10
Ealand N Lincs 45 A11
Ealing London 19 C8
Eals Northumb 62 H2
Eamont Bridge Cumb 57 D7
Earby Lancs 50 E5
Earcroft Blackburn 50 G2
Eardington Shrops 34 F3
Eardisland Hereford 25 C11
Eardisley Hereford 25 D10
Eardiston Shrops 33 C9
Eardiston Worcs 26 B3
Earith Cambs 29 A10
Earl Shilton Leics 35 F10
Earl Soham Suff 31 B9
Earl Sterndale Derbys 44 F4
Earl Stonham Suff 31 C8
Earle Northumb 71 H8
Earley Wokingham 18 D4
Earlham Norf 39 E8
Earlish Highld 85 B8
Earls Barton Northants 28 B5
Earls Colne Essex 30 F5
Earl's Croome Worcs 26 D5
Earl's Green Suff 31 B7
Earlsdon W Mid 35 H9
Earlsferry Fife 77 H7
Earlsfield Lincs 36 B5
Earlsford Aberds 89 E8
Earlsheaton W Yorks 51 G8
Earlsmill Moray 87 F12
Earlston Borders 70 G4
Earlston E Ayrs 67 C7
Earlswood Mon 15 B10
Earlswood Sur 19 G9
Earlswood Warks 27 A8
Earnley W Sus 11 E7
Earsairidh W Isles 84 J2
Earsdon T&W 63 F9
Earsham Norf 39 G9
Earswick York 52 D2
Eartham W Sus 11 D8
Easby N Yorks 58 F2
Easby N Yorks 59 F6
Easdale Argyll 72 B6
Easebourne W Sus 11 B7
Easenhall Warks 35 H10
Eashing Sur 18 G6
Easington Bucks 28 G3
Easington Durham 58 B5
Easington E Yorks 53 H9
Easington Northumb 71 G10
Easington Oxon 18 B3
Easington Oxon 27 E11
Easington Redcar 59 E8
Easington Colliery Durham 58 B5
Easington Lane T&W 58 B4
Easingwold N Yorks 51 C11
Easole Street Kent 21 F9
Eassie Angus 76 C6
East Aberthaw V Glam 14 E6
East Adderbury Oxon 27 E11
East Allington Devon 5 G8
East Anstey Devon 7 D7
East Appleton N Yorks 58 G3
East Ardsley W Yorks 51 G9
East Ashling W Sus 11 D7
East Auchronie Aberds 83 C10
East Ayton N Yorks 59 H10
East Bank Bl Gwent 25 H9
East Barkwith Lincs 46 D5
East Barming Kent 20 F4
East Barnby N Yorks 59 E9
East Barnet London 19 B9
East Barns E Loth 70 C6
East Barsham Norf 38 B5
East Beckham Norf 39 B7
East Bedfont London 19 D7
East Bergholt Suff 31 E7
East Bilney Norf 38 D5
East Blatchington E Sus 12 F3
East Boldre Hants 10 D2
East Brent Som 15 F9
East Bridgford Notts 36 A2
East Buckland Devon 6 C5
East Budleigh Devon 7 H9
East Burrafirth Shetland 96 H5
East Burton Dorset 9 F7
East Butsfield Durham 58 B2
East Butterwick N Lincs 46 B2
East Cairnbeg Aberds 83 F9
East Calder W Loth 69 D9
East Carleton Norf 39 E7
East Carlton Northants 36 G4
East Carlton W Yorks 51 E8
East Chaldon Dorset 9 F6
East Challow Oxon 17 C10
East Chiltington E Sus 12 E2
East Chinnock Som 8 C3
East Chisenbury Wilts 17 F8
East Clandon Sur 19 F7
East Claydon Bucks 28 F4
East Clyne Highld 93 J12
East Coker Som 8 C4
East Combe Som 7 C10
East Common N Yorks 52 F2
East Compton Som 16 G3
East Cottingwith E Yorks 52 E3
East Cowes IoW 10 E4
East Cowick E Yorks 52 G2
East Cowton N Yorks 58 F4
East Cramlington Northumb 63 F8
East Cranmore Som 16 G3
East Creech Dorset 9 F8
East Croachy Highld 81 A8
East Croftmore Highld 81 B11
East Curthwaite Cumb 56 B5
East Dean E Sus 12 G4
East Dean Hants 10 B1
East Dean W Sus 11 C8
East Down Devon 6 B5
East Drayton Notts 45 E11
East Ella Hull 53 G6
East End Dorset 9 E8
East End E Yorks 53 G8
East End Hants 10 B5
East End Hants 10 E2
East End Hants 17 E11
East End Herts 29 F11
East End Kent 13 C7
East End N Som 15 D10
East End Oxon 27 G10
East Farleigh Kent 20 F4
East Farndon Northants 36 G3
East Ferry Lincs 46 C2
East Fortune E Loth 70 C4
East Garston W Berks 17 D10
East Ginge Oxon 17 C11
East Goscote Leics 36 D2
East Grafton Wilts 17 E9
East Grimstead Wilts 9 B11
East Grinstead W Sus 12 C2
East Guldeford E Sus 13 D8
East Haddon Northants 28 B3
East Hagbourne Oxon 18 C2
East Halton N Lincs 53 H7
East Ham London 19 C11
East Hanney Oxon 17 B11
East Hanningfield Essex 20 A4
East Hardwick W Yorks 51 H10
East Harling Norf 38 G5
East Harlsey N Yorks 58 G5
East Harnham Wilts 9 B10
East Harptree Bath 16 F2
East Hartford Northumb 63 F8
East Harting W Sus 11 C6
East Hatley Cambs 29 C9
East Hauxwell N Yorks 58 G2
East Haven Angus 77 D8
East Heckington Lincs 37 A7
East Hedleyhope Durham 58 B2
East Hendred Oxon 17 C11
East Herrington T&W 58 A4
East Heslerton N Yorks 52 B5
East Hoathly E Sus 12 E4
East Horrington Som 16 G2
East Horsley Sur 19 F7
East Horton Northumb 71 G9
East Huntspill Som 15 G9
East Hyde C Beds 29 G8
East Ilkerton Devon 6 B6
East Ilsley W Berks 17 C11
East Keal Lincs 47 F7
East Kennett Wilts 17 E8
East Keswick W Yorks 51 E9
East Kilbride S Lanark 68 E5
East Kirkby Lincs 47 F7
East Knapton N Yorks 52 B4
East Knighton Dorset 9 F7
East Knoyle Wilts 9 A7
East Kyloe Northumb 71 G9
East Lambrook Som 8 C3
East Lamington Highld 87 D10
East Langdon Kent 21 G10
East Langton Leics 36 F3
East Langwell Highld 93 J10
East Lavant W Sus 11 D7
East Lavington W Sus 11 C8
East Layton N Yorks 58 F2
East Leake Notts 36 C1
East Learmouth Northumb 71 G7
East Leigh Devon 6 F5
East Lexham Norf 38 D4
East Lilburn Northumb 62 A6
East Linton E Loth 70 C4
East Liss Hants 11 B6
East Looe Corn 4 F3
East Lound N Lincs 45 C11
East Lulworth Dorset 9 F7
East Lutton N Yorks 52 C5
East Lydford Som 8 A4
East Mains Aberds 83 D8
East Malling Kent 20 F4
East March Angus 77 D7
East Marden W Sus 11 C7
East Markham Notts 45 E11
East Marton N Yorks 50 D5
East Meon Hants 10 B5
East Mere Devon 7 E8
East Mersea Essex 31 G7
East Mey Highld 94 C5
East Molesey Sur 19 E8
East Morden Dorset 9 E8
East Morton W Yorks 51 E6
East Ness N Yorks 52 B2
East Newton E Yorks 53 F8
East Norton Leics 36 E3
East Nynehead Som 7 D10
East Oakley Hants 18 F2
East Ogwell Devon 5 D9
East Orchard Dorset 9 C7
East Ord Northumb 71 E8
East Panson Devon 6 G2
East Peckham Kent 20 G3
East Pennard Som 16 H2
East Perry Cambs 29 B8
East Portlemouth Devon 5 H8
East Prawle Devon 5 H8
East Preston W Sus 11 D9
East Putford Devon 6 E2
East Quantoxhead Som 7 B10
East Rainton T&W 58 B4
East Ravendale NE Lincs 46 C6
East Raynham Norf 38 C4
East Rhidorroch Lodge Highld 86 B5
East Rigton W Yorks 51 E9
East Rounton N Yorks 58 F5
East Row N Yorks 59 E9
East Rudham Norf 38 C4
East Runton Norf 39 A7
East Ruston Norf 39 C9
East Saltoun E Loth 70 D3
East Sleekburn Northumb 63 E8
East Somerton Norf 39 D10
East Stockwith Lincs 45 C11
East Stoke Dorset 9 F7
East Stoke Notts 45 H11
East Stour Dorset 9 B7
East Stourmouth Kent 21 E9
East Stowford Devon 6 D5
East Stratton Hants 18 H2
East Studdal Kent 21 G10
East Suisnish Highld 85 E10
East Taphouse Corn 4 E2
East-the-Water Devon 6 D3
East Thirston Northumb 63 D7
East Tilbury Thurrock 20 D3
East Tisted Hants 10 A6
East Torrington Lincs 46 D5
East Tuddenham Norf 39 D6
East Tytherley Hants 10 B1
East Tytherton Wilts 16 D6
East Village Devon 7 F7
East Wall Shrops 33 F11
East Walton Norf 38 D3
East Wellow Hants 10 B2
East Wemyss Fife 76 H6
East Whitburn W Loth 69 D8
East Williamston Pembs 22 F5
East Winch Norf 38 D2
East Winterslow Wilts 9 A11
East Wittering W Sus 11 E6
East Witton N Yorks 58 H2
East Woodburn Northumb 62 E5
East Woodhay Hants 17 E11
East Worldham Hants 18 H4
East Worlington Devon 7 E6
East Worthing W Sus 11 D10
Eastbourne E Sus 12 G5
Eastbridge Suff 31 B11
Eastburn W Yorks 50 E6
Eastbury London 19 B7
Eastbury W Berks 17 D10
Eastby N Yorks 50 D6
Eastchurch Kent 20 D6
Eastcombe Glos 16 A5
Eastcote London 19 C8
Eastcote Northants 28 C3
Eastcote W Mid 35 H7
Eastcott Corn 6 E1
Eastcott Wilts 17 F7
Eastcourt Wilts 16 B6
Eastcourt Wilts 17 E9
Easter Ardross Highld 87 D9
Easter Balmoral Aberds 82 D4
Easter Boleskine Highld 81 A7
Easter Compton S Glos 16 C2
Easter Cringate Stirling 68 B6
Easter Davoch Aberds 82 C6
Easter Earshaig Dumfries 60 C6
Easter Fearn Highld 87 C9
Easter Galcantray Highld 87 G11
Easter Howgate Midloth 69 D11
Easter Howlaws Borders 70 F6
Easter Kinkell Highld 87 F8
Easter Lednathie Angus 76 A6
Easter Milton Highld 87 F12
Easter Moniack Highld 87 G8
Easter Ord Aberdeen 83 C10
Easter Quarff Shetland 96 K6
Easter Rhynd Perth 76 F4
Easter Row Stirling 75 H10
Easter Silverford Aberds 89 B7
Easter Skeld Shetland 96 J5
Easter Whyntie Aberds 88 B6
Eastergate W Sus 11 D8
Easterhouse Glasgow 68 D5
Eastern Green W Mid 35 G8

Glenhurich Highld 79 E11
Glenkerry Borders 61 B8
Glenkiln Dumfries 60 F4
Glenkindie Aberds 82 B6
Glenlatterach Moray 88 C1
Glenlee Dumfries 55 A9
Glenlichorn Perth 75 F10
Glenlivet Moray 82 A3
Glenlochsie Perth 82 F2
Glenloig N Ayrs 66 C2
Glenluce Dumfries 54 D5
Glenmallan Argyll 74 H5
Glenmarksie Highld 86 F6
Glenmassan Argyll 73 E10
Glenmavis N Lanark 68 D6
Glenmaye IoM 48 E2
Glenmidge Dumfries 60 E4
Glenmore Argyll 73 B7
Glenmore Highld 85 D9
Glenmore Lodge Highld 82 C1
Glenmoy Angus 77 A7
Glenogil Angus 77 A7
Glenprosen Lodge Angus 82 G4
Glenprosen Village Angus 82 G5
Glenquiech Angus 77 A7
Glenreasdell Mains Argyll 73 H7
Glenree N Ayrs 66 D2
Glenridding Cumb 56 E5
Glenrossal Highld 92 J7
Glenrothes Fife 76 G5
Glensanda Highld 79 G11
Glensaugh Aberds 83 F8
Glenshero Lodge Highld 81 D7
Glenstockadale Dumfries 54 C3
Glenstriven Argyll 73 F9
Glentaggart S Lanark 69 H7
Glentham Lincs 46 C4
Glentirranmuir Stirling 68 A5
Glenton Aberds 83 A8
Glentress Borders 69 G11
Glentromie Lodge Highld 81 D9
Glentrool Village Dumfries 54 B6
Glentruan IoM 48 B4
Glentruim House Highld 81 D8
Glentworth Lincs 46 D3
Glenuig Highld 79 D9
Glenurquhart Highld 87 E10
Glespin S Lanark 69 H7
Gletness Shetland 96 H6
Glewstone Hereford 26 F2
Glinton Pboro 37 E7
Glooston Leics 36 F3
Glororum Northumb 71 G10
Glossop Derbys 44 C4
Gloster Hill Northumb 63 C8
Gloucester Glos 26 G5
Gloup Shetland 96 C7
Glusburn N Yorks 50 E6
Glutt Lodge Highld 93 F12
Glutton Bridge Staffs 44 F4
Glympton Oxon 27 F11
Glyn-Ceiriog Wrex 33 B8
Glyn-cywarch Gwyn 41 G8
Glyn Ebwy = Ebbw Vale Bl Gwent 25 H8
Glyn-neath = Glynedd Neath 24 H5
Glynarthen Ceredig 23 B8
Glynbrochan Powys 32 G5
Glyncoch Rhondda 14 B6
Glyncorrwg Neath 14 B4
Glynde E Sus 12 F3
Glyndebourne E Sus 12 E3
Glyndyfrdwy Denb 33 A7
Glynedd = Glyn-neath Neath 24 H5
Glynogwr Bridgend 14 C5
Glyntaff Rhondda 14 C6
Glyntawe Powys 24 G5
Gnosall Staffs 34 C4
Gnosall Heath Staffs 34 C4
Goadby Leics 36 F3
Goadby Marwood Leics 36 C3
Goat Lees Kent 21 G7
Goatacre Wilts 17 D7
Goathill Dorset 8 C5
Goathland N Yorks 59 F9
Goathurst Som 8 A1
Gobernuisgach Lodge Highld 92 E7
Gobhaig W Isles 90 G5
Gobowen Shrops 33 B9
Godalming Sur 18 G6
Godley Gtr Man 44 C3
Godmanchester Cambs 29 A9
Godmanstone Dorset 8 E5
Godmersham Kent 21 F7
Godney Som 15 G10
Godolphin Cross Corn 2 F5
Godre'r-graig Neath 24 H4
Godshill Hants 9 C10
Godshill IoW 10 F4
Godstone Sur 19 F10
Godwinscroft Hants 9 E10
Goetre Mon 25 H10
Goferydd Anglesey 40 B4
Goff's Oak Herts 19 A10
Gogar Edin 69 C10
Goginan Ceredig 32 G2
Golan Gwyn 41 F7
Golant Corn 4 F2
Golberdon Corn 4 D4
Golborne Gtr Man 43 C9
Golcar W Yorks 51 H7
Gold Hill Norf 37 F11
Goldcliff Newport 15 C9
Golden Cross E Sus 12 E4
Golden Green Kent 20 G3
Golden Grove Carms 23 E10
Golden Hill Hants 10 E1
Golden Pot Hants 18 G4
Golden Valley Glos 26 F6
Goldenhill Stoke 44 G2
Golders Green London 19 C9
Goldhanger Essex 30 H6
Golding Shrops 33 E11
Goldington Bedford 29 C7
Goldsborough N Yorks 51 D9
Goldsborough N Yorks 59 E9
Goldsithney Corn 2 F4
Goldsworthy Devon 6 D2
Goldthorpe S Yorks 45 B8
Gollanfield Highld 87 F11
Golspie Highld 93 J11
Golval Highld 93 C11
Gomeldon Wilts 17 H8
Gomersal W Yorks 51 G8
Gomshall Sur 19 G7
Gonalston Notts 45 H10
Gonfirth Shetland 96 G5
Good Easter Essex 30 G3
Gooderstone Norf 38 E3
Goodleigh Devon 6 C5
Goodmanham E Yorks 52 E4
Goodnestone Kent 21 E7
Goodnestone Kent 21 F9
Goodrich Hereford 26 G2
Goodrington Torbay 5 F9
Goodshaw Lancs 50 G4
Goodwick = Wdig Pembs 22 C4
Goodworth Clatford Hants 17 G10
Goole E Yorks 52 G3
Goonbell Corn 2 E6
Goonhavern Corn 3 D6
Goose Eye W Yorks 50 E6
Goose Green Gtr Man 43 B8
Goose Green Norf 39 G7
Goose Green W Sus 11 C10
Gooseham Corn 6 E1
Goosey Oxon 17 B10
Goosnargh Lancs 50 F1
Goostrey Ches E 43 E10
Gorcott Hill Warks 27 B7
Gord Shetland 96 L6
Gordon Borders 70 F5
Gordonbush Highld 93 J11
Gordonsburgh Moray 88 B4
Gordonstoun Moray 88 B1
Gordonstown Aberds 88 C5
Gordonstown Aberds 89 E7
Gore Kent 21 F10
Gore Cross Wilts 17 F7
Gore Pit Essex 30 G5
Gorebridge Midloth 70 D2
Gorefield Cambs 37 D10
Gorey Jersey 11
Gorgie Edin 69 C11
Goring Oxon 18 C3
Goring-by-Sea W Sus 11 D10
Goring Heath Oxon 18 D3
Gorleston-on-Sea Norf 39 E11
Gornalwood W Mid 34 F5
Gorrachie Aberds 89 C7
Gorran Churchtown Corn 3 E8
Gorran Haven Corn 3 E9
Gorrenberry Borders 61 D10
Gors Ceredig 32 H2
Gorse Hill Swindon 17 C8
Gorsedd Flint 42 E4
Gorseinon Swansea 23 G10
Gorseness Orkney 95 G5
Gorsgoch Ceredig 23 A9
Gorslas Carms 23 E10
Gorsley Glos 26 F3
Gorstan Highld 86 E6
Gorstanvorran Highld 79 D11
Gorsteyhill Staffs 43 G10
Gorsty Hill Staffs 35 C7
Gortantaoid Argyll 64 A4
Gorton Gtr Man 44 C2
Gosbeck Suff 31 C8
Gosberton Lincs 37 B8
Gosberton Clough Lincs 37 C7
Gosfield Essex 30 F4
Gosford Hereford 26 B2
Gosforth Cumb 56 F2
Gosforth T&W 63 G8
Gosmore Herts 29 F8
Gosport Hants 10 E5
Gossabrough Shetland 96 E7
Gossington Glos 16 A4
Goswick Northumb 71 F9
Gotham Notts 35 B11
Gotherington Glos 26 F6
Gott Shetland 96 J6
Goudhurst Kent 12 C6
Goulceby Lincs 46 E6
Gourdas Aberds 89 D7
Gourdon Aberds 83 F10
Gourock Invclyd 73 F11
Govan Glasgow 68 D4
Govanhill Glasgow 68 D4
Goveton Devon 5 G8
Govilon Mon 25 G9
Gowanhill Aberds 89 B10
Gowdall E Yorks 52 G2
Gowerton Swansea 23 G10
Gowkhall Fife 69 B9
Gowthorpe E Yorks 52 D3
Goxhill E Yorks 53 E7
Goxhill N Lincs 53 G7
Goxhill Haven N Lincs 53 G7
Goytre Neath 14 C3
Grabhair W Isles 91 F8
Graby Lincs 37 C6
Grade Corn 2 H6
Graffham W Sus 11 C8
Grafham Cambs 29 B8
Grafham Sur 19 G7
Grafton Hereford 25 E11
Grafton N Yorks 51 C10
Grafton Oxon 17 A9
Grafton Shrops 33 D10
Grafton Worcs 26 B2
Grafton Flyford Worcs 26 C6
Grafton Regis Northants 28 D4
Grafton Underwood Northants 36 G5
Grafty Green Kent 20 G5
Graianrhyd Denb 42 G5
Graig Conwy 41 C10
Graig Denb 42 E3
Graig-fechan Denb 42 G4
Grain Medway 20 D5
Grainsby Lincs 46 C6
Grainthorpe Lincs 47 C7
Grampound Corn 3 E8
Grampound Road Corn 3 D8
Gramsdal W Isles 84 C3
Granborough Bucks 28 F4
Granby Notts 36 B3
Grandborough Warks 27 B11
Grandtully Perth 76 B2
Grange Cumb 56 E4
Grange E Ayrs 67 C7
Grange Medway 20 E4
Grange Mers 42 D5
Grange Perth 76 E5
Grange Crossroads Moray 88 C4
Grange Hall Moray 87 E13
Grange Hill Essex 19 B11
Grange Moor W Yorks 51 H8
Grange of Lindores Fife 76 F5
Grange-over-Sands Cumb 49 B4
Grange Villa Durham 58 A3
Grangemill Derbys 44 G6
Grangemouth Falk 69 B8
Grangepans Falk 69 B9
Grangetown Cardiff 15 D7
Grangetown Redcar 59 D6
Granish Highld 81 B11
Gransmoor E Yorks 53 D7
Granston Pembs 22 C3
Grantchester Cambs 29 C11
Grantham Lincs 36 B5
Grantley N Yorks 51 C8
Grantlodge Aberds 83 B9
Granton Dumfries 60 C6
Granton Edin 69 C11
Grantown-on-Spey Highld 82 A2
Grantshouse Borders 71 D7
Grappenhall Warr 43 D9
Grasby Lincs 46 B4
Grasmere Cumb 56 F5
Grasscroft Gtr Man 44 B3
Grassendale Mers 43 D6
Grassholme Durham 57 D11
Grassington N Yorks 50 C6
Grassmoor Derbys 45 F8
Grassthorpe Notts 45 F11
Grateley Hants 17 G9
Gratwich Staffs 34 B6
Graveley Cambs 29 B9
Graveley Herts 29 F9
Gravelly Hill W Mid 35 F7
Gravels Shrops 33 E9
Graven Shetland 96 F6
Graveney Kent 21 E7
Gravesend Herts 29 F11
Gravesend Kent 20 D3
Grayingham Lincs 46 C3
Grayrigg Cumb 57 G7
Grays Thurrock 20 D3
Grayshott Hants 18 H5
Grayswood Sur 11 A8
Graythorp Hrtlpl 58 D6
Grazeley Wokingham 18 E3
Greasbrough S Yorks 45 C8
Greasby Mers 42 D5
Great Abington Cambs 30 D2
Great Addington Northants 28 A6
Great Alne Warks 27 C8
Great Altcar Lancs 42 B6
Great Amwell Herts 29 G10
Great Asby Cumb 57 E8
Great Ashfield Suff 30 B6
Great Ayton N Yorks 59 E6
Great Baddow Essex 20 A4
Great Bardfield Essex 30 E3
Great Barford Bedford 29 C8
Great Barr W Mid 34 F6
Great Barrington Glos 27 G9
Great Barrow Ches W 43 F7
Great Barton Suff 30 B5
Great Barugh N Yorks 52 B3
Great Bavington Northumb 62 E5
Great Bealings Suff 31 D9
Great Bedwyn Wilts 17 E9
Great Bentley Essex 31 F8
Great Billing Northants 28 B5
Great Bircham Norf 38 B3
Great Blakenham Suff 31 C8
Great Blencow Cumb 56 C6
Great Bolas Telford 34 C2
Great Bookham Sur 19 F8
Great Bourton Oxon 27 D11
Great Bowden Leics 36 G3
Great Bradley Suff 30 C3
Great Braxted Essex 30 G5
Great Bricett Suff 31 C7
Great Brickhill Bucks 28 E6
Great Bridge W Mid 34 F5
Great Bridgeford Staffs 34 C4
Great Brington Northants 28 B3
Great Bromley Essex 31 F7
Great Broughton Cumb 56 C2
Great Broughton N Yorks 59 F6
Great Budworth Ches W 43 E9
Great Burdon Darl 58 E4
Great Burgh Sur 19 F9
Great Burstead Essex 20 B3
Great Busby N Yorks 58 F6
Great Canfield Essex 30 G2
Great Carlton Lincs 47 D8
Great Casterton Rutland 36 E6
Great Chart Kent 13 B8
Great Chatwell Staffs 34 D3
Great Chesterford Essex 30 D2
Great Cheverell Wilts 16 F6
Great Chishill Cambs 29 E11
Great Clacton Essex 31 G8
Great Cliff W Yorks 51 H9
Great Clifton Cumb 56 D2
Great Coates NE Lincs 46 B6
Great Comberton Worcs 26 D6
Great Corby Cumb 56 A6
Great Cornard Suff 30 D5
Great Cowden E Yorks 53 E8
Great Coxwell Oxon 17 B9
Great Crakehall N Yorks 58 G3
Great Cransley Northants 36 H4
Great Cressingham Norf 38 E4
Great Crosby Mers 42 C6
Great Cubley Derbys 35 B7
Great Dalby Leics 36 D3
Great Denham Bedford 29 D7
Great Doddington Northants 28 B5
Great Dunham Norf 38 D4
Great Dunmow Essex 30 F3
Great Durnford Wilts 17 H8
Great Easton Essex 30 F3
Great Easton Leics 36 F4
Great Eccleston Lancs 49 E4
Great Edstone N Yorks 52 A3
Great Ellingham Norf 38 F6
Great Elm Som 16 G4
Great Eversden Cambs 29 C10
Great Fencote N Yorks 58 G3
Great Finborough Suff 31 C7
Great Fransham Norf 38 D4
Great Gaddesden Herts 29 G7
Great Gidding Cambs 37 G7
Great Givendale E Yorks 52 D4
Great Glemham Suff 31 B10
Great Glen Leics 36 F2
Great Gonerby Lincs 36 B4
Great Gransden Cambs 29 C9
Great Green Norf 39 G8
Great Green Suff 30 C6
Great Habton N Yorks 52 B3
Great Hale Lincs 37 A7
Great Hallingbury Essex 30 G2
Great Hampden Bucks 18 A5
Great Harrowden Northants 28 A5
Great Harwood Lancs 50 F3
Great Haseley Oxon 18 A3
Great Hatfield E Yorks 53 E7
Great Haywood Staffs 34 C6
Great Heath W Mid 35 G9
Great Heck N Yorks 52 G1
Great Henny Essex 30 E5
Great Hinton Wilts 16 F6
Great Hockham Norf 38 F5
Great Holland Essex 31 G9
Great Horkesley Essex 30 E6
Great Hormead Herts 29 F10
Great Horton W Yorks 51 F7
Great Horwood Bucks 28 E4
Great Houghton Northants 28 C4
Great Houghton S Yorks 45 B8
Great Hucklow Derbys 44 E5
Great Kelk E Yorks 53 D7
Great Kimble Bucks 28 H5
Great Kingshill Bucks 18 B5
Great Langton N Yorks 58 G3
Great Leighs Essex 30 G4
Great Lever Gtr Man 43 B10
Great Limber Lincs 46 B5
Great Linford M Keynes 28 D5
Great Livermere Suff 30 A5
Great Longstone Derbys 44 E6
Great Lumley Durham 58 B3
Great Lyth Shrops 33 E10
Great Malvern Worcs 26 D4
Great Maplestead Essex 30 E5
Great Marton Blackpool 49 F3
Great Massingham Norf 38 C3
Great Melton Norf 39 E7
Great Milton Oxon 18 A3
Great Missenden Bucks 18 A5
Great Mitton Lancs 50 F3
Great Mongeham Kent 21 F10
Great Moulton Norf 39 F7
Great Munden Herts 29 F10
Great Musgrave Cumb 57 E9
Great Ness Shrops 33 D9
Great Notley Essex 30 F4
Great Oakley Essex 31 F8
Great Oakley Northants 36 G4
Great Offley Herts 29 F8
Great Ormside Cumb 57 E9
Great Orton Cumb 56 A5
Great Ouseburn N Yorks 51 C10
Great Oxendon Northants 36 G3
Great Oxney Green Essex 30 H3
Great Palgrave Norf 38 D4
Great Parndon Essex 29 H11
Great Paxton Cambs 29 B9
Great Plumpton Lancs 49 F3
Great Plumstead Norf 39 D9
Great Ponton Lincs 36 B5
Great Preston W Yorks 51 G10
Great Raveley Cambs 37 G8
Great Rissington Glos 27 G8
Great Rollright Oxon 27 E10
Great Ryburgh Norf 38 C5
Great Ryle Northumb 62 B6
Great Ryton Shrops 33 E10
Great Saling Essex 30 F4
Great Salkeld Cumb 57 C7
Great Sampford Essex 30 E3
Great Sankey Warr 43 D8
Great Saxham Suff 30 B4
Great Shefford W Berks 17 D10
Great Shelford Cambs 29 C11
Great Smeaton N Yorks 58 F4
Great Snoring Norf 38 B5
Great Somerford Wilts 16 C6
Great Stainton Darl 58 D4
Great Stambridge Essex 20 B5
Great Staughton Cambs 29 B8
Great Steeping Lincs 47 F8
Great Stonar Kent 21 F10
Great Strickland Cumb 57 D7
Great Stukeley Cambs 29 A9
Great Sturton Lincs 46 E6
Great Sutton Ches W 43 E6
Great Sutton Shrops 33 G11
Great Swinburne Northumb 62 F5
Great Tew Oxon 27 F10
Great Tey Essex 30 F5
Great Thurkleby N Yorks 51 B10
Great Thurlow Suff 30 C3
Great Torrington Devon 6 E3
Great Tosson Northumb 62 C6
Great Totham Essex 30 G5
Great Totham Essex 30 G5
Great Tows Lincs 46 C6
Great Urswick Cumb 49 B2
Great Wakering Essex 20 C6
Great Waldingfield Suff 30 D6
Great Walsingham Norf 38 B5
Great Waltham Essex 30 G3
Great Warley Essex 20 B2
Great Washbourne Glos 26 E6
Great Weldon Northants 36 G5
Great Welnetham Suff 30 C5
Great Wenham Suff 31 E7
Great Whittington Northumb 62 F6
Great Wigborough Essex 30 G6
Great Wilbraham Cambs 30 C2
Great Wishford Wilts 17 H7
Great Witcombe Glos 26 G6
Great Witley Worcs 26 B4
Great Wolford Warks 27 E9
Great Wratting Suff 30 D3
Great Wymondley Herts 29 F9
Great Wyrley Staffs 34 E5
Great Wytheford Shrops 34 D1
Great Yarmouth Norf 39 E11
Great Yeldham Essex 30 E4
Greater Doward Hereford 26 G2
Greatford Lincs 37 D6
Greatgate Staffs 35 A6
Greatham Hants 11 A6
Greatham Hrtlpl 58 D5
Greatham W Sus 11 C9
Greatstone on Sea Kent 13 D9
Greatworth Northants 28 D2
Greave Lancs 50 G4
Greeba IoM 48 D3
Green Denb 42 F3
Green End Bedford 29 C8
Green Hammerton N Yorks 51 D10
Green Lane Powys 33 F7
Green Ore Som 16 F2
Green St Green London 19 E11
Green Street Herts 19 B8
Greenbank Shetland 96 C7
Greenburn W Loth 69 D8
Greendikes Northumb 71 H9
Greenfield C Beds 29 E7
Greenfield Flint 42 E4
Greenfield Gtr Man 44 B3
Greenfield Highld 80 C4
Greenfield Oxon 18 B4
Greenford London 19 C8
Greengairs N Lanark 68 C6
Greenham W Berks 17 E11
Greenhaugh Northumb 62 E3
Greenhead Northumb 62 G2
Greenhill Falk 69 C7
Greenhill Kent 21 E8
Greenhill Leics 35 D10
Greenhill London 19 C8
Greenhills N Ayrs 67 A6
Greenhithe Kent 20 D2
Greenholm E Ayrs 67 C8
Greenholme Cumb 57 F7
Greenhouse Borders 61 A11
Greenhow Hill N Yorks 51 C7
Greenigoe Orkney 95 H5
Greenland Highld 94 D4
Greenlands Bucks 18 C4
Greenlaw Aberds 89 C6
Greenlaw Borders 70 F6
Greenlea Dumfries 60 F6
Greenloaning Perth 75 G11
Greenmount Gtr Man 43 A10
Greenmow Shetland 96 L6
Greenock Invclyd 73 F11
Greenock West Invclyd 73 F11
Greenodd Cumb 49 A3
Greenrow Cumb 56 A3
Greens Norton Northants 28 D3
Greenside T&W 63 G7
Greensidehill Northumb 62 B5
Greenstead Green Essex 30 F5
Greensted Essex 20 A2
Greenwich London 19 D10
Greet Glos 27 E7
Greete Shrops 26 A2
Greetham Lincs 47 E7
Greetham Rutland 36 D5
Greetland W Yorks 51 G6
Gregg Hall Cumb 56 G6
Gregson Lane Lancs 50 G1
Greinetobht W Isles 84 A3
Greinton Som 15 H10
Gremista Shetland 96 J6
Grenaby IoM 48 E2
Grendon Northants 28 B5
Grendon Warks 35 E8
Grendon Common Warks 35 F8
Grendon Green Hereford 26 C2
Grendon Underwood Bucks 28 F3
Grenofen Devon 4 D5
Grenoside S Yorks 45 C7
Greosabhagh W Isles 90 H6
Gresford Wrex 42 G6
Gresham Norf 39 B7
Greshornish Highld 85 C8
Gressenhall Norf 38 D5
Gressingham Lancs 50 C1
Gresty Green Ches E 43 G10
Greta Bridge Durham 58 E1
Gretna Dumfries 61 G9
Gretna Green Dumfries 61 G9
Gretton Glos 27 E7
Gretton Northants 36 F4
Gretton Shrops 33 F11
Grewelthorpe N Yorks 51 B8
Grey Green N Lincs 45 B11
Greygarth N Yorks 51 B7
Greynor Carms 23 F10
Greysouthen Cumb 56 D2
Greystoke Cumb 56 C6
Greystone Angus 77 C8
Greystone Dumfries 60 F5
Greywell Hants 18 F4
Griais W Isles 91 C9
Grianan W Isles 91 D9
Gribthorpe E Yorks 52 F3
Gridley Corner Devon 6 G2
Griff Warks 35 G9
Griffithstown Torf 15 B8
Grimbister Orkney 95 G4
Grimblethorpe Lincs 46 D6
Grimeford Village Lancs 43 A9
Grimethorpe S Yorks 45 B8
Griminis W Isles 84 C2
Grimister Shetland 96 D6
Grimley Worcs 26 B5
Grimness Orkney 95 J5
Grimoldby Lincs 47 D7
Grimpo Shrops 33 C9
Grimsargh Lancs 50 F1
Grimsbury Oxon 27 D11
Grimsby NE Lincs 46 A6
Grimscote Northants 28 C3
Grimscott Corn 6 F1
Grimsthorpe Lincs 36 C6
Grimston E Yorks 53 F8
Grimston Leics 36 C2
Grimston Norf 38 C3
Grimston York 52 D2
Grimstone Dorset 8 E5
Grinacombe Moor Devon 6 G3
Grindale E Yorks 53 B7
Grindigar Orkney 95 H6
Grindiscol Shetland 96 K6
Grindle Shrops 34 E3
Grindleford Derbys 44 E6
Grindleton Lancs 50 E3
Grindley Staffs 34 C6
Grindley Brook Shrops 33 A11
Grindlow Derbys 44 E5
Grindon Northumb 71 F8
Grindon Staffs 44 G4
Grindonmoor Gate Staffs 44 G4
Gringley on the Hill Notts 45 C11
Grinsdale Cumb 61 H9
Grinshill Shrops 33 C11
Grinton N Yorks 58 G1
Griomsidar W Isles 91 E8
Grishipoll Argyll 78 F4
Grisling Common E Sus 12 D3
Gristhorpe N Yorks 53 A6
Griston Norf 38 F5
Gritley Orkney 95 H6
Grittenham Wilts 17 C7
Grittleton Wilts 16 C5
Grizebeck Cumb 49 A2
Grizedale Cumb 56 G5
Grobister Orkney 95 F7
Groby Leics 35 E11
Groes Conwy 42 F3
Groes Neath 14 C3
Groes-faen Rhondda 14 C6
Groes-lwyd Powys 33 D8
Groesffordd Marli Denb 42 E3
Groeslon Gwyn 40 E6
Groeslon Gwyn 41 D7
Grogport Argyll 65 D9
Gromford Suff 31 C10
Gronant Flint 42 D3
Groombridge E Sus 12 C4
Grosmont Mon 25 F11
Grosmont N Yorks 59 F9
Groton Suff 30 D6
Grougfoot Falk 69 C9
Grouville Jersey 11
Grove Dorset 8 G6
Grove Kent 21 E9
Grove Notts 45 E11
Grove Oxon 17 B11
Grove Park London 19 D11
Grove Vale W Mid 34 F6
Grovesend Swansea 23 F10
Grudie Highld 86 E6
Gruids Highld 93 J8
Gruinard House Highld 86 B2
Grula Highld 85 F8
Gruline Argyll 79 G8
Grunasound Shetland 96 K5
Grundisburgh Suff 31 C9
Grunsagill Lancs 50 D3
Gruting Shetland 96 J4
Grutness Shetland 96 N6
Gualachulain Highld 74 C4
Gualin Ho. Highld 92 D6
Guardbridge Fife 77 F7
Guarlford Worcs 26 D5
Guay Perth 76 C3
Guestling Green E Sus 13 E7
Guestling Thorn E Sus 13 E7
Guestwick Norf 39 C6
Guestwick Green Norf 39 C6
Guide Blackburn 50 G3
Guide Post Northumb 63 E8
Guilden Morden Cambs 29 D9
Guilden Sutton Ches W 43 F7
Guildford Sur 18 G6
Guildtown Perth 76 D4
Guilsborough Northants 28 A3
Guilsfield Powys 33 D8
Guilton Kent 21 F9
Guineaford Devon 6 C4
Guisborough Redcar 59 E7
Guiseley W Yorks 51 E7
Guist Norf 38 C5
Guith Orkney 95 E6
Guiting Power Glos 27 F7
Gulberwick Shetland 96 K6
Gullane E Loth 70 B3
Gulval Corn 2 F3
Gulworthy Devon 4 D5
Gumfreston Pembs 22 F6
Gumley Leics 36 F2
Gummow's Shop Corn 3 D7
Gun Hill E Sus 12 E4
Gunby E Yorks 52 F3
Gunby Lincs 36 C5
Gundleton Hants 10 A5
Gunn Devon 6 C5
Gunnerside N Yorks 57 G11
Gunnerton Northumb 62 F5
Gunness N Lincs 46 A2
Gunnislake Corn 4 D5
Gunnista Shetland 96 J7
Gunthorpe Norf 38 B6
Gunthorpe Notts 36 A2
Gunthorpe Pboro 37 E7
Gunville IoW 10 F3
Gunwalloe Corn 2 G5
Gurnard IoW 10 E3
Gurnett Ches E 44 E3
Gurney Slade Som 16 G3
Gurnos Powys 24 H4
Gussage All Saints Dorset 9 C9
Gussage St Michael Dorset 9 C8
Guston Kent 21 G10
Gutcher Shetland 96 D7
Guthrie Angus 77 B8
Guyhirn Cambs 37 E9
Guyhirn Gull Cambs 37 E9
Guy's Head Lincs 37 C10
Guy's Marsh Dorset 9 B7
Guyzance Northumb 63 C8
Gwaenysgor Flint 42 D3
Gwalchmai Anglesey 40 C5
Gwaun-Cae-Gurwen Neath 24 G4
Gwaun-Leision Neath 24 G4
Gwbert Ceredig 22 B6
Gweek Corn 2 G6
Gwehelog Mon 15 A9
Gwenddwr Powys 25 D7
Gwennap Corn 2 F6
Gwenter Corn 2 H6
Gwernaffield Flint 42 F5
Gwernesney Mon 15 A10
Gwernogle Carms 23 C10
Gwernymynydd Flint 42 F5
Gwersyllt Wrex 42 G6
Gwespyr Flint 42 D4
Gwithian Corn 2 E4
Gwredog Anglesey 40 B6
Gwyddelwern Denb 42 H3
Gwyddgrug Carms 23 C9
Gwydyr Uchaf Conwy 41 D9
Gwynfryn Wrex 42 G5
Gwystre Powys 25 B7
Gwytherin Conwy 41 D10
Gyfelia Wrex 42 H6
Gyffin Conwy 41 C9
Gyre Orkney 95 H4
Gyrn-goch Gwyn 40 F6

H

Habberley Shrops 33 E9
Habergham Lancs 50 F4
Habrough NE Lincs 46 A5
Haceby Lincs 36 B6
Hacheston Suff 31 C10
Hackbridge London 19 E9
Hackenthorpe S Yorks 45 D8
Hackford Norf 39 E6
Hackforth N Yorks 58 G3
Hackland Orkney 95 F4
Hackleton Northants 28 C5
Hackness N Yorks 59 G10
Hackness Orkney 95 J4
Hackney London 19 C10
Hackthorn Lincs 46 D3
Hackthorpe Cumb 57 D7
Haconby Lincs 37 C7
Hacton London 20 C2
Hadden Borders 70 G6
Haddenham Bucks 28 H4
Haddenham Cambs 37 H10
Haddington E Loth 70 C4
Haddington Lincs 46 F3
Haddiscoe Norf 39 F10
Haddon Cambs 37 F7
Haddon Ches E 44 F3
Hade Edge W Yorks 44 B5
Hademore Staffs 35 E7
Hadfield Derbys 44 C4
Hadham Cross Herts 29 G11
Hadham Ford Herts 29 F11
Hadleigh Essex 20 C5
Hadleigh Suff 31 D7
Hadley Telford 34 D2
Hadley End Staffs 35 C7
Hadlow Kent 20 G3
Hadlow Down E Sus 12 D4
Hadnall Shrops 33 D11
Hadstock Essex 30 D2
Hady Derbys 45 E7
Hadzor Worcs 26 B6
Haffenden Quarter Kent 13 B7
Hafod-Dinbych Conwy 41 E10
Hafod-Iom Conwy 41 C10
Haggate Lancs 50 F4
Haggbeck Cumb 61 F10
Haggerston Northumb 71 F9
Haggrister Shetland 96 F5
Hagley Hereford 26 D2
Hagley Worcs 34 G5
Hagworthingham Lincs 47 F7
Haigh Gtr Man 43 B9
Haigh S Yorks 44 A6
Haigh Moor W Yorks 51 G8
Haighton Green Lancs 50 F1
Hail Weston Cambs 29 B8
Haile Cumb 56 F2
Hailes Glos 27 E7
Hailey Herts 29 G10
Hailey Oxon 27 G10
Hailsham E Sus 12 F4
Haimer Highld 94 D3
Hainault London 19 B11
Hainford Norf 39 D8
Hainton Lincs 46 D5
Hairmyres S Lanark 68 E5
Haisthorpe E Yorks 53 C7
Hakin Pembs 22 F3
Halam Notts 45 G10
Halbeath Fife 69 B10
Halberton Devon 7 E9
Halcro Highld 94 D4
Hale Gtr Man 43 D10
Hale Halton 43 D7
Hale Hants 9 C10
Hale Bank Halton 43 D7
Hale Street Kent 20 G3
Halebarns Gtr Man 43 D10
Hales Norf 39 F9
Hales Staffs 34 B3
Hales Place Kent 21 F8
Halesfield Telford 34 E3
Halesgate Lincs 37 C9
Halesowen W Mid 34 G5
Halesworth Suff 39 H9
Halewood Mers 43 D7
Halford Shrops 33 G10
Halford Warks 27 D9
Halfpenny Furze Carms 23 E7
Halfpenny Green Staffs 34 F4
Halfway Carms 24 E3
Halfway Carms 24 E5
Halfway W Berks 17 E11
Halfway Bridge W Sus 11 B8
Halfway House Shrops 33 D9
Halfway Houses Kent 20 D6
Halifax W Yorks 51 G6
Halket E Ayrs 67 A7
Halkirk Highld 94 E3
Halkyn Flint 42 E5
Hall Dunnerdale Cumb 56 G4
Hall Green W Mid 35 G7
Hall Green W Yorks 51 H9
Hall Grove Herts 29 G9
Hall of Tankerness Orkney 95 H6
Hall of the Forest Shrops 33 G8
Halland E Sus 12 E3
Hallaton Leics 36 F3
Hallatrow Bath 16 F3
Hallbankgate Cumb 61 H11
Hallen S Glos 15 C11
Halliburton Borders 70 F5
Hallin Highld 84 C7
Halling Medway 20 E4
Hallington Lincs 47 D7
Hallington Northumb 62 F5
Halliwell Gtr Man 43 A10
Halloughton Notts 45 G10
Hallow Worcs 26 C5
Hallrule Borders 61 B11
Halls E Loth 70 C5
Hall's Green Herts 29 F9
Hallsands Devon 5 H9
Hallthwaites Cumb 56 H3
Hallworthy Corn 4 C2
Hallyburton House Perth 76 D5
Hallyne Borders 69 F10
Halmer End Staffs 43 H10
Halmore Glos 16 A3
Halmyre Mains Borders 69 F10
Halnaker W Sus 11 D8
Halsall Lancs 42 A6
Halse Northants 28 D2
Halse Som 7 D10
Halsetown Corn 2 F4
Halsham E Yorks 53 G8
Halsinger Devon 6 C4
Halstead Essex 30 E5
Halstead Kent 19 E11
Halstead Leics 36 E3
Halstock Dorset 8 D4
Haltham Lincs 46 F6
Haltoft End Lincs 47 H7
Halton Bucks 28 G5
Halton Halton 43 D8
Halton Lancs 49 C5
Halton Northumb 62 G5
Halton W Yorks 51 F9
Halton Wrex 33 B9
Halton East N Yorks 50 D6
Halton Gill N Yorks 50 B4
Halton Holegate Lincs 47 F8
Halton Lea Gate Northumb 62 H2
Halton West N Yorks 50 D4
Haltwhistle Northumb 62 G3
Halvergate Norf 39 E10
Halwell Devon 5 F8
Halwill Devon 6 G3
Halwill Junction Devon 6 F3
Ham Devon 7 F11
Ham Glos 16 B3
Ham Highld 94 C4
Ham Kent 21 F10
Ham London 19 D8
Ham Shetland 96 K1
Ham Wilts 17 E10
Ham Common Dorset 9 B7
Ham Green Hereford 26 D4
Ham Green Kent 13 D7
Ham Green Kent 20 E5
Ham Green N Som 15 D11
Ham Green Worcs 27 B7
Ham Street Som 8 A4
Hamble-le-Rice Hants 10 D3
Hambleden Bucks 18 C4
Hambledon Hants 10 C5
Hambledon Sur 18 H6
Hambleton Lancs 49 E3
Hambleton N Yorks 52 F1
Hambridge Som 8 B2
Hambrook S Glos 16 D3
Hambrook W Sus 11 D6
Hameringham Lincs 47 F7
Hamerton Cambs 37 H7
Hametoun Shetland 96 K1
Hamilton S Lanark 68 E6
Hammer W Sus 11 A7
Hammerpot W Sus 11 D9
Hammersmith London 19 D9
Hammerwich Staffs 35 E6
Hammerwood E Sus 12 C3
Hammond Street Herts 19 A10
Hammoon Dorset 9 C7
Hamnavoe Shetland 96 E4
Hamnavoe Shetland 96 E6
Hamnavoe Shetland 96 F6
Hamnavoe Shetland 96 K5
Hampden Park E Sus 12 F5
Hamperden End Essex 30 E2
Hampnett Glos 27 G7
Hampole S Yorks 45 A9
Hampreston Dorset 9 E9
Hampstead London 19 C9
Hampstead Norreys W Berks 18 D2
Hampsthwaite N Yorks 51 D8
Hampton London 19 E8
Hampton Shrops 34 G3
Hampton Worcs 27 D7
Hampton Bishop Hereford 26 E2
Hampton Heath Ches W 43 H7
Hampton in Arden W Mid 35 G8
Hampton Loade Shrops 34 G3
Hampton Lovett Worcs 26 B5
Hampton Lucy Warks 27 C9
Hampton on the Hill Warks 27 B9
Hampton Poyle Oxon 28 G2
Hamrow Norf 38 C5
Hamsey E Sus 12 E3
Hamsey Green London 19 F10
Hamstall Ridware Staffs 35 D7
Hamstead IoW 10 E3
Hamstead W Mid 34 F6
Hamstead Marshall W Berks 17 E11
Hamsterley Durham 58 C2
Hamsterley Durham 63 H7
Hamstreet Kent 13 C9
Hamworthy Poole 9 E8
Hanbury Staffs 35 C7
Hanbury Worcs 26 B6
Hanbury Woodend Staffs 35 C7
Hanby Lincs 36 B6
Hanchurch Staffs 34 A4
Handbridge Ches W 43 F7
Handcross W Sus 12 D1
Handforth Ches E 44 D2
Handley Ches W 43 G7
Handsacre Staffs 35 D6
Handsworth S Yorks 45 D8
Handsworth W Mid 34 F6
Handy Cross Devon 6 D3
Hanford Stoke 34 A4
Hanging Langford Wilts 17 H7
Hangleton W Sus 11 D9
Hanham S Glos 16 D3
Hankelow Ches E 43 H9
Hankerton Wilts 16 B6
Hankham E Sus 12 F5
Hanley Stoke 44 H2
Hanley Castle Worcs 26 D5
Hanley Child Worcs 26 B3
Hanley Swan Worcs 26 D5
Hanley William Worcs 26 B3
Hanlith N Yorks 50 C5
Hanmer Wrex 33 B10
Hannah Lincs 47 E9
Hannington Hants 18 F2
Hannington Northants 28 A5
Hannington Swindon 17 B8
Hannington Wick Swindon 17 B8
Hansel Village S Ayrs 67 C6
Hanslope M Keynes 28 D5
Hanthorpe Lincs 37 C6
Hanwell London 19 C8
Hanwell Oxon 27 D11
Hanwood Shrops 33 E10
Hanworth London 19 D8
Hanworth Norf 39 B7
Happendon S Lanark 69 G7
Happisburgh Norf 39 B9
Happisburgh Common Norf 39 C9
Hapsford Ches W 43 E7
Hapton Lancs 50 F3
Hapton Norf 39 F7
Harberton Devon 5 F8
Harbertonford Devon 5 F8
Harbledown Kent 21 F8
Harborne W Mid 34 G6
Harborough Magna Warks 35 H10
Harbottle Northumb 62 C5
Harbury Warks 27 C10
Harby Leics 36 B3
Harby Notts 46 E2
Harcombe Devon 7 G10
Harden W Mid 34 E6
Harden W Yorks 51 F6
Hardenhuish Wilts 16 D6
Hardgate Aberds 83 C9
Hardham W Sus 11 C9
Hardingham Norf 38 E6
Hardingstone Northants 28 C4
Hardington Som 16 F4
Hardington Mandeville Som 8 C4
Hardington Marsh Som 8 D4
Hardley Hants 10 D3
Hardley Street Norf 39 E9
Hardmead M Keynes 28 D6
Hardrow N Yorks 57 G10
Hardstoft Derbys 45 F8
Hardway Hants 10 D5
Hardway Som 8 A6
Hardwick Bucks 28 G5
Hardwick Cambs 29 C10
Hardwick Norf 38 D2
Hardwick Norf 39 G8
Hardwick Northants 28 B5
Hardwick Notts 45 E10
Hardwick Oxon 27 H10
Hardwick Oxon 28 F2
Hardwick W Mid 35 F6
Hardwicke Glos 26 F6
Hardwicke Glos 26 G4
Hardwicke Hereford 25 D9
Hardy's Green Essex 30 F6
Hare Green Essex 31 F7
Hare Hatch Wokingham 18 D5
Hare Street Herts 29 F10
Hareby Lincs 47 F7
Hareden Lancs 50 D2
Harefield London 19 B7
Harehills W Yorks 51 F9
Harehope Northumb 62 A6
Haresceugh Cumb 57 B8
Harescombe Glos 26 G5
Haresfield Glos 26 G5
Hareshaw N Lanark 69 D7
Hareshaw Head Northumb 62 E4
Harewood W Yorks 51 E9
Harewood End Hereford 26 F2
Harford Carms 24 D3
Harford Devon 5 F7
Hargate Norf 39 F7
Hargatewall Derbys 44 E5
Hargrave Ches W 43 F7
Hargrave Northants 29 A7
Hargrave Suff 30 C4
Harker Cumb 61 G9
Harkland Shetland 96 E6
Harkstead Suff 31 E8
Harlaston Staffs 35 D8
Harlaw Ho. Aberds 83 A9
Harlaxton Lincs 36 B4
Harle Syke Lancs 50 F4
Harlech Gwyn 41 G7
Harlequin Notts 36 B2
Harlescott Shrops 33 D11
Harlesden London 19 C9
Harleston Devon 5 G8
Harleston Norf 39 G8
Harleston Suff 31 C7
Harlestone Northants 28 B4
Harley S Yorks 45 C7
Harley Shrops 34 E1
Harleyholm S Lanark 69 G8
Harlington C Beds 29 E7
Harlington London 19 D7
Harlington S Yorks 45 B8
Harlosh Highld 85 D7
Harlow Essex 29 G11
Harlow Hill N Yorks 51 D8
Harlow Hill Northumb 62 G6
Harlthorpe E Yorks 52 F3
Harlton Cambs 29 C10
Harman's Cross Dorset 9 F8
Harmby N Yorks 58 H2
Harmer Green Herts 29 G9
Harmer Hill Shrops 33 C10
Harmondsworth London 19 D7
Harmston Lincs 46 F3
Harnham Northumb 62 F6
Harnhill Glos 17 A7
Harold Hill London 20 B2
Harold Wood London 20 B2
Haroldston West Pembs 22 E3
Haroldswick Shetland 96 B8
Harome N Yorks 52 A2
Harpenden Herts 29 G8
Harpford Devon 7 G9
Harpham E Yorks 53 C6
Harpley Norf 38 C3
Harpley Worcs 26 B3
Harpole Northants 28 B3
Harpsdale Highld 94 E3
Harpsden Oxon 18 C4
Harpswell Lincs 46 D3
Harpur Hill Derbys 44 E4
Harpurhey Gtr Man 44 B2
Harraby Cumb 56 A6
Harrapool Highld 85 F11
Harrier Shetland 96 J1
Harrietfield Perth 76 E2
Harrietsham Kent 20 F5
Harrington Cumb 56 D1
Harrington Lincs 47 E7
Harrington Northants 36 G3
Harringworth Northants 36 F5
Harris Highld 78 B6
Harrogate N Yorks 51 D9
Harrold Bedford 28 C6
Harrow London 19 C8
Harrow on the Hill London 19 C8
Harrow Street Suff 30 E6
Harrow Weald London 19 B8
Harrowbarrow Corn 4 E4
Harrowden Bedford 29 D7
Harrowgate Hill Darl 58 E3
Harston Cambs 29 C11
Harston Leics 36 B4
Harswell E Yorks 52 E4
Hart Hrtlpl 58 C5
Hart Common Gtr Man 43 B9
Hart Hill Luton 29 F8
Hart Station Hrtlpl 58 C5
Hartburn Northumb 62 E6
Hartburn Stockton 58 E5
Hartest Suff 30 C5
Hartfield E Sus 12 C3
Hartford Cambs 29 A9
Hartford Ches W 43 E9
Hartford End Essex 30 G3
Hartfordbridge Hants 18 F4
Hartforth N Yorks 58 F2
Harthill Ches W 43 G8
Harthill N Lanark 69 D8
Harthill S Yorks 45 D8
Hartington Derbys 44 F5
Hartland Devon 6 D1
Hartlebury Worcs 26 A5
Hartlepool Hrtlpl 58 C6
Hartley Cumb 57 F9
Hartley Kent 13 C6
Hartley Kent 20 E3
Hartley Northumb 63 F9
Hartley Westpall Hants 18 F3
Hartley Wintney Hants 18 F4
Hartlip Kent 20 E5
Hartoft End N Yorks 59 G8
Harton N Yorks 52 C3
Harton Shrops 33 G10
Harton T&W 63 G9
Hartpury Glos 26 F4
Hartshead W Yorks 51 G7
Hartshill Warks 35 F9
Hartshorne Derbys 35 C9
Hartsop Cumb 56 E6
Hartwell Northants 28 C4
Hartwood N Lanark 69 E7
Harvieston Stirling 68 B4
Harvington Worcs 27 D7
Harvington Cross Worcs 27 D7
Harwell Oxon 17 C11
Harwich Essex 31 E9
Harwood Durham 57 C10
Harwood Gtr Man 43 A10
Harwood Dale N Yorks 59 G10
Harworth Notts 45 C10
Hasbury W Mid 34 G5
Hascombe Sur 18 G6
Haselbech Northants 36 H3
Haselbury Plucknett Som 8 C3
Haseley Warks 27 B9
Haselor Warks 27 C8
Hasfield Glos 26 F5
Hasguard Pembs 22 F3
Haskayne Lancs 42 B6
Hasketon Suff 31 C9
Hasland Derbys 45 F7
Haslemere Sur 11 A8
Haslingden Lancs 50 G3
Haslingfield Cambs 29 C11
Haslington Ches E 43 G10
Hassall Ches E 43 G10
Hassall Green Ches E 43 G10
Hassell Street Kent 21 G7
Hassendean Borders 61 A11
Hassingham Norf 39 E9
Hassocks W Sus 12 E1
Hassop Derbys 44 E6
Hastigrow Highld 94 D4
Hastingleigh Kent 13 B9
Hastings E Sus 13 F7
Hastingwood Essex 29 H11
Hastoe Herts 28 H6
Haswell Durham 58 B4
Haswell Plough Durham 58 B4
Hatch C Beds 29 D8
Hatch Hants 18 F3
Hatch Wilts 9 B8
Hatch Beauchamp Som 8 B2
Hatch End London 19 B8
Hatch Green Som 8 C2
Hatchet Gate Hants 10 D2
Hatching Green Herts 29 G8
Hatchmere Ches W 43 E8
Hatcliffe NE Lincs 46 B6
Hatfield Hereford 26 C2
Hatfield Herts 29 H9
Hatfield S Yorks 45 B10
Hatfield Worcs 26 C5
Hatfield Broad Oak Essex 30 G2
Hatfield Garden Village Herts 29 H9
Hatfield Heath Essex 30 G2
Hatfield Hyde Herts 29 G9
Hatfield Peverel Essex 30 G4
Hatfield Woodhouse S Yorks 45 B10
Hatford Oxon 17 B10
Hatherden Hants 17 F10
Hatherleigh Devon 6 F4
Hathern Leics 35 C10
Hatherop Glos 27 H8
Hathersage Derbys 44 D6
Hathershaw Gtr Man 44 B3
Hatherton Ches E 43 H9
Hatherton Staffs 34 D5
Hatley St George Cambs 29 C9
Hatt Corn 4 E4
Hattingley Hants 18 H3
Hatton Aberds 89 E10
Hatton Derbys 35 C8
Hatton Lincs 46 E5
Hatton Shrops 33 F10
Hatton Warks 27 B9
Hatton Warr 43 D8
Hatton Castle Aberds 89 D7
Hatton Heath Ches W 43 F7
Hatton of Fintray Aberds 83 B10
Hattoncrook Aberds 89 F8
Haugh E Ayrs 67 D7
Haugh Gtr Man 44 A3
Haugh Lincs 47 E8
Haugh Head Northumb 71 H9
Haugh of Glass Moray 88 E4
Haugh of Urr Dumfries 55 C11
Haugham Lincs 47 D7
Haughley Suff 31 B7
Haughley Green Suff 31 B7
Haughs of Clinterty Aberdeen 83 B10
Haughton Notts 45 E10
Haughton Shrops 33 C9
Haughton Shrops 34 D1
Haughton Shrops 34 E3
Haughton Shrops 34 F2
Haughton Staffs 34 C4
Haughton Castle Northumb 62 F5
Haughton Green Gtr Man 44 C3
Haughton Moss Ches E 43 G8
Haultwick Herts 29 F10
Haunn Argyll 78 G6
Haunn W Isles 84 G2
Haunton Staffs 35 D8
Hauxley Northumb 63 C8
Hauxton Cambs 29 C11
Havant Hants 10 D6
Haven Hereford 25 C11
Haven Bank Lincs 46 G6
Haven Side E Yorks 53 G7
Havenstreet IoW 10 E4
Havercroft W Yorks 45 A7
Haverfordwest = Hwlffordd Pembs 22 E4
Haverhill Suff 30 D3
Haverigg Cumb 49 B1
Havering-atte-Bower London 20 B2
Haveringland Norf 39 C7
Haversham M Keynes 28 D5
Haverthwaite Cumb 49 A3
Haverton Hill Stockton 58 D5
Hawarden = Penarlâg Flint 42 F6
Hawcoat Cumb 49 B2
Hawen Ceredig 23 B8
Hawes N Yorks 57 H10
Hawes' Green Norf 39 F8
Hawes Side Blackpool 49 F3
Hawford Worcs 26 B5
Hawick Borders 61 B11
Hawk Green Gtr Man 44 D3
Hawkchurch Devon 8 D2
Hawkedon Suff 30 C4
Hawkenbury Kent 12 C4
Hawkenbury Kent 13 B7
Hawkeridge Wilts 16 F5
Hawkerland Devon 7 H9
Hawkes End W Mid 35 G9
Hawkesbury S Glos 16 C4
Hawkesbury Warks 35 G9
Hawkesbury Upton S Glos 16 C4
Hawkhill Northumb 63 B8
Hawkhurst Kent 13 C6
Hawkinge Kent 21 H9
Hawkley Hants 10 B6
Hawkridge Som 7 C7
Hawkshead Cumb 56 G5
Hawkshead Hill Cumb 56 G5
Hawksland S Lanark 69 G7
Hawkswick N Yorks 50 B5
Hawksworth Notts 36 A3
Hawksworth W Yorks 51 E7
Hawksworth W Yorks 51 F8
Hawkwell Essex 20 B5
Hawley Hants 18 F5
Hawley Kent 20 D2
Hawling Glos 27 F7
Hawnby N Yorks 59 H6
Haworth W Yorks 50 F6
Hawstead Suff 30 C5
Hawthorn Durham 58 B5
Hawthorn Rhondda 15 C7
Hawthorn Wilts 16 E5
Hawthorn Hill Brack 18 D5
Hawthorn Hill Lincs 46 G6
Hawthorpe Lincs 36 C6
Hawton Notts 45 G11
Haxby York 52 D2
Haxey N Lincs 45 C11
Hay Green Norf 37 D11
Hay-on-Wye = Y Gelli Gandryll Powys 25 D9
Hay Street Herts 29 F10
Haydock Mers 43 C8
Haydon Dorset 8 C5
Haydon Bridge Northumb 62 G4
Haydon Wick Swindon 17 C8
Haye Corn 4 E4
Hayes London 19 C8
Hayes London 19 E11
Hayfield Derbys 44 D4
Hayfield Fife 69 A11
Hayhill E Ayrs 67 E7
Hayhillock Angus 77 C8
Hayle Corn 2 F4
Haynes C Beds 29 D7
Haynes Church End C Beds 29 D7
Hayscastle Pembs 22 D3
Hayscastle Cross Pembs 22 D4
Hayshead Angus 77 C9
Hayton Aberdeen 83 C11
Hayton Cumb 56 B3
Hayton Cumb 61 H11
Hayton E Yorks 52 E4
Hayton Notts 45 D11
Hayton's Bent Shrops 33 G11
Haytor Vale Devon 5 D8
Haywards Heath W Sus 12 D2
Haywood S Yorks 45 A9
Haywood Oaks Notts 45 G10
Hazel Grove Gtr Man 44 D3
Hazel Street Kent 12 C5
Hazelbank S Lanark 69 F7
Hazelbury Bryan Dorset 8 D6
Hazeley Hants 18 F4
Hazelhurst Gtr Man 44 B3
Hazelslade Staffs 34 D6
Hazelton Glos 27 G7
Hazelton Walls Fife 76 E6
Hazelwood Derbys 45 H7
Hazlemere Bucks 18 B5
Hazlerigg T&W 63 F8
Hazlewood N Yorks 51 D6
Hazon Northumb 63 C7
Heacham Norf 38 B2
Head of Muir Falk 69 B7
Headbourne Worthy Hants 10 A3
Headbrook Hereford 25 C10
Headcorn Kent 13 B7
Headingley W Yorks 51 F8
Headington Oxon 28 H2
Headlam Durham 58 E2
Headless Cross Worcs 27 B7
Headley Hants 18 E2
Headley Hants 18 H5
Headley Sur 19 F9
Headon Notts 45 E11
Heads S Lanark 68 F6
Heads Nook Cumb 61 H10
Heage Derbys 45 G7
Healaugh N Yorks 51 E10
Healaugh N Yorks 58 G1
Heald Green Gtr Man 44 D2
Heale Devon 6 B5
Heale Som 16 G3
Healey Gtr Man 50 H4
Healey N Yorks 51 A7
Healey Northumb 62 H6
Healing NE Lincs 46 A6
Heamoor Corn 2 F3
Heanish Argyll 78 G3
Heanor Derbys 45 H8
Heanton Punchardon Devon 6 C4
Heapham Lincs 46 D2
Hearthstane Borders 69 H10
Heasley Mill Devon 7 C6
Heast Highld 85 G11
Heath Cardiff 15 D7
Heath Derbys 45 F8
Heath and Reach C Beds 28 F6
Heath End Hants 18 E2
Heath End Sur 18 G5
Heath End Warks 27 B9
Heath Hayes Staffs 34 D6
Heath Hill Shrops 34 D3
Heath House Som 15 G10
Heath Town W Mid 34 F5
Heathcote Derbys 44 F5
Heather Leics 35 D9
Heatherfield Highld 85 D9
Heathfield Devon 5 D9
Heathfield E Sus 12 D4
Heathfield Som 7 D10
Heathhall Dumfries 60 F5
Heathrow Airport London 19 D7
Heathstock Devon 8 D1
Heathton Shrops 34 F4
Heatley Warr 43 D10
Heaton Lancs 49 C4
Heaton Staffs 44 F3
Heaton T&W 63 G8
Heaton W Yorks 51 F7
Heaton Moor Gtr Man 44 C2
Heaverham Kent 20 F2
Heaviley Gtr Man 44 D3
Heavitree Devon 7 G8
Hebburn T&W 63 G9
Hebden N Yorks 50 C6
Hebden Bridge W Yorks 50 G5
Hebron Anglesey 40 B6
Hebron Carms 22 D6
Hebron Northumb 63 E7
Heck Dumfries 60 E6
Heckfield Hants 18 E4
Heckfield Green Suff 39 H7
Heckfordbridge Essex 30 F6
Heckington Lincs 37 A7
Heckmondwike W Yorks 51 G8
Heddington Wilts 16 E6
Heddle Orkney 95 G4
Heddon-on-the-Wall Northumb 63 G7
Hedenham Norf 39 F9
Hedge End Hants 10 C3
Hedgerley Bucks 18 C6
Hedging Som 8 B2
Hedley on the Hill Northumb 62 H6
Hednesford Staffs 34 D6
Hedon E Yorks 53 G7
Hedsor Bucks 18 C6
Hedworth T&W 63 G9
Hegdon Hill Hereford 26 C2
Heggerscales Cumb 57 E10
Heglibister Shetland 96 H5
Heighington Darl 58 D3
Heighington Lincs 46 F4
Heights of Brae Highld 87 E8
Heights of Kinlochewe Highld 86 E3
Heilam Highld 92 C7
Heiton Borders 70 G6
Hele Devon 6 B4
Hele Devon 7 F8
Helensburgh Argyll 73 E11
Helford Corn 3 G6
Helford Passage Corn 3 G6
Helhoughton Norf 38 C4
Helions Bumpstead Essex 30 D3
Hellaby S Yorks 45 C9
Helland Corn 4 D1
Hellesdon Norf 39 D8
Hellidon Northants 28 C2
Hellifield N Yorks 50 D4
Hellingly E Sus 12 E4
Hellington Norf 39 E9
Hellister Shetland 96 J5
Helm Northumb 63 D7
Helmdon Northants 28 D2
Helmingham Suff 31 C8
Helmington Row Durham 58 C2
Helmsdale Highld 93 H13
Helmshore Lancs 50 G3
Helmsley N Yorks 52 A2
Helperby N Yorks 51 C10
Helperthorpe N Yorks 52 B5
Helpringham Lincs 37 A7
Helpston Pboro 37 E7
Helsby Ches W 43 E7
Helsey Lincs 47 E9
Helston Corn 2 G5
Helstone Corn 4 C1
Helton Cumb 57 D7
Helwith Bridge N Yorks 50 C4
Hemblington Norf 39 D9
Hemel Hempstead Herts 29 H7
Hemingbrough N Yorks 52 F2
Hemingby Lincs 46 E6
Hemingford Abbots Cambs 29 A9
Hemingford Grey Cambs 29 A9
Hemingstone Suff 31 C8
Hemington Leics 35 C10
Hemington Northants 37 G6
Hemington Som 16 F4
Hemley Suff 31 D9
Hemlington Mbro 58 E6
Hemp Green Suff 31 B10
Hempholme E Yorks 53 D6
Hempnall Norf 39 F8
Hempnall Green Norf 39 F8
Hempriggs House Highld 94 F5
Hempstead Essex 30 E3
Hempstead Medway 20 E4
Hempstead Norf 39 B7
Hempstead Norf 39 C10
Hempsted Glos 26 G5
Hempton Norf 38 C5
Hempton Oxon 27 E11
Hemsby Norf 39 D10
Hemswell Lincs 46 C3
Hemswell Cliff Lincs 46 D3
Hemsworth W Yorks 45 A8
Hemyock Devon 7 E10
Hen-feddau fawr Pembs 23 C7
Henbury Bristol 16 D2
Henbury Ches E 44 E2
Hendon London 19 C9
Hendon T&W 63 H10
Hendre Flint 42 F4
Hendre-ddu Conwy 41 D10
Hendreforgan Rhondda 14 C5
Hendy Carms 23 F10
Heneglwys Anglesey 40 C6
Henfield W Sus 11 C11
Henford Devon 6 G2
Henghurst Kent 13 C8
Hengoed Caerph 15 B7
Hengoed Powys 25 C9
Hengoed Shrops 33 B8
Hengrave Suff 30 B5
Henham Essex 30 F2
Heniarth Powys 33 E7
Henlade Som 8 B1
Henley Shrops 33 H11
Henley Som 8 A3
Henley Suff 31 C8
Henley W Sus 11 B7
Henley-in-Arden Warks 27 B8
Henley-on-Thames Oxon 18 C4
Henley's Down E Sus 12 E6
Henllan Ceredig 23 B8
Henllan Denb 42 F3
Henllan Amgoed Carms 22 D6
Henllys Torf 15 B8
Henlow C Beds 29 E8
Hennock Devon 5 C9
Henny Street Essex 30 E5
Henryd Conwy 41 C9
Henry's Moat Pembs 22 D5
Hensall N Yorks 52 G1
Henshaw Northumb 62 G3
Hensingham Cumb 56 E1
Henstead Suff 39 G10
Henstridge Som 8 C6
Henstridge Ash Som 8 B6
Henstridge Marsh Som 8 B6
Henton Oxon 18 A4
Henton Som 15 G10
Henwood Corn 4 D3
Heogan Shetland 96 J6
Heol-las Swansea 14 B2
Heol Senni Powys 24 F6
Heol-y-Cyw Bridgend 14 C5
Hepburn Northumb 62 A6
Hepple Northumb 62 C5
Hepscott Northumb 63 E8
Heptonstall W Yorks 50 G5
Hepworth Suff 30 A6
Hepworth W Yorks 44 B5
Herbrandston Pembs 22 F3
Hereford Hereford 26 D2
Heriot Borders 70 E2
Hermiston Edin 69 C10
Hermitage Borders 61 D11
Hermitage Dorset 8 D5
Hermitage W Berks 18 D2
Hermitage W Sus 11 D6
Hermon Anglesey 40 D5
Hermon Carms 23 C8
Hermon Carms 24 F3
Hermon Pembs 23 C7
Herne Kent 21 E8
Herne Bay Kent 21 E8
Herner Devon 6 D4
Hernhill Kent 21 E7
Herodsfoot Corn 4 E3
Herongate Essex 20 B3
Heronsford S Ayrs 54 A4
Herriard Hants 18 G3
Herringfleet Suff 39 F10
Herringswell Suff 30 A4
Hersden Kent 21 E9
Hersham Corn 6 F1
Hersham Sur 19 E8
Herstmonceux E Sus 12 E5
Herston Orkney 95 J5
Hertford Herts 29 G10
Hertford Heath Herts 29 G10
Hertingfordbury Herts 29 G10
Hesket Newmarket Cumb 56 C5
Hesketh Bank Lancs 49 G4
Hesketh Lane Lancs 50 E2
Heskin Green Lancs 49 H5
Hesleden Durham 58 C5
Hesleyside Northumb 62 E4
Heslington York 52 D2
Hessay York 51 D11
Hessenford Corn 4 F4
Hessett Suff 30 B6
Hessle E Yorks 52 G6
Hest Bank Lancs 49 C4
Heston London 19 D8
Hestwall Orkney 95 G3
Heswall Mers 42 D5
Hethe Oxon 28 F2
Hethersett Norf 39 E7
Hethersgill Cumb 61 G10
Hethpool Northumb 71 H7
Hett Durham 58 C3
Hetton N Yorks 50 D5
Hetton-le-Hole T&W 58 B4
Hetton Steads Northumb 71 G9
Heugh Northumb 62 F6
Heugh-head Aberds 82 B5
Heveningham Suff 31 A10
Hever Kent 12 B3
Heversham Cumb 49 A4
Hevingham Norf 39 C7
Hewas Water Corn 3 E8
Hewelsfield Glos 16 A2
Hewish N Som 15 E10
Hewish Som 8 D3
Heworth York 52 D2
Hexham Northumb 62 G5
Hextable Kent 20 D2
Hexton Herts 29 E8
Hexworthy Devon 5 D7
Hey Lancs 50 E4
Heybridge Essex 20 B3
Heybridge Essex 30 H5
Heybridge Basin Essex 30 H5
Heybrook Bay Devon 4 G6
Heydon Cambs 29 D11

Kinlocheil Highld 80 F1
Kinlochewe Highld 86 E3
Kinlochleven Highld 74 A4
Kinlochmoidart Highld 79 D10
Kinlochmorar Highld 79 B11
Kinlochmore Highld 74 A4
Kinlochspelve Argyll 79 J9
Kinloid Highld 79 C9
Kinloss Moray 87 E13
Kinmel Bay Conwy 42 D2
Kinmuck Aberds 83 B10
Kinmundy Aberds 83 B10
Kinnadie Aberds 89 D9
Kinnaird Perth 76 E5
Kinnaird Castle Angus 77 B9
Kinneff Aberds 83 F10
Kinnelhead Dumfries 60 C6
Kinnell Angus 77 B9
Kinnerley Shrops 33 C9
Kinnersley Hereford 25 D10
Kinnersley Worcs 26 D5
Kinnerton Powys 25 B9
Kinnesswood Perth 76 G4
Kinninvie Durham 58 D1
Kinnordy Angus 76 B6
Kinoulton Notts 36 B2
Kinross Perth 76 G4
Kinrossie Perth 76 D4
Kinsbourne Green Herts 29 G8
Kinsey Heath Ches E 34 A2
Kinsham Hereford 25 B10
Kinsham Worcs 26 E6
Kinsley W Yorks 45 A8
Kinson Bmouth 9 E9
Kintbury W Berks 17 E10
Kintessack Moray 87 E12
Kintillo Perth 76 F4
Kintocher Aberds 83 C7
Kinton Hereford 25 A11
Kinton Shrops 33 D9
Kintore Aberds 83 B9
Kintour Argyll 64 C5
Kintra Argyll 64 D4
Kintra Argyll 78 J6
Kintraw Argyll 73 C7
Kinuachdrachd Argyll 72 D6
Kinveachy Highld 81 B11
Kinver Staffs 34 G4
Kippax W Yorks 51 F10
Kippen Stirling 68 A5
Kippford or Scaur Dumfries 55 D11
Kirbister Orkney 95 F7
Kirbister Orkney 95 H4
Kirbuster Orkney 95 F3
Kirby Bedon Norf 39 E8
Kirby Bellars Leics 36 D3
Kirby Cane Norf 39 F9
Kirby Cross Essex 31 F9
Kirby Grindalythe N Yorks 52 C5
Kirby Hill N Yorks 51 C9
Kirby Hill N Yorks 58 F2
Kirby Knowle N Yorks 58 H5
Kirby-le-Soken Essex 31 F9
Kirby Misperton N Yorks 52 B3
Kirby Muxloe Leics 35 E11
Kirby Row Norf 39 F9
Kirby Sigston N Yorks 58 G5
Kirby Underdale E Yorks 52 D4
Kirby Wiske N Yorks 51 A9
Kirdford W Sus 11 B9
Kirk Highld 94 E4
Kirk Bramwith S Yorks 45 A10
Kirk Deighton N Yorks 51 D9
Kirk Ella E Yorks 52 G6
Kirk Hallam Derbys 35 A10
Kirk Hammerton N Yorks 51 D10
Kirk Ireton Derbys 44 G6
Kirk Langley Derbys 35 B8
Kirk Merrington Durham 58 C3
Kirk Michael IoM 48 C3
Kirk of Shotts N Lanark 69 D7
Kirk Sandall S Yorks 45 B10
Kirk Smeaton N Yorks 51 H11
Kirk Yetholm Borders 71 H7
Kirkabister Shetland 96 K6
Kirkandrews Dumfries 55 E9
Kirkandrews upon Eden Cumb 61 H9
Kirkbampton Cumb 61 H9
Kirkbean Dumfries 60 H5
Kirkbride Cumb 61 H8
Kirkbuddo Angus 77 C8
Kirkburn Borders 69 G11
Kirkburn E Yorks 52 D5
Kirkburton W Yorks 44 A5
Kirkby Lincs 46 C4
Kirkby Mers 43 C7
Kirkby N Yorks 59 F6
Kirkby Fleetham N Yorks 58 G3
Kirkby Green Lincs 46 G4
Kirkby In Ashfield Notts 45 G9
Kirkby-in-Furness Cumb 49 A2
Kirkby la Thorpe Lincs 46 H5
Kirkby Lonsdale Cumb 50 B2
Kirkby Malham N Yorks 50 C4
Kirkby Mallory Leics 35 E10
Kirkby Malzeard N Yorks 51 B8
Kirkby Mills N Yorks 59 H8
Kirkby on Bain Lincs 46 F6
Kirkby Overflow N Yorks 51 E9
Kirkby Stephen Cumb 57 F9
Kirkby Thore Cumb 57 D8
Kirkby Underwood Lincs 37 C6
Kirkby Wharfe N Yorks 51 E11
Kirkbymoorside N Yorks 59 H7
Kirkcaldy Fife 69 A11
Kirkcambeck Cumb 61 G11
Kirkcarswell Dumfries 55 E10
Kirkcolm Dumfries 54 C3
Kirkconnel Dumfries 60 B3
Kirkconnell Dumfries 60 G5
Kirkcowan Dumfries 54 C6
Kirkcudbright Dumfries 55 D9
Kirkdale Mers 42 C6
Kirkfieldbank S Lanark 69 F7
Kirkgunzeon Dumfries 55 C11
Kirkham Lancs 49 F4
Kirkham N Yorks 52 C3
Kirkhamgate W Yorks 51 G8
Kirkharle Northumb 62 E6
Kirkheaton Northumb 62 F6
Kirkheaton W Yorks 51 H7
Kirkhill Angus 77 A9
Kirkhill Highld 87 G8
Kirkhill Midloth 69 D11
Kirkhill Moray 88 E2
Kirkhope Borders 61 A9
Kirkhouse Borders 70 G2
Kirkiboll Highld 93 D8
Kirkibost Highld 85 G10
Kirkinch Angus 76 C6
Kirkinner Dumfries 55 D7
Kirkintilloch E Dunb 68 C5
Kirkland Cumb 56 E2
Kirkland Cumb 57 C8
Kirkland Dumfries 60 B3
Kirkland Dumfries 60 D4
Kirkleatham Redcar 59 D6
Kirklevington Stockton 58 F5
Kirkley Suff 39 F11
Kirklington N Yorks 51 A9
Kirklington Notts 45 G10
Kirklinton Cumb 61 G10
Kirkliston Edin 69 C10
Kirkmaiden Dumfries 54 F4
Kirkmichael Perth 76 B3
Kirkmichael S Ayrs 66 F6
Kirkmuirhill S Lanark 68 F6
Kirknewton Northumb 71 G8
Kirknewton W Loth 69 D10
Kirkney Aberds 88 E5
Kirkoswald Cumb 57 B7
Kirkoswald S Ayrs 66 F5
Kirkpatrick Durham Dumfries 60 F3
Kirkpatrick-Fleming Dumfries 61 F8
Kirksanton Cumb 49 A1
Kirkstall W Yorks 51 F8
Kirkstead Lincs 46 F5
Kirkstile Aberds 88 E5
Kirkstyle Highld 94 C5
Kirkton Aberds 83 A8
Kirkton Aberds 89 D6
Kirkton Angus 77 C7
Kirkton Angus 77 D7
Kirkton Borders 61 B11
Kirkton Dumfries 60 E5
Kirkton Fife 76 E6
Kirkton Highld 85 F13
Kirkton Highld 86 G2
Kirkton Highld 87 B10
Kirkton Highld 87 F10
Kirkton Perth 76 F2
Kirkton S Lanark 60 A5
Kirkton Stirling 75 G8
Kirkton Manor Borders 69 G11
Kirkton of Airlie Angus 76 B6
Kirkton of Auchterhouse Angus 76 D6
Kirkton of Auchterless Aberds 89 D7
Kirkton of Barevan Highld 87 G11
Kirkton of Bourtie Aberds 89 F8
Kirkton of Collace Perth 76 D4
Kirkton of Craig Angus 77 B10
Kirkton of Culsalmond Aberds 89 E6
Kirkton of Durris Aberds 83 D9
Kirkton of Glenbuchat Aberds 82 B5
Kirkton of Glenisla Angus 76 A5
Kirkton of Kingoldrum Angus 76 B6
Kirkton of Largo Fife 77 G7
Kirkton of Lethendy Perth 76 C4
Kirkton of Logie Buchan Aberds 89 F9
Kirkton of Maryculter Aberds 83 D10
Kirkton of Menmuir Angus 77 A8
Kirkton of Monikie Angus 77 D8
Kirkton of Oyne Aberds 83 A8
Kirkton of Rayne Aberds 83 A8
Kirkton of Skene Aberds 83 C10
Kirkton of Tough Aberds 83 B8
Kirktonhill Borders 70 E3
Kirktown Aberds 89 C10
Kirktown of Alvah Aberds 89 B6
Kirktown of Deskford Moray 88 B5
Kirktown of Fetteresso Aberds 83 E10
Kirktown of Mortlach Moray 88 E3
Kirktown of Slains Aberds 89 F10
Kirkurd Borders 69 F10
Kirkwall Orkney 95 G5
Kirkwhelpington Northumb 62 E5
Kirmington N Lincs 46 A5
Kirmond le Mire Lincs 46 C5
Kirn Argyll 73 F10
Kirriemuir Angus 76 B6
Kirstead Green Norf 39 F8
Kirtlebridge Dumfries 61 F8
Kirtleton Dumfries 61 E8
Kirtling Cambs 30 C3
Kirtling Green Cambs 30 C3
Kirtlington Oxon 27 G11
Kirtomy Highld 93 C10
Kirton Lincs 37 B9
Kirton Notts 45 F10
Kirton Suff 31 E9
Kirton End Lincs 37 A8
Kirton Holme Lincs 37 A8
Kirton in Lindsey N Lincs 46 C3
Kislingbury Northants 28 C3
Kites Hardwick Warks 27 B11
Kittisford Som 7 D9
Kittle Swansea 23 H10
Kitt's Green W Mid 35 G7
Kitt's Moss Gtr Man 44 D2
Kittybrewster Aberdeen 83 C11
Kitwood Hants 10 A5
Kivernoll Hereford 25 E11
Kiveton Park S Yorks 45 D8
Knaith Lincs 46 D2
Knaith Park Lincs 46 D2
Knap Corner Dorset 9 B7
Knaphill Sur 18 F6
Knapp Perth 76 D5
Knapp Som 8 B2
Knapthorpe Notts 45 G11
Knapton Norf 39 B9
Knapton York 52 D1
Knapton Green Hereford 25 C11
Knapwell Cambs 29 B10
Knaresborough N Yorks 51 D9
Knarsdale Northumb 57 A8
Knauchland Moray 88 C5
Knaven Aberds 89 D8
Knayton N Yorks 58 H5
Knebworth Herts 29 F9
Knedlington E Yorks 52 G3
Kneesall Notts 45 F11
Kneesworth Cambs 29 D10
Kneeton Notts 45 H11
Knelston Swansea 23 H9
Knenhall Staffs 34 B5
Knettishall Suff 38 G5
Knightacott Devon 6 C5
Knightcote Warks 27 C10
Knightley Dale Staffs 34 C4
Knighton Devon 4 G6
Knighton Leicester 36 E1
Knighton = Tref-y Clawdd Powys 25 A9
Knighton Staffs 34 A3
Knighton Staffs 34 C3
Knightswood Glasgow 68 D4
Knightwick Worcs 26 C4
Knill Hereford 25 B9
Knipton Leics 36 B4
Knitsley Durham 58 B2
Kniveton Derbys 44 G6
Knock Argyll 79 H8
Knock Cumb 57 D8
Knock Moray 88 C5
Knockally Highld 94 H3
Knockan Highld 92 H5
Knockandhu Moray 82 A4
Knockando Moray 88 D1
Knockando Ho. Moray 88 D2
Knockbain Highld 87 F9
Knockbreck Highld 84 B7
Knockbrex Dumfries 55 E8
Knockdee Highld 94 D3
Knockdolian S Ayrs 66 H4
Knockenkelly N Ayrs 66 D3
Knockentiber E Ayrs 67 C6
Knockespock Ho. Aberds 83 A7
Knockfarrel Highld 87 F8
Knockglass Dumfries 54 D3
Knockholt Kent 19 F11
Knockholt Pound Kent 19 F11
Knockie Lodge Highld 80 B6
Knockin Shrops 33 C9
Knockinlaw E Ayrs 67 C7
Knocklearn Dumfries 60 F3
Knocknaha Argyll 65 G7
Knocknain Dumfries 54 C2
Knockrome Argyll 72 F4
Knocksharry IoM 48 D2
Knodishall Suff 31 B11
Knolls Green Ches E 44 E2
Knolton Wrex 33 B9
Knolton Bryn Wrex 33 B9
Knook Wilts 16 G6
Knossington Leics 36 E4
Knott End-on-Sea Lancs 49 E3
Knotting Bedford 29 B7
Knotting Green Bedford 29 B7
Knottingley W Yorks 51 G11
Knotts Cumb 56 D6
Knotts Lancs 50 D3
Knotty Ash Mers 43 C7
Knotty Green Bucks 18 B6
Knowbury Shrops 26 A2
Knowe Dumfries 54 B6
Knowehead Dumfries 67 G9
Knowes of Elrick Aberds 88 C6
Knowesgate Northumb 62 E5
Knoweton N Lanark 68 E6
Knowhead Aberds 89 C9
Knowl Hill Windsor 18 D5
Knowle Bristol 16 D3
Knowle Devon 6 C3
Knowle Devon 7 F6
Knowle Devon 7 H9
Knowle Shrops 26 A2
Knowle W Mid 35 H7
Knowle Green Lancs 50 F2
Knowle Park W Yorks 51 E6
Knowlton Dorset 9 C9
Knowlton Kent 21 F9
Knowsley Mers 43 C7
Knowstone Devon 7 D7
Knox Bridge Kent 13 B6
Knucklas Powys 25 A9
Knuston Northants 28 B6
Knutsford Ches E 43 E10
Knutton Staffs 44 H2
Knypersley Staffs 44 G2
Kuggar Corn 2 H6
Kyle of Lochalsh Highld 85 F12
Kyleakin Highld 85 F12
Kylerhea Highld 85 F12
Kylesknoydart Highld 79 B11
Kylesku Highld 92 F5
Kylesmorar Highld 79 B11
Kylestrome Highld 92 F5
Kyllachy House Highld 81 A9
Kynaston Shrops 33 C9
Kynnersley Telford 34 D2
Kyre Magna Worcs 26 B3

L

La Fontenelle Guern 11
La Planque Guern 11
Labost W Isles 91 C7
Lacasaidh W Isles 91 E8
Lacasdal W Isles 91 D9
Laceby NE Lincs 46 B6
Lacey Green Bucks 18 B5
Lach Dennis Ches W 43 E10
Lackford Suff 30 A4
Lacock Wilts 16 E6
Ladbroke Warks 27 C11
Laddingford Kent 20 G3
Lade Bank Lincs 47 G7
Ladock Corn 3 D7
Lady Orkney 95 D7
Ladybank Fife 76 F6
Ladykirk Borders 71 F7
Ladysford Aberds 89 B9
Laga Highld 79 E9
Lagalochan Argyll 73 B7
Lagavulin Argyll 64 D5
Lagg Argyll 72 F4
Lagg N Ayrs 66 D2
Laggan Argyll 64 C3
Laggan Highld 79 D10
Laggan Highld 80 D4
Laggan Highld 81 D8
Laggan S Ayrs 54 A5
Lagganulva Argyll 78 G7
Laide Highld 91 H13
Laigh Fenwick E Ayrs 67 B7
Laigh Glengall S Ayrs 66 E6
Laighmuir E Ayrs 67 B7
Laindon Essex 20 C3
Lair Highld 86 G3
Lairg Highld 93 J8
Lairg Lodge Highld 93 J8
Lairg Muir Highld 93 J8
Lairgmore Highld 87 H8
Laisterdyke W Yorks 51 F7
Laithes Cumb 56 C6
Lake IoW 10 F4
Lake Wilts 17 H8
Lakenham Norf 39 E8
Lakenheath Suff 38 G3
Lakesend Norf 37 F11
Lakeside Cumb 56 H5
Laleham Sur 19 E7
Laleston Bridgend 14 D4
Lamarsh Essex 30 E5
Lamas Norf 39 C8
Lambden Borders 70 F6
Lamberhurst Kent 12 C5
Lamberhurst Quarter Kent 12 C5
Lamberton Borders 71 E8
Lambeth London 19 D10
Lambhill Glasgow 68 D4
Lambley Northumb 62 H2
Lambley Notts 45 H10
Lamborough Hill Oxon 17 A11
Lambourn W Berks 17 D10
Lambourne End Essex 19 B11
Lambs Green W Sus 19 H9
Lambston Pembs 22 E4
Lambton T&W 58 A3
Lamerton Devon 4 D5
Lamesley T&W 63 H8
Laminess Orkney 95 E7
Lamington Highld 87 D10
Lamington S Lanark 69 G8
Lamlash N Ayrs 66 C3
Lamloch Dumfries 67 G8
Lamonby Cumb 56 C6
Lamorna Corn 2 G3
Lamorran Corn 3 E7
Lampardbrook Suff 31 B9
Lampeter = Llanbedr Pont Steffan Ceredig 23 B10
Lampeter Velfrey Pembs 22 E6
Lamphey Pembs 22 F5
Lamplugh Cumb 56 D2
Lamport Northants 28 A4
Lamyatt Som 16 H3
Lana Devon 6 G2
Lanark S Lanark 69 F7
Lancaster Lancs 49 C4
Lanchester Durham 58 B2
Lancing W Sus 11 D10
Landbeach Cambs 29 B11
Landcross Devon 6 D3
Landerberry Aberds 83 C9
Landford Wilts 10 C1
Landford Manor Wilts 10 B1
Landimore Swansea 23 G9
Landkey Devon 6 C4
Landore Swansea 14 B2
Landrake Corn 4 E4
Landscove Devon 5 E8
Landshipping Pembs 22 E5
Landshipping Quay Pembs 22 E5
Landulph Corn 4 E5
Landwade Suff 30 B3
Lane Corn 3 C7
Lane End Bucks 18 B5
Lane End Cumb 56 G3
Lane End Dorset 9 E7
Lane End Hants 10 B4
Lane End IoW 10 F5
Lane End Lancs 50 E4
Lane Ends Lancs 50 D3
Lane Ends Lancs 50 F3
Lane Ends N Yorks 50 E5
Lane Head Derbys 44 E5
Lane Head Durham 58 E2
Lane Head Gtr Man 43 C9
Lane Head W Yorks 44 B5
Lane Side Lancs 50 G3
Laneast Corn 4 C3
Laneham Notts 46 E2
Lanehead Durham 57 B10
Lanehead Northumb 62 E3
Lanercost Cumb 61 G11
Laneshaw Bridge Lancs 50 E5
Lanfach Caerph 15 B8
Langar Notts 36 B3
Langbank Renfs 68 C2
Langbar N Yorks 51 D6
Langburnshiels Borders 61 C11
Langcliffe N Yorks 50 C4
Langdale Highld 93 E9
Langdale End N Yorks 59 G10
Langdon Corn 4 C4
Langdon Beck Durham 57 C10
Langdon Hills Essex 20 C3
Langdyke Fife 76 G6
Langenhoe Essex 31 G7
Langford C Beds 29 D8
Langford Devon 7 F9
Langford Essex 30 H5
Langford Notts 46 G2
Langford Oxon 17 A9
Langford Budville Som 7 D10
Langham Essex 31 E7
Langham Norf 38 A6
Langham Rutland 36 D4
Langham Suff 30 B6
Langhaugh Borders 69 G11
Langho Lancs 50 F3
Langholm Dumfries 61 E9
Langleeford Northumb 62 A5
Langley Ches E 44 E3
Langley Hants 10 D3
Langley Herts 29 F9
Langley Kent 20 F5
Langley Northumb 62 G4
Langley Slough 19 D7
Langley W Sus 11 B7
Langley Warks 27 B8
Langley Burrell Wilts 16 D6
Langley Common Derbys 35 B8
Langley Heath Kent 20 F5
Langley Lower Green Essex 29 E11
Langley Marsh Som 7 D9
Langley Park Durham 58 B3
Langley Street Norf 39 E9
Langley Upper Green Essex 29 E11
Langney E Sus 12 F5
Langold Notts 45 D9
Langore Corn 4 C4
Langport Som 8 B3
Langrick Lincs 46 H6
Langridge Bath 16 E4
Langridge Ford Devon 6 D4
Langrigg Cumb 56 B3
Langrish Hants 10 B6
Langsett S Yorks 44 B6
Langshaw Borders 70 G4
Langside Perth 75 F10
Langskaill Orkney 95 D5
Langstone Hants 10 D6
Langstone Newport 15 B9
Langthorne N Yorks 58 G3
Langthorpe N Yorks 51 C9
Langthwaite N Yorks 58 F1
Langtoft E Yorks 52 C6
Langtoft Lincs 37 D7
Langton Durham 58 E2
Langton Lincs 46 F6
Langton Lincs 47 E7
Langton N Yorks 52 C3
Langton by Wragby Lincs 46 E5
Langton Green Kent 12 C4
Langton Green Suff 31 A8
Langton Herring Dorset 8 F5
Langton Matravers Dorset 9 G9
Langtree Devon 6 E3
Langwathby Cumb 57 C7
Langwell Ho. Highld 94 H3
Langwell Lodge Highld 92 J4
Langwith Derbys 45 F9
Langwith Junction Derbys 45 F9
Langworth Lincs 46 E4
Lanivet Corn 3 C9
Lanlivery Corn 4 F1
Lanner Corn 2 F6
Lanreath Corn 4 F2
Lansallos Corn 4 F2
Lansdown Glos 26 F6
Lanteglos Highway Corn 4 F2
Lanton Borders 62 A2
Lanton Northumb 71 G8
Lapford Devon 7 F6
Laphroaig Argyll 64 D4
Lapley Staffs 34 D4
Lapworth Warks 27 A8
Larachbeg Highld 79 G9
Larbert Falk 69 B7
Larden Green Ches E 43 G8
Largie Aberds 88 E6
Largiemore Argyll 73 E8
Largoward Fife 77 G7
Largs N Ayrs 73 H11
Largybeg N Ayrs 66 D3
Largymore N Ayrs 66 D3
Larkfield Invclyd 73 F11
Larkhall S Lanark 68 E6
Larkhill Wilts 17 G8
Larling Norf 38 G5
Larriston Borders 61 D11
Lartington Durham 58 E1
Lary Aberds 82 C5
Lasham Hants 18 G3
Lashenden Kent 13 B7
Lassington Glos 26 F4
Lassodie Fife 69 A10
Lastingham N Yorks 59 G8
Latcham Som 15 G10
Latchford Herts 29 F10
Latchford Warr 43 D9
Latchingdon Essex 20 A5
Latchley Corn 4 D5
Lately Common Warr 43 C9
Lathbury M Keynes 28 D5
Latheron Highld 94 G3
Latheronwheel Highld 94 G3
Latheronwheel Ho. Highld 94 G3
Lathones Fife 77 G7
Latimer Bucks 19 B7
Latteridge S Glos 16 C3
Lattiford Som 8 B5
Latton Wilts 17 B7
Latton Bush Essex 29 H11
Lauchintilly Aberds 83 B9
Lauder Borders 70 F4
Laugharne Carms 23 E8
Laughterton Lincs 46 E2
Laughton E Sus 12 E4
Laughton Leics 36 G2
Laughton Lincs 37 B6
Laughton Lincs 46 C2
Laughton Common S Yorks 45 D9
Laughton en le Morthen S Yorks 45 D9
Launcells Corn 6 F1
Launceston Corn 4 C4
Launton Oxon 28 F3
Laurencekirk Aberds 83 F9
Laurieston Dumfries 55 C9
Laurieston Falk 69 C8
Lavendon M Keynes 28 C6
Lavenham Suff 30 D6
Laverhay Dumfries 61 D7
Laversdale Cumb 61 G10
Laverstock Wilts 9 A10
Laverstoke Hants 17 G11
Laverton Glos 27 E7
Laverton N Yorks 51 B8
Laverton Som 16 F4
Lavister Wrex 42 G6
Law S Lanark 69 E7
Lawers Perth 75 D9
Lawers Perth 75 E10
Lawford Essex 31 E7
Lawhitton Corn 4 C4
Lawkland N Yorks 50 C3
Lawley Telford 34 E2
Lawnhead Staffs 34 C4
Lawrenny Pembs 22 F5
Lawshall Suff 30 C5
Lawton Hereford 25 C11
Laxey IoM 48 D4
Laxfield Suff 31 A9
Laxfirth Shetland 96 H6
Laxfirth Shetland 96 J6
Laxford Bridge Highld 92 E5
Laxo Shetland 96 G6
Laxobigging Shetland 96 F6
Laxton E Yorks 52 G3
Laxton Northants 36 F5
Laxton Notts 45 F11
Laycock W Yorks 50 E6
Layer Breton Essex 30 G6
Layer de la Haye Essex 30 G6
Layer Marney Essex 30 G6
Layham Suff 31 D7
Laylands Green W Berks 17 E10
Laytham E Yorks 52 F3
Layton Blackpool 49 F3
Lazenby Redcar 59 D6
Lazonby Cumb 57 C7
Le Planel Guern 11
Le Skerne Haughton Darl 58 E4
Le Villocq Guern 11
Lea Derbys 45 G7
Lea Hereford 26 F3
Lea Lincs 46 D2
Lea Shrops 33 E10
Lea Shrops 33 G9
Lea Wilts 16 C6
Lea Marston Warks 35 F8
Lea Town Lancs 49 F4
Leabrooks Derbys 45 G8
Leac a Li W Isles 90 H6
Leachkin Highld 87 G9
Leadburn Midloth 69 E11
Leaden Roding Essex 30 G2
Leadenham Lincs 46 G3
Leadgate Cumb 57 B9
Leadgate Durham 58 A2
Leadgate T&W 63 H7
Leadhills S Lanark 60 B4
Leafield Oxon 27 G10
Leagrave Luton 29 F7
Leake N Yorks 58 G5
Leake Commonside Lincs 47 G7
Lealholm N Yorks 59 F8
Lealt Argyll 72 D5
Lealt Highld 85 B10
Leamington Hastings Warks 27 B11
Leamonsley Staffs 35 E7
Leamside Durham 58 B4
Leanaig Highld 87 F8
Leargybreck Argyll 72 F4
Leasgill Cumb 49 A4
Leasingham Lincs 46 H4
Leasingthorne Durham 58 D3
Leasowe Mers 42 C5
Leatherhead Sur 19 F8
Leatherhead Common Sur 19 F8
Leathley N Yorks 51 E8
Leaton Shrops 33 D10
Leaveland Kent 21 F7
Leavening N Yorks 52 C3
Leaves Green London 19 E11
Leazes Durham 63 H7
Lebberston N Yorks 53 A6
Lechlade-on-Thames Glos 17 B9
Leck Lancs 50 B2
Leckford Hants 17 H10
Leckfurin Highld 93 D10
Leckgruinart Argyll 64 B3
Leckhampstead Bucks 28 E4
Leckhampstead W Berks 17 D11
Leckhampstead Thicket W Berks 17 D11
Leckhampton Glos 26 G6
Leckie Highld 86 E3
Leckmelm Highld 86 B4
Leckwith V Glam 15 D7
Leconfield E Yorks 52 E6
Ledaig Argyll 74 D2
Ledburn Bucks 28 F6
Ledbury Hereford 26 E4
Ledcharrie Stirling 75 E8
Ledgemoor Hereford 25 C11
Ledicot Hereford 25 B11
Ledmore Highld 92 H5
Lednagullin Highld 93 C10
Ledsham Ches W 42 E6
Ledsham W Yorks 51 G10
Ledston W Yorks 51 G10
Ledston Luck W Yorks 51 F10
Ledwell Oxon 27 F11
Lee Argyll 78 J7
Lee Devon 6 B3
Lee Hants 10 C2
Lee Lancs 50 D1
Lee Shrops 33 B10
Lee Brockhurst Shrops 33 C11
Lee Clump Bucks 18 A6
Lee Mill Devon 5 F7
Lee Moor Devon 5 E6
Lee-on-the-Solent Hants 10 D4
Leeans Shetland 96 J5
Leebotten Shetland 96 L6
Leebotwood Shrops 33 F10
Leece Cumb 49 C2
Leechpool Pembs 22 E4
Leeds Kent 20 F5
Leeds W Yorks 51 F8
Leedstown Corn 2 F5
Leek Staffs 44 G3
Leek Wootton Warks 27 B9
Leekbrook Staffs 44 G3
Leeming N Yorks 58 H3
Leeming Bar N Yorks 58 G3
Lees Derbys 35 B8
Lees Gtr Man 44 B3
Lees W Yorks 50 F6
Leeswood Flint 42 F5
Legbourne Lincs 47 D7
Legerwood Borders 70 F4
Legsby Lincs 46 D5
Leicester Leicester 36 E1
Leicester Forest East Leics 35 E11
Leigh Dorset 8 D5
Leigh Glos 26 F5
Leigh Gtr Man 43 B9
Leigh Kent 20 G2
Leigh Shrops 33 E9
Leigh Sur 19 G9
Leigh Wilts 17 B7
Leigh Worcs 26 C4
Leigh Beck Essex 20 C5
Leigh Common Som 8 B6
Leigh Delamere Wilts 16 D5
Leigh Green Kent 13 C8
Leigh on Sea Southend 20 C5
Leigh Park Hants 10 D6
Leigh Sinton Worcs 26 C4
Leigh upon Mendip Som 16 G3
Leigh Woods N Som 16 D2
Leighswood W Mid 35 E6
Leighterton Glos 16 B5
Leighton N Yorks 51 B7
Leighton Powys 33 E8
Leighton Shrops 34 E2
Leighton Som 16 G4
Leighton Bromswold Cambs 37 H7
Leighton Buzzard C Beds 28 F6
Leinthall Earls Hereford 25 B11
Leinthall Starkes Hereford 25 B11
Leintwardine Hereford 25 A11
Leire Leics 35 F11
Leirinmore Highld 92 C7
Leiston Suff 31 B11
Leitfie Perth 76 C5
Leith Edin 69 C11
Leitholm Borders 70 F6
Lelant Corn 2 F4
Lelley E Yorks 53 F8
Lem Hill Worcs 26 A4
Lemmington Hall Northumb 63 B7
Lempitlaw Borders 70 G6
Lenchwick Worcs 27 D7
Lendalfoot S Ayrs 66 H4
Lendrick Lodge Stirling 75 G8
Lenham Kent 20 F5
Lenham Heath Kent 20 G6
Lennel Borders 71 F7
Lennoxtown E Dunb 68 C5
Lenton Lincs 36 B6
Lenton Nottingham 36 B1
Lentran Highld 87 G8
Lenwade Norf 39 D6
Leny Ho. Stirling 75 G9
Lenzie E Dunb 68 C5
Leoch Angus 76 D6
Leochel-Cushnie Aberds 83 B7
Leominster Hereford 25 C11
Leonard Stanley Glos 16 A5
Leorin Argyll 64 D4
Lepe Hants 10 E3
Lephin Highld 84 D6
Lephinchapel Argyll 73 D8
Lephinmore Argyll 73 D8
Leppington N Yorks 52 C3
Lepton W Yorks 51 H8
Lerryn Corn 4 F2
Lerwick Shetland 96 J6
Lesbury Northumb 63 B8
Leslie Aberds 83 A7
Leslie Fife 76 G5
Lesmahagow S Lanark 69 G7
Lesnewth Corn 4 B2
Lessendrum Aberds 88 D5
Lessingham Norf 39 C9
Lessonhall Cumb 56 A4
Leswalt Dumfries 54 C3
Letchmore Heath Herts 19 B8
Letchworth Herts 29 E9
Letcombe Bassett Oxon 17 C10
Letcombe Regis Oxon 17 C10
Letham Angus 77 C8
Letham Falk 69 B7
Letham Fife 76 F6
Letham Perth 76 E3
Letham Grange Angus 77 C9
Lethenty Aberds 89 D8
Letheringham Suff 31 C9
Letheringsett Norf 39 B6
Lettaford Devon 5 C8
Lettan Orkney 95 D8
Letterewe Highld 86 D2
Letterfearn Highld 85 F13
Letterfinlay Highld 80 D4
Lettermorar Highld 79 C10
Lettermore Argyll 78 G7
Letters Highld 86 C4
Letterston Pembs 22 D4
Lettoch Highld 82 B2
Lettoch Highld 87 H13
Letton Hereford 25 A10
Letton Hereford 25 D10
Letton Green Norf 38 E5
Letty Green Herts 29 G9
Letwell S Yorks 45 D9
Leuchars Fife 77 E7
Leuchars Ho. Moray 88 B2
Leumrabhagh W Isles 91 F8
Levan Invclyd 73 F11
Levaneap Shetland 96 G6
Levedale Staffs 34 D4
Leven E Yorks 53 E7
Leven Fife 76 G6
Levencorroch N Ayrs 66 D3
Levens Cumb 57 H6
Levens Green Herts 29 F10
Levenshulme Gtr Man 44 C2
Levenwick Shetland 96 L6
Leverburgh = An t-Ob W Isles 90 J5
Leverington Cambs 37 D10
Leverton Lincs 47 H8
Leverton Highgate Lincs 47 H8
Leverton Lucasgate Lincs 47 H8
Leverton Outgate Lincs 47 H8
Levington Suff 31 E9
Levisham N Yorks 59 G9
Levishie Highld 80 B6
Lew Oxon 27 H10
Lewannick Corn 4 C3
Lewdown Devon 4 C5
Lewes E Sus 12 E3
Leweston Pembs 22 D4
Lewisham London 19 D10
Lewiston Highld 81 A7
Lewistown Bridgend 14 C5
Lewknor Oxon 18 B4
Leworthy Devon 6 C5
Leworthy Devon 6 F2
Lewtrenchard Devon 4 C5
Lexden Essex 30 F6
Ley Aberds 83 B7
Ley Corn 4 E2
Leybourne Kent 20 F3
Leyburn N Yorks 58 G2
Leyfields Staffs 35 E8
Leyhill Bucks 18 A6
Leyland Lancs 49 G5
Leylodge Aberds 83 B9
Leymoor W Yorks 51 H7
Leys Aberds 89 C10
Leys Perth 76 D5
Leys Castle Highld 87 G9
Leys of Cossans Angus 76 C6
Leysdown-on-Sea Kent 21 D7
Leysmill Angus 77 C9
Leysters Pole Hereford 26 B2
Leyton London 19 C10
Leytonstone London 19 C10
Lezant Corn 4 D4
Leziate Norf 38 D2
Lhanbryde Moray 88 B2
Liatrie Highld 86 H5
Libanus Powys 24 F6
Libberton S Lanark 69 F8
Liberton Edin 69 D11
Liceasto W Isles 90 H6
Lichfield Staffs 35 E7
Lickey Worcs 34 H5
Lickey End Worcs 26 A6
Lickfold W Sus 11 B8
Liddel Orkney 95 K5
Liddesdale Highld 79 F10
Liddington Swindon 17 C9
Lidgate Suff 30 C4
Lidget S Yorks 45 B10
Lidget Green W Yorks 51 F7
Lidgett Notts 45 F10
Lidlington C Beds 28 E6
Lidstone Oxon 27 F10
Lieurary Highld 94 D2
Liff Angus 76 D6
Lifton Devon 4 C4
Liftondown Devon 4 C4
Lighthorne Warks 27 C10
Lightwater Sur 18 E6
Lightwood Stoke 34 A5
Lightwood Green Ches E 34 A2
Lightwood Green Wrex 33 A9
Lilbourne Northants 36 H1
Lilburn Tower Northumb 62 A6
Lilleshall Telford 34 D3
Lilley Herts 29 F8
Lilley W Berks 17 D11
Lilliesleaf Borders 61 A11
Lillingstone Dayrell Bucks 28 E4
Lillingstone Lovell Bucks 28 D4
Lillington Dorset 8 C5
Lillington Warks 27 B10
Lilliput Poole 9 E9
Lilstock Som 7 B10
Lilyhurst Shrops 34 D3
Limbury Luton 29 F7
Limebrook Hereford 25 B10
Limefield Gtr Man 44 A2
Limekilnburn S Lanark 68 E6
Limekilns Fife 69 B9
Limerigg Falk 69 C7
Limerstone IoW 10 F3
Limington Som 8 B4
Limpenhoe Norf 39 E9
Limpley Stoke Wilts 16 E4
Limpsfield Sur 19 F11
Limpsfield Chart Sur 19 F11
Linby Notts 45 G9
Linchmere W Sus 11 A7
Lincluden Dumfries 60 F5
Lincoln Lincs 46 E3
Lincomb Worcs 26 B5
Lincombe Devon 5 F8
Lindal in Furness Cumb 49 B2
Lindale Cumb 49 A4
Lindean Borders 70 G3
Lindfield W Sus 12 D2
Lindford Hants 18 H5
Lindifferon Fife 76 F6
Lindley W Yorks 51 H7
Lindley Green N Yorks 51 E8
Lindores Fife 76 F5
Lindridge Worcs 26 B3
Lindsell Essex 30 F3
Lindsey Suff 30 D6
Linford Hants 9 D10
Linford Thurrock 20 D3
Lingague IoM 48 E2
Lingards Wood W Yorks 44 A4
Lingbob W Yorks 51 F6
Lingdale Redcar 59 E7
Lingen Hereford 25 B10
Lingfield Sur 12 B2
Lingreabhagh W Isles 90 J5
Lingwood Norf 39 E9
Linicro Highld 85 B8
Linkenholt Hants 17 F10
Linkhill Kent 13 D7
Linkinhorne Corn 4 D4
Linklater Orkney 95 K5
Linksness Orkney 95 H3
Linktown Fife 69 A11
Linley Shrops 33 F9
Linley Green Hereford 26 C3
Linlithgow W Loth 69 C9
Linlithgow Bridge W Loth 69 C8
Linshiels Northumb 62 C4
Linsiadar W Isles 90 D7
Linsidemore Highld 87 B8
Linslade C Beds 28 F6
Linstead Parva Suff 39 H9
Linstock Cumb 61 H10
Linthwaite W Yorks 44 A5
Lintlaw Borders 71 E7
Lintmill Moray 88 B5
Linton Borders 70 H6
Linton Cambs 30 D2
Linton Derbys 35 D8
Linton Hereford 26 F3
Linton Kent 20 G4
Linton N Yorks 50 C5
Linton Northumb 63 D8
Linton W Yorks 51 E9
Linton-on-Ouse N Yorks 51 C10
Linwood Hants 9 D10
Linwood Lincs 46 D5
Linwood Renfs 68 D3
Lionacleit W Isles 84 D2
Lional W Isles 91 A10
Liphook Hants 11 A7
Liscard Mers 42 C6
Liscombe Som 7 C7
Liskeard Corn 4 E3
L'Islet Guern 11
Liss Hants 11 B6
Liss Forest Hants 11 B6
Lissett E Yorks 53 D7
Lissington Lincs 46 D5
Lisvane Cardiff 15 C7
Liswerry Newport 15 C9
Litcham Norf 38 D4
Litchborough Northants 28 C3
Litchfield Hants 17 F11
Litherland Mers 42 C6
Litlington Cambs 29 D10
Litlington E Sus 12 F4
Little Abington Cambs 30 D2
Little Addington Northants 28 A6
Little Alne Warks 27 B8
Little Altcar Mers 42 B6
Little Asby Cumb 57 F8
Little Assynt Highld 92 G4
Little Aston Staffs 35 E6
Little Atherfield IoW 10 F3
Little Ayre Orkney 95 J4
Little-ayre Shetland 96 G5
Little Ayton N Yorks 59 E6
Little Baddow Essex 30 H4
Little Badminton S Glos 16 C5
Little Ballinluig Perth 76 B2
Little Bampton Cumb 61 H8
Little Bardfield Essex 30 E3
Little Barford Bedford 29 C8
Little Barningham Norf 39 B7
Little Barrington Glos 27 G9
Little Barrow Ches W 43 E7
Little Barugh N Yorks 52 B3
Little Bavington Northumb 62 F5
Little Bealings Suff 31 D9
Little Bedwyn Wilts 17 E9
Little Bentley Essex 31 F8
Little Berkhamsted Herts 29 H9
Little Billing Northants 28 B5
Little Birch Hereford 26 E2
Little Blakenham Suff 31 D8
Little Blencow Cumb 56 C6
Little Bollington Ches E 43 D10
Little Bookham Sur 19 F8
Little Bowden Leics 36 G3
Little Bradley Suff 30 C3
Little Brampton Shrops 33 G9
Little Brechin Angus 77 A8
Little Brickhill M Keynes 28 E6
Little Brington Northants 28 B3
Little Bromley Essex 31 F7
Little Broughton Cumb 56 C2
Little Budworth Ches W 43 F8
Little Burstead Essex 20 B3
Little Bytham Lincs 36 D6
Little Carlton Lincs 47 D7
Little Carlton Notts 45 G11
Little Casterton Rutland 36 E6
Little Cawthorpe Lincs 47 D7
Little Chalfont Bucks 18 B6
Little Chart Kent 20 G6
Little Chesterford Essex 30 D2
Little Cheverell Wilts 16 F6
Little Chishill Cambs 29 E11
Little Clacton Essex 31 G8
Little Clifton Cumb 56 D2
Little Colp Aberds 89 D7
Little Comberton Worcs 26 D6
Little Common E Sus 12 F6
Little Compton Warks 27 E9
Little Cornard Suff 30 E5
Little Cowarne Hereford 26 C3
Little Coxwell Oxon 17 B9
Little Crakehall N Yorks 58 G3
Little Cressingham Norf 38 F4
Little Crosby Mers 42 B6
Little Dalby Leics 36 D3
Little Dawley Telford 34 E2
Little Dens Aberds 89 D10
Little Dewchurch Hereford 26 E2
Little Downham Cambs 37 G11
Little Driffield E Yorks 52 D6
Little Dunham Norf 38 D4
Little Dunkeld Perth 76 C3
Little Dunmow Essex 30 F3
Little Easton Essex 30 F3
Little Eaton Derbys 35 A9
Little Eccleston Lancs 49 E4
Little Ellingham Norf 38 F6
Little End Essex 20 A2
Little Eversden Cambs 29 C10
Little Faringdon Oxon 17 A9
Little Fencote N Yorks 58 G3
Little Fenton N Yorks 51 F11
Little Finborough Suff 31 C7
Little Fransham Norf 38 D5
Little Gaddesden Herts 28 G6
Little Gidding Cambs 37 G7
Little Glemham Suff 31 C10
Little Glenshee Perth 76 D2
Little Gransden Cambs 29 C9
Little Green Som 16 G4
Little Grimsby Lincs 47 C7
Little Gruinard Highld 86 C2
Little Habton N Yorks 52 B3
Little Hadham Herts 29 F11
Little Hale Lincs 37 A7
Little Hallingbury Essex 29 G11
Little Hampden Bucks 18 A5
Little Harrowden Northants 28 A5
Little Haseley Oxon 18 A3
Little Hatfield E Yorks 53 E7
Little Hautbois Norf 39 C8
Little Haven Pembs 22 E3
Little Hay Staffs 35 E7
Little Hayfield Derbys 44 D4
Little Haywood Staffs 34 C6
Little Heath W Mid 35 G9
Little Hereford Hereford 26 B2
Little Horkesley Essex 30 E6
Little Horsted E Sus 12 E3
Little Horton W Yorks 51 F7
Little Horwood Bucks 28 E4
Little Houghton Northants 28 C5
Little Houghton S Yorks 45 B8
Little Hucklow Derbys 44 E5
Little Hulton Gtr Man 43 B10
Little Humber E Yorks 53 G7
Little Hungerford W Berks 18 D2
Little Irchester Northants 28 B6
Little Kimble Bucks 28 H5
Little Kineton Warks 27 C10
Little Kingshill Bucks 18 B5
Little Langdale Cumb 56 F5
Little Langford Wilts 17 H7
Little Laver Essex 30 H2
Little Leigh Ches W 43 E9
Little Leighs Essex 30 G4
Little Lever Gtr Man 43 B10
Little London Bucks 28 G3
Little London E Sus 12 E4
Little London Hants 17 G10
Little London Hants 18 F3
Little London Lincs 37 C10
Little London Lincs 37 C8
Little London Norf 39 C7
Little London Powys 32 G6
Little Longstone Derbys 44 E5
Little Lynturk Aberds 83 B7
Little Malvern Worcs 26 D4
Little Maplestead Essex 30 E5
Little Marcle Hereford 26 E3
Little Marlow Bucks 18 C5
Little Marsden Lancs 50 F4
Little Massingham Norf 38 C3
Little Melton Norf 39 E7
Little Mill Mon 15 A9
Little Milton Oxon 18 A3
Little Missenden Bucks 18 B6
Little Musgrave Cumb 57 E9
Little Ness Shrops 33 D10
Little Neston Ches W 42 E5
Little Newcastle Pembs 22 D4
Little Newsham Durham 58 E2
Little Oakley Essex 31 F9
Little Oakley Northants 36 G4
Little Orton Cumb 61 H9
Little Ouseburn N Yorks 51 C10
Little Paxton Cambs 29 B8
Little Petherick Corn 3 B8
Little Pitlurg Moray 88 D4
Little Plumpton Lancs 49 F3
Little Plumstead Norf 39 D9
Little Ponton Lincs 36 B5
Little Raveley Cambs 37 H8
Little Reedness E Yorks 52 G4
Little Ribston N Yorks 51 D9
Little Rissington Glos 27 G8
Little Ryburgh Norf 38 C5
Little Ryle Northumb 62 B6
Little Salkeld Cumb 57 C7
Little Sampford Essex 30 E3
Little Sandhurst Brack 18 E5
Little Saxham Suff 30 B4
Little Scatwell Highld 86 F6
Little Sessay N Yorks 51 B10
Little Shelford Cambs 29 C11
Little Singleton Lancs 49 F3
Little Skillymarno Aberds 89 C9
Little Smeaton N Yorks 51 H11
Little Snoring Norf 38 B5
Little Sodbury S Glos 16 C4
Little Somborne Hants 10 A2
Little Somerford Wilts 16 C6
Little Stainforth N Yorks 50 C4
Little Stainton Darl 58 D4
Little Stanney Ches W 43 E7
Little Staughton Bedford 29 B8
Little Steeping Lincs 47 F8
Little Stoke Staffs 34 B5
Little Stonham Suff 31 B8
Little Stretton Leics 36 E2
Little Stretton Shrops 33 F10
Little Strickland Cumb 57 E7
Little Stukeley Cambs 37 H8
Little Sutton Ches W 42 E6
Little Tew Oxon 27 F10
Little Thetford Cambs 37 H11
Little Thirkleby N Yorks 51 B10
Little Thurlow Suff 30 C3
Little Thurrock Thurrock 20 D3
Little Torboll Highld 87 B10
Little Torrington Devon 6 E3
Little Totham Essex 30 G5
Little Toux Aberds 88 C5
Little Town Cumb 56 E4
Little Town Lancs 50 F2
Little Urswick Cumb 49 B2
Little Wakering Essex 20 C6
Little Walden Essex 30 D2
Little Waldingfield Suff 30 D6
Little Walsingham Norf 38 B5
Little Waltham Essex 30 G4
Little Warley Essex 20 B3
Little Weighton E Yorks 52 F5
Little Weldon Northants 36 G5
Little Welnetham Suff 30 B5
Little Wenlock Telford 34 E2
Little Whittingham Green Suff 39 H8
Little Wilbraham Cambs 30 C2
Little Wishford Wilts 17 H7
Little Witley Worcs 26 B4
Little Wittenham Oxon 18 B2
Little Wolford Warks 27 E9
Little Wratting Suff 30 D3
Little Wymington Bedford 28 B6
Little Wymondley Herts 29 F9
Little Wyrley Staffs 34 E6
Little Yeldham Essex 30 E4
Littlebeck N Yorks 59 F9
Littleborough Gtr Man 50 H5
Littleborough Notts 46 D2
Littlebourne Kent 21 F9
Littlebredy Dorset 8 F4
Littlebury Essex 30 E2
Littlebury Green Essex 29 E11
Littledean Glos 26 G3
Littleferry Highld 87 B11
Littleham Devon 5 C11
Littleham Devon 6 D3
Littlehampton W Sus 11 D9
Littlehempston Devon 5 E9
Littlehoughton Northumb 63 B8
Littlemill Aberds 82 D5
Littlemill E Ayrs 67 E7
Littlemill Highld 87 F12
Littlemill Northumb 63 B8
Littlemoor Dorset 8 F5
Littlemore Oxon 18 A2
Littleover Derby 35 B9
Littleport Cambs 38 G1
Littlestone on Sea Kent 13 D9
Littlethorpe Leics 35 F11
Littlethorpe N Yorks 51 C9
Littleton Ches W 43 F7
Littleton Hants 10 A3
Littleton Perth 76 D5
Littleton Som 8 A3
Littleton Sur 18 G6
Littleton Sur 19 E7
Littleton Drew Wilts 16 C5
Littleton-on-Severn S Glos 16 C2
Littleton Pannell Wilts 17 F7
Littletown Durham 58 B4
Littlewick Green Windsor 18 D5
Littleworth Bedford 29 D7
Littleworth Glos 16 A5
Littleworth Oxon 17 B10
Littleworth Staffs 34 D6
Littleworth Worcs 26 C5
Litton Derbys 44 E5
Litton N Yorks 50 B5
Litton Som 16 F2
Litton Cheney Dorset 8 E4
Liurbost W Isles 91 E8
Liverpool Mers 42 C6
Liverpool Airport Mers 43 D7
Liversedge W Yorks 51 G8
Liverton Devon 5 D9
Liverton Redcar 59 E8
Livingston W Loth 69 D9
Livingston Village W Loth 69 D9
Lixwm Flint 42 E4
Lizard Corn 2 H6
Llaingoch Anglesey 40 B4
Llaithddu Powys 33 G6
Llan Powys 32 E4
Llan Ffestiniog Gwyn 41 F9
Llan-y-pwll Wrex 42 G6
Llanaber Gwyn 32 D2
Llanaelhaearn Gwyn 40 F5
Llanafan Ceredig 24 A3
Llanafan-fawr Powys 24 C6
Llanallgo Anglesey 40 B6
Llanandras = Presteigne Powys 25 B10
Llanarmon Gwyn 40 G6
Llanarmon Dyffryn Ceiriog Wrex 33 B7
Llanarmon-yn-Ial Denb 42 G4
Llanarth Ceredig 23 A9
Llanarth Mon 25 G10
Llanarthne Carms 23 D10
Llanasa Flint 42 D4
Llanbabo Anglesey 40 B5
Llanbadarn Fawr Ceredig 32 G2
Llanbadarn Fynydd Powys 33 H7
Llanbadarn-y-Garreg Powys 25 D8
Llanbadoc Mon 15 B9
Llanbadrig Anglesey 40 A5
Llanbeder Newport 15 B9
Llanbedr Gwyn 32 C1
Llanbedr Powys 25 D8
Llanbedr Powys 25 F9
Llanbedr-Dyffryn-Clwyd Denb 42 G4
Llanbedr Pont Steffan = Lampeter Ceredig 23 B10
Llanbedr-y-cennin Conwy 41 D9
Llanbedrgoch Anglesey 41 B7
Llanbedrog Gwyn 40 G5
Llanberis Gwyn 41 D7
Llanbethêry V Glam 14 E6
Llanbister Powys 25 A8
Llanblethian V Glam 14 D5
Llanboidy Carms 23 D7
Llanbradach Caerph 15 B7
Llanbrynmair Powys 32 E4
Llancarfan V Glam 14 D6
Llancayo Mon 15 A9
Llancloudy Hereford 25 F11
Llancynfelyn Ceredig 32 F2
Llandaff Cardiff 15 D7
Llandanwg Gwyn 32 C1
Llandarcy Neath 14 B3
Llandawke Carms 23 E7
Llanddaniel Fab Anglesey 40 C6
Llanddarog Carms 23 E10
Llanddeiniol Ceredig 24 A2
Llanddeiniolen Gwyn 41 D7
Llandderfel Gwyn 32 B5
Llanddeusant Anglesey 40 B5
Llanddeusant Carms 24 F4
Llanddew Powys 25 E7
Llanddewi Swansea 23 H9
Llanddewi-Brefi Ceredig 24 C3
Llanddewi Rhydderch Mon 25 G10
Llanddewi Velfrey Pembs 22 E6
Llanddewi'r Cwm Powys 25 D7
Llanddoged Conwy 41 D10
Llanddona Anglesey 41 C7
Llanddowror Carms 23 E7
Llanddulas Conwy 42 E2
Llanddwywe Gwyn 32 C1
Llanddyfynan Anglesey 41 C7
Llandefaelog Fach Powys 25 E7
Llandefaelog-tre'r-graig Powys 25 F8
Llandefalle Powys 25 E8
Llandegai Gwyn 41 C7
Llandegfan Anglesey 41 C7
Llandegla Denb 42 G4
Llandegley Powys 25 B8
Llandegveth Mon 15 B9
Llandegwning Gwyn 40 G4
Llandeilo Carms 24 F3
Llandeilo Graban Powys 25 D7
Llandeilo'r Fan Powys 24 E5
Llandeloy Pembs 22 D3
Llandenny Mon 15 A10
Llandevenny Mon 15 C10
Llandewednock Corn 2 H6
Llandewi Ystradenny Powys 25 B8
Llandinabo Hereford 26 F2
Llandinam Powys 32 G6
Llandissilio Pembs 22 D6
Llandogo Mon 15 A11
Llandough V Glam 14 D5
Llandough V Glam 15 D7
Llandovery = Llanymddyfri Carms 24 E4
Llandow V Glam 14 D5
Llandre Carms 24 D3
Llandre Ceredig 32 G2
Llandrillo Denb 32 B6
Llandrillo-yn-Rhos Conwy 41 B10
Llandrindod = Llandrindod Wells Powys 25 B7
Llandrindod Wells = Llandrindod Powys 25 B7
Llandrinio Powys 33 D8
Llandudno Conwy 41 B9
Llandudno Junction = Cyffordd Llandudno Conwy 41 C9
Llandwrog Gwyn 40 E6
Llandybie Carms 24 G3
Llandyfaelog Carms 23 E9
Llandyfan Carms 24 G3
Llandyfriog Ceredig 23 B8
Llandyfrydog Anglesey 40 B6
Llandygwydd Ceredig 23 B7
Llandynan Denb 42 H4
Llandyrnog Denb 42 F4
Llandysilio Powys 33 D8
Llandyssil Powys 33 F7
Llandysul Ceredig 23 B9
Llanedeyrn Cardiff 15 C8
Llanedi Carms 23 F10
Llaneglwys Powys 25 E7
Llanegryn Gwyn 32 E1
Llanegwad Carms 23 D10
Llaneilian Anglesey 40 A6
Llanelian-yn-Rhos Conwy 41 C10
Llanelidan Denb 42 G4
Llanelieu Powys 25 E8
Llanellen Mon 25 G10
Llanelli Carms 23 G10
Llanelltyd Gwyn 32 D3
Llanelly Mon 25 G9
Llanelly Hill Mon 25 G9
Llanelwedd Powys 25 C7
Llanelwy = St Asaph Denb 42 E3
Llanenddwyn Gwyn 32 C1
Llanengan Gwyn 40 H4
Llanerchymedd Anglesey 40 B6
Llanerfyl Powys 32 E6
Llanfachraeth Anglesey 40 B5
Llanfachreth Gwyn 32 C3
Llanfaelog Anglesey 40 C5
Llanfaelrhys Gwyn 40 H4
Llanfaenor Mon 25 G11
Llanfaes Anglesey 41 C8
Llanfaes Powys 25 F7
Llanfaethlu Anglesey 40 B5
Llanfaglan Gwyn 40 D6
Llanfair Gwyn 32 C1
Llanfair-ar-y-bryn Carms 24 E5
Llanfair Caereinion Powys 33 E7
Llanfair Clydogau Ceredig 24 C3
Llanfair-Dyffryn-Clwyd Denb 42 G4
Llanfair Kilgheddin Mon 25 H10
Llanfair-Nant-Gwyn Pembs 22 C6
Llanfair Talhaiarn Conwy 42 E2
Llanfair Waterdine Shrops 33 H8
Llanfair-ym-Muallt = Builth Wells Powys 25 C7
Llanfairfechan Conwy 41 C8
Llanfairpwll-gwyngyll Anglesey 41 C7
Llanfairyneubwll Anglesey 40 C5
Llanfairynghornwy Anglesey 40 A5
Llanfallteg Carms 22 E6
Llanfaredd Powys 25 C7
Llanfarian Ceredig 32 H1
Llanfechain Powys 33 C7
Llanfechan Powys 24 C6
Llanfechell Anglesey 40 A5
Llanfendigaid Gwyn 32 E1
Llanferres Denb 42 F4
Llanfflewyn Anglesey 40 B5
Llanfihangel-ar-arth Carms 23 C9
Llanfihangel-Crucorney Mon 25 F10
Llanfihangel Glyn Myfyr Conwy 42 H2
Llanfihangel Nant Bran Powys 24 E6
Llanfihangel-nant-Melan Powys 25 C8
Llanfihangel Rhydithon Powys 25 B8
Llanfihangel Rogiet Mon 15 C10
Llanfihangel Tal-y-llyn Powys 25 F8
Llanfihangel-uwch-Gwili Carms 23 D9
Llanfihangel-y-Creuddyn Ceredig 32 H2
Llanfihangel-y-pennant Gwyn 32 E2
Llanfihangel-y-pennant Gwyn 41 F7
Llanfihangel-y-traethau Gwyn 41 G7
Llanfihangel-yn-Ngwynfa Powys 33 D6
Llanfihangel yn Nhowyn Anglesey 40 C5
Llanfilo Powys 25 E8
Llanfoist Mon 25 G9
Llanfor Gwyn 32 B5
Llanfrechfa Torf 15 B9
Llanfrothen Gwyn 41 F8
Llanfrynach Powys 25 F7
Llanfwrog Anglesey 40 B5
Llanfwrog Denb 42 G4
Llanfyllin Powys 33 D7
Llanfynydd Carms 23 D10
Llanfynydd Flint 42 G5
Llanfyrnach Pembs 23 C7
Llangadfan Powys 32 D6
Llangadog Carms 24 F4
Llangadwaladr Anglesey 40 D5
Llangadwaladr Powys 33 B7
Llangaffo Anglesey 40 D6
Llangain Carms 23 E8
Llangammarch Wells Powys 24 D6
Llangan V Glam 14 D5
Llangarron Hereford 26 F2
Llangasty Talyllyn Powys 25 F8
Llangathen Carms 23 D10
Llangattock Powys 25 G9
Llangattock Lingoed Mon 25 F10
Llangattock nigh Usk Mon 25 H10
Llangattock-Vibon-Avel Mon 25 G11
Llangedwyn Powys 33 C7
Llangefni Anglesey 40 C6
Llangeinor Bridgend 14 C5
Llangeitho Ceredig 24 C3
Llangeler Carms 23 C8
Llangelynin Gwyn 32 E1
Llangendeirne Carms 23 E9
Llangennech Carms 23 F10
Llangennith Swansea 23 G9
Llangenny Powys 25 G9
Llangernyw Conwy 41 D10
Llangian Gwyn 40 H4
Llanglydwen Carms 22 D6
Llangoed Anglesey 41 C8
Llangoedmor Ceredig 22 B6
Llangollen Denb 33 A8
Llangolman Pembs 22 D6
Llangors Powys 25 F8
Llangovan Mon 25 H11
Llangower Gwyn 32 B5
Llangrannog Ceredig 23 A8
Llangristiolus Anglesey 40 C6
Llangrove Hereford 26 G2
Llangua Mon 25 F10
Llangunllo Powys 25 A9
Llangunnor Carms 23 E9
Llangurig Powys 32 H5
Llangwm Conwy 32 A5
Llangwm Mon 15 A10
Llangwm Pembs 22 F4
Llangwnnadl Gwyn 40 G4
Llangwyfan Denb 42 F4
Llangwyfan-isaf Anglesey 40 D5
Llangwyllog Anglesey 40 C6
Llangwyryfon Ceredig 24 A2
Llangybi Ceredig 24 C3
Llangybi Gwyn 40 F6
Llangybi Mon 15 B9
Llangyfelach Swansea 14 B2
Llangynhafal Denb 42 F4
Llangynidr Powys 25 G8
Llangynin Carms 23 E7
Llangynog Carms 23 E8
Llangynog Powys 33 C6
Llangynwyd Bridgend 14 C4
Llanhamlach Powys 25 F7
Llanharan Rhondda 14 C6
Llanharry Rhondda 14 C6
Llanhennock Mon 15 B9
Llanhiledd = Llanhilleth Bl Gwent 15 A8
Llanhilleth = Llanhiledd Bl Gwent 15 A8
Llanidloes Powys 32 G5
Llaniestyn Gwyn 40 G4
Llanifyny Powys 32 G4
Llanigon Powys 25 E9
Llanilar Ceredig 24 A3
Llanilid Rhondda 14 C5
Llanilltud Fawr = Llantwit Major V Glam 14 E5
Llanishen Cardiff 15 C7
Llanishen Mon 15 A10
Llanllawddog Carms 23 D9
Llanllechid Gwyn 41 D8
Llanllowell Mon 15 B9
Llanllugan Powys 33 E6
Llanllwch Carms 23 E8
Llanllwchaiarn Powys 33 F7
Llanllwni Carms 23 C9
Llanllyfni Gwyn 40 E6
Llanmadoc Swansea 23 G9
Llanmaes V Glam 14 E5
Llanmartin Newport 15 C9
Llanmihangel V Glam 14 D5
Llanmorlais Swansea 23 G10
Llannefydd Conwy 42 E2
Llannon Carms 23 F10
Llannor Gwyn 40 G5
Llanon Ceredig 24 B2
Llanover Mon 25 H10
Llanpumsaint Carms 23 D9
Llanreithan Pembs 22 D3
Llanrhaeadr Denb 42 F3
Llanrhaeadr-ym-Mochnant Powys 33 C7
Llanrhian Pembs 22 C3
Llanrhidian Swansea 23 G9
Llanrhos Conwy 41 B9
Llanrhyddlad Anglesey 40 B5
Llanrhystud Ceredig 24 B2
Llanrosser Hereford 25 E9
Llanrothal Hereford 25 G11
Llanrug Gwyn 41 D7
Llanrumney Cardiff 15 C8
Llanrwst Conwy 41 D10
Llansadurnen Carms 23 E7
Llansadwrn Anglesey 41 C7
Llansadwrn Carms 24 E3
Llansaint Carms 23 F8
Llansamlet Swansea 14 B2
Llansannan Conwy 42 F2
Llansannor V Glam 14 D5
Llansantffraed Ceredig 24 B2
Llansantffraed Powys 25 F8
Llansantffraed Cwmdeuddwr Powys 24 B6
Llansantffraed-in-Elvel Powys 25 C7
Llansantffraid-ym-Mechain Powys 33 C8
Llansawel Carms 24 E3
Llansilin Powys 33 C8
Llansoy Mon 15 A10
Llanspyddid Powys 25 F7
Llanstadwell Pembs 22 F4
Llansteffan Carms 23 E8
Llanstephan Powys 25 D8
Llantarnam Torf 15 B9
Llanteg Pembs 22 E6
Llanthony Mon 25 F9
Llantilio Crossenny Mon 25 G10
Llantilio Pertholey Mon 25 G10
Llantood Pembs 22 B6
Llantrisant Anglesey 40 B5
Llantrisant Mon 15 B9
Llantrisant Rhondda 14 C6
Llantrithyd V Glam 14 D6
Llantwit Fardre Rhondda 14 C6
Llantwit Major = Llanilltud Fawr V Glam 14 E5
Llanuwchllyn Gwyn 41 G10
Llanvaches Newport 15 B10

Molehill Green Essex 30 F2
Molescroft E Yorks 52 E6
Molesden Northumb 63 E7
Molesworth Cambs 37 H6
Moll Highld 85 E10
Molland Devon 7 D7
Mollington Ches W 43 E6
Mollington Oxon 27 D11
Mollinsburn N Lanark 68 C6
Monachty Ceredig 24 B2
Monachylemore Stirling 75 F7
Monar Lodge Highld 86 G5
Monaughty Powys 25 B9
Monboddo House Aberds 83 F9
Mondynes Aberds 83 F9
Monevechadan Argyll 74 G4
Monewden Suff 31 C9
Moneydie Perth 76 E3
Moniaive Dumfries 60 D3
Monifieth Angus 77 D7
Monikie Angus 77 D7
Monimail Fife 76 F5
Monington Pembs 22 B6
Monk Bretton S Yorks 45 B7
Monk Fryston N Yorks 51 G11
Monk Sherborne Hants 18 F3
Monk Soham Suff 31 B9
Monk Street Essex 30 F3
Monken Hadley London 19 B9
Monkhopton Shrops 34 F2
Monkland Hereford 25 C11
Monkleigh Devon 6 D3
Monknash V Glam 14 D5
Monkokehampton Devon 6 F4
Monks Eleigh Suff 30 D6
Monk's Gate W Sus 11 B11
Monks Heath Ches E 44 E2
Monks Kirby Warks 35 G10
Monks Risborough Bucks 18 A5
Monkseaton T&W 63 F9
Monkshill Aberds 89 D7
Monksilver Som 7 C9
Monkspath W Mid 35 H7
Monkswood Mon 15 A9
Monkton Devon 7 F10
Monkton Kent 21 E9
Monkton Pembs 22 F4
Monkton S Ayrs 67 D6
Monkton Combe Bath 16 E4
Monkton Deverill Wilts 16 H5
Monkton Farleigh Wilts 16 E5
Monkton Heathfield Som 8 B1
Monkton Up Wimborne Dorset 9 C9
Monkwearmouth T&W 63 H9
Monkwood Hants 10 A5
Monmouth = Trefynwy Mon 26 G2
Monmouth Cap Mon 25 F10
Monnington on Wye Hereford 25 D10
Monreith Dumfries 54 E6
Monreith Mains Dumfries 54 E6
Mont Saint Guern 11
Montacute Som 8 C3
Montcoffer Ho. Aberds 89 B6
Montford Argyll 73 G10
Montford Shrops 33 D10
Montford Bridge Shrops 33 D10
Montgarrie Aberds 83 B7
Montgomery = Trefaldwyn Powys 33 F8
Montrave Fife 76 G6
Montrose Angus 77 B10
Montsale Essex 21 B7
Monxton Hants 17 G10
Monyash Derbys 44 F5
Monymusk Aberds 83 B8
Monzie Perth 75 E11
Monzie Castle Perth 75 E11
Moodiesburn N Lanark 68 C5
Moonzie Fife 76 F6
Moor Allerton W Yorks 51 F8
Moor Crichel Dorset 9 D8
Moor End E Yorks 52 F4
Moor End York 52 D2
Moor Monkton N Yorks 51 D11
Moor of Granary Moray 87 F13
Moor of Ravenstone Dumfries 54 E6
Moor Row Cumb 56 E2
Moor Street Kent 20 E5
Moorby Lincs 46 F6
Moordown Bmouth 9 E9
Moore Halton 43 D8
Moorend Glos 16 A4
Moorends S Yorks 52 H2
Moorgate S Yorks 45 C8
Moorgreen Notts 45 H8
Moorhall Derbys 45 E7
Moorhampton Hereford 25 D10
Moorhead W Yorks 51 F7
Moorhouse Cumb 61 H9
Moorhouse Notts 45 F11
Moorlinch Som 15 H9
Moorsholm Redcar 59 E7
Moorside Gtr Man 44 B3
Moorthorpe W Yorks 45 A8
Moortown Hants 9 D10
Moortown IoW 10 F3
Moortown Lincs 46 C4
Morangie Highld 87 C10
Morar Highld 79 B9
Morborne Cambs 37 F7
Morchard Bishop Devon 7 F6
Morcombelake Dorset 8 E3
Morcott Rutland 36 E5
Morda Shrops 33 C8
Morden Dorset 9 E8
Morden London 19 E9
Mordiford Hereford 26 E2
Mordon Durham 58 D4
More Shrops 33 F9
Morebath Devon 7 D8
Morebattle Borders 62 A3
Morecambe Lancs 49 C4
Morefield Highld 86 B4
Moreleigh Devon 5 F8
Morenish Perth 75 D8
Moresby Cumb 56 D1
Moresby Parks Cumb 56 E1
Morestead Hants 10 B4
Moreton Dorset 9 F7
Moreton Essex 30 H2
Moreton Mers 42 C5
Moreton Oxon 18 A3
Moreton Staffs 34 D3
Moreton Corbet Shrops 34 C1
Moreton-in-Marsh Glos 27 E9
Moreton Jeffries Hereford 26 D3
Moreton Morrell Warks 27 C10
Moreton on Lugg Hereford 26 D2
Moreton Pinkney Northants 28 D2
Moreton Say Shrops 34 B2
Moreton Valence Glos 26 H4
Moretonhampstead Devon 5 C8
Morfa Carms 23 E10
Morfa Carms 23 G10
Morfa Bach Carms 23 E8
Morfa Bychan Gwyn 41 G7
Morfa Dinlle Gwyn 40 E6
Morfa Glas Neath 24 H5
Morfa Nefyn Gwyn 40 F4
Morfydd Denb 42 H4
Morgan's Vale Wilts 9 B10
Moriah Ceredig 32 H2
Morland Cumb 57 D7
Morley Derbys 35 A9
Morley Durham 58 D2
Morley W Yorks 51 G8
Morley Green Ches E 44 D2
Morley St Botolph Norf 39 F6
Morningside Edin 69 C11
Morningside N Lanark 69 E7
Morningthorpe Norf 39 F8
Morpeth Northumb 63 E8
Morphie Aberds 77 A10
Morrey Staffs 35 D7
Morris Green Essex 30 E4
Morriston Swansea 14 B2
Morston Norf 38 A6
Mortehoe Devon 6 B3
Mortimer W Berks 18 E3
Mortimer West End Hants 18 E3
Mortimer's Cross Hereford 25 B11
Mortlake London 19 D9
Morton Cumb 56 A5
Morton Derbys 45 F8
Morton Lincs 37 C6
Morton Lincs 46 C2
Morton Lincs 46 F2
Morton Norf 39 D7
Morton Notts 45 G11
Morton S Glos 16 B3
Morton Shrops 33 C8
Morton Bagot Warks 27 B8
Morton-on-Swale N Yorks 58 G4
Morvah Corn 2 F3
Morval Corn 4 F3
Morvich Highld 80 A1
Morvich Highld 93 J10
Morville Shrops 34 F2
Morville Heath Shrops 34 F2
Morwenstow Corn 6 E1
Mosborough S Yorks 45 D8
Moscow E Ayrs 67 B7
Mosedale Cumb 56 C5
Moseley W Mid 34 F5
Moseley W Mid 35 G6
Moseley Worcs 26 C5
Moss Argyll 78 G2
Moss Highld 79 E9
Moss S Yorks 45 A9
Moss Wrex 42 G6
Moss Bank Mers 43 C8
Moss Edge Lancs 49 E4
Moss End Brack 18 D5
Moss of Barmuckity Moray 88 B2
Moss Pit Staffs 34 C5
Moss-side Highld 87 F11
Moss Side Lancs 49 F3
Mossat Aberds 82 B6
Mossbank Shetland 96 F6
Mossbay Cumb 56 D1
Mossblown S Ayrs 67 D7
Mossbrow Gtr Man 43 D10
Mossburnford Borders 62 B2
Mossdale Dumfries 55 B9
Mossend N Lanark 68 D6
Mosser Cumb 56 D3
Mossfield Highld 87 D9
Mossgiel E Ayrs 67 D7
Mosside Angus 77 B7
Mossley Ches E 44 F2
Mossley Gtr Man 44 B3
Mossley Hill Mers 43 D6
Mosstodloch Moray 88 C3
Mosston Angus 77 C8
Mossy Lea Lancs 43 A8
Mosterton Dorset 8 D3
Moston Gtr Man 44 B2
Moston Shrops 34 C1
Moston Green Ches E 43 F10
Mostyn Flint 42 D4
Mostyn Quay Flint 42 D4
Motcombe Dorset 9 B7
Mothecombe Devon 5 G7
Motherby Cumb 56 D6
Motherwell N Lanark 68 E6
Mottingham London 19 D11
Mottisfont Hants 10 B2
Mottistone IoW 10 F3
Mottram in Longdendale Gtr Man 44 C3
Mottram St Andrew Ches E 44 E2
Mouilpied Guern 11
Mouldsworth Ches W 43 E8
Moulin Perth 76 B2
Moulsecoomb Brighton 12 F2
Moulsford Oxon 18 C2
Moulsoe M Keynes 28 D6
Moulton Ches W 43 F9
Moulton Lincs 37 C9
Moulton N Yorks 58 F3
Moulton Northants 28 B4
Moulton Suff 30 B3
Moulton V Glam 14 D6
Moulton Chapel Lincs 37 D8
Moulton Eaugate Lincs 37 D9
Moulton St Mary Norf 39 E9
Moulton Seas End Lincs 37 C9
Mounie Castle Aberds 83 A9
Mount Corn 3 D6
Mount Corn 4 E2
Mount Highld 87 G12
Mount Bures Essex 30 E6
Mount Canisp Highld 87 D10
Mount Hawke Corn 2 E6
Mount Pleasant Ches E 44 G2
Mount Pleasant Derbys 35 D8
Mount Pleasant Derbys 45 H7
Mount Pleasant Flint 42 E5
Mount Pleasant Hants 10 E1
Mount Pleasant W Yorks 51 G8
Mount Sorrel Wilts 9 B9
Mount Tabor W Yorks 51 G6
Mountain W Yorks 51 F6
Mountain Ash = Aberpennar Rhondda 14 B6
Mountain Cross Borders 69 F10
Mountain Water Pembs 22 D4
Mountbenger Borders 70 H2
Mountfield E Sus 12 D6
Mountgerald Highld 87 E8
Mountjoy Corn 3 C7
Mountnessing Essex 20 B3
Mounton Mon 15 B11
Mountsorrel Leics 36 D1
Mousehole Corn 2 G3
Mousen Northumb 71 G10
Mouswald Dumfries 60 F6
Mow Cop Ches E 44 G2
Mowhaugh Borders 62 A4
Mowsley Leics 36 G2
Moxley W Mid 34 F5
Moy Highld 80 E6
Moy Highld 87 H10
Moy Hall Highld 87 H10
Moy Ho. Moray 87 E13
Moy Lodge Highld 80 E6
Moyles Court Hants 9 D10
Moylgrove Pembs 22 B6
Muasdale Argyll 65 D7
Much Birch Hereford 26 E2
Much Cowarne Hereford 26 D3
Much Dewchurch Hereford 25 E11
Much Hadham Herts 29 G11
Much Hoole Lancs 49 G4
Much Marcle Hereford 26 E3
Much Wenlock Shrops 34 E2
Muchalls Aberds 83 D11
Muchelney Som 8 B3
Muchlarnick Corn 4 F3
Muchrachd Highld 86 H5
Muckernich Highld 87 F8
Mucking Thurrock 20 C3
Muckleford Dorset 8 E5
Mucklestone Staffs 34 B3
Muckleton Shrops 34 C1
Muckletown Aberds 83 A7
Muckley Corner Staffs 35 E6
Muckton Lincs 47 D7
Mudale Highld 93 F8
Muddiford Devon 6 C4
Mudeford Dorset 9 E10
Mudford Som 8 C4
Mudgley Som 15 G10
Mugdock Stirling 68 C4
Mugeary Highld 85 E9
Mugginton Derbys 35 A8
Muggleswick Durham 58 B1
Muie Highld 93 J9
Muir Aberds 82 E2
Muir of Fairburn Highld 86 F7
Muir of Fowlis Aberds 83 B7
Muir of Ord Highld 87 F8
Muir of Pert Angus 77 D7
Muirden Aberds 89 C7
Muirdrum Angus 77 D8
Muirhead Angus 76 D6
Muirhead Fife 76 G5
Muirhead N Lanark 68 D5
Muirhead S Ayrs 66 C6
Muirhouselaw Borders 70 H5
Muirhouses Falk 69 B9
Muirkirk E Ayrs 68 H5
Muirmill Stirling 68 B6
Muirshearlich Highld 80 E3
Muirskie Aberds 83 D10
Muirtack Aberds 89 E9
Muirton Highld 87 E10
Muirton Perth 76 E4
Muirton Perth 76 F2
Muirton Mains Highld 86 F7
Muirton of Ardblair Perth 76 C4
Muirton of Ballochy Angus 77 A9
Muiryfold Aberds 89 C7
Muker N Yorks 57 G11
Mulbarton Norf 39 E7
Mulben Moray 88 C3
Mulindry Argyll 64 C4
Mullardoch House Highld 86 H5
Mullion Corn 2 H5
Mullion Cove Corn 2 H5
Mumby Lincs 47 E9
Munderfield Row Hereford 26 C3
Munderfield Stocks Hereford 26 C3
Mundesley Norf 39 B9
Mundford Norf 38 F4
Mundham Norf 39 F9
Mundon Essex 20 A5
Mundurno Aberdeen 83 B11
Munerigie Highld 80 C4
Muness Shetland 96 C8
Mungasdale Highld 86 B2
Mungrisdale Cumb 56 C5
Munlochy Highld 87 F9
Munsley Hereford 26 D3
Munslow Shrops 33 G11
Murchington Devon 5 C7
Murcott Oxon 28 G2
Murkle Highld 94 D3
Murlaggan Highld 80 D2
Murlaggan Highld 80 E5
Murra Orkney 95 H3
Murrayfield Edin 69 C11
Murrow Cambs 37 E9
Mursley Bucks 28 F5
Murthill Angus 77 B7
Murthly Perth 76 D3
Murton Cumb 57 D9
Murton Durham 58 B4
Murton Northumb 71 F8
Murton York 52 D2
Musbury Devon 8 E1
Muscoates N Yorks 52 A2
Musdale Argyll 74 E2
Musselburgh E Loth 70 C2
Muston Leics 36 B4
Muston N Yorks 53 B6
Mustow Green Worcs 26 A5
Mutehill Dumfries 55 E9
Mutford Suff 39 G10
Muthill Perth 75 F11
Mutterton Devon 7 F9
Muxton Telford 34 D3
Mybster Highld 94 E3
Myddfai Carms 24 F4
Myddle Shrops 33 C10
Mydroilyn Ceredig 23 A9
Myerscough Lancs 49 F4
Mylor Bridge Corn 3 F7
Mynachlog-ddu Pembs 22 C6
Myndtown Shrops 33 G9
Mynydd Bach Ceredig 32 H3
Mynydd-bach Mon 15 B10
Mynydd Bodafon Anglesey 40 B6
Mynydd-isa Flint 42 F5
Mynyddygarreg Carms 23 F9
Mynytho Gwyn 40 G5
Myrebird Aberds 83 D9
Myrelandhorn Highld 94 E4
Myreside Perth 76 E5
Myrtle Hill Carms 24 E4
Mytchett Sur 18 F5
Mytholm W Yorks 50 G5
Mytholmroyd W Yorks 50 G6
Myton-on-Swale N Yorks 51 C10
Mytton Shrops 33 D10

N

Na Gearrannan W Isles 90 C6
Naast Highld 91 J13
Naburn York 52 E1
Nackington Kent 21 F8
Nacton Suff 31 D9
Nafferton E Yorks 53 D6
Nailbridge Glos 26 G3
Nailsbourne Som 7 D11
Nailsea N Som 15 D10
Nailstone Leics 35 E10
Nailsworth Glos 16 B5
Nairn Highld 87 F11
Nalderswood Sur 19 G9
Nancegollan Corn 2 F5
Nancledra Corn 2 F3
Nanhoron Gwyn 40 G4
Nannau Gwyn 32 C3
Nannerch Flint 42 F4
Nanpantan Leics 35 D11
Nanpean Corn 3 D8
Nanstallon Corn 3 C9
Nant-ddu Powys 25 G7
Nant-glas Powys 24 B6
Nant Peris Gwyn 41 E8
Nant Uchaf Denb 42 G3
Nant-y-Bai Carms 24 D4
Nant-y-cafn Neath 24 H5
Nant-y-derry Mon 25 H10
Nant-y-ffin Carms 23 C10
Nant-y-moel Bridgend 14 B5
Nant-y-pandy Conwy 41 C8
Nanternis Ceredig 23 A8
Nantgaredig Carms 23 D9
Nantgarw Rhondda 15 C7
Nantglyn Denb 42 F3
Nantgwyn Powys 32 H5
Nantlle Gwyn 41 E7
Nantmawr Shrops 33 C8
Nantmel Powys 25 B7
Nantmor Gwyn 41 F8
Nantwich Ches E 43 G9
Nantycaws Carms 23 E9
Nantyffyllon Bridgend 14 B4
Nantyglo Bl Gwent 25 G8
Naphill Bucks 18 B5
Nappa N Yorks 50 D4
Napton on the Hill Warks 27 B11
Narberth = Arberth Pembs 22 E6
Narborough Leics 35 F11
Narborough Norf 38 D3
Nasareth Gwyn 40 E6
Naseby Northants 36 H2
Nash Bucks 28 E4
Nash Hereford 25 B10
Nash Newport 15 C9
Nash Shrops 26 A3
Nash Lee Bucks 28 H5
Nassington Northants 37 F6
Nasty Herts 29 F10
Nateby Cumb 57 F9
Nateby Lancs 49 E4
Natland Cumb 57 H7
Naughton Suff 31 D7
Naunton Glos 27 F8
Naunton Worcs 26 E5
Naunton Beauchamp Worcs 26 C6
Navenby Lincs 46 G3
Navestock Heath Essex 20 B2
Navestock Side Essex 20 B2
Navidale Highld 93 H13
Nawton N Yorks 52 A2
Nayland Suff 30 E6
Nazeing Essex 29 H11
Neacroft Hants 9 E10
Neal's Green Warks 35 G9
Neap Shetland 96 H7
Near Sawrey Cumb 56 G5
Neasham Darl 58 E4
Neath = Castell-Nedd Neath 14 B3
Neath Abbey Neath 14 B3
Neatishead Norf 39 C9
Nebo Anglesey 40 A6
Nebo Ceredig 24 B2
Nebo Conwy 41 E10
Nebo Gwyn 40 E6
Necton Norf 38 E4
Nedd Highld 92 F4
Nedderton Northumb 63 E8
Nedging Tye Suff 31 D7
Needham Norf 39 G8
Needham Market Suff 31 C7
Needingworth Cambs 29 A10
Needwood Staffs 35 C7
Neen Savage Shrops 34 H2
Neen Sollars Shrops 26 A3
Neenton Shrops 34 G2
Nefyn Gwyn 40 F5
Neilston E Renf 68 E3
Neinthirion Powys 32 E5
Neithrop Oxon 27 D11
Nelly Andrews Green Powys 33 E8
Nelson Caerph 15 B7
Nelson Lancs 50 F4
Nelson Village Northumb 63 F8
Nemphlar S Lanark 69 F7
Nempnett Thrubwell N Som 15 E11
Nene Terrace Lincs 37 E8
Nenthall Cumb 57 B9
Nenthead Cumb 57 B9
Nenthorn Borders 70 G5
Nerabus Argyll 64 C3
Nercwys Flint 42 F5
Nerston S Lanark 68 E5
Nesbit Northumb 71 G8
Ness Ches W 42 E6
Nesscliffe Shrops 33 D9
Neston Ches W 42 E5
Neston Wilts 16 E5
Nether Alderley Ches E 44 E2
Nether Blainslie Borders 70 F4
Nether Booth Derbys 44 D5
Nether Broughton Leics 36 C2
Nether Burrow Lancs 50 B2
Nether Cerne Dorset 8 E5
Nether Compton Dorset 8 C4
Nether Crimond Aberds 89 F8
Nether Dalgliesh Borders 61 C8
Nether Dallachy Moray 88 B3
Nether Exe Devon 7 F8
Nether Glasslaw Aberds 89 C8
Nether Handwick Angus 76 C6
Nether Haugh S Yorks 45 C8
Nether Heage Derbys 45 G7
Nether Heyford Northants 28 C3
Nether Hindhope Borders 62 B3
Nether Howecleuch S Lanark 60 B6
Nether Kellet Lancs 49 C5
Nether Kinmundy Aberds 89 D10
Nether Langwith Notts 45 E9
Nether Leask Aberds 89 E10
Nether Lenshie Aberds 89 D6
Nether Monynut Borders 70 D6
Nether Padley Derbys 44 E6
Nether Park Aberds 89 C10
Nether Poppleton York 52 D1
Nether Silton N Yorks 58 G5
Nether Stowey Som 7 C10
Nether Urquhart Fife 76 G4
Nether Wallop Hants 17 H10
Nether Wasdale Cumb 56 F3
Nether Whitacre Warks 35 F8
Nether Worton Oxon 27 E11
Netheravon Wilts 17 G8
Netherbrae Aberds 89 C7
Netherbrough Orkney 95 G4
Netherburn S Lanark 69 F7
Netherbury Dorset 8 E3
Netherby Cumb 61 F9
Netherby N Yorks 51 E9
Nethercote Warks 28 B2
Nethercott Devon 6 C3
Netherend Glos 16 A2
Netherfield E Sus 12 E6
Netherhampton Wilts 9 B10
Netherlaw Dumfries 55 E10
Netherley Aberds 83 D10
Netherley Mers 43 D7
Nethermill Dumfries 60 E6
Nethermuir Aberds 89 D9
Netherplace E Renf 68 E4
Netherseal Derbys 35 D8
Netherthird E Ayrs 67 E8
Netherthong W Yorks 44 B5
Netherthorpe S Yorks 45 D9
Netherton Angus 77 B8
Netherton Devon 5 D9
Netherton Hants 17 F10
Netherton Mers 42 B6
Netherton Northumb 62 C5
Netherton Oxon 17 B11
Netherton Perth 76 B4
Netherton Stirling 68 C4
Netherton W Mid 34 G5
Netherton W Yorks 44 A5
Netherton W Yorks 51 H8
Netherton Worcs 26 D6
Nethertown Cumb 56 F1
Nethertown Highld 94 C5
Netherwitton Northumb 63 D7
Netherwood E Ayrs 68 H5
Nethy Bridge Highld 82 A2
Netley Hants 10 D3
Netley Marsh Hants 10 C2
Netteswell Essex 29 G11
Nettlebed Oxon 18 C4
Nettlebridge Som 16 G3
Nettlecombe Dorset 8 E4
Nettleden Herts 29 G7
Nettleham Lincs 46 E4
Nettlestead Kent 20 F3
Nettlestead Green Kent 20 F3
Nettlestone IoW 10 E5
Nettlesworth Durham 58 B3
Nettleton Lincs 46 B5
Nettleton Wilts 16 D5
Neuadd Carms 24 F3
Nevendon Essex 20 B4
Nevern Pembs 22 B5
New Abbey Dumfries 60 G5
New Aberdour Aberds 89 B8
New Addington London 19 E10
New Alresford Hants 10 A4
New Alyth Perth 76 C5
New Arley Warks 35 G8
New Ash Green Kent 20 E3
New Barn Kent 20 E3
New Barnetby N Lincs 46 A4
New Barton Northants 28 B5
New Bewick Northumb 62 A6
New-bigging Angus 76 C5
New Bilton Warks 35 H10
New Bolingbroke Lincs 47 G7
New Boultham Lincs 46 E3
New Bradwell M Keynes 28 D5
New Brancepeth Durham 58 B3
New Bridge Wrex 33 A8
New Brighton Flint 42 F5
New Brighton Mers 42 C6
New Brinsley Notts 45 G8
New Broughton Wrex 42 G6
New Buckenham Norf 39 F6
New Byth Aberds 89 C8
New Catton Norf 39 D8
New Cheriton Hants 10 B4
New Costessey Norf 39 D7
New Cowper Cumb 56 B3
New Cross Ceredig 32 H2
New Cross London 19 D10
New Cumnock E Ayrs 67 E9
New Deer Aberds 89 D8
New Delaval Northumb 63 F8
New Duston Northants 28 B4
New Earswick York 52 D2
New Edlington S Yorks 45 C9
New Elgin Moray 88 B2
New Ellerby E Yorks 53 F7
New Eltham London 19 D11
New End Worcs 27 C7
New Farnley W Yorks 51 F8
New Ferry Mers 42 D6
New Fryston W Yorks 51 G10
New Galloway Dumfries 55 B9
New Gilston Fife 77 G7
New Grimsby Scilly 2 C2
New Hainford Norf 39 D8
New Hartley Northumb 63 F9
New Haw Sur 19 E7
New Hedges Pembs 22 F6
New Herrington T&W 58 A4
New Hinksey Oxon 18 A2
New Holkham Norf 38 B4
New Holland N Lincs 53 G6
New Houghton Derbys 45 F8
New Houghton Norf 38 C3
New Houses N Yorks 50 B4
New Humberstone Leicester 36 E2
New Hutton Cumb 57 G7
New Hythe Kent 20 F4
New Inn Carms 23 C9
New Inn Mon 15 A10
New Inn Pembs 22 C5
New Inn Torf 15 B9
New Invention Shrops 33 H8
New Invention W Mid 34 E5
New Kelso Highld 86 G2
New Kingston Notts 35 C11
New Lanark S Lanark 69 F7
New Lane Lancs 43 A7
New Lane End Warr 43 C9
New Leake Lincs 47 G8
New Leeds Aberds 89 C9
New Longton Lancs 49 G5
New Luce Dumfries 54 C4
New Malden London 19 E9
New Marske Redcar 59 D7
New Marton Shrops 33 B9
New Micklefield W Yorks 51 F10
New Mill Aberds 83 E9
New Mill Herts 28 G6
New Mill W Yorks 44 B5
New Mill Wilts 17 E8
New Mills Ches E 43 D10
New Mills Corn 3 D7
New Mills Derbys 44 D3
New Mills Powys 33 E6
New Milton Hants 9 E11
New Moat Pembs 22 D5
New Ollerton Notts 45 F10
New Oscott W Mid 35 F6
New Park N Yorks 51 D8
New Pitsligo Aberds 89 C8
New Polzeath Corn 3 B8
New Quay = Ceinewydd Ceredig 23 A8
New Rackheath Norf 39 D8
New Radnor Powys 25 B9
New Rent Cumb 56 C6
New Ridley Northumb 62 H6
New Road Side N Yorks 50 E5
New Romney Kent 13 D9
New Rossington S Yorks 45 C10
New Row Ceredig 24 A4
New Row Lancs 50 F2
New Row N Yorks 59 E7
New Sarum Wilts 9 A10
New Silksworth T&W 58 A4
New Stevenston N Lanark 68 E6
New Street Staffs 44 G4
New Street Lane Shrops 34 B2
New Swanage Dorset 9 F9
New Totley S Yorks 45 E7
New Town E Loth 70 C3
New Tredegar = Tredegar Newydd Caerph 15 A7
New Trows S Lanark 69 G7
New Ulva Argyll 72 E6
New Walsoken Cambs 37 E10
New Waltham NE Lincs 46 B6
New Whittington Derbys 45 E7
New Wimpole Cambs 29 D10
New Winton E Loth 70 C3
New Yatt Oxon 27 G10
New York Lincs 46 G6
New York N Yorks 51 C7
Newall W Yorks 51 E7
Newark Orkney 95 D8
Newark Pboro 37 E8
Newark-on-Trent Notts 45 G11
Newarthill N Lanark 68 E6
Newbarns Cumb 49 B2
Newbattle Midloth 70 D2
Newbiggin Cumb 49 C2
Newbiggin Cumb 56 D6
Newbiggin Cumb 56 G2
Newbiggin Cumb 57 B7
Newbiggin Cumb 57 D8
Newbiggin Durham 57 D11
Newbiggin N Yorks 57 G11
Newbiggin N Yorks 57 H11
Newbiggin-by-the-Sea Northumb 63 E9
Newbiggin-on-Lune Cumb 57 F9
Newbigging Angus 77 D7
Newbigging Angus 77 D7
Newbigging S Lanark 69 F9
Newbold Derbys 45 E7
Newbold Leics 35 D10
Newbold on Avon Warks 35 H10
Newbold on Stour Warks 27 D9
Newbold Pacey Warks 27 C9
Newbold Verdon Leics 35 E10
Newborough Anglesey 40 D6
Newborough Pboro 37 E8
Newborough Staffs 35 C7
Newbottle Northants 28 E2
Newbottle T&W 58 A4
Newbourne Suff 31 D9
Newbridge Caerph 15 B8
Newbridge Ceredig 23 A10
Newbridge Corn 2 F3
Newbridge Corn 4 E4
Newbridge Dumfries 60 F5
Newbridge Edin 69 C10
Newbridge Hants 10 C1
Newbridge IoW 10 F3
Newbridge Pembs 22 C4
Newbridge Green Worcs 26 E5
Newbridge-on-Usk Mon 15 B9
Newbridge on Wye Powys 25 C7
Newbrough Northumb 62 G4
Newbuildings Devon 7 F6
Newburgh Aberds 89 C9
Newburgh Aberds 89 F9
Newburgh Borders 61 B9
Newburgh Fife 76 F5
Newburgh Lancs 43 A7
Newburn T&W 63 G7
Newbury W Berks 17 E11
Newbury Park London 19 C11
Newby Cumb 57 D7
Newby Lancs 50 E4
Newby N Yorks 50 B3
Newby N Yorks 58 E6
Newby N Yorks 59 G11
Newby Bridge Cumb 56 H5
Newby East Cumb 61 H10
Newby West Cumb 56 A5
Newby Wiske N Yorks 58 H4
Newcastle Mon 25 G11
Newcastle Shrops 33 G8
Newcastle Emlyn = Castell Newydd Emlyn Carms 23 B8
Newcastle-under-Lyme Staffs 44 H2
Newcastle Upon Tyne T&W 63 G8
Newcastleton or Copshaw Holm Borders 61 E10
Newchapel Pembs 23 C7
Newchapel Powys 32 G5
Newchapel Staffs 44 G2
Newchapel Sur 12 B2
Newchurch Carms 23 D8
Newchurch IoW 10 F4
Newchurch Kent 13 C9
Newchurch Lancs 50 F4
Newchurch Mon 15 B10
Newchurch Powys 25 C9
Newchurch Staffs 35 C7
Newcott Devon 7 F11
Newcraighall Edin 70 C2
Newdigate Sur 19 G8
Newell Green Brack 18 D5
Newenden Kent 13 D7
Newent Glos 26 F4
Newerne Glos 16 A3
Newfield Durham 58 C3
Newfield Highld 87 D10
Newford Scilly 2 C3
Newfound Hants 18 F2
Newgale Pembs 22 D3
Newgate Norf 39 A6
Newgate Street Herts 19 A10
Newhall Ches E 43 H9
Newhall Derbys 35 C8
Newhall House Highld 87 E9
Newhall Point Highld 87 E10
Newham Northumb 71 H10
Newham Hall Northumb 71 H10
Newhaven Derbys 44 G5
Newhaven E Sus 12 F3
Newhaven Edin 69 C11
Newhey Gtr Man 44 A3
Newholm N Yorks 59 E9
Newhouse N Lanark 68 D6
Newick E Sus 12 D3
Newingreen Kent 13 C10
Newington Kent 20 E5
Newington Kent 21 E10
Newington Kent 21 H8
Newington Notts 45 C10
Newington Oxon 18 B3
Newington Shrops 33 G10
Newland Glos 26 H2
Newland Hull 53 F6
Newland N Yorks 52 G2
Newland Worcs 26 D4
Newlandrig Midloth 70 D2
Newlands Borders 61 D11
Newlands Highld 87 G10
Newlands Moray 88 C3
Newlands Northumb 62 H6
Newland's Corner Sur 19 G7
Newlands of Geise Highld 94 D2
Newlands of Tynet Moray 88 B3
Newlands Park Anglesey 40 B4
Newlandsmuir S Lanark 68 E5
Newlot Orkney 95 G6
Newlyn Corn 2 G3
Newmachar Aberds 83 B10
Newmains N Lanark 69 E7
Newmarket Suff 30 B3
Newmarket W Isles 91 D9
Newmill Borders 61 B10
Newmill Corn 2 F3
Newmill Moray 88 C4
Newmill of Inshewan Angus 77 A7
Newmills of Boyne Aberds 88 C5
Newmiln Perth 76 D4
Newmilns E Ayrs 67 C8
Newnham Cambs 29 C11
Newnham Glos 26 G3
Newnham Hants 18 F4
Newnham Herts 29 E9
Newnham Kent 20 F6
Newnham Northants 28 C2
Newnham Bridge Worcs 26 B3
Newpark Fife 77 F7
Newport Devon 6 C4
Newport E Yorks 52 F4
Newport Essex 30 E2
Newport Highld 94 H3
Newport IoW 10 F4
Newport = Casnewydd Newport 15 C9
Newport Norf 39 D11
Newport = Trefdraeth Pembs 22 C5
Newport Telford 34 D3
Newport-on-Tay Fife 77 E7
Newport Pagnell M Keynes 28 D5
Newpound Common W Sus 11 B9
Newquay Corn 3 C7
Newsbank Ches E 44 F2
Newseat Aberds 89 D10
Newseat Aberds 89 E7
Newsham N Yorks 51 A9
Newsham N Yorks 58 E2
Newsham Northumb 63 F9
Newsholme E Yorks 52 G3
Newsholme Lancs 50 D4
Newsome W Yorks 44 A5
Newstead Borders 70 G4
Newstead Northumb 71 H10
Newstead Notts 45 G9
Newthorpe N Yorks 51 F10
Newton Argyll 73 D9
Newton Borders 62 A1
Newton Bridgend 14 D4
Newton Cambs 29 D11
Newton Cambs 37 D10
Newton Cardiff 15 D8
Newton Ches W 43 E8
Newton Ches W 43 F7
Newton Ches W 43 G8
Newton Cumb 49 B2
Newton Derbys 45 G8
Newton Dorset 9 C6
Newton Dumfries 61 D7
Newton Dumfries 61 F8
Newton Gtr Man 44 C3
Newton Hereford 25 E10
Newton Hereford 26 C2
Newton Highld 87 E10
Newton Highld 87 G10
Newton Highld 92 F5
Newton Highld 94 F5
Newton Lancs 49 F4
Newton Lancs 50 B1
Newton Lancs 50 D2
Newton Lincs 36 B6
Newton Moray 88 B1
Newton Norf 38 D4
Newton Northants 36 G4
Newton Northumb 62 G6
Newton Notts 36 A2
Newton Perth 75 D11
Newton S Lanark 68 D5
Newton S Lanark 69 G8
Newton S Yorks 45 B9
Newton Staffs 34 C6
Newton Suff 30 D6
Newton Swansea 14 C2
Newton W Loth 69 C9
Newton Warks 35 H11
Newton Wilts 9 B11
Newton Abbot Devon 5 D9
Newton Arlosh Cumb 61 H7
Newton Aycliffe Durham 58 D3
Newton Bewley Hrtlpl 58 D5
Newton Blossomville M Keynes 28 C6
Newton Bromswold Northants 28 B6
Newton Burgoland Leics 35 E9
Newton by Toft Lincs 46 D4
Newton Ferrers Devon 4 G6
Newton Flotman Norf 39 F8
Newton Hall Northumb 62 G6
Newton Harcourt Leics 36 F2
Newton Heath Gtr Man 44 B2
Newton Ho. Aberds 83 A8
Newton Kyme N Yorks 51 E10
Newton-le-Willows Mers 43 C8
Newton-le-Willows N Yorks 58 H3
Newton Longville Bucks 28 E5
Newton Mearns E Renf 68 E4
Newton Morrell N Yorks 58 F3
Newton Mulgrave N Yorks 59 E8
Newton of Ardtoe Highld 79 D9
Newton of Balcanquhal Perth 76 F4
Newton of Falkland Fife 76 G5
Newton on Ayr S Ayrs 66 D6
Newton on Ouse N Yorks 51 D11
Newton-on-Rawcliffe N Yorks 59 G9
Newton-on-the-Moor Northumb 63 C7
Newton on Trent Lincs 46 E2
Newton Park Argyll 73 G10
Newton Poppleford Devon 7 H9
Newton Purcell Oxon 28 E3
Newton Regis Warks 35 E8
Newton Reigny Cumb 57 C6
Newton St Cyres Devon 7 G7
Newton St Faith Norf 39 D8
Newton St Loe Bath 16 E4
Newton St Petrock Devon 6 E3
Newton Solney Derbys 35 C8
Newton Stacey Hants 17 G11
Newton Stewart Dumfries 55 C7
Newton Tony Wilts 17 G9
Newton Tracey Devon 6 D4
Newton under Roseberry Redcar 59 E6
Newton upon Derwent E Yorks 52 E3
Newton Valence Hants 10 A6
Newtonairds Dumfries 60 E4
Newtongrange Midloth 70 D2
Newtonhill Aberds 83 D11
Newtonhill Highld 87 G8
Newtonmill Angus 77 A9
Newtonmore Highld 81 D9
Newtown Argyll 73 C9
Newtown Ches W 43 E8
Newtown Corn 2 G6
Newtown Cumb 56 B2
Newtown Cumb 61 G11
Newtown Derbys 44 D3
Newtown Devon 7 D6
Newtown Glos 16 A3
Newtown Glos 26 E6
Newtown Hants 10 B2
Newtown Hants 10 C4
Newtown Hants 10 C1
Newtown Hants 10 C5
Newtown Hants 10 D3
Newtown Hants 17 E11
Newtown Hereford 26 D3
Newtown Highld 80 C5
Newtown IoM 48 E3
Newtown IoW 10 E3
Newtown Northumb 62 C6
Newtown Northumb 71 G8
Newtown Northumb 71 H9
Newtown Poole 9 E9
Newtown = Y Drenewydd Powys 33 F7
Newtown Shrops 33 B10
Newtown Staffs 44 F4
Newtown Staffs 44 F3
Newtown Wilts 9 B8
Newtown Linford Leics 35 E11
Newtown St Boswells Borders 70 G4
Newtown Unthank Leics 35 E10
Newtyle Angus 76 C5
Neyland Pembs 22 F4
Niarbyl IoM 48 E2
Nibley S Glos 16 C3
Nibley Green Glos 16 B4
Nibon Shetland 96 F5
Nicholashayne Devon 7 E10
Nicholaston Swansea 23 H10
Nidd N Yorks 51 C9
Nigg Aberdeen 83 C11
Nigg Highld 87 D11
Nigg Ferry Highld 87 E10
Nightcott Som 7 D7
Nilig Denb 42 G3
Nine Ashes Essex 20 A2
Nine Mile Burn Midloth 69 E10
Nine Wells Pembs 22 D2
Ninebanks Northumb 57 A9
Ninfield E Sus 12 E6
Ningwood IoW 10 F2
Nisbet Borders 70 H5
Nisthouse Orkney 95 G4
Nisthouse Shetland 96 G7
Niton IoW 10 G4
Nitshill Glasgow 68 D4
No Man's Heath Ches W 43 H8
No Man's Heath Warks 35 E8
Noak Hill London 20 B2
Noblethorpe S Yorks 44 B6
Nobottle Northants 28 B3
Nocton Lincs 46 F4
Noke Oxon 28 G2
Nolton Pembs 22 E3
Nolton Haven Pembs 22 E3
Nomansland Devon 7 E7
Nomansland Wilts 10 C1
Noneley Shrops 33 C10
Nonikiln Highld 87 D9
Nonington Kent 21 F9
Noonsbrough Shetland 96 H4
Norbreck Blackpool 49 E3
Norbridge Hereford 26 D4
Norbury Ches E 43 H8
Norbury Derbys 35 A7
Norbury Shrops 33 F9
Norbury Staffs 34 C3
Nordelph Norf 38 E1
Norden Gtr Man 44 A2
Norden Heath Dorset 9 F8
Nordley Shrops 34 F2
Norham Northumb 71 F8
Norley Ches W 43 E8
Norleywood Hants 10 E2
Norman Cross Cambs 37 F7
Normanby N Lincs 52 H4
Normanby N Yorks 52 A3
Normanby Redcar 59 E6
Normanby-by-Spital Lincs 46 D4
Normanby by Stow Lincs 46 D2
Normanby le Wold Lincs 46 C5
Normandy Sur 18 F6
Norman's Bay E Sus 12 F5
Norman's Green Devon 7 F9
Normanstone Suff 39 F11
Normanton Derby 35 B9
Normanton Leics 36 A4
Normanton Lincs 46 H3
Normanton Notts 45 G11
Normanton Rutland 36 E5
Normanton W Yorks 51 G9
Normanton le Heath Leics 35 D9
Normanton on Soar Notts 35 C11
Normanton-on-the-Wolds Notts 36 B2
Normanton on Trent Notts 45 F11
Normoss Lancs 49 F3
Norney Sur 18 G6
Norrington Common Wilts 16 E5
Norris Green Mers 43 C6
Norris Hill Leics 35 D9
North Anston S Yorks 45 D9
North Aston Oxon 27 F11
North Baddesley Hants 10 C2
North Ballachulish Highld 74 A3
North Barrow Som 8 B5
North Barsham Norf 38 B5
North Benfleet Essex 20 C4
North Bersted W Sus 11 D8
North Berwick E Loth 70 B4
North Boarhunt Hants 10 C5
North Bovey Devon 5 C8
North Bradley Wilts 16 F5
North Brentor Devon 4 C5
North Brewham Som 16 H4
North Buckland Devon 6 B3
North Burlingham Norf 39 D9
North Cadbury Som 8 B5
North Cairn Dumfries 54 B2
North Carlton Lincs 46 E3
North Carrine Argyll 65 H7
North Cave E Yorks 52 F4
North Cerney Glos 27 H7
North Charford Wilts 9 C10
North Charlton Northumb 63 A7
North Cheriton Som 8 B5
North Cliff E Yorks 53 E8
North Cliffe E Yorks 52 F4
North Clifton Notts 46 E2
North Cockerington Lincs 47 C7
North Coker Som 8 C4
North Collafirth Shetland 96 E5
North Common E Sus 12 D2
North Connel Argyll 74 D2
North Cornelly Bridgend 14 C4
North Cotes Lincs 47 B7
North Cove Suff 39 G10
North Cowton N Yorks 58 F3
North Crawley M Keynes 28 D6
North Cray London 19 D11
North Creake Norf 38 B4
North Curry Som 8 B2
North Dalton E Yorks 52 D5
North Dawn Orkney 95 H5
North Deighton N Yorks 51 D9
North Duffield N Yorks 52 F2
North Elkington Lincs 46 C6
North Elmham Norf 38 C5
North Elmshall W Yorks 45 A8
North End Bucks 28 F5
North End E Yorks 53 F8
North End Essex 30 G3
North End Hants 17 E11
North End Lincs 37 A8
North End N Som 15 E10
North End Ptsmth 10 D5
North End Som 8 B1
North End W Sus 11 D10
North Erradale Highld 91 J12
North Fambridge Essex 20 B5
North Fearns Highld 85 E10
North Featherstone W Yorks 51 G10
North Ferriby E Yorks 52 G5
North Frodingham E Yorks 53 D7
North Gluss Shetland 96 F5
North Gorley Hants 9 C10
North Green Norf 39 G8
North Green Suff 31 B10
North Greetwell Lincs 46 E4
North Grimston N Yorks 52 C4
North Halley Orkney 95 H6
North Halling Medway 20 E4
North Hayling Hants 10 D6
North Hazelrigg Northumb 71 G9
North Heasley Devon 7 C6
North Heath W Sus 11 B9
North Hill Cambs 37 H10
North Hill Corn 4 D3
North Hinksey Oxon 27 H11
North Holmwood Sur 19 G8
North Howden E Yorks 52 F3
North Huish Devon 5 F8
North Hykeham Lincs 46 F3
North Johnston Pembs 22 E4
North Kelsey Lincs 46 B4
North Kelsey Moor Lincs 46 B4
North Kessock Highld 87 G9
North Killingholme N Lincs 53 H7
North Kilvington N Yorks 58 H5
North Kilworth Leics 36 G2
North Kirkton Aberds 89 C11
North Kiscadale N Ayrs 66 D3
North Kyme Lincs 46 G5
North Lancing W Sus 11 D10
North Lee Bucks 28 H5
North Leigh Oxon 27 G10
North Leverton with Habblesthorpe Notts 45 D11
North Littleton Worcs 27 D7
North Lopham Norf 38 G6
North Luffenham Rutland 36 E5
North Marden W Sus 11 C7
North Marston Bucks 28 F4
North Middleton Midloth 70 E2
North Middleton Northumb 62 A6
North Molton Devon 7 D6
North Moreton Oxon 18 C2
North Mundham W Sus 11 D7
North Muskham Notts 45 G11
North Newbald E Yorks 52 F5
North Newington Oxon 27 E11
North Newnton Wilts 17 F8
North Newton Som 8 A1
North Nibley Glos 16 B4
North Oakley Hants 18 F2
North Ockendon London 20 C2
North Ormesby Mbro 58 D6
North Ormsby Lincs 46 C6
North Otterington N Yorks 58 H4
North Owersby Lincs 46 C4
North Perrott Som 8 D3
North Petherton Som 8 A1
North Petherwin Corn 4 C3
North Pickenham Norf 38 E4
North Piddle Worcs 26 C6
North Poorton Dorset 8 E4
North Port Argyll 74 E3
North Queensferry Fife 69 B10
North Radworthy Devon 7 C6
North Rauceby Lincs 46 H4
North Reston Lincs 47 D7
North Rigton N Yorks 51 E8
North Rode Ches E 44 F2
North Roe Shetland 96 E5
North Runcton Norf 38 D2
North Sandwick Shetland 96 D7
North Scale Cumb 49 C1
North Scarle Lincs 46 F2
North Seaton Northumb 63 E8
North Shian Argyll 74 C2
North Shields T&W 63 G9
North Shoebury Southend 20 C6
North Shore Blackpool 49 F3
North Side Cumb 56 D2
North Side Pboro 37 F8
North Skelton Redcar 59 E7
North Somercotes Lincs 47 C8
North Stainley N Yorks 51 B8
North Stainmore Cumb 57 E10
North Stifford Thurrock 20 C3
North Stoke Bath 16 E4
North Stoke Oxon 18 C3
North Stoke W Sus 11 C9
North Street Hants 10 A5
North Street Kent 21 F7
North Street Medway 20 D5
North Street W Berks 18 D3
North Sunderland Northumb 71 G11
North Tamerton Corn 6 G2
North Tawton Devon 6 F5
North Thoresby Lincs 46 C6
North Tidworth Wilts 17 G9
North Togston Northumb 63 C8
North Tuddenham Norf 38 D6
North Walbottle T&W 63 G7
North Walsham Norf 39 B8
North Waltham Hants 18 G2
North Warnborough Hants 18 F4
North Water Bridge Angus 83 G8
North Watten Highld 94 E4
North Weald Bassett Essex 19 A11
North Wheatley Notts 45 D11
North Whilborough Devon 5 E9
North Wick Bath 16 E2
North Willingham Lincs 46 D5
North Wingfield Derbys 45 F8
North Witham Lincs 36 C5
North Woolwich London 19 D11
North Wootton Dorset 8 C5
North Wootton Norf 38 C2
North Wootton Som 16 G2
North Wraxall Wilts 16 D5
North Wroughton Swindon 17 C8
Northacre Norf 38 F5
Northallerton N Yorks 58 G4
Northam Devon 6 D3
Northam Soton 10 C3
Northampton Northants 28 B4
Northaw Herts 19 A9
Northbeck Lincs 37 A6
Northborough Pboro 37 E7
Northbourne Kent 21 F10
Northbridge Street E Sus 12 D6
Northchapel W Sus 11 B8
Northchurch Herts 28 H6
Northcott Devon 6 G2
Northdown Kent 21 D10
Northdyke Orkney 95 F3
Northend Bath 16 E4
Northend Bucks 18 B4
Northend Warks 27 C10
Northenden Gtr Man 44 C2
Northfield Aberdeen 83 C11
Northfield Borders 71 D8
Northfield E Yorks 52 G6
Northfield W Mid 34 H6
Northfields Lincs 36 E6
Northfleet Kent 20 D3
Northgate Lincs 37 C7
Northhouse Borders 61 C10
Northiam E Sus 13 D7
Northill C Beds 29 D8
Northington Hants 18 H2
Northlands Lincs 47 G7
Northlea Durham 58 A5
Northleach Glos 27 G8
Northleigh Devon 7 G10
Northlew Devon 6 G4
Northmoor Oxon 17 A11
Northmoor Green or Moorland Som 8 A2
Northmuir Angus 76 B6
Northney Hants 10 D6
Northolt London 19 C8
Northop Flint 42 F5
Northop Hall Flint 42 F5
Northorpe Lincs 37 B8
Northorpe Lincs 37 D6
Northorpe Lincs 46 C2
Northover Som 8 B4
Northover Som 15 H10
Northowram W Yorks 51 G7
Northport Dorset 9 F8
Northpunds Shetland 96 L6
Northrepps Norf 39 B8
Northstowe Cambs 29 B11
Northtown Orkney 95 J5
Northway Glos 26 E6
Northwich Ches W 43 E9
Northwick S Glos 16 C2
Northwold Norf 38 F3
Northwood Derbys 44 F6
Northwood IoW 10 E3
Northwood Kent 21 E10
Northwood London 19 B7
Northwood Shrops 33 B10
Northwood Green Glos 26 G4
Norton E Sus 12 F3
Norton Glos 26 F5
Norton Halton 43 D8
Norton Herts 29 E9
Norton IoW 10 F2
Norton Mon 25 G11
Norton Northants 28 B3
Norton Notts 45 E9
Norton Powys 25 B10
Norton S Yorks 51 H11
Norton Shrops 33 G10
Norton Shrops 34 E1
Norton Shrops 34 E3
Norton Stockton 58 D5
Norton Suff 30 B6
Norton W Sus 11 D8
Norton W Sus 11 E7
Norton Wilts 16 C5
Norton Worcs 26 C5
Norton Worcs 27 D7
Norton Bavant Wilts 16 G6
Norton Bridge Staffs 34 B4
Norton Canes Staffs 34 E6
Norton Canon Hereford 25 D10
Norton Corner Norf 39 C6
Norton Disney Lincs 46 G2
Norton East Staffs 34 E6
Norton Ferris Wilts 16 H4
Norton Fitzwarren Som 7 D10
Norton Green IoW 10 F2
Norton Hawkfield Bath 16 E2
Norton Heath Essex 20 A3
Norton in Hales Shrops 34 B3
Norton-in-the-Moors Stoke 44 G2
Norton-Juxta-Twycross Leics 35 E9
Norton-le-Clay N Yorks 51 B10
Norton Lindsey Warks 27 B9
Norton Malreward Bath 16 E3
Norton Mandeville Essex 20 A2
Norton-on-Derwent N Yorks 52 B3
Norton St Philip Som 16 F4
Norton sub Hamdon Som 8 C3
Norton Woodseats S Yorks 45 D7
Norwell Notts 45 F11
Norwell Woodhouse Notts 45 F11
Norwich Norf 39 E8
Norwick Shetland 96 B8
Norwood Derbys 45 D8
Norwood Hill Sur 19 G9
Norwoodside Cambs 37 F10
Noseley Leics 36 F3
Noss Shetland 96 M5
Noss Mayo Devon 4 G6
Nosterfield N Yorks 51 A8
Nostie Highld 85 F13
Notgrove Glos 27 F8
Nottage Bridgend 14 D4
Nottingham Nottingham 36 B1
Nottington Dorset 8 F5
Notton W Yorks 45 A7
Notton Wilts 16 E6
Nounsley Essex 30 G4
Noutard's Green Worcs 26 B4
Novar House Highld 87 E9
Nox Shrops 33 D10
Nuffield Oxon 18 C3
Nun Hills Lancs 50 G4
Nun Monkton N Yorks 51 D11
Nunburnholme E Yorks 52 E4
Nuncargate Notts 45 G9
Nuneaton Warks 35 F9
Nuneham Courtenay Oxon 18 B2
Nunney Som 16 G4
Nunnington N Yorks 52 B2
Nunnykirk Northumb 62 D6
Nunsthorpe NE Lincs 46 B6
Nunthorpe Mbro 59 E6
Nunthorpe York 52 D2
Nunton Wilts 9 B10
Nunwick N Yorks 51 B9
Nupend Glos 26 H4
Nursling Hants 10 C2
Nursted Hants 11 B6
Nutbourne W Sus 11 C9
Nutbourne W Sus 11 D6
Nutfield Sur 19 F10
Nuthall Notts 35 A11
Nuthampstead Herts 29 E11
Nuthurst W Sus 11 B10
Nutley E Sus 12 D3
Nutley Hants 18 G3
Nutwell S Yorks 45 B10
Nybster Highld 94 D5
Nyetimber W Sus 11 E7
Nyewood W Sus 11 B7
Nymet Rowland Devon 6 F6
Nymet Tracey Devon 7 F6
Nympsfield Glos 16 A5
Nynehead Som 7 D10
Nyton W Sus 11 D8

O

Oad Street Kent 20 E5
Oadby Leics 36 E2
Oak Cross Devon 6 G4
Oakamoor Staffs 35 A6
Oakbank W Loth 69 D9
Oakdale Caerph 15 B7
Oake Som 7 D10
Oaken Staffs 34 E4
Oakenclough Lancs 49 E5
Oakengates Telford 34 D3
Oakenholt Flint 42 E5
Oakenshaw Durham 58 C3
Oakenshaw W Yorks 51 G7
Oakerthorpe Derbys 45 G7
Oakes W Yorks 51 H7
Oakfield Torf 15 B9
Oakford Ceredig 23 A9
Oakford Devon 7 D8
Oakfordbridge Devon 7 D8
Oakgrove Ches E 44 F3
Oakham Rutland 36 E4
Oakhanger Hants 18 H4
Oakhill Som 16 G3
Oakhurst Kent 20 F2
Oakington Cambs 29 B11
Oaklands Herts 29 G9
Oaklands Powys 25 C7
Oakle Street Glos 26 G4
Oakley Bedford 29 C7
Oakley Bucks 28 G3
Oakley Fife 69 B9
Oakley Hants 18 F2
Oakley Oxon 18 A4
Oakley Poole 9 E9
Oakley Suff 39 H7
Oakley Green Windsor 18 D6
Oakley Park Powys 32 G5
Oakmere Ches W 43 F8
Oakridge Glos 16 A6
Oakridge Hants 18 F3
Oaks Shrops 33 E10
Oaks Green Derbys 35 B7
Oaksey Wilts 16 B6
Oakthorpe Leics 35 D9
Oakwoodhill Sur 19 H8
Oakworth W Yorks 50 F6
Oape Highld 92 J7
Oare Kent 21 E7
Oare Som 7 B7
Oare W Berks 18 D2
Oare Wilts 17 E8
Oasby Lincs 36 B6
Oathlaw Angus 77 B7
Oatlands N Yorks 51 D9
Oban Argyll 79 J11
Oban Highld 79 C11
Oborne Dorset 8 C5
Obthorpe Lincs 37 D6
Occlestone Green Ches W 43 F9
Occold Suff 31 A8
Ochiltree E Ayrs 67 D8
Ochtermuthill Perth 75 F11
Ochtertyre Perth 75 E11
Ockbrook Derbys 35 B10
Ockham Sur 19 F7
Ockle Highld 79 D8
Ockley Sur 19 H8
Ocle Pychard Hereford 26 D2
Octon E Yorks 52 C6
Octon Cross Roads E Yorks 52 C6
Odcombe Som 8 C4
Odd Down Bath 16 E4
Oddendale Cumb 57 E7
Odder Lincs 46 E3
Oddingley Worcs 26 C6
Oddington Glos 27 F9
Oddington Oxon 28 G2
Odell Bedford 28 C6
Odie Orkney 95 F7
Odiham Hants 18 F4
Odstock Wilts 9 B10
Odstone Leics 35 E9
Offchurch Warks 27 B10
Offenham Worcs 27 D7
Offham E Sus 12 E2
Offham Kent 20 F3
Offham W Sus 11 D9
Offord Cluny Cambs 29 B9
Offord Darcy Cambs 29 B9
Offton Suff 31 D7
Offwell Devon 7 G10
Ogbourne Maizey Wilts 17 D8
Ogbourne St Andrew Wilts 17 D8
Ogbourne St George Wilts 17 D9
Ogil Angus 77 A7
Ogle Northumb 63 F7
Ogmore V Glam 14 D4
Ogmore-by-Sea V Glam 14 D4
Ogmore Vale Bridgend 14 B5
Okeford Fitzpaine Dorset 9 C7
Okehampton Devon 6 G4
Okehampton Camp Devon 6 G4
Okraquoy Shetland 96 K6
Old Northants 28 A4
Old Aberdeen Aberdeen 83 C11
Old Alresford Hants 10 A4
Old Arley Warks 35 F8
Old Basford Nottingham 35 A11
Old Basing Hants 18 F3
Old Bewick Northumb 62 A6
Old Bolingbroke Lincs 47 F7
Old Bramhope W Yorks 51 E8
Old Brampton Derbys 45 E7
Old Bridge of Tilt Perth 81 G10
Old Bridge of Urr Dumfries 55 C10
Old Buckenham Norf 39 F6
Old Burghclere Hants 17 F11
Old Byland N Yorks 59 H6
Old Cassop Durham 58 C4
Old Castleton Borders 61 D11
Old Catton Norf 39 D8
Old Clee NE Lincs 46 B6
Old Cleeve Som 7 B9
Old Clipstone Notts 45 F10
Old Colwyn Conwy 41 C10
Old Coulsdon London 19 F10
Old Crombie Aberds 88 C5
Old Dailly S Ayrs 66 G5
Old Dalby Leics 36 C2
Old Deer Aberds 89 D9
Old Denaby S Yorks 45 C8
Old Edlington S Yorks 45 C9
Old Eldon Durham 58 D3
Old Ellerby E Yorks 53 F7
Old Felixstowe Suff 31 E10
Old Fletton Pboro 37 F7
Old Glossop Derbys 44 C4
Old Goole E Yorks 52 G3
Old Hall Powys 32 G5
Old Heath Essex 31 F7
Old Heathfield E Sus 12 D4
Old Hill W Mid 34 G5
Old Hunstanton Norf 38 A2
Old Hurst Cambs 37 H8
Old Hutton Cumb 57 H7
Old Kea Corn 3 E7
Old Kilpatrick W Dunb 68 C3
Old Kinnernie Aberds 83 C9
Old Knebworth Herts 29 F9
Old Langho Lancs 50 F3
Old Laxey IoM 48 D4
Old Leake Lincs 47 G8
Old Malton N Yorks 52 B3
Old Micklefield W Yorks 51 F10
Old Milton Hants 9 E11
Old Milverton Warks 27 B9
Old Monkland N Lanark 68 D6
Old Netley Hants 10 D3
Old Philpstoun W Loth 69 C9
Old Quarrington Durham 58 C4
Old Radnor Powys 25 C9
Old Rattray Aberds 89 C10
Old Rayne Aberds 83 A8
Old Romney Kent 13 D9
Old Sodbury S Glos 16 C4
Old Somerby Lincs 36 B5
Old Stratford Northants 28 D4
Old Thirsk N Yorks 51 A10
Old Town Cumb 50 A1
Old Town Cumb 57 B6
Old Town Northumb 62 D4
Old Town Scilly 2 C3
Old Trafford Gtr Man 44 C2
Old Tupton Derbys 45 F7
Old Warden C Beds 29 D8
Old Weston Cambs 37 H6
Old Whittington Derbys 45 E7
Old Wick Highld 94 E5
Old Windsor Windsor 18 D6
Old Wives Lees Kent 21 F7
Old Woking Sur 19 F7
Old Woodhall Lincs 46 F6
Oldany Highld 92 F4
Oldberrow Warks 27 B8
Oldborough Devon 7 F6
Oldbury Shrops 34 F3
Oldbury W Mid 34 G5
Oldbury Warks 35 F9
Oldbury-on-Severn S Glos 16 B3
Oldbury on the Hill Glos 16 C5
Oldcastle Bridgend 14 D5
Oldcastle Mon 25 F10
Oldcotes Notts 45 D9
Oldfallow Staffs 34 D5
Oldfield Worcs 26 B5
Oldford Som 16 F4
Oldham Gtr Man 44 B3
Oldhamstocks E Loth 70 C6
Oldland S Glos 16 D3
Oldmeldrum Aberds 89 F8
Oldshore Beg Highld 92 D4
Oldshoremore Highld 92 D5
Oldstead N Yorks 51 A11
Oldtown Aberds 83 A7
Oldtown of Ord Aberds 88 C6
Oldway Swansea 23 H10
Oldways End Devon 7 D7
Oldwhat Aberds 89 C8
Olgrinmore Highld 94 E2
Oliver's Battery Hants 10 B3
Ollaberry Shetland 96 E5
Ollerton Ches E 43 E10
Ollerton Notts 45 F10

Rho–Sly 149

Rhodiad Pembs 22 D2
Rhondda Rhondda 14 B5
Rhonehouse or Kelton Hill Dumfries 55 D10
Rhoose = Y Rhws V Glam 14 E6
Rhos-fawr Gwyn 40 G5
Rhos-goch Powys 25 D8
Rhos-hill Pembs 22 B6
Rhos-on-Sea Conwy 41 B10
Rhos-y-brithdir Powys 33 C7
Rhos-y-garth Ceredig 24 A3
Rhos-y-gwaliau Gwyn 32 B5
Rhos-y-llan Gwyn 40 G4
Rhos-y-Madoc Wrex 33 A9
Rhos-y-meirch Powys 25 B9
Rhosaman Carms 24 G4
Rhosbeirio Anglesey 40 A5
Rhoscefnhir Anglesey 41 C7
Rhoscolyn Anglesey 40 C4
Rhoscrowther Pembs 22 F4
Rhosesmor Flint 42 F5
Rhosgadfan Gwyn 41 E7
Rhosgoch Anglesey 40 B6
Rhoshirwaun Gwyn 40 H3
Rhoslan Gwyn 40 F6
Rhoslefain Gwyn 32 E1
Rhosllanerchrugog Wrex 42 H5
Rhosmaen Carms 24 F3
Rhosmeirch Anglesey 40 C6
Rhosneigr Anglesey 40 C5
Rhosnesni Wrex 42 G6
Rhosrobin Wrex 42 G6
Rhossili Swansea 23 H9
Rhosson Pembs 22 D2
Rhostryfan Gwyn 40 E6
Rhostyllen Wrex 42 H6
Rhosybol Anglesey 40 B6
Rhu Argyll 73 E11
Rhu Argyll 73 G7
Rhuallt Denb 42 E3
Rhuddall Heath Ches W 43 F8
Rhuddlan Ceredig 23 B9
Rhuddlan Denb 42 E3
Rhue Highld 86 B3
Rhulen Powys 25 D8
Rhunahaorine Argyll 65 D8
Rhuthun = Ruthin Denb 42 G4
Rhyd Gwyn 41 F8
Rhyd Powys 32 E5
Rhyd-Ddu Gwyn 41 E7
Rhyd-moel-ddu Powys 33 H6
Rhyd-Rosser Ceredig 24 B2
Rhyd-uchaf Gwyn 32 B5
Rhyd-wen Gwyn 32 D3
Rhyd-y-clafdy Gwyn 40 G5
Rhyd-y-fro Neath 24 H4
Rhyd-y-gwin Swansea 14 A2
Rhyd-y-meirch Mon 25 H10
Rhyd-y-meudwy Denb 42 G4
Rhyd-y-pandy Swansea 14 A2
Rhyd-y-sarn Gwyn 41 F8
Rhyd-yr-onen Gwyn 32 E2
Rhydaman = Ammanford Carms 24 G3
Rhydargaeau Carms 23 D9
Rhydcymerau Carms 23 C10
Rhydd Worcs 26 D5
Rhydding Neath 14 B3
Rhydfudr Ceredig 24 B2
Rhydlewis Ceredig 23 B8
Rhydlios Gwyn 40 G3
Rhydlydan Conwy 41 E10
Rhydness Powys 25 D8
Rhydowen Ceredig 23 B9
Rhydspence Hereford 25 D9
Rhydtalog Flint 42 G5
Rhydwyn Anglesey 40 B5
Rhydycroesau Powys 33 B8
Rhydyfelin Ceredig 32 H1
Rhydyfelin Rhondda 14 C6
Rhydymain Gwyn 32 C4
Rhydymwyn Flint 42 F5
Rhyl = Y Rhyl Denb 42 D3
Rhymney = Rhymni Caerph 25 H8
Rhymni = Rhymney Caerph 25 H8
Rhynd Fife 77 E7
Rhynd Perth 76 E4
Rhynie Aberds 82 A6
Rhynie Highld 87 D11
Ribbesford Worcs 26 A4
Ribblehead N Yorks 50 B3
Ribbleton Lancs 50 F1
Ribchester Lancs 50 F2
Ribigill Highld 93 D8
Riby Lincs 46 B5
Riby Cross Roads Lincs 46 B5
Riccall N Yorks 52 F2
Riccarton E Ayrs 67 C7
Richards Castle Hereford 25 B11
Richings Park Bucks 19 D7
Richmond London 19 D8
Richmond N Yorks 58 F2
Rickarton Aberds 83 E10
Rickinghall Suff 38 H6
Rickleton T&W 58 A3
Rickling Essex 29 E11
Rickmansworth Herts 19 B7
Riddings Cumb 61 F10
Riddings Derbys 45 G8
Riddlecombe Devon 6 E5
Riddlesden W Yorks 51 E6
Riddrie Glasgow 68 D5
Ridge Dorset 9 F8
Ridge Hants 10 C2
Ridge Wilts 9 A8
Ridge Green Sur 19 G10
Ridge Lane Warks 35 F8
Ridgebourne Powys 25 B7
Ridgehill N Som 15 E11
Ridgeway Cross Hereford 26 D4
Ridgewell Essex 30 D4
Ridgewood E Sus 12 E3
Ridgmont C Beds 28 E6
Riding Mill Northumb 62 G6
Ridleywood Wrex 43 G7
Ridlington Norf 39 B9
Ridlington Rutland 36 E4
Ridsdale Northumb 62 E5
Riechip Perth 76 C3
Riemore Perth 76 C3
Rienachait Highld 92 F3
Rievaulx N Yorks 59 H6
Rift House Hrtlpl 58 C5
Rigg Dumfries 61 G8
Riggend N Lanark 68 C6
Rigsby Lincs 47 E8
Rigside S Lanark 69 G7
Riley Green Lancs 50 G2
Rileyhill Staffs 35 D7
Rilla Mill Corn 4 D3
Rillington N Yorks 52 B4
Rimington Lancs 50 E4
Rimpton Som 8 B5
Rimswell E Yorks 53 G9
Rinaston Pembs 22 D4
Ringasta Shetland 96 M5
Ringford Dumfries 55 D9
Ringinglow S Yorks 44 D6
Ringland Norf 39 D7
Ringles Cross E Sus 12 D3
Ringmer E Sus 12 E3
Ringmore Devon 5 G7
Ringorm Moray 88 D2
Ring's End Cambs 37 E9
Ringsfield Suff 39 G10
Ringsfield Corner Suff 39 G10
Ringshall Herts 28 G6
Ringshall Suff 31 C7
Ringshall Stocks Suff 31 C7
Ringstead Norf 38 A3
Ringstead Northants 36 H5
Ringwood Hants 9 D10
Ringwould Kent 21 G10
Rinmore Aberds 82 B6
Rinnigill Orkney 95 J4
Rinsey Corn 2 G4
Riof W Isles 90 D6
Ripe E Sus 12 E4
Ripley Derbys 45 G7
Ripley Hants 9 E10
Ripley N Yorks 51 C8
Ripley Sur 19 F7
Riplingham E Yorks 52 F5
Ripon N Yorks 51 B9
Rippingale Lincs 37 C6
Ripple Kent 21 G10
Ripple Worcs 26 E5
Ripponden W Yorks 50 H6
Rireavach Highld 86 B3
Risabus Argyll 64 D4
Risbury Hereford 26 C2
Risby Suff 30 B4
Risca = Rhisga Caerph 15 B8
Rise E Yorks 53 E7
Riseden E Sus 12 C5
Risegate Lincs 37 C8
Riseholme Lincs 46 E3
Riseley Bedford 29 B7
Riseley Wokingham 18 E4
Rishangles Suff 31 B8
Rishton Lancs 50 F3
Rishworth W Yorks 50 H6
Rising Bridge Lancs 50 G3
Risley Derbys 35 B10
Risley Warr 43 C9
Risplith N Yorks 51 C8
Rispond Highld 92 C7
Rivar Wilts 17 E10
Rivenhall End Essex 30 G5
River Bank Cambs 30 B2
Riverhead Kent 20 F2
Rivington Lancs 43 A9
Roa Island Cumb 49 C2
Roachill Devon 7 D7
Road Green Norf 39 F8
Roade Northants 28 C4
Roadhead Cumb 61 F11
Roadmeetings S Lanark 69 F7
Roadside Highld 94 D3
Roadside of Catterline Aberds 83 F10
Roadside of Kinneff Aberds 83 F10
Roadwater Som 7 C9
Roag Highld 85 D7
Roath Cardiff 15 D7
Roberton Borders 61 B10
Roberton S Lanark 69 H8
Robertsbridge E Sus 12 D6
Roberttown W Yorks 51 G7
Robeston Cross Pembs 22 F3
Robeston Wathen Pembs 22 E5
Robin Hood W Yorks 51 G9
Robin Hood's Bay N Yorks 59 F10
Roborough Devon 4 E6
Roborough Devon 6 E4
Roby Mers 43 C7
Roby Mill Lancs 43 B8
Rocester Staffs 35 B7
Roch Pembs 22 D3
Roch Gate Pembs 22 D3
Rochdale Gtr Man 44 A2
Roche Corn 3 C8
Rochester Medway 20 E4
Rochester Northumb 62 D4
Rochford Essex 20 B5
Rock Corn 3 B8
Rock Northumb 63 A8
Rock W Sus 11 C10
Rock Worcs 26 A4
Rock Ferry Mers 42 D6
Rockbeare Devon 7 G9
Rockbourne Hants 9 C10
Rockcliffe Cumb 61 G9
Rockcliffe Dumfries 55 D11
Rockfield Highld 87 C12
Rockfield Mon 25 G11
Rockford Hants 9 D10
Rockhampton S Glos 16 B3
Rockingham Northants 36 F4
Rockland All Saints Norf 38 F5
Rockland St Mary Norf 39 E9
Rockland St Peter Norf 38 F5
Rockley Wilts 17 D8
Rockwell End Bucks 18 C4
Rockwell Green Som 7 D10
Rodborough Glos 16 A5
Rodbourne Swindon 17 C8
Rodbourne Wilts 16 C6
Rodbourne Cheney Swindon 17 C8
Rodd Hereford 25 B10
Roddam Northumb 62 A6
Rodden Dorset 8 F5
Rode Som 16 F5
Rode Heath Ches E 44 G2
Rodeheath Ches E 44 F2
Roden Telford 34 D1
Rodhuish Som 7 C9
Rodington Telford 34 D1
Rodley Glos 26 G4
Rodley W Yorks 51 F8
Rodmarton Glos 16 B6
Rodmell E Sus 12 F3
Rodmersham Kent 20 E6
Rodney Stoke Som 15 F10
Rodsley Derbys 35 A8
Rodway Som 15 H8
Rodwell Dorset 8 G5
Roe Green Herts 29 E10
Roecliffe N Yorks 51 C9
Roehampton London 19 D9
Roesound Shetland 96 G5
Roffey W Sus 11 A10
Rogart Highld 93 J10
Rogart Station Highld 93 J10
Rogate W Sus 11 B7
Rogerstone Newport 15 C8
Roghadal W Isles 90 J5
Rogiet Mon 15 C10
Rogue's Alley Cambs 37 E9
Roke Oxon 18 B3
Roker T&W 63 H10
Rollesby Norf 39 D10
Rolleston Leics 36 E3
Rolleston Notts 45 G11
Rolleston-on-Dove Staffs 35 C8
Rolston E Yorks 53 E8
Rolvenden Kent 13 C7
Rolvenden Layne Kent 13 C7
Romaldkirk Durham 57 D11
Romanby N Yorks 58 G4
Romannobridge Borders 69 F10
Romansleigh Devon 7 D6
Romford London 20 C2
Romiley Gtr Man 44 C3
Romsey Hants 10 B2
Romsey Town Cambs 29 C11
Romsley Shrops 34 G3
Romsley Worcs 34 H5
Ronague IoM 48 E2
Rookhope Durham 57 B11
Rookley IoW 10 F4
Rooks Bridge Som 15 F9
Roos E Yorks 53 F8
Roosebeck Cumb 49 C2
Rootham's Green Bedford 29 C8
Rootpark S Lanark 69 E8
Ropley Hants 10 A5
Ropley Dean Hants 10 A5
Ropsley Lincs 36 B5
Rora Aberds 89 C10
Rorandle Aberds 83 B8
Rorrington Shrops 33 E9
Roscroggan Corn 2 E5
Rose Corn 3 D6
Rose Ash Devon 7 D6
Rose Green W Sus 11 E8
Rose Grove Lancs 50 F4
Rose Hill E Sus 12 E3
Rose Hill Lancs 50 F4
Rose Hill Suff 31 D8
Roseacre Kent 20 F4
Roseacre Lancs 49 F4
Rosebank S Lanark 69 F7
Rosebrough Northumb 71 H10
Rosebush Pembs 22 D5
Rosecare Corn 4 B2
Rosedale Abbey N Yorks 59 G8
Roseden Northumb 62 A6
Rosefield Highld 87 F11
Rosehall Highld 92 J7
Rosehaugh Mains Highld 87 F9
Rosehearty Aberds 89 B9
Rosehill Shrops 34 B2
Roseisle Moray 88 B1
Roselands E Sus 12 F5
Rosemarket Pembs 22 F4
Rosemarkie Highld 87 F10
Rosemary Lane Devon 7 E10
Rosemount Perth 76 C4
Rosenannon Corn 3 C8
Rosewell Midloth 69 D11
Roseworth Stockton 58 D5
Roseworthy Corn 2 F5
Rosgill Cumb 57 E7
Roshven Highld 79 D10
Roskhill Highld 85 D7
Roskill House Highld 87 F9
Rosley Cumb 56 B5
Roslin Midloth 69 D11
Rosliston Derbys 35 D8
Rosneath Argyll 73 E11
Ross Dumfries 55 E9
Ross Northumb 71 G10
Ross Perth 75 E10
Ross-on-Wye Hereford 26 F3
Rossett Wrex 42 G6
Rossett Green N Yorks 51 D9
Rossie Ochill Perth 76 F3
Rossie Priory Perth 76 D5
Rossington S Yorks 45 C10
Rosskeen Highld 87 E9
Rossland Renfs 68 C3
Roster Highld 94 G4
Rostherne Ches E 43 D10
Rosthwaite Cumb 56 E4
Roston Derbys 35 A7
Rosyth Fife 69 B10
Rothbury Northumb 62 C6
Rotherby Leics 36 D2
Rotherfield E Sus 12 D4
Rotherfield Greys Oxon 18 C4
Rotherfield Peppard Oxon 18 C4
Rotherham S Yorks 45 C8
Rothersthorpe Northants 28 C4
Rotherwick Hants 18 F4
Rothes Moray 88 D2
Rothesay Argyll 73 G9
Rothiebrisbane Aberds 89 E7
Rothienorman Aberds 89 E7
Rothiesholm Orkney 95 F7
Rothley Leics 36 D1
Rothley Northumb 62 E6
Rothley Shield East Northumb 62 D6
Rothmaise Aberds 89 E6
Rothwell Lincs 46 C5
Rothwell Northants 36 G4
Rothwell W Yorks 51 G9
Rothwell Haigh W Yorks 51 G9
Rotsea E Yorks 53 D6
Rottal Angus 82 G5
Rotten End Suff 31 B10
Rottingdean Brighton 12 F2
Rottington Cumb 56 E1
Roud IoW 10 F4
Rough Close Staffs 34 B5
Rough Common Kent 21 F8
Rougham Norf 38 C4
Rougham Suff 30 B6
Rougham Green Suff 30 B6
Roughburn Highld 80 E5
Roughlee Lancs 50 E4
Roughley W Mid 35 F7
Roughsike Cumb 61 F11
Roughton Lincs 46 F6
Roughton Norf 39 B8
Roughton Shrops 34 F3
Roughton Moor Lincs 46 F6
Roundhay W Yorks 51 F9
Roundstonefoot Dumfries 61 C7
Roundstreet Common W Sus 11 B9
Roundway Wilts 17 E7
Rous Lench Worcs 27 C7
Rousdon Devon 8 E1
Routenburn N Ayrs 73 G10
Routh E Yorks 53 E6
Row Corn 4 D1
Row Cumb 56 H6
Row Heath Essex 31 G8
Rowanburn Dumfries 61 F10
Rowardennan Stirling 74 H6
Rowde Wilts 16 E6
Rowen Conwy 41 C9
Rowfoot Northumb 62 G2
Rowhedge Essex 31 F7
Rowhook W Sus 11 A10
Rowington Warks 27 B9
Rowland Derbys 44 E6
Rowlands Castle Hants 10 C6
Rowlands Gill T&W 63 H7
Rowledge Sur 18 G5
Rowlestone Hereford 25 F10
Rowley E Yorks 52 F5
Rowley Shrops 33 E9
Rowley Hill W Yorks 44 A5
Rowley Regis W Mid 34 G5
Rowly Sur 19 G7
Rowney Green Worcs 27 A7
Rownhams Hants 10 C2
Rowrah Cumb 56 E2
Rowsham Bucks 28 G5
Rowsley Derbys 44 F6
Rowstock Oxon 17 C11
Rowston Lincs 46 G4
Rowton Ches W 43 F7
Rowton Shrops 33 D9
Rowton Telford 34 D2
Roxburgh Borders 70 G6
Roxby N Lincs 52 H5
Roxby N Yorks 59 E8
Roxton Bedford 29 C8
Roxwell Essex 30 H3
Royal Leamington Spa Warks 27 B10
Royal Oak Darl 58 D3
Royal Oak Lancs 43 B7
Royal Tunbridge Wells Kent 12 C4
Royal Wootton Bassett Wilts 17 C7
Roybridge Highld 80 E4
Roydhouse W Yorks 44 A6
Roydon Essex 29 H11
Roydon Norf 38 C3
Roydon Norf 39 G6
Roydon Hamlet Essex 29 H11
Royston Herts 29 D10
Royston S Yorks 45 A7
Royton Gtr Man 44 B3
Rozel Jersey 11
Ruabon = Rhiwabon Wrex 33 A9
Ruaig Argyll 78 G3
Ruan Lanihorne Corn 3 E7
Ruan Minor Corn 2 H6
Ruarach Highld 80 A1
Ruardean Glos 26 G3
Ruardean Woodside Glos 26 G3
Rubery Worcs 34 H5
Ruckcroft Cumb 57 B7
Ruckhall Hereford 25 E11
Ruckinge Kent 13 C9
Ruckland Lincs 47 E7
Ruckley Shrops 33 E11
Rudbaxton Pembs 22 D4
Rudby N Yorks 58 F5
Ruddington Notts 36 B1
Rudford Glos 26 F4
Rudge Shrops 34 F4
Rudge Som 16 F5
Rudgeway S Glos 16 C3
Rudgwick W Sus 11 A9
Rudhall Hereford 26 F3
Rudheath Ches W 43 E9
Rudley Green Essex 20 A5
Rudry Caerph 15 C7
Rudston E Yorks 52 C6
Rudyard Staffs 44 G3
Rufford Lancs 49 H4
Rufforth York 51 D11
Rugby Warks 35 H11
Rugeley Staffs 34 D6
Ruglen S Ayrs 66 F5
Ruilick Highld 87 G8
Ruishton Som 8 B1
Ruisigearraidh W Isles 90 J4
Ruislip London 19 C7
Ruislip Common London 19 C7
Rumbling Bridge Perth 76 H3
Rumburgh Suff 39 G9
Rumford Corn 3 B7
Rumney Cardiff 15 D8
Runcorn Halton 43 D8
Runcton W Sus 11 D7
Runcton Holme Norf 38 E2
Rundlestone Devon 5 D6
Runfold Sur 18 G5
Runhall Norf 39 E6
Runham Norf 39 D10
Runham Norf 39 E11
Runnington Som 7 D10
Runsell Green Essex 30 H4
Runswick Bay N Yorks 59 E9
Runwell Essex 20 B4
Ruscombe Wokingham 18 D4
Rush Green London 20 C2
Rush-head Aberds 89 D8
Rushall Hereford 26 E3
Rushall Norf 39 G7
Rushall W Mid 34 E6
Rushall Wilts 17 F8
Rushbrooke Suff 30 B5
Rushbury Shrops 33 F11
Rushden Herts 29 E10
Rushden Northants 28 B6
Rushenden Kent 20 D6
Rushford Norf 38 G5
Rushlake Green E Sus 12 E5
Rushmere Suff 39 G10
Rushmere St Andrew Suff 31 D9
Rushmoor Sur 18 G5
Rushock Worcs 26 A5
Rusholme Gtr Man 44 C2
Rushton Ches W 43 F8
Rushton Northants 36 G4
Rushton Shrops 34 E2
Rushton Spencer Staffs 44 F3
Rushwick Worcs 26 C5
Rushyford Durham 58 D3
Ruskie Stirling 75 G9
Ruskington Lincs 46 G4
Rusland Cumb 56 H5
Rusper W Sus 19 H9
Ruspidge Glos 26 G3
Russell's Water Oxon 18 C4
Russel's Green Suff 31 A9
Rusthall Kent 12 C4
Rustington W Sus 11 D9
Ruston N Yorks 52 A5
Ruston Parva E Yorks 53 C6
Ruswarp N Yorks 59 F9
Rutherford Borders 70 G5
Rutherglen S Lanark 68 D5
Ruthernbridge Corn 3 C9
Ruthin = Rhuthun Denb 42 G4
Ruthrieston Aberdeen 83 C11
Ruthven Aberds 88 D5
Ruthven Angus 76 C5
Ruthven Highld 81 D9
Ruthven Highld 87 H11
Ruthven House Angus 76 C6
Ruthvoes Corn 3 C8
Ruthwell Dumfries 60 G6
Ruyton-XI-Towns Shrops 33 C9
Ryal Northumb 62 F6
Ryal Fold Blackburn 50 G2
Ryall Dorset 8 E3
Ryarsh Kent 20 F3
Rydal Cumb 56 F5
Ryde IoW 10 E4
Rye E Sus 13 D8
Rye Foreign E Sus 13 D7
Rye Harbour E Sus 13 E8
Rye Park Herts 29 G10
Rye Street Worcs 26 E4
Ryecroft Gate Staffs 44 F3
Ryehill E Yorks 53 G8
Ryhall Rutland 36 D6
Ryhill W Yorks 45 A7
Ryhope T&W 58 A5
Rylstone N Yorks 50 D5
Ryme Intrinseca Dorset 8 C4
Ryther N Yorks 52 F1
Ryton Glos 26 E4
Ryton N Yorks 52 B3
Ryton Shrops 34 E3
Ryton T&W 63 G7
Ryton-on-Dunsmore Warks 27 A10

S

Sabden Lancs 50 F3
Sacombe Herts 29 G10
Sacriston Durham 58 B3
Sadberge Darl 58 E4
Saddell Argyll 65 E8
Saddington Leics 36 F2
Saddle Bow Norf 38 D2
Saddlescombe W Sus 12 E1
Sadgill Cumb 57 F6
Saffron Walden Essex 30 E2
Sageston Pembs 22 F5
Saham Hills Norf 38 E5
Saham Toney Norf 38 E5
Saighdinis W Isles 84 B3
Saighton Ches W 43 F7
St Abbs Borders 71 D8
St Abb's Haven Borders 71 D8
St Agnes Corn 2 D6
St Agnes Scilly 2 D2
St Albans Herts 29 H8
St Allen Corn 3 D7
St Andrews Fife 77 F8
St Andrew's Major V Glam 15 D7
St Anne Ald 11
St Annes Lancs 49 G3
St Ann's Dumfries 60 D6
St Ann's Chapel Corn 4 D5
St Ann's Chapel Devon 5 G7
St Anthony-in-Meneage Corn 3 G6
St Anthony's Hill E Sus 12 F5
St Arvans Mon 15 B11
St Asaph = Llanelwy Denb 42 E3
St Athan V Glam 14 E6
St Aubin Jersey 11
St Austell Corn 3 D9
St Bees Cumb 56 E1
St Blazey Corn 4 F1
St Boswells Borders 70 G4
St Brelade Jersey 11
St Breock Corn 3 B8
St Breward Corn 4 D1
St Briavels Glos 16 A2
St Bride's Pembs 22 E3
St Brides Major V Glam 14 D4
St Bride's Netherwent Mon 15 C10
St Brides super Ely V Glam 14 D6
St Brides Wentlooge Newport 15 C8
St Budeaux Plym 4 F5
St Buryan Corn 2 G3
St Catherine Bath 16 D4
St Catherine's Argyll 73 C10
St Clears = Sanclêr Carms 23 E7
St Cleer Corn 4 E3
St Clement Corn 3 E7
St Clements Jersey 11
St Clether Corn 4 C3
St Colmac Argyll 73 G9
St Columb Major Corn 3 C8
St Columb Minor Corn 3 C7
St Columb Road Corn 3 D8
St Combs Aberds 89 B10
St Cross South Elmham Suff 39 G8
St Cyrus Aberds 77 A10
St David's Perth 76 E2
St David's = Tyddewi Pembs 22 D2
St Day Corn 2 E6
St Dennis Corn 3 D8
St Devereux Hereford 25 E11
St Dogmaels Pembs 22 B6
St Dogwells Pembs 22 D4
St Dominick Corn 4 E5
St Donat's V Glam 14 E5
St Edith's Wilts 16 E6
St Endellion Corn 3 B8
St Enoder Corn 3 D7
St Erme Corn 3 D7
St Erney Corn 4 F4
St Erth Corn 2 F4
St Ervan Corn 3 B7
St Eval Corn 3 C7
St Ewe Corn 3 E8
St Fagans Cardiff 15 D7
St Fergus Aberds 89 C10
St Fillans Perth 75 E9
St Florence Pembs 22 F5
St Genny's Corn 4 B2
St George Conwy 42 E2
St George's V Glam 14 D6
St Germans Corn 4 F4
St Giles Lincs 46 E3
St Giles in the Wood Devon 6 E4
St Giles on the Hth. Devon 6 G2
St Harmon Powys 24 A6
St Helen Auckland Durham 58 D2
St Helena Warks 35 E8
St Helen's E Sus 13 E7
St Helens IoW 10 F5
St Helens Mers 43 C8
St Helier Jersey 11
St Helier London 19 E9
St Hilary Corn 2 F4
St Hilary V Glam 14 D6
Saint Hill W Sus 12 C2
St Illtyd Bl Gwent 15 A8
St Ippollytts Herts 29 F8
St Ishmael's Pembs 22 F3
St Issey Corn 3 B8
St Ive Corn 4 E4
St Ives Cambs 29 A10
St Ives Corn 2 E4
St Ives Dorset 9 D10
St James South Elmham Suff 39 G9
St Jidgey Corn 3 C8
St John Corn 4 F5
St John's IoM 48 D2
St John's Jersey 11
St John's Sur 18 F6
St John's Worcs 26 C5
St John's Chapel Durham 57 C10
St John's Fen End Norf 37 D11
St John's Highway Norf 37 D11
St John's Town of Dalry Dumfries 55 A9
St Judes IoM 48 C3
St Just in Roseland Corn 3 F7
St Just Corn 2 F2
St Katherine's Aberds 89 E7
St Keverne Corn 3 G6
St Kew Corn 3 B9
St Kew Highway Corn 3 B9
St Keyne Corn 4 E3
St Lawrence Corn 3 C9
St Lawrence Essex 20 A6
St Lawrence IoW 10 G4
St Leonard's Bucks 28 H6
St Leonards Dorset 9 D10
St Leonards E Sus 13 F6
Saint Leonards S Lanark 68 E5
St Levan Corn 2 G2
St Lythans V Glam 15 D7
St Mabyn Corn 3 B9
St Madoes Perth 76 E4
St Margaret South Elmham Suff 39 G9
St Margaret's Hereford 25 E10
St Margarets Herts 29 G10
St Margaret's at Cliffe Kent 21 G10
St. Margaret's Hope Orkney 95 J5
St Mark's IoM 48 E2
St Martin Corn 4 F3
St Martins Corn 2 G6
St Martin's Jersey 11
St Martins Perth 76 D4
St Martin's Shrops 33 B9
St Mary Bourne Hants 17 F11
St Mary Church V Glam 14 D6
St Mary Cray London 19 E11
St Mary Hill V Glam 14 D5
St Mary Hoo Medway 20 D5
St Mary in the Marsh Kent 13 D9
St Mary's Jersey 11
St Mary's Orkney 95 H5
St Mary's Bay Kent 13 D9
St Maughans Mon 25 G11
St Mawes Corn 3 F7
St Mawgan Corn 3 C7
St Mellion Corn 4 E4
St Mellons Cardiff 15 C8
St Merryn Corn 3 B7
St Mewan Corn 3 D8
St Michael Caerhays Corn 3 E8
St Michael Penkevil Corn 3 E7
St Michael South Elmham Suff 39 G9
St Michael's Kent 13 C7
St Michaels Worcs 26 B2
St Michael's on Wyre Lancs 49 E4
St Minver Corn 3 B8
St Monans Fife 77 G8
St Neot Corn 4 E2
St Neots Cambs 29 B8
St Newlyn East Corn 3 D7
St Nicholas Pembs 22 C3
St Nicholas V Glam 14 D6
St Nicholas at Wade Kent 21 E9
St Ninians Stirling 68 A6
St Osyth Essex 31 G8
St Osyth Heath Essex 31 G8
St Ouens Jersey 11
St Owens Cross Hereford 26 F2
St Paul's Cray London 19 E11
St Paul's Walden Herts 29 F8
St Peter Port Guern 11
St Peter's Jersey 11
St Peter's Kent 21 E10
St Petrox Pembs 22 G4
St Pinnock Corn 4 E3
St Quivox S Ayrs 67 D6
St Ruan Corn 2 H6
St Sampson Guern 11
St Stephen Corn 3 D8
St Stephen's Corn 4 C4
St Stephens Corn 4 F5
St Stephens Herts 29 H8
St Teath Corn 4 C1
St Thomas Devon 7 G8
St Tudy Corn 4 D1
St Twynnells Pembs 22 G4
St Veep Corn 4 F2
St Vigeans Angus 77 C9
St Wenn Corn 3 C8
St Weonards Hereford 25 F11
Saintbury Glos 27 E8
Salcombe Devon 5 H8
Salcombe Regis Devon 7 H10
Salcott Essex 30 G6
Sale Gtr Man 43 C10
Sale Green Worcs 26 C6
Saleby Lincs 47 E8
Salehurst E Sus 12 D6
Salem Carms 24 F3
Salem Ceredig 32 G2
Salen Argyll 79 G8
Salen Highld 79 E9
Salesbury Lancs 50 F2
Salford C Beds 28 E6
Salford Gtr Man 44 C2
Salford Oxon 27 F9
Salford Priors Warks 27 C7
Salfords Sur 19 G9
Salhouse Norf 39 D9
Saline Fife 69 A9
Salisbury Wilts 9 B10
Sallachan Highld 74 A2
Sallachy Highld 86 H2
Sallachy Highld 93 J8
Salle Norf 39 C7
Salmonby Lincs 47 E7
Salmond's Muir Angus 77 D8
Salperton Glos 27 F7
Salph End Bedford 29 C7
Salsburgh N Lanark 69 D7
Salt Staffs 34 C5
Salt End E Yorks 53 G7
Saltaire W Yorks 51 F7
Saltash Corn 4 F5
Saltburn Highld 87 E10
Saltburn-by-the-Sea Redcar 59 D7
Saltby Leics 36 C4
Saltcoats Cumb 56 G2
Saltcoats N Ayrs 66 B5
Saltdean Brighton 12 F2
Salter Lancs 50 C2
Salterforth Lancs 50 E4
Salterswall Ches W 43 F9
Saltfleet Lincs 47 C8
Saltfleetby All Saints Lincs 47 C8
Saltfleetby St Clements Lincs 47 C8
Saltfleetby St Peter Lincs 47 D8
Saltford Bath 16 E3
Salthouse Norf 39 A6
Saltmarshe E Yorks 52 G3
Saltney Flint 43 F6
Salton N Yorks 52 B3
Saltwick Northumb 63 F7
Saltwood Kent 21 H8
Salum Argyll 78 G3
Salvington W Sus 11 D10
Salwarpe Worcs 26 B5
Salwayash Dorset 8 E3
Sambourne Warks 27 B7
Sambrook Telford 34 C3
Samhla W Isles 84 B2
Samlesbury Lancs 50 F1
Samlesbury Bottoms Lancs 50 G2
Sampford Arundel Som 7 E10
Sampford Brett Som 7 B9
Sampford Courtenay Devon 6 F5
Sampford Peverell Devon 7 E9
Sampford Spiney Devon 4 D6
Sampool Bridge Cumb 56 H6
Samuelston E Loth 70 C3
Sanachan Highld 85 D13
Sanaigmore Argyll 64 A3
Sanclêr = St Clears Carms 23 E7
Sancreed Corn 2 G3
Sancton E Yorks 52 F5
Sand Highld 86 B2
Sand Shetland 96 J5
Sand Hole E Yorks 52 F4
Sand Hutton N Yorks 52 D2
Sandaig Highld 85 H12
Sandal Magna W Yorks 51 H9
Sandale Cumb 56 B4
Sandbach Ches E 43 F10
Sandbank Argyll 73 E10
Sandbanks Poole 9 F9
Sandend Aberds 88 B5
Sanderstead London 19 E10
Sandfields Glos 26 F6
Sandford Cumb 57 E9
Sandford Devon 7 F7
Sandford Dorset 9 F8
Sandford IoW 10 F4
Sandford N Som 15 F10
Sandford S Lanark 68 F6
Sandford Shrops 34 B1
Sandford on Thames Oxon 18 A2
Sandford Orcas Dorset 8 B5
Sandford St Martin Oxon 27 F11
Sandfordhill Aberds 89 D11
Sandgate Kent 21 H8
Sandgreen Dumfries 55 D8
Sandhaven Aberds 89 B9
Sandhead Dumfries 54 E3
Sandhills Sur 18 H6
Sandhoe Northumb 62 G5
Sandholme E Yorks 52 F4
Sandholme Lincs 37 B9
Sandhurst Brack 18 E5
Sandhurst Glos 26 F5
Sandhurst Kent 13 D6
Sandhurst Cross Kent 13 D6
Sandhutton N Yorks 51 A9
Sandiacre Derbys 35 B10
Sandilands Lincs 47 D9
Sandilands S Lanark 69 G7
Sandiway Ches W 43 E9
Sandleheath Hants 9 C10
Sandling Kent 20 F4
Sandlow Green Ches E 43 F10
Sandness Shetland 96 H3
Sandon Essex 20 A4
Sandon Herts 29 E10
Sandon Staffs 34 B5
Sandown IoW 10 F4
Sandplace Corn 4 F3
Sandridge Herts 29 G8
Sandridge Wilts 16 E6
Sandringham Norf 38 C2
Sandsend N Yorks 59 E9
Sandside Ho. Highld 93 C12
Sandsound Shetland 96 J5
Sandtoft N Lincs 45 B11
Sandway Kent 20 F5
Sandwell W Mid 34 G6
Sandwich Kent 21 F10
Sandwick Cumb 56 E6
Sandwick Orkney 95 K5
Sandwick Shetland 96 L6
Sandwith Cumb 56 E1
Sandy C Beds 29 D8
Sandy Carms 23 F9
Sandy Bank Lincs 46 G6
Sandy Haven Pembs 22 F3
Sandy Lane Wilts 16 E6
Sandy Lane Wrex 33 A9
Sandycroft Flint 42 F6
Sandyford Dumfries 61 D8
Sandyford Stoke 44 G2
Sandygate IoM 48 C3
Sandyhills Dumfries 55 D11
Sandylands Lancs 49 C4
Sandypark Devon 5 C8
Sandysike Cumb 61 G9
Sangobeg Highld 92 C7
Sangomore Highld 92 C7
Sanna Highld 78 E7
Sanndabhaig W Isles 84 D3
Sanndabhaig W Isles 91 D9
Sannox N Ayrs 66 B3
Sanquhar Dumfries 60 C3
Santon N Lincs 46 A3
Santon Bridge Cumb 56 F3
Santon Downham Suff 38 G4
Sapcote Leics 35 F10
Sapey Common Hereford 26 B4
Sapiston Suff 38 H5
Sapley Cambs 29 A9
Sapperton Glos 16 A6
Sapperton Lincs 36 B6
Saracen's Head Lincs 37 C9
Sarclet Highld 94 F5
Sardis Carms 23 F10
Sarn Bridgend 14 C5
Sarn Powys 33 F8
Sarn Bach Gwyn 40 H5
Sarn Meyllteyrn Gwyn 40 G4
Sarnau Carms 23 E8
Sarnau Ceredig 23 A8
Sarnau Gwyn 32 B5
Sarnau Powys 25 E7
Sarnau Powys 33 D8
Sarnesfield Hereford 25 C10
Saron Carms 23 C8
Saron Carms 24 G3
Saron Denb 42 F3
Saron Gwyn 40 E6
Saron Gwyn 41 D7
Sarratt Herts 19 B7
Sarre Kent 21 E9
Sarsden Oxon 27 F9
Sarsgrum Highld 92 C6
Satley Durham 58 B2
Satron N Yorks 57 G11
Satterleigh Devon 6 D5
Satterthwaite Cumb 56 G5
Satwell Oxon 18 C4
Sauchen Aberds 83 B8
Saucher Perth 76 D4
Sauchie Clack 69 A7
Sauchieburn Aberds 83 G8
Saughall Ches W 42 E6
Saughtree Borders 61 D11
Saul Glos 26 H4
Saundby Notts 45 D11
Saundersfoot Pembs 22 F6
Saunderton Bucks 18 A4
Saunton Devon 6 C3
Sausthorpe Lincs 47 F7
Saval Highld 93 J8
Savary Highld 79 G9
Savile Park W Yorks 51 G6
Sawbridge Warks 28 B2
Sawbridgeworth Herts 29 G11
Sawdon N Yorks 59 H10
Sawley Derbys 35 B10
Sawley Lancs 50 E3
Sawley N Yorks 51 C8
Sawston Cambs 29 D11
Sawtry Cambs 37 G7
Saxby Leics 36 D4
Saxby Lincs 46 D4
Saxby All Saints N Lincs 52 H5
Saxelbye Leics 36 C3
Saxham Street Suff 31 B7
Saxilby Lincs 46 E2
Saxlingham Norf 38 B6
Saxlingham Green Norf 39 F8
Saxlingham Nethergate Norf 39 F8
Saxlingham Thorpe Norf 39 F8
Saxmundham Suff 31 B10
Saxon Street Cambs 30 C3
Saxondale Notts 36 B2
Saxtead Suff 31 B9
Saxtead Green Suff 31 B9
Saxthorpe Norf 39 B7
Saxton N Yorks 51 F10
Sayers Common W Sus 12 E1
Scackleton N Yorks 52 B2
Scadabhagh W Isles 90 H6
Scaftworth Notts 45 C10
Scagglethorpe N Yorks 52 B4
Scaitcliffe Lancs 50 G3
Scalasaig Argyll 72 D2
Scalby E Yorks 52 G4
Scalby N Yorks 59 G11
Scaldwell Northants 28 A4
Scale Houses Cumb 57 B7
Scaleby Cumb 61 G10
Scaleby Hill Cumb 61 G10
Scales Cumb 49 B2
Scales Cumb 56 D5
Scales Lancs 49 F4
Scalford Leics 36 C3
Scaling Redcar 59 E8
Scallastle Argyll 79 H9
Scalloway Shetland 96 K6
Scalpay W Isles 90 H7
Scalpay Ho. Highld 85 F11
Scalpsie Argyll 73 H9
Scamadale Highld 79 B10
Scamblesby Lincs 46 E6
Scamodale Highld 79 D11
Scampston N Yorks 52 B4
Scampton Lincs 46 E3
Scapa Orkney 95 H5
Scapegoat Hill W Yorks 51 H6
Scar Orkney 95 D7
Scarborough N Yorks 59 H11
Scarcliffe Derbys 45 F8
Scarcroft W Yorks 51 E9
Scarcroft Hill W Yorks 51 E9
Scardroy Highld 86 F5
Scarff Shetland 96 E4
Scarfskerry Highld 94 C4
Scargill Durham 58 E1
Scarinish Argyll 78 G3
Scarisbrick Lancs 43 A6
Scarning Norf 38 D5
Scarrington Notts 36 A3
Scartho NE Lincs 46 B6
Scarwell Orkney 95 F3
Scatness Shetland 96 M5
Scatraig Highld 87 H10
Scawby N Lincs 46 B3
Scawsby S Yorks 45 B9
Scawton N Yorks 51 A11
Scayne's Hill W Sus 12 D2
Scethrog Powys 25 F8
Scholar Green Ches E 44 G2
Scholes W Yorks 44 B5
Scholes W Yorks 51 F9
Scholes W Yorks 51 G7
School Green Ches W 43 F9
Scleddau Pembs 22 C4
Sco Ruston Norf 39 C8
Scofton Notts 45 D10
Scole Norf 39 H7
Scolpaig W Isles 84 A2
Scone Perth 76 E4
Sconser Highld 85 E10
Scoonie Fife 76 G6
Scoor Argyll 78 K7
Scopwick Lincs 46 G4
Scoraig Highld 86 B3
Scorborough E Yorks 52 E6
Scorrier Corn 2 E6
Scorton Lancs 49 E5
Scorton N Yorks 58 F3
Scotbheinn W Isles 84 C3
Scotby Cumb 61 H10
Scotch Corner N Yorks 58 F3
Scotforth Lancs 49 D4
Scothern Lincs 46 E4
Scotland Gate Northumb 63 E8
Scotlandwell Perth 76 G4
Scots' Gap Northumb 62 E6
Scotsburn Highld 87 D10
Scotscalder Station Highld 94 E2
Scotscraig Fife 77 E7
Scotston Aberds 83 F9
Scotston Perth 76 C2
Scotstoun Glasgow 68 D4
Scotstown Highld 79 E11
Scotswood T&W 63 G7
Scottas Highld 85 H12
Scotter Lincs 46 B2
Scotterthorpe Lincs 46 B2
Scottlethorpe Lincs 37 C6
Scotton Lincs 46 C2
Scotton N Yorks 51 D9
Scotton N Yorks 58 G2
Scottow Norf 39 C8
Scoughall E Loth 70 B5
Scoulag Argyll 73 H10
Scoulton Norf 38 E5
Scourie Highld 92 E4
Scourie More Highld 92 E4
Scousburgh Shetland 96 M5
Scrabster Highld 94 C2
Scrafield Lincs 47 F7
Scrainwood Northumb 62 C5
Scrane End Lincs 37 A9
Scraptoft Leics 36 E2
Scratby Norf 39 D11
Scrayingham N Yorks 52 C3
Scredington Lincs 37 A6
Scremby Lincs 47 F8
Scremerston Northumb 71 F9
Screveton Notts 36 A3
Scrivelsby Lincs 46 F6
Scriven N Yorks 51 D9
Scrooby Notts 45 C10
Scropton Derbys 35 B7
Scrub Hill Lincs 46 G6
Scruton N Yorks 58 G3
Sculcoates Hull 53 F6
Sculthorpe Norf 38 B4
Scunthorpe N Lincs 46 A2
Scurlage Swansea 23 H9
Sea Palling Norf 39 C10
Seaborough Dorset 8 D3
Seacombe Mers 42 C6
Seacroft Lincs 47 F9
Seacroft W Yorks 51 F9
Seadyke Lincs 37 B9
Seafield S Ayrs 66 D6
Seafield W Loth 69 D9
Seaford E Sus 12 G3
Seaforth Mers 42 C6
Seagrave Leics 36 D2
Seaham Durham 58 B5
Seahouses Northumb 71 G11
Seal Kent 20 F2
Sealand Flint 42 F6
Seale Sur 18 G5
Seamer N Yorks 52 A6
Seamer N Yorks 58 E5
Seamill N Ayrs 66 B5
Searby Lincs 46 B4
Seasalter Kent 21 E7
Seascale Cumb 56 F2
Seathorne Lincs 47 F9
Seathwaite Cumb 56 E4
Seathwaite Cumb 56 G4
Seatoller Cumb 56 E4
Seaton Corn 4 F4
Seaton Cumb 56 C2
Seaton Devon 8 F1
Seaton Durham 58 A4
Seaton E Yorks 53 E7
Seaton Northumb 63 F9
Seaton Rutland 36 F5
Seaton Burn T&W 63 F8
Seaton Carew Hrtlpl 58 D6
Seaton Delaval Northumb 63 F9
Seaton Ross E Yorks 52 E3
Seaton Sluice Northumb 63 F9
Seatown Aberds 88 B5
Seatown Dorset 8 E3
Seave Green N Yorks 59 F6
Seaview IoW 10 E5
Seaville Cumb 56 A3
Seavington St Mary Som 8 C3
Seavington St Michael Som 8 C3
Sebergham Cumb 56 B5
Seckington Warks 35 E8
Second Coast Highld 86 B2
Sedbergh Cumb 57 G8
Sedbury Glos 15 B11
Sedbusk N Yorks 57 G10
Sedgeberrow Worcs 27 E7
Sedgebrook Lincs 36 B4
Sedgefield Durham 58 D4
Sedgeford Norf 38 B3
Sedgehill Wilts 9 B7
Sedgley W Mid 34 F5
Sedgwick Cumb 57 H7
Sedlescombe E Sus 13 E6
Sedlescombe Street E Sus 13 E6
Seend Wilts 16 E6
Seend Cleeve Wilts 16 E6
Seer Green Bucks 18 B6
Seething Norf 39 F9
Sefton Mers 42 B6
Seghill Northumb 63 F8
Seifton Shrops 33 G10
Seighford Staffs 34 C4
Seilebost W Isles 90 H5
Seion Gwyn 41 D7
Seisdon Staffs 34 F4
Seisiadar W Isles 91 D10
Selattyn Shrops 33 B8
Selborne Hants 10 A6
Selby N Yorks 52 F2
Selham W Sus 11 B8
Selhurst London 19 E10
Selkirk Borders 70 H3
Sellack Hereford 26 F2
Sellafirth Shetland 96 D7
Sellibister Orkney 95 D8
Sellindge Kent 13 C9
Sellindge Lees Kent 13 C10
Selling Kent 21 F7
Sells Green Wilts 16 E6
Selly Oak W Mid 34 G6
Selmeston E Sus 12 F4
Selsdon London 19 E10
Selsey W Sus 11 E7
Selsfield Common W Sus 12 C2
Selsted Kent 21 G9
Selston Notts 45 G8
Selworthy Som 7 B8
Semblister Shetland 96 H5
Semer Suff 30 D6
Semington Wilts 16 E5
Semley Wilts 9 B7
Send Sur 19 F7
Send Marsh Sur 19 F7
Senghenydd Caerph 15 B7
Sennen Corn 2 G2
Sennen Cove Corn 2 G2
Sennybridge = Pont Senni Powys 24 F6
Serlby Notts 45 D10
Sessay N Yorks 51 B10
Setchey Norf 38 D2
Setley Hants 10 D2
Setter Shetland 96 E6
Setter Shetland 96 H5
Setter Shetland 96 J7
Settiscarth Orkney 95 G4
Settle N Yorks 50 C4
Settrington N Yorks 52 B4
Seven Kings London 19 C11
Seven Sisters Neath 24 H5
Sevenhampton Glos 27 F7
Sevenoaks Kent 20 F2
Sevenoaks Weald Kent 20 F2
Severn Beach S Glos 15 C11
Severn Stoke Worcs 26 D5
Severnhampton Swindon 17 B9
Sevington Kent 13 B9
Sewards End Essex 30 E2
Sewardstone Essex 19 B10
Sewardstonebury Essex 19 B10
Sewerby E Yorks 53 C7
Seworgan Corn 2 F6
Sewstern Leics 36 C4
Sezincote Glos 27 E8
Sgarasta Mhor W Isles 90 H5
Sgiogarstaigh W Isles 91 A10
Shabbington Bucks 28 H3
Shackerstone Leics 35 E9
Shackleford Sur 18 G6
Shade W Yorks 50 G5
Shadforth Durham 58 B4
Shadingfield Suff 39 G10
Shadoxhurst Kent 13 C8
Shadsworth Blackburn 50 G3
Shadwell Norf 38 G5
Shadwell W Yorks 51 F9
Shaftesbury Dorset 9 B7
Shafton S Yorks 45 A7
Shalbourne Wilts 17 E10
Shalcombe IoW 10 F2
Shalden Hants 18 G3
Shaldon Devon 5 D10
Shalfleet IoW 10 F3
Shalford Essex 30 F4
Shalford Sur 19 G7
Shalford Green Essex 30 F4
Shallowford Devon 6 B6
Shalmsford Street Kent 21 F7
Shalstone Bucks 28 E3
Shamley Green Sur 19 G7
Shandon Argyll 73 E11
Shandwick Highld 87 D11
Shangton Leics 36 F3
Shankhouse Northumb 63 F8
Shanklin IoW 10 F4
Shanquhar Aberds 88 E5
Shanzie Perth 76 B5
Shap Cumb 57 E7
Shapwick Dorset 9 D8
Shapwick Som 15 H10
Shardlow Derbys 35 B10
Shareshill Staffs 34 E5
Sharlston W Yorks 51 H9
Sharlston Common W Yorks 51 H9
Sharnbrook Bedford 28 C6
Sharnford Leics 35 F10
Sharoe Green Lancs 49 F5
Sharow N Yorks 51 B9
Sharp Street Norf 39 C9
Sharpenhoe C Beds 29 E7
Sharperton Northumb 62 C5
Sharpness Glos 16 A3
Sharpthorne W Sus 12 C2
Sharrington Norf 38 B6
Shatterford Worcs 34 G3
Shaugh Prior Devon 4 E6
Shavington Ches E 43 G10
Shaw Gtr Man 44 B3
Shaw W Berks 17 E11
Shaw Wilts 16 E5
Shaw Green Lancs 49 H5
Shaw Mills N Yorks 51 C8
Shawbury Shrops 34 C1
Shawdon Hall Northumb 62 B6
Shawell Leics 35 G11
Shawford Hants 10 B3
Shawforth Lancs 50 G4
Shawhead Dumfries 60 F4
Shawhill Dumfries 61 G8
Shawton S Lanark 68 F5
Shawtonhill S Lanark 68 F5
Shear Cross Wilts 16 G5
Shearington Dumfries 60 G6
Shearsby Leics 36 F2
Shebbear Devon 6 F3
Shebdon Staffs 34 C3
Shebster Highld 93 C13
Sheddens E Renf 68 E4
Shedfield Hants 10 C4
Sheen Staffs 44 F5
Sheepscar W Yorks 51 F9
Sheepscombe Glos 26 G5
Sheepstor Devon 5 E6
Sheepwash Devon 6 F3
Sheepway N Som 15 D10
Sheepy Magna Leics 35 E9
Sheepy Parva Leics 35 E9
Sheering Essex 30 G2
Sheerness Kent 20 D6
Sheet Hants 11 B6
Sheffield S Yorks 45 D7
Sheffield Bottom W Berks 18 E3
Sheffield Green E Sus 12 D3
Shefford C Beds 29 E8
Shefford Woodlands W Berks 17 D10
Sheigra Highld 92 C4
Sheinton Shrops 34 E2
Shelderton Shrops 33 H10
Sheldon Derbys 44 F5
Sheldon Devon 7 F10
Sheldon W Mid 35 G7
Sheldwich Kent 21 F7
Shelf W Yorks 51 G7
Shelfanger Norf 39 G7
Shelfield W Mid 34 E6
Shelfield Warks 27 B8
Shelford Notts 36 A2
Shellacres Northumb 71 F7
Shelley Essex 20 A2
Shelley Suff 31 E7
Shelley W Yorks 44 A6
Shellingford Oxon 17 B10
Shellow Bowells Essex 30 H3
Shelsley Beauchamp Worcs 26 B4
Shelsley Walsh Worcs 26 B4
Shelthorpe Leics 35 D11
Shelton Bedford 29 B7
Shelton Norf 39 F8
Shelton Notts 36 A3
Shelton Shrops 33 D10
Shelton Green Norf 39 F8
Shelve Shrops 33 F9
Shelwick Hereford 26 D2
Shenfield Essex 20 B3
Shenington Oxon 27 D10
Shenley Herts 19 A8
Shenley Brook End M Keynes 28 E5
Shenley Church End M Keynes 28 E5
Shenleybury Herts 19 A8
Shenmore Hereford 25 E10
Shennanton Dumfries 54 C6
Shenstone Staffs 35 E7
Shenstone Worcs 26 A5
Shenton Leics 35 E9
Shenval Highld 80 A6
Shenval Moray 82 A4
Shepeau Stow Lincs 37 D9
Shephall Herts 29 F9
Shepherd's Green Oxon 18 C4
Shepherd's Port Norf 38 B2
Shepherdswell Kent 21 G9
Shepley W Yorks 44 B5
Shepperdine S Glos 16 B3
Shepperton Sur 19 E7
Shepreth Cambs 29 D10
Shepshed Leics 35 D10
Shepton Beauchamp Som 8 C3
Shepton Mallet Som 16 G3
Shepton Montague Som 8 A5
Shepway Kent 20 F4
Sheraton Durham 58 C5
Sherborne Dorset 8 C5
Sherborne Glos 27 G8
Sherborne St John Hants 18 F3
Sherbourne Warks 27 B9
Sherburn Durham 58 B4
Sherburn N Yorks 52 B5
Sherburn Hill Durham 58 B4
Sherburn in Elmet N Yorks 51 F10
Shere Sur 19 G7
Shereford Norf 38 C4
Sherfield English Hants 10 B1
Sherfield on Loddon Hants 18 F3
Sherford Devon 5 G8
Sheriff Hutton N Yorks 52 C2
Sheriffhales Shrops 34 D3
Sheringham Norf 39 A7
Sherington M Keynes 28 D5
Shernal Green Worcs 26 B6
Shernborne Norf 38 B3
Sherrington Wilts 16 H6
Sherston Wilts 16 C5
Sherwood Green Devon 6 D4
Shettleston Glasgow 68 D5
Shevington Gtr Man 43 B8
Shevington Moor Gtr Man 43 A8
Shevington Vale Gtr Man 43 B8
Sheviock Corn 4 F4
Shide IoW 10 F3
Shiel Bridge Highld 80 B1
Shieldaig Highld 85 A13
Shieldaig Highld 85 C13
Shieldhill Dumfries 60 E6
Shieldhill Falk 69 C7
Shieldhill S Lanark 69 F9
Shielfoot Highld 79 E9
Shielhill Angus 77 B7
Shielhill Invclyd 73 F11
Shifford Oxon 17 A10
Shifnal Shrops 34 E3
Shilbottle Northumb 63 C7
Shildon Durham 58 D3
Shillingford Devon 7 D8
Shillingford Oxon 18 B2
Shillingford St George Devon 5 C10
Shillingstone Dorset 9 C7
Shillington C Beds 29 E8
Shillmoor Northumb 62 C4
Shilton Oxon 27 H9
Shilton Warks 35 G10
Shilvington Northumb 63 E7
Shimpling Norf 39 G7
Shimpling Suff 30 C5
Shimpling Street Suff 30 C5
Shincliffe Durham 58 B3
Shiney Row T&W 58 A4
Shinfield Wokingham 18 E4
Shingham Norf 38 E3
Shingle Street Suff 31 D10
Shinner's Bridge Devon 5 E8
Shinness Highld 93 H8
Shipbourne Kent 20 F2
Shipdham Norf 38 E5
Shipham Som 15 F10
Shiphay Torbay 5 E9
Shiplake Oxon 18 D4
Shipley Derbys 35 A10
Shipley Northumb 63 B7
Shipley Shrops 34 F4
Shipley W Sus 11 B10
Shipley W Yorks 51 F7
Shipley Shiels Northumb 62 D3
Shipmeadow Suff 39 G9
Shippea Hill Sta. Cambs 38 G2
Shippon Oxon 17 B11
Shipston-on-Stour Warks 27 D9
Shipton Glos 27 G7
Shipton N Yorks 52 D1
Shipton Shrops 34 F1
Shipton Bellinger Hants 17 G9
Shipton Gorge Dorset 8 E3
Shipton Green W Sus 11 D7
Shipton Moyne Glos 16 C5
Shipton on Cherwell Oxon 27 G11
Shipton Solers Glos 27 G7
Shipton-under-Wychwood Oxon 27 G9
Shiptonthorpe E Yorks 52 E4
Shirburn Oxon 18 B3
Shirdley Hill Lancs 42 A6
Shirebrook Derbys 45 F9
Shiregreen S Yorks 45 C7
Shirehampton Bristol 15 D11
Shiremoor T&W 63 F9
Shirenewton Mon 15 B10
Shireoaks Notts 45 D9
Shirkoak Kent 13 C8
Shirl Heath Hereford 25 C11
Shirland Derbys 45 G7
Shirley Derbys 35 A8
Shirley London 19 E10
Shirley Soton 10 C3
Shirley W Mid 35 H7
Shirrell Heath Hants 10 C4
Shirwell Devon 6 C4
Shirwell Cross Devon 6 C4
Shiskine N Ayrs 66 D2
Shobdon Hereford 25 B11
Shobnall Staffs 35 C8
Shobrooke Devon 7 F7
Shoby Leics 36 D2
Shocklach Ches W 43 H7
Shoeburyness Southend 20 C6
Sholden Kent 21 F10
Sholing Soton 10 C3
Shoot Hill Shrops 33 D10
Shop Corn 3 B7
Shop Corn 6 E1
Shop Corner Suff 31 E9
Shore Mill Highld 87 E10
Shoreditch London 19 C10
Shoreham Kent 20 E2
Shoreham-By-Sea W Sus 11 D11
Shoresdean Northumb 71 F8
Shoreswood Northumb 71 F8
Shoreton Highld 87 E9
Shorncote Glos 17 B7
Shorne Kent 20 D3
Short Heath W Mid 34 E5
Shortacombe Devon 4 C6
Shortgate E Sus 12 E3
Shortlanesend Corn 3 E7
Shortlees E Ayrs 67 C7
Shortstown Bedford 29 D7
Shorwell IoW 10 F3
Shoscombe Bath 16 F4
Shotatton Shrops 33 C9
Shotesham Norf 39 F8
Shotgate Essex 20 B4
Shotley Suff 31 E9
Shotley Bridge Durham 58 A1
Shotley Gate Suff 31 E9
Shotleyfield Northumb 58 A1
Shottenden Kent 21 F7
Shottermill Sur 11 A7
Shottery Warks 27 C8
Shotteswell Warks 27 D11
Shottisham Suff 31 D10
Shottle Derbys 45 H7
Shottlegate Derbys 45 H7
Shotton Durham 58 C5
Shotton Flint 42 F6
Shotton Northumb 71 G7
Shotton Colliery Durham 58 B4
Shotts N Lanark 69 D7
Shotwick Ches W 42 E6
Shouldham Norf 38 E2
Shouldham Thorpe Norf 38 E2
Shoulton Worcs 26 C5
Shover's Green E Sus 12 C5
Shrawardine Shrops 33 D10
Shrawley Worcs 26 B5
Shrewley Common Warks 27 B9
Shrewsbury Shrops 33 D10
Shrewton Wilts 17 G7
Shripney W Sus 11 D8
Shrivenham Oxon 17 C9
Shropham Norf 38 F5
Shrub End Essex 30 F6
Shucknall Hereford 26 D2
Shudy Camps Cambs 30 D3
Shulishadermor Highld 85 D9
Shurdington Glos 26 G6
Shurlock Row Windsor 18 D5
Shurrery Highld 93 D13
Shurrery Lodge Highld 93 D13
Shurton Som 7 B11
Shustoke Warks 35 F8
Shute Devon 7 F7
Shute Devon 8 E1
Shutford Oxon 27 D10
Shuthonger Glos 26 E5
Shutlanger Northants 28 C4
Shuttington Warks 35 E8
Shuttlewood Derbys 45 E8
Siabost bho Dheas W Isles 90 C7
Siabost bho Thuath W Isles 90 C7
Siadar W Isles 91 B8
Siadar Iarach W Isles 91 B8
Siadar Uarach W Isles 91 B8
Sibbaldbie Dumfries 61 E7
Sibbertoft Northants 36 G2
Sibdon Carwood Shrops 33 G10
Sibford Ferris Oxon 27 E10
Sibford Gower Oxon 27 E10
Sible Hedingham Essex 30 E4
Sibsey Lincs 47 G7
Sibson Cambs 37 F6
Sibson Leics 35 E9
Sibthorpe Notts 45 H11
Sibton Suff 31 B10
Sibton Green Suff 31 A10
Sicklesmere Suff 30 B5
Sicklinghall N Yorks 51 E9
Sid Devon 7 H10
Sidbury Devon 7 G10
Sidbury Shrops 34 G2
Sidcot N Som 15 F10
Sidcup London 19 D11
Siddick Cumb 56 C2
Siddington Ches E 44 E2
Siddington Glos 17 B7
Sidemoor Worcs 26 A6
Sidestrand Norf 39 B8
Sidford Devon 7 G10
Sidlesham W Sus 11 E7
Sidley E Sus 12 F6
Sidlow Sur 19 G9
Sidmouth Devon 7 H10
Sigford Devon 5 D8
Sigglesthorne E Yorks 53 E7
Sighthill Edin 69 C10
Sigingstone V Glam 14 D5
Signet Oxon 27 G9
Silchester Hants 18 E3
Sildinis W Isles 91 F7
Sileby Leics 36 D1
Silecroft Cumb 49 A1
Silfield Norf 39 F7
Silian Ceredig 23 A10
Silk Willoughby Lincs 37 A6
Silkstone S Yorks 44 B6
Silkstone Common S Yorks 44 B6
Silloth Cumb 56 A3
Sills Northumb 62 C4
Sillyearn Moray 88 C5
Siloh Carms 24 E4
Silpho N Yorks 59 G10
Silsden W Yorks 50 E6
Silsoe C Beds 29 E7
Silver End Essex 30 G5
Silverburn Midloth 69 D11
Silverdale Lancs 49 B4
Silverdale Staffs 44 H2
Silvergate Norf 39 C7
Silverhill E Sus 13 E6
Silverley's Green Suff 39 H8
Silverstone Northants 28 D3
Silverton Devon 7 F8
Silvington Shrops 34 H2
Silwick Shetland 96 J4
Simmondley Derbys 44 C4
Simonburn Northumb 62 F4
Simonsbath Som 7 C6
Simonstone Lancs 50 F3
Simprim Borders 71 F7
Simpson M Keynes 28 E5
Simpson Cross Pembs 22 E3
Sinclair's Hill Borders 71 E7
Sinclairston E Ayrs 67 E7
Sinderby N Yorks 51 A9
Sinderhope Northumb 57 A10
Sindlesham Wokingham 18 E4
Singdean Borders 61 C11
Singleborough Bucks 28 E4
Singleton Lancs 49 F3
Singleton W Sus 11 C7
Singlewell Kent 20 D3
Sinkhurst Green Kent 13 B7
Sinnahard Aberds 82 B6
Sinnington N Yorks 59 H8
Sinton Green Worcs 26 B5
Sipson London 19 D7
Sirhowy Bl Gwent 25 G8
Sisland Norf 39 F9
Sissinghurst Kent 13 C6
Sisterpath Borders 70 F6
Siston S Glos 16 D3
Sithney Corn 2 G5
Sittingbourne Kent 20 E6
Six Ashes Staffs 34 G3
Six Hills Leics 36 C2
Six Mile Bottom Cambs 30 C2
Sixhills Lincs 46 D5
Sixpenny Handley Dorset 9 C8
Sizewell Suff 31 B11
Skail Highld 93 E10
Skaill Orkney 95 E5
Skaill Orkney 95 G3
Skaill Orkney 95 H6
Skares E Ayrs 67 E8
Skateraw E Loth 70 C6
Skaw Shetland 96 G7
Skeabost Highld 85 D9
Skeabrae Orkney 95 F3
Skeeby N Yorks 58 F3
Skeffington Leics 36 E3
Skeffling E Yorks 53 H9
Skegby Notts 45 F8
Skegness Lincs 47 F9
Skelberry Shetland 96 M5
Skelbo Highld 87 B10
Skelbrooke S Yorks 45 A9
Skeldyke Lincs 37 B9
Skellingthorpe Lincs 46 E3
Skellister Shetland 96 H6
Skellow S Yorks 45 A9
Skelmanthorpe W Yorks 44 A6
Skelmersdale Lancs 43 B7
Skelmonae Aberds 89 E8
Skelmorlie N Ayrs 73 G10
Skelmuir Aberds 89 D9
Skelpick Highld 93 D10
Skelton Cumb 56 C6
Skelton E Yorks 52 G3
Skelton N Yorks 58 F1
Skelton Redcar 59 E7
Skelton York 52 D1
Skelton-on-Ure N Yorks 51 C9
Skelwick Orkney 95 D5
Skelwith Bridge Cumb 56 F5
Skendleby Lincs 47 F8
Skene Ho. Aberds 83 C9
Skenfrith Mon 25 F11
Skerne E Yorks 52 D6
Skeroblingarry Argyll 65 F8
Skerray Highld 93 C9
Skerton Lancs 49 C4
Sketchley Leics 35 F10
Sketty Swansea 14 B2
Skewen Neath 14 B3
Skewsby N Yorks 52 B2
Skeyton Norf 39 C8
Skiag Bridge Highld 92 G5
Skibo Castle Highld 87 C10
Skidbrooke Lincs 47 C8
Skidbrooke North End Lincs 47 C8
Skidby E Yorks 52 F6
Skilgate Som 7 D8
Skillington Lincs 36 C4
Skinburness Cumb 61 H7
Skinflats Falk 69 B8
Skinidin Highld 84 D7
Skinnet Highld 93 C8
Skinningrove Redcar 59 D8
Skipness Argyll 73 H7
Skippool Lancs 49 E3
Skipsea E Yorks 53 D7
Skipsea Brough E Yorks 53 D7
Skipton N Yorks 50 D5
Skipton-on-Swale N Yorks 51 B9
Skipwith N Yorks 52 F2
Skirbeck Lincs 37 A9
Skirbeck Quarter Lincs 37 A9
Skirlaugh E Yorks 53 F7
Skirling Borders 69 G9
Skirmett Bucks 18 C4
Skirpenbeck E Yorks 52 D3
Skirwith Cumb 57 C8
Skirza Highld 94 D5
Skulamus Highld 85 F11
Skullomie Highld 93 C9
Skyborry Green Shrops 25 A9
Skye of Curr Highld 82 A1
Skyreholme N Yorks 51 C6
Slackhall Derbys 44 D4
Slackhead Moray 88 B4
Slad Glos 26 H5
Slade Devon 6 B4
Slade Pembs 22 E4
Slade Green London 20 D2
Slaggyford Northumb 57 A8
Slaidburn Lancs 50 D3
Slaithwaite W Yorks 44 A4
Slaley Northumb 62 H5
Slamannan Falk 69 C7
Slapton Bucks 28 F6
Slapton Devon 5 G9
Slapton Northants 28 D3
Slatepit Dale Derbys 45 F7
Slattocks Gtr Man 44 B2
Slaugham W Sus 12 D1
Slaughterford Wilts 16 D5
Slawston Leics 36 F3
Sleaford Hants 18 H5
Sleaford Lincs 46 H4
Sleagill Cumb 57 E7
Sleapford Telford 34 D2
Sledge Green Worcs 26 E5
Sledmere E Yorks 52 C5
Sleightholme Durham 57 E11
Sleights N Yorks 59 F9
Slepe Dorset 9 E8
Slickly Highld 94 D4
Sliddery N Ayrs 66 D2
Sligachan Hotel Highld 85 F9
Slimbridge Glos 16 A4
Slindon Staffs 34 B4
Slindon W Sus 11 D8
Slinfold W Sus 11 A10
Sling Gwyn 41 D8
Slingsby N Yorks 52 B2
Slioch Aberds 88 E5
Slip End C Beds 29 G7
Slip End Herts 29 E9
Slipton Northants 36 H5
Slitting Mill Staffs 34 D6
Slochd Highld 81 A10
Slockavullin Argyll 73 D7
Sloley Norf 39 C8
Sloothby Lincs 47 E8
Slough Slough 18 D6
Slough Green W Sus 12 D1
Sluggan Highld 81 A10
Slumbay Highld 85 E13
Slyfield Sur 18 F6

Slyne Lancs 49 C4
Smailholm Borders 70 G5
Small Dole W Sus 11 C11
Small Hythe Kent 13 C7
Smallbridge Gtr Man 50 H5
Smallburgh Norf 39 C9
Smallburn Aberds 89 D10
Smallburn E Ayrs 68 H5
Smalley Derbys 35 A10
Smallfield Sur 12 B2
Smallridge Devon 8 D2
Smannell Hants 17 G10
Smardale Cumb 57 F9
Smarden Kent 13 B7
Smarden Bell Kent 13 B7
Smeatharpe Devon 7 E10
Smeeth Kent 13 C9
Smeeton Westerby Leics 36 F2
Smercleit W Isles 84 G2
Smerral Highld 94 G3
Smethwick W Mid 34 G6
Smirisary Highld 79 D9
Smisby Derbys 35 D9
Smith Green Lancs 49 D4
Smithfield Cumb 61 G10
Smithincott Devon 7 E9
Smith's Green Essex 30 F2
Smithstown Highld 85 A12
Smithton Highld 87 G10
Smithy Green Ches E 43 E10
Smockington Leics 35 G10
Smoogro Orkney 95 H4
Smythe's Green Essex 30 G6
Snaigow House Perth 76 C3
Snailbeach Shrops 33 E9
Snailwell Cambs 30 B3
Snainton N Yorks 52 A5
Snaith E Yorks 52 G2
Snape N Yorks 51 A8
Snape Suff 31 C10
Snape Green Lancs 43 A6
Snarestone Leics 35 E9
Snarford Lincs 46 D4
Snargate Kent 13 D8
Snave Kent 13 D9
Snead Powys 33 F9
Sneath Common Norf 39 G7
Sneaton N Yorks 59 F9
Sneatonthorpe N Yorks 59 F10
Snelland Lincs 46 D4
Snelston Derbys 35 A7
Snettisham Norf 38 B2
Sniseabhal W Isles 84 E2
Snitter Northumb 62 C6
Snitterby Lincs 46 C3
Snitterfield Warks 27 C9
Snitton Shrops 34 H1
Snodhill Hereford 25 D10
Snodland Kent 20 E3
Snowden Hill S Yorks 44 B6
Snowdown Kent 21 F9
Snowshill Glos 27 E7
Snydale W Yorks 51 H10
Soar Anglesey 40 C5
Soar Carms 24 F3
Soar Devon 5 H8
Soar-y-Mynydd Ceredig 24 C4
Soberton Hants 10 C5
Soberton Heath Hants 10 C5
Sockbridge Cumb 57 D7
Sockburn Darl 58 F4
Soham Cambs 30 A2
Soham Cotes Cambs 38 H1
Solas W Isles 84 A3
Soldon Cross Devon 6 E2
Soldridge Hants 10 A5
Sole Street Kent 20 E3
Sole Street Kent 21 G7
Solihull W Mid 35 H7
Sollers Dilwyn Hereford 25 C11
Sollers Hope Hereford 26 E3
Sollom Lancs 49 H4
Solva Pembs 22 D2
Somerby Leics 36 D3
Somerby Lincs 46 B4
Somercotes Derbys 45 G8
Somerford Dorset 9 E10
Somerford Keynes Glos 17 B7
Somerley W Sus 11 E7
Somerleyton Suff 39 F10
Somersal Herbert Derbys 35 B7
Somersby Lincs 47 E7
Somersham Cambs 37 H9
Somersham Suff 31 D7
Somerton Oxon 27 F11
Somerton Som 8 B3
Sompting W Sus 11 D10
Sonning Wokingham 18 D4
Sonning Common Oxon 18 C4
Sonning Eye Oxon 18 D4
Sontley Wrex 42 H6
Sopley Hants 9 E10
Sopwell Herts 29 H8
Sopworth Wilts 16 C5
Sorbie Dumfries 55 E7
Sordale Highld 94 D3
Sorisdale Argyll 78 E5
Sorn E Ayrs 68 H4
Sornhill E Ayrs 67 C8
Sortat Highld 94 D4
Sotby Lincs 46 E6
Sots Hole Lincs 46 F5
Sotterley Suff 39 G10
Soudley Shrops 34 C3
Soughton Flint 42 F5
Soulbury Bucks 28 F5
Soulby Cumb 57 E9
Souldern Oxon 28 E2
Souldrop Bedford 28 B6
Sound Ches E 43 H9
Sound Shetland 96 H5
Sound Shetland 96 J6
Sound Heath Ches E 43 H9
Soundwell S Glos 16 D3
Sourhope Borders 62 A4
Sourin Orkney 95 E5
Sourton Devon 6 G4
Soutergate Cumb 49 A2
South Acre Norf 38 D4
South Allington Devon 5 H8
South Alloa Falk 69 A7
South Ambersham W Sus 11 B8
South Anston S Yorks 45 D9
South Ascot Windsor 18 E6
South Ballachulish Highld 74 B3
South Balloch S Ayrs 66 G6
South Bank Redcar 59 D6
South Barrow Som 8 B4
South Beach Gwyn 40 G5
South Benfleet Essex 20 C4
South Bersted W Sus 11 D8
South Brent Devon 5 E7
South Brewham Som 16 H4
South Broomhill Northumb 63 D8
South Burlingham Norf 39 E9
South Cadbury Som 8 B5
South Cairn Dumfries 54 C2
South Carlton Lincs 46 E3
South Cave E Yorks 52 F5
South Cerney Glos 17 B7
South Chard Som 8 D2
South Charlton Northumb 63 A7
South Cheriton Som 8 B5
South Cliffe E Yorks 52 F4
South Clifton Notts 46 E2
South Cockerington Lincs 47 D7
South Cornelly Bridgend 14 C4
South Cove Suff 39 G10
South Creagan Argyll 74 C2
South Creake Norf 38 B4
South Croxton Leics 36 D2
South Croydon London 19 E10
South Dalton E Yorks 52 E5
South Darenth Kent 20 E2
South Duffield N Yorks 52 F2
South Elkington Lincs 46 D6
South Elmsall W Yorks 45 A8
South End Bucks 28 F5
South End Cumb 49 C2
South End N Lincs 53 G7
South Erradale Highld 85 A12
South Fambridge Essex 20 B5
South Fawley W Berks 17 C10
South Ferriby N Lincs 52 G5
South Garth Shetland 96 D7
South Garvan Highld 80 F1
South Glendale W Isles 84 G2
South Godstone Sur 19 G10
South Gorley Hants 9 C10
South Green Essex 20 B3
South Green Kent 20 E5
South-haa Shetland 96 E5
South Ham Hants 18 F3
South Hanningfield Essex 20 B4
South Harting W Sus 11 C6
South Hatfield Herts 29 H9
South Hayling Hants 10 E6
South Hazelrigg Northumb 71 G9
South Heath Bucks 18 A6
South Heighton E Sus 12 F3
South Hetton Durham 58 B4
South Hiendley W Yorks 45 A7
South Hill Corn 4 D4
South Hinksey Oxon 18 A2
South Hole Devon 6 D1
South Holme N Yorks 52 B2
South Holmwood Sur 19 G8
South Hornchurch London 20 C2
South Hykeham Lincs 46 F3
South Hylton T&W 63 H9
South Kelsey Lincs 46 C4
South Kessock Highld 87 G9
South Killingholme N Lincs 53 H7
South Kilvington N Yorks 51 A10
South Kilworth Leics 36 G2
South Kirkby W Yorks 45 A8
South Kirkton Aberds 83 C9
South Kiscadale N Ayrs 66 D3
South Kyme Lincs 46 H5
South Lancing W Sus 11 D10
South Leigh Oxon 27 H10
South Leverton Notts 45 D11
South Littleton Worcs 27 D7
South Lopham Norf 38 G6
South Luffenham Rutland 36 E5
South Malling E Sus 12 E3
South Marston Swindon 17 C8
South Middleton Northumb 62 A5
South Milford N Yorks 51 F10
South Millbrex Aberds 89 D8
South Milton Devon 5 G8
South Mimms Herts 19 A9
South Molton Devon 6 D6
South Moreton Oxon 18 C2
South Mundham W Sus 11 D7
South Muskham Notts 45 G11
South Newbald E Yorks 52 F5
South Newington Oxon 27 E11
South Newton Wilts 9 A9
South Normanton Derbys 45 G8
South Norwood London 19 E10
South Nutfield Sur 19 G10
South Ockendon Thurrock 20 C2
South Ormsby Lincs 47 E7
South Otterington N Yorks 58 H4
South Owersby Lincs 46 C4
South Oxhey Herts 19 B8
South Perrott Dorset 8 D3
South Petherton Som 8 C3
South Petherwin Corn 4 C4
South Pickenham Norf 38 E4
South Pool Devon 5 G8
South Port Argyll 74 E3
South Radworthy Devon 7 C6
South Rauceby Lincs 46 H4
South Raynham Norf 38 C4
South Reston Lincs 47 D8
South Runcton Norf 38 E2
South Scarle Notts 46 F2
South Shian Argyll 74 C2
South Shields T&W 63 G9
South Shore Blackpool 49 F3
South Somercotes Lincs 47 C8
South Stainley N Yorks 51 C9
South Stainmore Cumb 57 E10
South Stifford Thurrock 20 D3
South Stoke Oxon 18 C2
South Stoke W Sus 11 D9
South Street E Sus 12 E2
South Street Kent 21 E7
South Street Kent 21 F8
South Street London 19 F11
South Tawton Devon 6 G5
South Thoresby Lincs 47 E8
South Tidworth Wilts 17 G9
South Town Hants 18 H3
South View Hants 18 F3
South Walsham Norf 39 D9
South Warnborough Hants 18 G4
South Weald Essex 20 B2
South Weston Oxon 18 B4
South Wheatley Corn 4 B3
South Wheatley Notts 45 D11
South Whiteness Shetland 96 J5
South Widcombe Bath 16 F2
South Wigston Leics 36 F1
South Willingham Lincs 46 D5
South Wingfield Derbys 45 G7
South Witham Lincs 36 D5
South Wonston Hants 17 H11
South Woodham Ferrers Essex 20 B5
South Wootton Norf 38 C2
South Wraxall Wilts 16 E5
South Zeal Devon 6 G5
Southall London 19 D8
Southam Glos 26 F6
Southam Warks 27 B11
Southampton Soton 10 C3
Southborough Kent 12 B4
Southbourne Bmouth 9 E10
Southbourne W Sus 11 D6
Southburgh Norf 38 E5
Southburn E Yorks 52 D5
Southchurch Southend 20 C6
Southcott Wilts 17 F8
Southcourt Bucks 28 G5
Southdean Borders 62 C2
Southdene Mers 43 C7
Southease E Sus 12 F3
Southend Argyll 65 H7
Southend W Berks 18 D2
Southend Wilts 17 D8
Southend-on-Sea Southend 20 C5
Southernden Kent 20 G5
Southerndown V Glam 14 D4
Southerness Dumfries 60 H5
Southery Norf 38 F2
Southfield Northumb 63 F8
Southfleet Kent 20 D3
Southgate Ceredig 32 H1
Southgate London 19 B9
Southgate Norf 39 C7
Southgate Swansea 23 H10
Southill C Beds 29 D8
Southleigh Devon 7 G11
Southminster Essex 20 B6
Southmoor Oxon 17 B10
Southoe Cambs 29 B8
Southolt Suff 31 B8
Southorpe Pboro 37 E6
Southowram W Yorks 51 G7
Southport Mers 49 H3
Southpunds Shetland 96 L6
Southrepps Norf 39 B8
Southrey Lincs 46 F5
Southrop Glos 17 A8
Southrope Hants 18 G3
Southsea Ptsmth 10 E5
Southstoke Bath 16 E4
Southtown Norf 39 E11
Southtown Orkney 95 J5
Southwaite Cumb 56 B6
Southwark London 19 D10
Southwater W Sus 11 B10
Southwater Street W Sus 11 B10
Southway Som 15 G11
Southwell Dorset 8 G5
Southwell Notts 45 G10
Southwick Hants 10 D5
Southwick Northants 36 F6
Southwick T&W 63 H9
Southwick Wilts 16 F5
Southwick W Sus 11 D11
Southwold Suff 39 H11
Southwood Norf 39 E9
Southwood Som 8 A4
Soval Lodge W Isles 91 E8
Sower Carr Lancs 49 E3
Sowerby N Yorks 51 A10
Sowerby W Yorks 50 G6
Sowerby Bridge W Yorks 51 G6
Sowerby Row Cumb 56 C5
Sowood W Yorks 51 H6
Sowton Devon 7 G8
Soyal Highld 87 B8
Spa Common Norf 39 B8
Spacey Houses N Yorks 51 D9
Spadeadam Farm Cumb 61 F11
Spalding Lincs 37 C8
Spaldington E Yorks 52 F3
Spaldwick Cambs 29 A8
Spalford Notts 46 F2
Spanby Lincs 37 B6
Sparham Norf 39 D6
Spark Bridge Cumb 49 A3
Sparkford Som 8 B5
Sparkhill W Mid 35 G6
Sparkwell Devon 5 F6
Sparrow Green Norf 38 D5
Sparrowpit Derbys 44 D4
Sparsholt Hants 10 A3
Sparsholt Oxon 17 C10
Spartylea Northumb 57 B10
Spaunton N Yorks 59 H8
Spaxton Som 7 C11
Spean Bridge Highld 80 E4
Spear Hill W Sus 11 C10
Speen Bucks 18 B5
Speen W Berks 17 E11
Speeton N Yorks 53 B7
Speke Mers 43 D7
Speldhurst Kent 12 B4
Spellbrook Herts 29 G11
Spelsbury Oxon 27 F10
Spelter Bridgend 14 B4
Spencers Wood Wokingham 18 E4
Spennithorne N Yorks 58 H2
Spennymoor Durham 58 C3
Spetchley Worcs 26 C5
Spetisbury Dorset 9 D8
Spexhall Suff 39 G9
Spey Bay Moray 88 B3
Speybridge Highld 82 A2
Speyview Moray 88 D2
Spilsby Lincs 47 F8
Spindlestone Northumb 71 G10
Spinkhill Derbys 45 E8
Spinningdale Highld 87 C9
Spirthill Wilts 16 D6
Spital Hill S Yorks 45 C10
Spital in the Street Lincs 46 D3
Spithurst E Sus 12 E3
Spittal Dumfries 54 D6
Spittal E Loth 70 C3
Spittal Highld 94 E3
Spittal Northumb 71 E9
Spittal Pembs 22 D4
Spittal Stirling 68 B4
Spittal of Glenmuick Aberds 82 E5
Spittal of Glenshee Perth 82 F3
Spittalfield Perth 76 C4
Spixworth Norf 39 D8
Splayne's Green E Sus 12 D3
Spofforth N Yorks 51 D9
Spon End W Mid 35 H9
Spon Green Flint 42 F5
Spondon Derby 35 B10
Spooner Row Norf 39 F6
Sporle Norf 38 D4
Spott E Loth 70 C5
Spratton Northants 28 A4
Spreakley Sur 18 G5
Spreyton Devon 6 G5
Spridlington Lincs 46 D4
Spring Vale S Yorks 44 B6
Spring Valley IoM 48 E3
Springburn Glasgow 68 D5
Springfield Dumfries 61 G9
Springfield Essex 30 H4
Springfield Fife 76 F6
Springfield Moray 87 F13
Springfield W Mid 35 G6
Springhill Staffs 34 E5
Springholm Dumfries 55 C11
Springkell Dumfries 61 F8
Springside N Ayrs 67 C6
Springthorpe Lincs 46 D2
Springwell T&W 63 H8
Sproatley E Yorks 53 F7
Sproston Green Ches W 43 F10
Sprotbrough S Yorks 45 B9
Sproughton Suff 31 D8
Sprouston Borders 70 G6
Sprowston Norf 39 D8
Sproxton Leics 36 C4
Sproxton N Yorks 52 A2
Spurstow Ches E 43 G8
Spynie Moray 88 B2
Squires Gate Blackpool 49 F3
Srannda W Isles 90 J5
Sronphadruig Lodge Perth 81 F9
Stableford Shrops 34 F3
Stableford Staffs 34 B4
Stacey Bank S Yorks 44 C6
Stackhouse N Yorks 50 C4
Stackpole Pembs 22 G4
Staddiscombe Plym 4 F6
Staddlethorpe E Yorks 52 G4
Stadhampton Oxon 18 B3
Stadhlaigearraidh W Isles 84 E2
Staffield Cumb 57 B7
Staffin Highld 85 B9
Stafford Staffs 34 C5
Stagsden Bedford 28 D6
Stainburn Cumb 56 D2
Stainburn N Yorks 51 E8
Stainby Lincs 36 C5
Staincross S Yorks 45 A7
Staindrop Durham 58 D2
Staines-upon-Thames Sur 19 D7
Stainfield Lincs 37 C6
Stainfield Lincs 46 E5
Stainforth N Yorks 50 C4
Stainforth S Yorks 45 A10
Staining Lancs 49 F3
Stainland W Yorks 51 H6
Stainsacre N Yorks 59 F10
Stainsby Derbys 45 F8
Stainton Cumb 57 D6
Stainton Cumb 57 H7
Stainton Durham 58 E1
Stainton Mbro 58 E5
Stainton N Yorks 58 G2
Stainton S Yorks 45 C9
Stainton by Langworth Lincs 46 E4
Stainton le Vale Lincs 46 C5
Stainton with Adgarley Cumb 49 B2
Staintondale N Yorks 59 G10
Stair Cumb 56 D4
Stair E Ayrs 67 D7
Stairhaven Dumfries 54 D5
Staithes N Yorks 59 E8
Stake Pool Lancs 49 E4
Stakeford Northumb 63 E8
Stalbridge Dorset 8 C6
Stalbridge Weston Dorset 8 C6
Stalham Norf 39 C9
Stalham Green Norf 39 C9
Stalisfield Green Kent 20 F6
Stalling Busk N Yorks 57 H11
Stallingborough NE Lincs 46 A5
Stalmine Lancs 49 E3
Stalybridge Gtr Man 44 C3
Stambourne Essex 30 E4
Stambourne Green Essex 30 E4
Stamford Lincs 36 E6
Stamford Bridge Ches W 43 F7
Stamford Bridge E Yorks 52 D3
Stamfordham Northumb 62 F6
Stanah Cumb 56 E5
Stanborough Herts 29 G9
Stanbridge C Beds 28 F6
Stanbridge Dorset 9 D9
Stanbrook Worcs 26 D5
Stanbury W Yorks 50 F6
Stand Gtr Man 43 B10
Stand N Lanark 68 D6
Standburn Falk 69 C8
Standeford Staffs 34 E5
Standen Kent 13 B7
Standford Hants 11 A7
Standingstone Cumb 56 C2
Standish Gtr Man 43 A8
Standlake Oxon 17 A10
Standon Hants 10 B3
Standon Herts 29 F10
Standon Staffs 34 B4
Stane N Lanark 69 E7
Stanfield Norf 38 C5
Stanford C Beds 29 D8
Stanford Kent 13 C10
Stanford Bishop Hereford 26 C3
Stanford Bridge Worcs 26 B4
Stanford Dingley W Berks 18 D2
Stanford in the Vale Oxon 17 B10
Stanford-le-Hope Thurrock 20 C3
Stanford on Avon Northants 36 H1
Stanford on Soar Notts 35 C11
Stanford on Teme Worcs 26 B4
Stanford Rivers Essex 20 A2
Stanfree Derbys 45 E8
Stanghow Redcar 59 E7
Stanground Pboro 37 F7
Stanhoe Norf 38 B4
Stanhope Borders 69 H10
Stanhope Durham 57 C11
Stanion Northants 36 G5
Stanley Derbys 35 A10
Stanley Durham 58 A2
Stanley Lancs 43 B7
Stanley Perth 76 D4
Stanley Staffs 44 G3
Stanley W Yorks 51 G9
Stanley Common Derbys 35 A10
Stanley Gate Lancs 43 B7
Stanley Hill Hereford 26 D3
Stanlow Ches W 43 E7
Stanmer Brighton 12 F2
Stanmore Hants 10 B3
Stanmore London 19 B8
Stanmore W Berks 17 D11
Stannergate Dundee 77 D7
Stanningley W Yorks 51 F8
Stannington Northumb 63 F8
Stannington S Yorks 45 D7
Stansbatch Hereford 25 B10
Stansfield Suff 30 C4
Stanstead Suff 30 D5
Stanstead Abbotts Herts 29 G10
Stansted Kent 20 E3
Stansted Airport Essex 30 F2
Stansted Mountfitchet Essex 30 F2
Stanton Glos 27 E7
Stanton Mon 25 F10
Stanton Northumb 63 E7
Stanton Staffs 44 H5
Stanton Suff 30 A6
Stanton by Bridge Derbys 35 C9
Stanton-by-Dale Derbys 35 B10
Stanton Drew Bath 16 E2
Stanton Fitzwarren Swindon 17 B8
Stanton Harcourt Oxon 27 H11
Stanton Hill Notts 45 F8
Stanton in Peak Derbys 44 F6
Stanton Lacy Shrops 33 H10
Stanton Long Shrops 34 F1
Stanton-on-the-Wolds Notts 36 B2
Stanton Prior Bath 16 E3
Stanton St Bernard Wilts 17 E7
Stanton St John Oxon 28 H2
Stanton St Quintin Wilts 16 D6
Stanton Street Suff 30 B6
Stanton under Bardon Leics 35 D10
Stanton upon Hine Heath Shrops 34 C1
Stanton Wick Bath 16 E3
Stanwardine in the Fields Shrops 33 C10
Stanwardine in the Wood Shrops 33 C10
Stanway Essex 30 F6
Stanway Glos 27 E7
Stanway Green Suff 31 A9
Stanwell Sur 19 D7
Stanwell Moor Sur 19 D7
Stanwick Northants 28 A6
Stanwick-St-John N Yorks 58 E2
Stanwix Cumb 61 H10
Stanydale Shetland 96 H4
Staoinebrig W Isles 84 E2
Stape N Yorks 59 G8
Stapehill Dorset 9 D9
Stapeley Ches E 43 H9
Stapenhill Staffs 35 C8
Staple Kent 21 F9
Staple Som 7 B10
Staple Cross E Sus 13 D6
Staple Fitzpaine Som 8 C1
Staplefield W Sus 12 D1
Stapleford Cambs 29 C11
Stapleford Herts 29 G10
Stapleford Leics 36 D4
Stapleford Lincs 46 G2
Stapleford Notts 35 B10
Stapleford Wilts 17 H7
Stapleford Abbotts Essex 20 B2
Stapleford Tawney Essex 20 B2
Staplegrove Som 7 D11
Staplehay Som 7 D11
Staplehurst Kent 13 B6
Staplers IoW 10 F4
Stapleton Bristol 16 D3
Stapleton Cumb 61 F11
Stapleton Hereford 25 B10
Stapleton Leics 35 F10
Stapleton N Yorks 58 E3
Stapleton Shrops 33 E10
Stapleton Som 8 B3
Stapley Som 7 E10
Staploe Bedford 29 B8
Staplow Hereford 26 D3
Star Fife 76 G6
Star Pembs 23 C7
Star Som 15 F10
Stara Orkney 95 F3
Starbeck N Yorks 51 D9
Starbotton N Yorks 50 B5
Starcross Devon 5 C10
Stareton Warks 27 A10
Starkholmes Derbys 45 G7
Starlings Green Essex 29 E11
Starston Norf 39 G8
Startforth Durham 58 E1
Startley Wilts 16 C6
Stathe Som 8 B2
Stathern Leics 36 B3
Station Town Durham 58 C5
Staughton Green Cambs 29 B8
Staughton Highway Cambs 29 B8
Staunton Glos 26 F4
Staunton Glos 26 G2
Staunton in the Vale Notts 36 A4
Staunton on Arrow Hereford 25 B10
Staunton on Wye Hereford 25 D10
Staveley Cumb 56 G6
Staveley Cumb 56 H5
Staveley Derbys 45 E8
Staveley N Yorks 51 C9
Staverton Devon 5 E8
Staverton Glos 26 F5
Staverton Northants 28 B2
Staverton Wilts 16 E5
Staverton Bridge Glos 26 F5
Stawell Som 15 H9
Staxigoe Highld 94 E5
Staxton N Yorks 52 B6
Staylittle Powys 32 F4
Staynall Lancs 49 E3
Staythorpe Notts 45 G11
Stean N Yorks 51 B6
Stearsby N Yorks 52 B2
Steart Som 15 G8
Stebbing Essex 30 F3
Stebbing Green Essex 30 F3
Stedham W Sus 11 B7
Steele Road Borders 61 D11
Steen's Bridge Hereford 26 C2
Steep Hants 10 B6
Steep Marsh Hants 11 B6
Steeple Dorset 9 F8
Steeple Essex 20 A6
Steeple Ashton Wilts 16 F6
Steeple Aston Oxon 27 F11
Steeple Barton Oxon 27 F11
Steeple Bumpstead Essex 30 D3
Steeple Claydon Bucks 28 F3
Steeple Gidding Cambs 37 G7
Steeple Langford Wilts 17 H7
Steeple Morden Cambs 29 D9
Steeton W Yorks 50 E6
Stein Highld 84 C7
Steinmanhill Aberds 89 D7
Stelling Minnis Kent 21 G8
Stemster Highld 94 D3
Stemster Ho. Highld 94 D3
Stenalees Corn 3 D9
Stenhousemuir Falk 69 B7
Stenigot Lincs 46 D6
Stenness Shetland 96 F4
Stenscholl Highld 85 B9
Stenso Orkney 95 F4
Stenson Derbys 35 C9
Stenton E Loth 70 C5
Stenton Fife 76 H5
Stenwith Lincs 36 B4
Stepaside Pembs 22 F6
Stepping Hill Gtr Man 44 D3
Steppingley C Beds 29 E7
Stepps N Lanark 68 D5
Sterndale Moor Derbys 44 F5
Sternfield Suff 31 B10
Sterridge Devon 6 B4
Stert Wilts 17 F7
Stetchworth Cambs 30 C3
Stevenage Herts 29 F9
Stevenston N Ayrs 66 B5
Steventon Hants 18 G2
Steventon Oxon 17 B11
Stevington Bedford 28 C6
Stewartby Bedford 29 D7
Stewarton Argyll 65 G7
Stewarton E Ayrs 67 B7
Stewkley Bucks 28 F5
Stewton Lincs 47 D7
Steyne Cross IoW 10 F5
Steyning W Sus 11 C10
Steynton Pembs 22 F4
Stibb Corn 6 E1
Stibb Cross Devon 6 E3
Stibb Green Wilts 17 E9
Stibbard Norf 38 C5
Stibbington Cambs 37 F6
Stichill Borders 70 G6
Sticker Corn 3 D8
Stickford Lincs 47 G7
Sticklepath Devon 6 G5
Stickney Lincs 47 G7
Stiffkey Norf 38 A5
Stifford's Bridge Hereford 26 D4
Stillingfleet N Yorks 52 E1
Stillington N Yorks 52 C1
Stillington Stockton 58 D4
Stilton Cambs 37 G7
Stinchcombe Glos 16 B4
Stinsford Dorset 8 E6
Stirchley Telford 34 E3
Stirkoke Ho. Highld 94 E5
Stirling Aberds 89 D11
Stirling Stirling 68 A6
Stisted Essex 30 F4
Stithians Corn 2 F6
Stittenham Highld 87 D9
Stivichall W Mid 35 H9
Stixwould Lincs 46 F5
Stoak Ches W 43 E7
Stobieside S Lanark 68 G5
Stobo Borders 69 G10
Stoborough Dorset 9 F8
Stoborough Green Dorset 9 F8
Stobshiel E Loth 70 D3
Stobswood Northumb 63 D8
Stock Essex 20 B3
Stock Green Worcs 26 C6
Stock Wood Worcs 27 C7
Stockbridge Hants 10 A2
Stockbury Kent 20 E5
Stockcross W Berks 17 E11
Stockdalewath Cumb 56 B5
Stockerston Leics 36 F4
Stockheath Hants 10 D6
Stockiemuir Stirling 68 B4
Stocking Pelham Herts 29 F11
Stockingford Warks 35 F9
Stockland Devon 8 D1
Stockland Bristol Som 15 G8
Stockleigh English Devon 7 F7
Stockleigh Pomeroy Devon 7 F7
Stockley Wilts 17 E7
Stocklinch Som 8 C2
Stockport Gtr Man 44 C2
Stocksbridge S Yorks 44 C6
Stocksfield Northumb 62 G6
Stockton Hereford 26 B2
Stockton Norf 39 F9
Stockton Shrops 33 E8
Stockton Shrops 34 F3
Stockton Warks 27 B11
Stockton Wilts 16 H6
Stockton Heath Warr 43 D9
Stockton-on-Tees Stockton 58 E5
Stockton on Teme Worcs 26 B4
Stockton on the Forest York 52 D2
Stodmarsh Kent 21 E9
Stody Norf 39 B6
Stoer Highld 92 G3
Stoford Som 8 C4
Stoford Wilts 17 H7
Stogumber Som 7 C9
Stogursey Som 7 B11
Stoke Devon 6 D1
Stoke Hants 10 D6
Stoke Hants 17 F11
Stoke Medway 20 D5
Stoke Suff 31 D8
Stoke Abbott Dorset 8 D3
Stoke Albany Northants 36 G4
Stoke Ash Suff 31 A8
Stoke Bardolph Notts 36 A2
Stoke Bliss Worcs 26 B3
Stoke Bruerne Northants 28 D4
Stoke by Clare Suff 30 D4
Stoke-by-Nayland Suff 30 E6
Stoke Canon Devon 7 G8
Stoke Charity Hants 17 H11
Stoke Climsland Corn 4 D4
Stoke D'Abernon Sur 19 F8
Stoke Doyle Northants 36 G6
Stoke Dry Rutland 36 F4
Stoke Farthing Wilts 9 B9
Stoke Ferry Norf 38 F3
Stoke Fleming Devon 5 G9
Stoke Gabriel Devon 5 F9
Stoke Gifford S Glos 16 D3
Stoke Golding Leics 35 F9
Stoke Goldington M Keynes 28 D5
Stoke Green Bucks 18 C6
Stoke Hammond Bucks 28 F5
Stoke Heath Shrops 34 C2
Stoke Holy Cross Norf 39 E8
Stoke Lacy Hereford 26 D3
Stoke Lyne Oxon 28 F2
Stoke Mandeville Bucks 28 G5
Stoke Newington London 19 C10
Stoke on Tern Shrops 34 C2
Stoke-on-Trent Stoke 44 H2
Stoke Orchard Glos 26 F6
Stoke Poges Bucks 18 C6
Stoke Prior Hereford 26 C2
Stoke Prior Worcs 26 B6
Stoke Rivers Devon 6 C5
Stoke Rochford Lincs 36 C5
Stoke Row Oxon 18 C3
Stoke St Gregory Som 8 B2
Stoke St Mary Som 8 B1
Stoke St Michael Som 16 G3
Stoke St Milborough Shrops 34 G1
Stoke sub Hamdon Som 8 C3
Stoke Talmage Oxon 18 B3
Stoke Trister Som 8 B6
Stoke Wake Dorset 9 D6
Stokeford Dorset 9 F7
Stokeham Notts 45 E11
Stokeinteignhead Devon 5 D10
Stokenchurch Bucks 18 B4
Stokenham Devon 5 G9
Stokesay Shrops 33 G10
Stokesby Norf 39 D10
Stokesley N Yorks 59 F6
Stolford Som 15 G8
Ston Easton Som 16 F3
Stondon Massey Essex 20 A2
Stone Bucks 28 G4
Stone Glos 16 B3
Stone Kent 13 D8
Stone Kent 20 D2
Stone S Yorks 45 D9
Stone Staffs 34 B5
Stone Worcs 34 H4
Stone Allerton Som 15 F10
Stone Bridge Corner Pboro 37 E8
Stone Chair W Yorks 51 G7
Stone Cross E Sus 12 F5
Stone Cross Kent 21 F10
Stone-edge Batch N Som 15 D10
Stone House Cumb 57 H9
Stone Street Kent 20 F2
Stone Street Suff 30 E6
Stone Street Suff 39 G9
Stonebroom Derbys 45 G8
Stoneferry Hull 53 F7
Stonefield S Lanark 68 E5
Stonegate E Sus 12 D5
Stonegate N Yorks 59 F8
Stonegrave N Yorks 52 B2
Stonehaugh Northumb 62 F3
Stonehaven Aberds 83 E10
Stonehouse Glos 26 H5
Stonehouse Northumb 62 H2
Stonehouse S Lanark 68 F6
Stoneleigh Warks 27 A10
Stonely Cambs 29 B8
Stoner Hill Hants 10 B6
Stone's Green Essex 31 F8
Stonesby Leics 36 C4
Stonesfield Oxon 27 G10
Stonethwaite Cumb 56 E4
Stoney Cross Hants 10 C1
Stoney Middleton Derbys 44 E6
Stoney Stanton Leics 35 F10
Stoney Stoke Som 8 A6
Stoney Stratton Som 16 H3
Stoney Stretton Shrops 33 E9
Stoneybreck Shetland 96 N8
Stoneyburn W Loth 69 D8
Stoneygate Aberds 89 E10
Stoneygate Leicester 36 E2
Stoneyhills Essex 20 B6
Stoneykirk Dumfries 54 E3
Stoneywood Aberdeen 83 B10
Stoneywood Falk 68 B6
Stonganess Shetland 96 C7
Stonham Aspal Suff 31 C8
Stonnall Staffs 35 E6
Stonor Oxon 18 C4
Stonton Wyville Leics 36 F3
Stony Cross Hereford 26 D4
Stony Stratford M Keynes 28 D4
Stonyfield Highld 87 D9
Stoodleigh Devon 7 E8
Stopes S Yorks 44 D6
Stopham W Sus 11 C9
Stopsley Luton 29 F8
Stores Corner Suff 31 D10
Storeton Mers 42 D6
Stornoway W Isles 91 D9
Storridge Hereford 26 D4
Storrington W Sus 11 C9
Storrs Cumb 56 G5
Storth Cumb 49 A4
Storwood E Yorks 52 E3
Stotfield Moray 88 A2
Stotfold C Beds 29 E9
Stottesdon Shrops 34 G2
Stoughton Leics 36 E2
Stoughton Sur 18 F6
Stoughton W Sus 11 C7
Stoul Highld 79 B10
Stoulton Worcs 26 D6
Stour Provost Dorset 9 B6
Stour Row Dorset 9 B7
Stourbridge W Mid 34 G5
Stourpaine Dorset 9 D7
Stourport on Severn Worcs 26 A5
Stourton Staffs 34 G4
Stourton Warks 27 E9
Stourton Wilts 9 A6
Stourton Caundle Dorset 8 C6
Stove Orkney 95 E7
Stove Shetland 96 L6
Stoven Suff 39 G10
Stow Borders 70 F3
Stow Lincs 37 B6
Stow Lincs 46 D2
Stow Bardolph Norf 38 E2
Stow Bedon Norf 38 F5
Stow cum Quy Cambs 30 B2
Stow Longa Cambs 29 A8
Stow Maries Essex 20 B5
Stow-on-the-Wold Glos 27 F8
Stowbridge Norf 38 E2
Stowe Shrops 25 A10
Stowe-by-Chartley Staffs 34 C6
Stowe Green Glos 26 H2
Stowell Som 8 B5
Stowford Devon 4 C5
Stowlangtoft Suff 30 B6
Stowmarket Suff 31 C7
Stowting Kent 13 B10
Stowupland Suff 31 C7
Straad Argyll 73 G9
Strachan Aberds 83 D8
Stradbroke Suff 31 A9
Stradishall Suff 30 C4
Stradsett Norf 38 E2
Stragglethorpe Lincs 46 G3
Straid S Ayrs 66 G4
Straith Dumfries 60 E4
Straiton Edin 69 D11
Straiton S Ayrs 67 F6
Straloch Aberds 89 F8
Straloch Perth 76 A3
Stramshall Staffs 35 B6
Strang IoM 48 E3
Stranraer Dumfries 54 C3
Stratfield Mortimer W Berks 18 E3
Stratfield Saye Hants 18 E3
Stratfield Turgis Hants 18 F3
Stratford London 19 C10
Stratford St Andrew Suff 31 B10
Stratford St Mary Suff 31 E7
Stratford Sub Castle Wilts 9 A10
Stratford Tony Wilts 9 B9
Stratford-upon-Avon Warks 27 C8
Strath Highld 85 A12
Strath Highld 94 E4
Strathan Highld 80 D1
Strathan Highld 92 G3
Strathan Highld 93 C8
Strathaven S Lanark 68 F6
Strathblane Stirling 68 C4
Strathcanaird Highld 92 J4
Strathcarron Highld 86 G2
Strathcoil Argyll 79 H9
Strathdon Aberds 82 B5
Strathellie Aberds 89 B10
Strathkinness Fife 77 F7
Strathmashie House Highld 81 D7
Strathmiglo Fife 76 F5
Strathmore Lodge Highld 94 F3
Strathpeffer Highld 86 F7
Strathrannoch Highld 86 D6
Strathtay Perth 76 B2
Strathvaich Lodge Highld 86 D6
Strathwhillan N Ayrs 66 C3
Strathy Highld 93 C11
Strathyre Stirling 75 F8
Stratton Corn 4 A3
Stratton Dorset 8 E5
Stratton Glos 17 A7
Stratton Audley Oxon 28 F3
Stratton on the Fosse Som 16 F3
Stratton St Margaret Swindon 17 C8
Stratton St Michael Norf 39 F8
Stratton Strawless Norf 39 C8
Stravithie Fife 77 F8
Streat E Sus 12 E2
Streatham London 19 D10
Streatley C Beds 29 F7
Streatley W Berks 18 C2
Street Lancs 49 D5
Street N Yorks 59 F8
Street Som 15 H10
Street Dinas Shrops 33 B9
Street End Kent 21 F8
Street End W Sus 11 E7
Street Gate T&W 63 H8
Street Lydan Wrex 33 B10
Streethay Staffs 35 D7
Streetlam N Yorks 58 G4
Streetly W Mid 35 F6
Streetly End Cambs 30 D3
Strefford Shrops 33 G10
Strelley Notts 35 A11
Strensall York 52 C2
Stretcholt Som 15 G8
Strete Devon 5 G9
Stretford Gtr Man 44 C2
Strethall Essex 29 E11
Stretham Cambs 30 A2
Strettington W Sus 11 D7
Stretton Ches W 43 G7
Stretton Derbys 45 F7
Stretton Rutland 36 D5
Stretton Staffs 34 D4
Stretton Staffs 35 C8
Stretton Warr 43 D9
Stretton Grandison Hereford 26 D3
Stretton-on-Dunsmore Warks 27 A11
Stretton-on-Fosse Warks 27 E9
Stretton Sugwas Hereford 25 D11
Stretton under Fosse Warks 35 G10
Stretton Westwood Shrops 34 F1
Strichen Aberds 89 C9
Strines Gtr Man 44 D3
Stringston Som 7 B10
Strixton Northants 28 B6
Stroat Glos 16 B2
Stromeferry Highld 85 E13
Stromemore Highld 85 E13
Stromness Orkney 95 H3
Stronaba Highld 80 E4
Stronachlachar Stirling 75 F7
Stronchreggan Highld 80 F2
Stronchrubie Highld 92 H5
Strone Argyll 73 E10
Strone Highld 80 E3
Strone Highld 81 A7
Strone Involyd 73 F11
Stronmilchan Argyll 74 E4
Strontian Highld 79 E11
Strood Medway 20 E4
Strood Green Sur 19 G9
Strood Green W Sus 11 A10
Strood Green W Sus 11 B9
Stroud Glos 26 H5
Stroud Hants 10 B6
Stroud Green Essex 20 B5
Stroxton Lincs 36 B5
Struan Highld 85 E8
Struan Perth 81 G10
Strubby Lincs 47 D8
Strumpshaw Norf 39 E9
Strutherhill S Lanark 68 F6
Struy Highld 86 H6
Stryt-issa Wrex 42 H5
Stuartfield Aberds 89 D9
Stub Place Cumb 56 G2
Stubbington Hants 10 D4
Stubbins Lancs 50 H3
Stubbs Cross Kent 13 C8
Stubbs Green Norf 39 F9
Stubb's Green Norf 39 E8
Stubhampton Dorset 9 C8
Stubton Lincs 46 H2
Stuckgowan Argyll 74 G6
Stuckton Hants 9 C10
Stud Grn. Windsor 18 D5
Studham C Beds 29 G7
Studland Dorset 9 F9
Studley Warks 27 B7
Studley Wilts 16 D6
Studley Roger N Yorks 51 B8
Stump Cross Essex 30 D2
Stuntney Cambs 38 H1
Sturbridge Staffs 34 B4
Sturmer Essex 30 D3
Sturminster Marshall Dorset 9 D8
Sturminster Newton Dorset 9 C6
Sturry Kent 21 E8
Sturton N Lincs 46 B3
Sturton by Stow Lincs 46 D2
Sturton le Steeple Notts 45 D11
Stuston Suff 39 H7
Stutton N Yorks 51 E10
Stutton Suff 31 E8
Styal Ches E 44 D2
Styrrup Notts 45 C10
Suainebost W Isles 91 A10
Suardail W Isles 91 D9
Succoth Aberds 88 E4
Succoth Argyll 74 G5
Suckley Worcs 26 C4
Suckquoy Orkney 95 K5
Sudborough Northants 36 G5
Sudbourne Suff 31 C11
Sudbrook Lincs 36 A5
Sudbrook Mon 15 C11
Sudbrooke Lincs 46 E4
Sudbury Derbys 35 B7
Sudbury London 19 C8
Sudbury Suff 30 D5
Suddie Highld 87 F9
Sudgrove Glos 26 H6
Suffield N Yorks 59 G10
Suffield Norf 39 B8
Sugnall Staffs 34 B3
Suladale Highld 85 C8
Sulaisiadar W Isles 91 D10
Sulby IoM 48 C3
Sulgrave Northants 28 D2
Sulham W Berks 18 D3
Sulhamstead W Berks 18 E3
Sulland Orkney 95 D6
Sullington W Sus 11 C9
Sullom Shetland 96 F5
Sullom Voe Oil Terminal Shetland 96 F5
Sully V Glam 15 E7
Sumburgh Shetland 96 N6
Summer Bridge N Yorks 51 C8
Summer-house Darl 58 E3
Summercourt Corn 3 D7
Summerfield Norf 38 B3
Summergangs Hull 53 F7
Summerleaze Mon 15 C10
Summersdale W Sus 11 D7
Summerseat Gtr Man 43 A10
Summit Gtr Man 44 B3
Summertown Oxon 28 H2
Sunbury-on-Thames Sur 19 E8
Sundaywell Dumfries 60 E4
Sunderland Argyll 64 B3
Sunderland Cumb 56 C3
Sunderland T&W 63 H9
Sunderland Bridge Durham 58 C3
Sundhope Borders 70 H2
Sundon Park Luton 29 F7
Sundridge Kent 19 F11
Sunipol Argyll 78 F6
Sunk Island E Yorks 53 H8
Sunningdale Windsor 18 E6
Sunninghill Windsor 18 E6
Sunningwell Oxon 17 A11
Sunniside Durham 58 C2
Sunniside T&W 63 H8
Sunnyhurst Blackburn 50 G2
Sunnylaw Stirling 75 H10
Sunnyside W Sus 12 C2
Sunton Wilts 17 F9
Surbiton London 19 E8
Surby IoM 48 E2
Surfleet Lincs 37 C8
Surfleet Seas End Lincs 37 C8
Surlingham Norf 39 E9
Sustead Norf 39 B7
Susworth Lincs 46 B2
Sutcombe Devon 6 E2
Suton Norf 39 F6
Sutors of Cromarty Highld 87 E11
Sutterby Lincs 47 E7
Sutterton Lincs 37 B8
Sutton C Beds 29 D9
Sutton Cambs 37 H10
Sutton Kent 21 G10
Sutton London 19 E9
Sutton Mers 43 C8
Sutton N Yorks 51 G10
Sutton Norf 39 C9
Sutton Notts 36 B3
Sutton Notts 45 D10
Sutton Oxon 27 H11
Sutton Pboro 37 F6
Sutton S Yorks 45 A9
Sutton Shrops 34 B2
Sutton Shrops 34 G3
Sutton Som 8 A5
Sutton Staffs 34 C3
Sutton Suff 31 D10
Sutton Sur 19 G7
Sutton W Sus 11 C8
Sutton at Hone Kent 20 D2
Sutton Bassett Northants 36 G3
Sutton Benger Wilts 16 D6
Sutton Bonington Notts 35 C11
Sutton Bridge Lincs 37 C10
Sutton Cheney Leics 35 E10
Sutton Coldfield W Mid 35 F7
Sutton Courtenay Oxon 18 B2
Sutton Crosses Lincs 37 C10
Sutton Grange N Yorks 51 B8
Sutton Green Sur 19 F7
Sutton Howgrave N Yorks 51 B9
Sutton In Ashfield Notts 45 G8
Sutton-in-Craven N Yorks 50 E6
Sutton in the Elms Leics 35 F11
Sutton Ings Hull 53 F7
Sutton Lane Ends Ches E 44 E3
Sutton Leach Mers 43 C8
Sutton Maddock Shrops 34 E3
Sutton Mallet Som 15 H9
Sutton Mandeville Wilts 9 B8
Sutton Manor Mers 43 C8
Sutton Montis Som 8 B5
Sutton on Hull Hull 53 F7
Sutton on Sea Lincs 47 D9
Sutton-on-the-Forest N Yorks 52 C1
Sutton on the Hill Derbys 35 B8
Sutton on Trent Notts 45 F11
Sutton St Edmund Lincs 37 D9
Sutton St James Lincs 37 D9
Sutton St Nicholas Hereford 26 D2
Sutton Scarsdale Derbys 45 F8
Sutton Scotney Hants 17 H11
Sutton under Brailes Warks 27 E10
Sutton-under-Whitestonecliffe N Yorks 51 A10
Sutton upon Derwent E Yorks 52 E3
Sutton Valence Kent 20 G5
Sutton Veny Wilts 16 G5
Sutton Waldron Dorset 9 C7
Sutton Weaver Ches W 43 E8
Sutton Wick Bath 16 F2
Swaby Lincs 47 E7
Swadlincote Derbys 35 D9
Swaffham Norf 38 E4
Swaffham Bulbeck Cambs 30 B2
Swaffham Prior Cambs 30 B2
Swafield Norf 39 B8
Swainby N Yorks 58 F5
Swainshill Hereford 25 D11
Swainsthorpe Norf 39 E8
Swainswick Bath 16 E4
Swalcliffe Oxon 27 E10
Swalecliffe Kent 21 E8
Swallow Lincs 46 B5
Swallowcliffe Wilts 9 B8
Swallowfield Wokingham 18 E4
Swallownest S Yorks 45 D8
Swallows Cross Essex 20 B3
Swan Green Ches W 43 E10
Swan Green Suff 31 A9
Swanage Dorset 9 G9
Swanbister Orkney 95 H4
Swanbourne Bucks 28 F5
Swanland E Yorks 52 G5
Swanley Kent 20 E2
Swanley Village Kent 20 E2
Swanmore Hants 10 C4
Swannington Leics 35 D10
Swannington Norf 39 D7
Swanscombe Kent 20 D3
Swansea = Abertawe Swansea 14 B2
Swanton Abbott Norf 39 C8
Swanton Morley Norf 38 D6
Swanton Novers Norf 38 B6
Swanton Street Kent 20 F5
Swanwick Derbys 45 G8
Swanwick Hants 10 D4
Swarby Lincs 36 A6
Swardeston Norf 39 E8
Swarister Shetland 96 E7
Swarkestone Derbys 35 C9
Swarland Northumb 63 C7
Swarland Estate Northumb 63 C7
Swarthmoor Cumb 49 B2
Swathwick Derbys 45 F7
Swaton Lincs 37 B7
Swavesey Cambs 29 B10
Sway Hants 10 E1
Swayfield Lincs 36 C5
Swaythling Soton 10 C3
Sweet Green Worcs 26 B3
Sweetham Devon 7 G7
Sweethouse Corn 4 E1
Sweffling Suff 31 B10
Swepstone Leics 35 D9
Swerford Oxon 27 E10
Swettenham Ches E 44 F2
Swetton N Yorks 51 B7
Swffryd Caerph 15 B8
Swiftsden E Sus 12 D6
Swilland Suff 31 C8
Swillington W Yorks 51 F9
Swimbridge Devon 6 D5
Swimbridge Newland Devon 6 C5
Swinbrook Oxon 27 G9
Swinderby Lincs 46 F2
Swindon Glos 26 F6
Swindon Staffs 34 F4
Swindon Swindon 17 C8
Swine E Yorks 53 F7
Swinefleet E Yorks 52 G3
Swineshead Bedford 29 B7
Swineshead Lincs 37 A8
Swineshead Bridge Lincs 37 A8
Swiney Highld 94 G4
Swinford Leics 36 H1
Swinford Oxon 27 H11
Swingate Notts 35 A11
Swingfield Minnis Kent 21 G9
Swingfield Street Kent 21 G9
Swinhoe Northumb 71 H11
Swinhope Lincs 46 C6
Swining Shetland 96 G6
Swinithwaite N Yorks 58 H1
Swinnow Moor W Yorks 51 F8
Swinscoe Staffs 44 H5
Swinside Hall Borders 62 B3
Swinstead Lincs 36 C6
Swinton Borders 71 F7
Swinton Gtr Man 43 B10
Swinton N Yorks 51 B8
Swinton N Yorks 52 B3
Swinton S Yorks 45 C8
Swintonmill Borders 71 F7
Swithland Leics 35 D11
Swordale Highld 87 E8
Swordland Highld 79 B10
Swordly Highld 93 C10
Sworton Heath Ches E 43 D9
Swydd-ffynnon Ceredig 24 B3
Swynnerton Staffs 34 B4
Swyre Dorset 8 F4
Sychtyn Powys 32 E5
Syde Glos 26 G6
Sydenham London 19 D10
Sydenham Oxon 18 A4
Sydenham Damerel Devon 4 D5
Syderstone Norf 38 B4
Sydling St Nicholas Dorset 8 E5
Sydmonton Hants 17 F11
Syerston Notts 45 H11
Syke Gtr Man 50 H4
Sykehouse S Yorks 52 H2
Sykes Lancs 50 D2
Syleham Suff 39 H8
Sylen Carms 23 F10
Symbister Shetland 96 G7
Symington S Ayrs 67 C6
Symington S Lanark 69 G8
Symonds Yat Hereford 26 G2
Symondsbury Dorset 8 E3
Synod Inn Ceredig 23 A9
Syre Highld 93 E9
Syreford Glos 27 F7
Syresham Northants 28 D3
Syston Leics 36 D2
Syston Lincs 36 A5
Sytchampton Worcs 26 B5
Sywell Northants 28 B5

T

Taagan Highld 86 E3
Tabost W Isles 91 F8
Tabost W Isles 91 A10
Tackley Oxon 27 F11
Tacleit W Isles 90 D6
Tacolneston Norf 39 F7
Tadcaster N Yorks 51 E10
Taddington Derbys 44 E5
Taddiport Devon 6 E3
Tadley Hants 18 E3
Tadlow C Beds 29 D9
Tadmarton Oxon 27 E10
Tadworth Sur 19 F9
Tafarn-y-gelyn Denb 42 F4
Tafarnau-bach Bl Gwent 25 G8
Taff's Well Rhondda 15 C7
Tafolwern Powys 32 E4
Tai Conwy 41 D9
Tai-bach Powys 33 C7
Tai-mawr Conwy 32 A5
Tai-Ucha Denb 42 G3
Taibach Neath 14 B3
Taigh a Ghearraidh W Isles 84 A2
Tain Highld 87 C10
Tain Highld 94 D4
Tainant Wrex 42 H5
Tainlon Gwyn 40 E6
Tai'r-Bull Powys 24 F6
Tairbeart = Tarbert W Isles 90 G6
Tairgwaith Neath 24 G4
Takeley Essex 30 F2
Takeley Street Essex 30 F2
Tal-sarn Ceredig 23 A10
Tal-y-bont Ceredig 32 G2
Tal-y-Bont Conwy 41 D9
Tal-y-bont Gwyn 32 C1
Tal-y-bont Gwyn 41 C8
Tal-y-cafn Conwy 41 C9
Tal-y-llyn Gwyn 32 E3
Tal-y-wern Powys 32 E4
Talachddu Powys 25 E7
Talacre Flint 42 D4
Talardd Gwyn 32 C4
Talaton Devon 7 G9
Talbenny Pembs 22 E3
Talbot Green Rhondda 14 C6
Talbot Village Poole 9 E9
Tale Devon 7 F9
Talerddig Powys 32 E5
Talgarreg Ceredig 23 A9
Talgarth Powys 25 E8
Talisker Highld 85 E8
Talke Staffs 44 G2
Talkin Cumb 61 H11
Talla Linnfoots Borders 61 A7
Talladale Highld 86 D2
Tallarn Green Wrex 33 A10
Tallentire Cumb 56 C3
Talley Carms 24 E3
Tallington Lincs 37 E6
Talmine Highld 93 C8
Talog Carms 23 D8
Talsarn Carms 24 F4
Talsarnau Gwyn 41 G8
Talskiddy Corn 3 C8
Talwrn Anglesey 40 C6
Talwrn Wrex 42 H5
Talybont-on-Usk Powys 25 F8
Talygarn Rhondda 14 C6
Talyllyn Powys 25 F8
Talysarn Gwyn 40 E6
Talywain Torf 15 A8
Tame Bridge N Yorks 58 F6
Tamerton Foliot Plym 4 E5
Tamworth Staffs 35 E8
Tan Hinon Powys 32 G4
Tan-lan Conwy 41 D9
Tan-lan Gwyn 41 F8
Tan-y-bwlch Gwyn 41 F8
Tan-y-fron Conwy 42 F2
Tan-y-graig Anglesey 41 C7
Tan-y-graig Gwyn 40 G5
Tan-y-groes Ceredig 23 B7
Tan-y-pistyll Powys 33 C6
Tan-yr-allt Gwyn 40 E6
Tandem W Yorks 51 H7
Tanden Kent 13 C8
Tandridge Sur 19 F10
Tanerdy Carms 23 D9
Tanfield Durham 63 H7
Tanfield Lea Durham 58 A2
Tangasdal W Isles 84 J1
Tangiers Pembs 22 E4
Tangley Hants 17 F10
Tanglwst Carms 23 C8
Tangmere W Sus 11 D8
Tangwick Shetland 96 F4
Tankersley S Yorks 45 B7
Tankerton Kent 21 E8
Tannach Highld 94 F5
Tannachie Aberds 83 E9
Tannadice Angus 77 B7
Tannington Suff 31 B9
Tansley Derbys 45 G7
Tansley Knoll Derbys 45 F7
Tansor Northants 37 F6
Tantobie Durham 58 A2
Tanton N Yorks 58 E6
Tanworth-in-Arden Warks 27 A8
Tanygrisiau Gwyn 41 F8
Tanyrhydiau Ceredig 24 B4
Taobh a Chaolais W Isles 84 G2
Taobh a' Ghlinne W Isles 91 F8
Taobh a Thuath Loch Aineort W Isles 84 F2
Taobh a Tuath Loch Baghasdail W Isles 84 F2
Taobh Tuath W Isles 90 J4
Taplow Bucks 18 C6
Tapton Derbys 45 E7
Tarbat Ho. Highld 87 D10
Tarbert Argyll 65 C7
Tarbert Argyll 72 E5
Tarbert Argyll 73 G7
Tarbert = Tairbeart W Isles 90 G6
Tarbet Argyll 74 G6
Tarbet Highld 79 B10
Tarbet Highld 92 E4
Tarbock Green Mers 43 D7
Tarbolton S Ayrs 67 D7
Tarbrax S Lanark 69 E9
Tardebigge Worcs 27 B7
Tarfside Angus 82 F6
Tarland Aberds 82 C6
Tarleton Lancs 49 G4
Tarlogie Highld 87 C10
Tarlscough Lancs 43 A7
Tarlton Glos 16 B6
Tarnbrook Lancs 50 D1
Tarporley Ches W 43 F8
Tarr Som 7 C10
Tarrant Crawford Dorset 9 D8
Tarrant Gunville Dorset 9 C8
Tarrant Hinton Dorset 9 C8
Tarrant Keyneston Dorset 9 D8
Tarrant Launceston Dorset 9 D8
Tarrant Monkton Dorset 9 D8
Tarrant Rawston Dorset 9 D8
Tarrant Rushton Dorset 9 D8
Tarrel Highld 87 C11
Tarring Neville E Sus 12 F3
Tarrington Hereford 26 D3
Tarsappie Perth 76 E4
Tarskavaig Highld 85 H10
Tarves Aberds 89 E8
Tarvie Highld 86 F7
Tarvie Perth 76 A3
Tarvin Ches W 43 F7
Tasburgh Norf 39 F8
Tasley Shrops 34 F2
Taston Oxon 27 F10
Tatenhill Staffs 35 C8
Tathall End M Keynes 28 D5
Tatham Lancs 50 C2
Tathwell Lincs 47 D7
Tatling End Bucks 19 C7
Tatsfield Sur 19 F11
Tattenhall Ches W 43 G7
Tattenhoe M Keynes 28 E5
Tatterford Norf 38 C4
Tattersett Norf 38 B4
Tattershall Lincs 46 G6
Tattershall Bridge Lincs 46 G5
Tattershall Thorpe Lincs 46 G6
Tattingstone Suff 31 E8
Tatworth Som 8 D2
Taunton Som 7 D11
Taverham Norf 39 D7
Tavernspite Pembs 22 E6
Tavistock Devon 4 D5
Taw Green Devon 6 G5
Tawstock Devon 6 D4
Taxal Derbys 44 E4
Tay Bridge Dundee 77 E7
Tayinloan Argyll 65 D7
Taymouth Castle Perth 75 C10
Taynish Argyll 72 E6
Taynton Glos 26 F4
Taynton Oxon 27 G9
Taynuilt Argyll 74 D3
Tayport Fife 77 E7
Tayvallich Argyll 72 E6
Tealby Lincs 46 C5
Tealing Angus 77 D7
Teangue Highld 85 H11
Teanna Mhachair W Isles 84 B2
Tebay Cumb 57 F8
Tebworth C Beds 28 F6
Tedburn St Mary Devon 7 G7
Teddington Glos 26 E6
Teddington London 19 D8
Tedstone Delamere Hereford 26 C3
Tedstone Wafre Hereford 26 C3
Teeton Northants 28 A3
Teffont Evias Wilts 9 A8
Teffont Magna Wilts 9 A8
Tegryn Pembs 23 C7
Teigh Rutland 36 D4
Teigncombe Devon 5 C7
Teigngrace Devon 5 D9
Teignmouth Devon 5 D10
Telford Telford 34 E2
Telham E Sus 13 E6
Tellisford Som 16 F5
Telscombe E Sus 12 F3
Telscombe Cliffs E Sus 12 F2
Templand Dumfries 60 E6
Temple Corn 4 D2
Temple Glasgow 68 D4
Temple Midloth 70 E2
Temple Balsall W Mid 35 H8
Temple Bar Carms 23 E10
Temple Bar Ceredig 23 A10
Temple Cloud Bath 16 F3
Temple Combe Som 8 B6
Temple Ewell Kent 21 G9
Temple Grafton Warks 27 C8
Temple Guiting Glos 27 F7
Temple Herdewyke Warks 27 C10
Temple Hirst N Yorks 52 G2
Temple Normanton Derbys 45 F8
Temple Sowerby Cumb 57 D8
Templehall Fife 69 A11
Templeton Devon 7 E7
Templeton Pembs 22 E6
Templeton Bridge Devon 7 E7
Templetown Durham 58 A2
Tempsford C Beds 29 C8
Ten Mile Bank Norf 38 F2
Tenbury Wells Worcs 26 B2
Tenby = Dinbych-y-Pysgod Pembs 22 F6
Tendring Essex 31 F8
Tendring Green Essex 31 F8
Tenston Orkney 95 G3
Tenterden Kent 13 C7
Terling Essex 30 G4
Ternhill Shrops 34 B2
Terregles Banks Dumfries 60 F5
Terrick Bucks 28 H5
Terrington N Yorks 52 B2
Terrington St Clement Norf 37 D11
Terrington St John Norf 37 D11
Teston Kent 20 F4
Testwood Hants 10 C2
Tetbury Glos 16 B5
Tetbury Upton Glos 16 B5
Tetchill Shrops 33 B9
Tetcott Devon 6 G2
Tetford Lincs 47 E7
Tetney Lincs 47 B7
Tetney Lock Lincs 47 B7
Tetsworth Oxon 18 A3
Tettenhall W Mid 34 E4
Teuchan Aberds 89 E10
Teversal Notts 45 F8
Teversham Cambs 29 C11
Teviothead Borders 61 C10
Tewel Aberds 83 E10
Tewin Herts 29 G9
Tewkesbury Glos 26 E5
Teynham Kent 20 E6
Thackthwaite Cumb 56 D3
Thainston Aberds 83 F8
Thakeham W Sus 11 C10
Thame Oxon 28 H4
Thames Ditton Sur 19 E8
Thames Haven Thurrock 20 C4
Thamesmead London 19 C11
Thanington Kent 21 F8
Thankerton S Lanark 69 G8
Tharston Norf 39 F7
Thatcham W Berks 18 E2
Thatto Heath Mers 43 C8
Thaxted Essex 30 E3
The Aird Highld 85 C9
The Arms Norf 38 F4
The Bage Hereford 25 D9
The Balloch Perth 75 F11
The Barony Orkney 95 F3
The Bog Shrops 33 F9
The Bourne Sur 18 G5
The Braes Highld 85 E10
The Broad Hereford 25 B11
The Butts Som 16 G4
The Camp Glos 26 H6
The Camp Herts 29 H8
The Chequer Wrex 33 A10
The City Bucks 18 B4
The Common Wilts 9 A11
The Craigs Highld 86 B7
The Cronk IoM 48 C3
The Dell Suff 39 F10
The Den N Ayrs 66 A6
The Eals Northumb 62 E3
The Eaves Glos 26 H3
The Flatt Cumb 61 F11
The Four Alls Shrops 34 B2
The Garths Shetland 96 B8
The Green Cumb 49 A1
The Green Wilts 9 A7
The Grove Dumfries 60 F5
The Hall Shetland 96 D8
The Haven W Sus 11 A9
The Heath Norf 39 C7
The Heath Suff 31 E8
The Hill Cumb 49 A1
The Howe Cumb 56 H6
The Howe IoM 48 F1
The Hundred Hereford 26 B2
The Lee Bucks 18 A6
The Lhen IoM 48 B3
The Marsh Powys 33 F9
The Marsh Wilts 17 C7
The Middles Durham 58 A3
The Moor Kent 13 D6
The Mumbles = Y Mwmbwls Swansea 14 C2
The Murray S Lanark 68 E5
The Neuk Aberds 83 D9
The Oval Bath 16 E4
The Pole of Itlaw Aberds 89 C6
The Quarry Glos 16 B4
The Rhos Pembs 22 E5
The Rock Telford 34 E2
The Ryde Herts 29 H9
The Sands Sur 18 G5
The Stocks Kent 13 D8
The Throat Wokingham 18 E5
The Vauld Hereford 26 D2
The Wyke Shrops 34 E3
Theakston N Yorks 58 H4
Thealby N Lincs 52 H4
Theale Som 15 G10
Theale W Berks 18 D3
Thearne E Yorks 53 F6
Theberton Suff 31 B11
Theddingworth Leics 36 G2
Theddlethorpe All Saints Lincs 47 D8
Theddlethorpe St Helen Lincs 47 D8
Thelbridge Barton Devon 7 E6
Thelnetham Suff 38 H6
Thelveton Norf 39 G7
Thelwall Warr 43 D9
Themelthorpe Norf 39 C6
Thenford Northants 28 D2
Therfield Herts 29 E10
Thetford Lincs 37 D7
Thetford Norf 38 G4
Theydon Bois Essex 19 B11
Thickwood Wilts 16 D5
Thimbleby Lincs 46 F6
Thimbleby N Yorks 58 G5
Thingwall Mers 42 D5
Thirdpart N Ayrs 66 B4
Thirlby N Yorks 51 A10
Thirlestane Borders 70 F4
Thirn N Yorks 58 H3
Thirsk N Yorks 51 A10
Thirtleby E Yorks 53 F7
Thistleton Lancs 49 F4

Thistleton Rutland 36 D5
Thistley Green Suff 38 H2
Thixendale N Yorks 52 C4
Thockrington Northumb 62 F5
Tholomas Drove Cambs 37 E9
Tholthorpe N Yorks 51 C10
Thomas Chapel Pembs 22 F6
Thomas Close Cumb 56 B6
Thomastown Aberds 88 E5
Thompson Norf 38 F5
Thomshill Moray 88 C2
Thong Kent 20 D3
Thongsbridge W Yorks 44 B5
Thoralby N Yorks 58 H1
Thoresway Lincs 46 C5
Thorganby Lincs 46 C6
Thorganby N Yorks 52 E2
Thorgill N Yorks 59 G8
Thorington Suff 31 A11
Thorington Street Suff 31 E7
Thorlby N Yorks 50 D5
Thorley Herts 29 G11
Thorley Street Herts 29 G11
Thorley Street IoW 10 F2
Thormanby N Yorks 51 B10
Thornaby-on-Tees Stockton 58 E5
Thornage Norf 38 B6
Thornborough Bucks 28 E4
Thornborough N Yorks 51 B8
Thornbury Devon 6 F3
Thornbury Hereford 26 C3
Thornbury S Glos 16 B3
Thornbury W Yorks 51 F7
Thornby Northants 36 H2
Thorncliffe Staffs 44 G4
Thorncombe Dorset 8 D2
Thorncombe Dorset 9 D7
Thorncombe Street Sur 19 G7
Thorncote Green C Beds 29 D8
Thorncross IoW 10 F3
Thorndon Suff 31 B8
Thorndon Cross Devon 6 G4
Thorne S Yorks 45 A10
Thorne St Margaret Som 7 D9
Thorner W Yorks 51 E9
Thorney Notts 46 E2
Thorney Pboro 37 E8
Thorney Crofts E Yorks 53 G8
Thorney Green Suff 31 B7
Thorney Hill Hants 9 E10
Thorney Toll Pboro 37 E9
Thornfalcon Som 8 B1
Thornford Dorset 8 C5
Thorngrumbald E Yorks 53 G8
Thornham Norf 38 A3
Thornham Magna Suff 31 A8
Thornham Parva Suff 31 A8
Thornhaugh Pboro 37 E6
Thornhill Cardiff 15 C7
Thornhill Cumb 56 F2
Thornhill Derbys 44 D5
Thornhill Dumfries 60 D4
Thornhill Soton 10 C3
Thornhill Stirling 75 H9
Thornhill W Yorks 51 H8
Thornhill Edge W Yorks 51 H8
Thornhill Lees W Yorks 51 H8
Thornholme E Yorks 53 C7
Thornley Durham 58 C4
Thornley Durham 58 C2
Thornliebank E Renf 68 E4
Thorns Suff 30 C4
Thorns Green Ches E 43 D10
Thornsett Derbys 44 D4
Thornthwaite Cumb 56 D4
Thornthwaite N Yorks 51 D7
Thornton Angus 76 C6
Thornton Bucks 28 E4
Thornton E Yorks 52 E3
Thornton Fife 76 H5
Thornton Lancs 49 E3
Thornton Leics 35 E10
Thornton Lincs 46 F6
Thornton Mbro 58 E5
Thornton Mers 42 B6
Thornton Northumb 71 F8
Thornton Pembs 22 F4
Thornton W Yorks 51 F7
Thornton Curtis N Lincs 53 H6
Thornton Heath London 19 E10
Thornton Hough Mers 42 D6
Thornton in Craven N Yorks 50 E5
Thornton-le-Beans N Yorks 58 G4
Thornton-le-Clay N Yorks 52 C2
Thornton-le-Dale N Yorks 52 A4
Thornton le Moor Lincs 46 C4
Thornton-le-Moor N Yorks 58 H4
Thornton-le-Moors Ches W 43 E7
Thornton-le-Street N Yorks 58 H5
Thornton Rust N Yorks 57 H11
Thornton Steward N Yorks 58 H2
Thornton Watlass N Yorks 58 H3
Thorntonhall S Lanark 68 E4
Thorntonloch E Loth 70 C6
Thorntonpark Northumb 71 F8
Thornwood Common Essex 19 A11
Thornydykes Borders 70 F5
Thoroton Notts 36 A3
Thorp Arch W Yorks 51 E10
Thorpe Derbys 44 G5
Thorpe E Yorks 52 E5
Thorpe Lincs 47 D8
Thorpe N Yorks 50 C6
Thorpe Norf 39 F10
Thorpe Notts 45 H11
Thorpe Sur 19 E7
Thorpe Abbotts Norf 39 H7
Thorpe Acre Leics 35 C11
Thorpe Arnold Leics 36 C3
Thorpe Audlin W Yorks 51 H10
Thorpe Bassett N Yorks 52 B4
Thorpe Bay Southend 20 C6
Thorpe by Water Rutland 36 F4
Thorpe Common Suff 31 E9
Thorpe Constantine Staffs 35 E8
Thorpe Culvert Lincs 47 F8
Thorpe End Norf 39 D8
Thorpe Fendykes Lincs 47 F8
Thorpe Green Essex 31 F8
Thorpe Green Suff 30 C6
Thorpe Hesley S Yorks 45 C7
Thorpe in Balne S Yorks 45 A9
Thorpe in the Fallows Lincs 46 D3
Thorpe Langton Leics 36 F3
Thorpe Larches Durham 58 D4
Thorpe-le-Soken Essex 31 F8
Thorpe le Street E Yorks 52 E4
Thorpe Malsor Northants 36 H4
Thorpe Mandeville Northants 28 D2
Thorpe Market Norf 39 B8
Thorpe Marriot Norf 39 D7
Thorpe Morieux Suff 30 C6
Thorpe on the Hill Lincs 46 F3
Thorpe St Andrew Norf 39 E8
Thorpe St Peter Lincs 47 F8
Thorpe Salvin S Yorks 45 D9
Thorpe Satchville Leics 36 D3
Thorpe Thewles Stockton 58 D5
Thorpe Tilney Lincs 46 G5
Thorpe Underwood N Yorks 51 D10
Thorpe Waterville Northants 36 G6
Thorpe Willoughby N Yorks 52 F1
Thorpeness Suff 31 C11
Thorrington Essex 31 F7
Thorverton Devon 7 F8
Thrandeston Suff 39 H7
Thrapston Northants 36 H5
Thrashbush N Lanark 68 D6
Threapland Cumb 56 C3
Threapland N Yorks 50 C5
Threapwood Ches W 43 H7
Threapwood Staffs 34 A6
Three Ashes Hereford 26 F2
Three Bridges W Sus 12 C1
Three Burrows Corn 2 E6
Three Chimneys Kent 13 C7
Three Cocks Powys 25 E8
Three Crosses Swansea 23 G10
Three Cups Corner E Sus 12 D5
Three Holes Norf 37 E11
Three Leg Cross E Sus 12 C5
Three Legged Cross Dorset 9 D9
Three Oaks E Sus 13 E7
Threehammer Common Norf 39 D9
Threekingham Lincs 37 B6
Threemile Cross Wokingham 18 E4
Threemilestone Corn 3 E6
Threemiletown W Loth 69 C9
Threlkeld Cumb 56 D5
Threshfield N Yorks 50 C5
Thrigby Norf 39 D10
Thringarth Durham 57 D11
Thringstone Leics 35 D10
Thrintoft N Yorks 58 G4
Thriplow Cambs 29 D11
Throckenholt Lincs 37 E9
Throcking Herts 29 E10
Throckley T&W 63 G7
Throckmorton Worcs 26 D6
Throphill Northumb 63 E7
Thropton Northumb 62 C6
Throsk Stirling 69 A7
Throwleigh Devon 6 G5
Throwley Kent 20 F6
Thrumpton Notts 35 B11
Thrumster Highld 94 F5
Thrunton Northumb 62 B6
Thrupp Glos 16 A5
Thrupp Oxon 27 G11
Thrushelton Devon 4 C5
Thrussington Leics 36 D2
Thruxton Hants 17 G9
Thruxton Hereford 25 E11
Thrybergh S Yorks 45 C8
Thulston Derbys 35 B10
Thundergay N Ayrs 66 B1
Thundersley Essex 20 C4
Thundridge Herts 29 G10
Thurcaston Leics 36 D1
Thurcroft S Yorks 45 D8
Thurgarton Norf 39 B7
Thurgarton Notts 45 H10
Thurgoland S Yorks 44 B6
Thurlaston Leics 35 F11
Thurlaston Warks 27 A11
Thurlbear Som 8 B1
Thurlby Lincs 37 D7
Thurlby Lincs 46 F3
Thurleigh Bedford 29 C7
Thurlestone Devon 5 G7
Thurloxton Som 8 A1
Thurlstone S Yorks 44 B6
Thurlton Norf 39 F10
Thurlwood Ches E 44 G2
Thurmaston Leics 36 E2
Thurnby Leics 36 E2
Thurne Norf 39 D10
Thurnham Kent 20 F5
Thurnham Lancs 49 D4
Thurning Norf 39 C6
Thurning Northants 37 G6
Thurnscoe S Yorks 45 B8
Thurnscoe East S Yorks 45 B8
Thursby Cumb 56 A5
Thursford Norf 38 B5
Thursley Sur 18 H6
Thurso Highld 94 D3
Thurso East Highld 94 D3
Thurstaston Mers 42 D5
Thurston Suff 30 B6
Thurstonfield Cumb 61 H9
Thurstonland W Yorks 44 A5
Thurton Norf 39 E9
Thurvaston Derbys 35 B8
Thuxton Norf 38 E6
Thwaite N Yorks 57 G10
Thwaite Suff 31 B8
Thwaite St Mary Norf 39 F9
Thwaites W Yorks 51 E6
Thwaites Brow W Yorks 51 E6
Thwing E Yorks 53 B6
Tibbermore Perth 76 E3
Tibberton Glos 26 F4
Tibberton Telford 34 C2
Tibberton Worcs 26 C6
Tibenham Norf 39 G7
Tibshelf Derbys 45 F8
Tibthorpe E Yorks 52 D5
Ticehurst E Sus 12 C5
Tichborne Hants 10 A4
Tickencote Rutland 36 E5
Tickenham N Som 15 D10
Tickhill S Yorks 45 C9
Ticklerton Shrops 33 F10
Ticknall Derbys 35 C9
Tickton E Yorks 53 E6
Tidcombe Wilts 17 F9
Tiddington Oxon 18 A3
Tiddington Warks 27 C9
Tidebrook E Sus 12 D5
Tideford Corn 4 F4
Tideford Cross Corn 4 E4
Tidenham Glos 16 B2
Tideswell Derbys 44 E5
Tidmarsh W Berks 18 D3
Tidmington Warks 27 E9
Tidpit Hants 9 C9
Tidworth Wilts 17 G9
Tiers Cross Pembs 22 E4
Tiffield Northants 28 C3
Tifty Aberds 89 D7
Tigerton Angus 77 A8
Tigh-na-Blair Perth 75 F10
Tighnabruaich Argyll 73 F8
Tighnafiline Highld 91 J13
Tigley Devon 5 E8
Tilbrook Cambs 29 B7
Tilbury Thurrock 20 D3
Tilbury Juxta Clare Essex 30 D4
Tile Cross W Mid 35 G7
Tile Hill W Mid 35 H8
Tilehurst Reading 18 D3
Tilford Sur 18 G5
Tilgate W Sus 12 C1
Tilgate Forest Row W Sus 12 C1
Tillathrowie Aberds 88 E4
Tilley Shrops 33 C11
Tillicoultry Clack 76 H2
Tillingham Essex 20 A6
Tillington Hereford 25 D11
Tillington W Sus 11 B8
Tillington Common Hereford 25 D11
Tillyarblet Angus 83 G7
Tillybirloch Aberds 83 C8
Tillycorthie Aberds 89 F9
Tillydrine Aberds 83 D8
Tillyfour Aberds 83 B8
Tillyfourie Aberds 83 B8
Tillygarmond Aberds 83 D8
Tillygreig Aberds 89 F8
Tillykerrie Aberds 89 F8
Tilmanstone Kent 21 F10
Tilney All Saints Norf 38 D1
Tilney High End Norf 38 D1
Tilney St Lawrence Norf 37 D11
Tilshead Wilts 17 G7
Tilstock Shrops 33 B11
Tilston Ches W 43 G7
Tilstone Fearnall Ches W 43 F8
Tilsworth C Beds 28 F6
Tilton on the Hill Leics 36 E3
Timberland Lincs 46 G5
Timbersbrook Ches E 44 F2
Timberscombe Som 7 B8
Timble N Yorks 51 D7
Timperley Gtr Man 43 D10
Timsbury Bath 16 F3
Timsbury Hants 10 B2
Timsgearraidh W Isles 90 D5
Timworth Green Suff 30 B5
Tincleton Dorset 9 E6
Tindale Cumb 62 H2
Tingewick Bucks 28 E3
Tingley W Yorks 51 G8
Tingrith C Beds 29 E7
Tingwall Orkney 95 F4
Tinhay Devon 4 C4
Tinshill W Yorks 51 F8
Tinsley S Yorks 45 C8
Tintagel Corn 4 C1
Tintern Parva Mon 15 A11
Tintinhull Som 8 C4
Tintwistle Derbys 44 C4
Tinwald Dumfries 60 E6
Tinwell Rutland 36 E6
Tipperty Aberds 89 F9
Tipsend Norf 37 F11
Tipton W Mid 34 F5
Tipton St John Devon 7 G9
Tiptree Essex 30 G5
Tir-y-dail Carms 24 G3
Tirabad Powys 24 D5
Tiraghoil Argyll 78 J6
Tirley Glos 26 F5
Tirphil Caerph 15 A7
Tirril Cumb 57 D7
Tisbury Wilts 9 B8
Tisman's Common W Sus 11 A9
Tissington Derbys 44 G5
Titchberry Devon 6 D1
Titchfield Hants 10 D4
Titchmarsh Northants 36 H6
Titchwell Norf 38 A3
Tithby Notts 36 B2
Titley Hereford 25 B10
Titlington Northumb 63 B7
Titsey Sur 19 F11
Tittensor Staffs 34 B4
Tittleshall Norf 38 C4
Tiverton Ches W 43 F8
Tiverton Devon 7 E8
Tivetshall St Margaret Norf 39 G7
Tivetshall St Mary Norf 39 G7
Tividale W Mid 34 F5
Tivy Dale S Yorks 44 B6
Tixall Staffs 34 C5
Tixover Rutland 36 E5
Toab Orkney 95 H6
Toab Shetland 96 M5
Toadmoor Derbys 45 G7
Tobermory Argyll 79 F8
Toberonochy Argyll 72 C6
Tobha Mor W Isles 84 E2
Tobhtarol W Isles 90 D6
Tobson W Isles 90 D6
Tocher Aberds 89 E6
Tockenham Wilts 17 D7
Tockenham Wick Wilts 17 C7
Tockholes Blackburn 50 G2
Tockington S Glos 16 C3
Tockwith N Yorks 51 D10
Todber Dorset 9 B7
Todding Hereford 33 H10
Toddington C Beds 29 F7
Toddington Glos 27 E7
Todenham Glos 27 E9
Todhills Cumb 61 G9
Todlachie Aberds 83 B8
Todmorden W Yorks 50 G5
Todrig Borders 61 B10
Todwick S Yorks 45 D8
Toft Cambs 29 C10
Toft Lincs 37 D6
Toft Hill Durham 58 D2
Toft Hill Lincs 46 F6
Toft Monks Norf 39 F10
Toft next Newton Lincs 46 D4
Toftrees Norf 38 C4
Tofts Highld 94 D5
Toftwood Norf 38 D5
Togston Northumb 63 C8
Tokavaig Highld 85 G11
Tokers Green Oxon 18 D4
Tolastadh a Chaolais W Isles 90 D6
Tolastadh bho Thuath W Isles 91 C10
Toll Bar S Yorks 45 B9
Toll End W Mid 34 F5
Toll of Birness Aberds 89 E10
Tolland Som 7 C10
Tollard Royal Wilts 9 C8
Tollbar End W Mid 35 H9
Toller Fratrum Dorset 8 E4
Toller Porcorum Dorset 8 E4
Tollerton N Yorks 51 C11
Tollerton Notts 36 B2
Tollesbury Essex 30 G6
Tolleshunt D'Arcy Essex 30 G6
Tolleshunt Major Essex 30 G6
Tolm W Isles 91 D9
Tolpuddle Dorset 9 E6
Tolvah Highld 81 D10
Tolworth London 19 E8
Tomatin Highld 81 A10
Tombreck Highld 87 H9
Tomchrasky Highld 80 B4
Tomdoun Highld 80 C3
Tomich Highld 80 A5
Tomich Highld 87 D9
Tomich House Highld 87 G8
Tomintoul Aberds 82 D3
Tomintoul Moray 82 B3
Tomnaven Moray 88 E4
Tomnavoulin Moray 82 A4
Ton-Pentre Rhondda 14 B5
Tonbridge Kent 20 G2
Tondu Bridgend 14 C4
Tonfanau Gwyn 32 E1
Tong Shrops 34 E3
Tong W Yorks 51 F8
Tong Norton Shrops 34 E3
Tonge Leics 35 C10
Tongham Sur 18 G5
Tongland Dumfries 55 D9
Tongue Highld 93 D8
Tongue End Lincs 37 D7
Tongwynlais Cardiff 15 C7
Tonna Neath 14 B3
Tonwell Herts 29 G10
Tonypandy Rhondda 14 B5
Tonyrefail Rhondda 14 C6
Toot Baldon Oxon 18 A2
Toot Hill Essex 20 A2
Toothill Hants 10 C2
Top of Hebers Gtr Man 44 B2
Topcliffe N Yorks 51 B10
Topcroft Norf 39 F8
Topcroft Street Norf 39 F8
Toppesfield Essex 30 E4
Toppings Gtr Man 43 A10
Topsham Devon 5 C10
Torbay Torbay 5 F10
Torbeg N Ayrs 66 D2
Torboll Farm Highld 87 B10
Torbrex Stirling 68 A6
Torbryan Devon 5 E9
Torcross Devon 5 G9
Tore Highld 87 F9
Torinturk Argyll 73 G7
Torksey Lincs 46 E2
Torlum W Isles 84 C2
Torlundy Highld 80 F3
Tormarton S Glos 16 D4
Tormisdale Argyll 64 C2
Tormitchell S Ayrs 66 G5
Tormore N Ayrs 66 C1
Tornagrain Highld 87 G10
Tornahaish Aberds 82 C4
Tornaveen Aberds 83 C8
Torness Highld 81 A7
Toronto Durham 58 C2
Torpenhow Cumb 56 C4
Torphichen W Loth 69 C8
Torphins Aberds 83 C8
Torpoint Corn 4 F5
Torquay Torbay 5 E10
Torquhan Borders 70 F3
Torran Argyll 73 C7
Torran Highld 85 D10
Torran Highld 87 D10
Torrance E Dunb 68 C5
Torrans Argyll 78 J7
Torranyard N Ayrs 67 B6
Torre Torbay 5 E10
Torridon Highld 86 F2
Torridon Ho. Highld 85 C13
Torrin Highld 85 F10
Torrisdale Highld 93 C9
Torrisdale-Square Argyll 65 E8
Torrish Highld 93 H12
Torrisholme Lancs 49 C4
Torroble Highld 93 J8
Torry Aberdeen 83 C11
Torry Aberds 88 E4
Torryburn Fife 69 B9
Torterston Aberds 89 D10
Torthorwald Dumfries 60 F6
Tortington W Sus 11 D9
Tortworth S Glos 16 B4
Torvaig Highld 85 D9
Torver Cumb 56 G4
Torwood Falk 69 B7
Torworth Notts 45 D10
Tosberry Devon 6 D1
Toscaig Highld 85 E12
Toseland Cambs 29 B9
Tosside N Yorks 50 D3
Tostock Suff 30 B6
Totaig Highld 84 C7
Totaig Highld 85 F13
Tote Highld 85 D9
Totegan Highld 93 C11
Tothill Lincs 47 D8
Totland IoW 10 F2
Totnes Devon 5 E9
Toton Notts 35 B11
Totronald Argyll 78 F4
Totscore Highld 85 B8
Tottenham London 19 B10
Tottenhill Norf 38 D2
Tottenhill Row Norf 38 D2
Totteridge London 19 B9
Totternhoe C Beds 28 F6
Tottington Gtr Man 43 A10
Totton Hants 10 C2
Touchen End Windsor 18 D5
Tournaig Highld 91 J13
Toux Aberds 89 C9
Tovil Kent 20 F4
Tow Law Durham 58 C2
Toward Argyll 73 G10
Towcester Northants 28 D3
Towednack Corn 2 F3
Tower End Norf 38 D2
Towersey Oxon 28 H4
Towie Aberds 82 B6
Towie Aberds 89 B8
Towiemore Moray 88 D3
Town End Cambs 37 F10
Town End Cumb 49 A4
Town Row E Sus 12 C4
Town Yetholm Borders 71 H7
Townend W Dunb 68 C3
Towngate Lincs 37 D7
Townhead Cumb 57 C7
Townhead Dumfries 55 E9
Townhead S Ayrs 66 F5
Townhead S Yorks 44 B5
Townhead of Greenlaw Dumfries 55 C10
Townhill Fife 69 B10
Townsend Bucks 28 H4
Townsend Herts 29 H8
Townshend Corn 2 F4
Towthorpe York 52 D2
Towton N Yorks 51 F10
Towyn Conwy 42 E2
Toxteth Mers 42 D6
Toynton All Saints Lincs 47 F7
Toynton Fen Side Lincs 47 F7
Toynton St Peter Lincs 47 F8
Toy's Hill Kent 19 F11
Trabboch E Ayrs 67 D7
Traboe Corn 2 G6
Tradespark Highld 87 F11
Tradespark Orkney 95 H5
Trafford Park Gtr Man 43 C10
Trallong Powys 24 F6
Tranent E Loth 70 C3
Tranmere Mers 42 D6
Trantlebeg Highld 93 D11
Trantlemore Highld 93 D11
Tranwell Northumb 63 E7
Trapp Carms 24 G3
Traprain E Loth 70 C4
Traquair Borders 70 G2
Trawden Lancs 50 F5
Trawsfynydd Gwyn 41 G9
Tre-Gibbon Rhondda 14 A5
Tre-Taliesin Ceredig 32 F2
Tre-vaughan Carms 23 D9
Tre-wyn Mon 25 F10
Trealaw Rhondda 14 B6
Treales Lancs 49 F4
Trearddur Anglesey 40 C4
Treaslane Highld 85 C8
Trebanog Rhondda 14 B6
Trebanos Neath 14 A3
Trebartha Corn 4 D3
Trebarwith Corn 4 C1
Trebetherick Corn 3 B8
Treborough Som 7 C9
Trebudannon Corn 3 C7
Trebullett Corn 4 D4
Treburley Corn 4 D4
Trebyan Corn 4 E1
Trecastle Powys 24 F5
Trecenydd Caerph 15 C7
Trecwn Pembs 22 C4
Trecynon Rhondda 14 A5
Tredavoe Corn 2 G3
Treddiog Pembs 22 D3
Tredegar Bl Gwent 25 H8
Tredegar Newydd = New Tredegar Caerph 15 A7
Tredington Glos 26 F6
Tredington Warks 27 D9
Tredinnick Corn 3 B8
Tredomen Powys 25 E8
Tredunnock Mon 15 B9
Tredustan Powys 25 E8
Treen Corn 2 G2
Treeton S Yorks 45 D8
Tref-Y-Clawdd = Knighton Powys 25 A9
Trefaldwyn = Montgomery Powys 33 F8
Trefasser Pembs 22 C3
Trefdraeth Anglesey 40 C6
Trefdraeth = Newport Pembs 22 C5
Trefecca Powys 25 E8
Trefechan Ceredig 32 G1
Trefeglwys Powys 32 F5
Trefenter Ceredig 24 B3
Treffgarne Pembs 22 D4
Treffynnon = Holywell Flint 42 E4
Treffynnon Pembs 22 D3
Trefgarn Owen Pembs 22 D3
Trefil Bl Gwent 25 G8
Trefilan Ceredig 23 A10
Trefin Pembs 22 C3
Treflach Shrops 33 C8
Trefnanney Powys 33 D8
Trefnant Denb 42 E3
Trefonen Shrops 33 C8
Trefor Gwyn 40 F5
Trefor Anglesey 40 B5
Treforest Rhondda 14 C6
Trefriw Conwy 41 D9
Trefynwy = Monmouth Mon 26 G2
Tregadillett Corn 4 C3
Tregaian Anglesey 40 C6
Tregare Mon 25 G11
Tregaron Ceredig 24 C3
Tregarth Gwyn 41 D8
Tregeare Corn 4 C3
Tregeiriog Wrex 33 B7
Tregele Anglesey 40 A5
Tregidden Corn 3 G6
Treglemais Pembs 22 D3
Tregole Corn 4 B2
Tregonetha Corn 3 C8
Tregony Corn 3 E8
Tregoss Corn 3 C8
Tregoyd Powys 25 E9
Tregroes Ceredig 23 B9
Tregurrian Corn 3 C7
Tregynon Powys 33 F6
Trehafod Rhondda 14 B6
Treharris M Tydf 14 B6
Treherbert Rhondda 14 B5
Trekenner Corn 4 D4
Treknow Corn 4 C1
Trelan Corn 2 H6
Trelash Corn 4 B2
Trelassick Corn 3 D7
Trelawnyd Flint 42 E3
Trelech Carms 23 C7
Treleddyd-fawr Pembs 22 D2
Trelewis M Tydf 15 B7
Treligga Corn 4 C1
Trelights Corn 3 B8
Trelill Corn 3 B8
Trelissick Corn 3 F7
Trellech Mon 26 H2
Trelleck Grange Mon 15 A10
Trelogan Flint 42 D4
Trelystan Powys 33 E8
Tremadog Gwyn 41 F7
Tremail Corn 4 C2
Tremain Ceredig 23 B7
Tremaine Corn 4 C3
Tremar Corn 4 E3
Trematon Corn 4 F4
Tremeirchion Denb 42 E3
Trenance Corn 3 C7
Trenarren Corn 3 E9
Trench Telford 34 D2
Treneglos Corn 4 C3
Trenewan Corn 4 F2
Trent Dorset 8 C4
Trent Vale Stoke 34 A4
Trentham Stoke 34 A4
Trentishoe Devon 6 B5
Treoes V Glam 14 D5
Treorchy = Treorci Rhondda 14 B5
Treorci = Treorchy Rhondda 14 B5
Tre'r-ddôl Ceredig 32 F2
Trerulefoot Corn 4 F4
Tresaith Ceredig 23 A7
Tresawle Corn 3 E7
Trescott Staffs 34 F4
Trescowe Corn 2 F4
Tresham Glos 16 B4
Tresillian Corn 3 E7
Tresinwen Pembs 22 B4
Treskinnick Cross Corn 4 B3
Tresmeer Corn 4 C3
Tresparrett Corn 4 B2
Tresparrett Posts Corn 4 B2
Tressait Perth 75 A11
Tresta Shetland 96 D8
Tresta Shetland 96 H5
Treswell Notts 45 E11
Trethosa Corn 3 D8
Trethurgy Corn 3 D9
Tretio Pembs 22 D2
Tretire Hereford 26 F2
Tretower Powys 25 F8
Treuddyn Flint 42 G5
Trevalga Corn 4 C1
Trevalyn Wrex 43 G6
Trevanson Corn 3 B8
Trevarren Corn 3 C8
Trevarrian Corn 3 C7
Trevarrick Corn 3 E8
Trevaughan Carms 22 E6
Treveighan Corn 4 D1
Trevellas Corn 2 D6
Treverva Corn 3 F6
Trevethin Torf 15 A8
Trevigro Corn 4 E4
Treviscoe Corn 3 D8
Trevone Corn 3 B7
Trewarmett Corn 4 C1
Trewassa Corn 4 C2
Trewellard Corn 2 F2
Trewen Corn 4 C3
Trewennack Corn 2 G5
Trewern Powys 33 D8
Trewethern Corn 3 B9
Trewidland Corn 4 F3
Trewint Corn 4 B2
Trewint Corn 4 C3
Trewithian Corn 3 F7
Trewoofe Corn 2 G3
Trewoon Corn 3 D8
Treworga Corn 3 E7
Treworlas Corn 3 F7
Treyarnon Corn 3 B7
Treyford W Sus 11 C7
Trezaise Corn 3 D8
Triangle W Yorks 50 G6
Trickett's Cross Dorset 9 D9
Triffleton Pembs 22 D4
Trimdon Durham 58 C4
Trimdon Colliery Durham 58 C4
Trimdon Grange Durham 58 C4
Trimingham Norf 39 B8
Trimley Lower Street Suff 31 E9
Trimley St Martin Suff 31 E9
Trimley St Mary Suff 31 E9
Trimpley Worcs 34 H3
Trimsaran Carms 23 F9
Trimstone Devon 6 B3
Trinafour Perth 75 A10
Trinant Caerph 15 A8
Tring Herts 28 G6
Tring Wharf Herts 28 G6
Trinity Angus 77 A9
Trinity Jersey 11
Trisant Ceredig 32 H3
Trislaig Highld 80 F2
Trispen Corn 3 D7
Tritlington Northumb 63 D8
Trochry Perth 75 C11
Trodigal Argyll 65 F7
Troed-rhiwdalar Powys 24 C6
Troedyraur Ceredig 23 B8
Troedyrhiw M Tydf 14 A6
Tromode IoM 48 E3
Trondavoe Shetland 96 F5
Troon Corn 2 F5
Troon S Ayrs 66 C6
Trosaraidh W Isles 84 G2
Trossachs Hotel Stirling 75 G8
Troston Suff 30 A5
Trottiscliffe Kent 20 E3
Trotton W Sus 11 B7
Troutbeck Cumb 56 D5
Troutbeck Cumb 56 F6
Troutbeck Bridge Cumb 56 F6
Trow Green Glos 26 H2
Trowbridge Wilts 16 F5
Trowell Notts 35 B10
Trowle Common Wilts 16 F5
Trowley Bottom Herts 29 G7
Trows Borders 70 G5
Trowse Newton Norf 39 E8
Trudoxhill Som 16 G4
Trull Som 7 D11
Trumaisgearraidh W Isles 84 A3
Trumpan Highld 84 B7
Trumpet Hereford 26 E3
Trumpington Cambs 29 C11
Trunch Norf 39 B8
Trunnah Lancs 49 E3
Truro Corn 3 E7
Trusham Devon 5 C9
Trusley Derbys 35 B8
Trusthorpe Lincs 47 D9
Trysull Staffs 34 F4
Tubney Oxon 17 B11
Tuckenhay Devon 5 F9
Tuckhill Shrops 34 G3
Tuckingmill Corn 2 E5
Tuddenham Suff 30 A4
Tuddenham St Martin Suff 31 D8
Tudeley Kent 20 G3
Tudhoe Durham 58 C3
Tudorville Hereford 26 F2
Tudweiliog Gwyn 40 G4
Tuesley Sur 18 G6
Tuffley Glos 26 G5
Tufton Hants 17 G11
Tufton Pembs 22 D5
Tugby Leics 36 E3
Tugford Shrops 34 G1
Tullibardine Perth 76 F2
Tullibody Clack 75 H11
Tullich Argyll 73 B9
Tullich Highld 81 A8
Tullich Muir Highld 87 D10
Tulliemet Perth 76 B2
Tulloch Aberds 83 F9
Tulloch Aberds 89 E8
Tulloch Perth 76 E3
Tulloch Castle Highld 87 E8
Tullochgorm Argyll 73 D8
Tulloes Angus 77 C8
Tullybannocher Perth 75 E10
Tullybelton Perth 76 D3
Tullyfergus Perth 76 C5
Tullymurdoch Perth 76 B4
Tullynessle Aberds 83 B7
Tumble Carms 23 E10
Tumby Woodside Lincs 46 G6
Tummel Bridge Perth 75 B10
Tunga W Isles 91 D9
Tunstall E Yorks 53 F9
Tunstall Kent 20 E5
Tunstall Lancs 50 B2
Tunstall N Yorks 58 G3
Tunstall Norf 39 E10
Tunstall Stoke 44 G2
Tunstall Suff 31 C10
Tunstall T&W 58 A4
Tunstead Derbys 44 E5
Tunstead Gtr Man 44 B4
Tunstead Norf 39 C8
Tunworth Hants 18 G3
Tupsley Hereford 26 D2
Tupton Derbys 45 F7
Tur Langton Leics 36 F3
Turgis Green Hants 18 F3
Turin Angus 77 B8
Turkdean Glos 27 G8
Turleigh Wilts 16 E5
Turn Lancs 50 H4
Turnastone Hereford 25 E10
Turnberry S Ayrs 66 F5
Turnditch Derbys 44 H6
Turners Hill W Sus 12 C2
Turners Puddle Dorset 9 E7
Turnford Herts 19 A10
Turnhouse Edin 69 C10
Turnworth Dorset 9 D7
Turriff Aberds 89 C7
Turton Bottoms Blackburn 50 H3
Turves Cambs 37 F9
Turvey Bedford 28 C6
Turville Bucks 18 B4
Turville Heath Bucks 18 B4
Turweston Bucks 28 E3
Tushielaw Borders 61 B9
Tutbury Staffs 35 C8
Tutnall Worcs 26 A6
Tutshill Glos 15 B11
Tuttington Norf 39 C8
Tutts Clump W Berks 18 D2
Tuxford Notts 45 E11
Twatt Orkney 95 F3
Twatt Shetland 96 H5
Twechar E Dunb 68 C5
Tweedmouth Northumb 71 E8
Tweedsmuir Borders 60 A6
Twelve Heads Corn 3 E6
Twemlow Green Ches E 43 F10
Twenty Lincs 37 C7
Twerton Bath 16 E4
Twickenham London 19 D8
Twigworth Glos 26 F5
Twineham W Sus 12 E1
Twinhoe Bath 16 F4
Twinstead Essex 30 E5
Twinstead Green Essex 30 E5
Twiss Green Warr 43 C9
Twiston Lancs 50 E4
Twitchen Devon 7 C6
Twitchen Shrops 33 H9
Two Bridges Devon 5 D7
Two Dales Derbys 44 F6
Two Mills Ches W 42 E6
Twycross Leics 35 E9
Twyford Bucks 28 F3
Twyford Derbys 35 C9
Twyford Hants 10 B3
Twyford Leics 36 D3
Twyford Lincs 36 C5
Twyford Norf 38 C6
Twyford Wokingham 18 D4
Twyford Common Hereford 26 E2
Twyn-y-Sheriff Mon 25 H11
Twynholm Dumfries 55 D9
Twyning Glos 26 E5
Twyning Green Glos 26 E6
Twynllanan Carms 24 F4
Twynmynydd Carms 24 G3
Twywell Northants 36 H5
Ty-draw Conwy 41 E10
Ty-hen Carms 23 D8
Ty-hen Gwyn 40 G3
Ty-mawr Anglesey 40 B6
Ty Mawr Carms 23 B10
Ty Mawr Cwm Conwy 42 H2
Ty-nant Conwy 32 A5
Ty-nant Gwyn 32 C5
Ty-uchaf Powys 32 C6
Tyberton Hereford 25 E10
Tyburn W Mid 35 F7
Tycroes Carms 24 G3
Tycrwyn Powys 33 D7
Tydd Gote Lincs 37 D10
Tydd St Giles Cambs 37 D10
Tydd St Mary Lincs 37 D10
Tyddewi = St David's Pembs 22 D2
Tyddyn-mawr Gwyn 41 F7
Tye Green Essex 29 H11
Tye Green Essex 30 F2
Tye Green Essex 30 E2
Tyldesley Gtr Man 43 B9
Tyler Hill Kent 21 E8
Tylers Green Bucks 18 B6
Tylorstown Rhondda 14 B6
Tylwch Powys 32 G5
Tyn-y-celyn Wrex 33 B7
Tyn-y-coed Shrops 33 C8
Tyn-y-fedwen Powys 33 B7
Tyn-y-ffridd Powys 33 B7
Tyn-y-graig Powys 25 C7
Tŷ'n-y-groes Conwy 41 C9
Ty'n-y-maes Gwyn 41 D8
Tyn-y-pwll Anglesey 40 B6
Ty'n-yr-eithin Ceredig 24 B3
Tyncelyn Ceredig 24 B3
Tyndrum Stirling 74 D6
Tyne Tunnel T&W 63 G9
Tyneham Dorset 9 F7
Tynehead Midloth 70 E2
Tynemouth T&W 63 G9
Tynewydd Rhondda 14 B5
Tyninghame E Loth 70 C5
Tynron Dumfries 60 D4
Tynygongl Anglesey 41 B7
Tynygraig Ceredig 24 B3
Tŷ'r-felin-isaf Conwy 41 D10
Tyrie Aberds 89 B9
Tyringham M Keynes 28 D5
Tythecott Devon 6 E3
Tythegston Bridgend 14 D4
Tytherington Ches E 44 E3
Tytherington S Glos 16 C3
Tytherington Som 16 G4
Tytherington Wilts 16 G6
Tytherleigh Devon 8 D2
Tywardreath Corn 4 F1
Tywyn Conwy 41 C9
Tywyn Gwyn 32 E1

U

Uachdar W Isles 84 C2
Uags Highld 85 E12
Ubbeston Green Suff 31 A10
Ubley Bath 16 F2
Uckerby N Yorks 58 F3
Uckfield E Sus 12 D3
Uckington Glos 26 F6
Uddingston S Lanark 68 D5
Uddington S Lanark 69 G7
Udimore E Sus 13 E7
Udny Green Aberds 89 F8
Udny Station Aberds 89 F9
Udston S Lanark 68 E5
Udstonhead S Lanark 68 F6
Uffcott Wilts 17 D8
Uffculme Devon 7 E9
Uffington Lincs 37 E6
Uffington Oxon 17 C10
Uffington Shrops 33 D11
Ufford Pboro 37 E6
Ufford Suff 31 C9
Ufton Warks 27 B10
Ufton Nervet W Berks 18 E3
Ugadale Argyll 65 F8
Ugborough Devon 5 F7
Uggeshall Suff 39 G10
Ugglebarnby N Yorks 59 F9
Ughill S Yorks 44 C6
Ugley Essex 30 F2
Ugley Green Essex 30 F2
Ugthorpe N Yorks 59 E8
Uidh W Isles 84 J1
Uig Argyll 73 E10
Uig Highld 84 C6
Uig Highld 85 B8
Uigen W Isles 90 D5
Uigshader Highld 85 D9
Uisken Argyll 78 K6
Ulbster Highld 94 F5
Ulceby Lincs 47 E8
Ulceby N Lincs 46 A5
Ulceby Skitter N Lincs 46 A5
Ulcombe Kent 20 G5
Uldale Cumb 56 C4
Uley Glos 16 B4
Ulgham Northumb 63 D8
Ullapool Highld 86 B4
Ullenhall Warks 27 B8
Ullenwood Glos 26 G6
Ulleskelf N Yorks 51 E11
Ullesthorpe Leics 35 G11
Ulley S Yorks 45 D8
Ullingswick Hereford 26 D2
Ullinish Highld 85 E8
Ullock Cumb 56 D2
Ulnes Walton Lancs 49 H5
Ulpha Cumb 56 G3
Ulrome E Yorks 53 D7
Ulsta Shetland 96 E6
Ulva House Argyll 78 H7
Ulverston Cumb 49 B2
Ulwell Dorset 9 F9
Umberleigh Devon 6 D5
Unapool Highld 92 F5
Unasary W Isles 84 F2
Underbarrow Cumb 56 G6
Undercliffe W Yorks 51 F7
Underhoull Shetland 96 C7
Underriver Kent 20 F2
Underwood Notts 45 G8
Undy Mon 15 C10
Unifirth Shetland 96 H4
Union Cottage Aberds 83 D10
Union Mills IoM 48 E3
Union Street E Sus 12 C6
Unstone Derbys 45 E7
Unstone Green Derbys 45 E7
Unthank Cumb 56 C6
Unthank Cumb 57 B8
Unthank Cumb 57 C7
Unthank End Cumb 56 C6
Up Cerne Dorset 8 D5
Up Exe Devon 7 F8
Up Hatherley Glos 26 F6
Up Holland Lancs 43 B8
Up Marden W Sus 11 C6
Up Nately Hants 18 F3
Up Somborne Hants 10 A2
Up Sydling Dorset 8 D5
Upavon Wilts 17 F8
Upchurch Kent 20 E5
Upcott Hereford 25 C10
Upend Cambs 30 C3
Upgate Norf 39 D7
Uphall W Loth 69 C9
Uphall Station W Loth 69 C9
Upham Devon 7 F7
Upham Hants 10 B4
Uphampton Worcs 26 B5
Uphill N Som 15 F9
Uplawmoor E Renf 68 E3
Upleadon Glos 26 F4
Upleatham Redcar 59 E7
Uplees Kent 20 E6
Uploders Dorset 8 E4
Uplowman Devon 7 E9
Uplyme Devon 8 E2
Upminster London 20 C2
Upnor Medway 20 D4
Upottery Devon 7 F11
Upper Affcot Shrops 33 G10
Upper Ardchronie Highld 87 C9
Upper Arley Worcs 34 G3
Upper Arncott Oxon 28 G3
Upper Astrop Northants 28 E2
Upper Badcall Highld 92 E4
Upper Basildon W Berks 18 D2
Upper Beeding W Sus 11 C10
Upper Benefield Northants 36 G5
Upper Bighouse Highld 93 D11
Upper Boddington Northants 27 C11
Upper Borth Ceredig 32 G2
Upper Boyndlie Aberds 89 B9
Upper Brailes Warks 27 E10
Upper Breakish Highld 85 F11
Upper Breinton Hereford 25 D11
Upper Broadheath Worcs 26 C5
Upper Broughton Notts 36 C2
Upper Bucklebury W Berks 18 E2
Upper Burnhaugh Aberds 83 D10
Upper Caldecote C Beds 29 D8
Upper Catesby Northants 28 C2
Upper Chapel Powys 25 D7
Upper Church Village Rhondda 14 C6
Upper Chute Wilts 17 F9
Upper Clatford Hants 17 G10
Upper Clynnog Gwyn 40 F6
Upper Cumberworth W Yorks 44 B6
Upper Cwm-twrch Powys 24 G4
Upper Cwmbran Torf 15 B8
Upper Dallachy Moray 88 B3
Upper Dean Bedford 29 B7
Upper Denby W Yorks 44 B6
Upper Denton Cumb 62 G2
Upper Derraid Highld 87 H13
Upper Dicker E Sus 12 F4
Upper Dovercourt Essex 31 E9
Upper Druimfin Argyll 79 F8
Upper Dunsforth N Yorks 51 C10
Upper Eathie Highld 87 E10
Upper Elkstone Staffs 44 G4
Upper End Derbys 44 E4
Upper Farringdon Hants 18 H4
Upper Framilode Glos 26 G4
Upper Glenfintaig Highld 80 E4
Upper Gornal W Mid 34 F5
Upper Gravenhurst C Beds 29 E8
Upper Green Mon 25 G10
Upper Green W Berks 17 E10
Upper Grove Common Hereford 26 F2
Upper Hackney Derbys 44 F6
Upper Hale Sur 18 G5
Upper Halistra Highld 84 C7
Upper Halling Medway 20 E3
Upper Hambleton Rutland 36 E5
Upper Hardres Court Kent 21 F8
Upper Hartfield E Sus 12 C3
Upper Haugh S Yorks 45 C8
Upper Heath Shrops 34 G1
Upper Hellesdon Norf 39 D8
Upper Helmsley N Yorks 52 D2
Upper Hergest Hereford 25 C9
Upper Heyford Northants 28 C3
Upper Heyford Oxon 27 F11
Upper Hill Hereford 25 C11
Upper Hopton W Yorks 51 H7
Upper Horsebridge E Sus 12 E4
Upper Hulme Staffs 44 F4
Upper Inglesham Swindon 17 B9
Upper Inverbrough Highld 87 H11
Upper Killay Swansea 23 G10
Upper Knockando Moray 88 D1
Upper Lambourn W Berks 17 C10
Upper Leigh Staffs 34 B6
Upper Lenie Highld 81 A7
Upper Lochton Aberds 83 D8
Upper Longdon Staffs 35 D6
Upper Lybster Highld 94 G4
Upper Lydbrook Glos 26 G3
Upper Maes-coed Hereford 25 E10
Upper Midway Derbys 35 C8
Upper Milovaig Highld 84 D6
Upper Minety Wilts 17 B7
Upper Mitton Worcs 26 A5
Upper North Dean Bucks 18 B5
Upper Obney Perth 76 D3
Upper Ollach Highld 85 E10
Upper Padley Derbys 44 E6
Upper Pollicott Bucks 28 G4
Upper Poppleton York 52 D1
Upper Quinton Warks 27 D8
Upper Ratley Hants 10 B2
Upper Rissington Glos 27 G9
Upper Rochford Worcs 26 B3
Upper Sandaig Highld 85 G12
Upper Sanday Orkney 95 H6
Upper Sapey Hereford 26 B3
Upper Saxondale Notts 36 B2
Upper Seagry Wilts 16 C6
Upper Shelton C Beds 28 D6
Upper Sheringham Norf 39 A7
Upper Skelmorlie N Ayrs 73 G11
Upper Slaughter Glos 27 F8
Upper Soudley Glos 26 G3
Upper Stondon C Beds 29 E8
Upper Stowe Northants 28 C3
Upper Stratton Swindon 17 C8
Upper Street Hants 9 C10
Upper Street Norf 39 D9
Upper Street Norf 39 D9
Upper Street Suff 31 E8
Upper Strensham Worcs 26 E6
Upper Sundon C Beds 29 F7
Upper Swell Glos 27 F8
Upper Tean Staffs 34 B6
Upper Tillyrie Perth 76 G4
Upper Tooting London 19 D9
Upper Tote Highld 85 C10
Upper Town N Som 15 E11
Upper Treverward Shrops 33 H8
Upper Tysoe Warks 27 D10
Upper Upham Wilts 17 D9
Upper Wardington Oxon 27 D11
Upper Weald M Keynes 28 E5
Upper Weedon Northants 28 C3
Upper Wield Hants 18 H3
Upper Winchendon Bucks 28 G4
Upper Witton W Mid 35 F6
Upper Woodend Aberds 83 B8
Upper Woodford Wilts 17 H8
Upper Wootton Hants 18 F2
Upper Wyche Hereford 26 D4
Upperby Cumb 56 A6
Uppermill Gtr Man 44 B3
Uppersound Shetland 96 J6
Upperthong W Yorks 44 B5
Upperthorpe N Lincs 45 B11
Upperton W Sus 11 B8
Uppertown Derbys 45 F7
Uppertown Highld 94 C5
Uppertown Orkney 95 J5
Uppingham Rutland 36 F4
Uppington Shrops 34 E1
Upsall N Yorks 58 H5
Upshire Essex 19 A11
Upstreet Kent 21 E9
Upthorpe Suff 30 A6
Upton Cambs 37 H7
Upton Ches W 43 F7
Upton Corn 4 B3
Upton Dorset 8 F6
Upton Dorset 9 E8
Upton Hants 10 C2
Upton Hants 17 F10
Upton Leics 35 F9
Upton Lincs 46 D2
Upton Mers 42 D5
Upton Norf 39 D9
Upton Northants 28 B4
Upton Notts 45 E11
Upton Notts 45 G11
Upton Oxon 18 C2
Upton Pboro 37 E7
Upton Slough 18 D6
Upton Som 7 D8
Upton W Yorks 45 A8
Upton Bishop Hereford 26 F3
Upton Cheyney S Glos 16 E3
Upton Cressett Shrops 34 F2
Upton Cross Corn 4 D3
Upton Grey Hants 18 G3
Upton Hellions Devon 7 F7
Upton Lovell Wilts 16 G6
Upton Magna Shrops 34 D1
Upton Noble Som 16 H4
Upton Pyne Devon 7 G8
Upton St Leonard's Glos 26 G5
Upton Scudamore Wilts 16 G5
Upton Snodsbury Worcs 26 C6
Upton upon Severn Worcs 26 D5
Upton Warren Worcs 26 B6
Upwaltham W Sus 11 C8
Upware Cambs 30 A2
Upwell Norf 37 E10
Upwey Dorset 8 F5
Upwood Cambs 37 G8
Uradale Shetland 96 K6
Urafirth Shetland 96 F5
Urchfont Wilts 17 F7
Urdimarsh Hereford 26 D2
Ure Shetland 96 F4
Ure Bank N Yorks 51 B9
Urgha W Isles 90 H6
Urishay Common Hereford 25 E10
Urlay Nook Stockton 58 E4
Urmston Gtr Man 43 C10
Urpeth Durham 58 A3
Urquhart Highld 87 F8
Urquhart Moray 88 B2
Urra N Yorks 59 F6
Urray Highld 87 F8
Ushaw Moor Durham 58 B3
Usk = Brynbuga Mon 15 A9
Usselby Lincs 46 C4
Usworth T&W 63 H9
Utkinton Ches W 43 F8
Utley W Yorks 50 E6
Uton Devon 7 G7
Utterby Lincs 47 C7
Uttoxeter Staffs 35 B6
Uwchmynydd Gwyn 40 H3
Uxbridge London 19 C7
Uyeasound Shetland 96 C7
Uzmaston Pembs 22 E4

V

Valley Anglesey 40 C4
Valley Truckle Corn 4 C1
Valleyfield Dumfries 55 D9
Valsgarth Shetland 96 B8
Valtos Highld 85 B10
Van Powys 32 G5
Vange Essex 20 C4
Varteg Torf 25 H9
Vatten Highld 85 D7
Vaul Argyll 78 G3
Vaynor M Tydf 25 G7
Veensgarth Shetland 96 J6
Velindre Powys 25 E8
Vellow Som 7 C9
Veness Orkney 95 F6
Venn Green Devon 6 E2
Venn Ottery Devon 7 G9
Vennington Shrops 33 E9
Venny Tedburn Devon 7 G7
Ventnor IoW 10 G4
Vernham Dean Hants 17 F10
Vernham Street Hants 17 F10
Vernolds Common Shrops 33 G10
Verwood Dorset 9 D9
Veryan Corn 3 F8
Vicarage Devon 7 H11
Vickerstown Cumb 49 C1
Victoria Corn 3 C8
Victoria S Yorks 44 B5
Vidlin Shetland 96 G6
Viewpark N Lanark 68 D6
Vigo Village Kent 20 E3
Vinehall Street E Sus 13 D6
Vine's Cross E Sus 12 E4
Viney Hill Glos 26 H3
Virginia Water Sur 18 E6
Virginstow Devon 6 G2
Vobster Som 16 G4
Voe Shetland 96 E5
Voe Shetland 96 G6
Vowchurch Hereford 25 E10
Voxter Shetland 96 F5
Voy Orkney 95 G3

W

Wackerfield Durham 58 D2
Wacton Norf 39 F7
Wadbister Shetland 96 J6
Wadborough Worcs 26 D6
Waddesdon Bucks 28 G4
Waddingham Lincs 46 C3
Waddington Lancs 50 E3
Waddington Lincs 46 F3
Wadebridge Corn 3 B8
Wadeford Som 8 C2
Wadenhoe Northants 36 G6
Wadesmill Herts 29 G10
Wadhurst E Sus 12 C5
Wadshelf Derbys 45 E7
Wadsley S Yorks 45 C7
Wadsley Bridge S Yorks 45 C7
Wadworth S Yorks 45 C9
Waen Denb 42 F4
Waen Denb 42 F2
Waen Fach Powys 33 D8
Waen Goleugoed Denb 42 E3
Wag Highld 93 G13
Wainfleet All Saints Lincs 47 G8
Wainfleet Bank Lincs 47 G8
Wainfleet St Mary Lincs 47 G9
Wainfleet Tofts Lincs 47 G8
Wainhouse Corner Corn 4 B2
Wainscott Medway 20 D4
Wainstalls W Yorks 50 G6
Waitby Cumb 57 F9
Waithe Lincs 46 B6
Wake Lady Green N Yorks 59 G7
Wakefield W Yorks 51 G9
Wakerley Northants 36 F5
Wakes Colne Essex 30 F5
Walberswick Suff 31 A11
Walberton W Sus 11 D8
Walbottle T&W 63 G7
Walcot Lincs 37 B6
Walcot N Lincs 52 G4
Walcot Shrops 33 G9
Walcot Swindon 17 C8
Walcot Telford 34 D1
Walcot Green Norf 39 G7
Walcote Leics 36 G1
Walcote Warks 27 C8
Walcott Lincs 46 G5
Walcott Norf 39 B9
Walden N Yorks 50 A6
Walden Head N Yorks 50 A5
Walden Stubbs N Yorks 52 H1
Waldersey Cambs 37 E10
Walderslade Medway 20 E4
Walderton W Sus 11 C6
Walditch Dorset 8 E3
Waldley Derbys 35 B7
Waldridge Durham 58 A3
Waldringfield Suff 31 D9
Waldringfield Heath Suff 31 D9
Waldron E Sus 12 E4
Wales S Yorks 45 D8
Walesby Lincs 46 C5
Walesby Notts 45 E10
Walford Hereford 25 A10
Walford Hereford 26 F2
Walford Shrops 33 C10
Walford Heath Shrops 33 D10
Walgherton Ches E 43 H9
Walgrave Northants 28 A5
Walhampton Hants 10 E2
Walk Mill Lancs 50 F4
Walkden Gtr Man 43 B10
Walker T&W 63 G8
Walker Barn Ches E 44 E3
Walker Fold Lancs 50 E2
Walkerburn Borders 70 G2
Walkeringham Notts 45 C11
Walkerith Lincs 45 C11
Walkern Herts 29 F9
Walker's Green Hereford 26 D2
Walkerville N Yorks 58 G3
Walkford Dorset 9 E11
Walkhampton Devon 4 E6
Walkington E Yorks 52 F5
Walkley S Yorks 45 D7
Wall Northumb 62 G5
Wall Staffs 35 E7
Wall Bank Shrops 33 F11
Wall Heath W Mid 34 G4
Wall under Heywood Shrops 33 F11
Wallaceton Dumfries 60 E4
Wallacetown S Ayrs 66 F5
Wallacetown S Ayrs 66 D6
Wallands Park E Sus 12 E3
Wallasey Mers 42 C6
Wallcrouch E Sus 12 C5
Wallingford Oxon 18 C3
Wallington Hants 10 D4
Wallington Herts 29 E9
Wallington London 19 E9
Wallis Pembs 22 D5
Walliswood Sur 19 H8
Walls Shetland 96 J4
Wallsend T&W 63 G8
Wallston V Glam 15 D7
Wallyford E Loth 70 C2
Walmer Kent 21 F10
Walmer Bridge Lancs 49 G4
Walmersley Gtr Man 44 A2
Walmley W Mid 35 F7
Walpole Suff 31 A10
Walpole Cross Keys Norf 37 D11
Walpole Highway Norf 37 D11
Walpole Marsh Norf 37 D10
Walpole St Andrew Norf 37 D11
Walpole St Peter Norf 37 D11
Walsall W Mid 34 F6
Walsall Wood W Mid 34 E6
Walsden W Yorks 50 G5
Walsgrave on Sowe W Mid 35 G9
Walsham le Willows Suff 30 A6
Walshaw Gtr Man 43 A10
Walshford N Yorks 51 D10
Walsoken Cambs 37 D10
Walston S Lanark 69 F9
Walsworth Herts 29 E8
Walters Ash Bucks 18 B5
Walterston V Glam 14 D6
Walterstone Hereford 25 F10
Waltham Kent 21 G8
Waltham NE Lincs 46 B6
Waltham Abbey Essex 19 A10
Waltham Chase Hants 10 C4
Waltham Cross Herts 19 A10
Waltham on the Wolds Leics 36 C4
Waltham St Lawrence Windsor 18 D5
Walthamstow London 19 C10
Walton Cumb 61 G11
Walton Derbys 45 F7
Walton Leics 36 G1
Walton M Keynes 28 E5
Walton Mers 42 C6
Walton Pboro 37 E7
Walton Powys 25 C9
Walton Som 15 H10
Walton Staffs 34 B4
Walton Suff 31 E9
Walton Telford 34 D1
Walton W Yorks 51 E10
Walton W Yorks 51 H9
Walton Warks 27 C9
Walton Cardiff Glos 26 E6
Walton East Pembs 22 D5
Walton-in-Gordano N Som 15 D10
Walton-le-Dale Lancs 50 G1
Walton-on-Thames Sur 19 E8
Walton on the Hill Staffs 34 C5
Walton on the Hill Sur 19 F9
Walton-on-the-Naze Essex 31 F9
Walton on the Wolds Leics 36 D1
Walton-on-Trent Derbys 35 D8
Walton West Pembs 22 E3
Walwen Flint 42 E5
Walwick Northumb 62 F5
Walworth Darl 58 E3
Walworth Gate Darl 58 D3
Walwyn's Castle Pembs 22 E3
Wambrook Som 8 D1
Wanborough Sur 18 G6
Wanborough Swindon 17 C9
Wandsworth London 19 D9
Wangford Suff 39 H10
Wanlockhead Dumfries 60 B4
Wansford E Yorks 53 D6
Wansford Pboro 37 F6
Wanstead London 19 C11
Wanstrow Som 16 G4
Wanswell Glos 16 A3
Wantage Oxon 17 C10
Wapley S Glos 16 D4
Wappenbury Warks 27 B10
Wappenham Northants 28 D3
Warbleton E Sus 12 E5
Warblington Hants 10 D6
Warborough Oxon 18 B2
Warboys Cambs 37 G9
Warbreck Blackpool 49 F3
Warbstow Corn 4 B3
Warburton Gtr Man 43 D10
Warcop Cumb 57 E9
Ward End W Mid 35 G7
Ward Green Suff 31 B7
Warden Kent 21 D7
Warden Northumb 62 G5
Wardhill Orkney 95 F7
Wardington Oxon 27 D11
Wardlaw Borders 61 B8
Wardle Ches E 43 G9
Wardle Gtr Man 50 H5
Wardley Rutland 36 E4
Wardlow Derbys 44 E5
Wardy Hill Cambs 37 G10
Ware Herts 29 G10
Ware Kent 21 E9
Wareham Dorset 9 F8
Warehorne Kent 13 C8
Waren Mill Northumb 71 G10
Warenford Northumb 71 H10
Warenton Northumb 71 G10
Wareside Herts 29 G10
Waresley Cambs 29 C9
Waresley Worcs 26 A5
Warfield Brack 18 D5
Warfleet Devon 5 F9
Wargrave Wokingham 18 D4
Warham Norf 38 A5
Warhill Gtr Man 44 C3
Wark Northumb 62 F4
Wark Northumb 71 G7
Warkleigh Devon 6 D5
Warkton Northants 36 H4
Warkworth Northants 27 D11
Warkworth Northumb 63 C8
Warlaby N Yorks 58 G4
Warland W Yorks 50 G5
Warleggan Corn 4 E2
Warlingham Sur 19 F10
Warmfield W Yorks 51 G9
Warmingham Ches E 43 F10
Warmington Northants 37 F6
Warmington Warks 27 D11
Warminster Wilts 16 G5
Warmlake Kent 20 F5
Warmley S Glos 16 D3
Warmley Tower S Glos 16 D3
Warmonds Hill Northants 28 B6
Warmsworth S Yorks 45 B9
Warmwell Dorset 9 F6
Warndon Worcs 26 C5
Warnford Hants 10 B5
Warnham W Sus 11 A10
Warninglid W Sus 11 B11
Warren Ches E 44 E2
Warren Pembs 22 G4
Warren Heath Suff 31 D9
Warren Row Windsor 18 C5
Warren Street Kent 20 F6
Warrington M Keynes 28 C5
Warrington Warr 43 D9
Warsash Hants 10 D3
Warslow Staffs 44 G4
Warter E Yorks 52 D4
Warthermarske N Yorks 51 B8
Warthill N Yorks 52 D2
Wartling E Sus 12 F5
Wartnaby Leics 36 C3
Warton Lancs 49 B4
Warton Lancs 49 G4
Warton Northumb 62 C6
Warton Warks 35 E8
Warwick Warks 27 B9
Warwick Bridge Cumb 61 H10
Warwick on Eden Cumb 61 H10
Wasbister Orkney 95 E4
Wasdale Head Cumb 56 F3
Wash Common W Berks 17 E11
Washaway Corn 3 C9
Washbourne Devon 5 F8
Washfield Devon 7 E8
Washfold N Yorks 58 F1
Washford Som 7 B9
Washford Pyne Devon 7 E7
Washingborough Lincs 46 E4
Washington T&W 63 H9
Washington W Sus 11 C10
Wasing W Berks 18 E2
Waskerley Durham 58 B1
Wasperton Warks 27 C9
Wasps Nest Lincs 46 F4
Wass N Yorks 52 B1
Watchet Som 7 B9
Watchfield Oxon 17 B9
Watchfield Som 15 G9
Watchgate Cumb 57 G7
Watchhill Cumb 56 B3
Watcombe Torbay 5 E10
Watendlath Cumb 56 E4
Water Devon 5 C8
Water Lancs 50 G4
Water End E Yorks 52 F3
Water End Herts 19 A9
Water End Herts 29 G7
Water Newton Cambs 37 F7
Water Orton Warks 35 F7
Water Stratford Bucks 28 E3
Water Yeat Cumb 56 H4
Waterbeach Cambs 29 B11
Waterbeck Dumfries 61 F8
Waterden Norf 38 B4
Waterfall Staffs 44 G4
Waterfoot E Renf 68 E4
Waterfoot Lancs 50 G4
Waterford Herts 29 G10
Waterhead Cumb 56 F5
Waterhead Dumfries 61 D7
Waterheads Borders 69 E11
Waterhouses Durham 58 B2
Waterhouses Staffs 44 G4
Wateringbury Kent 20 F3
Waterloo Gtr Man 44 B3
Waterloo Highld 85 F11
Waterloo Mers 42 C6
Waterloo N Lanark 69 E7
Waterloo Norf 39 D8
Waterloo Perth 76 D3
Waterloo Poole 9 E9
Waterloo Shrops 33 B11
Waterloo Port Gwyn 40 D6
Waterlooville Hants 10 D5
Watermeetings S Lanark 60 B5
Watermillock Cumb 56 D6
Waterperry Oxon 28 H3
Waterrow Som 7 D9
Water's Nook Gtr Man 43 B9
Waters Upton Telford 34 D2
Watersfield W Sus 11 C9
Waterside Aberds 89 F10
Waterside Blackburn 50 G3
Waterside Cumb 56 B4
Waterside E Ayrs 67 B7
Waterside E Ayrs 67 F7
Waterside E Dunb 68 C5
Waterside E Renf 68 E4
Waterstock Oxon 28 H3
Waterston Pembs 22 F4
Watford Herts 19 B8
Watford Northants 28 B3
Watford Gap Staffs 35 E7
Wath N Yorks 51 B9
Wath N Yorks 51 C7
Wath N Yorks 52 B2
Wath Brow Cumb 56 E2
Wath upon Dearne S Yorks 45 B8
Watlington Norf 38 D2
Watlington Oxon 18 B3
Watnall Notts 45 H9
Watten Highld 94 E4
Wattisfield Suff 31 A7
Wattisham Suff 31 C7
Wattlesborough Heath Shrops 33 D9
Watton E Yorks 52 D6
Watton Norf 38 E5
Watton at Stone Herts 29 G10
Wattston N Lanark 68 C6
Wattstown Rhondda 14 B6
Wauchan Highld 80 E1
Waulkmill Lodge Orkney 95 H4
Waun Powys 32 E4
Waun-y-clyn Carms 23 F9
Waunarlwydd Swansea 14 B2
Waunclunda Carms 24 E3
Waunfawr Gwyn 41 E7
Waungron Swansea 23 F10
Waunlwyd Bl Gwent 25 H8
Wavendon M Keynes 28 E6
Waverbridge Cumb 56 B4
Waverton Ches W 43 F7
Waverton Cumb 56 B4
Wavertree Mers 43 D6
Wawne E Yorks 53 F6
Waxham Norf 39 C10
Waxholme E Yorks 53 G9
Way Kent 21 E10
Way Village Devon 7 E7
Wayfield Medway 20 E4
Wayford Som 8 D3
Waymills Shrops 34 A1
Wayne Green Mon 25 G11
Wdig = Goodwick Pembs 22 C4
Weachyburn Aberds 89 C6
Weald Oxon 17 A10
Wealdstone London 19 C8
Weardley W Yorks 51 E8
Weare Som 15 F10
Weare Giffard Devon 6 D3
Wearhead Durham 57 C10
Weasdale Cumb 57 F8
Weasenham All Saints Norf 38 C4
Weasenham St Peter Norf 38 C4
Weatherhill Sur 12 B2
Weaverham Ches W 43 E9
Weaverthorpe N Yorks 52 B5
Webheath Worcs 27 B7
Wedderlairs Aberds 89 E8
Wedderlie Borders 70 E5
Weddington Warks 35 F9
Wedhampton Wilts 17 F7
Wedmore Som 15 G10
Wednesbury W Mid 34 F5
Wednesfield W Mid 34 E5
Weedon Bucks 28 G5
Weedon Bec Northants 28 C3
Weedon Lois Northants 28 D3
Weeford Staffs 35 E7
Week Devon 7 E6
Week St Mary Corn 4 B3
Weeke Hants 10 A3
Weekley Northants 36 G4
Weel E Yorks 53 F6
Weeley Essex 31 F8
Weeley Heath Essex 31 F8
Weem Perth 75 C11
Weeping Cross Staffs 34 C5
Weethley Gate Warks 27 C7
Weeting Norf 38 G3
Weeton E Yorks 53 G9
Weeton Lancs 49 F3